Early medieval militarisation

Early medieval militarisation

Edited by Ellora Bennett, Guido M. Berndt,
Stefan Esders and Laury Sarti

MANCHESTER UNIVERSITY PRESS

Copyright © Manchester University Press 2021

While copyright in the volume as a whole is vested in Manchester University Press, copyright in individual chapters belongs to their respective authors, and no chapter may be reproduced wholly or in part without the express permission in writing of both author and publisher.

Published by Manchester University Press
Oxford Road, Manchester M13 9PL

www.manchesteruniversitypress.co.uk

British Library Cataloguing-in-Publication Data
A catalogue record for this book is available from the British Library

ISBN 978 1 5261 3862 0 hardback
ISBN 978 1 5261 7180 1 paperback

First published 2021
Paperback published 2023

The publisher has no responsibility for the persistence or accuracy of URLs for any external or third-party internet websites referred to in this book, and does not guarantee that any content on such websites is, or will remain, accurate or appropriate.

Typeset
by New Best-set Typesetters Ltd

Contents

List of figures	page viii
List of contributors	x
Preface	xii
Abbreviations	xiii

1 Introducing early medieval militarisation, 400–900 1
Laury Sarti, Ellora Bennett, Guido M. Berndt and Stefan Esders

PART I: THE MILITARY AND SOCIETY

2 Soldier and civilian in the Byzantine Empire *c.* 600–*c.* 900: a militarised society? 31
Philip Rance

3 The *exercitus Gothorum* in Italy: a professional army in a demilitarised society? 48
Kai Grundmann

4 Military organisation as an indicator of militarisation (and demilitarisation) in Lombard Italy 63
Guido M. Berndt

5 The 'dark matter' evidence for Alfredian military reforms in their ninth-century context 80
Ryan Lavelle

PART II: WARFARE AND SOCIETY

6 War and the transformation of society in early Byzantine Arabia 99
Conor Whately

7 The role of the military factor in the political and
  administrative shaping of the Visigothic kingdom
  (sixth to seventh centuries) 115
  Pablo Poveda Arias
8 Recent archaeological research on fortifications in France,
  Belgium and Switzerland, 750–1000 130
  Luc Bourgeois
9 *Gens Germana gente ferocior*: Lombards and warfare
  between representation and reality 152
  Stefano Gasparri
10 The blinkers of militarisation: Charles the Bald, Lothar I
   and the Vikings 164
   Simon Coupland

PART III: ETHICS OF WAR

11 Manlike discipline and loyalty against the 'enemies of God':
   some observations on the militarised frontier society of
   eastern *Francia* around 600 181
   Stefan Esders
12 Swords in Christian hands: reflections on the emergence of
   the 'Schwertmission' in the early Middle Ages 196
   Uta Heil
13 'Holy wars'? 'Religious wars'? The perception of religious
   motives of warfare against non-Christian enemies in
   ninth-century chronicles 211
   Hans-Werner Goetz

PART IV: PERCEPTIONS OF THE WARRIOR

14 Change of habit equals change of values? Burials of 'military
   men' between 300 and 500 231
   Benjamin Hamm
15 Warlike and heroic virtues in the post-Roman world 253
   Edward James
16 Military equipment in late antique and early medieval female
   burial evidence: a reflection of 'militarisation'? 266
   Susanne Brather-Walter
17 The construction of the enemy in pre-Viking England 283
   Ellora Bennett
18 Warriors and warlike kings in the *Gesta Karoli* of Notker
   the Stammerer 299
   Thomas Wittkamp

19 Early medieval 'warrior' images and the concept of
    Gefolgschaft 314
    Michel Summer

20 Conclusion – militarisation: process or discourse? 331
    Guy Halsall

Select bibliography 346
Index 359

List of figures

8.1 A: Proposal for the reconstruction of the Carolingian gate of Pont-de-Bonne (Belgium, Modave) (aSEHS Studio / Cercle archéologique Hesbaye-Condroz). B: Villejoubert (France, Charente), 'Andone', reconstruction seen from the west (infography M. Linlaud). C: Périgueux (France, Dordogne), Porte de Mars. Gallo-Roman structures and transformations of the tenth to twelfth centuries (infography H. Gaillard and Y. Laborie). D: The moated site of Pineuilh (France, Gironde), 'La Mothe' in 975–83 (infography C. Morineau and K. Sammour, Cireve). *pages* 132–133

8.2 The fortified monasteries and collegial churches of the Carolingian Empire: a state of knowledge (map L. Bourgeois). 134

8.3 Saint-Dizier-Leyrenne (France, Creuse), 'Murat', plan of the *oppidum* and excavated areas (map R. Jonvel). 137

8.4 Proposal for a reconstitution of the *castrum* of Saint-Martin de Tours (France, Indre-et-Loire) (map E. Marot). 141

8.5 Saint John Abbey, Müstair (Switzerland, Canton Grisons). The tower is on the right (Wikipedia Commons). 142

8.6 Axonometry of the residential building of Mayenne (France, Mayenne) *c.* 900 (infography J.-C. Fossey / Craham, after Early). 143

8.7 The *roca* of Niozelles (France, Alpes-de-Haute-Provence), first phase (J.-M. Gassend, IRAA/CNRS, after D. Mouton). 144

List of figures

14.1 Cemeteries of the time between 300 and 500. Based on the author's research of 2014 cemeteries examined. In 340 necropolises one or more burial containing weaponry were detected. These concentrate foremost along the frontiers of the late Roman Empire but can also be found in central provinces in the Iberian Peninsula, northern Italy and the Balkans (map B. Hamm) — 232

14.2 The diagram gives an impression of the chronological development of weapon-burials in the time between 300 and 500. — 233

14.3 Share of graves with spatha within the weapons inventory of the observation period — 237

14.4 Late Roman burial scene with gravestone, which is inspired by finds from Aquileia and Longeau (Drawing kindly provided by L. Hamm) — 240

16.1 Meshed rings, former part of a chain mail — 270

16.2 Washer, former part of a lance head — 270

16.3 The distribution of late antique female graves with military belts (from Hamm 2018) — 273

16.4 The distribution of seventh-century decorated discs with 'horseman with a lance' (from Brather-Walter 2013) — 276

19.1 Distribution of 'wolf warrior' images (© Michael Kempf) — 317

19.2 Distribution of 'warrior procession' images (© Michael Kempf) — 318

List of contributors

Ellora Bennett, DPhil Candidate at the Freie Universität Berlin

Guido M. Berndt, Research Fellow at the Freie Universität Berlin

Luc Bourgeois, Professor of Medieval Archaeology at the Université de Caen – Basse-Normandie, Centre Michel de Boüard – Centre de recherches archéologiques et historiques anciennes et médiévales

Susanne Brather-Walter, Research Fellow at the Albert-Ludwigs-Universität Freiburg

Simon Coupland, Affiliated Scholar at the MacDonald Institute for Archaeological Research, University of Cambridge

Stefan Esders, Professor of Late Antique and Early Medieval History at the Freie Universität Berlin

Stefano Gasparri, Emeritus Professor of Medieval History at the Università Ca' Foscari Venezia

Hans-Werner Goetz, Emeritus Professor of Medieval History at the University of Hamburg

Kai Grundmann, Independent Scholar, Berlin

Guy Halsall, Honorary Professor in the Department of Archaeology at Durham University

Benjamin Hamm, PhD Candidate at the Albert-Ludwigs-Universität Freiburg

Uta Heil, Professor of Church History at the University of Vienna

Edward James, Emeritus Professor of Medieval History at the University College Dublin

Ryan Lavelle, Professor of Early Medieval History at the University of Winchester

Pablo Poveda Arias, Postdoctoral Research Associate at the Universität Hamburg

Philip Rance, Research Associate at the Freie Universität Berlin

Laury Sarti, Lecturer at the Albert-Ludwigs-Universität Freiburg

Michel Summer, PhD Candidate at Trinity College Dublin

Conor Whately, Associate Professor of Classics at the University of Winnipeg

Thomas Wittkamp, PhD Candidate at the Carl-von-Ossietzky Universität Oldenburg

Preface

The present volume assembles a selection of studies, the majority of which emerged from three different gatherings organised within the framework of a project funded by the Fritz-Thyssen Foundation and located at the Freie Universität Berlin, which was directed by Laury Sarti and Stefan Esders. The aim of the project was to study 'The militarisation of early medieval societies' by analysing its 'Nature, control and perception in a west-European comparison' (January 2016–June 2020). It was conducted in cooperation with Ryan Lavelle from the University of Winchester and Philipp von Rummel from the German Archaeological Institute (DAI). A workshop on 'Military organisation and society in the post-Roman world' (August 2016) and a conference entitled 'Reflections of a militarised world? Perceptions and conceptions of war and the military in the early Middle Ages (c. 500–1000)' (September 2017) were both held at the Freie Universität Berlin, while a third gathering on 'Early medieval militarisation. An archaeological perspective' (November 2019) took place at the University of Freiburg (im-Breisgau). It was organised in cooperation with the Institute for the Archaeology of the Middle Ages at the University of Freiburg. We would like to thank Anna Gehler-Rachůnek, Maria-Elena Kammerlander, Jean-Michel Klopp, Pia Lucas and Alexander Schie for their assistance throughout these meetings. In addition, one series of sessions was organised within the framework of the Leeds International Medieval Congress 2017 entitled 'The other look at early medieval societies – the phenomenon of militarisation', followed in 2018 by a Round Table discussion on 'The militarisation of early medieval societies'. We would like to thank all the speakers and attendants of these gatherings for their contributions to the subject. In addition, we would like to thank Meredith Carroll from Manchester University Press for bringing this volume to press and the external reviewers for their many useful suggestions for improvement.

Ellora Bennett, Guido M. Berndt, Stefan Esders and Laury Sarti

Abbreviations

AE	l'Année épigraphique
AHDE	Anuario de Historia del Derecho Español
AM	Archéologie médiévale
ASC	The Anglo-Saxon Chronicle
BASOR	Bulletin of the American Schools of Oriental Research
BG	De Bello Gothico
BMGS	Byzantine and Modern Greek Studies
BT	Bosworth-Toller Anglo-Saxon Dictionary
Bucema	Bulletin du Centre d'études médiévales d'Auxerre
CCSL	Corpus Christianorum: Series Latina
CSEL	Corpus Scriptorum Ecclesiasticorum Latinorum
CDL	Codice Diplomatico Longobardo
CG	Château Gaillard
Chron. Caesar	Chronica Caesaraugustana
Chron. Moz. a. 754	Chronica mozarabica of 754
Chron	Chronica
CIL	Corpus Inscriptionum Latinarum
CISAM	Centro Italiano di Studi sull'Alto Medioevo
DLH	Decem Libri Historiarum
EME	Early Medieval Europe
Epist. Wisigoth	Epistulae Wisigothicae
GCS	Die griechischen christlichen Schriftsteller der ersten Jahrhunderte
Get	Getica
HAMA	Collection Haut Moyen Âge
HE	Bede, Historia Ecclesiastica gentis Anglorum
Hist. Wambae	Historia Wambae

In Glor. Confess	*In Gloria Confessorum*
IGLSyr	Inscriptions grecques et latines de la Syrie
Isid. Hisp., *Etym*	Isidore of Seville, *Etymologiae*
Isid. Hisp., *Hist*	Isidore of Seville, *Historiae*
Iust. Nov	Iustinianus Novellae
JECS	*Journal of Early Christian Studies*
JRA	*Journal of Roman Archaeology*
LV	*Leges Visigothorum*
MGH	*Monumenta Germaniae Historica*
AA	*Auctores antiquissimi*
Capit	*Capitularia regum Francorum*
EE	*Monumenta Germaniae Historica, Epistolae*
Epp	*Epistulae*
LL	*Leges*
SRG	*Scriptores rerfum Germanicarum in usum scholarum separatim editi*
SRG, NS	*Scriptores rerum Germanicarum, Nova series*
SRL	*Scriptores rerum Langobardicarum et Italicarum saec. VI.-IX*
SRM	*Scriptores rerum Merovingicarum*
SS	*Scriptores*
SS rer. Merov	*Monumenta Germaniae Historica, Scriptores rerum Merovingicarum*
Not. dign	*Notitia Dignitatum*
PL	*Patrologia Latina*
P. Ness	Excavations at Nessana
P. Petra	The Petra Papyri
Ps.-Josh	Pseudo-Joshua the Stylite, *The Chronicle of Pseudo-Joshua the Stylite*
Ps.-Zach HE	Pseudo-Zachariah Rhetor, *The Chronicle of Pseudo-Zachariah Rhetor*
PPUAES	Publications of the Princeton University Archaeological Expeditions to Syria in 1904–1905 and 1909. Division III, Greek and Latin Inscriptions in Syria
Procop. *Anec*	Procopius *Anecdota*
Procop. *BG*	Procopius of Caesarea, *Bellum Gothicum*
Procop. *Hist. Arc*	Procopius of Caesarea, *Historia Arcana*
RAO	*Revue archéologique de l'Ouest*
RAP	*Revue archéologique de Picardie*
RBPH	*Revue belge de philologie et d'histoire*
Reg. Epist	*Registrum Epistularum*

RGA	*Reallexikon der Germanischen Altertumskunde*
S	Electronic Sawyer. Online Catalogue of Anglo-Saxon charters
SCI	*Scripta Classica Israelica*
SEG	Supplementum Epigraphicum Graecum
VSF	*Vita Sancti Fructuosi*
VSPE	*Vitas Sanctorum Patrum Emeretensium*
ZRG GA	*Zeitschrift der Savigny-Stiftung für Rechtsgeschichte, Germanistische Abteilung*

1

Introducing early medieval militarisation, 400–900

Laury Sarti, Ellora Bennett, Guido M. Berndt and Stefan Esders

The military in the Frankish world, Anglo-Saxon England and Lombard Italy

Europe at the turn from Antiquity to the Middle Ages underwent a gradual evolution that may be characterised as militarisation. Depending on the geographic situation, historic background and military organisation, this process progressed at different rates and to different degrees. In north-eastern Gaul, for example, Romans and non-Romans lived for centuries in close contact both east and west of the Roman frontier. While the empire expanded, its frontiers were increasingly fortified. Armies were recruited from the population both inside and outside of the Roman territory, while those without Roman civic rights became part of the auxiliaries (*foederati*, *laeti*) and received such rights at the end of their service.[1] Thus, the provinces of Gaul and Germany created large recruiting pools for the Roman army. While other provinces paid the recruitment tax in gold as a substitute, it was the Gallic provinces that furnished 'bodies'.[2] Despite laws forbidding the marriage of soldiers,[3] many among those based in the border regions established families. These families lived in nearby *canabae* or *vici*, which soon became also the homes of farmers, artisans and tradesmen. The border that has attracted most scholarly attention is the north-western Rhine–Danube frontier which was home to a large number of military camps, among which places such as the *castra Bonnensia* (Bonn) or *Vindobona* (Vienna) grew into impressive settlements. From the later fourth century, these communities began to bury rather than cremate their dead and to furnish graves with weapons, one among the most impressive cemeteries being Krefeld-Gellep (between modern Duisburg and Düsseldorf).[4] In contrast to the more central regions of the Roman Empire, this border population lived in close proximity to the potential threat of military violence and the military itself, a living condition that had only become the norm for Gaul's more central regions since the end of the *pax Romana* and the breakdown of the Roman *limes* in 406/7.

How did these changes impact society? While the sources describing life in Roman Gaul in further detail are rather meagre, subsequent testimonies portray a world that was increasingly characterised by military conflicts: the Goths expanded from southern Toulouse, where they had been settled in 418, while regular Burgundian inroads took place in the east, and Frankish conquests affected the north. The emerging kingdoms surrounded the remaining Roman territories, including the so-called kingdom of Soissons, which around 486 was conquered by the young king Clovis I and incorporated into the Frankish realm.[5] Paradoxically, the late Roman separation between military and civil office-holding had not only allowed the senatorial aristocracy to survive and maintain its civil values well into the fifth century, it also offered non-Romans the opportunity to advance a faster career within the military sector alone and to establish themselves as a new elite.[6] While most of the barbarian kingdoms emerged within already highly militarised late Roman societies, it is only in the face of the fifth-century confrontations that we also have evidence for the militarisation of the Roman senatorial elite.[7]

The Frankish kingdoms that absorbed most of Gaul over the course of the sixth century display a great variety of phenomena that are relevant here. The sources reveal a society wherein military conflicts could be fought out more or less anywhere, where forces were regularly assembled *ad hoc* from the local population and office-bearers were in charge of both military and civil functions. The kings retained small professional troops referred to in our sources as *antrustiones* and apparently organised as a *numerus*,[8] which could be complemented by the recruitment of troops on a large scale from among the cities of Gaul.[9] It also appears that some parts of the late Roman army based in Gaul became integrated within the Frankish army along with their military lands and resources.[10] The most striking feature of militarisation, however, is the fact that most of the law-codes drafted in the sixth and seventh centuries under Frankish rule presuppose a general obligation of the free adult men to perform military service.[11] As it is inconceivable that men were sent to war without prior military training, the potential recruitment of the entire male population premises that this had somewhat become part of every boy's education. Although a document contained in the *Formularies of Angers* (nr. 37) mentioning a father thanking his son for having served in his place speaks for the existence of a specific strategy (for example, list of names to allow service in alternation or the drawing of lots) used to prevent the simultaneous recruitment of every suitable male of a certain region, this still suggests a far higher degree of militarisation of society than we encounter in the late Roman period. The *bannus*, a fine meant to punish the failure to follow a call to join the Frankish army whose application is mentioned in the narrative sources in reference to exceptional cases, i.e. when it was applied to ecclesiastical dependents,[12] was introduced to make sure that the lower rank and file complied with their military duties. Besides, the written and archaeological sources attest to the high esteem and significance attributed to military roles and identities – which were particularly prominent among the elite – ideals of manliness (*virilitas*) and usefulness (*utilitas*) being strongly linked to military skills and exploits, and even spiritual writings like homilies or hagiography now referred to military values and concepts.[13] The Frankish law-codes are full of references to military concepts such as *wergild* or to offenses that were seen as diminishing a person's embodied honour.[14]

The success of the Frankish kingdom which eventually absorbed most other barbarian kingdoms cannot be explained without the huge military resources that were available in Gaul and now became concentrated in the hands of Clovis and his successors. The same may be said with reference to the early Carolingians whose military expansion and imperial consolidation rested on the mobilisation of human and other resources they found in the conquered territories[15] as demonstrated, for example, by the large Carolingian armies recruited for campaigning against the Lombards and Avars.[16] Moreover, there is ample evidence for the Carolingian rulers exerting military taxes such as the *heribannus* from among those parts of the population that were not recruited for their mostly annual campaigns.[17]

The situation of Britain was different inasmuch as it was defined by the region's remote and insular location. The Roman conquest and expansion, led by the military and trailed by Roman trade, administration and customs, allowed for the diffusion of *Romanitas* through the elites into the tribal communities.[18] Yet, the conquest did not encompass the entire island of Britain; the Scottish Highlands never came under direct Roman control, and neither were parts of modern Wales and Cornwall fully integrated into the province.[19] This resulted in border regions not dissimilar to those on the continent, with soldiers stationed at military outposts and leading social and economic lives in the adjacent *vici*. Military forts were generally consigned to the north and west of the island whilst the south and east remained more civil in character, giving the impression of two distinct 'zones'.[20]

The degradation of Roman administrative infrastructure and the gradual removal of Roman forces, the completion of which has been traditionally dated to *c.* 410 AD,[21] were followed by a partial abandonment of Roman ways, including towns and coinage.[22] Indeed, the extent to which Britain was less Romanised than Gaul is revealed through the rapid resurgence of military tribal societies, although these post-Roman British kingdoms capitalised on the physical remains of Roman military infrastructure, particularly in the north.²³ The lack of written sources between the late Roman period and the arrival of the 'Anglo-Saxons' shrouds the intervening years in uncertainty. According to the narrative of the British monk Gildas († 570), the Saxons were invited to the island as a safeguard against the raids of Picts and Scots but turned on their employers, effectively initiating the *adventus Saxonum*.²⁴ The Northumbrian monk Bede, writing in the eighth century, built on this narrative and supplemented certain details, such as the Anglian, Saxon and Jutish origins of the arriving forces.²⁵ Whilst the narratives of Gildas and Bede contain plausible grains of truth, reality was certainly far more complex.²⁶ By the end of the sixth century, nascent kingdoms had formed, based around warrior-kings and their retinues.²⁷ Clearly, the transformation of Roman Britain to Anglo-Saxon England followed a markedly different path to the empire's 'successor states' in mainland Europe, making the question of militarisation as a force for societal change all the more complex.

The manner by which fighting men were recruited in Anglo-Saxon England remains opaque but a number of theories have been posed, ranging from the idea that all 'free' farmers were gathered by mass levy, to warfare being the sole prerogative of aristocratic elites.²⁸ Either way, there were no large professional armies until the ninth-century military reforms of Alfred the Great.²⁹ It was not until the laws of King Ine of Wessex (688–726) that any form of military service was mentioned in legislation. These laws laid out the fine for not attending the army (*fyrdwite*), stating the amounts owed from landed and unlanded nobles and *ceorls* (free farmers).³⁰ Whilst this has been taken by some to mean that the *ceorl* participated in warfare *en masse*,³¹ Richard Abels argued in 1988 that Ine's law referred only to those who were expected to attend the army and did not do so, rather than referring to an overarching system that included all free farmers. This interpretation is vital to his overall thesis that Anglo-Saxon armies were primarily aristocratic in composition, based on intertwined bonds of lordship.³² This notion, which continues to be both influential and controversial, contrasts with those of nineteenth- and other twentieth-century scholars whose interpretations of army organisation was fundamentally rooted in the paradigm that all free men had a duty to perform military service.³³ A significant development took place in eighth-century Mercia, wherein kings Æthelbald (716–57) and Offa (757–96) began to reserve the rights to construction of fortresses and bridges and military service from all land, including bookland.³⁴ This ensured that these lands remained militarily useful, with one fighting man being owed from every five hides by the eleventh century.³⁵ This suggests an overall shift from personal bonds of lordship to land-ownership as the predominate factor in recruiting fighting men. Overall, since the 1990s, scholarly opinion has tended to favour the idea of small, generally aristocratic forces rather than mass levies. Nonetheless, the role of non-aristocratic fighters continues to invite debate, particularly in relation to defensive warfare that required the mobilisation of local forces and resources.[36] In such cases, it is difficult to determine how far elites relied on local *ad hoc* recruitment and, in turn, the extent to which the recruitment pool was experienced in, or prepared for, the conduct of war.

Warfare was integral to socio-political structures and, integrally, warfare shaped the framework through which the Anglo-Saxons viewed their world. Furnished graves, found in numerous inhumation cemeteries and burial mounds such as Buckland, Dover and Sutton Hoo[37] reveal the extent to which warfare and military symbols governed rituals based on the perceptions and expectations of communities and society at large, with nearly one-half of identifiably male burials containing weapons (so-called warrior-graves).[38] Such evidence is at odds with the interpretations of scholars such as Abels who have argued for primarily aristocratic forces.[39] Indeed, the permeation of these tools and symbols in grave-goods reflects for larger parts of society the extent to which distinct 'civilian' and 'military' spheres were lacking, in contrast to the 'zoning' of the island during Roman occupation. It therefore appears that warfare and military values were in close physical and mental proximity throughout the communities of Anglo-Saxon England, because participation in warfare and the immediacy of violence had ripple effects that impacted the life experiences and perceptions of fighters and non-fighters alike.

In contrast to the Anglo-Saxon realms, the Lombard kingdom was founded in the former heartland of the Roman Empire. Lombard domains soon emerged north and south of the Byzantine territories linking Rome with Ravenna and the Pentapolis, thus transforming Italy into a frontier zone. The sources that explicitly refer to the military are meagre. Apart from brief mentions in works like Gregory of Tours' *Histories*,[40] the only consecutive narrative source is the late eighth-century *Historia Langobardorum* of Paul the Deacon († 799).[41] The temporal distance between Paul's own time and most of his narratives, and the fact that it only occasionally focuses on the military, makes it a particularly difficult source for the study of militarisation. Still, the evidence, and the collected laws (*leges Langobardorum*) in particular, are able to provide some important information on the basic organisational structure of the Lombard army, contemporary military values and the *wergild*.[42] They suggest a strong hierarchisation of the Lombard military based in the former Roman *civitates* thus providing access to city-based infrastructures and resources.[43] It was headed by the respective *rex Langobardorum*, to which *duces* and *gastalds* were subordinated, high-ranking military leaders who were responsible for recruiting fighters *ad hoc* in their respective territories. The responsibilities and obligations of the military officers below these ranks are difficult to grasp.[44] The *exercitales* and *arimanni* referred to in the Lombard laws clearly show that military settlements must have played a crucial role in the distribution of such obligations.[45] While the Roman system of a 'stately' tax collection appears to have been maintained to a considerable extent in the Byzantine parts of Italy beyond the year 600, it seems less clear whether the Lombard kings continued to exact taxes.[46] Similarly to the Byzantine areas of Italy,[47] the family-household appears to have played a central role in the period that followed, as the respective expenditure was measured by the property of the individual family,[48] combining several *massaria* to furnish a recruit.[49] While all free Lombards were obliged to perform military service, individual families had the option of sending only one member at once. Still, those recruited and those who stayed home were jointly responsible for the equipment of the *arimannus*. The social structures of the Lombard kingdom, however, underwent significant changes until the eighth century. The seventh-century edict of King Rothari attests that many descendants of those Lombards who had come to Italy in the sixth century had fallen into economic crisis, as since the beginning of the seventh century the possibilities for obtaining spoils of war had diminished considerably due to lack of military activity. In the eighth century, the military performance of rulers such as Aistulf, whose army conquered the exarchate of Ravenna, once more appears to have been based on the recruitment of larger parts of the local population,[50] although there is no evidence suggesting that the initial situation when all free Lombards were warriors (*arimannus, exercitales*) was restored.[51]

The early history of the Lombard kingdom was determined by its military campaigns, the significance of which decreased up to the seventh century, but resurfaced in the eighth century. The external and internal interests of the Lombard kingdom were largely secured by the maintenance of strong armies as Lombard Italy could only be ruled by taking into account the interests of the powerful magnates and by securing the territory against foreign enemies. In northern and central Italy, the *exarchate* of Ravenna paid ambitious Lombards willing to change sides for their own benefit to promote insurgencies, while the Franks and the Pope strove to gain as much power as possible. In the south, the duchies of Spoleto and Benevento emerged as largely independent lordships which from the end of the sixth century posed a significant limitation to the Lombard royal power.[52] In consequence, the Lombard *duces* were constantly engaged in military and diplomatic activities against both external enemies and internal rivals. The sources attest that Lombard society, in particular in this earlier phase, was fairly militarised. The *Historia Langobardorum*, for example, includes several episodes stressing the efficiency, bravery and masculinity of the early Lombards as outstanding warriors.[53] The significance attributed to the military is confirmed by the archaeological evidence with a large number of warrior-graves that could include complete sets of military equipment (sword, lance and shield) which are evidenced from the Lombard invasion in the late 560s until the middle of the seventh century. Although the interpretation of these finds remains controversial, they do attest to the significance the community responsible for these burials attributed to the military identity of their dead.

This short survey using only three examples shows how the relation between the military and the civil population changed as a consequence of an increase in military conflicts inside former Roman territory, a largely militarised secular elite and the installation of armies that were based on a variety of recruitment modes – including large numbers of people who were recruited *ad hoc*. Settlements on 'military land', mostly composed of property formerly belonging to the Roman fisc, represented one possible basis for the recruitment of troops.[54] But what were the consequences of the fact that late and post-Roman military men could contract lawful marriages and hand down the military lands they had from their kings?[55] It introduced a profound change that had a crucial impact on the relationship between warfare and society. Although the Anglo-Saxon, the Frankish and the Lombard kingdoms differed significantly in view of their Roman heritage, the fact that men were often recruited from their families to join battles that were mainly fought in some proximity of their homeland was always associated with an altered perception of military activity and related values, an evolution that was not limited to those who fought but affected society as a whole. Thus, the issue of marriage underlines the importance of considering militarisation as a process that affected families and society as a whole in a fundamental way. The early medieval kingdoms also attest to a regionalisation of late Roman state structures: disconnected from the late antique exchange system, where 'bodies' and 'payments' could be compensated by different provinces on an empire-wide base, the post-Roman *regna* had to rely primarily on human and other resources that were available within their territories.[56]

'Militarisation' as an alternative term to 'barbarisation' and 'Germanisation'

Until recently, the social changes described above were largely characterised as a process of 'Germanisation' or 'barbarisation'.[57] Both concepts postulate the existence of distinguishable peoples with different ways of living, values and cultures: civilised Romans on the one hand, and warlike Germans or barbarians on the other. In consequence, weapon burials found near the Roman frontier, for example, were labelled as 'Germanic', regardless of whether they were interpreted as the burials of *laeti*[58] or *foederati*[59] fighting as part of the Roman auxiliaries, while unfurnished graves were understood to be the remains of a Roman population.[60] From this perspective, the civilised Roman world had been overrun by warlike barbarians, which influenced societies from outside by threatening their borders and from within through their presence in the Roman army.

Historians and archaeologists today mostly agree that such a strict distinction between Romans and barbarians neither corresponds to late Roman nor to early medieval reality.[61] As Heiko Steuer convincingly argued, the empire was largely responsible for the military role these outer people developed over time by setting up their frontiers and by recruiting in large numbers from outside of these.[62] Other archaeologists have pointed to the fact that furnished burials largely emerged around the Roman *limes*, with some cemeteries outside the official frontier but a majority inside the (former) Roman territory. Guy Halsall, later followed by scholars like Frans Theuws and Monika Alkemade, stressed that weapon burials could not have been the sole work of barbarians given their location inside Roman territory. They conclude that these burials were the product of situations wherein the positions of local elites were contested and of the struggles for power this implied.[63] In consequence, these graves cannot have belonged to a particular ethnic group. Subsequent studies like those by Irene Barbiera and Bonnie Effros question whether archaeological remains allow for making ethnic distinctions in the first place, stressing that very different reasons may have entailed that objects found in a burial were deposed where later generations found them.[64] Most researchers thus agree now that these graves should not be strictly linked to barbarians or 'Germanic' people, but to a distinct society that emerged due to the particular situation at the late Roman frontier.[65] This society was characterised by factors such as the prevalence of the military, potential exposure to armed violence and close contact between those who fought and the remaining civilian population. Consequently, instead of speaking of 'Germanisation' or 'barbarisation', these changes more recently have been characterised as the results of a process of 'militarisation'.[66]

Thinking about the transition between Antiquity and the Middle Ages has significantly changed since the international project on the 'Transformation of the Roman world' funded by the European Science Foundation (1993–98).[67] It focused on questions related to empire and kingdoms, the *gentes* and their settlements, everyday production and distribution, as well as the world of ideas and belief, and it argued that the transition towards the medieval era was a long-term process largely taking place inside the (late) Roman world. It opposed the opinion represented until that time by a majority of scholars that the Roman world had fallen due to decay and calamity, a model at the centre of which the external barbarian threat and the Roman inability to stand their ground were decisive factors. Although the project resulted in a sustainable alternative model that is able to take account of the complexities that led to the end of the Roman world, warfare and military violence – being at the centre of the contested scholarship – were not integrated as factors into the new model. While warfare had been considered as a significant factor in the framework of the now largely refuted thesis of an abrupt breakdown of Western imperial power as a consequence of the early fourth-century barbarian inroads, the mentioned project failed to consider that warfare needs to be factored in as an essential force for long-term societal change when discussing questions related to the thesis of a protracted process of transformation. While cities and settlements can be rebuilt after being destroyed, the constant confrontation with military violence attested since the end of the *pax romana* not only affected the population and its infrastructure, but also left long-lasting impressions on contemporaries' perceptions, priorities, values and beliefs.

Defining militarisation

In a study on 'Defining military culture',[68] which although largely based on observations related to modern history aims at providing a 'model to be applied across time and space' (p. 41), Peter H. Wilson defines militarisation as 'militarism viewed as a process', while 'militarism' refers to the mental and cultural willingness to embark on war and 'militarisation' to the capacity to wage war. He distinguishes between political militarisation, referring to the 'extent to which state structure is geared for war', social militarisation, as 'the proportion of the population incorporated into military institutions, and […] involved in other preparations for war', economic militarisation, as a matter of resource mobilisation, and cultural militarisation, referring to the wider 'presence of military culture in society beyond military institutions', which may 'extend from passive acceptance to active endorsement and promotion of military values' (p. 40). By stressing that a 'militarised' state is materially organised to make war although not necessarily governed by soldiers nor 'men readily prepared to use violence' (p. 40), Wilson argues that a militarised society does not necessarily need to be characterised by the use of violence or the active waging of war.

In a seminal paper on 'The militarisation of Roman Society' published in 1997, Edward James proposed a definition that already combined the different aspects addressed by Wilson:

> By a militarised society I mean a society in which there is no clear distinction between soldier and civilian, nor between military officer and government official; where the head of state is also commander-in-chief of the army; where all adult free men have the right to carry weapons; where a certain group or class of people (normally the aristocracy) is expected, by reason of birth, to participate in the army; where the education of the young thus often involves a military element; where the symbolism of warfare and weaponry is prominent in official and private life, and the warlike and heroic virtues are glorified; and where warfare is a predominant government expenditure and/or a major source of economic profit.[69]

James herewith provides a multi-layered definition that goes beyond a society's external factors as it includes both structural and mentality related features: the first implies characteristics like the lack of differentiation between the military and the civil, such as officials bearing military and civil functions, as well as the prominent display of weapons and military training of children. As has become apparent from the historical sketch above, the 'right to carry weapons' needs to be supplemented by the obligation to military service, which generally applies to the adult free male population. The mentality related aspects consider the significance attributed to weapons, military symbolism, martial skills and exploits, including ideals like manliness or honour, and the predominantly military identity of the (secular) elite.[70] The definition is sufficiently flexible to be applied to differing societies, which is important if several regions or historic periods are to be studied or compared. James' definition of militarisation addresses every area of early medieval life and thus will be used as a basis for the subsequent chapters. It is a useful tool to describe and analyse a process of change. Historians may resort to it to analyse long-term developments inside a society and its political system. It not only helps to study the significance and repercussions of warfare as a factor for the transformation of the Roman world, it also has the benefit that it allows considerations of these changes without having to resort to an oversimplified model of Romans opposing barbarians/Germanics or defining the observed changes as a product of the clash of such opposing people and their respective cultures.[71] To this end, militarisation should not be understood as referring to a static condition but to a historical process that neither has to be linear nor mono-causal. It becomes a useful tool if conceived as a means to describe and analyse what happened in the context of a specific period and region, and why a society underwent these changes, rather than as a means to define a society with a hard set of criteria or to attempt to determine its supposed 'degree of militarisation'. This also implies that James' criteria do not necessarily have to apply altogether or at the same moment to a specific case, and that one criterion can become more or less important over time. Thus, the essential question to be asked when using the concept of militarisation as an analytical tool is not to define when this process started or ended – particularly as there is hardly a society in history that is entirely demilitarised or unaffected by the military – but what factors and historical processes affected a society in between and how these were (inter)related. Still, any study needs to define a starting and ending point relevant to the investigations to be undertaken. In terms of early medieval militarisation, the starting point should be the largely militarised provincial societies of the late Roman Empire, a process that was significantly and decisively intensified inside the barbarian kingdoms, while the terminal point should be the ninth century, when new tendencies of professionalisation of the military, new recruitment modes and new types of warfare are attested throughout Europe.

While the term 'militarisation' may be used to refer to a process by which state and society became more closely dominated by military ideas, it could also involve a process of 'de-differentiation' on certain levels, as things could not be separated from one another in a manner as clear-cut as late Roman distinctions between 'military' and 'civil' would suggest. If we look at these societies, we can observe how military values and concepts of behaviour entered social practice and political discourse. Militarisation is thus a helpful tool to understand how the political and social organisation developed new differentiations that were essentially based and rooted in a society that underwent profound changes. The rise of the concept of *wergild* is a case in point.

Although militarisation refers to the role attributed to warfare, the military, warlike rituals, behaviour and related values, a militarised society does not necessarily need to be a society at war. The Roman world of the Principate was largely civil and the seventh-century Lombards, just like the late Merovingians, did not wage as many wars as their predecessors; still, none of these circumstances should imply that these societies were 'less militarised'. It should also be noted that being under military threat does not equal going to war: both have a significantly different effect on a society. Furthermore, although the early medieval clergy were supposed to refrain from military violence, they clearly underwent a process of militarisation that can be traced from the fourth and beyond the eighth century.[72] Thus, the fact that warfare, the military and warlike values significantly shaped the society in question and contemporaries' relationship to warfare, their values and their perception of violence are more important factors in defining a militarised society than the intensity of military violence.

Studying militarisation

The early medieval military has only recently regained the attention of researchers. B. S. Bachrach's 1972 and 2001 studies remain to this date the only monographic investigations specifically focusing on the Merovingian and Carolingian military organisations, respectively.[73] Regarding the Lombard armies, research is limited to scattered articles and comparative treatments in books that use a wider geographic and temporal perspective,[74] while the (later) Anglo-Saxon military has been treated in further depth in Ryan Lavelle's *Alfred's wars*.[75] More recent monographic studies provide a comparative perspective, which increasingly include society within discussions of the military, most prominently Guy Halsall's *Warfare and society*.[76] Although several recent studies have dealt with the warrior,[77] the military functions of the elite[78] and the role of violence,[79] the phenomenon of early medieval militarisation still lacks thorough investigation. Relevant research is restricted to several articles dealing with the frontier region of late Roman Gaul and the aforementioned weapon graves.[80]

In view of the above, militarisation can be studied using two complementary approaches. The first is to consider a society's external relation to the military and warfare, which includes the military organisation and recruitment strategies, (potential) military roles of the local population and the elite and the relationship between the military and society. Important sources, alongside historiographical narratives, include law-codes, hagiography and archaeology. Remains of architecture like *castra*/forts, city walls, roads or common housing help us to better understand a society, its everyday presentation and how it reacted and/or related to (potential) military threat or violence. The second approach focuses on contemporary ideas, perceptions and values related to warfare and the military. This includes methods developed in the context of the history of mentality (*histoire des mentalités*), which searches for common patterns of behaviour and thought[81] (as far as the available sources allow), the study of ideas as presented by medieval authors in their works, as proposed by the study of semantic fields (*Begriffsgeschichte*) and discourse analysis[82] and as part of a history of perceptions (*Vorstellungsgeschichte*).[83] Alongside sources mentioned in relation to the first approach, poetry, letters and iconography are particularly pertinent. The remaining paragraphs aim at presenting some introductory thoughts by discussing methodological approaches to study early medieval appreciations of military abilities and participation, military roles and identities, and contemporary conceptions of honour.

Burial evidence is essential for understanding the early medieval appraisal of military abilities and participation. Although furnished burials are restricted both regionally and temporally, they provide information for estimating the contemporary significance attributed to a military identity and related functions; an assessment that applies to a majority of those individuals who participated in the burial ceremony. The aforementioned fifth- to seventh-century weapon burials, which were part of the so-called row graves (*Reihengräber*) largely found in regions adjacent to the (former) Roman frontiers including Gaul, Anglo-Saxon England and Lombard Italy, are an important source for the study of the significance attributed to military identities and functions. Weapons were very expensive and therefore not deposited without good reason. Moreover, given that funerary rituals generally aimed at expressing some kind of appreciation for the departed, it appears most unlikely that attendees deposited these objects if they carried a negative connotation. Although the percentage of weapon graves varies significantly from site to site, these burials do inevitably attest that a military identity and function were considered desirable and appreciated. This does not imply that the deceased had acted as, or considered himself, a warrior when alive. As Heinrich Härke emphasised in reference to the Anglo-Saxon evidence, weapons found in burials do not necessarily reflect contemporary armament, nor do they prove that the deceased had actually fought in a battle.[84] Dawn Hadley and Jenny Moore added that these 'weapon burials do not signify actual warriors so much as "warrior status"', and that 'weapons had a symbolic meaning beyond that of their functional role'.[85] This means that warrior identity was significant beyond an individual's military role or implication. This particularly applies to those individuals whose bodies were found in high-status burials, graves that tend to contain the largest variety and number of weapons. Given the quality of these objects, these burials must have belonged to the upper social layer. This again implies that these burials testify to the significance this group attributed to its military role and identity.

Words and ideas expressed in writing represent further puzzle-pieces that, when put together, carry useful information about how one author and (at least a major part of) his expected audience perceived the world. Although there are always components specific to one particular author, the second approach allows the study of perceptions of a group that extends beyond the authors themselves. Moreover, the examination of words and conceptions, as testified in the sources, allows for the assessment of (potentially shared) bias, prejudice, partiality and implicitness, which is particularly useful when working on a period with so few sources as the earlier Middle Ages – when written evidence itself often lacks statements explicitly relating to questions about which we would like to know more. A word or a concept analysed on the *longue durée* in a representative set of sources allows for the examination of how the carried meanings, connotations and (implicit and explicit) ideas changed over time, while considering the relevant historical background may help understanding why these alterations occurred. This method, however, is only practicable for a limited set of terms whose meanings evolved over the period and inside the geographic analytical scope. Given that words referring to core aspects related to long-term transformations tend to change their meaning as a consequence of their external evolutions, studying these terms and their change in meaning provides potentially new evidence with which to assess long-term outer and inner evolutions and processes. For the assessment of early medieval militarisation, this applies to words like *honor*, *virilitas* or *milites*, and to concepts like reputation, military identity or peace.

One important structural feature of a militarised society is the lack of differentiation between the military and the civil, an aspect that is closely related to contemporaries' military identity. It is notable that in the Merovingian sources terms like *bellator*, *belliger*, *proeliator* or *pugnator*, which clearly define a person as a warrior, are largely used, if at all, to refer to a restricted or distinguished part of society. In the Merovingian sources, this is applied to the early Franks, their kings and military men who were either in the immediate proximity of a ruler as a member of his retinue or were at least closely associated with a king.[86] Although this could be explained by the fact that the sources scarcely mention non-elite individuals, the rare usage and the virtual lack of plural uses (with a few exceptions) is noteworthy, as it reinforces the impression that military roles were considered particularly important by those belonging to the upper secular strata.

More revealing is the term *miles* itself, the standard word in Roman sources used to refer to a soldier. Although it does appear sporadically in Italy and Britain to refer to military men,[87] for reasons we shall try to hypothesise, Merovingian and early Carolingian sources using it in reference to contemporary Frankish secular men only do so to refer to custodians of prisoners.[88] It is not until the ninth century that it once more progressively refers to fighters. The interesting question is: why? The term *miles* obviously carried a strong reference to (full-time) service, the *militia*, a meaning that appears to have been considered inappropriate after the Roman army system had broken down in Gaul. This would explain why, after the abolishment of the Roman standing armies in Gaul, the term *miles* was used only to refer to the aforementioned civic functionaries. As opposed to the part-time fighters called to arms only when needed, these *milites* fulfilled the criteria of armed permanent service. This explanation also sits well with the fact that the ancient meaning of *miles* was retained in Ostrogothic Italy, wherein a professional army remained in place at least until the Lombard conquest, thus inviting no reason for the term to change in meaning. In Britain, on the other hand, Latin ceased to be used as a vernacular from as early as the sixth century, when it was mainly used as a (more static) language of the learned elite.[89] This likely prevented the adaptation of the Latin term to the current situation, and thus from reflecting a transition from an institutionalised Roman to an Anglo-Saxon military organisation largely based on *ad hoc* recruitment.

Neither *miles* nor terms like *bellator* were commonly used in the Merovingian sources to refer to a large body of fighters. It is noteworthy that the ordinary members of an army were generally referred to by using more vague words such as *viri*, *homines* or, in a Latin adaption of the vernacular, *leudes*, and in the case of an actual campaign, as *exercitus*.[90] Evidently, there was no need to define these men more specifically by referring to their military identity. Although every man could be considered a potential warrior, a military identity was only noted more explicitly when the designated individual was performing a military function during a specific moment (such as during a campaign). The long-term change in the use of *miles* thus does not only support the significance of the elite's military identity, but also attests that this was less the case for the large majority of secular men. For them, the transition from civil to military was more fluid, as their military role was not necessarily a long-term occupation that would support the further elaboration of a shared military identity. Against the backdrop of the ongoing debate about early medieval ethnic identity,[91] it should be noted that the importance of warfare for creating and reaffirming the ethnic identity of 'we-groups' has also been emphasised by anthropological studies.[92] The blurred transition and distinctions between the 'military' and the 'civil' population entailed that ethnic identities became increasingly important as a potential reference not only for the military elites but for the entire population.[93] Low-end burials support the impression of a gradual intensity of identification with the military, given that weapons tend to feature less prominently and in a larger variance. Thus, the evidence helps to confirm two important criteria for defining militarisation in a society: the merging of the civil and the military, and the significance of a military identity for the elite.

The last criterion to address here is the early medieval significance of honour. The ancient meaning of the corresponding Latin term *honor* is generally taken for granted, and thus willingly translated accordingly. However, in contrast to the Roman sources, Merovingian authors do not use the Latin term *honor* to refer to an individual's appreciation as a full and esteemed member of society, i.e. an honour any man owns until he eventually loses it. From the late fifth and until the seventh century, Frankish sources mostly use the term *honor* to designate an official function or to refer to glory and fame.[94] There are other terms that do refer to a notion that matches the modern definition of honour. While several of the Roman implications of *honor* as referring to office-holding were maintained and eventually became transformed into medieval terminology,[95] post-Roman 'honourableness', as opposed to the late Roman conception of a more civic notion implied within the term *honor*, was increasingly associated with action and physical skills. Thus, the term *honor* was gradually substituted by words like *virilitas*, *fortitudo* or *utilitas*. As revealed by deeper analysis, the notion of honour carried within these terms clearly implied that proof was required through physical activity, preferably in a military context. This altered notion of honour is confirmed where injured honour is mentioned (*iniuria*).[96] This was generally done by depriving a man of his liberty of action (for example by bonding) or by damaging his outward appearance (for example by disrobement or mutilation).[97] Both implied harm to a man's physical integrity and constitution and would hinder his ability to be active. The evidence thus does not only support the importance of honour, it also proves that physical and military performance were considered significant criteria in defining honourableness, which altogether entailed a change in the vocabulary used to refer to the same notion. The verbal evidence thus demonstrates that at least some Frankish notions of honour were intrinsically tied to the expectation of (physical) activity, meaning that honour was not only an important criterion to define the need for action, it was defined by action. A comparable conclusion could be drawn from an analysis of the term *virilitas* referring to manliness.

To conclude, as the concept of militarisation may be applied to a society as a whole, virtually every source may be used to investigate the phenomenon and its underlying processes. This includes evidence related to the general living conditions, like archaeological findings, findings that although inexplicit, still do speak for themselves. The same applies to the meanings carried by words and designations. Although the approaches we have stressed here are limited to selected pieces of evidence and notions, the evidence gathered therewith may help to uncover historic processes that tend to remain uncommented on by contemporary sources. The few examples discussed here support the idea that perceptions and conceptions as attested by the archaeological evidence or expressed in the written sources are able to reflect current outer situations and recent changes. As contemporaries' views, expectations and thinking were shaped by their own outer world, any significant outer change was likely to have an effect on how related elements were assessed, perceived and described. A comprehensive investigation of relevant evidence thus represents a useful approach not only to assess a society's militarisation, but also to understand the underlying historical processes.

Presentation of the volume

This volume presents a large variety of case studies related to militarisation in the different regions of the early medieval world. It expands beyond the geographic examples discussed in the present introduction by including investigations on Gothic Italy and Spain, northern Europe with the Vikings, and the Byzantine world. The volume's organisation reflects the considerations presented above in reference to its definition and methodological approaches. The first two sections collect studies that focus on the structural features of militarisation by discussing aspects like military organisation and structures, recruitment strategies and related taxes, military infrastructure, tendencies of militarisation and demilitarisation, the relationship between those who fought and society, and the role of the military in and the impact of the waging of war on society. The third and fourth sections gather studies related to mentalities, particularly the ethics of war and the perception of the warrior. They include studies on the significance of Christian ethics and notions in the assessment of military participation, notions of loyalty and discipline, the perception and depiction of the warrior, military virtues, and the role attributed to military features discovered in male and female burials. The volume closes with a comparative conclusion discussing the notion of militarisation as a means to deal with the complexity of the changes societies in Europe underwent from late Antiquity by considering its potential limits and benefits with reference to the case studies presented in the different chapters. Although the thematic and geographic scope of the collected studies is very broad, a single volume is not able to cover every aspect that may be related to the subject of militarisation. For example, issues surrounding the gendered experience of militarisation brought into focus by Susanne Brather-Walter's Chapter 16 prove to be highly informative to the overall picture of militarised societies. Thus, the present volume provides solid groundwork with many questions open for future investigations.

Notes

1 A. D. Lee, 'The army', in A. Cameron and P. Garnsey (eds), *The Cambridge ancient history*, vol. 13. *The late empire AD 337–425* (Cambridge: Cambridge University Press, 1998), pp. 211–37, here pp. 222–4. Questions related to the complexity of barbarian legal status are discussed by R. W. Mathisen, '*Peregrini, barbari*, and *cives Romani*. Concepts of citizenship and the legal identity of barbarians in the later Roman Empire', *American Historical Review*, 111 (2006), 1011–40.

2 Ammianus Marcellinus, *Historia Romana* XV,12, XV,3; see S. Esders, 'Nordwestgallien um 500. Von der militarisierten spätrömischen Provinzgesellschaft zur erweiterten Militäradministration des merowingischen Königtums', in M. Meier and S. Patzold (eds), *Chlodwigs Welt. Organisation von Herrschaft um 500*, Roma aeterna, 3 (Stuttgart: Steiner, 2014), pp. 339–61, pp. 341–3.

3 B. Campbell, 'The marriage of soldiers under the empire', *The Journal of Roman Studies*, 68 (1978), 153–66; S. E. Phang, *The marriage of Roman soldiers (13 BC–AD 235). Law and family in the Imperial Army*, Columbia Studies in the Classical Tradition, 24 (Leiden: Brill, 2001).

4 R. Pirling and M. Siepen, *Die Funde aus den römischen Gräbern von Krefeld-Gellep*, Germanische Denkmäler der Völkerwanderungszeit, 20 (Stuttgart: Franz Steiner, 2006), with further references.

5 P. J. Geary, *Before France and Germany. The creation and transformation of the Merovingian world* (New York: Oxford University Press, 1988), pp. 77–116.

6 A. Demandt, 'Der spätrömische Militäradel', *Chiron*, 10 (1980), 606–36.

7 A. Schwarcz, 'Senatorische Heerführer im Westgotenreich im 5. Jahrhundert', in F. Vallet and M. Kazanski (eds), *La noblesse romaine et les chefs barbares du IIIe au VIIe siècles* (Saint-Germain-en-Laye: Association française d'archéologie mérovingienne, 1995), pp. 49–54.

8 Marculf, Formula I, 18. See B. S. Bachrach, *Early Carolingian warfare. Prelude to empire* (Philadelphia: University of Pennsylvania Press, 2001), pp. 68–71; D. Gaspar, 'The concept "in numeros referri" in the Roman Army', *Acta archaeologica Academiae Scientiarum Hungaricae* 21 (1974), 113–16.

9 B. S. Bachrach, *Merovingian military organization, 481–751* (Minneapolis: University of Minnesota Press, 1972), pp. 42–73; Bachrach, *Early Carolingian warfare*, pp. 51–68. See also L. Sarti, 'The military and its role in Merovingian society' in B. Effors and I. Moreira (eds), *Oxford handbook of the Merovingian world* (Oxford: Oxford University Press, 2020), pp. 255–77.

10 Procopius, *Wars* 5, 12, 9; B. S. Bachrach, 'Military lands in historical perspective', *Haskins Society Journal*, 9 (1997), 95–122. See also T. B. Anderson, 'Roman military colonies in Gaul, Salian ethnogenesis and the forgotten meaning of Pactus Legis Salicae 59.5', *Early Medieval Europe*, 4 (1995), pp. 129–44.

11 S. Esders, 'Late Roman military law in the Bavarian code', *clio@themis. Revue électronique d'histoire du droit* 10 (2016) (La forge du droit. Naissance des identités juridiques en Europe, IVe–XIIIe siècles): www.cliothemis.com/IMG/pdf/3-_Esders-2.pdf (accessed 28 September 2019).

12 Bachrach, *Early Carolingian warfare*, p. 29; L. Sarti, *Perceiving war and the military in early Christian Gaul (ca. 400–700 A.D.)*, Early Middle Ages Series, 22 (Leiden/Boston: Brill, 2013), p. 26. See also M. Innes, *State and society in the early Middle Ages. The middle Rhine Valley, 400–1000* (Cambridge: Cambridge University Press, 2008), pp. 153–6.

13 Sarti, *Perceiving war*, pp. 13–45, 249–88, and 315–57; Sarti 'Die spätantike Militärpräsenz und die Entstehung einer militarisierten 'Grenzgesellschaft' in der nordwesteuropäischen *limes*-Region' in C. Rass (ed.), *Militärische Migration vom*

14 See L. Bothe, S. Esders and H. Nijdam (eds), *Wergild, compensation and penance. The monetary logic of early medieval conflict resolution* (Leiden: Brill, 2021, forthcoming).
15 Bachrach, *Early Carolingian warfare*.
16 W. Pohl, *The Avars. A steppe empire in central Europe, 567–822* (Ithaca: Cornell University Press, 2018), pp. 376–89.
17 S. Esders, '"Öffentliche" Abgaben und Leistungen im Übergang von der Spätantike zum Frühmittelalter. Konzeptionen und Befunde', in T. Kölzer and R. Schieffer (eds), *Von der Spätantike zum frühen Mittelalter. Kontinuitäten und Brüche, Konzeptionen und Befunde* (Ostfildern: Thorbecke, 2009), pp. 189–244, at pp. 227–33 (also on Merovingian models for this); W. Goffart, 'Defensio Patriae as a Carolingian military obligation', *Francia*, 43 (2016), 21–40. The size of Carolingian armies is a matter of dispute. For a maximum view, see B. S. Bachrach and C. R. Bowlus, 'Heerwesen', *RGA*, 14 (1999), 120–36; much more pessimistic is T. Reuter, 'Plunder and tribute in the Carolingian empire', *Transactions of the Royal Historical Society* 5th ser., 35 (1985), 75–94; T. Reuter, 'The end of Carolingian Military expansion', in P. Godman and R. Collins (eds), *Charlemagne's heir. New perspectives on the reign of Louis the Pious (814–840)* (Oxford: Oxford University Press, 1990), pp. 391–405.
18 N. J. Higham, *Rome, Britain and the Anglo-Saxons* (London: Routledge, 1992), p. 18.
19 For a more optimistic view on Romanisation in Britain, see R. White, 'Fortress, forts, and the impact of the Roman army in the West Midlands', in R. White and M. Hodder (eds), *Clash of cultures? The Romano-British period in the West Midlands* (Oxford: Oxbow, 2018), pp. 15–32.
20 A. Sargent, 'The north-south divide revisited. Thoughts on the character of Roman Britain', *Britannia*, 33 (2002), 219–26.
21 Higham, *Rome*, p. 17.
22 See B. Ward-Perkins, 'Why did the Anglo-Saxons not become more British?', *The English Historical Review*, 115 (2000), 513–33, here 528. M. Fafinski, *Via Britannica. The Roman infrastructural past in Late Roman and early medieval Britain* (Amsterdam: Amsterdam University Press, forthcoming).
23 K. R. Dark, 'A sub-Roman re-defence of Hadrian's wall?', *Britannia*, 23 (1992), 111–20.
24 Gildas, *The ruin of Britain, and other works*, ed. M. Winterbottom (London: Dodo Press, 1978); J. Campbell (ed.), *The Anglo-Saxons* (London: Penguin, 1991), p. 23.
25 *HE* I,15. *Historia ecclesiastica gentis Anglorum*, eds. B. Colgrave and R. A. B. Mynors (Oxford: Clarendon Press, 1969).
26 For particularly thought-provoking re-assessments of the Anglo-Saxon migrations, see G. Halsall, *Worlds of Arthur. Facts and fictions of the Dark Ages* (Oxford: Oxford University Press, 2013); S. Oosthuizen, *The emergence of the English* (York: ARC Humanities Press, 2019).

27 B. Yorke, *Kings and kingdoms of early Anglo-Saxon England* (London: Routledge, 1990), pp. 9–10 and 15–16.
28 The former view was favoured in the late nineteenth to early twentieth-century, and developed by Sir Frank Stenton. F. M. Stenton, *Anglo-Saxon England* (Oxford: Oxford University Press, 1971), pp. 290–1. Aristocratic forces were favoured by H. Munro Chadwick and Eric John in 1907 and 1960 respectively. See G. Williams, 'Military institutions and royal power', in M. P. Brown and C. A. Farr (eds), *Mercia. An Anglo-Saxon kingdom in Europe* (Leicester: Leicester University Press, 2001), pp. 295–309, at p. 296.
29 See Ryan Lavelle's Chapter 5 in this volume. R. Abels, *Alfred the Great. War, kingship and culture in Anglo-Saxon England* (London: Routledge, 1998), pp. 195–8.
30 Ine § 51, in F. Liebermann, *Die Gesetze der Angelsachsen* (Berlin: Halle a.S.: Max Niemeyer, 1903).
31 This was firmly Stenton's view. Stenton, *Anglo-Saxon England*, p. 290.
32 R. Abels, *Lordship and military obligation in Anglo-Saxon England* (Berkeley: University of California Press, 1988).
33 For helpful historiographic overviews, see Williams, 'Military institutions and royal power'; R. Lavelle, *Alfred's wars. Sources and interpretation of Anglo-Saxon warfare in the Viking Age* (Woodbridge: Boydell and Brewer, 2010), pp. 47–110.
34 N. P. Brooks, 'The development of military obligations in eighth- and ninth-century England', in P. Clemoes and K. Hughes (eds), *England before the conquest. Studies in primary sources presented to Dorothy Whitelock* (Cambridge: Cambridge University Press, 1971), pp. 69–84; G. Williams, 'Military obligations and Mercian supremacy in the eighth century', in D. Hill and M. Worthington (eds), *Æthelbald and Offa. Two eighth–century kings of Mercia* (Oxford: BAR British Series 383, 2005), pp. 103–10.
35 This conclusion is based on the evidence from the Berkshire entry in the Domesday Book. C. W. Hollister, 'The five-hide unit and the Old English military obligation', *Speculum*, 36 (1961), 61–74. (62). See also Lavelle, *Alfred's wars*, pp. 55–106.
36 Williams, 'Military institutions and royal power', pp. 300–9.
37 V. I. Evison, *The Buckland Anglo-Saxon cemetery. English Heritage* (London: Historic Buildings and Monuments Commission for England. Archaeological Report No. 3, 1987); K. Parfitt and T. Anderson, *Buckland Anglo-Saxon cemetery, Dover. Excavations 1994* (Ashford: Canterbury Archaeological Trust, 2012). The historiography of the Sutton Hoo ship-burial is vast. A few works are as follows; T. D. Kendrick, E. Kitzinger, and D. Allen, 'The Sutton Hoo finds', *The British Museum Quarterly*, 13 (1939), ii and 111–136; F. P. Magoun Jr., 'The Sutton Hoo ship-burial. A chronological bibliography', *Speculum*, 29 (1954), 116–24; J. B. Bessinger Jr., 'The Sutton Hoo ship-burial. A chronological bibliography, part two', *Speculum*, 33 (1958), 515–22; M. Biddle, A. Binns, J. M. Cameron, D. M. Metcalf, R. I. Page, C. Sparrow and F. L. Warren, 'Sutton Hoo published. A review', *Anglo-Saxon England*, 6 (1977), 249–65; J. Urbanus, 'The ongoing tale of Sutton Hoo', *Archaeology*, 67 (2014), 48–51.
38 H. Härke, '"Warrior graves"? The background of the Anglo-Saxon weapon burial rite', *Past and Present*, 126 (1990), 22–43, here 25.

39 Of particular note is E. John, *Orbis Britanniae and other studies* (Leicester: University of Leicester Press, 1966).
40 For example, Gregory, *Libri historiarum* IV,42, IV,44, V,26, VII,42, IX,29, X,3, ed. B. Krusch, *Gregorii Turonensis Opera. Libri historiarum X, MGH SRM*, 1,1 (Hanover; Hahnsche Buchhandlung, 1937).
41 *Paul the Deacon. History of the Lombards*, trans. W. D. Foulke and E. Peters (Philadelphia: University of Pennsylvania Press, 1974).
42 *The Lombard laws*, trans. K. F. Drew, Sources of Medieval History (Philadelphia: University of Pennsylvania Press, 1973).
43 See Berndt's Chapter in 4 this volume.
44 See M. Zerjadtke, *Das Amt 'Dux' in Spätantike und frühem Mittelalter. Der 'ducatus' im Spannungsfeld zwischen römischem Einfluss und eigener Entwicklung*, RGA Ergänzungsbände, 110 (Berlin: De Gruyter, 2018), pp. 167–211.
45 J. Jarnut, 'Beobachtungen zu den langobardischen *arimanni* und *exercitales*', *Zeitschrift der Savigny-Stiftung für Rechtsgeschichte, Germanistische Abteilung*, 38 (1971), pp. 1–28.
46 W. Pohl, '*Per hospites divisi*. Wirtschaftliche Grundlagen der langobardischen Ansiedlung in Italien', *Römische Historische Mitteilungen*, 43 (2001), 179–226.
47 A. Guillou, 'Des collectivités rurales à la collectivité urbaine en Italie méridionale byzantine (VIe–XIe siècle)', *Bulletin de correspondance hellénique*, 100 (1976), 315–25.
48 S. Gasparri, 'Strutture militari e legami di dipendenza in Italia in età longobardo e carolingia', *Rivista Storica Italiana*, 98 (1986), 664–726, at 705–7.
49 Esders, '"Öffentliche" Abgaben und Leistungen', pp. 213–14.
50 P. S. Leicht, 'König Aistulfs Heeresgesetze', in *Miscellanea Academica Berolinensia. Gesammelte Abhandlungen zur Feier des 250jährigen Bestehens der Deutschen Akademie der Wissenschaften zu Berlin*, Vol. II/1 (Berlin: Akademie-Verlag, 1950), pp. 97–102.
51 S. Esders, 'Die *Capitula de expeditione Corsicana* Lothars I. vom Februar 825. Überlieferung, historischer Kontext, Textrekonstruktion und Zielsetzung', *Quellen und Forschungen aus italienischen Archiven und Bibliotheken*, 98 (2018), 91–144, at 118–40.
52 See related contributions in *I Longobardi dei ducati di Spoleto e Benevento* (Atti del XVI Congresso Internazionale di Studi sull'Alto Medioevo), 2 vols (Spoleto: CISAM, 2003).
53 C. Heath, *The narrative worlds of Paul the Deacon. Between empires and identities in Lombard Italy* (Amsterdam: Amsterdam University Press, 2017).
54 See Bachrach, 'Military lands in historical perspective', with further references.
55 R. W. Mathisen, '*Provinciales, gentiles*, and marriages between Romans and barbarians in the late Roman Empire', *Journal of Roman Studies* 99 (2009), 140–55.
56 Esders, 'Nordwestgallien um 500', pp. 343–4.
57 For example, W. Baetke, *Die Aufnahme des Christentums durch die Germanen. Ein Beitrag zur Frage der Germanisierung des Christentums* (Darmstadt: Wissenschaftliche Buchgesellschaft, 1962); J. Ropert, 'Mentalité religieuse et regression

culterelle dans la Gaule franque au Ve–VIIIe siècle', *Les Cahiers de Tunésie*, 24 (1976), 45–68, here 49–50; J. C. Russell, *The Germanization of early medieval Christianity. A sociohistorical approach to religious transformation* (New York: Oxford University Press, 1995); J. Arce, 'Dress control in late Antiquity. Codex Theodosianus 14.10.1–4', in A. Köb and P. Riedel (eds), *Kleidung und Repräsentation in Antike und Mittelalter*, MittelalterStudien, 7 (Munich: Fink, 2005), pp. 33–44. See also R. Le Jan, 'Austrasien – Versuch einer Begriffsdefinition', in A. Wieczorek, P. Périn, K. von Welck and W. Menghin (eds), *Die Franken, Wegbereiter Europas. 5. bis 8. Jahrhundert n. Chr.*, 2nd edn (Berlin: Philipp von Zabern, 1997), pp. 222–6, here p. 222, referring to the Germanisation of names in Austria; M. Heinzelmann: 'Wandlungen des Heiligentypus in der Merowingerzeit? Eine Stellungnahme', in D. Hägermann, W. Haubrichs and J. Jarnut (eds), *Akkulturation. Probleme einer germanisch-romanischen Kultursynthese in Spätantike und frühem Mittelalter*, RGA Ergänzungsbände, 41 (Berlin: De Gruyter, 2004), pp. 335–9, here p. 338, referring to the 'Germanisation' of the seventh-century saints, according to earlier research.

58 J. Werner, 'Zur Entstehung der Reihengräberzivilisation. Ein Beitrag zur Methode der frühgeschichtlichen Archäologie', *Archaeologia Geographica*, 1 (1950), 23–32.

59 H. W. Böhme, *Germanische Grabfunde des 4. bis 5. Jahrhunderts zwischen unterer Elbe und Loire. Studien zur Chronologie und Bevölkerungsgeschichte*, Münchner Beiträge zur Vor- und Frühgeschichte, 19 (Munich: C. H. Beck, 1974).

60 E. Salin, *La civilisation merovingienne d'après les sépultures, les textes et le laboratoire*. Vol. 1: *Les Idées et les faits* (Paris: Editions Picard, 1949), pp. 213–16; Werner, 'Reihengräberzivilisation', 23–32; V. Bierbrauer, 'Romanen im fränkischen Siedelgebiet' in Wieczorek et al. (eds), *Die Franken*, pp. 110–20.

61 L. Buchet, in 'Die Landnahme der Franken in Gallien aus der Sicht der Anthropologen', in Wieczorek et al. (eds), *Die Franken*, vol. 2, pp. 662–7, here p. 666, already pointed out that the people mentioned in the sources should rather be understood as military or political groups than ethnicities. B. Effros, *Merovingian mortuary archaeology and the making of the early Middle Ages*, The Transformation of the Classical Heritage, 35 (Berkeley: University of California Press, 2003), pp. 106–8 also stresses that making ethnic distinctions from an archaeological point of view is most problematic.

62 H. Steuer, 'Kriegerbanden und Heerkönige. Krieg als Auslöser der Entwicklung zum Stamm und Staat im ersten Jahrtausend n. Chr. in Mitteleuropa. Überlegungen zu einem theoretischen Modell', in W. Heizmann, J. Hoops, H. Beck and K. Düwel (eds), *Runica, Germanica, Mediaevalia. Gewidmet Klaus Düwel*, RGA Ergänzungsbände, 37 (Berlin: De Gruyter, 2003), pp. 824–53. See also W. Pohl, 'Perceptions of barbarian violence', in H. A. Drake (ed.), *Violence in late Antiquity. Perceptions and practices* (Aldershot: Routledge, 2007), pp. 15–26.

63 G. Halsall, 'The origin of the Reihengräberzivilisation. Forty years on' in J. Drinkwater and H. Elton (eds), *Fifth-century Gaul. A crisis of identity?* (Cambridge: Cambridge University Press, 1992), pp. 196–207; F. Theuws and M. Alkemade, 'A kind of mirror for men. Sword depositions in late antique

northern Gaul' in F. Theuws und J. L. Nelson (eds), *Rituals of power. From late Antiquity to the early Middle Ages*, Transformation of the Roman World, 8 (Leiden: Brill, 2000), pp. 401–76.

64 B. Effros, *Caring for body and soul. Burial and the afterlife in the merovingian world* (Pennsylvania: Pennsylvania State University Press, 2002), in particular pp. 41–2; I. Barbiera, 'Remembering the warriors. Weapon burials and tombstones between Antiquity and the early Middle Ages in northern Italy', in W. Pohl and G. Heydemann (eds), *Post-Roman transitions. Christian and barbarian identities in the early medieval west* (Turnhout: Brepols, 2013), pp. 407–36.

65 The same can be said for the Slavs, see F. Curta, *The making of the Slavs. History and archaeology of the lower Danube Region, ca. 500–700* (Cambridge: Cambridge University Press, 2002).

66 See Theuws, 'Grave Goods', p. 309, using the terms of 'Germanisation' and 'militarisation' synonymously.

67 See I. N. Wood, 'Report. The European Science Foundation's programme on the Transformation of the Roman World and emergence of early medieval Europe', *Early Medieval Europe*, 6:2 (1997), 217–27.

68 P. H. Wilson, 'Defining military culture', *The Journal of Military History*, 72:1 (2007), 11–41, in particular 40–1.

69 E. James, 'The militarisation of Roman society, 400–700' in A. N. Jørgensen and B. L. Clausen (eds), *Military aspects of Scandinavian society in a European perspective AD 1–1300* (Copenhagen: Publications from the National Museum, 1997), pp. 19–24, here p. 19.

70 Militarisation thus can apply to people with a military function or status as well as to procedures involving weapons or warlike symbolism.

71 See in particular the thesis of medieval society being the result of an amalgamation of Roman, Christian and barbarian elements still inherent, i.e. in M. Perry, M. Chase, J. Jacob, M. Jacob, J. W. Daly, J. R. Jacob, M.C. Jacob and T. H. von Laue (eds), *Western civilization. Ideas, politics, and society*. Vol. 1: *To 1789*, 11th edn (Boston: Cengage Learning, 2015), p. 197.

72 See, e.g., F. Prinz, *Klerus und Krieg im früheren Mittelalter. Untersuchungen zur Rolle der Kirche beim Aufbau der Königsherrschaft*, Monographien zur Geschichte des Mittelalters, 2 (Stuttgart: Hiersemann, 1971); C. J. Holdsworth, '"An airier aristocracy". The saints at war', in R. R. Davies, J. Martindale, S. Gunn, J. C. Heim, P. J. Marshall, J. Gillingham, P. Cross and D. Crouch (eds), *Transactions of the Royal Historical Society. Sixth series* (Cambridge: Cambridge University Press, 1996), pp. 103–22; T. Scharff, *Die Kämpfe der Herrscher und der Heiligen. Krieg und historische Erinnerung in der Karolingerzeit*, Symbolische Kommunikation in der Vormoderne (Habil. Univ. Münster 2000, Darmstadt: Wissenschaftliche Buchgesellschaft 2002); D. S. Bachrach, *Religion and the conduct of war c. 300–1215*, Warfare in History (Woodbridge: Boydell Press, 2003). For an alternative perspective, see W. Goffart, 'Conspicuous by absence. Heroism in the early Frankish era (6th-7th cent.)', in T. Pàroli (ed.), *La funzione dell'eroe germanico. Storicità, metafora, paradigma*, Philologia: Saggi – richerche – edizioni 2 (Rome: Calamo, 1995), pp. 41–56.

73 Bachrach, *Merovingian military organization*; Bachrach, *Early Carolingian Warfare*.
74 For example, G. Tabacco, *I liberi del re nell'Italia carolingia e postcarolingia* (Spoleto: Fondazione CISAM, 1966); O. Bertolini, 'Ordinamenti militari e strutture sociali dei Longobardi in Italia', in *Ordinamenti militari in Occidente nell'alto medioevo*, Settimane di studio del Centro italiano di studi sull'alto medioevo 15 (Spoleto: Centro italiano di studi sull'alto Medioevo, 1968), pp. 429–608; Jarnut, 'Beobachtungen zu den langobardischen arimanni und exercitales'; S. Gasparri, 'La questione degli arimanni', *Bullettino dell'Istituto Storico Italiano per il Medioevo*, 87 (1978), 121–53; Gasparri, 'Strutture militari'.
75 Lavelle, *Alfred's wars*. Further important studies include, e.g., M. Powicke, *Military obligation in medieval England. A study in liberty and duty* (Oxford: Clarendon Press, 1962); C. W. Hollister, 'Military obligation in late Saxon and Norman England', in *Ordinamenti militari in Occidente nell'alto medioevo*, Settimane di studio del Centro italiano di studi sull'alto medioevo 15 (Spoleto: Centro italiano di studi sull'alto Medioevo, 1968), pp. 169–86; Abels, *Lordship and military obligation*; N. Brooks, 'The development of military obligations in eighth- and ninth-century England', in A. E. Pelteret David (ed.), *Anglo-Saxon history. Basic readings* (New York: Garland Publishing, 2000), pp. 83–105; R. Abels, 'Alfred the Great, the micel hæðen here and the Viking Threat', in T. Reuter (ed.), *Alfred the Great. Papers from the eleventh-centenary conference*, Studies in Early Medieval Britain (Aldershot: Routledge, 2003), pp. 265–79; G. Williams, 'Military obligations'; I. N. Wood, 'Land tenure and military obligations in the Anglo-Saxon and Merovingian kingdoms. The evidence of Bede and Boniface in context', *Bulletin of International Medieval Research*, 9–10 (2005), 3–22; R. Abels, 'Household men, mercenaries and Vikings in Anglo-Saxon England', in J. France (ed.), *Mercenaries and paid men. The mercenary identity in the Middle Ages*, History of Warfare, 47 (Leiden: Brill, 2008), pp. 143–65; S. Bassett, 'Divide and rule? The military infrastructure of eighth- and ninth-century Mercia', *Early Medieval Europe*, 15:1 (2007), 53–85.
76 G. Halsall, *Warfare and society in the barbarian west, 450–900*, Warfare and History (London: Routledge, 2003). Comparable approaches may be found, e.g. in I. Steffelbauer, 'Barbaren und Könige. Krieg und Gesellschaft im nachrömischen Westen', in C. Kaindel and A. Obenaus (eds), *Krieg im mittelalterlichen Abendland*, Krieg und Gesellschaft (Vienna: Mandelbaum, 2010), pp. 11–38; Sarti, *Perceiving war*; Sarti. 'The military and its role'. Referring to the early medieval military more generally, see, e.g., T. Reuter, 'The recruitment of armies in the early Middle Ages. What can we know?', in A. N. Jørgensen and B. L. Clausen (eds), *Military aspects of Scandinavian society in a European perspective AD 1–1300* (Copenhagen: National Museum, 1997), pp. 32–7; B. S. Bachrach: *Charlemagne's early campaigns (768–777). A diplomatic and military analysis*, History of Warfare, 82 (Leiden: Brill, 2013); L. I. R. Petersen, *Siege warfare and military organization in the successor states (400–800 AD). Byzantium, the west and Islam* (Leiden: Brill, 2013). Not restricted to the early Middle

Ages, e.g., P. Contamine, *Histoire militaire de la France. Des origines à 1715*, Histoire militaire de la France, 1 (Paris: Presses Universitaires de France, 1992); H. J. Nicholson, *Medieval warfare. Theory and practice of war in Europe, 300–1500* (New York: Palgrave Macmillan, 2004); M. Prietzel, *Krieg im Mittelalter* (Darmstadt: Wissenschaftliche Buchgesellschaft, 2006); H.-H. Kortüm, *Kriege und Krieger, 500–1500* (Stuttgart: Kohlhammer, 2010); D. S. Bachrach and B. S. Bachrach: *Warfare in medieval Europe, c. 400–c. 1453* (London: Routledge, 2017)

77 See, e.g., A. Veit, 'Warlord. Nutzen und Mängel einer negativen Kategorie', in T. Jäger and R. Beckmann (eds), *Handbuch Kriegstheorien* (Wiesbaden: Verlag für Sozialwissenschaften, 2011), pp. 487–97.

78 For example, Demandt, 'Der spätrömische Militäradel'; A. Cowell, *The medieval warrior aristocracy. Gifts, violence, performance, and the sacred* (Suffolk: Boydell & Brewer, 2007); L. Sarti, 'Eine Militärelite im merowingischen Gallien? Versuch einer Eingrenzung, Zuordnung und Definition', *Mitteilungen des Instituts für Österreichische Geschichtsforschung*, 124:2 (2016), 271–95.

79 For example, G. Halsall (ed.), *Violence and society in the early Medieval West* (Woodbridge: The Boydell Press, 1998); B. D. Shaw, 'War and violence', in G. W. Bowersock, P. Brown and O. Graba (ed.), *Late Antiquity. A guide to the post-classical world* (Cambridge: Harvard University Press, 1999), pp. 130–69; R. W. Kaeuper, *Violence in medieval society* (Woodbridge, Suffolk: Boydell Press, 2000); H. A. Drake (ed.), *Violence in late Antiquity. Perceptions and practices* (Aldershot: Ashgate, 2007); L. J. Swift, 'Early Christian views on violence, war, and peace', in K. A. Raaflaub (ed.), *War and peace in the ancient world* (Malden: Blackwell, 2007), pp. 279–96; W. C. Brown, *Violence in medieval Europe* (Harlow: Longman, 2010); P. Allen and N. Bronwen, *Crisis management in late Antiquity (410–590 CE). A survey of the evidence from episcopal letters*, Suppl. Vigiliae Christianae (Leiden: Brill, 2013); H.-H. Kortüm, 'Militärische Gewaltkultur. Eine Problemskizze', in M. Becher, S. Airlie, B. Segelken and T. Urbach (eds), *Kaiser und Kalifen. Karl der Große und die Mächte am Mittelmeer um 800* (Darmstadt: Zabern Philipp, 2014), pp. 130–43.

80 See D. Whittaker, 'Landlords and warlords in the later Roman Empire', in J. Rich and G. Shipley (eds), *War and society in the Roman world* (London: Routledge, 1993), pp. 277–302; P. van Ossel, 'L'insécurité et militarisation en Gaul du nord au bas-empire. L'exemple des campagnes', *Revue du Nord*, 77 (1995), 27–36; R. Brulet, 'La militarisation de la Gaule du Nord au bas-empire et des petites agglomérations urbaines de Farmars et de Bavay', *Revue du Nord*, 77 (1995), 55–70; James, 'Militarisation of Roman Society'; J.-C. Routier and F. Thuillier, 'Les témoins d'occupation germanique de la villa gallo-romaine de Zouafques (France) et leur apport dans le contexte de la militarisation de la Gaule du nord au bas-empire', in F. Vermeulen and H. Thoen (eds), *Archaeology in confrontation. Aspects of Roman military presence in the northwest* (Gent: Academic Press, 2004), pp. 371–92; G. Halsall, 'Die Militarisierung Nordgalliens. Föderaten und 'Föderatengräber', in S. Burmeister (ed.), *2000 Jahre Varusschlacht. Imperium*,

Konflikt, Mythos (Stuttgart: Theiss, 2009), pp. 270–7; Esders, 'Nordwestgallien um 500', pp. 339–61; Sarti, 'Die spätantike Militärpräsenz'.

81 See J. Le Goff, 'Les mentalités. Une histoire ambiguë', in J. Le Goff and P. Nora (eds), *Faire de l'Histoire*, vol. 3 (Paris: Gallimard, 1974), pp. 76–94; F. Graus (ed.), *Mentalitäten im Mittelalter. Methodische und inhaltliche Probleme* (Sigmaringen: Thorbecke, 1987); R. Schneider, 'Mittelalterliche Mentalitäten als Forschungsproblem. Eine skizzierende Zusammenfassung' in F. Graus (ed.), *Mentalitäten im Mittelalter. Methodische und inhaltliche Probleme* (Sigmaringen: Thorbecke, 1987), pp. 319–32; H.-H. Kortüm, *Menschen und Mentalitäten. Einführung in die Vorstellungswelten des Mittelalters* (Berlin: De Gruyter, 1996); K. Neumann, *Das Fremde verstehen – Grundlagen einer kulturanthropologischen Exegese*, vol. 2 (Münster: Lit, 2000); C. Brinker-von-der-Heyde, 'Mentalität, historische Anthropologie und Literatur. Zu Möglichkeiten und Grenzen der Interdisziplinarität der Mediävistik', *Jahrbuch der Oswald von Wolkenstein Gesellschaft*, 12 (2000), 65–81; P. Dinzelbacher, *Religiosität und Mentalität des Mittelalters* (Klagenfurt: KITAB, 2003).

82 M. Bevir and H. E. Bödeker (eds), *Begriffsgeschichte, Diskursgeschichte, Metapherngeschichte* (Göttingen: Wallstein-Verlag, 2002); C. Dutt, *Herausforderungen der Begriffsgeschichte* (Heidelberg: Winter, 2003); H. U. Gumbrecht, *Dimension und Grenzen der Begriffsgeschichte* (Paderborn: Fink, 2006); C. Dutt, 'Historische Semantik als Begriffsgeschichte. Theoretische Grundlagen und paradigmatische Anwendungsfelder' in J. Riecke (ed.), *Historische Semantik* (Berlin: De Gruyter, 2011), pp. 37–50; E. Müller and F. Schmieder, *Begriffsgeschichte und historische Semantik. Ein kritisches Kompendium*, Suhrkamp Taschenbuch Wissenschaft (Berlin: Suhrkamp, 2016).

83 H.-W. Goetz, '"Vorstellungsgeschichte". Menschliche Vorstellungen und Meinungen als Dimension der Vergangenheit. Bemerkungen zu einem jüngeren Arbeitsfeld der Geschichtswissenschaft als Beitrag zu einer Methodik der Quellenauswertung', *Archiv für Kulturgeschichte*, 61 (1979), 253–71.

84 Härke, 'Warrior graves?'; Härke, *Angelsächsische Waffengräber des 5. bis 7. Jahrhunderts*, Zeitschrift für Archäologie des Mittelalters, Beiheft 6 (Bonn: Rheinland-Verlag, 1992).

85 D. M. Hadley and J. M. Moore, 'Death makes the man? Burial rite and the construction of masculinities in the early Middle Ages', in J. C. Jeffrey and B. Wheeler (eds), *Masculinity in medieval Europe* (London: Taylor & Francis, 1998), pp. 21–38, at p. 31. Compare H. W. Böhme; *Germanische Grabfunde des 4. bis 5. Jahrhunderts zwischen unterer Elbe und Loire. Studien zur Chronologie und Bevölkerungsgeschichte*, Münchner Beiträge zur Vor- un Frühgeschichte, 19 (Munich: Beck, 1974) arguing that '[d]ie Waffenbeigabensitte im spätrömischen Gallien [...] scheint vielmehr von neu angekommenen Germanen ausgebildet worden zu sein, die erstmals in direkte Berührung mit der römischen Welt kamen und sich ihres Kriegertums und ihres sozialen Status innerhalb des spätantiken Staates bewußt wurden' (p. 165).

86 For example, *bellator* referring to the Trojans as Frankish ancestors in 'Liber Historiae Francorum', c. 1, ed. B. Krusch, *Fredegarii et aliorum Chronica*.

Vitae Sanctorum, MGH SRM, 2 (Hanover: Hahnsche Buchhandlung, 1888), pp. 215–328; referring to Charles Martel in *Continuationes*, c. 14 and 20, ed. Krusch, *Fredegarii et aliorum Chronica*; *belliger* only used in reference to the Frankish kings, Venantius, *Carmen* 9.1, l. 102 and 9.5, l. 5, ed. F. Leo, *Venanti Honori Clementiani Fortunati presbyteri italici. Opera poetica, MGH AA*, 4,1 (Berlin: Weidmannsche Buchhandlung, 1881); *Continuationes* c. 13 and 20; *proeliator* referring to the warriors in near vicinity of Clovis at Gregory, *Libri historiarum* 2,27; *pugnator* used to refer to the ancient Macedonians in *Chronicarum quae dictuntur Fredegarii* 2,4, in ed. Krusch, *Fredegarii et aliorum Chronica*; referring to King Clovis, Gregory, *Libri historiarum* 2,12; *Liber Historiae Francorum*, c. 7, and *Chronicarum quae dictuntur Fredegarii* 3,12; referring to Clovis' retinue *Liber Historiae Francorum* c. 10; the officials at the court of Sigibert III, *Chronicarum quae dictuntur Fredegarii* 4,87; and high-ranking weapon bearers in *Chronicarum quae dictuntur Fredegarii* 4,55.

87 For example, *HE* II,2, II,9, IV,22, V,10, V,19.
88 Gregory, *Libri historiarum* V,58; Gregory, *Liber vitae patrum* IV,3, VII,4 ed. B. Krusch and W. Arndt, *Gregorii Turonensis opera. Miracula et opera minora, MGH SRM* 1,2 (Hanover: Hahnsche Buchhandlung, 1969); Gregory, *De passione et virtutibus sancti Martini episcopi* I.21, eds Krusch and Arndt, *Gregorii Turonensis*; Venantius Fortunatus, *Vita sancti Albini* c. 12, ed. Krusch, *Venanti Honori Clementiani Fortunati presbyteri italici. Opera pedestria, MGH AA* 4,2 (Berlin: Weidmannsche Buchhandlung, 1885); Fortunatus, *Vita sancti Germani* c. 180–1, ed. Krusch, *Venanti Honori Clementiani Fortunati*; Jonas of Bobbio, *Vita sancti Columbani* I,19, I.20, ed. B. Krusch, *Ionae Vitae sanctorum Columbani, Vedastis, Iohannis* (Hanover: Hahnsche Buchhandlung, 1905), pp. 144–294; Dado of Rouen, *Vita Eligii episcopi Noviomagensis* II,15, ed. B. Krusch, *Passiones vitaeque sanctorum aevi Merovingici, MGH SS rer. Merov.*, 4, pp. 663–742. For a more elaborate discussion, see L. Sarti, 'Der fränkische *miles*. Weder Soldat noch Ritter', *Frühmittelalterliche Studien*, 52:1 (2018), 99–117.
89 G. Knappe, 'The rhetorical aspect of grammar teaching in Anglo-Saxon England', *Rhetorica. A Journal of the History of Rhetoric*, 17 (1999), 1–34, here 3.
90 On *leudes* and its meanings, see W. Haubrichs, '*Leudes, fara, faramanni* and *farones*. Zur Semantik der Bezeichnungen für einige am Konsenshandeln beteiligte Gruppen', in V. Epp and C. Meyer (eds), *Recht und Konsens im frühen Mittelalter*, Vorträge und Forschungen 82 (Ostfildern: Thorbecke, 2016), pp. 235–69, at pp. 236–47, who also points to the interesting fact that the term *leudes*, which most often refers to a collective of militarily relevant individuals, is often rendered in Latin by the institutional term *exercitus*. See also Sarti, 'Eine Militärelite', pp. 278–9.
91 See A. Gillett (ed.), *On barbarian identity. Critical approaches to ethnicity in the early Middle Ages*, Studies in the Early Middle Ages, 4 (Turnhout: Brepols, 2002); W. Pohl, *Die ethnische Wende des Frühmittelalters und ihre Auswirkungen auf Ostmitteleuropa* (Leipzig: Leipziger Universitätsverlag, 2008). On the importance of Christianity in the formation of new identities, a process that

always involves larger parts of a population, see Pohl and Heydemann (eds), *Post-Roman transitions*.

92 G. Elwert, 'Nationalismus und Ethnizität. Über die Bildung von Wir-Gruppen', *Kölner Zeitschrift für Soziologie und Sozialpsychologie*, 41 (1989), 440–64.

93 On the importance of the military recruitment of *pagenses* for the formation of ethnic identities within kingdoms and *regna*, see particularly K. F. Werner, 'Völker und *regna*', in C. Brühl and B. Schneidmüller (eds), *Beiträge zur mittelalterlichen reichs- und Nationsbildung in Deutschland und Frankreich* (Munich: Oldenbourg, 1997), pp. 15–43.

94 *Honor* referring to an official function, e.g. Fortunatus, *Carmen* VII,16, ll. 11, 17 and 35; *Chronicarum quae dictuntur Fredegarii* III,58; *Passio Praeiecti episcopi et martyris Arverni* c. 23, ed. Krusch, *Passiones vitaeque sanctorum aevi Merovingici*, MGH SRM, 5 (Hanover: Hahnsche Buchhandlung, 1910), pp. 225–48. Referring to glory and fame, e.g. *Epistulae Austrasiacae* 22 and 26, ed. W. Gundlach, *Epistolae Merowingici et Karolini aevi*, vol. 1, MGH EE, 3 (Berlin: Weidmannsche Buchhandlung, 1892), pp. 110–53; Fortunatus, *Carmen* VII,16, l. 46, VIII,21, ll. 13–14. For a more elaborate discussion, see L. Sarti, 'Militärische Wertvorstellungen und männliche Identität im merowingischen Gallien' in A. Fößel (ed.), *Gewalt, Krieg und Gender im Mittelalter* (Bern: Lang, 2020), pp. 29–45.

95 See also J. F. Niermeyer, 'De semantiek van *honor* en de oorsprong van het heerlijk gezag', in J. W. Wolters, D. Th. Enklaar and W. Jappe Alberts (eds), *Dancwerc opstellen aangeboden aan Prof. Dr. D. Th. Enklaar ter gelegenheid van zijn vijfenzestigste verjaardag* (Groningen: Wolters, 1959), pp. 56–63; P. W. A. Immink, '*Honor*, heerlijkheid en koningsgezag', Tijdschrift voor Geschiedenis, 74 (1961), 285–308.

96 On the legal sources, see G. Jerouschek, 'Busse, Strafe und Ehre im frühen Mittelalter. Ein Beitrag zu Entstehung und Begründung peinlichen Strafens', in P. Landau, H. Nehlsen and M. Schmoeckel (eds), *Karl von Amira zum Gedächtnis* (Frankfurt am Main: Lang, 1999), pp. 231–43. On embodied honour in *wergild* tariffs, see the contributions in Bothe, Nijdam and Esders (eds), *Wergild, compensation and penance*.

97 For example, Gregory, *Libri historiarum* II,42, V,25, V,39, VI,35, VII,38, VIII,29, XI,9; *Chronicarum quae dictuntur Fredegarii* IV,28, IV,38. On other punishments of a more dishonouring nature, see, e.g., J.-M. Moeglin. '*Harmiscara – harmschar – hachée*. Le dossier des rituels d'humiliation et de soumission au Moyen Âge', *Archivum latinitatis medii aevi*, 54 (1996), 11–65.

PART I

THE MILITARY AND SOCIETY

2

Soldier and civilian in the Byzantine Empire c. 600–c. 900: a militarised society?

Philip Rance

Scholars of the Byzantine Empire have long discerned evidence of overt and pervasive 'militarisation' from the mid-seventh century, broadly defined by the increasingly military character and practices of imperial governance and administration, the prominence of military status, roles and values in society and culture, and the subordination of economic resources and production to military priorities, largely in response to the existential threat posed by expansionist Islam. The evidence leaves plenty of room for definitional disputes and differing interpretations – and permits no easy solutions. Although few would conceive 'militarisation' as a binary contest between 'military' and 'civil' parties, the varying impact of this multifaceted process is most apparent in soldier–civilian interactions in several interconnected spheres. Older scholarship, primarily concerned with institutional structures, sought to establish how and when the authority of military personnel extended to civil, fiscal and judicial affairs. Debate focused especially on the origin, nature and development of territorialised military-fiscal jurisdictions, traditionally termed the *'theme* system', which scholarly consensus now views as one stage of a protracted evolution of Byzantine armed forces, regionalised power and provincial elites.[1] While Roman armies had for centuries chosen or endorsed emperors, a concurrent 'militarisation' of politics – or 'politicisation' of armies – is evident in sharply escalating military unrest – civil wars, usurpations and rebellions – after c. 650, and especially 695–726, as provincial armies competed to elevate their own imperial candidates. Easier to describe than to explain, their fluctuating alignments variously reflected factional interests, regional particularism and patronage networks.[2] From this era also, a more explicitly theorised Byzantine imperial ideology accorded soldiers a special 'constitutional' position within the body politic as guardians of dynastic legitimacy and defenders of the Christian empire.[3] 'Militarisation' of regional economies and environments is discernible in routine – sometimes ruthless – prioritisation of defence in the state's allocation of revenue, resources and labour, as well as the economic imprint of soldiers, both institutionally, as state-salaried consumer, market and employer, and individually, through landownership/-holding.[4] One could also include here military interventions in religious life, insofar as the emperor's longer-term role as guarantor of Orthodoxy drew soldiers into Church politics, interconfessional disputes and suppression of heterodoxy, in this period most notably during two episodes of state-sponsored Iconoclasm (730–87, 815–42).[5] Beyond identifying soldiers' functions within the broader dimensions of the state apparatus, less easily distinguishable aspects of this complex picture relate to 'military sociology': how the backgrounds, status, presence and behaviour of soldiers, on and off duty, affected the socio-economic patterns, cultural complexion and power relationships of urban and rural communities. In this short chapter, I attempt to adjust the focus of enquiry onto some less discussed microdynamics of 'militarisation', by considering the place of soldiers in the society, economy and culture of provincial towns and villages, where most soldiers resided, and how their localisation and rootedness in civilian life, through origin, kinship, property and lived experience, shaped social relationships between *c.* 600 and *c.* 900. These three centuries constitute a relatively 'dark' age, framed by the more brightly lit sixth and tenth centuries. By its nature the source material, often reflecting civilian perspectives and furnishing little direct testimony to soldiers' attitudes or self-perceptions, allows only general trends to be traced, while some basic questions remain unresolved. Although it will be necessary to draw comparative evidence from prior and subsequent documentation, the intention is to examine this period in its own terms, and not as an appendix to late Antiquity nor a preface to later developments.

Military organisation *c.* 600-*c.* 900

Prolonged warfare during the first half of the seventh century radically transformed Anatolia into the Byzantine empire's military, fiscal and demographic heartland. Intensive Byzantine–Persian conflict (602–28) led to unprecedented Persian conquests of Byzantine provinces in Mesopotamia, Syria, Palestine and Egypt, and devastating inroads into Anatolia. A corresponding collapse of fragile Byzantine control in the Balkans largely constrained imperial territory there to coastal strongholds. Although aggressive campaigning (622–28) by Heraclius (r. 610–41) momentarily restored Byzantine ascendancy in the Near East, the nascent onslaught of militant Islam upon the exhausted empire from the early 630s resumed the vast, rapid and now irreversible territorial losses. In *c.* 637–40, Byzantine forces again withdrew north of the Taurus and Anti-Taurus ranges. They left behind the relatively urbanised and heavily fortified frontier zone of Mesopotamia, Syria and Palestine, where Roman/Byzantine troops had ordinarily been based for six centuries. In Anatolia, in contrast, cities and towns were fewer and sparser, military infrastructure deficient and few troops were regularly stationed. The remnants of Byzantine field armies were billeted or cantoned across Asia Minor in a series of *ad hoc* or emergency measures that, over time, acquired permanence. Insofar as patterns of deployment can be discerned, units were allocated to districts selected primarily on the basis of logistical capacity.[6] In response to recurrent and penetrative Muslim invasions from the 640s, localised 'defence-in-depth' strategies reduced cities and towns of Anatolia to fortified centres, serving as control points, depots and refuges. From the 720s a more stable, attritional Byzantine–Muslim frontier culture emerged, characterised by endemic predatory and punitive raiding, until Byzantine forces gradually assumed an offensive stance from the 920s.[7] Against this backdrop of long-term urban shrinkage and civic impoverishment, the dispersal of armies throughout Asia Minor was one aspect of a broader 'provincialisation' or 'ruralisation' of Byzantine administration, society and culture that had important consequences for both soldiers and the dynamics of town and village life.[8] The empire's armed forces were now distributed in territorial commands, typically termed 'generalships' (*stratēgiai, stratēgides*), whose armies soon acquired regional identities, associations and perspectives, underpinned by localised recruitment and supply. In the early ninth century, as a consequence of poorly documented developments, military-fiscal divisions called *themata* first emerge, wherein military governors (*stratēgoi*) exercised enhanced competence in civil affairs through new fiscal-administrative structures and personnel. Recent studies have discarded the long-term and near-universal tendency of modern scholarship to retroject the concept and/or terminology of the *thema* into preceding centuries.[9]

The circumstances and consequences of this 'territorialisation' of armies remain obscure. During the military-fiscal crisis of mid-/late seventh century, it appears that the government, struggling to pay armies in coin owing to a greatly reduced tax-base, supplied, equipped and remunerated soldiers largely in kind through levies of produce, materials and labour, in effect regularising emergency measures.[10] Limited evidence from the mid-eighth to tenth centuries suggests that most soldiers of provincial or 'thematic' armies then belonged to a broad category of peasant freeholders, often labelled 'farmer-soldiers', though the terms *stratiōtēs*, 'soldier', and *strateia*, 'military service/obligation', gradually embraced a wider range of military-fiscal contexts. Soldiers seemingly met part or most of their basic military expenses, including arms, equipment and horses, from their own or family's resources, typically cultivatable land. In return, a soldier received service-related remuneration and legal privileges, while his household benefited, directly or indirectly, from fiscal exemptions. Soldiers' ownership or possession of land has elicited scholarly controversy, particularly regarding the origin, status and significance of 'military properties' (*stratiōtika ktēmata*) first attested in more abundant tenth-century documentation. If localised recruitment, from the 640s/650s, transformed a unit's character and ties to neighbouring civilian communities within a generation or two, individual soldiers, whether quartered in encampments, billeted on inhabitants or living in their own households, may have initially obtained land locally by diverse private means – purchase, gift, marriage, inheritance or appropriation.[11] Although untraceable in Anatolia, such processes are documented papyrologically in Byzantine-controlled Italy, where garrisons became embedded in provincial society and landholding from the late sixth to eighth centuries.[12] An alternative hypothesis that the state systematically apportioned imperial or appropriated estates to soldiers, around the mid-seventh century, as a means of maintaining armies, is not supported by nor consistent with the evidence. Legal and historical sources from the mid-eighth/early ninth centuries indicate that neither a *stratiōtēs* nor his *strateia* was bound to a property. It is not until mid-tenth-century legislation, which sought to protect 'military properties' against alienation by provincial magnates, that one can discern a conceptual extension of *strateia* from a personal obligation incumbent upon a *stratiōtēs* to a liability attached to the land that sustained him.[13]

While provincial soldiers continued to form by far the greater part of imperial forces, in c. 743/4 Constantine V (r. 741–75) instituted the *tagmata*, permanently constituted units based in Constantinople and its hinterland. Successive emperors augmented the number of *tagmata*, but their total manpower remained proportionally small. Originally intended as centrally controlled guard units and a political counterweight to provincial armies, *tagmata* quickly evolved into zealously loyal 'security forces' and an elite nucleus of imperial expeditions. The social backgrounds and motivations of those enlisting in *tagmata* were more diverse: they included sons of Constantinopolitan and provincial elites, alongside provincial/thematic soldiers and, later, non-Byzantine warriors, attracted to the capital by superior remuneration, conditions of service and opportunities for advancement. The relationship between *tagmata* and land is more obscure, though at least some tagmatic soldiers, when not on active service, lived on landholdings near Constantinople.[14]

In post-Roman Western Europe, pervasive blurring of the roles and identities of soldier and civilian becomes a defining characteristic of 'militarisation', evinced in non-soldiers bearing arms and/or imitating martial dress or behaviour. Corresponding developments in Byzantine territory are harder to discern. Law codes selectively reprise the Augustan *lex Iulia de vi publica* prohibiting private citizens from carrying weapons in public, though exceptional circumstances and legal ambivalence periodically militated enforcement of penalties.[15] Justinianic legislation prohibited private manufacture, transportation and sale of all but the most rudimentary weaponry. From the mid-seventh century, although production of arms and armour seemingly shifted from state-run manufactories to contracted provincial workshops, the state largely retained control over distribution, while expense also constrained illicit access.[16] Unremarkably, when attacked or besieged, a city's inhabitants, including sometimes women and children, actively participated in communal defence, both alongside soldiers and in their absence, a well-attested phenomenon throughout Antiquity. Outside such emergency expedients, however, evidence for standing urban or local 'militias' – itself a multivalent and value-laden term – is slight and ambiguous, but could point to partial institutionalising of self-defence in regions afflicted by longer-term insecurity.[17] Beyond specific urban contexts, isolated references (*c*. 708–9 and 811) to apparently *ad hoc* levies of poor 'rustics' are variously interpreted as peasant *militia*, light-armed irregulars or civilian labour.[18] Only in the early tenth century is there potential evidence for broader, state-sanctioned measures to promote military capabilities among civilians. In his *Taktika* (*c*. 905), Leo VI (r. 886–912) ordains that ideally all 'men not registered for military service (*astrateutoi*)', or at least one per household, obtain a bow and practise archery so as to be able to harass enemy raiders in their locality. Derivative military literature reproduces these regulations, but contemporary and subsequent historical sources offer no evidence of their implementation.[19] It will become clear below that the status of 'soldier' remained distinct from civilian in Byzantine law and administrative practice, not least because it determined eligibility for legal privileges and fiscal immunities.

Who was a 'soldier'? And why?

The basic institution of Byzantine rural society was the village (*chōrion*, *ktēsis*), which was both a community of freeholders – varying in status and wealth but sharing space, environment and identity – and a mostly self-regulating fiscal-administrative unit with communal tax liabilities.[20] Provincial soldiers generally exhibit a high degree of socio-cultural homogeneity and cohesion. Increasingly embedded in the Anatolian countryside, by the 670s/680s soldiers and their families became closely integrated into rural communities by kinship, personal associations, property and culture, and acquired emotional and generational attachments to localities.[21] As products of highly localised and familial recruitment, and commanded by local junior officers, it is assumed that soldiers, notwithstanding their comparative prosperity and professional vested interests, shared the opinions and beliefs of the provincial populace. With the decline of provincial cities and towns as political-administrative centres and the demise of late Roman urban elites, armies remained a setting for regular large-scale gatherings and thus became institutional foci for expressions of popular approbation or discontent, and self-conscious intermediaries between the provinces and Constantinople.[22] As protectors of their communities, soldiers could evoke emotive responses: worshippers at rural churches and shrines would encounter memorials to soldiers killed in combat, indicative of a commemorative sensibility that combined parochial origin with universal heroic status.[23]

Scholarship has generally inferred that the primary basis of military service was hereditary obligation, imposed on soldiers' sons or heirs, apparently (re)introduced before the early eighth century (see below). Voluntary enlistment and, to a lesser extent, foreign mercenaries were also sources of manpower, varying according to date and circumstance. There is no legal evidence for conscription, but the possibility of compulsion in raising 'volunteers' cannot be excluded. A 'military household' (*stratiōtikos oikos*) was one in which a male member was registered as a *stratiōtēs* in army muster-rolls and/or tax-registers.[24] Until the late ninth/tenth century, an ethos of personal and familial service seemingly persisted. Evidence from fifth-/sixth-century Egypt and seventh-/eighth-century Byzantine Italy indicates that, in some areas, military status, considered more a privilege than a burden, was monopolised by local 'military families'.[25] If age or disability prevented a registered *stratiōtēs* from serving in person, a son or other member of that household could take his place. In certain circumstances, custom allowed a soldier to commute the notional value of his *strateia* into a cash payment, with which the government could hire a replacement. The earliest evidence for this practice, mostly implicit, concerns late eighth-/ninth-century cases of selective commutation where personal *strateia* was impossible, such as juvenile sons of deceased soldiers.[26] By the later eighth century, a distinction emerges within provincial armies between a core of 'select' (*epilektoi*) soldiers, who served on a semi-permanent basis and participated in long-distance campaigns, and a 'territorial'-type force, which usually served seasonally and/or regionally. By the mid-tenth, all *stratiōtai* in a *thema*, by collective preference or government imposition, might pay rather than serve in person, particularly on overseas expeditions.[27] Legal sources accordingly distinguish the *stratiōtēs*, the registered 'soldier', from the *strateuomenos*, the 'man (actually) serving', mirroring a shift from personal *strateia* by the head of a 'military household', his son or kinsman towards substitution by an unconnected volunteer from the same or another *thema* or a foreign mercenary.[28] In these circumstances, 'soldiers' who did not serve personally are not easily distinguishable from civilians, except for their entitlement to certain fiscal-judicial privileges. From the 960s, as Byzantine strategic priorities shifted from regionalised defence to piecemeal reconquest, the state increasingly preferred to commute the *strateia* of seasonal thematic farmer-soldiers as a means of funding full-time 'professional' armies, comprising *tagmata*, 'select' thematic soldiers and foreign contingents, trained in sophisticated tactics and furnished with specialised weaponry. A generalised policy of fiscalising the military obligations of thematic *stratiōtai* gradually transformed their *strateia* into a purely fiscal liability, in effect a selective military tax, while thematic armies declined in significance and ultimately fade from the historical record around the mid-eleventh century.[29]

The legal status of a *stratiōtēs* entailed certain benefits with regard to his person, family and property.[30] Soldiers enjoyed long-standing judicial immunities and testamentary privileges unique to their profession.[31] Outside a cadre of full-time salaried personnel in each *thema*, part-time thematic soldiers received pay (*roga*) and rations (*sitēresia*, *sitēseis*) only for periods of active service. Fragmentary evidence and variable pay rates frustrate calculation of 'average earnings'.[32] By the mid-eighth century, thematic soldiers were, in principle, also responsible for procuring their weaponry, armour and mount, which were their own heritable property.[33] In contrast, *tagmata* received annual salaries and monthly rations and fodder, and were issued with clothing, equipment, arms and horses.[34] For both categories, material rewards of campaigning offered additional sources of income; a law codified in 741 enjoined equal distribution of booty between men and officers.[35] The fiscal advantages of being a soldier are most apparent with respect to his landed property, which he cultivated either in person, with or through his relatives, or as a rentier landlord via tenants and/or waged or unfree labour. As previously indicated, soldiers quartered in Anatolia from the 640s could have variously acquired private land as a natural consequence of their long-term integration into rural society, while the legal basis of *strateia* remained personal rather than tenurial until the mid-tenth century. Soldiers' landholdings were territorially, fiscally and familially interlinked with the properties of civilian neighbours. Like other rural inhabitants, soldiers paid the land-tax (*dēmosion telos*) and hearth-tax (*kapnikon*), taxes relating to persons and livestock, and associated surtaxes (*parakolouthēmata*) and supplemental communal levies.[36] However, the property of a 'military household' enjoyed exemption from diverse secondary charges, including obligatory provision of food and lodging for officials (*kaniskion*), the billeting of military personnel (*mitaton*), requisitions and compulsory sale of produce and livestock, and unremunerated labour-services (*angareiai*), which were a regular, degrading and financially onerous burden on the majority of peasants.[37] This was at least the status of soldiers as prescribed in imperial legislation and military ordinances, but the same sources allude to potential disjuncture between legal theory and social practice. Leo VI envisaged circumstances in which soldiers, though exempt from private labour-services that peasants owed to landlords, might be required to contribute unpaid labour to state construction projects – roads, bridges, ships or fortifications.[38] Mid-tenth-century complaints about oppressive civil authorities, even if rhetorically exaggerated, articulate imperial concerns about dilution or abuse of soldiers' privileges.[39]

Equality with regard to legal status and fiscal privileges did not mean equivalence of income or assets. There were always wealthier and poorer *stratiōtai*, even in the same unit, with increasing differentiation according to rank, regiment and professional environment. The limited data, mostly from the tenth century, furnish few figures susceptible to statistical analysis, especially given divergent modern estimates of land values and agricultural yields. Nevertheless, the evidence suggests that, on the whole, thematic soldiers should be classed among better-off peasantry, and in some cases even as lesser 'gentry', who possessed substantial allotments of cultivatable land. At any time, however, a significant proportion of *stratiōtai* was less prosperous, while some are called 'poor', a relative distinction that usually signified inability to fulfil military obligations rather than destitution. Fluctuating fortunes and diverse circumstances – economic, agrarian, military – could quickly reduce some soldiers to hardship, suggestive of a borderline status between subsistence and surplus.[40] Socio-economic stratification is manifest in different ways, some superficial, others affecting operational capabilities and requiring material assistance from the state and/or community. The saint who gives his horse to an 'exceedingly poor' soldier becomes a *topos* of ninth-/tenth-century hagiographical literature.[41] A ninth-/tenth-century letter of uncertain authorship petitions the fisc on behalf of a soldier's impoverished widow, who possesses 'no horse, no quiver or helmet or sword' with which to equip her only son.[42] Rare official data on rates of commutation acknowledge the existence of soldiers 'wholly without means', who nevertheless pay half the standard fee.[43] Contemporary sources distinguish a self-supporting category of thematic soldiers, who provided their own campaign provisions, from the majority who received rations from the state. Similarly, some soldiers could afford a servant(s), others pooled resources in order to share one.[44] Early tenth-century officers charged with selecting troops from a muster of registered thematic manpower were instructed to consider not only age, physique and morale, but also a soldier's ability to equip and maintain himself.[45] The implications of soldiers' relative wealth or poverty therefore stretched far beyond their own households.

'Militarisation' of social relations

Soldiers routinely interacted with civilians in the course of their diverse duties: policing and internal security; supporting civil, fiscal and juridical authorities; enforcement of imperial religious policies; in-transit demands for foodstuffs, livestock, fuel, billets and labour-services – all circumstances open to abuse and exploitation.[46] Outside official contexts, however, the localisation of soldiers in civilian communities, together with soldiers' dependence on their own resources, fostered a more far-reaching 'militarisation' of social relations. Three examples follow.

First, at a microcosmic, familial level, the impact of 'militarisation' can be discerned in the nature and composition of 'military households', classified as the residence of a registered *stratiōtēs*. Space forbids examination of current scholarly assumptions about the primarily heritable character of military service;[47] it must suffice here to indicate that the evidence for a legal hereditary obligation is scant and ambiguous, while Byzantine law-codes are strikingly silent with regard to potential infringements (at least compared to late Roman legislation).[48] Leaving this issue to one side, it was clearly advantageous for a household to acquire and retain 'military' status: in addition to a soldier's pay, rewards and booty, the attendant fiscal exemptions greatly benefited a registered property. Doubtless many 'military households' comprised nuclear families exploiting patrimonial land, but military-fiscal calculations encouraged alternative arrangements whereby a household chose, though was not obliged, to maintain a *stratiōtēs*, apparently because it was mutually advantageous. A judicial ruling of *c.* 741 concerns a *stratiōtēs* who had been living in his wife's parental home; while his father-in-law funded his equipment and service-related expenses, the soldier contributed military-derived income to the household. The ruling adjudicated compensation due to the family when the soldier decided to leave and live elsewhere.[49] By means of similar 'military-marital' policies, the government sought to assimilate foreign manpower into Anatolian *themata* by inducing military or civilian households with widowed or unmarried women to accept fugitive or captive warriors as sons-in-law. This was accomplished either by imperial edict, whereby Theophilos (r. 829–42) accommodated reportedly *c.* 14,000 Khurramites in 834, or by offering exceptional tax exemptions, as mid-tenth-century regulations specify for Christianised Arab prisoners.[50] Some households endeavoured to keep the fiscal benefits of 'military' status after the death of a registered soldier. A widow could register an infant son as the '*stratiōtēs*' and pay a commuted fee until he became old enough to serve in person. Some studies adduce this practice as evidence of hereditary military obligation, but the sources may equally record a voluntary, financially-motivated procedure.[51] Similarly, an obscurely reported 'pitiable and inhuman exaction (*exapaitēsis*) on behalf of the deceased', long imposed on soldiers' widows but abolished by Empress Eirene in *c*. 801, is plausibly explained as the commuted fee charged for an infant '*stratiōtēs*' or, if the widow was childless, the loss of military-fiscal privileges by a household that was no longer eligible.[52] The distinction between hereditary and economic motivations is sometimes blurred: a Justinianic law, reiterated by Maurice in 594 and again in the *Basilika* (*c*. 892), permitted the eldest son of a soldier killed in action to inherit his father's rank and pay, but this measure was explicitly intended to secure the family against poverty rather than as a mechanism of recruitment . As elsewhere, apparent heredity occurs not by legal principle but as a consequence of fiscal incentives.[53]

Second, as previously outlined, sources from the eighth/ninth century onwards document impoverished *stratiōtai* unable to fulfil military obligations. In cases of severe penury, mid-tenth-century legislation clarifies an existing procedure, of unspecified date, whereby the state granted a soldier temporary exemption (*adōreia*) from his *strateia* until his fortunes revived; in the meantime he performed less financially onerous garrison duties with light-armed 'auxiliaries' (*apelatai*).[54] Before this last resort, however, other fiscal-administrative mechanisms required communities to assist local soldiers. Although much remains uncertain, the earliest evidence concerns a measure introduced by Nikephoros I (r. 802–11), as documented in a single hostile and textually problematic source. In *c*. 809/10, Nikephoros forcibly resettled soldiers from Asia Minor to recently recovered territory in Macedonia and Greece. Some relocated soldiers were compelled to sell ancestral properties. Seemingly in this context, 'in addition ... [Nikephoros] ordered that poor men were to serve in the army and be equipped by their fellow-villagers, also furnishing to the Treasury 18½ *nomismata* per man and his public taxes as a joint liability'.[55] Communal liability for paying the taxes of an insolvent or absconded (civilian) fellow villager was a long-standing principle of Roman/Byzantine taxation.[56] Nikephoros' innovation apparently made the village, as a fiscal unit, collectively responsible for supporting resident soldiers who, though evidently in possession of taxable property, were (temporarily?) unable to bear the cost of their military equipment and ordinary tax liabilities. Nikephoros presumably aimed to ensure that thematic armies had sufficient fiscally viable and properly equipped troops.[57] A century later (*c*. 905), a similar principle of 'communal solidarity and collaboration', albeit differently applied and justified, underlies Leo VI's authorisation of *ad hoc* levies on wealthier civilian households in order to provide poorer thematic soldiers with horses, service-related expenses and even basic equipment prior to a campaign.[58] The longer-term operation of Nikephoros' reform is implied by mid-tenth-century laws, which indicate that if the landholding of a *stratiōtēs* could no longer sustain his *strateia*, the state compulsorily allocated civilian landholders from the same village as temporary *syndotai*, 'contributors', who were required to assist him, materially or through labour, in performing his military service. Only after this measure had failed was exemption (*adōreia*) granted.[59] Furthermore, Constantine VII's *Novel* on soldiers' landholdings (*c.* 947) affirmed the preferential claim of *syndotai* to that 'military property', if it should eventually fall vacant or be reassigned, on condition that they, though civilians, became singly or proportionately liable for the attached *strateia*, as a commuted monetary equivalent rather than actual service.[60] In these ways, therefore, responsibility for funding a soldier(s) could be shifted directly and personally onto his civilian neighbours.

Third, some sources equate wealthy *stratiōtai* with provincial *dynatoi*, 'the powerful', who are accordingly able to use status, wealth and force to overawe rural society.[61] Although contemporary documentation contains no specific cases, parallels may be drawn with late Roman evidence of soldiers abusing their state-sanctioned monopoly of violence to intimidate and harass civilians.[62] In contrast, 'poor' soldiers, especially in rural areas far from the scrutiny of Constantinople, were vulnerable to coercion or exploitation by local elites. Anxieties about unlawful employment of military personnel (re)surface in mid-eighth-century legislation, which reprises Justininiac injunctions against soldiers entering into tenurial contracts or taking positions on private estates that might distract from or conflict with their military duties.[63] If this legislative reiteration signifies circumstantial correspondence with Justinian's reign, when seigneurial retinues periodically disturbed even the Constantinopolitan hinterland, then we may glimpse here eighth-century soldiers acting as 'military muscle' and contracting themselves to landowners/-holders as stewards, rent-collectors and bodyguards.[64] Certainly, the imperial government later became increasingly concerned about impoverished soldiers joining unauthorised paramilitary retinues. This problem became acute by the early tenth century with the rise of aristocratic clans, predominantly military in origin and character, who combined provincial landownership with imperial office-holding to dominate certain regions, particularly the central Anatolian plateau. Leo VI (*c.* 905) and Constantine VII (*c.* 947) financially penalised army officers and unspecified '*dynatoi*' who took *stratiōtai* into their personal service. They also forbade senior officers to exempt *stratiōtai* from their *strateia* in return for 'gifts', which, by implication, included surrendering land. As thematic officers were often members of regional landed families, both measures addressed threats posed by an ascendant military aristocracy, which sought to coerce or entice *stratiōtai* into becoming dependent tenants (*paroikoi*) or armed retainers, a process accelerated by severe famine across Anatolia in 927–28.[65] The government feared that these officer-magnates would use enlarged retinues of kinsmen and clients to further their territorial and political ambitions, reflected in the proliferation of large estates, inter-clan feuding and, ultimately, attempts at imperial power.[66]

Conclusions

This brief chapter can hardly do justice to the complexity and significance of the subject but permits some general observations. The distinction between 'soldier' and civilian, in terms of legal status, privileges and exemptions, remained clearly demarcated, but the intricacies of the Byzantine military-fiscal apparatus meant that terminological and functional ambiguities existed in reality: some 'soldiers' rarely if ever performed military service in person; some civilians were assigned or voluntarily undertook military-fiscal obligations. Correspondingly, although many soldiers enjoyed professional status and relative wealth, more striking are the ways in which other soldiers' poverty and vulnerability shaped social relations. Soldiers' rootedness in village communities with communal tax liabilities, and their dependence on private or familial resources to fulfil their *strateia*, made possible a partial transfer of military-fiscal obligations onto civilian neighbours. More broadly, the very presence of soldiers in rural society affected its cultural complexion and local power relationships. This we can call 'militarisation'. Conversely, with an emerging 'professionalisation' of Byzantine armies from the late ninth/early tenth century, and a general policy of fiscalising the *strateia* of thematic soldiers, one can discern the beginnings of a longer-term 'demilitarisation' of the empire's indigenous manpower.

Notes

1 See surveys of scholarship in J. Haldon, 'Military service, military lands, and the status of soldiers: current problems and interpretations', *Dumbarton Oaks Papers*, 47 (1993), 1–67, at 3–11; C. Zuckerman, 'Learning from the enemy and more: studies in the "dark centuries" of Byzantium', *Millennium*, 2 (2005), 79–136, at 125–9.

2 Conception and legitimation of military unrest: Y. Stouraitis, 'Civil war in the Christian empire', pp. 92–123; soldiers' motivation and roles: P. Rance, 'The army in peace time: the social status and function of soldiers', pp. 394–439, at

429–33, both in Y. Stouraitis (ed.), *A companion to the Byzantine culture of war ca. 300–1204* (Leiden: Brill, 2018).
3 For example, Leo VI, *Taktika* 11.9; 20.209; Constantine VII, *Novel* (c. 947), pref. (Svoronos 118).
4 J. Haldon, 'The army and the economy: the allocation and redistribution of surplus wealth in the Byzantine state', *Mediterranean Historical Review*, 7:2 (1992), 133–53; Rance, 'Army', pp. 412–21.
5 Bibliography in Rance, 'Army', pp. 425–9.
6 Haldon, 'Military service', pp. 13–15; J. Haldon, *Byzantium in the seventh century. The transformation of a culture* (Cambridge: Cambridge University Press, 2nd edn, 1997), pp. 147–9, 229–32.
7 J. Haldon, *Warfare, State and society in the Byzantine world, 565–1204* (London: UCL Press, 1999), pp. 60–6, 71–83; A. Eger, *The Islamic-Byzantine frontier: interaction and exchange among Muslim and Christian communities* (London: Tauris, 2015).
8 L. Brubaker and J. Haldon, *Byzantium in the iconoclast era, c. 680–850* (Cambridge: Cambridge University Press, 2011), pp. 22–6.
9 Zuckerman, 'Learning', pp. 125–34; Brubaker and Haldon, *Iconoclast era*, pp. 723–71; J. Haldon, 'A context for the two evil deeds: Nikephoros I and the origins of the *themata*', in O. Delouis, S. Métivier and P. Pagès (eds), *Le Saint, Le Moine et le Paysan. Mélanges d'histoire byzantine offerts à Michel Kaplan* (Paris: Sorbonne, 2016), pp. 245–65.
10 R.-J. Lilie, 'Die zweihundertjährige Reform: Zu den Anfängen der Themenorganisation im 7. und 8. Jahrhundert', *Byzantinoslavica*, 45 (1984), 27–39, 190–201, at 32–4; M. Hendy, *Studies in the Byzantine monetary economy c. 300–1450* (Cambridge: Cambridge University Press, 1985), pp. 414–20, 496–9, 619–62; Haldon, 'Military service', pp. 11–18; Haldon, *Seventh century*, pp. 147–9, 220–44; N. Oikonomides, *Fiscalité et exemption fiscale à Byzance (IXe-XIe s.)* (Athens: EIE, 1996), pp. 70–2; W. Brandes, *Finanzverwaltung in Krisenzeiten. Untersuchungen zur byzantinischen Administration im 6.-9. Jahrhundert* (Frankfurt: Löwenklau-Gesellschaft, 2002), pp. 239–365; Brubaker and Haldon, *Iconoclast era*, pp. 464–74, 682–705, 726–8; F. Curta, 'Coins and burials in dark age Greece. Archaeological remarks on the Byzantine "Reconquista"', in R. Kostova (ed.), Средновековният Човек и Неговият Свят (Veliko Trnovo: Faber, 2014), pp. 55–86.
11 Lilie, 'Die zweihundertjährige Reform', pp. 191–8; Hendy, *Monetary economy*, pp. 417–20, 645–51, 659–62; N. Oikonomides, 'Middle-Byzantine provincial recruits. Salary and armament', in J. Duffy and J. Peradotto (eds), *Gonimos. Neoplatonic and Byzantine studies presented to Leendert G. Westerink at 75* (Buffalo: Arethusa, 1988), pp. 121–36; Haldon, *Seventh century*, pp. 242–4, 249–51.
12 T. S. Brown, *Gentlemen and officers. Imperial administration and aristocratic power in Byzantine Italy, AD 554–800* (Rome: British School at Rome, 1984), pp. 101–8, 194–6.
13 Haldon, 'Military service', pp. 21–7, 54–5.

14 For example, *Vita Petri Atroae* §110 (Laurent 163–5). See M. Kaplan, 'La place des soldats dans la société villageoise byzantine (VIIe-Xe siècles)', in *Le combattant au Moyen Âge* (Paris: Sorbonne, 1995), pp. 45–55, at 46–7; M. Kaplan, *Les hommes et la terre à Byzance du VIe au XIe siècle. Propriété et exploitation du sol* (Paris: Sorbonne, 1992), pp. 235–6; J. Haldon, *Byzantine praetorians. An administrative, institutional, and social survey of the Opsikion and Tagmata, c. 580–900* (Bonn: Habelt, 1984), pp. 297–9, 325.

15 *Digest* 48.6; *Codex Justinianus* 11.47.1 (= *Codex Theodosianus* 15.15.1 [364]); also 9.12.10 (468). Exception for self-defence: 3.27.1 (= *Codex Theodosianus* 9.14.2 [391]). See selective reiteration in *Basilika* 60.18.20, 29; 39.16.

16 Justinian: *Novel* 85 (539). Post-seventh century: Haldon, *Warfare*, pp. 139–41; Brubaker and Haldon, *Iconoclast era*, pp. 682–705.

17 C. Makrypoulias, 'Civilians as combatants in Byzantium', in J. Koder and I. Stouraitis (eds), *Byzantine war ideology between Roman Imperial concept and Christian religion* (Vienna: ÖAW, 2012), pp. 109–20; L. I. R. Petersen, *Siege warfare and military organization in the successor states (400–800 AD)* (Leiden: Brill, 2013), pp. 67–74, 139–47, 336–43, 604.

18 Theophanes, *Chronographia* 377.2–5, 490.4–7 (De Boor); Nikephoros, *Breviarium* 44.9–11 (Mango 106), with Makrypoulias, 'Civilians', p. 116; Petersen, *Siege*, pp. 145–6, 695–7.

19 Leo, *Taktika* 11.41, 20.81. Nikephoros Ouranos' *Taktika* (*c.* 1000) paraphrases both passages; in the absence of a critical edition, I consulted the relevant manuscripts: *Constantinopolitanus gr.* (TSMK Gİ) 36, p. 154; *Monacensis gr.* 452, fol. 22r, 96v.

20 Kaplan, *Les hommes*, pp. 89–134, 185–280, 399–408; Oikonomides, *Fiscalité*, pp. 24–151; N. Oikonomides 'The social structure of the Byzantine countryside in the first half of the Xth century', *Byzantina Symmeikta*, 10 (1996), 105–25; J. Lefort, 'The rural economy, seventh-twelfth centuries', in A. Laiou (ed.) *The economic history of Byzantium: from the seventh through the fifteenth century* (Washington, DC: Dumbarton Oaks, 2002), pp. 231–310; J. Lefort, C. Morrisson and J.-P. Sodini (eds), *Les villages dans l'empire byzantine (IVe-XVe siècle)* (Paris: Lethielleux, 2005); M. Kaplan, 'Les villageois aux premiers siècles byzantins (VIe-Xe siècles): une société homogène?', in M. Kaplan (ed.), *Byzance: Villes et campagnes* (Paris: Picard, 2006), pp. 14–30; M. Kaplan, 'Les élites rurales byzantines. Historiographie et sources', *Mélanges de l'École française de Rome – Moyen Âge*, 124:2 (2012), 299–312.

21 D. Krallis, 'Popular political agency in Byzantium's villages and towns', *Byzantina Symmeikta*, 28 (2018), 11–48, at 25–7.

22 Haldon, *Seventh century*, pp. 99–124, 371–4; Brubaker and Haldon, *Iconoclast era*, pp. 22–9, 625–9.

23 Eighth-/tenth-century examples: F. Trombley, 'War, society and popular religion in Byzantine Anatolia (6th-13th centuries)', in S. Lampakis (ed.), *Η Βυζαντινή Μικρά Ασία (6ος-12ος αι.)* (Athens: EIE/IBE, 1998), pp. 97–139, at 129–30; Krallis, 'Popular political agency', pp. 30–41.

24 D. Górecki, 'The *Strateia* of Constantine VII. The legal status, administration and historical background', *Byzantinische Zeitschrift*, 82 (1989), 157–76, at 164–7; Haldon, 'Military service', pp. 27–8.
25 Italy: Brown, *Gentlemen and officers*, pp. 82–108. Egypt: J. Keenan, 'Evidence for the Byzantine Army in the Syene Papyri', *Bulletin of the American Society of Papyrologists*, 27 (1990), 139–50; M. Whitby, 'Recruitment in Roman armies from Justinian to Heraclius (ca. 565–615)', in A. Cameron (ed.), *The Byzantine and early Islamic Near East 3: states, resources and armies* (Princeton: Darwin Press, 1995), pp. 61–124, at 70–2, 79–80.
26 P. Lemerle, *The agrarian history of Byzantium from the origins to the twelfth century: the sources and the problems* (Galway: Galway University Press, 1979), pp. 143–5; Haldon, 'Military service', pp. 23–4, 32–3; Oikonomides, 'Provincial recruits', pp. 135–6.
27 Constantine VII, *De administrando imperio* 51–2 (Moravcsik/Jenkins 256: 51.199–52.16); *De cerimoniis* 2.45 (Reiske 666.16–667.1).
28 Lemerle, *Agrarian history*, pp. 124–8, 148–9; J. F. Haldon, *Recruitment and conscription in the Byzantine army c. 550–950* (Vienna: Verlag der ÖAW, 1979), pp. 49–62.
29 P. Lemerle, *Cinq Études sur le XIe siècle byzantin* (Paris: CNRS, 1977), pp. 267–71; Lemerle, *Agrarian history*, pp. 223–9; G. Dagron and H. Mihăescu, *Le Traité sur la guérilla (De velitatione) de l'empereur Nicéphore Phocas (963–969)* (Paris: CNRS, 1986), pp. 183–6, 262–4, 280–3; Kaplan, *Les hommes*, pp. 252–5; Haldon, 'Military service', pp. 32–9, 49–53, 60–4; Haldon, *Warfare*, pp. 124–5; Oikonomides, *Fiscalité*, pp. 37–40, 117–19.
30 Haldon, 'Military service'; Oikonomides, 'Provincial recruits'; Oikonomides, *Fiscalité*, pp. 37–40, 117–19; Górecki, '*Strateia*'; Kaplan, *Les hommes*, pp. 233–7.
31 Haldon, 'Military service', pp. 21–3, 42–3, 53–6; Dagron and Mihăescu, *Traité*, pp. 260–74.
32 W. Treadgold, *Byzantium and its army* (Stanford: Stanford University Press, 1995), pp. 118–57 offers extensive calculations on military pay; Haldon, *Warfare*, pp. 126–8 is more cautious; also Lilie, 'Die zweihundertjährige Reform', pp. 198–201.
33 Lemerle, *Agrarian history*, pp. 146–9; Oikonomides, 'Provincial recruits', pp. 121–34; Dagron and Mihăescu, *Traité*, pp. 260–4.
34 Haldon, *Byzantine praetorians*, pp. 307–23.
35 *Ekloga* 18.1 (Burgmann 244.945–58)
36 Oikonomides, *Fiscalité*, pp. 24–36, 46–84.
37 *Ibid.*, pp. 85–121.
38 Leo VI, *Taktika* 20.71, with Oikonomides, *Fiscalité*, p. 110; differently interpreted by J. Haldon, *A critical commentary on the* Taktika *of Leo VI* (Washington, DC: Dumbarton Oaks, 2014), pp. 142, 428.
39 Dagron and Mihăescu, *Traité*, pp. 259–74.
40 Bibliography in Rance, 'Army', pp. 412–16.
41 For example, Niketas, *Vita S. Philareti* §3 (Rydén 72–4); *Vita Eustratii* §13 (Papadopoulos-Kerameus 377).

42 J. Darrouzès, *Épistoliers byzantins du Xe siècle* (Paris: IFEB, 1960) pp. 130–1 (II.50).
43 Constantine VII, *De administrando imperio* 51–2 (Moravcsik/Jenkins 256: 51.199–52.16); *De cerimoniis* 2.45 (Reiske 666.16–667.1).
44 Lemerle, *Agrarian history*, pp. 146–9; Dagron and Mihăescu, *Traité*, pp. 261, 267–9; Haldon, 'Military service', p. 24; Kaplan, *Les hommes*, pp. 238–46; Kaplan, 'La place', pp. 49–51.
45 Leo VI, *Taktika* 4.1, 3; 18.149. See Dagron and Mihăescu, *Traité*, pp. 262–9, 275–80; Kaplan, *Les hommes*, pp. 238–46.
46 Rance, 'Army', pp. 417–29 with bibliography.
47 For example, Haldon, *Recruitment*, pp. 35–40, 79–80; Lilie, 'Die zweihundertjährige Reform', pp. 193, 199–201; Haldon, 'Military service', pp. 20, 23–8, 32–7; 'Nikephoros', pp. 251–3, 257.
48 I plan to examine this question in a separate study.
49 D. Simon, 'Byzantinische Hausgemeinschaftsverträge', in F. Baur, K. Larenz and F. Wieacker (eds) *Beiträge zur europäischen Rechtsgeschichte und zum geltenden Zivilrecht: Festgabe für J. Sontis* (Munich: Beck, 1977), pp. 91–128, at 94, with discussion at 95–100. See Oikonomides, 'Provincial recruits', pp. 130–4; Haldon, 'Military service', pp. 21–3; M. T. G. Humphreys, *Law, power, and imperial ideology in the iconoclast era c. 680–850* (Oxford: Oxford University Press, 2015), pp. 135–8.
50 Khurramites: W. Treadgold, *The Byzantine revival, 780–842* (Stanford: Stanford University Press 1988), pp. 282–3. Arab captives: Constantine VII, *De cerimoniis* 2.49 (Reiske 694.22–695.14).
51 See bibliography at note 26.
52 Theodore Studite, *Epistulae* 7.61–3 (Fatouros 26). Haldon, 'Military service', pp. 23–5, 33 discusses various interpretations.
53 *Codex Justinianus* 12.47.3 = *Basilika* 57.7.3; compare Theophylact Simocatta, *Historiae* 7.1.7 (De Boor); Theophanes, *Chronographia* 274.12–16 (De Boor); see Whitby, 'Recruitment', pp. 79–81.
54 Constantine VII, *Novel* (c. 947) A.9 (Svoronos 121–2); Constantine VII, *De cerimoniis* 2.49 (Reiske 696.1–9); *Peira* 36.2 (Zepos IV 143). See Lemerle, *Agrarian history*, pp. 119–20, 135–6. For a different interpretation of *adōreia*: Górecki, '*Strateia*', pp. 169–71; Haldon, 'Military service', pp. 30–2; D. Górecki, 'Constantine VII's *Peri tōn stratiotōn*', *Greek, Roman and Byzantine Studies*, 48 (2009), 135–54, at 143–5, 150–1.
55 Theophanes, *Chronographia* 486.10–26 (De Boor), quoting 486.23–6.
56 Gorecki, '*Strateia*', pp. 166–7.
57 Lemerle, *Agrarian history*, pp. 62–4; Kaplan, *Les hommes*, pp. 237–8; Haldon, 'Military service', pp. 25–6; Brubaker and Haldon, *Iconoclast era*, pp. 746–50; Haldon, 'Nikephoros'.
58 Leo VI, *Taktika* 4.1; 18.123–4; 20.205.
59 Constantine VII, *Novel* (c. 947) B.2 (Svoronos 123.101); Romanos II, *Novel* (962) C.1 (Svoronos 149.36, 51); Constantine VII, *De cerimoniis* 2.49 (Reiske 695.21–696.1). See Lemerle, *Cinq Études*, pp. 265–7; *Agrarian history*, pp. 134–6;

Haldon, *Recruitment*, pp. 49–53; Górecki, '*Strateia*', pp. 167–9; Kaplan, 'La place', pp. 52–4; Górecki, 'Constantine', pp. 146–52.
60 Constantine VII, *Novel* (*c.* 947) A.8, B.2 (Svoronos 121, 123). Bibliography in Rance, 'Army', pp. 407–10.
61 R. Morris, 'The powerful and the poor in tenth-century Byzantium: law and reality', *Past and Present*, 73 (1976), 3–27, at 23–6; Haldon, 'Military service', pp. 56–8; Kaplan, 'La place', pp. 46–51.
62 Bibliography in Rance 'Army', pp. 417–21.
63 *Ekloga* 12.6 (Burgmann 212.618–22); *Nomos Stratiotikos* §§55–6 (Ashburner), compare *Codex Justinianus* 4.65.31 (458), 35 (530); 12.35.15 (458), 16 (472–4).
64 For example, Justinian, *Novel* 116 (542), with D. Feissel and I. Kaygusuz, 'Un mandement impérial du VIe siècle dans une inscription d'Hadrianoupolis d'Honoriade', *Travaux et Mémoires*, 9 (1985), 397–419.
65 Leo VI, *Taktika* 8.26; 19.19; Constantine VII, *Novel* (*c.* 947) C.1–3 (Svoronos 124–6). See Lemerle, *Agrarian history*, pp. 122–4; Dagron and Mihăescu, *Traité*, pp. 268, 282–3; Haldon, *Commentary*, p. 221.
66 See selectively P. Magdalino, 'The Byzantine aristocratic *oikos*', in M. Angold (ed.), *The Byzantine aristocracy: IX to XIII centuries* (Oxford: BAR 221, 1984), pp. 92–111; J.-C. Cheynet, *Pouvoir et contestations à Byzance (963–1210)* (Paris: Sorbonne, 1990), pp. 207–37, 249–313; J. Howard-Johnston, 'Crown lands and the defence of imperial authority in the tenth and eleventh centuries', *Byzantinische Forschungen*, 21 (1995), 75–100.

3

The *exercitus Gothorum* in Italy: a professional army in a demilitarised society?

Kai Grundmann

The Ostrogothic army in Italy has received some scholarly attention, especially with regards to its ethnicity, identity and settlement. This chapter, however, attempts to shift the focus onto the organisation, administration and actual operation of the military. It is important to note that this includes the *exercitus Gothorum*, but is not limited to it. There were other military forces at the disposal of the Gothic kings; their different organisation and operation also led to different modes of interaction with civilians. Those differences shed some new light on how the military, including its institutions and personnel, was perceived by the civilians and how the Gothic kings attempted to structure their interactions in times of peace. The same differences highlight the ideal of a civilian population which – in contrast to other successor kingdoms – ceded all soldierly activities to professional military forces. This chapter will explore whether there was lack of differentiation between soldier and civilian and an overlap of civilian and military duties for state officials, two main characteristics of militarisation, applied to the Gothic kingdom in Italy. The Gothic Wars of 535–62, with their usually violent and rapacious treatment of civilians, will not be in the chapter's focus, as its very dynamic developments require a separate analysis.

While the *exercitus Gothorum* served as the king's main military force, other forces can be identified. Most prominent are the palace guards: *silentiarii, domestici, scholarii*. In a well-known chapter of his *Secret History*, Procopius of Caesarea describes them as a remnant of previous times, denies any military (combat) value, and goes as far as to say 'nothing military remained except the name of the army [στρατείας ὄνομα]' (trans. Dewing).[1] A similar case might be made for the *excubitores* who are noted by Ennodius.[2] The fact that these troops seemed to have had a civilian oversight, and thus did not fall under a military office,[3] reinforces their non-military nature. It also means they were not part of the *exercitus Gothorum*, which fell under different authorities and (military) officers. Though they were apparently taking over some watch duties,[4] prompting the idea they might be capable combat formations,[5] it is clear that they were no longer the elite soldiers who had previously borne the name.

The role of the guards should not be seen as simple sentry duties alone. Obviously, they represented an element of continuity, for similar formations had served in the western Roman Empire for centuries. Theoderic went to great lengths to emphasise the continuation of imperial traditions under his rule,[6] and maintaining palace guards helped to propagate that message. It certainly smoothed the transition of power, as the palace guards could not be labelled 'barbarian'. On the contrary, inferring from Procopius, it seems possible that these guards were the sons of well-off Romans. Standing post in high-visibility areas close to the centres of power might also provide social prestige besides the considerable pay, which would have been attractive to some of the Roman aristocracy. Moreover, the presence of guard regiments served to tie the civilian elites even closer to the king by giving them a job at the court.

This also explains why Justinian disbanded these troops. Procopius may have us believe that Justinian acted out of greed and lack of money alone,[7] but largely ceremonial palace guards were only useful in the capital, i.e. near the ruler. Indeed, Justinian maintained similar units in his capital, units that would have been useless in a military context if Procopius is to be believed.[8] His very harsh statements on guards units, east and west, should be taken with a grain of salt. But the civilian oversight, the non-combat nature of their mission and the tight connection to Roman aristocracy is interesting in that the line between civilian and military was definitely blurred in this case. To make a definite statement about the nature of this formation, we would have to know its size and details about its deployment, and having such units and the military in close proximity to the ruler is significant in and of itself in a monarchy, as many examples including Alexander's companion cavalry or the Wachregiment Berlin prove – even if the combat value was low. However, the process of transforming military units into essentially non-combat institutions was not unique; Mommsen has observed a similar decline of the late Roman guard troops, and the sources to be discussed here indicate that this was the case in Italy, too.[9]

The troops on the borders represent a different development. It is not entirely certain whether the Gothic kings continued the late Roman separation of the field army (*comitatenses*) and the dedicated border troops, the *limitanei*, as some scholars have proposed.[10] Guy Halsall pointed out that no formation under Gothic rule was ever referred to as *limitanei*.[11] Nonetheless, Servatus, *dux* of the two Raetian provinces, evidently had his own troops, commanding a military unit called the *Breones*.[12] This term describes a local mountain people who had been Romanised quite some time before,[13] and who likely formed an entity different from the Goths who primarily served the *exercitus Gothorum*. Considering Raetia served as the 'bars and bolts of Italy',[14] and played a vital role in the overall border defence strategy,[15] the use of locals to secure the area functionally equals the use of *limitainei*, especially as they seem to be operationally limited to their region. Despite the substantial troop movements during the Gothic Wars, no Raetian units are seen in Italy.

The letters of Cassiodorus allow us to understand how these military forces would have reacted to enemy incursions, at least in theory. We do not know the armament or tactics of the border-guarding *limitanei*, but, apparently, they were not expected to hold out against noteworthy forces. Delaying the enemy advance by harassment in the mountains, perhaps blocking passes, and defending key fortresses were the prime tasks of the border defenders. Despite the fancy words of Theoderic about Raetia being the bars and bolts of Italy, he was aware that an army could break through. The *tractus Italiae*, the chain of fortresses at the foot of the Southern Alps, was reinforced; two fortresses, Verruca and Dertona, are well-known. They, too, were not designed to stop an invading force. The fortresses served a dual purpose: to shelter the civil population but also to deny shelter to others. This forced a foreign army to invest part of their resources to forage, leaving them exposed to the elements and to an impending counter-attack.[16] It was the field army which needed to strike and ultimately repel the invader.

This strategy had severe consequences for the border regions. The Gothic field army, while highly mobile by the standards of late Antiquity, could never react in time to cross the Alps and protect the provinces of Raetia against smaller incursions. Unless a great invasion happened, the locals were on their own, civilian and military alike; and Theoderic made sure they knew it. However, there was the shadow of hierarchy (or perhaps rather a functional equivalent to it), to use a term from political science. In case of a full-scale invasion, but also in the event of a major uprising, Theoderic and his troops *could* act with terrifying efficiency, as demonstrated in many theatres of war.[17] This kind of deterrent meant the locals would need to fight most of their small battles alone when subjected to a raid, and it would require the inclusion of civilians at least in support roles. While Theoderic's system of indirect presence, which at times may have been little more than symbolic domination, did nothing to prevent small-scale incursions, it was a credible enough threat to stabilise the region on a grander scale, while leaving it largely independent. It is thus not a symptom of military weakness, as has been argued when reviewing the apparently low quality and numbers of the ducal troops.[18] Fending off small-scale incursions rather than full-scale invasions was precisely what local border guards were supposed to do. In the end, the borders gained some stability, and the heartlands gained their bars and bolts.[19]

Best documented is the *exercitus Gothorum*. If it is true that the border guards and the palace guards formed separate entities, the *exercitus Gothorum* effectively took the role of the late Roman *comitatenses* as the mobile strike force. Such a design should not come as a great surprise with Theoderic having been the commander of a Roman federate force and having been trained in Constantinople. The late Roman context offers a sensible background for the military organisation.

But perhaps the most striking characteristic of the field army is its professionalism. Scholars increasingly refer to late Roman armies as professional, though not always with clear definitions of the term.[20] Samuel Huntington's seminal *Soldier and the State* is helpful because it defines 'profession' as a 'peculiar type of functional group with highly specialised characteristics'. Those characteristics are 'expertise', 'corporateness' and 'responsibility'. Huntington firmly asserts professionalism is what distinguishes the modern soldiers from 'warriors of previous ages'.[21] While caution is indeed required when applying these criteria to the Gothic army, it is remarkable how well they fit, at least when we read Cassiodorus's *Variae*.

The *Variae* are notoriously difficult to interpret, partially due to debates on the date and intention of their publication.[22] Without doubt Cassiodorus presents an idealised view of the Ostrogothic kingdom, including its army. This ideal, however, is interesting in and of itself for it reflects Huntington's professionalism: the 'expertise' of the soldiers is evidenced by their exclusive limitation on military service; they are even protected from doing civilian work.[23] In fact, it is a life-long commitment.[24] We know of basic training as well as advanced and specialised training by more experienced officers.[25] Warfare may not have been as complex as it is in the digital age, but the skills for successfully mastering its challenges had to be taught and learned. Procopius, for example, emphasises the high skill level of Belisarius' elite troops acting as horse archers, shock cavalry and siege experts.[26] The use of untrained (and poorly equipped) personnel in an open field battle during the Gothic Wars proved disastrous,[27] although they seemed to be capable enough to man walls. Even a small number of military specialists could make a decisive difference when two otherwise untrained forces met.[28] All this implies the institutionalised transfer of professional knowledge to military personnel.

'Responsibility' can also be found. 'The client of every profession is society'[29] – and this is strongly connected to what Amory termed 'civilitas-ideology' and similarly to what Wiemer called 'Integration durch Separation':

the idea that the Goths (i.e. the soldiers in Amory's diction) defend the Romans (i.e. the civilians) and the Graeco-Roman patterned state they maintain. 'Think what a life of hardship the soldier leads in those frontier places for the general safety' (trans. Hodgkins)[30] and similar notions are legion in the *Variae*.[31] Of course, this is where Cassiodorus is at his peak in idealising the interaction between civilians and the military. It has even been argued that the civilians were constantly mistreated and consequently welcomed Belisarius in 535,[32] though this view conflates the experiences of common civilians (who certainly did not receive any better treatment by east Roman troops) and those of senatorial rank.[33] While some friction is undeniably evident even in the *Variae*, such as when an officer needs to be reminded that his troops are to protect the civilians,[34] the effect of the propagation of the ideal itself should not be underestimated. The very fact that the king, commander-in-chief, publicly and repeatedly insisted on certain moral standards could not be ignored by any officer without good reason, and it allowed judgement of the army by those standards. However, the army's leadership did not rely on moral standard setting alone, additionally arguing for a different rationality: if the civilians were robbed, they could hardly generate the revenues required to finance the soldiers' payments, especially the *donativum*.[35] Furthermore, the soldiers were supplied with ample provisions when marching through friendly territories, so they did not need to forage. This seems to have been a very important concern judging by the large number of *Variae* detailing such orders.[36] Whatever the motive, the army command was perfectly aware of its responsibility to protect, and rationalised this responsibility morally as well as economically.

Huntington's last point is 'corporateness':

> the sense of organic unity and consciousness of themselves as a group apart from laymen [...] Membership in the professional organisation, along with the possession of special expertise and the acceptance of special responsibility, thus becomes a criterion of professional status, publicly distinguishing the professional man from the layman.[37]

This is perhaps the most influential characteristic of the field army. It was often called *excercitus noster*,[38] the king's own men, and, conversely, the soldiers reciprocated by calling Theoderic *rex noster*,[39] implying a close relationship of the soldiers to the ruler. This is unlike the civilian offices, which are never addressed in a similar way by Theoderic. There are also no *romani nostri* in the language of the Gothic kings, despite Theoderic occasionally being called *dominus noster* by civilian elites in an imitation of imperial habit.[40] Civilians were furthermore not allowed to bear military-grade armaments.[41] Indeed, it is possible that soldiers carried a sword in public, as Theoderic himself most likely did.[42] Thus, it has been proposed that there must have been some other ways to physically distinguish between Goth and Roman in order to enforce such a law.[43]

However the ethnic difference is not the important issue here, as Theoderic merely renewed a Valentinianic ban which had been temporarily lifted by Maiorian in order to defend Rome.[44] And indeed there was another way to tell the difference between civilian and soldier: clothing. Again, there was an older law prohibiting the *populus* from wearing military clothing, especially combat boots (*tzangae*) and trousers (*bracae*).[45] Older interpretations of this law being directed against barbarian influences have long been discarded in favour of an attempt to protect the civilian sphere against military influences.[46] Such military clothing was to be expected in the case of the Gothic soldiers. The *cingulum*, the military belt, further helped identify a soldier; without it, his appearance was considered incomplete – bordering nakedness.[47] Sporting a beard might have been military habitus as well. The 'Gothic beard' as described by Ennodius[48] can be seen in ethnic terms. But why would Ennodius make fun of his friend Jovinianus for having such a beard? As a staunch supporter of Theoderic the Goth's rule, he probably did not chastise someone for following 'Gothic' trends based on ethnicity alone. It is more plausible that he objected to a civilian adopting a military style, indicating that the visual distinction between the two spheres had been internalised by at least a part of the civilian elite. This further illustrates how strong the separation actually was. The issue of the beard is a difficult one because Ennodius' description does actually not match the depiction of Theoderic's facial hair on the famous triple *solidus*. Theoderic's moustache itself, however, is certainly not 'barbarian', though some scholars assume as much,[49] but rather an expression of late Roman military habitus.[50]

Another distinction from the civilian sphere was that soldiers had their own jurisdiction, exclusively exercised by military officers. The *comites provinciarum* dealt with most problems in peace time, the *duces* acted to excursions and on campaign and the *comites Gothorum* were responsible for cases involving civilians and soldiers while being provided with civilian legal advisors.[51] Despite the military officer's supremacy, it is clear that the jurisdiction was organised with the premise of clearly determining who belonged to the professional army and who did not.

The soldiers even had their own language, the *lingua nostra*. Its precise nature remains subject to debate. It might have been Gothic, though it was never addressed as such in our sources; it might have been a 'military pidgin' language. Whatever it was, it factored heavily into the creation and stabilisation of group cohesion.[52] It had to be learned, too, like any other (military) skill.[53]

On top of all that is a superimposed ethnicity, being the *exercitus Gothorum*, but this identity did not always override other ethnic identities within the army. We know of Gepids, Rugians, Heruls, Huns and individual Romans serving in this army;[54] and this is before considering the huge number of defectors during the Gothic Wars, again including a variety of ethnicities. The specific Gothic ethnicity, from the army's point of view, worked as an overarching identity that supported the common military identity. As such, it is but one tool in a much larger box of tools separating the soldiers from the civilians.

The separation of the military and the civilian spheres thus had many levels: functional, in that it exclusively focused on warfare; habitual, in the right to bear arms, military clothing, insignia and perhaps facial hair; legal, having their own jurisdiction; linguistic thanks to the *lingua nostra*; and pseudo-ethnic by being called *exercitus gothorum*. A spatial separation may be argued as well, but touches upon the controversial subject of how the Goths were settled in Italy, i.e. whether they had tight clusters of settlements or were dispersed over all of Italy.[55] In any case, the separation of the spheres appears to be profound and far more pronounced than in the case of border troops or palace guards. Even though an ethnically defined line between Goth and Roman might be blurry at times, the line between soldier and civilian is clearer.

The *exercitus Gothorum* rarely interacted with civilians, as will be explored later, but was very much focused on the king, and not just because he was nominally the commander-in-chief. The Gothic kings were also the head of state, but their interaction with the field army was more akin to that of an army group commander like Belisarius. When he was younger, Theoderic rode at the head of his troops, charging right into the enemy lines.[56] His leadership style suggested a close personal relationship between king and army, even if, in reality, this was rarely the case. Of the three successors to the throne who were not murdered by their own people, two died in battle at the head of their troops. This style was called 'Germanic',[57] and indeed the Roman head of state would not leave his capital, much less fight in battle. Yet, just as the Gothic kings fought on the frontlines, so too did Justinian's army group commanders. Theoderic also wore clothes handmade by his family, as would most of his soldiers, further reinforcing the image of a close relationship between them.[58] Although the term *conmilitio* is not used, as it would be in Roman imperial tradition, all this appears somewhat stereotypical especially as Roman historiography and panegyrics used the motive of family-made clothing to praise the ruler's modesty; this goes back to Augustus.[59]

Most illustrative is the practice of the *donativum*, the special yearly payment, which Theoderic could have sent to his troops. But he did not. Instead, he insisted on his soldiers coming to him and receiving their money in Ravenna, no doubt face-to-face.[60] Even when Theoderic was not present, his presence was imagined, as described by Ennodius in a panegyric on Theoderic:

> Remember, comrades, on whose orders we are here. None of you shall believe that the eyes of the king, for whose honor we fight, are far away from you. Even when our spears blot out the sky, it will not go unnoticed who used his weapon with extraordinary courage. (Trans. based on Ch. Rohr)[61]

Perhaps the promised reward was also handed out personally. Indeed, the famous triple-solidus depicting Theoderic was actually modified to be worn as a fibula, fastening the cloak – another important part of military clothing. Thus, the owner carried the image of the king at all times.[62]

However, the obligation worked both ways. Leaving aside Theoderic taking care of the impoverished blind soldier Anduit[63] and similar tropes of a good ruler, the instances of military unrest are far more interesting as their consequences potentially impacted on the civilian populace. At least two of Theoderic's *comites* were disloyal to the point of planning a coup. The available information is extremely sparse, with only a few mentions in the anonymus *Excerpta Valesiani* chronicling the reign of Theoderic: 'Odoin, his governor, plotted against him. When Theoderic learned of it, he had Odoin beheaded in the palace which is called Sessorium'[64]; and, in another short chronicle, 'Coming to Milan King Theoderic killed governor Petia.'[65] The information on Odoin is repeated in the chronicles of Prosper of Aquitaine, although misdated.[66] We are certainly confronted with a meaningful event. It happened in the year 500; Theoderic was celebrating this *tricennalia* in Rome. And being a *comes* in Rome, Odoin belonged to the upper most echelons of the army. Thus, a high-ranking officer plotted against the king and was executed in the year of a major celebration, and the response from our (civilian) sources is minimal. In the other instance the silence is even greater, since we only know that Theoderic went to Milan and killed Petia.[67]

Despite the remarkable lack of documentation of these conflicts we may draw some conclusions. The executions of the officers mentioned above are sometimes seen as some kind of court intrigue as power-plays behind the scenes might explain the lack of evidence.[68] But that is not what happened. No one was executed at the court in Ravenna. Petia and Odoin were Theoderic's men, governing Rome and Milan in his stead, and he personally went to those places to deal with them. More importantly, he likely did not execute the officers in public. The Sessorium may not have been a restricted military area but neither was it a public space like the Circus.[69] Public executions or humiliations were common in late Antiquity; putting down enemies publicly was partly a tool of political communication between the triumphant ruler and the city population and aristocracy.[70]

A similar demonstration of power was well within Theoderic's reach, yet he abstained from involving the civilian sphere. It looks like he handled the executions as internal military affairs, which had nothing to do with the citizens of Rome or Milan, and which required Theoderic to act not as the head of state, deputy of the eastern emperor or pseudo-emperor of the west, but as the army's commander-in-chief. This offers an explanation for the lack of documentation from our civilian sources who could offer no further insight – another indication of how little they knew or cared about the military. It also explains why Theoderic was administering the executions personally. On the one hand, there is the possibility that the local soldiers could not be trusted, and on the other hand – more importantly – since the relationship between the commander and his troops was imaged as a close and personal face-to-face relationship in a special group, it makes perfect sense to end it face-to-face.

The civilian perception of the army is difficult to assess. Not only does it seem they were largely demilitarised in the heartlands, having little contact with the army, much less combat training or equipment, for example,[71] it is also true that our sources usually deal with conflict situations. As mentioned before, the prime cause for those conflicts was a large group of soldiers moving through friendly territory. The logistical challenges of supplying an army on the march were substantial: the weekly ration for 5,000 men equalled the produce from 70 acres of farmland and 90 oxen. These numbers have been estimated for a Principate-era Roman legion; although sixth century sources have been used for this estimate,[72] they are by no means final. But they do provide an impression of how much strain was put on the population when an army crossed their lands. It thus comes as no surprise that Cassiodorus' letters address this problem more often than any other civil–military interaction.[73] Equally unsurprisingly, they invariably present successful prevention and resolution mechanisms to the credit of the wise king. The solutions were sensible enough and display considerable experience in handling exactly this kind of problem. The soldiers were either given supplies directly or received money to buy them on the way.[74] It seems that occasionally even the prices were regulated to the benefit of the civilians, but that could be an exception granted for Rome alone.[75] The only time the field army almost fully assembled was before the gates of Rome when raising Vitiges on the shield. This is probably no coincidence, as Rome was a logistical hub receiving huge amounts of provisions on a daily basis.[76]

If Cassiodorus wanted to emphasise the army's peaceful integration, it seems strange that he would choose to portray the relation of the civilian population and the soldiers primarily through using examples of friction. Perhaps it was such a considerable problem that it could not be glossed over, or perhaps Cassiodorus consciously contrasted the attempts to rein in the soldiers with the events of the Gothic Wars and its rampant, unchecked violence committed by soldiers on both sides.

In peace time, encounters between civilians and soldiers were relatively uncommon. The numbers of the field army were simply too low, whatever stance one takes in the debate about the absolute numbers. Even the incredible number of 150,000 soldiers in the field army given by Procopius[77] would still mean a small proportion of the overall population. The operational formations of the armies on both sides as described by Procopius are usually much smaller and estimates of the total number range from 20,000 to 30,000 soldiers.[78] Most cities, for example, only had a small garrison, if any. Naples only received troops when Belisarius landed in Italy, i.e. when a hostile force directly threatened this strategically important city.[79] Neither did Theoderic place a garrison in Rome, but his successor Theodahad did, and this garrison was ordered to keep a low profile and was put under the command of an officer with a reputation for maintaining discipline among the ranks.[80]

Due to their 'expertise' as part of their professionalism, i.e. their exclusive preoccupation with warfare, the soldiers would rarely have reasons to interact with civilians. And if they did, their 'corporateness' made them stand out – much more so than any ethnic or pseudo-traits like Gothic beards. Unlike ethnic identity, both the ascription of a professional military identity as well as its self-attribution were relatively stable regardless of the ethnicity, loyalty or religion of the individual. Furthermore, ethnicity is almost a non-issue in civil–military interactions. This is not unlike the eastern Roman Empire where a similar observation can be made.[81] Indeed, had it not been for the ethnikon *Gothorum* in the labelling of the army, we would have little reason to think of it in ethnic terms. Separated from the rest of the Italian society on many levels by its professionalism, the interaction with this relatively small and highly mobile group was limited and often brutal.

There are some caveats to consider. The clear-cut separation between soldier and civilian may work for the field army to a certain extent. This separation would be less clear in the border regions, considering the overall strategy of the border defence as outlined above, and we know that civilians could be commissioned to help build fortifications[82] and to bolster the defence of city walls.[83] Having taken an oath of loyalty to the Gothic king, which originated from the Roman military oath of allegiance, they could be legally expected to provide such support.[84] Lastly, the three-fold organisation pattern of the military probably collapsed quickly during the Gothic Wars.

Nonetheless, we can observe three different modes of civil–military interaction based on the organisation patterns of the different parts of Theoderic's military forces, and the degree of professionalism of these forces.

Most intriguingly, these differences are reflected on the civilian side, although largely dictated by geography: the necessary interaction of border troops and the local population might also have led to a decreasing distinction between the two, unlike in mainland Italy. Here, Theoderic achieved perhaps the most profound separation between soldiers (Gothic or not) and civilians in late Antiquity. And as long as his rule ensured security and peace, Italian society did not exhibit many of the key traits of militarisation as attested elsewhere in the west.

Notes

1 Procop. *Hist. Arc.* 26,27–28: Ἰταλίαν γὰρ Θευδέριχος ἑλὼν τοὺς ἐν τῷ Ῥώμης Παλατίῳ στρατευομένους αὐτοῦ εἴασεν, ὅπως τι διασώζοιτο πολιτείας ἐνταῦθα τῆς παλαιᾶς ἴχνος, μίαν ἀπολιπὼν σύνταξιν ἐς ἡμέραν ἑκάστῳ. ἦσαν δὲ οὗτοι παμπληθεῖς ἄγαν. οἵ τε γὰρ σιλεντιάριοι καλούμενοι καὶ δομέστικοι καὶ σχολάριοι ἐν αὐτοῖς ἦσαν, οἷς δὴ ἄλλο οὐδὲν ἀπελέλειπτο ἢ τὸ τῆς στρατείας ὄνομα μόνον, καὶ ἡ σύνταξις αὕτη ἐς τὸ ἀποζῆν ἀποχρῶσα μόλις αὐτοῖς, ἅπερ ἔς τε παῖδας καὶ ἀπογόνους Θευδέριχος αὐτοὺς παραπέμπειν ἐκέλευσε. *Procopius. The Anecdoata or Secret History*, trans. H. B. Dewing (Cambridge: Harvard University Press, 1935), p. 310–12.
2 Ennodius, *ep.* 2,27, 6,21. F. Vogel (ed.), *Magni Felicis Ennodii opera, MGH AA*, 7 (Berlin: Weidmannsche Buchhandlung, 1895, p. 75; 225.
3 Cass., *Variae* 6,6,1; 8,12,8. T. Mommsen (ed.), *Cassiodori Senatoris Variae, MGH AA*, 12 (Berlin: Weidmannsche Buchhandlung, 1894), p. 179; 243.
4 Cass., *Var.* 1,10,2.
5 P. Amory, *People and identity* (Cambridge: Cambridge University Press 1997), p. 92.
6 J. Arnold, *Theoderic and the Roman Imperial restoration* (Cambridge: Cambridge University Press, 2014).
7 Procop., *Hist. Arc.* 26,28.
8 Procop., *Hist. Arc.* 24,21.
9 Th. Mommsen, 'Das römische Militärwesen seit Diocletian', *Hermes*, 24 (1889), 195–279, here 224–5.
10 P. Heather, 'Gens and Regnum among the Ostrogoths', in H.-W. Goetz, J. Jarnut and W. Pohl (eds), *Regna and Gentes. The relationship between late antique and early medieval peoples and kingdoms* (Leiden: Brill, 2003), p. 118; H. Wolfram, *Die Goten* (Munich: C.H. Beck, 2001), p. 300.
11 G. Halsall, 'The Ostrogothic military', in J. Arnold, S. Bjornlie and K. Sessa (eds), *Companion to Ostrogothic Italy* (Leiden: Brill, 2016), pp. 173–99, here p. 186.
12 Cass., *Var.* 1,11,2.
13 F. Glaser, 'Castra und Höhensiedlungen in Kärnten und Nordtirol', in H. Steuer and V. Bierbrauer (eds), *Höhensiedlungen zwischen Antike und Mittelalter von den Ardennen bis zur Adria* (Berlin: De Gruyter, 2008), pp. 613–14.

14 Cass., *Var.* 7,4,2.
15 Wolfram, *Die Goten*, pp. 315–17. Also F. Beyerle, 'Süddeutschland in der politischen Konzeption Theoderich des Großen', in T. Mayer (ed.), *Vorträge und Forschungen* (Darmstadt: WBG, 1962), pp. 66–71, putting a greater emphasis on Alemannia.
16 Cass., *Var.* 1,17.
17 T. Börzel and T. Risse, 'Governance without a state', *Regulation and Governance*, 4 (2010), 115–18. The concept itself needs some adaption to work for the late Antiquity since it was developed for describing the relationship between present-day non-state actors and the state, especially in non-hierarchical rulemaking. Even disregarding the vexed question of whether 'states' existed in Antiquity (see, e.g., S. Patzold, 'Human Security, fragile Staatlichkeit und Governance im Frühmittelalter', *Geschichte und Gesellschaft*, 38 (2012), 406–22), decision- and rulemaking was predominantly hierarchical. However, having a greater power – which by its sheer potential to markedly exert influence already affects local processes – is something that can be observed in late antique Raetia as well. This works as a functional equivalent to a shadow of hierarchy.
18 D. Claude, 'Studien zu Handel und Wirtschaft im italischen Ostgotenreich', *Münsterische Beiträge zur antiken Handelsgeschichte*, 15 (1996), 42–75, here 74.
19 Such a design would be supported by research highlighting the continuity of substructures in the duchy itself, rather than that of overlaying superregional (pseudo-)imperial structures of the late Roman, Gothic or Frankish administrations, and the importance of the ducal, rather than imperial, identity for the local population. S. Esders, 'Spätantike und frühmittelalterliche Dukate', in H. Fehr and I. Heitmeier (eds), *Die Anfänge Bayerns* (St. Ottilien: Eos, 2012), pp. 425–62.
20 A. Sarantis, 'Waging war in late Antiquity', in N. Christie and A. Sarantis (eds), *War and warfare in late Antiquity* (Leiden: Brill, 2013), *passim*; D. Parnell, *Justinian's men. Careers and relationships of Byzantine army officers 518–610* (London: Palgrave Macmillan, 2017), p. 1; P. Heather, *Rome resurgent. War and empire in the age of Justinian* (Oxford: Oxford University Press, 2018), p. 44.
21 S. Huntington, *The soldier and the state* (Cambridge: Harvard University Press, 1957), pp. 7–10.
22 Most prominently, S. Bjornlie, *Politics and tradition between Rome, Ravenna and Constantinople* (Cambridge: Cambridge University Press 2013), pp. 329–33; its critical review by H.-U. Wiemer, *Sehepunkte*, 13.11.2013; sehepunkte.de/2013/11/22995.html (accessed 14 January 2020).
23 Cass., *Var.* 5,29; 5,30.
24 Cass., *Var.* 5,36.
25 Cass., *Var.* 1,40; also Ennod., *Pan.* 83. *Der Theoderich-Panegyricus des Ennodius*, ed. and trans. C. Rohr (Hanover: Hahn, 1995), p. 256.
26 Procop., *Bella* 1,1,6–17. *Procopius History of the Wars*, trans. H. B. Dewing (Cambridge: Harvard University Press, 1935), p. 4–8
27 Procop., *Bella* 5,28,18; 5,29,26.

28 Procop., *Bella* 7,22.
29 Huntingon, 'Soldier and the state', p. 9.
30 Cass., *Var.* 2,5,2: *Decet enim cogitare de militis transactione, qui pro generali quiete finalibus locis noscitur insudare.*
31 Cass., *Var.* 1,40,4; 12,5,4; 3,38,2.
32 J. Moorhead, 'Italian loyalties during Justinian's Gothic War', *Byzantion*, 53 (1983), 575–96, here 592–3.
33 M. Kouroumali, 'The Justinianic reconquest of Italy. Imperial campaigns and local responses', in N. Christie and A. Sarantis (eds), *War and warfare in late Antiquity* (Leiden: Brill, 2013), pp. 977–86.
34 Cass., *Var.* 3,38,2: *vivat noster exercitus civiliter cum Romanis: prosit eis destinata defensio nec aliquid illos a nostris sinatis pati, quos ab hostili nitimur oppressione liberari*; also *Var.* 4,49; 5,26.
35 Cass., *Var.* 8,26,4.
36 Cass., *Var.* 2,5; 4,13; 5,11; 5,26; 8,27; 12,18.
37 Huntingon, 'Soldier and the state', p. 10.
38 Cass., *Var.* 1,4,17; 2,8,1; 2,15,2; 3,36,2; 3,42,2; 3,43,3; 4,36,2; 7,4,3; 8,10,8; 9,14,4.
39 Ennod., *Pan.* 65.
40 ILS 827. H. Dessau (ed.), *Inscriptiones Latinae Selectae*, 1 (Berlin: Weidmannsche Buchhandlung, 1892), p. 184.
41 *An. Val.* 2,83. *Aus der Zeit Theoderichs des Großen. Einleitung, Text, Übersetzung und Kommentar einer anonymen Quelle*, ed. and trans. I. König (Darmstadt: WBG, 1997), p. 90.
42 G. M. Berndt, 'The Goths drew their swords together. Individual and collective acts of violence by Gothic warlords and their war bands', in J. Rogge (ed.), *Killing or being killed. Bodies in battle. Perspectives on fighters in the Middle Ages*, Mainzer Historische Kulturwissenschaften, 38 (Bielefeld: Transcript, 2017), pp. 15–41, here p. 32.
43 Parnell, *Justinian's men*, p. 47.
44 *CTh* 15,15,1; *Nov. Val.* 9.; Nov. Mai. 8. T. Mommsen and P. Meyer (ed.), *Theodosiani Libri XVI cum Constitutionibus Sirmondianis et Leges Novellae ad Theodosianum Pertinentes, Lateinisch* (Berlin: Weidmannsche Buchhandlung, 1905), p. 832.
45 *CTh* 14,10.
46 P. von Rummel, *Habitus barbarus. Kleidung und Repräsentation spätantiker Eliten im 4. und 5. Jahrhundert* (Berlin: De Gruyter, 2007), p. 166.
47 A. Goltz, 'Der nackte Theoderich', in S. Bießenecker (ed.), *Und sie erkannten, dass sie nackt waren* (Bamberg: University of Bamberg Press, 2008), pp. 387–412, here pp. 400–2.
48 Ennod., *Carm.* 2,57–9. F. Vogel (ed.), *Magni Felicis Ennodii opera*, MGH AA, 7 (Berlin: Weidmannsche Buchhandlung, 1895), p. 157.
49 J. H. W. F. Liebeschütz, *East and west in late Antiquity. Invasion, settlement, ethnogenesis and conflicts of religion* (Leiden: Brill 2015), pp. 158–9.
50 J. Arnold, 'Theoderic's invincible mustache', *Journal of Late Antiquity*, 6 (2013), 152–83, here 158–60.

51 G. Maier, *Amtsträger und Herrscher in der Romania Gothica* (Stuttgart: Franz Steiner, 2005), pp. 207–22; 236.
52 B. Swain, 'Goths and Gothic identity in the Ostrogothic kingdom', in J. Arnold, S. Bjornlie and K. Sessa (eds) *Companion to Ostrogothic Italy* (Leiden: Brill, 2016), pp. 209–33, here pp. 222–24.
53 Cass., *Var.* 8,21.
54 P. Heather, *The Goths* (Malden: Wiley-Blackwell, 1996), pp. 173–4; H. Wolfram, *Gotische Studien* (Munich: C.H. Beck 2005), p. 258.
55 Halsall, 'The Ostrogothic military', pp. 189–90; P. Porena, *L'Insediamento degli Ostrogoti in Italia* (Roma: Bretschneider 2012), p. 132.
56 Ennod., *Pan.* 33, 44–5.
57 M. Vitiello, 'Motive germanischer Kultur und Prinzipien des gotischen Königtums im Panegyricus des Ennodius', *Hermes*, 133 (2005), 100–5, here 113–15.
58 Ennod., *Pan.* 44.
59 Suet., *Aug.* 73. *Sueton. Die Kaiserviten*, ed. and trans. H. Martinet (Düsseldorf: Artemis & Winkler, 1997), p. 269.
60 Maier, *Amtsträger*, pp. 170–1.
61 Ennod., *Pan.* 65: *meministis, socii, cuius ad haec loca conmeastis imperio. nemo absentes credat regis nostri oculos, pro cuius fama dimicandum est. si caelum lancearum imber obtexerit, qui fortius telum iecerit non latebit.*
62 M. Radnoti-Alföldi, 'Das Goldmultiplum Theoderichs des Großen', in H. Bellen and H.-M. Kaenel (eds), *Gloria Romanorvm* (Stuttgart: Franz Steiner, 2001), pp. 204–14, here p. 213.
63 Cass., *Var.* 5,29.
64 *An. Val.* 2,68–9: *Odoin comes eius insidiabatur ei. Dum haec cognovisset, in palatio quod appellatur Sessorium caput eius amputari praecepit.*
65 *Auct. Havn.* a. 514: *Theudoricus rex Mediolanium veniens Petiam comitem interfecit.*
66 *Auct. Havn.* a. 504.
67 Possibly identical with Pitzias, compare Wolfram, *Die Goten*, p. 486, n. 15.
68 A. Plassmann, 'Interessenvertretung und Intrigen am ostgotischen Königshof', in M. Becher and A. Plassmann (eds), *Streit am Hof im frühen Mittelalter* (Göttingen: V&R Unipress, 2011), pp. 75–94, here p. 77, n. 8; A. Goltz, *Barbar-König-Tyrann Das Bild Theoderichs des Großen in der Überlieferung des 5. bis 9. Jahrhunderts*, Millenium-Studien, 12 (Berlin: De Gruyter, 2007), p. 350.
69 E. Wirbelauer, *Zwei Päpste in Rom* (Munich: Utz, 1993), p. 34; S. Dieffenbach, *Römische Erinnerungsräume. Heiligenmemoria und kollektive Identitäten im Rom des 3. bis 5. Jahrhunderts n. Chr.* (Berlin: De Gruyter, 2007), p. 175.
70 H. Börm, 'Justinians Triumph und Belisars Erniedrigung', *Chiron*, 43 (2013), 63–91, here 84–88.
71 J. H. W. G. Liebeschuetz, 'The Romans demilitarised. The evidence of Procopius', *SCI*, 15 (1996), 230–9.
72 A. Goldsworthy, *The Roman army at war* (Oxford: Oxford University Press, 1996), pp. 291–2.
73 Cass., *Var.* 1,4,17; 2,8,1; 2,15,2; 3,36,2; 3,42,2; 3,43,3; 4,36,2; 7,4,3; 8,10,8; 9,14,4.

74 Cass., *Var.* 2,5; 4,13; 5,11; 5,26; 8,27; 12,18.
75 Cass., *Var.* 10,18.
76 S. Barnish, 'Pigs, plebeians and potentates. Rome's economic hinterland, c. AD 350–600', *Papers of the British School at Rome*, 55 (1987), 157–85, here 160–5.
77 C. Whately, *Battles and generals. Combat, culture, and didacticism in Procopius' Wars* (Leiden: Brill, 2015), pp. 173–4.
78 T. Burns, 'Calculating Ostrogothic army and population', *Ancient World*, 1 (1978), 187–90.
79 Procop., *Bella* 5,8,8.
80 Cass., *Var.* 10,18.
81 Parnell, *Justinian's men*, pp. 201–2.
82 Cass., *Var.* 1,17 and 1,28.
83 Procop., *Bella* 5,8,41.
84 S. Esders, *Sacramentum fidelitatis. Treueidleistung, Militärorganisation und Formierung mittelalterlicher Staatlichkeit* (Habilitationsschrift Bochum, 2003), p. 94.

4

Military organisation as an indicator of militarisation (and demilitarisation) in Lombard Italy

Guido M. Berndt

Anyone today attempting to write about the history of the Lombards risks repeating a story that has been told many times before.[1] Irrespective of one's research foci, whether political, social, religious, cultural or military, the main difficulty remains the nature of the surviving sources, or rather their limited number. When it comes to the question of militarisation of early medieval societies,[2] the Lombard case provides some interesting perspectives because one can combine the findings from the written sources with a remarkable amount of archaeological material.[3]

This chapter aims to show at least one method of assessing the degree of militarisation and/or demilitarisation in Lombard Italy, and to shed some light on the mechanisms that determined these processes. Militarisation has been subject to cursory examination in the past, but has been somewhat neglected in modern research,[4] even though there seems to be a consensus that the 'Lombards were a people of warriors, and war was a normal feature of life for all free men'.[5]

The point of departure here is the short but seminal article by Edward James, in which he compiled a series of criteria to define a militarised society.[6] When applying this concept to the society of Lombard Italy, the following features match remarkably well: (1) there was no clear demarcation between military and civilian responsibilities; for instance, in the most important offices, such as the *duces* and *gastaldi*; (2) there was a widespread proliferation of weapons in large parts of the free male population that were expected to serve in the army; (3) there was a high level of recognition of military capabilities, activities and values; (4) weapons were not only used in warfare, but also for certain ceremonies and rituals, thus having some symbolic meaning; for example, the handing over of a lance[7] to a chosen candidate on the occasion of his accession to the throne; (5) the head of the society was also the supreme commander of the army and usually participated personally in campaigns.[8]

Our understanding of Lombard society depends considerably on their military organisation and the question of who was obliged to serve in their armies. With this question, we encounter the undeniable difficulty that in fact only a small section of the entire Italian society can be analysed in some detail due to the perspectives of the surviving written sources. It is essential to make clear from the outset that, with the exception of Paul the Deacon's *Historia Langobardorum*,[9] we lack any coherent narrative of noteworthy length between the end of the sixth and the end of the eighth centuries. In all readings of this text, one must keep in mind that Paul was primarily a storyteller with his own agenda, not a military historian. We can at least agree that Paul, who had served at different royal and ducal courts before he withdrew from public life, gave a 'rich and varied response to the experiences and ideas that he encountered', as Christopher Heath recently pointed out.[10] To this main source, some further texts – chronicles, saints' lives, charters and inscriptions – can be added. In view of a 200-year history of the Lombards in Italy, it can hardly be supposed that in terms of militarisation a static and homogeneous picture emerges. Rather, different trends and developments are observable, leading to the sources depicting differing degrees of militarisation. Thus, in addition to increasing militarisation tendencies, most notably in the early years of the Lombard's presence in Italy, demilitarisation trends are also discernible, especially in the final decades of the Lombard kingdom. Moreover, as identities in human societies are constantly changing, we must also consider that the identity/identities of the Lombards changed during the course of these two centuries.[11] Furthermore, spatial factors likely played a considerable role. In border duchies, as for instance Friuli, a higher degree of militarisation can be observed than in regions that were only occasionally affected by armed conflict.[12]

When the Lombards entered Italy in 568, they did not appear from nowhere. For several decades, they had been living on the periphery of the Roman Empire where they occasionally came into contact with the Roman authorities.[13] Before the Italian invasion,[14] when still dwelling in *Pannonia*,[15] a considerable number of Lombard warriors had been engaged as Roman *foederati* and mercenaries in the ongoing military conflicts in the Balkans, thus gaining experience with the Roman military.[16] Most significantly, large contingents of Lombard warriors were recruited for the Gothic Wars of the Emperor Justinian I (r. 527–65).[17] Thus, research has recognised Roman influences on the political and military organisation of the Lombards.[18] In 1984, Tom Brown in his book *Gentlemen and officers* argued that the separation of the military and civil spheres in Italy, which had been maintained for centuries, began to erode as early as the fifth century.[19] After the fall of the Gothic kingdom[20] and the re-establishment of Roman authority in the middle of the sixth century (to some extent visible through Justinian's *Pragmatic Sanction*, promulgated in August 554),[21] in the newly created office of the exarchate of Ravenna, military and civil responsibilities were merged.[22] A similar development can be observed for the Lombard office of the *dux*, created in the early days of occupation.[23] Furthermore, the disappearance of the traditional civil senatorial aristocracy opened space for a new military aristocracy.[24] Brown was also able to prove that in the second half of the sixth century about 10 per cent of the participants in land transactions in the territories of Ravenna were military officials, whereas throughout the seventh century, this proportion rose to around 75 per cent.[25] It is reasonable to assume that similar developments were taking place in the parts of Italy dominated by the Lombards, as Byzantine and Lombard Italy were intertwined in many ways, even if we lack explicit sources on this matter for the Lombards.

In the context of the first conquests, Paul the Deacon writes that the Lombards were organised in *farae*.[26] This highly debated term was once believed to denote clan or family groups; however, they contained elements of military followings.[27] At the top of one *fara* was an individual commander, who appears to have had the power to act to some degree independently from the warrior-king.[28] In most of the major towns conquered, Alboin,[29] the Lombard military leader, installed a *dux* as head of the new administration.[30] The first reported case is *Forum Iulii* (Cividale del Friuli), where Gisulf, a nephew of Alboin who had served as 'master of the horse' (*strator erat, quem lingua propria marpahis appellant*), was invested. Strikingly, Gisulf imposed conditions before taking the office by claiming the right to choose some contingents (*farae*) to stay with him, as well as valuable horses.[31] Alboin generously granted these requests, whereupon the corresponding groups settled in *Forum Iulii* and its surroundings. What we might infer from this case is that Alboin was apparently unable to simply order his followers to accept commands; rather, he had to negotiate on matters like this. Besides creating a new Lombard administration in the *civitas* and commanding his warriors, one important task assigned to Gisulf was the defence of the Friulian territories and of the Julian Alps ('traditional' gateways to Italy for many barbarians). However, it would certainly be exaggerated to suggest that this story demonstrated that the leaders of the *farae* became the first *duces* of Lombard Italy.[32] *Farae* as a form of military organisation apparently fell out of use at some point between the Lombard settlement and the decade of the interregnum (574–84). When precisely this change took place, or what it precisely involved, remains unclear. Whatever the case, there are no sources indicating that by the time of Authari (r. 584–90)[33] or Agilulf (r. 590–615), the Lombards were keeping up the *fara*-system as an organisational unit for their military apparatus.[34]

Judging from the Lombard *leges*, landed wealth became increasingly important during the seventh century. The *Edictum Rothari* and the laws of subsequent kings present the Lombards as landowners in many of their chapters.[35] This indicates that sometime between the invasion of 568 and before 643, Lombard warriors had made use of opportunities to acquire land (as *hospites*), thus retaining their military obligations. The *arimanni* (Lomb.) or *exercitales* (Lat.) were organised corporately as free men fighting for their *rex* or *dux*, for their people and their territory.[36] At the same time, one can observe increasing social segregation. During the seventh century, families or households with multiple sons were required to send only one of them to join the army, whereas the other could stay at home to take care of the family's properties. He would also have had to take care of his brother's equipment and military supply. In return, he was entitled to a share of the profits of war.[37]

The core of the Lombard army was composed of the capable male members of the *gens Langobardorum*. However, Paul the Deacon improves the generalised reports of the contemporary chronicles by providing an important detail for the understanding of the character of the Lombard military.[38] He writes that Gepids, Bulgarians, Sarmatians, Suebians and people from *Pannonia* and *Noricum* joined forces with the Lombards. Paul also particularly emphasises the role of Saxon warriors in the conquest of Italy.[39] Therefore, the Lombard army, like many other warrior groups in the time of the transition from late Antiquity to the early Middle Ages, was polyethnic, even though it is not clear what practical consequences (if any) this mixture had for the military organisation that developed in Italy after 568. Apparently, in the first Italian years, the Roman population played no role in this organisation, even if the Latin term *dux* was used for military commanders as early as in the 570s.

The sources indicate that the invasion and occupation of large parts of northern Italy were not difficult tasks for the Lombard warriors and, apparently, no large battles had to be fought.[40] The Lombards advanced constantly, with the one exception that Alboin needed almost three years to conquer Pavia, the city that the Lombards would some decades later establish as their capital.[41] However, almost no military resistance is reported for many of the other north Italian cities.[42] They were able to capture Vicenza, Verona and Milan in the Po plain. Furthermore, a number of smaller posts in the Alpine foothills were taken from the Byzantines. Likewise, in middle and southern Italy, Lombard armies occupied large territories, resulting in the foundation of the two duchies of Spoleto and Benevento.[43] Henceforth, the organisation of the Lombard kingdom clearly was based upon the *civitates*, usually governed by dukes (and later *gastalds*). It is obvious that the Lombard's grand strategy was to get hold of a network of fortified towns in northern Italy.[44] In Italy, the Lombards were compelled to adopt new methods of warfare that included siege warfare and strategies to maintain the newly conquered fortified cities and strongholds. They must have acquired the skills to take fortifications, either through onrush or lengthy siege and blockades, both of which required engineering, logistical capabilities and planning, indicating a high degree of professionalisation.[45] Henceforth, Lombard units were mainly stationed in the cities, but also at strongholds and forts (*castra*).[46] Unfortunately, no written source tells us *how* the Lombards aquired these skills.

Neither in the time of Alboin nor of his successor Cleph (r. 572–74) was there *one* distinct Lombard warrior confederation. After the latter's assassination, the Lombard *duces*, increasingly acting as warlords or *condottieri*, refused to elect a common leader for an entire decade. Paul the Deacon reports that during this period, Lombard Italy was governed by thirty-five dukes, although this number seems exaggerated. He names only five explicitly, those of Pavia, Bergamo, Brescia, Trento and Cividale.[47] We might add to this list Milan, Turin, Spoleto and Benevento;[48] however, there are no sources for the many other important cities conquered by the Lombards.

In the first years after the invasion, many magnates were willingly turned over or bribed by the Byzantine authorities and henceforth no longer fought for the Lombards.[49] Indeed, Lombard warriors repeatedly served in the Byzantine army, with some of them rising to high ranks.[50] The letter-collection of Gregory the Great preserves some names of Lombard warriors fighting for the Byzantines.[51] The emperor also payed money to the Lombards' enemies. The Byzantine chronicler Menander Protector writes that Tiberius II (r. 574–82) paid 3,000 pounds of gold to the Franks to persuade them to fight in Italy against the Lombards, but that he also paid the Lombards to agree to a peace treaty.[52] Clearly, there was no ethnic cohesion or consensus among the powerful Lombard magnates.

Throughout the seventh century, reports of military conflicts become less frequent. The sources record three large battles fought by Lombard warriors against foreign enemies, which resulted in two victories and one defeat.[53] Of course, one must also take into account the fact that many small-scale military operations and skirmishes took place within the kingdom, in many cases triggered by the constant struggles for the Lombard throne and the aspirations of power-hungry *duces*.[54] The most prominent example is the usurpation of Alahis against King Cunincpert, a conflict that grew into a civil war. The Battle of Coronate took place in 689 and resulted in Alahis and most of his warriors losing their lives.[55]

In the eighth century, the military basis of social identity was still widespread, as might be inferred from a charter written in 730, in which the citizens of Siena were collectively referred to as an *exercitus*. However, it must be admitted that it is not easy to follow in detail the developments of the Lombard's military organisation from the 'ethnic' warrior groups of the years around 600 to the armies of the last Lombard kings. Nevertheless, in the first half of the eighth century, Lombard warriors must still have had a good reputation as reliable warriors, as Charles Martel, the mayor of the palace of *Francia*, called for military assistance in 737. King Liutprand (r. 712–44) led an army to support the fight against the Saracens, but seems to have arrived in southern France too late to get involved in the confrontation.[56]

From the middle of the eighth century onwards, new military conflicts arose in Italy. On the one hand, Lombard kings launched several campaigns against the Byzantines, leading to the conquest of Ravenna in 751; on the other, Frankish armies became increasingly involved and were sent to Italy to support the Pope, who could no longer rely upon aid from the emperor against increasing military threats.[57] This growing danger of Frankish interferences apparently caused some Lombard military men to withdraw from their general obligation to serve in the army.[58] Consequently, King Aistulf (r. 749–56) tried to counteract this development by proclaiming a series of laws to restructure the Lombard army.[59] The immediate effects of this reform are unknown. However, the warrior identity was clearly upheld, since a large number of the elite in the kingdom still identified as Lombards, i.e. free men serving in the army of the king. The first years of the reign of the last Lombard king Desiderius (r. 757–74) were initially quite peaceful, which may lead to the conclusion that due to inactivity, the Lombard armies gradually lost their military experience and confidence.[60] The reasons for some of these shifts of loyalty are not always clear, but they may have been reactions to a king's inability to satisfy the aspirations of members of the military aristocracy. The fact that the downfall of the kingdom in 774 faced no significant resistance might also indicate the fragmentation of the Lombard armies, whose warriors were apparently no longer willing to support their king or protect their kingdom.[61]

Due to the survival of the Lombard laws (*leges Langobardorum*) and some charters, we have some material that complements the rather vague descriptions of the narrative sources and helps to shine light on the developments of the Lombard military during the two centuries of their rule in Italy. These laws were codified and promulgated in the year 643 by King Rothari (r. 636–52),[62] and later extended and supplemented by subsequent Lombard kings.[63] Combining the available information, the following rough picture[64] can be drawn: initially, the Lombard *exercitus* was composed of all the capable men who followed Alboin from *Panonnia* to Italy, regardless of their original ethnic affiliation.[65] However, by the 570s this coherent picture is muddied by the fact that a considerable number of warriors defected from the Lombard army to place themselves in the service of Roman commanders, who obviously provided the necessary financial incentives for them to do so. They presumably took with them their military followers and dependants. For those who remained on the Lombard side, it seems that military service was mandatory. The *Edictum Rothari* clearly describes the *exercitus* as the most important political community of the realm. The first chapter orders capital punishment for anyone attempting to murder the king. Chapters 4 to 7 dictate severe punishment for those supporting enemies of the Lombard kingdom, thereby demonstrating that these laws were intended to stabilise the kingdom. Chapter 21 regulates the obligation of the warriors (*exercitales*) to join the army on campaign: 20 *solidi* are to be paid by those who refuse to follow the *rex* or *dux*. This is a clear sign of inculcation of loyalty that was demanded from every free Lombard and therefore another attempt to avoid unrest within the kingdom. Furthermore, with the codification of the law, Rothari underlined the Lombard's claim to rule Italy legitimately.

At the head of the social as well as the military hierarchy was the *rex Langobardorum*, who was personally responsible for the appointment of the high military offices. The office of *dux* was conferred for a lifetime and linked to supreme command over the available military men of the respective duchy.[66] These dukes were aristocrats and office holders, in charge of armies and responsible for the defence of the kingdom. Nonetheless, they frequently tried to enlarge their own power and territories at the expense of either other magnates or the king. Both externally and internally, the interests of the Lombard kingdom could only be secured through the maintenance of strong armies. Leadership of these troops fell within the sphere of responsibility of either the king or the *duces*.

Over the seventh century, a competing elite emerged, namely the *gastaldi*, who – endowed with royal authority – assumed military, legal and administrative functions in the Lombard kingdom. They apparently reported directly to the king and could therefore act as a counterweight to the dukes in local politics. As stated, both the dukes and *gastalds* combined military and civilian responsibilities. Furthermore, we know a series of terms for subordinate military offices, such as for the chamberlain or constable (Lomb. *marpahis*, Lat. *strator*),[67] some kind of district governor (*rector, quem >sculdahis< lingua propria dicunt*),[68] and the bearer of the royal lance, or the royal arm-bearer (*scilpor, hoc est armiger*).[69] For other official titles, it is not possible to determine exactly which areas of responsibility they covered. This is the case with the *antepor*,[70] the *hostiarius, mariscalc* (marshal?)[71] and the *scaffardus*.[72] In addition to these offices, the king must also have had various agents who represented his authority in his domains – the towns and villages (referred to as *missus, spatharius, maior domus* and *waldeman*).[73]

The *sculdahis* may have fulfilled certain judicial functions, but they were also responsible for military duties. Furthermore, the military character of the office seems to have been preserved in the title of *centinus* or *centenaries*.[74] Finally, *saltarii*,[75] *decani*[76] and *actores*[77] are to be located at the lowest level of the military hierarchy, probably tasked with policing duties in the broadest sense. The majority of warriors were under the command of either a *dux* or a *gastaldus*, who led them in the event of war within the king's *exercitus* and united them under his supreme command. Aside from the traditional armies, special military forces (some of them in the function of bodyguards) existed around the dukes and some rich landowners, and, of course, at the king's court. These retinues were called *gasindii* and their importance should not be underestimated.[78]

For the Lombard armies of the eighth century, there are a few chapters in the *leges* that provide insight into recruitment practices. King Ratchis (r. 744–49/756–57) enacted that everyone should appear at the military assembly on horseback equipped with shield and spear to support their local judge when summoned to the king. Additionally, Aistulf (r. 749–56) enacted two laws which directly concerned military organisation. These chapters explain in some detail that the right to carry arms – or rather its obligation – was connected to a man's relative wealth. Aistulf's laws, which some scholars interpret as traces of a fundamental military reform,[79] divided Lombard landowners into different groups depending on the size of their properties. Wealthier men were expected to own one corslet, a horse, a shield and a lance. The less wealthy had to be equipped and ready to fight with the same equipment, minus the corslet. Finally, the 'poorer men' (*homines minores*, apparently people whose property was worth less than a plot of 40 acres of land) were only required to have a shield, quiver and bow and arrows to hand.[80] Aistulf's intention may have been to strengthen the military capacities of the Lombards during a time of rising conflict with the Byzantines and the Franks. Whatever the case, it is clear that eighth-century Lombard Italy was primarily organised along socio-economic lines.

From the middle of the eighth century onwards, Frankish–Lombard relations intensified and became increasingly hostile. It is not easy to explain to what extent the following political instability seemingly contributed to a demilitarisation of Lombard society. As the popes repeatedly called upon Frankish armies for help against the expanding Lombards, a series of military encounters occurred. Following the Lombard takeover of Ravenna in 751,[81] Pepin (the Short) campaigned in Italy against King Aistulf, whose troops had expanded into the *ducatus Romanus*. The Frankish army advanced through the passes of the Alps, defeated Aistulf, and besieged him in Pavia. The Lombards had to obtain peace on condition of surrendering Ravenna and all of their most recent Italian conquests. However, on Pepin's withdrawal, Aistulf burst forth again, laid siege to Rome and looted the surrounding country. The Frankish army returned to Italy and defeated the Lombards a second time. A third major conflict occurred during the reign of Charlemagne, who had been bestowed the title *patricius Romanorum* by the Pope. In 773, he started a prolonged military campaign that finally led to the surrender of King Desiderius and the fall of the Lombard kingdom. It would only seem logical that the military encounters in the final decades of the Lombard kingdom would find a loud echo in the contemporary sources. Remarkably, this is not the case.

Notes

The research leading to this chapter was funded by the Fritz Thyssen Stiftung (Cologne) within the framework of the project 'The militarisation of early medieval societies' at the Freie Universität Berlin as well as the German Research Foundation (DFG), with its Center for Advanced Studies 2496 'Migration and mobility in late Antiquity and the early Middle Ages' at the University of Tübingen. I am grateful to Ellora Bennett and James Harland for the revision of my English and to Laury Sarti whose comments on earlier drafts of this chapter have improved it.

1 There are some valuable overviews: P. Delogu, 'Il regno longobardo', in G. Galasso (ed.), *Storia d'Italia*, I (Torino: Utet, 1980), pp. 2–216; J. Jarnut, *Geschichte der Langobarden*, Urban-Taschenbücher, 339 (Stuttgart: Kohlhammer, 1982); N. Christie, *The Lombards. The ancient Longobards* (Malden, MA: Blackwell, 1995); S. Gasparri, *Italia longobarda. Il regno, i Franchi, il papato* (Rome: Laterza, 2012).

2 Research has acknowledged the importance of this phenomenon; see, e.g., C. Wickham, *The inheritance of Rome. A history of Europe from 400 to 1000* (London: Penguin Books, 2010), p. 200: 'Overall, in fact, the major change in political culture was not Germanization but militarization: the age of a dominant military aristocracy began in the fifth and sixth centuries, and continued throughout the West for more than a millennium.' See also W. Pohl, 'Invasions and ethnic identity', in C. La Rocca (ed.), *Italy in the early Middle Ages 476–1000*, Short Oxford History of Italy (Oxford: Oxford University Press, 2002), pp. 11–33, here p. 13: 'The gradual militarization of the Roman world meant that civil society increasingly lost its control over the armed forces.'

3 I discuss the value of this material and some (of the rare) visual representations in 'The armament of Lombard warriors in Italy. Some historical and archaeological approaches', in R. Krause and S. Hansen (eds), *Materialisierung*

von Konflikten. Beiträge der Dritten Internationalen LOEWE-Konferenz vom 24. bis 27. September 2018 in Fulda, Universitätsforschungen zur prähistorischen Archäologie, 346 = Prähistorische Konfliktforschung, 4 (Bonn: Habelt, 2019), pp. 299–322.

4 The latest update: J. Jarnut, 'Zum Stand der Langobardenforschung', in W. Pohl and P. Erhart (eds), *Die Langobarden. Herrschaft und Identität*, Forschungen zur Geschichte des Mittelalters, 9 (Vienna: Akademie, 2005), pp. 11–19.

5 D. Harrison, 'Dark Age migrations and subjective ethnicity. The example of the Lombards', *Skandia*, 57 (2008), 19–36, here 30. A very useful synthesis of the military developments in Italy during the Middle Ages is provided by P. Grilli, *Cavalieri e popoli in armi. Le instituzioni nell'Italia medievale* (Rome-Bari: Laterza, 2008), with a chapter on the Lombard period, pp. 19–35. He describes the Lombards as 'un popolo guerriero' (here p. 22).

6 See E. James, 'The militarisation of Roman society, 400–700', in A. N. Jørgensen and B. L. Clausen (eds), *Military aspects of Scandinavian society in a European perspective AD 1–1300* (Copenhagen: National Museum, 1997), pp. 19–24 and the introduction to this volume.

7 Paul the Deacon, *Historia Langobardorum* (hereafter *HL*), ed. L. Bethmann and G. Waitz, *MGH SRL* (Hanover: Hahn, 1878), pp. 12–187, VI,55.

8 Paul the Deacon reports many different occasions when Lombard *reges* personally led their armies (*HL* II,14: Alboin conquers *Venetia*; II,25: Alboin conquers Liguria and takes Milan; II,26: Alboin conquers Tuscany; III,32: Authari's military expedition to Southern Italy; IV,28: Agilulf takes Cremona and Mantua; IV,45: the conquests of King Rothari; V,5: Grimoald defeats a Frankish army; V,7: Grimoald leads his army to support Benevento against Emperor Constans II; V,21: Grimoald tricks Avar warriors in Friuli; V,27 Grimoald destroys Forum Populi; V,28: Grimoald destroys Oderzo; V,41: Cunincpert defeats Alahis; VI, 49: The conquests of King Liutprand; VI,54: Liutprand helps the Franks against the Saracenes). The Frankish Royal Annals (*Annales regni Francorum*, ed. R. Rau, *Quellen zur karolingischen Reichsgeschichte*, 1, Ausgewählte Quellen zur deutschen Geschichte des Mittelalters = Freiherr vom Stein-Gedächtnisausgabe, 5 [Darmstadt: Wissenschaftliche Buchgesellschaft, 1955], pp. 9–155) report for the year 755 that King Aistulf fought at the head of his army against the Frankish invaders lead by Pepin (the Short).

9 The *HL* was written at the very end of the eighth century, at a time when the Lombard kingdom of Italy had already been vanquished by the armies of Charlemagne (774). Paul the Deacon was a Lombard from Cividale del Friuli, born in the 720s. At the time of writing, he was a highly experienced monk in the famous monastery of Montecassino. Generally, his History dealt with the origins of the Lombards, their vast migrations, their settlement in Italy and the deeds of their kings and dukes up to the death of Liutprand in 744. The literature on Paul the Deacon and his oeuvre is vast. An up-to-date overview is provided by C. Heath, *The narrative worlds of Paul the Deacon. Between empires and identities in Lombard Italy* (Amsterdam: Amsterdam University Press, 2017), pp. 20–37.

10 Heath, *The narrative worlds*, here p. 256.
11 F. Borri, 'Romans growing beards. Identity and historiography in seventh-century Italy', *Viator*, 15 (2014), 39–72.
12 M. Brozzi, *Il ducato langobardo di Friuli* (Udine: Grafiche Fulvio Spa, 1981).
13 The earliest Roman sources, for instance Velleius Paterculus, Strabo and Tacitus, recognised the military character of the Lombards. Cassius Dio in his *Roman History* writes about 6,000 Lombards crossing the Danube in search of booty during of the Marcomannic War. Some 300 years later, Lombard name reappears in the written sources. They are recorded as occupying the so-called *Rugiland* in 489, where they got into serious military conflicts with the Heruls, finally vanquishing their realm. See J. Jarnut, 'Die langobardische Herrschaft über Rugiland und ihre politischen Hintergründe', in R. Bratož (ed.), *Westillyricum und Nordostitalien in der spätrömischen Zeit* (Ljubljana: National Museum, 1996), pp. 207–13.
14 N. Christie, 'Invasion or invitation? The Longobard occupation of northern Italy, AD 568–69', *Romanobarbarica*, 11 (1991), 79–108.
15 N. Christie, 'Pannonia. Foundations of Langobardic power and identity', in G. Ausenda, P. Delogu and C. Wickham (eds), *The Langobards before the Frankish conquest. An ethnographic perspective* (Woodbridge: Boydell & Brewer, 2009), pp. 6–29. In the middle of the sixth century, the 'Pannonian Lombards' were faced with the danger of a growing hegemony of the Avars in the Danube basin. The strategy of Emperor Justinian I to allow the Avars to expand into that region was driven by the idea that they would counter and weaken other barbarian groups there. This strategy turned out to be successful, as the Lombards in the upcoming struggles for dominance in Pannonia realised that they would not prevail.
16 F. Wozniak, 'Byzantine diplomacy and the Lombard-Gepidic wars', *Balkan Studies*, 20 (1979), 139–58; W. Pohl, 'The empire and the Lombards. Treaties and negotiations in the sixth century', in W. Pohl (ed.), *Kingdoms of the empire. The integration of barbarians in late Antiquity.* The Transformation of the Roman World, 1 (Leiden: Brill, 1997), pp. 75–134.
17 Following Procopius, *Gothic Wars* IV,26,12 (ed. J. Haury, *Opera omnia*, vol. II: *De Bellis libris V-III* [Leipzig: Teubner, 1905; repr. 1963]; Procopius, *The wars of Justinian*, trans. by H. B. Dewing, rev. and modernised, with an introduction and notes, by A. Kaldellis [Indianapolis: Hackett, 2014]), no less than 5,500 Lombards (2,500 warriors and 3,000 fighting servants) served in the armies of General Narses. Therefore, one can assume that at least these warriors knew parts of Italy already before 568 and may have served as scouts in Alboin's army. For the Lombard–Byzantine entanglements, see K. P. Christou, *Byzanz und die Langobarden. Von der Ansiedlung in Pannonien bis zur endgültigen Anerkennung, 500–680* (Athens: Historical Publications St. D. Basilopoulos, 1991); W. Pohl, 'Die Langobarden in Pannonien und Justinians Gotenkrieg', in D. Bialeková and J. Zabojník (eds), *Ethnische und kulturelle Verhältnisse an der mittleren Donau im 6.-11. Jahrhundert* (Bratislava: Veda, 1996), pp. 27–36. Already in 546/7, the Byzantines had recognised the Lombards' presence in Pannonia as military and political allies under their leader Audoin, by granting

them 'the city of Noricum and the strongholds of Pannonia' (Procopius, *Gothic Wars* II,33).

18 G. P. Bognetti, 'L'influsso delle istituzioni militari romane sulle istituzioni longobarde del secolo VI e la nature della fara', in G. P. Bognetti (ed.), *L'età longobarda* 3 (Milan: Editore Giuffrè, 1967), pp. 3–46; S. Gasparri, 'I barbari, l'impero, l'esercito e il caso dei Longobardi', in F. Botta and L. Loschavio (eds) *Civitas, Arma, Iura. Organizzazioni militari, istituzioni giuridiche e strutture sociali alle origini dell'Europa, secc. III-VIII* (Lecce: Edizioni Grifo, 2015), pp. 91–102, here p. 98: 'L'organizzazione politica longobarda era dunque quella dei reparti militari federati dell'impero'.

19 T. S. Brown, *Gentlemen and officers. Imperial administration and aristocratic power in Byzantine Italy AD 554–800* (London: British School at Rome, 1984).

20 S. J. B. Barnish, 'Transformation and survival in the Western senatorial aristocracy, c. AD 400–700', *Papers of the British School at Rome*, 56 (1988), 120–55, here 120: 'Yet, it notoriously failed to recover from the Gothic wars as it had from earlier disasters; and, by the time of Gregory the Great, it [the senate] was a shadow of its former self.'

21 *Pragmatica sanctio pro petitione Vigilii*, ed. F. Bluhme, *MGH LL*, 5 (Hanover: Hahn, 1875–79), pp. 170–5.

22 Still essential for understanding the administration of Byzantine Italy are C. Diehl, *L'administration byzantine dans l'exarchat de ravenne, 568–751*. Bibliothèque des écoles francaise d'Athene et de Rome, fasc. 53 (Paris: Thorin, 1888), and L. M. Hartmann, *Untersuchungen zur Geschichte der byzantinischen Verwaltung in Italien, 540–750* (Leipzig: Hirzel, 1889); see also F. E. Shlosser, 'The exarchates of Africa and Italy', *Jahrbuch der Österreichischen Byzantinistik*, 53 (2003), 27–45, here at 33: 'Who the first exarch was, we may never know. The role that Narses played in Italy may have been that of exarch in all but name.'

23 See M. Zerjadtke, *Das Amt "Dux" in Spätantike und frühem Mittelalter. Der "ducatus" im Spannungsfeld zwischen römischem Einfluss und eigener Entwicklung*, RGA supplements, 110 (Berlin: De Gruyter, 2019) with a chapter on the Lombard *duces*, pp. 167–211.

24 In the sense of M. Humphries, 'Italy, AD 425–605', in A. Cameron, B. Ward-Perkins and M. Whitby (eds), *The Cambridge Ancient History*, vol. 14: *Late Antiquity. Empire and successors, AD 425–600* (Cambridge: Cambridge University Press, 2001), pp. 525–51, here pp. 539–40.

25 Brown, *Gentlemen and officers*, here p. 63

26 Paulus Diaconus, *HL* II,9.

27 There is no space here to present the details of the debate on the *farae*. It can easily be comprehended in J. Jarnut, 'Die Landnahme der Langobarden in Italien aus historischer Sicht', in M. Müller-Wille and R. Schneider (ed.), *Ausgewählte Probleme europäischer Landnahmen des Früh- und Hochmittelalters. Methodische Grundlagendiskussionen im Grenzbereich zwischen Archäologie und Geschichte*, Vorträge und Forschungen, 41 (Sigmaringen: Jan Thorbecke,

1993), pp. 173–94, here p. 185: 'Diese Fahrtgemeinschaften waren identisch mit den Untereinheiten des langobardischen *exercitus*, die nach dem Einmarsch in Italien wichtige *civitates* und *castra* besetzten und beherrschten.' I generally agree with Jarnut's interpretation. See also H. Beck, M. Pfister and R. Wenskus, 'Fara', in *RGA*, 8 (1994), 193–205.

28 This is proved by the fact that at the time when Alboin was carrying out the siege of Pavia (the town that would later become the Lombard capital), significant parts of the invading army left him heading for territories further south, finally leading to the foundation of the duchies of Spoleto and Benevento. Furthermore, some Lombard warriors tried to secure their livelihood through uncontrolled looting raids. This desertion surely weakened Alboin's army and delayed the progress of conquering the northern territories.

29 On Alboin, see the comprehensive study F. Borri, *Alboino. Frammenti di un racconto (s. VI-XI)* (Rome: Viella, 2016).

30 This office remained a characteristic feature of the Lombard kingdom. There was a constant tension between the centralising impulses of sovereign power and the aspirations for autonomy of the *duces*.

31 *HL* II,9.

32 S. Gasparri, *I duchi longobardi*, Studi Storici, 109 (Rome: Istituto storico italiano per il Medio Evo, 1978).

33 Authari took the title of *Flavius*, and thus created a meaningful link between himself and former Italian rulers Odoacer and Theoderic. No source tells us who exactly was involved in the election and what happened during the convention (a *gairethinx* – literally 'gathering of spears')? Ideally, this gathering of all the free Lombard men was meant to represent the Lombard *exercitus* as well as the Lombard people. However, one would be mistaken to imagine it as a kind of democratic gathering of equal warriors, but rather one by the powerful aristocrats.

34 The *Edictum Rothari* of 643 mentions *fara* only once (177). *Leges Langobardorum*, ed. F. Bluhme, *MGH LL*, 4 (Hanover: Hahn, 1868), p. 41; K. F. Drew, *The Lombard laws*, Sources of Medieval History (Philadelphia: University of Pennsylvania Press, 1973), pp. 83–4.

35 Jarnut, 'Landnahme', here p. 192.

36 J. Jarnut, 'Beobachtungen zu den langobardischen arimanni und exercitales', *ZRG GA*, 88 (1971), 1–28; S. Gasparri, 'La questione degli arimanni', *Bullettino dell'Istituto Storico Italiano per il Medioevo*, 87 (1978), 121–53.

37 *Edictum Rothari* 167 (pp. 38–9).

38 For example, Marius of Avenches, *Chronicon* ad a. 569 (ed. T. Mommsen, *MGH AA*, 11 [Berlin: Weidmann, 1894], pp. 225–39, here p. 238). 'In this year, the king of the Lombards Alboin, with all his forces, left and burned his homeland Pannonia, and, in an expedition that included wives and his entire people, took possession of Italy.' (trans. A. C. Murray, *From Roman to Merovingian Gaul: A reader* [Peterborough: Broadview Press, 1999, pp. 100–8, here p. 107]).

39 *HL* II,6. Those Saxons who had accompanied Alboin's Lombards into Italy remained distinct and departed from Italy a decade later, see Gregory of Tours, *DLH* IV,42 and V,15 (ed. B. Krusch and W. Levison, *MGH SRM*, 1/1 [Hannover: Hahn, 2nd edn 1951), here pp. 175–6 and p. 213. Paul the Deacon later states that a Bulgar warrior group took service with the Lombards in Italy and was given land on the frontier to defend. Eventually they became a part of the Lombard military (*HL* V,29).

40 See S. Gasparri's Chapter 9 in this volume.

41 S. Gasparri, 'Pavia Longobarda', in E. Gabba, S. Gasparri, A. A. Settia, F. E. Consolino, E. Cau, M. A. Casagrande Mazzoli, A. P. Schioppa, P. J. Hudson, D. Vicini, A. S. Malacart and V. Lanzani (eds) *Storia di Pavia II. L'alto medioevo* (Milan: Banca del Monte di Lombardia, 1987), pp. 19–65; G. P. Brogiolo, 'Capitali e residenze regie nell'Italia longobarda', in *Sedes regiae, ann. 400–800*, ed. G. Ripoll and J. M. Gurt (Barcelona: Reial Acadèmia de Bones Lletres, 2000), pp. 132–62. It is worth mentioning that no Byzantine relief operations are recorded.

42 Indeed, some of the north Italian cities seem to have opened their gates to the Lombards in order to first protect their inhabitants and (maybe), second, in the hope of future cooperation from which they could benefit. Furthermore, civil unrest in northern Italy, and still ongoing Ostrogothic resistance, handicapped Byzantine counter-attacks.

43 C. Azzara, 'Spoleto e Benevento e il regno longobardo d'Italia', in *I Longobardi dei ducati di Spoleto e Benevento*. Atti del XVI Congresso Internazionale di Studi sull'Alto Medioevo, Spoleto, 20–23 ottobre 2002, Benevento, 24–27 ottobre 2002, vol 1 (Spoleto: Fondazione CISAM, 2003), pp. 105–23.

44 Emperor Maurice trusted in the strategy of paying one warrior king or warlord to attack another. He also chased the Franks to attack the Lombards and drive them out of Italy.

45 L. I. R. Petersen, *Siege warfare and military organization in the Successor States, 400–800 AD. Byzantium, the West and Islam*, History of Warfare, 91 (Leiden: Brill, 2013), pp. 188–90.

46 For the debate on how and where the Lombards settled, see N. Christie, 'From bones to homes. Looking for the Longobards', *Accordia Research Papers*, 5 (1994), 97–114; S. Brather: 'Dwelling and settlement among the Lombards', in G. Ausenda, P. Delogu and C. Wickham (eds), *The Langobards before the Frankish conquest. An ethnographic perspective* (Woodbridge: Boydell & Brewer, 2009), pp. 30–68. On the *castra*, see N. Christie, 'The castra of Paul the Deacon and the Longobard frontier in Friuli', in *Paolo Diacono e il Friuli altomedievale (secc. VI-X)*, Atti del XIV congresso internazionale di studi sull'alto medioevo (Spoleto: CISAM, 2001, pp. 231–51.

47 *HL* II,32. See S. Dick, 'Langobardi per annos decem regem non habentes, sub ducibus fuerunt. Formen und Entwicklung der Herrschaftsorganisation bei den Langobarden. Eine Skizze', in W. Pohl and P. Erhart (eds), *Die Langobarden. Herrschaft und Identität*, Forschungen zur Geschichte des Mittelalters, 9 (Vienna: Akademie, 2005), pp. 335–43.

48 Zerjadtke, *Das Amt "Dux"*, pp. 174–5.
49 S. Gasparri, 'Compétion ou collaboration? Les Lombards, les Romains et les évêques jusq'au milieu du VIIe siècle', in R. Le Jan, G. Bührer-Thierry and S. Gasparri (eds), *Coopétiton. Rivaliser, coopérer dans les sociétés du Haut Moyen Âge*, Haut Moyen Âge, 31 (Turnhout: Brepols, 2018), pp. 39–47.
50 A prominent case is Droctulf. Some stages of his military career are recorded in an epitaph endowed to him in the Basilica of San Vitale (Ravenna), reported by Paul the Deacon (*HL* III,19). Also Theophylact Simocatta (trans. M. and M. Whitby, *The history of Theophylact Simocatta* [Oxford: Clarendon Press, 1986]) preserves some glimpses of his military engagements for the Byzantines (II,17,9–10, pp. 67–8).
51 For example, *ep*. V,36 (Nordulf), *Registrum Epistolarum*, ed. P. Ewald and L. M. Hartmann, *MGH Epp.* 1–2 (Berlin: Weidmann, 1891-9), pp. 317–20; *The letters of Gregory the Great*, trans. J. R. C. Martyn, Mediaeval Sources in Translation (Toronto: Pontifical Institute of Mediaeval Studies, 2004), pp. 348–51.
52 Menander Protector, *Fragments* (ed. R. Blockley, *The History of Menander the Guardsman. Introductory essay, text, translation, and historiographical notes* [Liverpool: Francis Cairns, 1985], *fr.* 22 (*Exc. De Leg. Gent.* 25), p. 196/197.
53 1) The Battle of Scultenna in 643 between the army of Rothari and the army of the Byzantine exarch Isacius; 2) the Battle of Forino (Campania) in 663 between the army of Romuald of Benevento, son of King Grimoald, and the Byzantine army of Emperor Constans II in which the Romans again suffered a crushing defeat (*HL* V,10); and 3) the four-day battle at the *Fluvius Frigidus* in 664, in which the Lombard warriors under the command of *dux* Lupus were beaten by Avar warriors who thereafter heavily plundered in Friuli (*HL* V,19).
54 G. M. Berndt, 'Insurgency and counter-insurgency in Lombard Italy (c AD 600–700)', in C. Heath and R. Houghton (eds), *Conflict and violence in Medieval Italy, 568–1154* (Amsterdam: Amsterdam University Press, forthcoming).
55 *HL* V,41.
56 *HL* VI,54. Indeed, the Lombards had been in more or less close alliance with the Franks since *c.* 600.
57 W. Pohl, 'Das Papsttum und die Langobarden', in M. Becher and J. Jarnut (eds), *Der Dynastiewechsel von 751. Vorgeschichte, Legitimationsstrategien und Erinnerung* (Münster: Scriptorium, 2004), pp. 145–62, here p. 156. See also B. S. Bachrach, *Charlemagne's early campaigns (768–777). A diplomatic and military analysis*, History of Warfare, 82 (Leiden: Brill, 2013), especially the chapter 'The unwanted war' (pp. 246–309).
58 See S. Gasparri's Chapter 9 in this volume.
59 G. Halsall, *Warfare and society in the barbarian West, 450–900* (London: Routledge, 2003), here p. 83.
60 *Ibid.*, here p. 36.
61 S. Gasparri, 'The fall of the Lombard kingdom. Facts, memory and propaganda', in S. Gasparri (ed.), *774 – ipotesi su una transizione*, Atti del seminario di Poggibonsi, 16–18 febbraio 2006 (Turnhout: Brepols, 2008), pp. 41–65.

62 The edict was surely issued in order to enforce the allegiance of the Lombards to their king, and to strengthen Lombard identity on the eve of a war against the Romans. However, when analysing its stipulations, one should keep in mind that 'there is little agreement in interpretation of the nature of Rothari's edict [...] and the extent to which it demonstrates the cultural milieu of Italo-Lombard society in the mid-seventh century,' see N. Everett, 'Literacy and the law in Lombard government', *EME*, 9 (2000), 93–127, here 96.

63 C. Azzara, 'Introduzione al testo', in C. Azzara and S. Gasparri (eds), *Le Leggi dei Longobardi. Storia, Memoria e Diritto di un Popolo Germanico* (Rome: Viella, 2005).

64 The lengthy study of the Lombard's military organisation by Ottorino Bertolini is still the best starting point on this matter: 'Ordinamenti militari e strutture sociali dei langobardi in Italia', in *Ordinamenti militari in Occidente nell'alto medievo*. Settimane di studio del Centro italiano di studi sull'alto medioevo 15 (Spoleto: Fondazione CISAM, 1968), pp. 429–629.

65 Bertolini, 'Ordinamenti', p. 498 states, surely correctly, that the Lombards did not have precise written rules on military service before the legislation promulgated by King Aistulf.

66 Gasparri, *I duchi longobardi*; Zerjadtke, *Das Amt "Dux"*, pp. 167–84.

67 *HL* II,9.

68 *HL* VI,24

69 *HL* II,28.

70 *CDL*, II, ed. L. Schiaparelli, Fonti per la storia d'Italia, 63 (Roma: Istituto storico italiano per il medioevo, 1933), no. 226, p. 274.

71 *CDL*, II, no. 253, p. 334 (*Ansifrid marisscalco*).

72 D. Harrison, 'The Lombards in the early Carolingian epoch', in P. L. Butzer, M. Kerner and W. Oberschelp (eds), *Charlemagne and his heritage. 1200 years of civilization and science in Europe*. Vol. 1: *Scholarship, worldview and understanding* (Turnhout: Brepols, 1997), pp. 125–54, here pp. 132–3.

73 Ibid., p. 133; e.g. *CDL*, I, ed. L. Schiaparelli, Fonti per la storia d'Italia, 62 (Roma: Istituto storico italiano per il medioevo, 1929), no. 17, p. 50 (*Ambrosius inluster maiordomus*); *CDL*, III/1, ed. C. Brühl and H. Zielinski, Fonti per la storia d'Italia, 64/1 (Roma: Istituto storico italiano per il medioevo, 1973), no. 41, p. 241–2 (*Albonus uualdeman*).

74 *CDL*, I, no. 19, p. 73; Bertolini, 'Ordinamenti', pp. 490–1; H. Krug, 'Untersuchungen zum Amt des centenarius-Schultheiß' (I), in *ZRG GA*, 87 (1970), 1–31; (II), in *ZRG GA*, 88 (1971), 29–109.

75 Bertolini, 'Ordinamenti', pp. 440–2.

76 For example, *CDL*, II., no. 184, p. 164.

77 *Aistulfi leges* 7; *CDL* II, no. 218, p. 252 (*Amantinus ... actor domni regis*).

78 G. von Olberg, *Die Bezeichnungen für soziale Stände, Schichten und Gruppen in den Leges barbarorum*, Arbeiten zur Frühmittelalterforschung, 11 (Berlin: De Gruyter, 1991), p. 118.

79 P. S. Leicht, 'König Aistulfs Heergesetze', *Miscellanea Academia Berolinensia*, 11/1 (1950), 97–102.

80 See S. Gasparri's Chapter 9 in this volume.
81 Strikingly, this capture is very poorly documented in the written sources. Neither Paul the Deacon nor Agnellus of Ravenna explicitly mention the conquest of Ravenna. The Roman *Liber Pontificalis* suggests that Aistulf also conquered various Roman cities in the exarchate, but is not very specific about which these were. The fall of Ravenna is partly a deduction from the approaches that Pope Zacharias (741–52) makes to the Franks and a document of 7 July 751 *in palatio Ravennate*.

5

The 'dark matter' evidence for Alfredian military reforms in their ninth-century context

Ryan Lavelle

The reign of Alfred the Great, king of the southern English kingdom of the West Saxons from 871–99, is often presented in adulatory terms: defeat, followed by military victories and systematic military reform reaching through all social strata, leading to no less than the establishment of foundations for a wider English kingdom. The question of whether such an assessment can be fairly attributed to the reign of Alfred is not a new one; it is addressed recently, for example, in an essay on Alfred's military leadership presented as part of the *Festschrift* for Bernard Bachrach.[1] Here, however, I attempt to reflect on what might be considered strictly contemporary written sources for the late ninth century. This affords consideration of how historical perceptions of an early medieval society which may be considered 'militarised' are determined by later expectations. At the heart of this chapter is the question of why we tend to place so much emphasis on the period 871–99, seeing it as a turning point. Many assumptions on this come down to perceptions of Alfred today. Indeed, my own 2010 work on late Anglo-Saxon warfare, *Alfred's wars*, started from the assumption that the responses to military crises during the reign of Alfred determined the shape of the society for the following two centuries.[2]

Although we may occasionally see further from the shoulders of giants, a well-worn path sometimes limits our view. In the nineteenth century, it was a comparatively easy matter for historians to write of Anglo-Saxon military reform and link it directly to Alfred in the sort of adulatory fashion noted above. Such was the case with the popular historian John Richard Green's 1883 *Conquest of England*, who I quoted back in 2010:

> It was the thinning of their own ranks in the hour of victory which forced Æthelred [I] to conventions such as that of Nottingham, and Ælfred to conventions such as that of Exeter. The Dane in fact had changed the whole conditions of existing warfare. His forces were really standing armies, and a standing army of some sort was needed to meet them.[3]

While I must admit that my choice of Green to represent Victorian orthodoxy provided something of a straw man, the narrative sequence he presented is instructive. Here was the clear historical problematisation of a crisis leading to a solution – and ultimately to resolution. In some ways this narrative has been influential, encompassing the notion of Viking activity as that of a 'standing army' against that of a late Anglo-Saxon state forced to grow up in the face of the external threat which the Vikings presented.

I start from the premise that there is sufficient evidence to consider a 'militarised' society in England in the early tenth century (i.e. after the death of King Alfred). This militarisation may be seen as being in response to the pressures of external threat and the development of cohesion of the structures of society, the latter being a pre-Conquest version of what Michael Mann has characterised as 'infrastructural power' in the 'extensive power' of the state.[4] What is in question is how far the assumptions of that militarisation can be extended, in the case of a late ninth-century society based in southern England, to a single figure. The strictly contemporary evidence for military organisation, reform and campaigning under Alfred is reviewed in the following pages, using this to reflect on the less-strictly-contemporary evidence. Therefore, the process of looking around the period provides a sense of an Alfredian reform. Here, the astrophysical term 'dark matter' is pertinent, defined by the *Oxford English Dictionary* as 'matter which has not been directly detected but whose existence is postulated to account for the dynamical behaviour of galaxies or the universe'.[5] The borrowing of such a term relevant to the nature of time and space itself may be a little presumptuous in its application to a fuzzy bit of history in an obscure corner of Europe, but I hope a little presumptuousness may be forgiven. If we were only able to measure it, Alfred's effect on the 'dynamical behaviour' of the tenth century may be a manifestation of Alfredian 'dark matter' of the ninth- and early tenth-century evidence.[6]

This chapter takes a tripartite approach, concentrating on the written evidence for the period: 1) contemporary ninth-century evidence which can be reasonably considered 'Alfredian'; 2) sources which could be thought of as evidence of the immediate influence of Alfredian reform; and 3) evidence for the continuity of a military society of sorts both before and after Alfred. From these issues, particularly the final theme, it may be possible to consider the ways in which a military elite can be reconciled with the development of a system with a wider sense of military obligation. Here it must be admitted that although there is a range of archaeological evidence relating to early medieval warfare which can sometimes be tied to the ninth- and tenth-century period, a genuinely interdisciplinary perspective is beyond the remit of this chapter.[7] However, some points relating to the development of fortifications will be noted as appropriate, particularly in discussion of the Burghal Hidage.

The 'Alfredian' evidence

What is meant by 'strictly Alfredian' is itself difficult to define in the light of questions of Alfredian authorship and the post-900 writing of the *Anglo-Saxon Chronicle* (hereafter *ASC*),[8] even if the question of the 'authenticity of Asser' is less problematic than it was briefly considered to be. Nonetheless, the surviving corpus of evidence remains slim: five key sets of evidence concerning warfare during the time of Alfred's reign are in the narrative written sources. I divide them here between what they are discussing as much as by the type of source.

Battles and military encounters in the Anglo-Saxon Chronicle

What can be considered an 'official' set of records for the West Saxon kingdom is in two sets of annals in the *ASC* relating to the reign of Alfred: the 'Common Stock' relating to the period to 893; and additions of a period *c.* 893 running through to the end of the reign of Alfred's son, Edward the Elder, suggesting that even if the late Alfredian annals were written during Alfred's reign they were copied at the orders of his son or those close to him.[9] A series of military victories are recorded under the years 871, 878, 892–93, 894, and there is evidence of *eventual* defeat of a Viking naval force in the *ASC*'s entry for 896.[10] Here, the sense of the West Saxon military victory is given significant emphasis, particularly contrasted with occasions when the Vikings defeated the Anglo-Saxons. Discussion of the definition of a *folc gefeoht*, translated somewhat opaquely by Dorothy Whitelock as 'general engagement', in 871 is particularly illuminating in this respect. The *ASC* seems to define this as the battles requiring participation of the king with all army units of ealdormen – in turn, thegns and followers, so the 'whole people' (*folc*). This record casts some light on the notion of a militarised society, wherein *folc* seems to be applied as an adjective, and may relate, as Ellora Bennett notes in Chapter 17 of this volume, to a concept of 'public' war: *bellum publicum*.[11] A number of *gefeohtan* which included royal princes (*æthelings*) and single ealdormen were not 'counted' (*rīman*). Here it is worth noting that the Old English word *rīman* means more than enumerating together and also refers to notions of describing 'in succession';[12] although Joseph Bosworth's *Anglo-Saxon dictionary* used the 871 *ASC* entry to consider the notion of enumeration, this supplementary meaning for *rīman* may reveal something of the *ASC*'s role as an official record, implying that the writer was excluding the B-team matches while copying up information which led to the 871 annal.[13]

Further comment is warranted: there is as much on peace-making as on the organisation of warfare, particularly taking into account the fact that there is a surviving version of a peace treaty between Alfred and his Viking opponent, Guthrum.[14]

Asser's Life of King Alfred on the Battle of Ashdown (871)

The narrative of military encounters provided by the Welsh monk and biographer of King Alfred, Asser of St David's (later bishop of Sherborne), usually reflects the narrative of the events in the 'Common Stock' of the *ASC* up to 887, which makes sense in view of his claim to have written his *Vita Ælfredi* in or soon after 893.[15] However, there are two cases where his perspective differs significantly. The description of the deployment before and events during the battle at Ashdown, probably along the range of hills of that name now in Oxfordshire, provide something of a departure from Asser's usual narrative of Alfred as a pious ruler. Alfred, here a prince of the royal house, is referred to in terms which suggest that Asser wished to see him as the successor of his brother, King Æthelred I. Alfred leads a charge like a 'wild boar' against one wing of a Viking army before his brother King Æthelred, at that time finishing taking mass in a tent, has been able to deploy his own force.[16] Alfred may have been too impetuous with a potential loss only just averted: a description which established that Alfred was a warlike prince could have been a means of spinning an event which was too important to be ignored entirely. Abels is inclined to take a kinder view, albeit still one which emphasises Æthelred's tactical ingenuity over that of his brother. Abels notes that the king's pause prior to the battle may have been 'a form of echelon tactics', Alfred moving forward while the king's force remained in reserve.[17] The evidence of the forces organised according to their leaders provided in Asser's account is clearly valuable in an Alfredian context, but the question of the extent of Alfred's agency in the organisation means that we should be careful about how far it is demonstrative of his direct role in military reform.

Fortresses in narrative sources

Æthelweard, who wrote a Latin version of the *ASC*, probably with access to an earlier version of that source (and justifying his inclusion here, despite being a later tenth-century author), provides some useful details of the combat undertaken by a band of followers with Alfred in 878. Perhaps more significant is Æthelweard's account of the defence of a fortress in the south-west of England by Odda, one of Alfred's ealdormen.[18] This fortification was described by Asser in terms which suggest that it was a former Iron Age hillfort, and is referred to as *Arx Cynuit*. The fortress of *Cynuit* was a place from which the West Saxon force who had gathered there were able to attack the Viking army which besieged them.[19] The *ASC* alludes to *Cynuit* but does not discuss it in any detail, perhaps because the leadership provided by the ealdorman did not suit the royal narrative of the *ASC*, but the breaking of the siege may have been a decisive moment for the West Saxon kingdom in 878: Barbara Yorke suggests that it was inspirational for the development of a later system of fortifications in Wessex.[20]

Elsewhere, the *ASC* demonstrates ambiguity with regard to the record of fortresses during the reign of Alfred. The sites used for over-wintering by Vikings in the 870s – Reading, London, Torksey, Repton and Wareham – are not referred to in terms of fortification. While much has been made of the fact that excavations at Torksey have revealed a military force which did not require ditches or ramparts for its security, we are at least aware that Repton and possibly also Wareham were defensible sites which may well have been modified through additional fortification.[21] In contrast, other sites used by Vikings in the 880s and 890s were referred to in terms of their value *as* fortifications and some details were provided by the Chronicler of the defensive work undertaken.[22] References to the use of fortifications by Alfred's forces – Athelney in 878, an as-yet unidentified fortification in the *Andredesweald* in 892, and fortifications generally in 893 – show that the West Saxons had begun to pay attention to fortifications in terms of their own strategic interests.[23] There is some indication, too, that Asser was concerned with this when referring to the campaigns of rebuilding.[24] Courtnay Konshuh has noted these references in relation to a campaign of exhortation, that the *ASC*'s message (and with it Asser's message) was related to a notion that the subjects of the king needed to work or suffer the consequences, a message that was commensurate with notions of reform associated with the court of Alfred.[25]

The organisation of forces in the **Anglo-Saxon Chronicle**

One of the *ASC*'s references to fortifications, in the 893 annal, regards the West Saxon forces being divided between being 'at home' (*æt ham*) and 'out' (*ute*), with the exception of those who were to guard the fortresses (*þe þa burga healdan scolden*). This is the clearest single reference to something like a standing army and has been read as such on a few occasions.[26] It is interesting that this reference is tied to a specific episode wherein the West Saxon force, led – according to Æthelweard – by the king's son Edward the

Elder, left a siege of a Viking force encamped on an islet on the Thames before they were able to press home an advantage. Both the *ASC* and Æthelweard are very clear about this matter – the terms of service were up.[27]

What can we make of these sources? While each episode discussed above could be extrapolated and argued as individual cases, because of the focus on the years 871, 878, 892–93, 894 and 896, the inescapable conclusion is that the sum total of historical examples remains effectively five or six cases of evidence. There are no charters relating to the organisation of armies in any way that might lead us to think that here was a moment of change to military organisation – at least not in Wessex (a Mercian case is discussed below). Taken on its own, the decisive moment of military action can be credited to Ealdorman Odda rather than the king – a matter which might suggest why it had been spun in the *ASC* to imply Alfred's own agency.[28] The *ASC*'s 893 entry, without which we probably would not pin the notion of military reforms to Alfred at all, has an iconic status of sorts.

To the above set of 'strictly contemporary' evidence may be added the minor reference to military organisation in the form of a clause promulgated in the lawcode of King Alfred, probably during the 880s:

> [40.1] If any of this [i.e. forcible entry into a king, cleric or freeman's enclosure] happens when the army has been called out, or in the Lenten fast, the compensations are to be doubled.[29]

That single legal clause pales into insignificance compared to the range of such references in other law-codes, such as those of Æthelstan, Æthelred and Cnut.[30] So the question of the Alfredian contribution to military defence may justifiably be subjected to the same sort of sceptical pressures as some scholars, Malcolm Godden foremost amongst them, have imposed on Alfredian authorship, relating us to the issue so beloved of undergraduate essays: 'Was Alfred really The Great?'[31] It must be acknowledged that although a number of important Old English texts date from very close to or during Alfred's reign, much of Alfred's intellectual reputation relies on the twelfth-century comments of William of Malmesbury. It was William whose *Gesta Regum*, using Asser's foundation as a reputation-builder for Alfred, attributed the authorship of many texts to the king himself.[32] In looking at the origins of aspects of government, William attributes the organisation of hundreds and tithings as areas of governance to Alfred himself.[33]

This is hardly what could be termed even remotely 'Alfredian' evidence and it is perhaps because of William that we have so much of the sense of Alfredian civic governance, a notion which was popular amongst nineteenth-century commentators.[34] But if William's account has any value with regard to military matters, it still serves to show the emergence of Alfredian 'dark matter': Æthelweard used the word *centurias* to refer to ninth-century troops and there are some links between the sort of local organisation outlined by William and the military organisation of the ninth and tenth centuries which are worth pursuing. At the heart of the evidence is the organisation of fortifications. Something happens in Alfred's reign, and we see the ripples of it in the document known, since Frederick Maitland named it as such in the late nineteenth century, as the *Burghal Hidage*.

The post-Alfredian evidence

A great deal has been written on the *Burghal Hidage*, to the extent that in 2012 John Baker and Stuart Brookes could make claim, with some justification, to have gone *Beyond the Burghal Hidage*.[35] What the document records is the number of hides referring to each town (*burh*) in southern England; the 'B' recension includes a calculation of a total number of hides relating to Wessex, as well as hides belonging to the Mercian fortifications of Warwick and Worcester; while a formula in the 'A' recension of the document relates to the number of men who can maintain (and perhaps also defend) a particular length of wall.

> For an acre's breadth *on wealstillinge 7 to þære wære* [i.e. the maintenance and defence of wall], are required 16 hides: if each hide be manned by one man, then may each pole [of wall] be set with four men.[36]

The 'A' recension continues with details of what was required for 12 furlongs of wall circuit (1,920 hides), noting the key formula of the additional amount needed for more than this (160 men per furlong). If this calculation was directly linked to the hidages of each town recorded in the document, as a result of the study of that document's formula, we might consider the significance of the hidages associated with the list of towns in the *Burghal Hidage* (Table 5.1).

Could this compilation of information itself be considered an *Alfredian* achievement? Again, I come back to the iconic status of references in the *ASC*. With the weight of Alfredian expectation, when the *Burghal Hidage* surfaced at the end of the nineteenth century, it was broadly attributed to Alfred.[37] The attribution has swung back and forth over some time. A significant Alfredian attribution is that of Jeremy Haslam, who in 2006 linked the *Burghal Hidage* directly with the organisation of Alfred's kingdom in 878–79.[38] In a 2013 publication, Richard Abels tied it to the period between 878 and 883, though his reading is not as certain as that of Haslam in linking all the fortifications to an Alfredian phase.[39]

Table 5.1 Fortifications named in the *Burghal Hidage*, in the order in which they appear, and the hidage measurements associated with each fortress

Name of fortress	Shire	Hidage assigned
Eorpeburnan	Unknown (Sussex?)	324
Hastings	Sussex	500
Lewes	Sussex	1,300
Burpham	Sussex	720
Chichester	Sussex	1,500
Portchester	Hants	500
Southampton	Hants	150
Winchester	Hants	2,400
Wilton	Wilts.	1,400
Chisbury	Wilts.	700 [or 500?]
Shaftesbury	Dors.	700 [or 500?]
Twynham (Christchurch)	Dors. (formerly Hants)	470
Wareham	Dors.	1,600
Bridport	Dors.	760
Exeter	Devon	734
Halwell	Devon	400
Lydford	Devon	140
Pilton	Devon	360
Watchet	Som.	513
Axbridge	Som.	400
Lyng	Som.	100
Langport	Som.	600
Bath	Som.	1,000
Malmesbury	Wilts.	1,200
Cricklade	Wilts.	1,400
Oxford	Oxon.	1,500
Wallingford	Oxon. (formerly Berks.)	2,400
Buckingham	Bucks.	1,600
Sashes (Shaftesey)	Berks.	1,000
Eashing	Surrey	600
Southwark	Surrey	1,800

The strongest sense of the *indirect* nature of any link with Alfred is provided by the fact that it includes fortifications that were never part of Alfred's kingdom but which only came into the orbit of Alfred's family after 914, during the reign of Alfred's son, Edward the Elder: Worcester, Buckingham and Warwick – suggesting that if the *Burghal Hidage* had any function in the forms in which it survived, it was as an administrative document for Edward's court. It should be added, however, that the common text of the list of fortifications for Wessex plus Surrey and Sussex in all versions of the manuscript, which 'has its own diplomatic entity as a text',[40] may reveal something of ninth-century conditions.

The one charter that does explicitly link military organisation to Alfred's reign relates to the Mercian kingdom, to Worcester, where the ealdorman Æthelred and his wife Æthelflaed, Alfred's daughter, seem to have been establishing a fortress, albeit a fortress with a religious community.[41] Dating from some point between 884 and the end of the ninth century, this was evidently a charter which related to the rights associated with the defence of a *burh*, so in some sense was a 'military' document. Reference to the witness of the assembly of the Mercians, the *witan*, places the tenurial and governmental interests in this document squarely to a point when it is relevant to the Mercian rather than the West Saxon kingdom. However, the charter does take us to a 'dark matter' for Alfred, as it also relates to the authority of King Alfred, in the period after the Battle of Edington, in 878, when a peace treaty existed with the Vikings.[42] As Nicholas Brooks noted in the late 1970s, there were significant differences in the actions of the Vikings' movements into the West Saxon kingdom. Prior to 878, they moved into Wessex with impunity and it was not until the 890s that resurgent Viking campaigns become visible, but Viking armies were (apparently) small and operating at the edges of the kingdom, particularly in Kent.[43] Here, if there is a gravitational pull of Alfredian 'dark matter', it is worth noting that Kent did not have a system of hides as a system of local land administration, and the *Burghal Hidage* did not include Kentish fortifications. It is worth admitting here to the significance of the existence of a Viking threat around Gloucestershire in 879 noted by Jeremy Haslam.[44] Although his reading of events of the construction of a system of fortifications in the space of single year is probably an overstatement, the crucial initiative that was required at a point of crisis is not, and the initiative of urban reform for the *burh* of Worcester is relevant here.

It seems entirely plausible, indeed likely, that the figures in the *Burghal Hidage* document represented some sort of reconfiguration of an existing system. That the total number of hides in the *Burghal Hidage* equate to the number of hides in the equivalent shires in the south of England recorded in *Domesday Book* for 1066–86 suggests that there was a fixed number of hides in the kingdom through the Anglo-Saxon period.[45] Even allowing for the fact that particularly pushy landholders might argue for a 'beneficial hidation' of the liabilities of their own estates, the overall resources of the kingdom remained stable. Crucially, the *Burghal Hidage* is an indication that there was a record of this for an administrator to work with according to circumstances. The *Burghal Hidage* may ultimately reveal more about an idealised sense of control, but showed that administrators were employed to work with the figures associated with the kingdom. Even if the document in the form in which it now survives is read as a product of the tenth century, we can read its earlier roots from it and argue that the initial stage in the employment of administrators on it was a product of King Alfred's court; thus, as John Baker and Stuart Brookes have noted, if the *Burghal Hidage* reflects stages in the changes to defensive mechanisms in the West Saxon kingdom, it may be able to detect a shift from frontier to defence in depth, for example.[46]

A militarised society in ninth-century Wessex?

It is when we come to assess the militarised nature of West Saxon society by the end of the ninth century that we may be able to perceive something significant. David Pratt has emphasised the ideological significance of military reforms, demonstrating that the military agenda should not be divorced from its religious and social context.[47] Such issues as the renovation of Roman walls in defended towns went beyond the practicalities of design and function: urban rebuilding projected a message of *Romanitas* associated with Christian Rome attributed to *Staatlichkeit*. In this manner the projection of royal authority became, in some sense, an urban phenomenon, a matter which may go some way to explaining the emphasis on urban defences apparent in the late ninth century drawing on through the tenth and even the early eleventh centuries.[48]

Reform thus had intrinsic military and Christian elements, and this is how we can understand it in a Carolingian framework that needed the Viking threat and what Nicholas Brooks called 'the Crucible of Defeat' in order for the reorganisation of a Christian society more widely – its militarisation, indeed – to work. Three orders of society are emphasised in the Old English translation of Boethius's *Consolation of Philosophy* associated with Alfred. There is a conception of rulership which saw fighting men as an essential tool for a king, part of society between those who prayed and those who worked: a king 'ought to have praying men, fighting men, and working men' (*gebedmen ond ferdmen ond weorcmen*). 'Without these,' the text goes on to say, 'he may not possess those tools nor without those tools may he bring about any of the things which he was commanded to do.'[49]

Thus, a warrior ethic – perhaps heightened in the face of a pagan Viking threat – could be seen as something fundamentally Christian. At the level of elite values, perhaps it was being redefined but, if so, it was still redefined within the framework of lordship. In 1988, Richard Abels highlighted the possession of bookland and a military revolution which had emerged in the eighth and ninth centuries in Mercia and Wessex, i.e. in a period prior to significant Viking invasions.[50] Bookland had been associated with a select military force which was aristocratic by its nature, consisting of lords and their followers.[51] Such a force was unable to match the mobility of Viking attacks. If we have come back to Green's narrative, highlighted at the beginning of this chapter, it is with good reason. Here, the important moment in West Saxon history under Alfred is indeed the 893 entry of the *ASC*, which recorded the division of the West Saxons' military force:

> The king had divided his army [*his fierd*] into two, such that they were always half at home, half out, apart from the men who were to guard the *burhs* [*butan þæm mannum þe þa burga healdan scolden*].[52]

A modified system of military organisation was at work. But we need not be so dogmatic in holding on to that '893 moment' as a solitary keystone for an understanding of a militarised society in Wessex. The link between military service and landholding is associated with the end of the Anglo-Saxon period. The Domesday folios for Berkshire record a pre-Conquest obligation which was due when the king despatched an army (*expeditio* – i.e. the equivalent of the Old English *fyrd*). From every five hides, one *miles* (i.e. a warrior) went out. The entry records that 'for his supplies [*victus*] or pay [*stipendium*] from each hide was given to him 4s for 2 months. This money was not sent to the king but was given to the *milites*'.[53]

Although any inferences can only be drawn out with regard to Berkshire, this Domesday entry does reveal some connection between the holding of land and royal service. It is an important inference, hinting at the continuity of Anglo-Saxon administrative systems with a link between Alfred's Wessex and eleventh-century southern England. If the *Burghal Hidage* provided for one man per hide or equivalent, it presumably also included the workforce available to work on the maintenance of the fortifications, and those who were available to defend them.

The reconciliation here is that of a 'one man per hide' formula in the *Burghal Hidage* with that of later one-man-per-5-hide assessments. If the Berkshire *Domesday* provision is extrapolated, with 4 shillings per hide equating with 20 shillings for a five-hide holding, the 20 shillings (240 d.) to be given for two months' service could have provided one penny per day for four men over sixty days. If a penny in some way equated to a day's skilled wage, the five-hide provision of the Berkshire *Domesday* customs perhaps had a link, even if only indirectly, with the one-man-per-hide provision of the *Burghal Hidage*.

In attempting to square a circle in this chapter, between the high participation ratio evident in the *Burghal Hidage* and the ninth-century account of the manning of *burhs* with a warrior who was to all intents and purposes a knight in the eleventh, the significance of some Alfredian 'dark matter' may be illuminated. The resources available at both of these points were very similar but they were evidently deployed in different ways. John Richard Green's straw man, set up at the beginning of this chapter, may ultimately still be standing. His narrative may have been exaggerated, but the process of investigation is an instructive one. In some ways the transformative process which is evident after the end of the ninth century may be revealing of the response to the need to allow for a wider participation in warfare during the course of the late ninth century itself – no less than a process of militarisation with far-reaching consequences for the nature of kingship and its relationship with society as a whole.

Notes

1 R. Abels, 'Reflections on Alfred the Great as a military leader', in G. I. Halfond (ed.), *The medieval way of war. Studies in medieval military history in honor of Bernard S. Bachrach* (Farnham: Ashgate, 2015), pp. 47–63.
2 R. Lavelle, *Alfred's wars. Sources and interpretations of Anglo-Saxon warfare in the Viking Age* (Woodbridge: Boydell, 2010), pp. 10–11.
3 J. R. Green, *The conquest of England* (London: Macmillan & Co., 1883), p. 135; see further discussion of his context in Lavelle, *Alfred's wars*, pp. 49–51.
4 M. Mann, *The sources of social power*, Vol. 1. *A history of power from the beginning to AD 1760* (Cambridge: Cambridge University Press, 1986; rev. edn, 2012), p. 170; although G. Molyneaux, *The formation of the English kingdom in the tenth century* (Oxford: Oxford University Press, 2015), esp. pp. 86–115, considers the limits of military organisation in the early tenth century, his review of evidence still shows a number of military obligations by the time of Æthelstan.
5 *Oxford English Dictionary*, online edition (Oxford: Oxford University Press, 2019) *s.v.* 'dark, *adj.*' oed.com/view/Entry/47295 (accessed 14 May 2019).
6 I owe the notional assessment of 'dark matter', a term first employed in 1922, in early medieval material to a chapter on 'The dark matter of Arthur', in G. Halsall's *Worlds of Arthur* (Oxford: Oxford University Press, 2013), pp. 157–81, and Andrew Lowerre's assessment, in an unpublished paper, of the Domesday economy of the eleventh century, '"Dark matter" in Domesday Book', presented at the *Conquests. 1016 and 1066* conference, Univ. of Oxford, July 2016.
7 See perspectives taken by, for example, A. Reynolds, 'Archaeological correlates for Anglo-Saxon military activity in comparative perspective', in J. Baker, S. Brookes and A. Reynolds (eds), *Landscapes of defence in early medieval Europe* (Turnhout: Brepols, 2013), pp. 1–38, T. J. T. Williams, 'The place of slaughter. Exploring the West Saxon battlescape', and J. Baker and S. Brookes, 'Landscapes of violence in early medieval Wessex. Towards a reassessment of

Anglo-Saxon strategic landscapes', both in R. Lavelle and S. Roffey (eds), *Danes in Wessex. The Scandinavian impact on southern England, c.800-c.1100* (Oxford: Oxbow, 2016), pp. 35–55 and 70–86.

8   C. Plummer (ed.), *Two of the Saxon chronicles parallel with supplementary extracts from the others* (Oxford: Oxford University Press, 2 vols, 1892–99), vol. 1; *The Anglo-Saxon Chronicle. A Revised Translation*, trans. D. Whitelock, with D. C. Douglas and S. I. Tucker (London: Eyre and Spottiswoode, 1961; rev. edn, 1965). Quotations are from the A MS of the *ASC* unless otherwise indicated, though references also note where the same text (notwithstanding variant spellings) is included in other MSS of the *ASC*.

9   A. D. Jorgensen, 'Introduction. Reading the Anglo-Saxon Chronicle', in A. D. Jorgensen (ed.), *Reading the Anglo-Saxon Chronicle. Language, literature, history* (Turnhout: Brepols, 2010), pp. 1–28, here pp. 11–14.

10 *ASC* 878, 892–93, and 896.

11 See Bennett, Chapter 17.

12 J. Bosworth and T. N. Toller, *An Anglo-Saxon dictionary* (Oxford: Oxford University Press, 1898), p. 799.

13 On the compilation of this annal, see Lavelle, *Alfred's wars*, pp. 264–5.

14 F. Liebermann (ed.), *Die Gesetze der Angelsachsen* (Halle: Max Niemeyer, 3 vols, 1903–16), vol. 1, pp. 128–9; see my comments in 'Towards a political contextualization of pacemaking and peace agreements in Anglo-Saxon England', in D. Wolfthal (ed.), *Peace and negotiation. Strategies for coexistence in the Middle Ages and the Renaissance* (Turnhout: Brepols, 2000), pp. 39–55.

15 Asser, *Vita Alfredi*, ch. 91: *Asser's life of King Alfred, together with the Annals of Saint Neots erroneously ascribed to Asser*, ed. W. H. Stevenson (Oxford: Clarendon, 1906), p. 76; *Alfred the Great. Asser's Life of King Alfred and other contemporary sources*, trans. S. D. Keynes and M. Lapidge (Harmondsworth: Penguin, 1983), p. 101. Keynes and Lapidge comment on the use of the *ASC* at pp. 55–6.

16 Asser, chs 37–9, pp. 28–31; trans. Keynes and Lapidge, pp. 78–80.

17 Abels 'Reflections on Alfred', pp. 50–1. I am grateful to both Richard Abels and Barbara Yorke for discussion on this point.

18 *Chronicon Æthelweardi. The Chronicle of Æthelweard*, ed. and trans. A. Campbell (London: Nelson, 1962), p. 43. On Æthelweard's likely source, see E. Barker, 'The Anglo-Saxon Chronicle used by Æthelweard', *Bulletin of the Institute of Historical Research* 40 (1967), 74–91

19 Asser, ch. 54, pp. 43–4; trans. Keynes and Lapidge, pp. 83–4. This is normally considered to have been at Countisbury (Devon), but other candidates have been proposed, such as Great Torrington: N. Arnold, 'The site of the Battle of *Cynuit*, 878', *Report and Transactions of the Devonshire Association*, 145 (2013), 7–30.

20 See B. Yorke, 'West Saxon fortifications in the ninth century. The perspective of the written sources', in Baker, Brookes and Reynolds (eds), *Landscapes of defence in early medieval Europe*, pp. 91–109, here at pp. 95–7 and 103.

21 ASC 871, 872, 873, 874, 875 and 876. On the unfortified site of Torksey, D. M. Hadley and J. D. Richards, 'The winter camp of the Viking Great Army, AD 872–3, Torksey, Lincolnshire', *Antiquaries Journal*, 96 (2016), 23–67; on the fortified enclosure at Repton, M. Biddle and B. Kjølbye-Biddle, 'Repton and the "Great Heathen Army", 873–4', in J. Graham-Campbell, R. Hall, J. Jesch and D. N. Parsons (eds), *Vikings and the Danelaw. Select papers from the proceedings of the thirteenth Viking Congress, Nottingham and York, 21–30 August 1997* (Oxford: Oxbow, 2001), pp. 45–96. On Wareham, picking up a suggestion from Shane McLeod, see my *Alfred's wars*, p. 229, n. 76.

22 For example, ASC 885 (Rochester) 892 (Milton), 893 (Benfleet).

23 ASC 878, 892 and 893. The fortification in 892 may be equated with the *Eorpeburnan* of the *Burghal Hidage*: for the identification of Rye (Sussex) as *Eorpeburnan*, see F. Kitchen, 'The *Burghal Hidage*. Towards the identification of *Eorpeburnan*', *Medieval Archaeology*, 28 (1984), 175–8.

24 Asser, ch. 91, ed. Stevenson, pp. 77–9; trans. Keynes and Lapidge, pp. 101–2.

25 C. Konshuh, "Warfare and authority in the Anglo-Saxon Chronicle" (PhD dissertation, University of Winchester, 2014 [forthcoming as *Anglo-Saxon Chronicles. Writing English identity*]); see also N. Christie, 'Creating defended communities in later Saxon Wessex', in C. Konshuh and H. Herold (eds), *Fortified settlements in early Medieval Europe. Defended communities of the 8th–10th centuries* (Oxford: Oxbow, 2016), pp. 52–67. See also D. Pratt, *The political thought of King Alfred the Great* (Cambridge: Cambridge University Press, 2007).

26 ASC 893; this famously compares with the reference to the division of the Amazons' army in *The Old English Orosius*, ed. J. Bately, Early English Text Society Supplementary Series, 6 (Oxford: Oxford University Press, 1980), I.10, p. 30.

27 Æthelweard, *Chronicon*, pp. 49–50; see R. P. Abels, *Lordship and military obligation in Anglo-Saxon England* (London: University of California Press, 1988), pp. 62–6.

28 See R. Lavelle, 'Places I'll remember. Reflections on Alfred, Asser and the power of memory in the West Saxon Landscape', in A. Langlands and R. Lavelle (eds), *The land of the English kin. Studies in Wessex and Anglo-Saxon England in honour of Professor Barbara Yorke* (Leiden: Brill, 2020), pp. 312–35, at 325–6.

29 Liebermann, *Gesetze*, vol. 1, pp. 74–5; *English Historical Documents. Vol. 1: c.500–1042*, trans. D. Whitelock (London: Eyre & Spottiswoode, 1955; 2nd edn, 1979), p. 415.

30 For summaries of this material, see Lavelle, *Alfred's wars*, pp. 47–140.

31 See M. R. Godden 'Did Alfred write anything?', *Medium Ævum*, 76:1 (2007), 1–23; and the discussion of these debates in N. G. Discenza and P. E. Szarmach (eds), *A companion to Alfred the Great* (Leiden: Brill, 2015), particularly J. Bately's contribution, 'Alfred as author and translator', pp. 113–42.

32 William of Malmesbury, *Gesta Regum Anglorum. The history of the English Kings, Volume 1*, ed. and trans. R. M. Thomson, M. Winterbottom and R. A. B. Mynors (Oxford: Oxford University Press, 1998), pp. 180–2.

33 *Ibid.*, p. 188; see Lavelle, *Alfred's wars*, p. 101.

34 B. Yorke, *The King Alfred millenary in Winchester, 1901*, Hampshire Papers, 17 (Winchester: Hampshire County Council, 1999).
35 J. Baker and S. Brookes, *Beyond the Burghal Hidage. Anglo-Saxon civil defence in the Viking Age* (Leiden: Brill, 2012). pp. 1–12.
36 A. R. Rumble, 'An edition and translation of the *Burghal Hidage*, together with recension C of the Tribal Hidage', and 'Diplomatic sub-sections', in D. Hill and A. R. Rumble (eds), *The defence of Wessex. The Burghal Hidage and Anglo-Saxon fortifications* (Manchester: Manchester University Press, 1996), pp. 14–35, and 69–74. Translations here are from Lavelle, *Alfred's wars*, p. 211.
37 For example, C. Oman, 'Alfred as warrior', in A. Bowker (ed.), *Alfred the Great* (London: Adam and Charles Black, 1899), pp. 117–48, at pp. 142–3.
38 J. Haslam, 'King Alfred and the Vikings. Strategies and tactics 876–886 AD', *Anglo-Saxon Studies in Archaeology and History*, 13 (2006), 122–54.
39 R. Abels, 'The costs and consequences of Anglo-Saxon civil defence, 878–1066', in Baker, Brookes and Reynolds (eds), *Landscapes of defence in early medieval Europe*, pp. 195–222.
40 Rumble, 'An edition and translation of the Burghal Hidage', p. 72.
41 F. E. Harmer (ed.), *Select English historical documents of the ninth and tenth centuries* (Cambridge: Cambridge University Press), pp. 22–3; catalogued in *Anglo-Saxon Charters. An annotated list and bibliography*, ed. P. H. Sawyer (London: Royal Historical Society, 1968), no. 223. Electronic edition available online at esawyer.org.uk (accessed 3 March 2020).
42 Above, pp. 82–3.
43 N. P. Brooks, 'England in the ninth century. The crucible of defeat', *Transactions of the Royal Historical Society*, 5th ser., 29 (1979), 1–20.
44 Haslam, 'King Alfred and the Vikings'.
45 N. P. Brooks, 'The administrative background to the Burghal Hidage', in D. Hill and A. R. Rumble (eds), *The defence of Wessex. The Burghal Hidage and Anglo-Saxon fortifications* (Manchester: Manchester University Press, 1996), pp. 128–50.
46 J. Baker and S. Brookes, 'From frontier to border. The evolution of northern West Saxon territorial delineation in the ninth and tenth centuries', *Anglo-Saxon Studies in Archaeology and History*, 17 (2011), 108–23.
47 Pratt, *Political thought*, pp. 93–111.
48 Lavelle, *Alfred's wars*, p. 10, discussing D. Hill, 'The origins of Alfred's urban policies', in T. Reuter (ed.), *Alfred the Great. Papers from the eleventh-centenary conferences* (Farnham: Ashgate, 2003), pp. 219–33.
49 W. J. Sedgefield (ed.), *King Alfred's Old English version of Boethius De consolatione philosophiae* (Oxford: Clarendon, 1899), ch. 17, p. 40.
50 Abels, *Lordship and military obligation*, pp. 60–2.
51 *Ibid.*, pp. 20–2, argues for a link between the *Königsfreie*, 'King's Free', influential for a number of post-war German historians, and the high-status military service in pre-Viking England. The *Königsfreie* model was being substantially dismantled by the time at which Abels wrote (for a review in English, see D. M. Hadley, *The northern Danelaw. Its social structure, c. 800–1100* [London: Leicester

University Press, 2000], pp. 43–9), though it should be acknowledged that Abels' reading of the link between elite status and military service did not itself depend on the *Königsfreihe* model.
52 *ASC* 893. See above, pp. 84–5.
53 *Great Domesday Book*, fol. 56c, in P. Morgan (ed. and trans.), *Domesday Book. Berkshire* (Chichester: Phillimore, 1979), entry B 10. The translation is my own, from *Alfred's wars*, p. 56, and the discussion herein summarises my assessment of the evidence in that volume, pp. 60–1.

PART II

WARFARE AND SOCIETY

6

War and the transformation of society in early Byzantine Arabia

Conor Whately

The focus of this chapter is militarisation in early Byzantine Arabia, or as the region was later known, Palaestina Tertia. The evidence is plentiful; however, little of it is narrative, with the majority comprising inscriptions, papyri, imperial edicts and detailed excavation reports. Space precludes a detailed treatment of the topic, and so what follows will be little more than a skeletal outline of some of the most pertinent characteristics of the militarisation of sixth-century Rome's south-east frontier.

Before I turn to the evidence, such as we have it, I want to set out the parameters of this chapter, and in particular what I mean when I refer to militarisation. My starting point is the four definitions of militarisation offered by Wilson: political, economic, social and cultural.[1] In this chapter, for the sake of brevity, I will focus on three: economic militarisation – 'resource mobilisation';[2] political militarisation – 'the extent to which state structure is geared for war';[3] and social militarisation – 'the proportion of the population incorporated into military institutions'.[4] In a previous study of militarisation amongst the elite and sixth-century Roman world at large, I focused on social and cultural militarisation; here, rather, the focus is on the lower levels of society in the south-east corner of the empire, which roughly corresponds to modern Israel and Jordan, especially the areas east and south of the Dead Sea and into the Negev. As in the previous case, my emphasis is on the sixth century.

The evidence for this part of the empire is relatively varied in its quantity and quality. The physical remains of numerous fortifications fill the countryside, which are, in turn, complemented by two significant collections of papyri and some substantive inscriptions. What wars the Roman Empire fought in the sixth century, however, were fought elsewhere, to the north in Syria, Turkey and the Caucasus, and far to the west in Africa, Italy and the Balkans. In fact, this part of the empire would not witness large-scale armed conflict until the first half of the seventh, first – and partially – at the hands of the Sasanians, and later at the hands of the invading Arab tribes. In the wake of their conquests in the early seventh century, the Sasanians occupied these lands for nearly two decades.[5] By 629, though the Persians had been expunged, the recently re-established outposts of Roman power were faced with a new and graver threat. After victories in places like Tabuk and negotiated surrenders in places like Aqaba, the invasion of Rome's eastern provinces would shift north towards the Wadi Mujib and beyond. In 636, the Arabs defeated the Romans in the Battle of Yarmuk, which effectively brought an end to Roman authority in this part of the world.[6]

Those wars came later than the period I am concerned with here, but if we broaden our perspective to include low-intensity conflict (LIC) the picture changes. There is little reason to doubt the existence of LIC in the south-east in the sixth century. A number of comments in late antique travelogues imply as much, as do some comparative anecdotes from more recent centuries.[7] It is these multitudinous skirmishes that likely had the greatest impact on whatever physical evidence of militarisation we might find in this part of the empire, a point which has generated a great deal of debate, and which is worth setting out here. To establish its intensity, however, we need to go back to the period when most of these forts were constructed, the late third and early fourth centuries, and look at the assorted explanations that have been proffered to explain their construction.

Political militarisation

There is perhaps no better physical manifestation of the region's political militarisation than the presence of dozens of fortifications, which include a handful of legionary forts, several fortlets and innumerable towers. The function of these structures has attracted a great deal of attention, and Castro has recently provided a thorough overview of the various positions, so I will not say much beyond providing a concise overview.[8] There are two dominant positions: Parker's view that the network of fortifications was constructed for the purposes of defending Roman territory from external forces, and Graf's that they were to protect against internal forces.[9] There is a third position, however, recently strongly reiterated by Castro, which does not see the two as mutually exclusive.[10] Though focusing specifically on the southern sector of Arabia Petraea, a region running roughly from Petra to Aqaba, Castro pointed to the reuse of older Nabataean fortifications and the construction of newer structures in the wake of unrest in the third century, both internal and external. What is more, the forts tended to follow important lines of communication. Much of this political militarisation took place at the end of the third century crisis, as a number of inscriptions make clear. Dedicatory inscriptions have been found at Qasr Bshir, Udhruh and Yotvata, for instance.[11]

Their construction and occupation in the late third and fourth centuries are not in question.[12] The difficulty lies in trying to determine how many of these structures were still in use in the sixth century, a subject that has engendered a good deal of debate. Only some of these fortifications have been subject to detailed excavations. In many instances, the dating of these sites has been limited to consideration of surface ceramic finds, and much of this was carried out many decades ago. On that basis, the following sites were occupied in the sixth century: Qasr el-Baik, Qasr el-Aseikhin, Qasr el-Azraq, Umm el-Jimal, Umm el-Quttein, Deir el-Kahf, Khirbet es-Samra, Qasr el-Hallabat, Khirbet ez-Zona, Umm er-Rasas, Lower Muhattet el-Haj, Upper Muhattet el-Haj, Qasr Bshir, Khirbet el-Fityan, el-Lejjun, Qasr el-Bint, Da'ajaniya, Udhruh, Rujm es-Sadaqa, Humayma, Khirbet el-Qirana, Khirbet el-Khalde, Qasr el Kithara, Upper Zohar, En Boqeq, Mampsis, Mezad Tamar, Nessana, Avdat and Beersheba.

During the middle of the sixth century, if not a decade or two earlier, there is good reason to suppose that there was some reshuffling of Roman forces in the region. We have incontrovertible evidence that a small number of these fortifications continued in use in the sixth century. A now lost inscription from Qasr el-Hallabat highlighted some of the renovation work carried out during the reign of Justinian.[13] A few other inscriptions point to additional building work in the region in the sixth century, including an inscription from modern Ma'an, which highlights fortification work in 547/548.[14] A handful of *metata* (military hostels), which Trombley has connected with army movements, witnessed some construction work.[15] Plenty of towers were fortified too in the sixth century, particularly to the north into Syria and the south-eastern corner of Turkey.[16]

The construction work itself would have required significant bodies of men and materiel. While there is no direct evidence for the construction of the fortifications in Arabia, there is some for fortifications further north in Syria and Mesopotamia. During the reign of Anastasius, the then governor (*praeses*) of Oshroene spent a considerable amount of money on repairing the walls of Edessa.[17] Additionally, the emperor (Anastasius) gave money to the local bishop to finance its upkeep. The construction of the Roman fortress at Dara involved imperial architects,[18] and it involved stonecutters, masons, craftsmen, slaves and peasants – but there were also supervisors and foremen.[19] In fact, the demand for workers was so great that there were labour shortages in other places undergoing major fortification development, like Resafa.[20] In smaller places, like Tanoutia, local officials, possibly even the local presbyter, paid for work on the fortifications.[21] They are unlikely to have had access to imperial works like those at bigger centres, such as Dara and Resafa. Places like Qasr el-Hallabat and el-Lejjun, some distance from wars to the north, are also unlikely to have had access to the imperial workers. When it came to materials, there was a tendency to use what was available, which is why places like Qasr el-Azraq were built with basalt stones and el-Lejjun with limestone and largely, most likely, local labour.

What is less clear is when these fortifications were abandoned. Part of the trouble is that a contentious comment made by Procopius in his *Secret History* has been used to suggest that there was a widespread demobilisation of Roman military forces in the region in the early sixth century, if not earlier. Some have connected this to Justinian's re-organisation of the military early in his reign, a process which allowed him to wage war on multiple fronts.[22] The gist of his comments is that Justinian's payments to the *limitanei* fell five years in arrears, and that they later lost their classification as legitimate soldiers.[23] This then has been connected to the abandonment of a range of sites throughout Jordan.[24]

The trouble is, we know that *limitanei* continued in use for some time thereafter, appearing in Justinian's administrative legislation regarding the conquest of Vandal Africa.[25] They show up in the Beersheba edict, which dates to the reign of Justinian and which lists soldiers from around the Transjordan.[26] They even appear in some of Justinian's edicts, particularly Novel 103 for Palestine, dated to 536, which is significant, even if it does not concern Palestine III where Nessana lay.[27] Evidence like this points to their continued use in the region. It would then hold that their fortifications were in use too. There is, for instance, good reason to suppose that el-Lejjun was in use until 551.[28] In some areas like the Negev and Sinai, new fortifications were constructed.[29] What is more, arguments that places like Qasr el-Hallabat changed with respect to their function and ownership have proven suspect.[30] These fortifications, then, provide physical evidence for political militarisation in the sixth century.

There were limits to the political organisation in the region, for the fortifications tell only part of the story. Another important facet of political militarisation is the role of the military in the administration of the relevant provinces, especially Arabia and Palestine, both the subject of Justinianic novels, and Phoenice Libanensis, the subject of an edict. Paragraph 102, dated to 536, concerns some changes to the *moderator* of Arabia's purview. Intriguingly, near the beginning, the novel states that the military command, the *dux*, had been 'conducting the business of the civil office', and this law is meant, in large part, to stop this.[31] Near the end of the second section of the law, it is quite explicit about the consequences of the *dux* overstepping his responsibilities and getting embroiled in civilian affairs – he will be stripped of command. On the other hand, the *moderator* was assigned some soldiers of his own that were to be independent of those soldiers serving under the *dux*, to say nothing of those fighting under the Arab phylarch. So while the military was not to step into civilian matters, the civilian administration was to be allowed some military support of its own, even if the law is not explicit about what this might entail.

The subsequent novel, 103, which is also dated to 536, is concerned with Palestine, and it provides a little more detail about the responsibilities of the different parties. In this case, the proconsul would be responsible for civil matters, the *dux* for military ones, as with the previous novel on Arabia. That said, it also stipulates that the proconsul has the option of using the soldiers stationed in the province should he need to, and these soldiers would be independent of those already under his command, which the local *dux* and *magister militum* could not themselves use.

Finally, also dated to 536 and to be grouped with the previous two, is the edict concerning Phoenice Libanensis, which takes matters a step further: where the previous two novels assign the respective officials some soldiers to carry out their tasks, this edict assigns the governor a specific regiment, the *Tertiodalmatae*, which is to be replaced if the unit is transferred for some other purpose decreed by the emperor. Assuming it is the same unit, it appears in the *Notitia Dignitatum* as a unit of *equites* serving under the *Magister Militum per Orientem*.[32] As in previous cases, if the local *dux* interferes in civil matters, he is to be stripped of command.

While the rights and responsibilities of the two parts of the administration, civilian and military, are, for all intents and purposes, to be kept separate, soldiers, as a general group, seem capable of operating in both capacities. Both administrators in the province are to be given soldiers to carry out their duties – but the distinction between military and civil administration is to be maintained. In this sphere, then, Justinian worked to bring a halt to the militarisation of administration that the legislation implies was an issue.

Economic militarisation

To address economic militarisation is to address resource mobilisation. Fortunately, we have a handful of documents, in the form of inscriptions, papyri and the physical materials of sites like el-Lejjun, that illuminate just this.

Let us start with el-Lejjun. This legionary fort has been the site of significant excavations, and much of the material recovered came in the form of the faunal and floral remains.[33] Not only has this illuminated the types of things that the fort's residents were consuming, but it has also given us a good idea about where all of it came from. By all accounts, both barley and wheat were cultivated and processed locally, while legumes were not.[34] While some olives and grapes were grown locally, they seem to have been used for consumption at the dinner table. At the same time, the presence of amphorae implies that some wine and oil was imported, though not in great quantities.[35] Not only were plants produced locally, so too were animals raised on site. This included sheep and goats, as well as chickens, cattle and pigs (domestic livestock).[36] Plenty of other animals were found too, but it seems it was the domestic livestock that was consumed by the soldiers, for they were found in much higher quantities.[37] Of the animals consumed, sheep and goats were the most prominent in terms of numbers, with sheep outnumbering goats. Toplyn argued that they were raised primarily to produce meat, and that they were primarily consumed locally.[38] This mirrors what we find in other parts of the region, for sheep and goats were staples of meat production in late antique Caesarea and further north at Androna in Syria.[39] As noted, pork was consumed on site too, though as a supplement to the sheep and goats. Pork was consumed by soldiers in other parts of the empire, like Egypt, at this time.[40] Poultry seem to have been consumed in considerable numbers too. All in all, the impression is that meat was a big part of the soldiers' diet and that quite a lot of it was obtained locally, at least here at el-Lejjun.[41] This relative abundance of local production and consumption of wheat and barley, assorted fruit and meat on site shows that, when it comes to food, a significant proportion of the local resources were for the military, a clear case of economic militarisation at this specific locale: el-Lejjun and its environs.

Toplyn characterised the economy of the el-Lejjun and neighbouring locations like Qasr Bshir and Da'janiya as self-sufficient to a large degree.[42] While it might be tempting to see this production as undertaken by soldiers for soldiers, it is worth stressing that it was not only soldiers living at this location, for we have good evidence for the presence of civilians, even if they are members of the wider military community (family members), at least in part.[43] El-Lejjun housed a legion, the *legio IV Martia*, and in late Antiquity they numbered close to 1,500 men, which is what it might have been in the fourth century AD. By the start of the sixth century, the legions had close to 1,200 soldiers, but we do not know how many were at el-Lejjun.[44] The *vicus*, where much of the broader military community are likely to have lived in the fourth century, seems to have been abandoned by the sixth.[45] This means many or most of the inhabitants were living in the fortress – and so largely involved in this food production.

I want to turn now to the documentary evidence, and we are quite well off in this regard too. At least three papyri from Nessana seem to deal explicitly with the extraction of resources from the town for the use of the military. One of those documents, P. Ness. 3.35, the so-called levy of camels (though it is also a levy of camel-riders), contains lists of camels and camel-riders, 30 of the former, and 34 of the latter, enlisted for a variety of different tasks. Some are assigned to *priores* (officers) of the camp, some are assigned to the staff members of the duke, some to the church and its (possible) priest, and some for an unknown expedition. Another document, P. Ness. 3.37, the so-called account of military camels, includes a list of camels assigned to individual soldiers, each grouped under at least eight *dekarchs* – only seven of which are named – and *dekarchies*, one of the smallest divisions in the sixth-century military.[46] At least two of the soldiers, if not two of the *dekarchies*, are to be dispatched to Egypt, for reasons unknown.[47] Another is to be sent to Caesarea.[48] Collectively, then, these two documents reveal that the village of Nessana was to provide men and materiel for a range of official tasks, with some of those tasks some distance away (Egypt), at least relatively speaking. We just do not know, at least explicitly, what they were for.

One papyrus, that might be some sort of account of taxes owing/paid, lists nine towns from the region, at least six of which had a military presence at some stage in late Antiquity: Nessana, Eboda, Chermoula, Birosaba, Malaatha and Birsamis.[49] Nessana and Eboda aside, the latter the location of a fort with an unknown garrison,[50] the other four are all listed in the *Notitia Dignitatum* under the *Dux Palaestinae*: Chermoula hosted the Equites Scutarii Illyriciani (*Not. dign. or.* 34.20), Birosaba the Equites Dalmatae Illyriciani (*Not. dign. or.* 34.18), Malaatha the Cohors Prima Flavia (*Not. dign. or.* 34.45), and Birsamis the Equites Thamudeni Illyriciani (*Not. dign. or.* 34.22). Of the others, Elusa was a major administrative centre, while Mampsis and Sobila were other towns in the region. All were required to provide something (we do not know what – we just have the numbers), and it could well have been taxes (money or some product in kind?) for the military. Fortunately, there are some other documents from Nessana that illuminate something of the tax regime in place, though only one dates to the Roman period (i.e. pre-Islamic conquest). Based on this evidence and what is known of the village's physical remains, O'Sullivan has calculated that around 550 the residents were being taxed both in cash (gold) and in kind (wheat), a practice in keeping with other locales, like Antaeopolis in Egypt.[51] At Nessana, he concluded that 62 per cent of the tax was paid in gold (solidi) and 38 per cent in grain units. This would work out to a tax rate of 3.5 solidi per household per year, with the people working 115 days per year. While we could not say how much of this tax would go towards military activities, there is every reason to suppose that it was a significant portion, perhaps between 25 per cent and 35 per cent of the state's budget.[52]

The Beersheba edict allows us to look at the mobilisation of resources beyond the local level to the regional one. This edict, to which the just mentioned papyrus from Nessana is often compared,[53] also names a few regional centres including some of those listed here, like Elusa and Mampsis. The second fragment of the edict lists over a dozen sites from the region, many identifiable locales in the region, like Adroa, Zoora and Ammatha, all close to Petra.[54] It lists the number of solidi per site to be distributed to *douloi*, whom di Segni takes to mean low-ranking soldiers (i.e. frontier soldiers).[55] Di Segni has made a good case that the reconstituted edict details the collection of taxes for the *duces* of Palestine. In turn, the duke used the taxes to pay for a range of things connected to pilgrimage, like wages for escorts and the upkeep of hostels.[56]

The general picture is that a significant portion of the population of the select communities that we have considered in the region were responsible in some way or other for providing resources for the military, whether that be in the form of taxation (cash or kind), men or even animals.

Social militarisation

We now shift from economic to social militarisation, and I will start with the one site that allows us to probe social militarisation on a local level. The mass of papyri from Nessana detail select activities in the lives of the local military community. Though a far from complete sample in a collection which privileges soldiers over civilians, there are plenty of papyri that name soldiers and their families alike.

I have limited myself to the datable papyri from the sixth century. Those from the seventh century and later do not name soldiers, and it seems that the unknown military unit was no longer in operation.[57] It is also the case that many of the known soldiers are recorded in only a few papyri. I counted 78 soldiers at Nessana, and 131 civilians somehow connected to Nessana's soldiers. Of those 131 individuals, only 6 are women. These are from a total of 868 named individuals, at least so far as I could tell. Unfortunately, the information about the individuals is not as straightforward as we might like. An exceedingly high proportion of the civilians in the papyri are only there because several of the soldiers used patronymics in their names.[58] What is more, the documents that we do have are not as diverse a group as we might like either.[59] That said, a small number of soldiers seem to be operating in an official capacity. 'Aziz, son of Stephan (P. Ness. 3.35.5), was one of the officers involved in the camel and camel-rider levy. Seven *dekarchs* are listed on the account of military camels: Abdallas, son of Ei...; Hermogenes; John, son of Abraham; Wa'li; Sergius, son of Ammonius;

Sergius, son of ...ios; and Stephan, son of Zunayn. There is one other named *dekarch*, a George, son of Patrick, who is listed on a document that details some sort of payment, though it is fragmentary.[60] Perhaps more importantly, the bulk of the papyri concern private matters involving soldiers. We have, for instance, the release of a soldier (P. Ness. 3.15), divisions of property (P. Ness. 3.16, 21), two marriage contracts (P. Ness. 3.18, 20), a partition of inheritance (P. Ness. 3.22) and a loan of money (P. Ness. 3.26). These kinds of documents point to a group of local soldiers of Nessana closely involved in civilian life.

Beyond considering the proportion of the population who are soldiers and what duties we find them performing with civilians, there is perhaps no better way to illustrate, albeit indirectly, the social militarisation of the soldiery in the region in the sixth century than by considering just how many civilians from the total listed lived beside the soldiers as their neighbours. Although, as noted, the sample is quite small, a few of the documents from Nessana concern the division of property, and these extensive papyri often give the layout and neighbours of the estate under consideration.[61] What they reveal is that at least some of Nessana's soldiers were fully ensconced in the village, often living shoulder-to-shoulder with their civilian neighbours.

We now move from one well-documented site to another, namely Petra, which did not have a military presence of its own, but which was in the same, wider, region.[62] The Petra papyri list, for example, several Flavii – a name associated with governmental officials and soldiers in sixth-century Egypt but applicable to Palestine.[63] To give but a few examples, we find a Flavius Eustathius (P. Petra 1.1), a Flavius Dusarius (P. Petra 1.2), Flavius Patricius (P. Petra 1.3), a Flavius Valens (P. Petra 1.7), a Flavius Ailian (P. Petra 4.46) and a Flavius Isakios (P.Petr. 5.35, 78). Besides the possible officers and ex-officers, there are also the certain officers. A few *priores* are named in the papyri, including a Flavius Nonnus (P. Petra 4.37), a George (P. Petra 4.46) and a Flavius Barachos (P. Petr. 4.43.147, 156).

In some cases, we cannot say unequivocally where the men were based. In other cases, we can; one papyrus, the longest one at Petra, P. Petra. 4.39, names a Beothos, who was a *prior* of Kastron Zadakathon, the nearest site with a military presence.[64] Zadakathon was home to an *equites promoti indigenae*, at least in the fifth century.[65] This papyrus also lists a phylarch, so betraying more evidence of a military presence, even if it was an allied one. Zadakathon appears in a number of other papyri,[66] as does the word *kastron*.[67] There is even one papyrus that mentions a regiment (unit), but it is too fragmentary to specify which one.[68] Two more also refer to an *arithmos*, though they too are fragmentary.[69] Two of the documents involve the marriage of a soldier named Thomas, an *embathmos* from Zadakathon, to a woman named Kyra.[70] Yet another *kastron* appears in two papyri: Ammatha, which like Zadakathon appears in the Beersheba edict, as noted above.[71] In the *Notitia*, it is listed as the home of an *Ala Antana dromedariorum*.[72] In one of those papyri, we also meet a Flavius Dusarius, a former prefect of Kastron Ammatha.[73] Though *ala* seems to appear in one of the papyri on which Ammatha is named, it seems to be in reference to Zadakathon.[74] While representing only a fraction of the total number of papyri from Petra, they do point to an active military presence far beyond their more firmly established spheres of influence – or at least operations.[75]

We now move from the papyrological to the epigraphical evidence, which is plentiful. Indeed, there are far more inscriptions from late Antique Arabia and Palestine (350–750 CE) than there were for the Roman period (50 BCE–350 CE).[76] In many instances, we cannot deduce the presence of military personnel, for they do not usually indicate the careers of individuals. In other cases, by looking for Flavii amongst the datable inscriptions we can get an impression of the relative presence of soldiers amongst the civilians. One, dated to 529 and from Scythopolis, celebrates the restoration of the city's walls thanks to the beneficence of a Flavius Arsenius.[77] A fragmentary inscription from Beersheba gives the title *scribendarius*, though it is not clear what the inscription is for.[78]

There are the fragments of the edict of Anastasius, some of which have been found at Bosra,[79] some at Qasr el-Hallabat[80] and at other spots around the Near East.[81] Although some fragments are small, like the one from Bosra, others are more complete, like the edict from Cyrenaica in north Africa.[82] The edict from Qasr el-Hallabat in Jordan covers a diverse range of tasks, including reports sent to Constantinople (Part I, Chapter 11, lines 43–75), soldiers profiting unjustly (Part I, Chapter 11, lines 110–121), the specific rights of soldiers (Part II) and even protection of the soldiers from extortion (Part IV).[83] The edict from Cyrenaica, long since edited and published, even contains details surrounding the billeting of soldiers and the impact of this on civilian–soldier interactions.[84] The provisions concerned with billeting and extortion in particular point to the involvement of the wider population in military matters. At the same time, collectively, these edicts set out some of the significant challenges involving the integration of the frontier soldiers into the various communities.

Before we close, one more note. Above, in the section on political militarisation, I discussed the construction of a variety of structures concerned with military matters. While many were paid for by the state in some capacity or other, in many cases the construction work was implemented by clergymen.[85] Whether the evidence for the efforts of clerics represents social militarisation or something else is another matter. Suffice to say, it is evidence of civilians taking a concerted interest in military affairs, even if it is borne out of necessity – safety and security, a concern of a number of sixth-century inscriptions.[86]

Conclusion

This chapter has only scratched the surface of the broader subject of militarisation in the region. There is more evidence that could be brought to bear: some of the visual evidence (mosaics) might prove useful – fortified representations of cities in mosaics, for instance. At the same time, most of what I have done is to present in outline much of the evidence for militarisation without examining it in close detail; moreover, my choice of sites has been selective.

It would be useful to know what proportion of the region was composed of soldiers; the evidence is insufficient and incomplete. Plus, many of the soldiers were concentrated in specific spots and so not evenly distributed across the region. Some have tried to estimate the population of some of the major centres in the region, as well as the smaller villages. Millar argues that there was one soldier for every one hundred civilians in the Near East during the high imperial era, though that encompasses a much broader area than the one under discussion here.[87] Given the lower troop total in Roman Arabia, Kennedy argues the ratio was closer to 200:1, though he notes that this too might be an exaggeration.[88] A better bet for late Antiquity might be to look to late Roman Palestine, which reached its peak in terms of population and number of settlements in the sixth century, the period with which we are concerned here; this included expansion into previously underpopulated areas.[89] Population estimates range between one and four million, the highest total until the twentieth century.[90] In turn, those inhabitants were largely spread between nearly 700 sites. Nessana, the site with the best-documented soldiers in the region, had a population that ranged between 1,000 and 3,000 by most accounts.[91] The unnamed local unit probably had between 100 and 500 soldiers.[92] That would make for a ratio of 1:10 on the high end and 1:30 on the low end. Either way, this would give Nessana a much higher proportion of soldiers than the region as a whole, at least if it was anything like Arabia. The military sites in the southern Hauran (north Jordan), like Umm el-Jimal, Umm el-Quttein and Deir el-Kahf, deserve closer consideration and might well have had similar soldier to civilian ratios.

For all my discussion of militarisation, by the end it might seem that I have devoted very little to the impact of war, which I had promised at the start. This is in part because the larger wars which the Romans fought, of which there were a few, were waged to the north and far to the west. Indeed, what conflict there was in the region was of a low intensity, particularly the raids conducted by groups of Arab tribesmen. There is good reason to suppose that even this was overblown.[93] Though studies of militarisation in the pre-modern world have usually focused on the Greek and Roman worlds, and for the late antique and medieval worlds, the west, this chapter reveals that the evidence for the Roman or Byzantine east deserves greater consideration.

Notes

1. P. Wilson, 'Defining military culture', *The Journal of Military History*, 72 (2008), 49–57, here 40–1; C. Whately, 'Militarization or rise of a distinct military culture? The east Roman ruling elite in the sixth century', in D. Boatright and S. O'Brien (eds), *Warfare and society in the ancient eastern mediterranean* (Oxford: BAR Archaeopress, 2013), pp. 49–57.
2. *Ibid.*, 41.
3. *Ibid.*, 40.
4. *Ibid.*, 40.
5. W. Kaegi, *Byzantium and the early Islamic conquests* (Cambridge: Cambridge University Press, 1992).
6. For an engaging overview of the conquest, see R. Hoyland, *In God's path* (Oxford: Oxford University Press, 2015). For a detailed analysis of the difficult sources for the early seventh century geo-political events involving the Roman Empire, see J. Howard-Johnston, *Witness to a world crisis* (Oxford: Oxford University Press, 2010).
7. See D. Caner, *History and hagiography from the late antique Sinai* (Liverpool: Liverpool University Press, 2010) and W. Ward, *Mirage of the Saracen* (Berkeley: University of California Press, 2015).
8. M. Castro, *The function of the Roman army in southern Arabia Petraea* (Oxford: Archaeopress, 2018), pp. 22–33.
9. T. Parker (ed.), *Romans and Saracens. A history of the Arabian frontier* (Winona Lake: ASOR, 1986); D. Graf, 'Rome and the Saracens. Reassessing the Nomadic menace', in T. Fahd (ed.), *L'Arabie préislamique et son environnement historique* (Leiden: Brill, 1989), pp. 341–400; D. Graf, 'The Saracens and the defense of the Arabian frontier', *BASOR*, 229 (1978), 1–26.
10. Castro, *Roman Army*.
11. CIL 3.14149 (Qasr Bshir); Kennedy and Fallahat (2008 – Udhruh); AE 1986, 699 (Yotvata).
12. R. R. Burns, 'Diocletian's fortifications of Syria and Arabia', in S. Lieu and P. McKechnie (eds), *Aspects of the Roman East, Volume II* (Turnhout: Brepols, 2016), pp. 1–77, discusses the frontier in the early fourth century. The dates of the structures are discussed by Parker, *Romans and Saracens*, S. Gregory, *Roman military architecture on the eastern frontier* (Amsterdam: Hakkert, 1997), and

D. Kennedy, *The Roman army in Jordan* (London: Council for British Research on the Levant, 2004).
13 PPUAES IIIa 2,18.
14 IGLSyr 4, 1809.
15 F. Trombley, 'War and society in rural Syria c. 502–613 A.D. Observations on the epigraphy', *BMGS* (1997), 154–209, here 164. See IGLS 4, 1610; 4, 1952; 5, 2155.
16 IGLSyr 4, 1598; IGLSyr 4, 1607; IGLSyr 13,1 9130; PPUAES IIIB, 860, 872, 992, 1117.
17 Ps.-Josh. Styl. 91.
18 Zach. *HE* 7.6.b.
19 Zach. *HE* 7.6.c. See too J. Crow, 'Fortifications and urbanism in late Antiquity. Thessaloniki and other eastern cities', in L. Lavan (ed.), *Recent research in late antique urbanism* (Portsmouth, RI: *JRA* Supplement Series), pp. 89–105; E. Zanini, 'Technology and ideas. Architects and master-builders in the Byzantine world', in L. Lavan, E. Zanini and A. Sarantis (eds), *Technology in transition, A. D. 300–630* (Leiden: Brill, 2008), pp. 381–405.
20 C. Hof, *Die Stadtmauer* (Wiesbaden: Harrassowitz Verlag, 2020).
21 IGLSyr 4, 1619, 1631.
22 C. Koehn, *Justinian und die Armee des frühen Byzanz* (Berlin: De Gruyter, 2018).
23 Procop. *Anec.* 24.12–13.
24 B. De Vries, *Umm el-Jimal. A frontier town and its landscape in northern Jordan*, vol. 1 (Portsmouth, RI: Journal of Roman Archaeology, 1998); I. Shahid, *Byzantium and the Arabs in the sixth century* (Washington, DC: Dumbarton Oaks, 2002); I. Arce, 'Severan *castra*, tetrarchic *quadriburgia*, Justinian *coenobia*, and Ghassanid *diyarat*. Patterns of transformation of *limes arabicus* forts during late Antiquity', in R. Collins and M. Weber (eds), *Roman military architecture on the frontiers. Armies and their architecture in late Antiquity* (Oxford: Oxbow, 2015), pp. 98–122.
25 *Cod. Iust.* 1.27.2.8; Procop. *Wars* 4.8.21.
26 L. Di Segni, 'The Beersheba tax edict reconsidered in the light of a newly discovered fragment', *SCI*, 23 (2004), 136. See too Malalas (18.2) for their presence in Syria in 527.
27 Iust. Nov. 103.3.1.
28 C. Whately, 'el-Lejjūn. Logistics and localisation on Rome's east frontier in the 6th c.', in A. Sarantis and N. Christie (eds), *War and warfare in late Antiquity. Current perspectives* (Brill: Leiden, 2013), pp. 893–924.
29 Ward, *Mirage*, 119.
30 P. Casey, 'Justinian, the *limitanei*, and Arab-Byzantine relations in the 6th c.', *JRA*, 9 (1996), 214–22; R. Harper, *Upper Zohar, an early Byzantine fort in Palaestina Tertia* (Oxford: Oxford University Press, 1997); D. Genequand, 'The archaeological evidence for the Jafnids and the Nasrids', in G. Fisher (ed.), *Arabs and empires before Islam* (Oxford: Oxford University Press, 2015), pp. 172–213.
31 Nov. 102, pr. Trans. Miller.

32 *Not. dign.* or. 7.27.
33 T. Parker (ed.), *The Roman frontier in central Jordan. Final report on the* limes arabicus *project, 1980–1989* (Washington, DC: Dumbarton Oaks Press, 2006).
34 P. Crawford, 'The plant remains', in T. Parker (ed.), *The Roman frontier in central Jordan. Final report on the* limes arabicus *project, 1980–1989* (Washington, DC: Dumbarton Oaks Press, 2006), pp. 453–61, here p. 460.
35 Parker (*The Roman frontier in central Jordan*, p. 356) had noted the relative absence of imported amphorae.
36 M. Toplyn, 'Livestock and *limitanei*: The zooarchaeological evidence', in T. Parker (ed.), *The Roman frontier in central Jordan. Final report on the* limes arabicus *project, 1980–1989* (Washington, DC: Dumbarton Oaks Press, 2006), pp. 464–7.
37 *Ibid.*, pp. 467–9.
38 *Ibid.*, p. 478.
39 C. R. Cope, 'Faunal remains and butchery practices from Byzantine and Islamic contexts', in K. G. Holum, A. Raban and J. Patrich (eds), *Caesarea Papers 2, Herod's Temple, the provincial governor's Praetorium and granaries, the later harbor, a gold coin hoard, and other studies* (Portsmouth, RI: Journal of Roman Archaeology, 1999), p. 407.
40 B. Haug, 'Military pork: two receipts for rations', *ZPE* 160 (2007), 215–219.
41 Toplyn, 'Livestock', p. 504.
42 *Ibid.*, p. 507.
43 C. Whately, 'Soldiers and their families on the late Roman frontier in central Jordan', in G. Wrightson (ed.), *The many faces of war in the ancient world* (Newcastle: Cambridge Scholars Publishing, 2015), pp. 283–301.
44 F. Onur, 'The Anastasian military decree from Perge in Pamphylia: Revised 2nd Edition', *Gephyra*, 14 (2017), 133–212.
45 P. Crawford and S. T. Parker, 'The east *vicus* building (Area P)', in T. Parker (ed.), *The Roman frontier in central Jordan. Final report on the* limes arabicus *project, 1980–1989* (Washington, DC: Dumbarton Oaks Press, 2006), pp. 247–57.
46 Note the comments of C. Whately, 'Combat motivation at the end of Antiquity', in G. Greatrex and S. Janniard (eds), *The world of Procopius* (Paris: De Boccard, 2018), pp. 185–213, here p. 191.
47 P. Ness. 3.37.33, 40.
48 P. Ness. 3.37.15.
49 P. Ness. 3.39.
50 Gregory, *Military architecture*, pp. 436–41; Kennedy, *Roman army*, p. 224.
51 S. O'Sullivan, 'Fiscal evidence from the Nessana papyri', in P. Sijpsteijn and A. Schubert (eds), *Documents and the history of the early Islamic world* (Leiden: Brill, 2015), pp. 56–57.
52 See the discussions of M. Hendy, *Studies in the Byzantine monetary economy* (Cambridge: Cambridge University Press, 1985), pp. 164–78.
53 Di Segni, 'Beersheba', 138, n. 20.
54 *Ibid.*, pp. 151–2.
55 *Ibid.*, pp. 150–1; Ward, *Mirage*, 125–6.

56 Di Segni, 'Beersheba', p. 150.
57 See C. Whately, 'Camels, soldiers, and pilgrims in sixth century Nessana', *Scripta Classica Israelica*, 35 (2016), 121–35.
58 While many, most, even all of these fathers might have been resident in Nessana, we have no way of knowing; it is also possible that none of the fathers were from the town.
59 Note Caner's (*Sinai*, p. 45) comments.
60 P. Ness. 3.38.1.
61 P. Ness. 3.16, 21, 22, 31.
62 On the army in and around Petra, see Z. Fiema, 'Late antique Petra and its hinterland. Recent research and new interpretations', in J. H. Humphrey (ed.), *The Roman and Byzantine near East*, vol. 3 (Portsmouth, RI: Journal of Roman Archaeology, 2002), pp. 191–252.
63 J. Keenan, 'The names Flavius and Aurelius as status designations in later Roman Egypt', *ZPE*, 11 (1973), 33–63; 'The names Flavius and Aurelius as status designations in later Roman Egypt', *ZPE*, 13 (1974), 283–304.
64 All of the papyri that comprise volume four of the five-volume collection of Petra papyri are concerned with affairs in Zadakathon in some way or other. See A. Arjava, M. Buchholz, T. Gagos and M. Kaimo, *The Petra Papyri IV* (Amman: ACOR, 2011), pp. ix, 27–8).
65 *Not. dign.* or. 34.24; Kennedy, *Roman army*, pp. 176–7; Fiema, 'Petra', p. 211.
66 P. Petra 3.23; 4.37, 39, 42, 43, 46, 49; 5.52, 59, 69.
67 P. Petra 3.23; 4.36, 37, 39, 41, 42, 43; 5.59, 61, 69.
68 P. Petra 5.58.78.
69 P. Petra 3.37fr; 5.SW.86.
70 P. Petra 4.42. The only other place where this mysterious rank appears is at Nessana in P. Ness. 3.24.
71 Di Segni, 'Beersheba', pp. 151–2.
72 *Not. dign.* or. 34.33.
73 P. Petra 3.23.5. In the other there is a Flavius Valens, a tax collector, which in itself highlights the difficulty in determining whether a Flavius was a soldier or a member of the civil service (i.e. it was used in either case).
74 P. Petra 5.59.5. It names a Flavius Monaxius, a *prior* of the *ala* of Kastron Zadakathon.
75 According to A. Arjava ('People of Petra', in A. Arjava, J. Frösen, J. Kaimio (eds), *Petra Papyri V* (Amman: ACOR, 2018), p. 1), they can only identify about 100 individuals from Petra, with another 50 who might be different persons. This is a much smaller number than at Nessana, even though it involves many more papyri. Some of the papyri at Nessana list a large number of people, which in turn skews the numbers.
76 L. Di Segni, 'Late antique inscriptions in the provinces of *Palaestina* and *Arabia*. Realities and change', in K. Bolle, C. Machado, and C. Witschel (eds), *The epigraphic cultures of late Antiquity* (Stuttgart: Franz Steiner Verlag, 2017), pp. 287–320.
77 SEG 8, 34.

78 SEG 36, 1335.
79 IGLSyr 13,1 9046.
80 SEG 32, 1554.
81 Some edicts even found their way into the *Codex Iustinianus* (12.35.18).
82 SEG 9, 356, 414.
83 A more detailed summary of this not-yet-fully-reconstructed inscription can be found in D. Feissel, 'The reconstructed text. A unique document on military administration in the late Roman East', in I. Arce, D. Feissel and T. Weber (eds), *The Edict of Anastasius I. (AD 491–517), An Interim Report* (Amman: Daad, 2014), pp. 33–5.
84 See chapter 10 of the edict for the discussion of billeting.
85 Trombley, 'War', p. 164.
86 IGLSyr 4, 1610: PPUAES IIIB 992 (safety), 993 (defence of safety).
87 F. Millar, *The Roman Near East* (Cambridge, MA: Harvard University Press, 1993), here p. 527.
88 D. Kennedy, *Gerasa and the Decapolis* (London: Duckworth, 2007), pp. 115–16. On the Roman military in Jordan, see Kennedy, *The Roman army in Jordan*, pp. 44–53.
89 D. Bar, 'Population, settlement and economy in late Roman and Byzantine Palestine (70–641 AD)', *Bulletin of the School of Oriental and African Studies*, 67 (2004), 307–20; D. Bar, 'Frontier and periphery in late antique Palestine', *Greek, Roman, and Byzantine Studies*, 44 (2004), 69–92.
90 G. Avni, *The Byzantine-Islamic transition in Palestine* (Oxford: Oxford University Press, 2014), p. 36.
91 G. Ruffini, 'Village life and family power in late antique Nessana', *Transactions of the American Philological Association*, 141 (2011), 201–25, here pp. 203–4.
92 Whately, 'Nessana'.
93 M. MacDonald, 'Nomads and the Hawran in the late hellenistic and Roman periods. A reassessment of the epigraphic evidence', *Syria*, 70 (1993), 303–413.

7

The role of the military factor in the political and administrative shaping of the Visigothic kingdom (sixth to seventh centuries)

Pablo Poveda Arias

Historiography tends to acknowledge the military nature of the formation process of the Visigothic kingdom in Hispania, given the credibility granted by the sources to armed conquest.[1] The military component is thus likely to have presented an essential determinant of the kingdom's political dynamics, which implies a certain degree of militarisation of the Visigothic society,[2] a trend that may be observed throughout the post-imperial west.[3] However, this military factor of Visigothic politics and administration has not yet been considered by historians. For instance, when it comes to portraying Visigothic kingship, scholars tend to neglect the social nature of military determinants by prioritising ideological or symbolic components.[4] Some studies deny a militarising element of the administrative system until the reforms of Chindaswinth and Recceswinth (642–72).[5] The following pages discuss the impact of waging war on shaping the royal institutions and on the kings' politics[6] to argue that militarisation was an important factor for the higher Visigothic administrative cadres.

Impact and instrumentalisation of war and the military in the assertion of royal power

I would like to explore the role of the military in the consolidation of Visigothic royal power. Attaining victory was important as it helped legitimise a ruler. Prestige gained on the battlefield strengthened his power and ensured a tangible influence in other political spheres of action.[7] The legitimising role of war is reflected in sources such as John of Biclaro and Isidore of Seville, listing the most outstanding royal victories. They use military success, whether obtained in offensive or defensive campaigns, as a literary *topos* in addition to other virtues that define the good king (Isid. Hisp. *Hist.* 64),[8] an idea that is also reflected in legal texts.⁹ The very existence of the Visigothic kingdom and its monarchy is related to its numerous military victories.¹⁰

Thus, kings exalted these victories. The most paradigmatic case is contained in the *Historia Wambae*, which recounts the triumph of the monarch over the rebel Paulus. The victories of the king acquire a religious significance by being interpreted as a divine design that substantially influenced Wamba's legitimacy, thus placing him on an equal footing with the kings of the Old Testament.¹¹ The same principle can be applied to understand the interest of other kings in playing down, or even consigning to oblivion, the triumphs of other Gothic figures who competed with them in terms of military prestige. This attitude can be observed in Suintila, to whom we can attribute a true attempt of *damnatio memoriae* against the *dux* Rechila and his victories during Sisebut's rule.¹² In addition, warfare also had a legitimising value for kings through its benefits, such as loot or prestige, which the Gothic aristocracy in particular obtained through their participation in successful military campaigns.¹³

In view of the role played by war as a royal legitimiser, it is not far-fetched to suggest that a particular king would make conscious use of military action, at least in the case of offensive campaigns, for the sake of staying in power.¹⁴ After all, military activity ultimately depended on the *rex*'s decisions, which is why it may be expected that it was undertaken in consideration of his own personal interests.¹⁵ Hence, the Visigothic kings engaged in war to gain legitimacy in the midst of continued competition for the throne among different factions; a threat that was by no means trivial. This can be observed in the numerous testimonies of failed or successful royal murders and usurpation attempts.¹⁶ The existence of these parallel powers forced the *reges* to engage in constant military activity to draw attention to their virtues as warriors and, therefore, to rise as worthy leaders above their rivals.¹⁷ On the other hand, war diverted internal competition towards common goals, which consolidated a ruler's power. Military victories would have been celebrated precisely with the intention of reasserting royal authority over these opposing aristocratic factions.¹⁸ Moreover, warfare could be used to increase royal wealth.¹⁹ War loot could contribute to asserting royal power from a symbolic and material point of view.²⁰

Liuvigild (569–86) clearly perceived all these pathways involving the instrumentalisation of war against the prevailing panorama of political competition.²¹ He was the best exponent of the warrior king and reaper of military success.²² Isidore, in praising his military legacy,²³ believed that Liuvigild devoted a large part of his rule to military activity precisely to avoid internal threats and to deflect political tensions towards other targets, and thus stresses the impact of the king's victories in winning the support of his people.²⁴ Interest in maintaining regular military activity was also common under Liuvigild's predecessors, Theudis (531–48), Agila (549–55) and Athanagild (555–67).[25] A certain correlation can be established between moments of greater offensive impetus and contexts of royal weakness. Offensive military activity was particularly intense in the early years of reigns, a moment when royal legitimacy was still contested, as attested by the many internal revolts against the ruling monarchs.[26] The later military initiatives of kings Liuvigild, Witteric (603–10), Gundemar (610–12), Sisebut (612–21) and Suintila (621–31) against imperial enclaves in Hispania or northern peoples can be understood in a similar vein.[27] Comparable dynamics are also plain in later periods. For example, a military campaign organised by King Chindaswinth (642–53) is evidenced in a funerary inscription just a few months after his accession to power.[28] Paulo's insurrection took Wamba (672–80) by surprise while he was waging a campaign against the Vascones shortly after ascending to the throne.[29] King Egica (687–702) also led the kingdom's troops during the first years of his rule in a context of clear internal weakness and confrontation.[30] Lastly, Roderic (710–11), a king who openly challenged the faction of his predecessor,[31] is mentioned as fighting against the Vascones after ascending to the Visigothic throne.[32] In short, Visigothic kings were compelled to undertake offensive campaigns on a regular basis, striving for prestige and authority through the open display of their skills on the battlefield.

The military factor's potential to legitimate and strengthen royal status was even more important as a tool for those aspiring to eventually become kings themselves. This appears to have been the case with Theudis, who accumulated enormous military power in the years before becoming king in 531.[33] Specifically, Theudis devoted this time to gathering a powerful military band.[34] After all, having a large number of followers was in itself an indicator of a leader's military and political potential.[35] Likewise, it is likely that Theudigisel's (548–49) military skills and his efficiency in leading the Goths to victory, specifically against the Franks (Isid. Hisp., *Hist.* 41), were what determined his royal promotion.[36] Some years later, in 584/5, Reccared (586–601) is known to have commanded the Visigothic troops in a successful campaign against Guntram's Frankish army.[37] His ultimate goal was to be the prime candidate in the royal succession. This does not mean, however, that other determinants did not influence his accession to power,[38] but we must stress the importance of this military factor as one of the springboards that allowed him to reach royal status. The military capabilities of some of his successors must have played an equally decisive role, as was the case with Witteric and Suintila (Isid. Hisp., *Hist.* 58; 62).

In other cases, the data available are not as precise as far as kings' feats before reaching the throne is concerned. However, these monarchs certainly can be credited with having an eminent military origin, since many of them came from the most important military hierarchy in the kingdom. For instance, Theudis' leap to the throne took place when commanding the Ostrogothic troops in Hispania.[39] Liuva (568–72) also acquired royal power while he was a military leader, in this case in Septimania (Isid. Hisp., *Hist.* 48). A military origin may also be attributed to Sisebut and Sisenand (631–36).[40] This martial component is not ruled out even for subsequent kings whose activities prior to occupying the throne are only sparsely recorded.[41] Thus, there is a clear hint of military determinism in the promotion to royalty of a certain individual. Kings mostly accessed the highest rank in the kingdom from an outstanding military position, or at least after having excelled in this sphere. In short, a scenario wherein any Visigothic general, with a minimum of military prestige and social support, could stand for the throne with high chances of success developed before a monarchy that had never been able to perpetuate a fixed system of royal succession.[42]

Nevertheless, the legitimising role of victory in war was not as effective in times of royal strength, that is, when a *rex* managed to consolidate his power against internal enemies or, at least, strengthen it by drawing from other sources of authority. This allows us to establish a correlation between these contexts and periods of inactivity in terms of offensive military action. Likewise, this could be used to explain the substantial decrease in the number of military campaigns waged by Liuvigild after the unprecedentedly intense years that characterised the beginning of his rule. In some cases, there even seems to be a certain reluctance to engage in these types of actions. This would explain, for example, Reccared's lack of interest throughout his rule, especially after his consolidation on the throne in 589,[43] in organising offensive and conquering campaigns against the Byzantine enclaves of the peninsular south-east, or the areas occupied by the northern peoples.[44] Instead, Reccared's military policy was reduced to securing positions and defending what he already had (Isid. Hisp., *Hist.* 55).[45] Sisebut adopted a similar attitude. Despite intensifying his military efforts against the imperial forces in the early years of his rule,[46] his negotiations with Caesarius on the release of prisoners of war suggest he eventually ceased fighting the Byzantines.[47] Thus, I think that Sisebut discontinued his attempts against the peninsular south-east when he no longer saw it as profitable,[48] especially while he enjoyed a consolidated position.[49] Here, it was not in the kings' interest to risk their political and military capital through unnecessary offensive military campaigns, especially if they were at risk of ending in defeat. Still, the major royal duty of protecting the kingdom was unaffected by this, which becomes particularly clear in times of royal strength.[50]

War only had a legitimising effect when it brought continuous successes. If it did not, and the ruling king failed to stand out on the battlefield, it would have the opposite effect. In fact, according to the sources, the military defeats of a specific *rex* discredited and delegitimised him as a ruler (Isid. Hisp., *Hist*. 58). It is even possible to establish a last chronological correlation, in this case between the military failures of certain kings and their subsequent fall and/or murder, especially during the earlier reigns. For example, Gesaleic (507–11) is portrayed by sources as a king who lacked the political and military skills to consolidate the throne. His defeats against the Franks and Burgundians eroded his social base of support, thus paving the way for Theodoric the Ostrogoth to rise above him and promote his grandson Amalaric (511–31).[51] The latter was not so militarily fortunate either when he began his independent rule, to the extent that no military victories can be attributed to him. On the contrary, the only warlike action of which we have evidence ended in defeat for the Visigoths. The sources themselves link this failure to his murder.[52] Amalaric's great rival Theudis replaced him, who, despite important victories in the early years of his reign, suffered a serious defeat against the Byzantines in *Septem* (the current town of Ceuta) (Isid. Hisp., *Hist*. 42). Such failure left the Visigoths vulnerable to potential imperial raids, consequently stirring restlessness among certain sectors of the Gothic aristocracy and leading to substantial erosion of Theudis' social support. This would explain his subsequent murder at the hands of his own people in 548.[53] Another such case is that of Agila who, whilst waging a campaign against Cordoba in 550, suffered a crushing defeat (Isid. Hisp., *Hist*. 45). Obviously, such misfortunes would have weakened Agila's political and military credibility, a situation upon which his rivals capitalised to rearrange and close ranks around an alternative pretender to the throne: Athanagild.[54] In the case of Witteric, the military prestige that determined his royal promotion must have gradually evaporated over his reign in the light of his lack of noteworthy military feats, which likely contributed to his murder in 610 (Isid. Hisp., *Hist*. 58). This does not mean that military defeat was the ultimate cause for the fall of these kings, although it was the catalyst that triggered the destabilisation among political factions. In other words, defeat would have seriously undermined the political capital of a particular *rex*, discrediting him and, consequently, weakening him; two factors that would provide rivals with greater chances of success in the struggle for power.

With all this in mind, it appears that Visigothic royal supremacy and power primarily originated from the status and quality of military leadership.[55] A particularly curious event related to this topic is when Witteric proceeded to remove young Liuva from the throne: he cut off his right hand (Isid. Hisp., *Hist*. 57). The severed hand was the one used to hold the weapon, such that, if our hypothesis proves correct, its loss would have meant incapacitating Liuva symbolically and literally as a warrior and, by extension, as *rex*.[56] In short, all this evidence proves that the Visigothic kingship's ancestral warlike nature persisted over time,[57] remaining one of the main pillars of royal authority, even when it was underpinned by other foundations.[58]

The early militarisation of the administration in the Visigothic kingdom

Given that the authority of Visigothic kings emanated in particular from their capacity as military leaders, it seems obvious that this premise also extended to other spheres of the kingdom's political functions, such as its administrative structure. However, the historiography disregards, and in some cases even rejects, such an idea, to the extent of only perceiving a process of militarisation of Visigothic administration after Chindaswinth and Recceswinth's reforms in the mid-seventh century.[59] Clearly, historians' endeavours over the last decades to deny any hint of the 'Germanic' in Visigothic society have contributed to the blindness around this topic. However, to attribute a military nature to the kingdom's administration, or to society in general, from its very beginning, does not necessarily imply the assumption or perpetuation of traits of an allegedly Germanic origin.[60] Instead, a more pragmatic, adaptive and innovative behaviour is preferably attributed to post-Roman societies. The Visigothic monarchy projected onto the civil administration those command structures that it controlled best, in particular the military. Likewise, the fact that Visigothic power in Hispania gained its legitimacy through the military is in itself a reason for the reproduction of military hierarchies within the scope of civil government and, therefore, for an early militarisation of Visigothic administration.

The clearest expression of this early interdependence between the civil and the military spheres is arguably the figure of the *comes ciuitatis*,[61] originally established by the Roman Empire to take charge of the defence of its cities.[62] Later, in the Visigothic kingdom of Toulouse, their military power was fused with other functions of a more civil nature as a logical consequence of the prevailing climate of insecurity.[63] During the phase that began with the defeat at Vouillé, their civil prerogatives increased, originally in the area of justice,[64] and subsequently in others areas of a fiscal nature.[65] While one might reasonably assume that the original military element of the *comes* became blurred within its civil governance duties,[66] it is likely that the position's military function, connected to the armed conquest that contributed to the making of the kingdom, was actually what legitimised its civil functions.[67] While it is true that the *leges antiquae* that have been preserved mark a difference between the figures of *comes ciuitatis* and *comes exercitus* (LV IX,2, 6),[68] this does not necessarily imply that the nature of each position was different, or that the first office did not have a prominently military profile. Another law conveys that urban *comites* were responsible for collecting the compensation required as a punishment for taking bribes from military defectors. Likewise, the same law establishes that the amount gathered was to be distributed among the troops, which I assume was to be carried about by the same *comes ciuitatis* who received such payment (*LV* IX,2,1). Hence, the office of *comes ciuitatis* appears to be acting within a scope corresponding to military action, thus evidencing the martial nature of such a position.[69] This would also explain the allocation of coercive powers over the army if troops plundered the kingdom's lands (*LV* VIII,1,9). Had it been a primarily civilian position, it would have been difficult to justify such powers over military personnel. For this, the troops had to acknowledge his authority, which depended on the person concerned being ranked above the army as a military commander. We also do not reject the idea that the delegation to a *comes* of government functions over a city might derive from a previous office such as that of *comes exercitus*. It is also possible that a *comes ciuitatis* could have taken over the command of the troops and, while on campaign outside his territory, be treated as *comes exercitus*. Nevertheless, there are no supporting data for this last option beyond the Merovingian parallel, where such dynamics did operate.[70] In short, although the military role of the *comes ciuitatis* is the least emphasised in the sources,[71] all the civil functions of this figure were derived precisely from its military condition.[72] In other words, civil duties would have had their origin in the military sphere and not the other way around. Indeed, it is possible that from quite early on, by virtue of this military authority, the *comes* gradually took over the judiciary and policing functions that had until then been performed by the *iudex*, who would finally become either assimilated or relegated by the *comes*.[73] In the end, the Visigothic monarchy established a militarised administration on a local scale in which the *comes ciuitatis* – a figure of eminent military origin – was its main agent of power.[74]

Another position that offers clear proof of the kingdom's early militarisation is the *dux*. In this case, the historiography has not questioned its military nature as the highest-ranking commanding position of the kingdom's military hierarchy, below the *rex* alone. In fact, the primary role of this figure was to lead the kingdom's troops.[75] Besides this, the category of *dux* included the most powerful individuals of the kingdom, with a permanent title and, sometimes, even without delegated command functions.[76] In view of the relevance of the military for the increasing of kings' political capital, it could be argued that such a high position and capacity for influence on the kingdom's government stemmed, first of all, from their feats performed as commanders on the battlefield.[77] These skills are conveyed by the portrait drawn by the *Vitas Sanctorum Patrum Emeretensium* (*VSPE*) for *dux* Claudius, whose bravery, skills and experience on the battlefield are highlighted (*VSPE*

V,10,32–6).⁷⁸ We can thus present a close relationship between a person's military capacities and the holding of the high position of *dux*, which could ultimately lead the individual to perform important functions in the ruling of the kingdom. The problems relating the title of *dux* do not, however, concern its military function, which is acknowledged in the historiography, but instead the origin of its civil prerogatives. Historians tend to deny the allocation of civil prerogatives until well into the seventh century, coinciding with the alleged late militarisation process of Visigothic administration. In fact, the arguments used to reject the early conflation of the *dux*'s civil and military functions are largely based on the delayed legal acknowledgement of this figure's judicial and fiscal powers.⁷⁹ However, it is not clear whether the *dux* previously did not enjoy the capacity to act at the civil level. For example, where the delivery of justice is concerned, the *VSPE* also convey the idea that the *dux* Claudius, who at the same time was acting as the most important military commander in the community of Merida and its surroundings, performed civil functions, at least from time to time. This would explain why Bishop Masona of Merida called said *dux* to discuss his concerns about the Arian Bishop Sunna and his cronies, who intended to murder Masona in the early years of Reccared's reign. Likewise, after thwarting Sunna's plan, Claudius appears as responsible for communicating and ensuring compliance with the legal sentences issued by Reccared, which were in fact suggested by the *dux* himself (*VSPE* V,11,27–33; 49–55).⁸⁰ There is even early and exceptional legal confirmation for these types of responsibilities in an alleged law established by Liuvigild, in which the Visigothic *dux* is allocated judicial powers pertaining to the punishment of slave prostitutes (*LV* III,4,17). As for taxation, Abilio Barbero and Marcelo Vigil evidenced *duces* in the *Vita Sancti Fructuosi* engaging in tax collection activities from the second third of the seventh century, at least in peripheral regions such as in El Bierzo (*VSF,* 2,1–5).⁸¹ It is indeed possible that, while they were engaged in military missions, *duces* would temporarily take on the collection of tax aimed at covering possible expenses without the mediation of royal power.

I consider that the reason that these civil powers did not obtain legal sanction until quite late is that their allocation was connected to the emergence or exceptional nature of the rank of *dux* from the fifth century onwards.⁸² For example, predominately military powers were delegated to *Salla*, a Visigothic *dux* under Euric's rule, to act as general-in-chief of the area around Merida.⁸³ During the period that began with the Visigothic defeat at Vouillé, certain *duces* may also have been granted an originally military office under this type of exceptional circumstance. This can be observed, for example, around Merida while Claudius was performing his task in the area, where political and social tensions had been a constant since Liuvigild's rule.⁸⁴ Against this background, it is easy to understand why Reccared sought to control and maintain order in an area that was quite prone to conflict by naming a delegate power agent with enough weight and coercive power to rise above any other instance of local authority.⁸⁵ *Dux* Claudius' original office would have therefore been military. Hereafter, *duces* gradually acquired additional powers as a pragmatic response to circumstantial needs that arose over the course of their missions, thus making it clear that the assumption of such prerogatives always originated from their supreme authority in the sphere of military activity. If such civil assignments were not reflected earlier in legislation, it was precisely due to the temporary nature that always characterised *duces*' missions;⁸⁶ either because they performed their function during the course of military campaigns or because these were taken as a result of exceptional situations.⁸⁷ Bearing all this in mind, what happened after the mid-seventh century was actually the legal confirmation of a reality that had prevailed *de facto* until that time as a response to specific and exceptional circumstances.⁸⁸ In sum, the alleged late militarisation of the Visigothic administration was nothing but an update of the legislation, accepting the reality of the time but adapting it to the specific necessities that led to its promulgation.⁸⁹ Thus, throughout the entire period, *duces* played roles as military chiefs who could acquire extraordinary powers and the capacity to intervene at other levels of civil activity only in emergency situations requiring a military and coercive response.

In short, we conclude that the military component that characterised the development of the Hispanic-Visigothic kingdom was built into its political and administrative structure from the very beginning. As far as the monarchy itself is concerned, warfare in general was a highly effective instrument for the legitimisation and perpetuation of Visigothic kings' authority. Specifically, we consider that martial activity could provide the *rex* with military capital that, skilfully used, could be amortised to impose on the continuing atmosphere of internal competition and extend his power to other spheres of action. On the other hand, our brief analysis of the Visigothic administration has revealed its early militarisation, at least where the most important positions are concerned; a phenomenon that is supported by the strong military component and background of their roles and players. We can therefore finish by stating that the civil power exercised by kings, *duces* and *comites* stemmed first and foremost from their military command and capacity.

Notes

My most sincere thanks to Ellora Bennett, Laury Sarti, Rebecca A. Devlin and the anonymous referees, whose valuable comments and suggestions have contributed to the improvement and enhancement of this chapter. The content of the above is the sole responsibility of the author. This work was partially supported by the Ministry of Science, Innovation and Universities [Research Project HAR2016-76094-C4-4-R].

1. Isid. Hisp., *Etym.* XVIII,2,1, ed. J. Oroz and M. A. Marcos (Madrid: Biblioteca de Autores Cristianos, 2009), p. 1218; *Hist. De laude Spaniae*, 26–30; 67; 69, ed. C. Rodríguez (León: Centro de Estudios e Investigación 'San Isidoro', 1975), pp. 170, 284, 286. See M. R. Valverde, *Ideología, simbolismo y ejercicio del poder real en la monarquía visigoda. Un proceso de cambio* (Salamanca: Ediciones Universidad de Salamanca, 2000), pp. 154–6.
2. Emphasising the transformative role of war in post-imperial societies, G. Halsall, *Barbarian migrations and the Roman west, 376–568* (Cambridge: Cambridge University Press, 2007), p. 11. Our definition of 'militarised society' is that suggested in E. James, 'The militarisation of Roman society, 400–700', in A. N. Jørgensen and B. L. Blausen (eds), *Military aspects of Scandinavian society in a European perspective, AD 1–1300* (Copenhagen: Copenhagen National Museum, 1997), pp. 19–24, here pp. 19–20.
3. James, 'The militarisation'; P. Heather, 'Elite militarisation and the post-Roman West', in G. Bonamente and R. Lizzi Testa (eds), *Istituzioni, carismi ed esercizio del potere (IV-VI secolo d.C.)* (Bari: Edipuglia, 2010), pp. 245–65.
4. On this, see Valverde, *Ideología*.
5. L. A. García Moreno, 'Estudios sobre la organización administrativa del reino visigodo de Toledo', *AHDE*, 44 (1974), 1–155, here 149–55.
6. Applying this idea to the entirety of the early medieval western monarchies: G. Halsall, *Warfare and society in the barbarian west, 450–900* (London: Routledge, 2003), pp. 25–6.
7. This role of war has already been adduced by other authors, both for the Visigothic case (Halsall, *Warfare*, pp. 136–7) and on a broader level (L. Sarti, *Perceiving war and the military in early Christian Gaul (ca. 400–700 A.D.)* (Leiden: Brill, 2013), p. 221). From an anthropological point of view, H. J. M. Claessen, 'Changing legitimacy', in R. Cohen and J. D. Toland (eds), *State formation and political legitimacy* (Oxford: Transaction Books, 1988), pp. 23–44, here p. 27.
8. M. McCormick, *Eternal victory. Triumphal rulership in late Antiquity, Byzantium and the early medieval west* (Cambridge: Cambridge University Press, Éd. De la Maison des Sciences de l'Homme, 1990), pp. 323–7; Valverde, *Ideología*, pp. 211–12.
9. *LV* I, 2, 6, ed. K. Zeumer, *MGH Legum sectio* I, t. I (Hanover: Hahn, 1902), p. 42.
10. M. Reydellet, *La royauté dans la littérature latine de Sidoine Apollinaire à Isidore de Séville* (Roma: École Française de Rome, 1981), pp. 514–23.
11. G. García Herrero, 'Julián de Toledo y la realeza visigoda', *Antigüedad y Cristianismo*, 8 (1991), 201–55, here 245–6.
12. L. A. García Moreno, 'La oposición a Suintila. Iglesia, monarquía y nobleza en el reino visigodo', *Polis*, 3 (1991), 13–24, here 17–18.

13 P. Poveda Arias, 'Hacia la unidad de Hispania? Explicaciones sociales a las ofensivas militares visigodas en la península ibérica (siglos VI-VIII)', *Gladius*, 40 (2020), 73–92.
14 The same arguments from an anthropological point of view are provided in M. S. Sahlins, 'Poor man, rich man, big-man, chief. Political types in Melanesia and Polynesia', *Comparative Studies in Society and History*, 5 (1963), 285–303, here 254–5; R. B. Ferguson, 'Ten points on war', *Social Analysis*, 52 (2008), 32–49, pp. here 44–6.
15 *Ibid*.
16 Echoing this situation: Greg. Tur., *DLH* III, 30, ed. B. Krusch and W. Levison, *MGH SRM*, t. I, p. I (Hanover: Hahn, 1951), p. 126; Fredeg., *Chron.*, III,42, ed. N. Desgrugillers (Clermont-Ferrand: Éditions Paleo, 2011), p. 48; IV,82, ed. O. Devillers and J. Meyers (Turnhout: Brepols, 2001), p. 184. See A. Besga Marroquín, 'El 'morbo gótico'. Tópico o realidad?', *Letras de Deusto*, 26 (2007), 135–44.
17 Sahlins, 'Poor man', p. 289.
18 McCormick, *Eternal victory*, pp. 302–3.
19 M. Hardt, 'Royal treasures and representation in the early Middle Ages', in W. Pohl and H. Reimitz (eds), *Strategies of distinction. The construction of ethnic communities, 300–800* (Leiden: Brill, 1998), pp. 255–80, here p. 267. We know that the king received a rather large part of the booty. Isid. Hisp., *Etym.* V,7,2; *Hist.* 49; 51.
20 See R. Le Jan, 'Les élites au haut Moyen Âge. Approche sociologique et anthropologique', in F. Bougard, H.-W. Goetz and R. Le Jan (eds), *Théorie et pratiques des élites au haut Moyen Âge. Conception, perception et réalisation* (Turnhout: Brepols, 2012), pp. 69–100, here p. 81.
21 Showing the political difficulties of his rule: Ioh. Bicl., *Chron.* 50; 54, ed. C. Cardelle de Hartmann, *CCSL*, 173A (Turnhout: Brepols, 2001), pp. 70–1; 86; Isid. Hisp., *Hist.* 51.
22 Greg. Tur., *In Glor. Confess.* 12,6–12, ed. B. Krusch, *MGH SRM*, t. I, p. II (Hanover: Hahn, 1885), p. 305; Ioh. Bicl., *Chron.* 12; 17; 27; 32; 35; Isid. Hisp., *Hist.* 49.
23 M. Reydellet, *La royauté*, p. 530.
24 Isid. Hisp., *Hist.* 49, short version, 3–4; long version, 5–8. As further support for our argument, see C. Martin, *La géographie du pouvoir dans l'Espagne visigothique* (Villeneuve d'Ascq: Presses Universitaires du Septentrion, 2003), p. 313.
25 *Chron. Caesar.* 6a, ed. C. Cardelle de Hartmann, *CCSL*, 173A (Turnhout: Brepols, 2001), p. 61; Greg. Tur., *DLH* IV, 8; Isid. Hisp., *Hist.* 41–2.
26 H. J. Diesner, 'Bandas de criminales, bandidos y usurpadores en la España visigoda', *Hispania Antiqua*, 8 (1978), 129–42.
27 On campaigns against the empire: Isid. Hisp., *Hist.* 58–9; 61–3; *Chron.* 415; 416b, ed. J. C. Martín, *CCSL*, 112 (Turnhout: Brepols, 2003), p. 204; Fredeg., *Chron.* IV,33; *Chron. Moz. a. 754*, 13, 4, ed. J. E. López Pereira (León: Centros de Estudios e Investigación 'San Isidoro', 2009), p. 184. As evidence of the

expeditions against the peoples of the peninsular north: Isid. Hisp., *Hist.* 59; 61; 63; Fredeg., *Chron.* IV,33; Siseb. *Epistvla Sisebvti regis Gothorum missa ad Isidorvm de Libro Rotarvm*, 5–8, ed. J. Fontaine (Paris: Institut d'Études Augustiniennes, 2002), p. 329.

28 See E. Moreno Resano, 'La representación épica del combate y de la muerte del guerrero en el epitafio de Opilano (año 642)', *Habis*, 42 (2011), 299–316.

29 Iul. Tol., *Hist. Wambae* 10, ed. W. Levison, *CCSL*, 74 (Turnhout: Brepols, 1976), p. 226. Halsall, *Warfare*, p. 136; A. Isla, *Ejército, sociedad y política en la península ibérica entre los siglos VII y XI* (Madrid: CSIC-Ministerio de Defensa, 2010) p. 46.

30 *Ibid.*, 66–7. See P. Poveda Arias, 'Relectura de la supuesta crisis del fin del reino visigodo de Toledo. Una aproximación al reinado de Egica a través de sus fuentes legales', *AHDE*, 85 (2015), 13–46.

31 P. C. Díaz and P. Poveda, '"*Qui patrie excidium intulerunt*". Hispania 711. Explicaciones desesperadas para un colapso inesperado', *Reti Medievali*, 17 (2016), 191–218, here 212–13.

32 Isla, *Ejército*, p. 117.

33 See P. C. Díaz and M. R. Valverde, 'Goths confronting Goths. Ostrogothic political relations in Hispania', in S. J. Barnish and F. Marazzi (eds), *The Ostrogoths. From the migration period to the sixth century* (Woodbridge: The Boydell Press, 2007), pp. 353–86, here p. 369.

34 Procop., *BG* V,12,50–51, ed. H. B. Dewing (London and Cambridge MA: William Heinemann Ltd., Harvard University Press, 1952), p. 130.

35 A. Barbero and M. Vigil, *La formación del feudalismo en la Península Ibérica* (Barcelona: Crítica, 1978), p. 39.

36 Iord., *Get.* LVIII,303; *Chron. Caesar.* 133a; Isid. Hisp., *Hist.* 44; Fredeg., *Chron.* III,42.

37 Greg. Tur., *DLH* VI,30; Ioh. Bicl., *Chron.* 74.

38 Greg. Tur., *DLH* VIII,46; IX,1; Ioh. Bicl., *Chron.* 79; Fredeg., *Chron.* IV,6; *VSPE* V, 9. See S. Castellanos, *Los godos y la cruz. Recaredo y la unidad de 'Spania'* (Madrid: Alianza Editorial, 2007).

39 Iord., *Get.* LVIII,302, ed. F. Giunta and A. Grillone (Roma, Istituto Storico Italiano per il Medio Evo, 1991), p. 124; Procop., *BG*, V,12,50–54.

40 As regards the former, this is suggested by Isidore of Seville himself, who attributes to Sisebut outstanding military skills. Isid. Hisp., *Hist.* 61. Regarding Sisenand, see García Moreno, 'La oposición', p. 23.

41 This could have been the case with Egica, who held the title of *dux*. *Conc. XIII Tol.* (a. 683), *Subscriptiones*, 795, ed. G. Martínez and F. Rodríguez (Madrid: CSIC, 2002), p. 266. See García Moreno, *El fin del reino visigodo de Toledo* (Madrid: Universidad Autónoma, 1975), p. 195. Highlighting this military origin for Wamba, Isla, *Ejército*, p. 46.

42 On this subject, see Valverde, *Ideología*, pp. 275–81.

43 See Castellanos, *Los godos*.

44 We only have evidence of small-scale actions, organised as a response to previous incursions. Isid. Hisp., *Hist.* 54.

45 P. C. Díaz, 'El siglo VI en Gallia e Hispania a través de las fuentes escrita', *Zona Arqueológica*, 11 (2008), 380–91, here 360. In fact, regarding international affairs, the king prioritised the diplomatic over the military route when addressing disputes. See M. Vallejo Girvés, 'The treaties between Justinian and Athanagild and the legality of the Byzantine possession on the Iberian Peninsula', *Byzantion*, 66 (1996), 208–18, here 209.
46 J. Wood, 'Defending Byzantine Spain. Frontiers and diplomacy', *EME*, 18 (2012), 292–319, here 318.
47 *Epist. Wisigoth.* II, ed. J. Gil (Sevilla: Universidad de Sevilla, 1991), pp. 5–6.
48 Isid. Hisp., *Hist.* 61 conveys a more propaganda-based reasoning.
49 On the mechanisms used to achieve it, see Valverde, *Ideología*, pp. 264–5.
50 P. Cazier, *Isidore de Séville et la naissance de l'Espagne catholique* (Paris: Beauchesne, 1994), p. 298.
51 Isid. Hisp., *Hist.* 37; *Chron. Caesar.* 94b. Shortly after, Gesaleic lost his life attempting to regain power. *Chron. Caesar.* 94a; Isid. Hisp., *Hist.* 38.
52 The sources fail to agree on whether the murder was committed by the Franks or by the Goths. *Chron. Caesar.* 11a; Iord., *Get.* LVIII,302; Greg. Tur., *DLH* III,10; Isid. Hisp., *Hist.* 40; Fredeg., *Chron.* III,30; III, 41. Nevertheless, it would not be unreasonable to attribute his death to his own people, which would have been consistent with the climate of internal tension described in Isid. Hisp., *Hist.* 40.
53 *Chron. Caesar.* 133a, 794–5; Isid. Hisp., *Hist.* 43. In a similar vein, M. Vallejo Girvés, *Hispania y Bizancio. Una relación desconocida* (Madrid: Akal, 2012), p. 118.
54 Iord., *Get.* LVIII,303; *Chron. Caesar.* 144a; Isid. Hisp., *Hist.* 43.
55 This affords the suggestion of a link between a Visigothic king's good governance and his military talents. Halsall, *Warfare*, pp. 25–6 and p. 136.
56 Similarly, punishment was delivered to those who dared to plot against the ruling king. Ioh. Bicl., *Chron.* 87; 93.
57 See H. Wolfram, *History of Goths* (Berkeley: California University Press, 1988).
58 See P. C. Díaz and M. R. Valverde, 'The theoretical strength and practical weakness of the Visigothic monarchy of Toledo', in F. Theuws and J. L. Nelson (eds), *Rituals of power. From late Antiquity to the early Middle Ages* (Leiden: Brill, 2000), pp. 59–93.
59 Barbero and Vigil, *La formación*; García Moreno, 'Estudios', pp. 149–55 are the main exponents of this line. In the Merovingian case, by contrast, this militarisation of administration has been acknowledged since the emergence of the *regnum Francorum*. Sarti, *Perceiving war*, pp. 32–41.
60 This approach disregards the militarisation of late imperial elites. Halsall, *Barbarian migrations*, pp. 492–6. Added to this is the militarisation of the administrative cadres of the late Roman Empire. See R. MacMullen, *Soldier and civilian in the later Roman Empire* (Cambridge, MA: Harvard University Press, 1963).
61 Halsall, *Warfare*, p. 31.
62 C. Sánchez-Albornoz, 'El gobierno de las ciudades de España del siglo V al X', in C. Sánchez-Albornoz (ed.) *Estudios sobre las instituciones medievales españolas* (México D.F.: UNAM, 1965), p. 617.

63 García Moreno, 'Estudios', pp. 8–9. Extending this phenomenon to the administration of Toulouse, Valverde, *Ideología*, p. 88.
64 *LV* III,4, 17; III,6, 1; VI,1, 1; VII,1, 5; VII,4, 2; VIII,4, 26; IX,1, 20. See Martin, *La géographie*, p. 162.
65 See Sánchez-Albornoz, 'El gobierno', pp. 626–8.
66 Compare P. D. King, *Law and society in the Visigothic kingdom* (Cambridge: Cambridge University Press, 1972), p. 75.
67 The military nature of the office of *comes* is clearly confirmed in the *VSPE*, where it is explicitly stated that *comites ciuitatum* customarily carried weapons inside the city. *VSPE* V, 10, 43–50, ed. A. Maya, *CCSL*, 116 (Turnhout: Brepols, 1992), pp. 83–4.
68 Compare García Moreno, 'Estudios', p. 10; James, 'The militarisation'.
69 In a similar vein, laws *LV* IX, 2, 3–5. Compare García Moreno, 'Estudios', p. 76.
70 Greg. Tur., *DLH* IV,30; VII,13. S. Barnwell, *Emperor, prefects and kings. The Roman West, 395–565* (London: Duckworth, 1992), pp. 110–11. Perhaps the case of Witteric, who held the position of *comes ciuitatis* before coming to the throne, can be set as the Visigothic exponent.
71 Ultimately, such military functions would have been performed only on an occasional basis. The legal nature of most of the available testimonies, which basically deal with civil issues, may also have influenced the relativisation of the *comites ciuitatum*'s military office.
72 Compare Martin, *La géographie*, pp. 162–3.
73 See Sánchez-Albornoz, 'El gobierno'; García Moreno, 'Estudios', p. 10. Nevertheless, the term *iudex* would at the time become a polysemous word, used to refer to individuals holding different positions. King, *Law*, pp. 99–101; Martin, *La géographie*, p. 151.
74 Such dynamics find a quite eloquent parallel in the Merovingian kingdoms. S. Esders, 'Nordwestgallien um 500. Von der militarisierten spätromischen Provinzgesellschaft zur erweiterten Militäradministration des merowingischen Königtums', in M. Meier and S. Patzold (eds), *Chlodwigs Welt. Organisation von Herrschaft um 500* (Stuttgart: Franz Steiner, 2014), pp. 339–61, here 354–5.
75 These are the contexts where *duces* are mentioned more frequently. Martin, *La géographie*, p. 168. These exclusively military figures could be the ones referred to in *VSF* 14, 27–31, ed. M. C. Díaz y Díaz (Braga: Empresa do Diário do Minho, 1974), p. 106.
76 As of the second half of the seventh century, references to *duces* increase, being especially frequent in the palatial milieu. A. Isla, 'El *officium palatinum* visigodo. Entorno regio y poder aristocrático', *Hispania*, 62 (2002), 823–48, here 841–3; Martin, *La géographie*, p. 170.
77 In a similar vein, Isla, 'El *officium*', 844. This is also how we understand honorary *duces*, whose title was not attached to any specific military or political functions. *Ibid.*, 837–43.
78 In a similar vein: Greg. Magn., *Reg. Epist.* IX,230, 10–12, ed. D. L. Norberg (Turnhout: Brepols, 1982), pp. 811–12.

79 See García Moreno, 'Estudios', pp. 120–4.
80 See I. Wood, 'Social relations in the Visigothic kingdom from the fifth to the seventh century. The example of Mérida', in P. Heather (ed.), *The Visigoths. From the migration period to the seventh century. An ethnographic perspective* (San Marino: The Boydell Press, 1999), pp. 191–223, here p. 200.
81 A. Barbero and M. Vigil, 'Algunos aspectos de la feudalización del reino visigodo en relación con su organización financiera y militar', in *Visigodos, cántabros y vascones en los orígenes sociales de la Reconquista* (Pamplona: Urgoiti, 2012), pp. 81–7.
82 Barnwell, *Emperor*, pp. 79–80.
83 See P. C. Díaz, *El reino suevo (411–585)* (Madrid: Akal, 2011), p. 121.
84 S. Castellanos, 'The significance of social unanimity in a Visigothic hagiography. Keys to an ideological screen', *JECS*, 11 (2003), 387–419.
85 This is also expressed by Martin, *La géographie*, p. 169. This is also how Claudius' having an armed body under his command can be explained. *VSPE* V, 11, 8, 38–42. We understand the presence of Visigothic *duces* in *Gallaecia* in the context that followed the conquest of the Suebi kingdom as having a similar purpose. Ioh. Bicl., *Chron.* 76. P. C. Díaz, 'El esquema provincial en el contexto administrativo de la monarquía visigoda', *Mélanges de la Casa de Velázquez*, 49 (2019), 77–108, here 87.
86 We thus reject the alleged territorial nature of its command, as well as the very existence of *duces prouinciae*. Díaz, 'El esquema', pp. 94–8. Compare García Moreno, 'Estudios', pp. 149–55; Martin, *La géographie*, pp. 167–75.
87 In a similar vein: Díaz, 'El esquema', pp. 94–8. A situation that would, in a certain way, resemble the one that prevailed in the Merovingian kingdoms. B. Dumézil, *Servir l'État barbare dans la Gaule franque: Du fonctionnariat antique à la noblesse médiévale, IVe-IXe siècle* (Paris: Tallandier, 2013), p. 181.
88 Compare Martin, *La géographie*, pp. 176–80.
89 See Poveda Arias, 'Relectura'.

8

Recent archaeological research on fortifications in France, Belgium and Switzerland, 750–1000

Luc Bourgeois

Carolingian fortifications have been a neglected subject in French research for a long time: archaeologists have focused on both Roman walls and medieval castles and, with the exception of two chapters devoted to the early Middle Ages in Gabriel Fournier's innovative work,[1] the centuries before the year 1000 are almost entirely absent from any comprehensive study on medieval fortification published to this day. This situation is not only the result of the scarcity of information but also of a preconception about the decline of fortification techniques after the end of the Roman Empire in the west. The same trends have long prevailed in Belgian and Swiss investigations.

Since 1990, however, the situation has started to change: excavations have increased in number and the question of places of power in the early Middle Ages is now at the centre of historians' and archaeologists' focus. Yet, only a very fragmentary assessment can be drawn from these surveys, which I propose to articulate here under three main topics: the impact of the past on defensive constructions between 750 and the tenth century; the emergence of new categories of fortified settlements at that time; and, finally, the architectural innovations that generated the classical castle around the year 1000. The aim of this chapter is not to provide a new synthesis on Carolingian fortification; it is limited to introducing recent and sometimes unpublished archaeological work carried out in three contemporary countries, which roughly correspond to the western part of the Frankish Empire.

The legacy of the past

Carolingian fortification appears to be strongly rooted in several distinct traditions. The maintenance or resurgence of fortification techniques inherited from Protohistory, which disappeared from the Roman world but remained very much alive in eastern and northern Europe, are now documented throughout the Carolingian area. Many *oppida* then experienced reoccupation, such as the Belgian hillfort of Modave (Figure 8.1.A – see also 8.1.B, 8.1.C and 8.1.D).[2] Furthermore, new fortifications used old architectural forms. These are in particular the ramparts related to the Iron Age *murus gallicus*, made up of interwoven timbers filled with earth or stone and sometimes preceded by a masonry wall;[3] forts closed by voluntarily vitrified ramparts, as in Saint-Dizier-Leyrenne (Creuse);[4] or *Zangentor*-type gates, already known in the Hallstatt period, which increased in number at the end of the Carolingian era (Figure 8.2).[5]

However, Roman fortification was a greater source of inspiration during the Carolingian era. This imitation was a symbolic choice, not only because this architecture was regarded as an ideal model, but also because it materialised the seats of power legitimised in the past. In the context of the Carolingian *Renovatio* and at a time when poliorcetic treatises such as Vegetius' *De re militari* were often copied,[6] this fidelity to Antiquity is also found in religious architecture until the early eleventh century. The wall built on the Vatican hill between 848 and 852 thus reproduces – on a scale reduced by half – the Aurelian wall that surrounded the city of Rome from the third century.[7] The *castrum* of Saint-Martin de Tours, completed in 918 or shortly before, illustrates the same imitation process: this is demonstrated by the construction techniques, the presence of towers at regular intervals, the large bays allowing the use of artillery or the doors opening to the four cardinal points (Figure 8.1.B).[8]

Some fortifications that differ relatively from ancient architecture also borrow some details from models dating back to before the Middle Ages. For instance, around 970, the crenellation of the rural residence of the Counts of Angoulême in Andone (Villejoubert, Charente) was clearly inspired by the Hellenistic and Roman traditions (Figure 8.1.B).[9] Around 900, the vast tower built in Mayenne by the Counts of Maine also recalled Roman architecture in many ways. This building bears the marks of another way of reclaiming the past: marking the heart of a new central place, it incorporates within its walls large Roman blocks transported from the former regional capital of Jublains, undoubtedly intended to materialise the continuity of power (Figure 8.1.C).[10] In all these cases, the necessities of defence are mixed with symbolic considerations.

The near complete disappearance of flanking towers has long been considered, especially in France, as typical of fortification in the early Middle Ages. This argument has long since been demolished by archaeologists working in German-speaking lands where flanking towers and projecting towers have been identified in large numbers from the ninth and tenth

132 Warfare and society

Figure 8.1 A: Proposal for the reconstruction of the Carolingian gate of Pont-de-Bonne (Belgium, Modave)
B: Villejoubert (France, Charente), 'Andone', reconstruction seen from the west

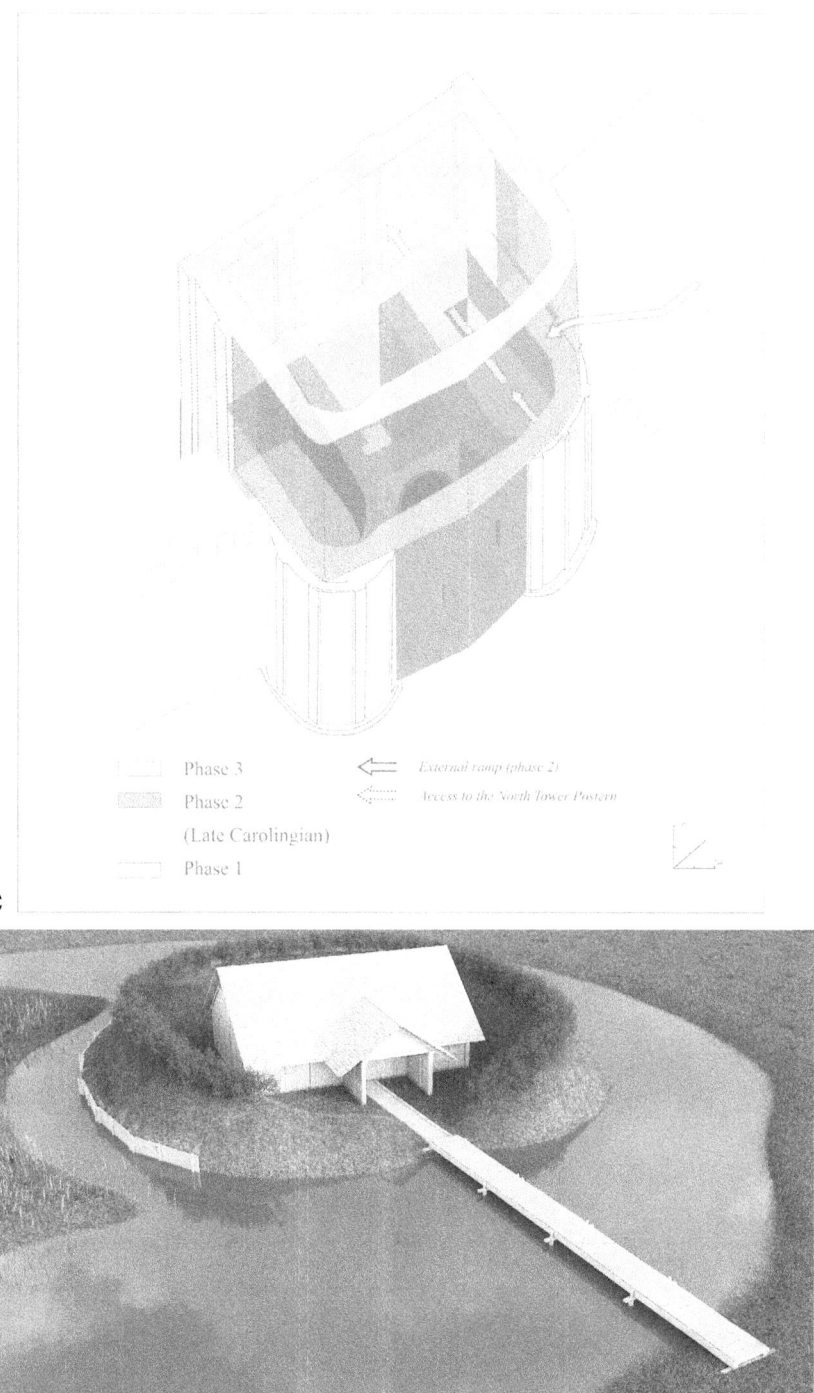

Figure 8.1, cont'd C: Périgueux (France, Dordogne), Porte de Mars. Gallo-Roman structures and transformations of the tenth to twelfth centuries
D: The moated site of Pineuilh (France, Gironde), 'La Mothe' in 975–83

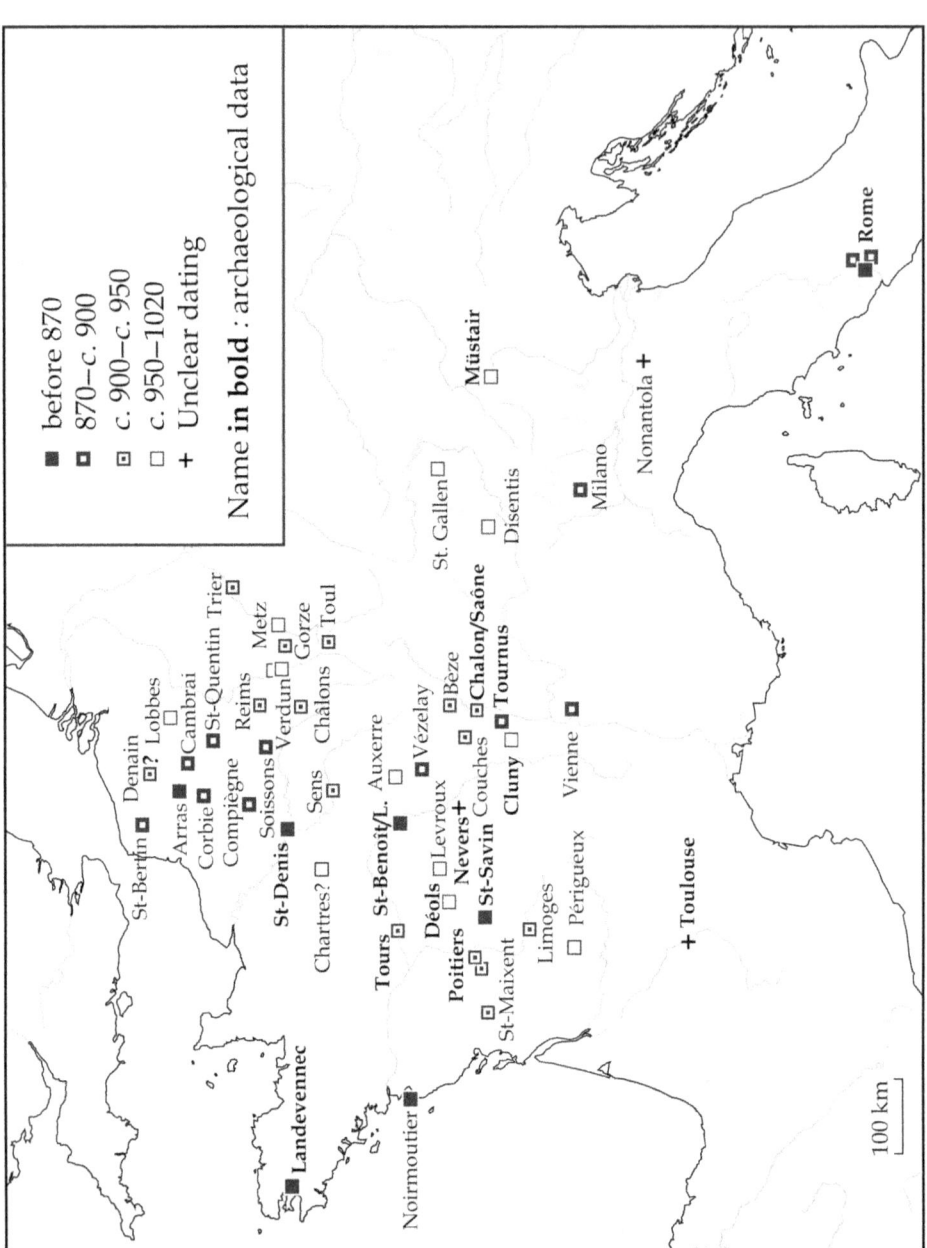

Figure 8.2 The fortified monasteries and collegial churches of the Carolingian Empire: a state of knowledge

centuries.[11] While masonry curtains now appear more frequently, it is also known that a few Carolingian curtain walls present towers established at regular intervals, such as the *castrum* of Saint-Martin de Tours already mentioned (Figure 8.1.B). Elsewhere, quadrangular towers are integrated, from time to time, within key places within the enclosing wall, such as in the early tenth-century example discovered at Château-Thierry (Aisne);[12] sometimes, the curved plan of the walls makes the presence of towers superfluous, as in the *castrum* of Andone at the end of the same century (Figure 8.1.B).[13]

With the exception of a few imitations of *Zangentor*-type towers or gates between two towers of Roman tradition, the gates are often simple openings in the walls. In front of them, the wooden bridges are static but assembled in such a way as to allow them to be dismantled quickly in case of danger (Figure 8.1.A).[14] Therefore, the defence of most of these fortifications can only be exercised from their upper parts. They are then reinforced by various obstacles placed in front of the curtain wall, such as long flat or sloping glacis that leave the attackers uncovered (Figure 8.1.B),[15] possible pointed posts (*cippi*) as identified along the scarp of Boves[16] castle, or several successive ditches alternating with earth mounds, as documented for several castles.[17] Introducing water into these ditches could lead to major hydraulic works, as in Saint-Denis where the canalisation of the nearby river and a water regulation system were documented during the time of Charles the Bald (Figure 8.3).[18] These Carolingian defensive elements are therefore not particularly different from those described by Vitruvius or Vegetius. The *ekphraseis* in Carolingian written sources might not be mere imitations of roman writers; they could in many cases correspond to an architectural reality.

The fortifications of late Antiquity, which surround most of the main Roman towns and a number of small towns, have long been studied solely as Roman monuments.[19] However, they were the main defences of these towns for much of the Middle Ages, sometimes until the modern period, and recent archaeological investigation shows frequent refurbishments to the defences in order to stay abreast of both the developing city and fighting techniques.

Conflicts led to the destruction (often very partial and temporary) of some fortifications: the reconquest of Aquitaine by Pepin the Short between 760 and 768 thus forced Duke Waïfre to render several urban fortifications unusable, though they were quickly restored by the victor.[20] But periods of peace might lead to their disappearance, either because of a lack of maintenance or because they were partly dismantled to allow the city to expand. In Tours (Indre-et-Loire), a breach in the *castrum*, which occurred in the fifth to sixth centuries, seems to have existed until the Carolingian period.

The neighbouring ditch was then used as a cemetery.[21] In the 820s, the Archbishop of Reims Ebbon (816–35) obtained the emperor's agreement to pull down a section of the city walls to rebuild the cathedral; the chronicler Flodoard explained this type of action as due to the prevailing peace in the Frankish world at that time. Barely half a century later, Archbishop Fulco (883–900), adopting the converse approach, used the stones of a ruined church to restore the city walls.[22]

Restoration of urban walls increased after the death of Louis the Pious (840) and continued throughout the tenth century. Archaeology reveals a number of examples of this work: in Rouen (Seine-Maritime) the city walls were extensively restored during the reign of King Eudes (888–98);[23] new square towers were added to the walls of Poitiers (Vienne) and Autun (Saône-et-Loire).[24] In Orléans (Loiret), the urban walls were also largely rebuilt.[25] The new Carolingian ditches of Toulouse (Haute-Garonne)[26] or the doubling of the ditch of the Portes mordelaises in Rennes (Ille-et-Vilaine)[27] are other examples of this periodic maintenance.

The extension of some cities as early as the tenth century sometimes led to an increase in the area enclosed, as in Metz (Moselle) where the wall extended as far as the Seille River,[28] due to the creation of new fortifications to defend the dynamic suburbs that had developed outside the walls: in Verdun (Meuse), the merchant district was already protected by walls at that time.[29]

Conversely, the difficulty of defending ancient fortifications that were too large or in too poor condition and the multiplication of competing powers in cities often led to the creation of smaller fortified spaces within the walls, such as around Nantes Cathedral (Loire-Atlantique) around 900.[30] These fortified enclosures established within the city sometimes reused ancient monuments: this was the fate, at an early date, of the amphitheatre of Nîmes (Gard), transformed into a fortification before the seventh century, which housed the residence of the viscount in 876 and 898.[31]

This phenomenon is even more common for city gates. The main Roman gate of Périgueux (Dordogne) was closed in the tenth century to become the residence of a lay aristocrat; this forced the bishop to open a new access to his cathedral.[32] Fortified settlements are documented earlier in some cities: in Orléans, each of the two courtyards of a residential (royal?) complex occupied from the Merovingian period to the early ninth century were thus associated with a stone tower.[33]

But it is also necessary to move away from cities and consider other forms of fortification. In several French regions, many *oppida* founded or reoccupied between the fourth and sixth centuries have been excavated since the 1990s.[34] Long considered temporary shelters, these rural fortifications appear today in all their diversity: aristocratic residences, centres of artisanal

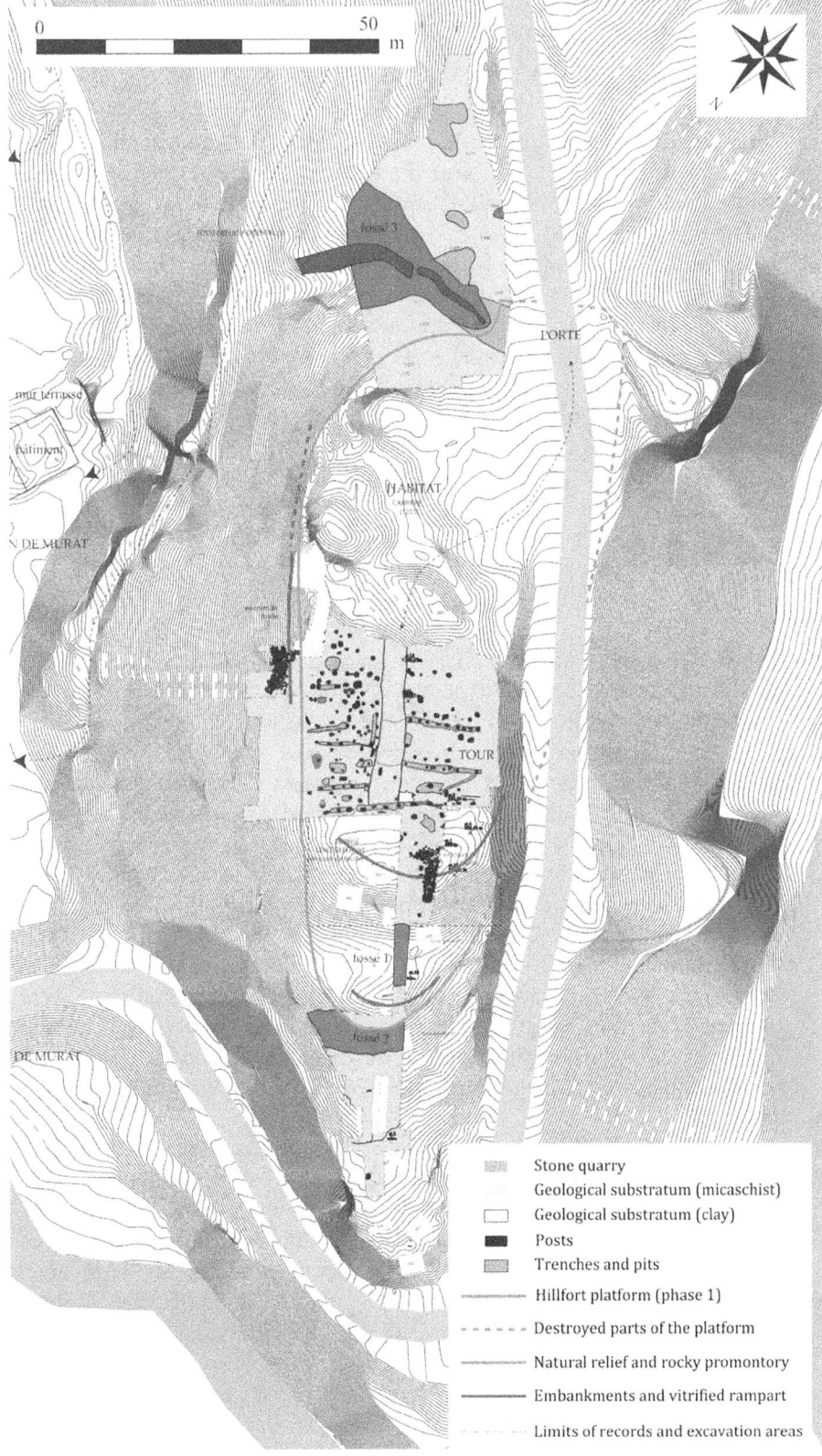

Figure 8.3 Saint-Dizier-Leyrenne (France, Creuse), 'Murat', plan of the *oppidum* and excavated areas

production or real towns. Indeed, they mark the adaptation of the geography of power to the new political and economic realities that emerged from the end of the Roman Empire.[35] Near the Mediterranean coast, most of these hillforts did not survive the sixth century. On the other hand, in Auvergne or Limousin, the numerous fortifications of this kind besieged by Pepin the Short during his conquest of Aquitaine show a continuity in the strategic points after the middle of the eighth century.[36] Similarly, the large fortifications inherited from late Antiquity that punctuate the Loire basin constitute the basis of the most important medieval castles in this region: Champtoceaux, Chinon, Amboise and Blois. It is no longer possible to think about the organisation of Carolingian defence without taking into account these networks of public fortifications, which have yet to be identified in many other French regions.

Two new categories of settlements: fortified bridges and fortified monasteries

The Carolingian period was not only marked by continuities, however. It also saw the emergence of new categories of fortified settlements, in particular fortifications associated with bridges and monasteries.

The building programme of fortified bridges to block Francia's main navigable rivers comes at a particular moment in Carolingian history, when Charles the Bald and his successor Charles the Fat tried, between 860 and 880, to resist the incursions of the great Viking fleets. However, this type of monument was not completely new; indeed, as early as 789, Charlemagne ordered the construction of a bridge over the Elbe river, the access to which was defended by two castles.[37] The royal capitulars and narrative sources enable us to set out the steps of this programme:[38] first in 862, on the Marne, the fortified bridge of Trilbardou was built, next were those of Charenton, reactivated in 865,[39] and Auvers, on the Oise, restored the same year;[40] then on the River Loire, came the fortification of the old bridge of Ponts-de-Cé[41] and, finally, that of the bridge over the River Seine at Paris.[42]

The largest monument in this series, and the only one examined through archaeological research, is another structure built on the Seine, near Pîtres (Eure): its bridgeheads were located in Igoville and Pont-de-l'Arche.[43] Its construction was initiated in June 864. Despite the particular form of financing, achieved through dedicated taxation and mobilisation of the men of the kingdom, work progressed slowly. The construction site was occupied by a Viking fleet in 865 and it was not until 869 that a Frankish garrison was assigned to the fortification, which was completed at the earliest in

873. It stopped a Viking fleet in 876 but did not prevent the siege of Paris in 885.[44]

This work, admired by contemporaries, consisted of a wooden bridge about 400 m long, possibly ending in porch towers. Each end was occupied by a *castellum*. Archaeological excavations in Igoville, since the 1970s, have identified both a structure about 270 m long bounded by a wide ditch and a clay and timber rampart with a stone facing and a palisade.[45] The *castellum* established on the left bank has not been excavated, but the current maps of Pont-de-l'Arche retain the layout of a primitive enclosure that probably equates to the Carolingian structure.[46]

While this construction programme did not always have the expected results, further fortification works were undertaken on most of these strategic sites from the Carolingian period.

The defence of monasteries and canonical communities in the ninth and tenth centuries is another phenomenon that has not yet been systematically studied.[47] The 49 cases currently identified in the Carolingian region are scattered between Brittany and central Italy. Outside the area studied here, this phenomenon also occurred east of the Rhine from the middle of the ninth century (Figure 8.2). While the monks and canons initially chose flight or sought refuge in fortified sites near their monasteries, the construction of the *castrum* of Noirmoutier on the order of Louis the Pious (824–30) constitutes the oldest well-dated monastic fortification.[48] In the following four decades, new fortified sites remained rare and scattered between the shores of the Atlantic and Rome. Later, the construction of monastic fortifications reached its first significant peak between 869 (Saint-Denis) and the 890s. In northern France and Burgundy, these were part of a more general fortification policy against the 'great Norman army'. The second decade of the tenth century saw the completion of two new projects, Saint-Martin de Tours (Figure 8.4) and Sainte-Colombe de Sens.

Saint-Martial de Limoges was also fortified during the reign of Charles the Simple. The monastic *castra* established in Poitou at the end of the 930s are clearly the result of a policy of the first dukes of Aquitaine. The multiplication of new constructions in Lotharingia and on its margins, between 922 and 953, is commonly attributed to the Hungarian raids; however, the fortification of the monasteries of Lobbes (around 970) or Saint-Paul and Saint-Vanne of Verdun (after 973–85 and 971–pre 986) is too late to be associated with this group. Furthermore, the construction or restoration of monastic or canonical fortifications has been documented for all subsequent centuries; it was thus a long-term process that existed in various political contexts.

In Carolingian written sources, these fortifications are often justified by formulas such as *Propter infestationem paganorum* or *causa persecutionis*

Nortmannorum. The Saracen, Viking and Hungarian threats obviously played a role in the development of this kind of fortification: the construction of this type of feature in Saint-Martin de Tours commenced just after an attack, for example (Figure 8.4).[49] Nevertheless, barbarians are easy to blame and other causes must also be sought.

The first is the control of the territory by kings and princes.[50] Indeed, Carolingian politics turned some monasteries or canonical communities into regional control centres run by lay abbots or bishops acting as agents of the king. Indeed, most of the religious houses of the Carolingian Empire that received fortification in the second half of the ninth and tenth centuries previously enjoyed royal protection, or even constituted sovereign residences.[51]

With a different chronology from one region to another, the benefits of royal abbeys and colleges tended to become hereditary fiefdoms attached to county honours, thus participating in the emergence of principalities as the bases of independent authority. It seems obvious that the Robertians or the new leaders of Aquitaine and Flanders consolidated the power and influence of their family through the control of the fortified abbeys.

The fortification of religious houses also reflects local political competition. The monastery of Lobbes was fortified around 970 by Rathier of Verona as part of his rivalry with Abbot Folcuin and his allies.[52] Therefore, these defences should not be considered solely as means of protecting religious people; like any other castles, they were defended by garrisons led by laymen and integrated into regional defence systems.

Finally, in some cases, the fortification of a religious community was part of a larger project to establish a new city. From 918 onwards, the *castrum* of Saint-Martin de Tours became the centre of a new city, competing with the old city of Tours.[53]

The protection of monastic or canonical communities by fortifications took various forms. It sometimes consisted of the enlargement of the enclosure of a city to include a community originally established outside the ramparts. For instance, in Cambrai, Bishop Odilon integrated the monastery of Saint-Aubert into the city walls between 888 and 901.[54] However, the creation of an autonomous enclosure was more frequent and, in rare cases, led to movement of the abbey to a site that was easier to defend, as in Vézelay.[55] On occasion, a simple fortified point was established in the middle of the buildings, such as the dungeon adjoining the church of Müstair (Grisons, Switzerland) between 957/58 and 961 (Figure 8.5).[56] Finally, castles were sometimes established near monasteries to control and defend them, as in Charroux (Vienne) where the *advocatus* erected a fortification on the margins of the monastery's immunity in the second half of the tenth century.[57]

Recent archaeological research on fortifications 141

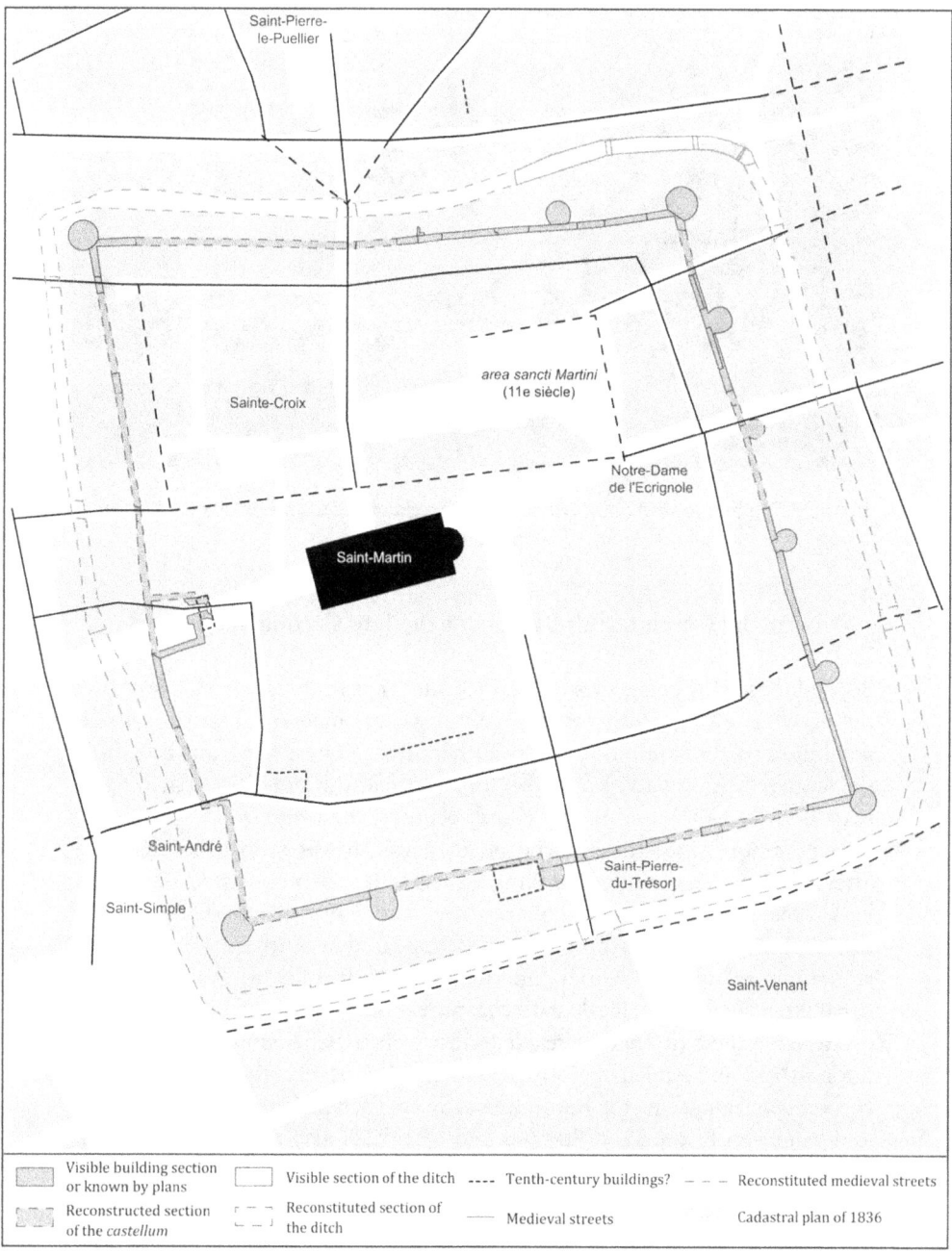

Figure 8.4 Proposal for a reconstitution of the *castrum* of Saint-Martin de Tours (France, Indre-et-Loire)

Figure 8.5 Saint John Abbey, Müstair (Switzerland, Canton Grisons). The tower is on the right.

Some new architectural forms of the late Carolingian period

Beyond these new categories of fortified sites, recent discoveries have shown the early date of many features of the classical medieval castle, formerly attributed to the late tenth to eleventh century. Thus, the transition from the large reception hall to the keep took place at the end of the Carolingian era. As early as the end of the eighth century, the *Granusturm* of Aachen Palace demonstrates the association of a vast tower with a hall. Shortly after 900, the rectangular building of Mayenne also consisted of a large hall above a storage level, a square tower and a stair tower (Figure 8.6).[58] But it was not until 920–50 that towers appeared in northern France which superimposed the residential functions of a palace on to their defensive capabilities. In Picardy, Flodoard's chronicle – now confirmed by archaeology – attests to the existence of residential towers at Château-Thierry in 924, Laon in 939 and Amiens before 950.[59] In addition, recently obtained radiocarbon determinations for Burgundian towers such as La Marche (775–943) and Semur-en-Brionnais (780–986 and 892–921) also give early dates.[60]

Further south, it would seem that it was not until the second half of the tenth century that large towers were documented – without achieving the dimensions of northern examples. The quadrangular structures of La Truque de Maurélis,[61] Saissac,[62] Ultrera[63] or the surprising hexagonal tower recently discovered in Allemagne-en-Provence/Notre-Dame[64] bear witness to their diversity. At the same time, some halls built on a cellar – a classic architectural

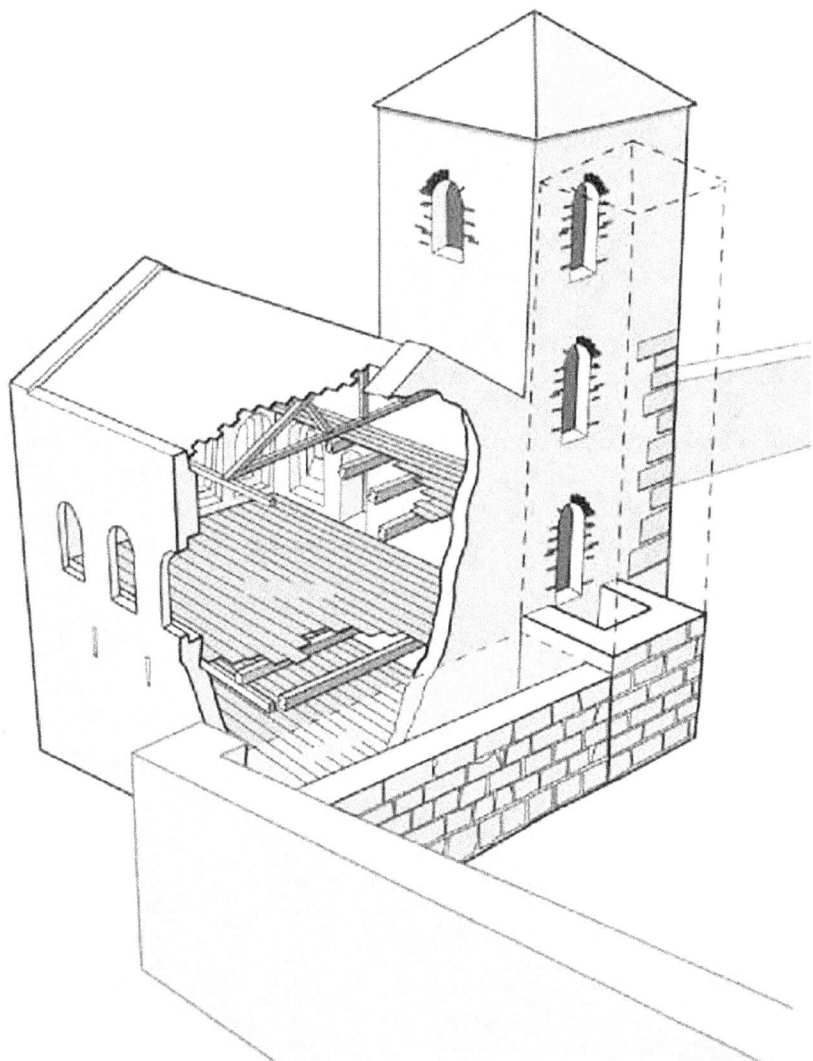

Figure 8.6 Axonometry of the residential building of Mayenne (France, Mayenne) c. 900

model since the eighth century[65] – were gradually transformed into towers from the end of the tenth century onwards, as shown by the examples of Doué-la-Fontaine,[66] Douai[67] and Ivry-la-Bataille, among others.[68] Some stone houses present in a number of elite sites in the south of France also underwent reconstruction in the form of a tower around the year 1000.[69]

Similarly, the emblematic character of the motte – an artificial earth mound which has long been considered in French historiography as the material proof of a 'révolution de l'an mil' – needs to be revised. Among the oldest examples, Boves (Picardy) is now attributed to the first half or mid-tenth century[70] and the modest mound of the first state of Montfélix (Chavot, Marne) probably corresponds to the foundation of the *castrum* in 952.[71] Depending on the context, the elevation of part of the *castrum* took the form of an artificial earth mound or used a rocky peak. These categories exist both in the north and south of the current French territory. The *mota* and *roca* of the texts therefore equated to two variants of the same logic, i.e. elevating the most symbolic part of a castle. On the other hand, these bases are not necessarily topped with a tower and a chemise, as is often claimed: the motte of Boves shelters a series of wooden buildings; while in Provence, simple houses without chemises crown the first states of Niozelles (Figure 8.7) and La Moutte in Allemagne-en-Provence.[72]

Ringworks raise other questions: these very basic shapes have transcended space and time. They increased in number at the end of the ninth and tenth

Figure 8.7 The *roca* of Niozelles (France, Alpes-de-Haute-Provence), first phase

centuries but on such diverse scales that it is impossible to gather them together in a homogeneous group. For example, the large ringworks built in Bergues and Bourbourg (north) or Veurnes (west Flanders, Belgium) have long been interpreted as the *castella recens facta* conceived against the Viking Great Army between 879 and 892 and have been related to similar fortifications built in Zeeland.[73] A recent re-evaluation of these sites has nevertheless shown that the creators, foundation dates and successive functions of these fortifications were relatively diverse. The many D-shaped fortifications, located against a river or seashore and often placed in the centre of later cities, are only one variant of these large ringforts.[74]

At the other end of the hierarchy, numerous small ringforts founded from the tenth century are evidence of the small elites' settlements. Their defences seem ostentatious rather than effective. Built from 973, the fortified house of Pineuilh, on the banks of the Dordogne river, illustrates this more modest category (Figure 8.1.D).[75] Near Paris, structures of this type appear to have been integrated into some villages, such as those of La Grande-Paroisse[76] (Seine-et-Marne). Between the Loire and the Garonne, recent archaeological excavations have also revealed elite residences built above underground galleries, which are surrounded by a modest discontinuous ditch (for example at Saint-Projet-Saint-Constant, Charente).[77] These sites – and many others – already embody the principles that will be observed by the residences of the small elites over the following centuries.

Final thoughts

Even though the increase in archaeological excavations from the 1990s has enabled an increase in our documentation of early medieval fortifications, this development has mainly concerned the two bookends of the period, i.e. the fifth to sixth centuries and the tenth century. Thus, information from the beginning of the Carolingian period remains relatively scarce and research should now focus on sites occupied in the eighth and ninth centuries.

In France, the castralisation of aristocratic housing was long dated to around the year 1000 and considered to be a consequence of the development of feudalism. Nowadays, it appears that the multiplication of fortifications occurred at different rates according to the region, but it is clearly between 860 and 950 that we can spot a first expansion.[78] Although Viking, Saracen and then Hungarian raids led to the construction of castles, it was probably more the internal struggles that marked the end of the Carolingian period and the birth of principalities that led to the proliferation of fortified sites.

We do now have many examples that illustrate the very progressive transition from unprotected residences to more or less fortified settlements.

This evolution requires surveys that explore the sites over time and within their environment. Indeed, whatever their size, Carolingian fortifications should not be considered isolated structures: they often constituted the defensive elements of polyfocal elite complexes: near the city of Liège (Belgium), the Carolingian estate included the palaces of Herstal and Jupille as well as the castle of Chèvremont, whose church is said to have received the tomb of Pippin II in 714;[79] in Aurillac (Cantal), the *castrum* where Count Gerald lived overlooked a *curtis* that was transformed into a monastery around 894;[80] in Douai (Nord), the *castrum* took over a large royal estate and its port;[81] and so on. On a more modest scale, the isolated towers that multiplied on the Languedoc coast from the 930s onwards were one of the components of a rural estate, as shown by the expression *villa cum turre* used in the texts and the example of this type studied in Teulet (Le Pouget, Hérault).[82] In many cases, therefore, Carolingian fortifications must be replaced in a landscape of power that includes several sites with complementary functions.

On the other hand, many fortifications took over a central place located nearby: the *portus* of Quentovic gradually gave way to the *castrum* of Montreuil;[83] the emergence of fortified sites in Pontoise (Val-d'Oise) and Corbeil (Essonne) led to the displacement of the neighbouring *vici*,[84] and so on. Decoding this changing materialisation of places of power seems essential to gain a better understanding of the nature of the changes that were happening at the end of the first millennium. The rise of the militarisation of the elites led to an increasingly marked integration of residential structures (*palatium*, *curtis*, *villa*) and fortifications (curtain walls, dungeons, mottes): at the end of the Carolingian era, fortified sites, power centres and elite residences had merged into the same architectural programmes.

Notes

I am grateful to Diane Rego, Patrick Ottaway and the editors of this volume for their contribution to the translation and to the institutions and individuals listed in the illustrations for permission to reproduce the materials for which they hold copyright.

1. G. Fournier, *Le château dans la France médiévale. Essai de sociologie monumentale* (Paris: Aubier-Montaigne, 1978), ch. II and III.
2. E. Delye (ed.), *Les fortifications celtique et carolingienne du Rocher du Vieux-Château à Pont-de-Bonne (Modave, Belgique)*, Bulletin du Cercle archéologique Hesbaye-Condroz, 32 (Amay: CAHC, 2016).
3. Igoville (Eure) in the ninth century: V. Carpentier and C. Marcigny (eds), *Le fort de Limaye à Igoville (Eure). Un pont fortifié sur la Seine normande, de l'âge*

viking à la guerre de Cent ans (Caen: Presses universitaires de Caen, in press), or the Camp de Péran, Pledran, Côtes d'Armor, at the beginning of the tenth century: J.-P. Nicolardot and P. Guigon, 'Une forteresse du xe siècle. Le camp de Peran à Pledran (Côtes-d'Armor)', *RAO*, 8 (1991), 123–57 have provided such constructions.

4 R. Jonvel, 'Le site fortifié carolingien de Murat "Les Tours"', in A.-M. Cocula and M. Combet (eds), *Châteaux et spectacles* (Bordeaux: Ausonius, 2018), pp. 345–75.

5 For example, Modave and Bressilien (Paule, Côtes-d'Armor): J. Le Gall, 'Une résidence aristocratique des viiie-ixe siècles au cœur de la Bretagne. L'enceinte de Bressilien à Paule (Côtes-d'Armor)', in P.-Y. Laffont (ed.), *Les élites et leurs résidences en Bretagne au Moyen Âge* (Rennes: PUR, 2014), pp. 125–38.

6 P. Richardot, *Végèce et la culture militaire au Moyen Âge (v^e-xve siècles)* (Paris: Economica, 1998).

7 *Liber pontificalis*, ed. L. Duchesne, 3 vols. (Paris: Société de l'Histoire de France, 1886–1892), vol. II, Leo IV, pp. 115–33.

8 L. Bourgeois and É. Marot, 'Une piste de recherche pour la fortification des ixe-xe siècles: l'imitation de l'antique', in P. Mignot et J.-M. Poisson (eds), *Archéologie des résidences aristocratiques du xe siècle en* Francia Media (Namur: Agence wallone du patrimoine, forthcoming).

9 L. Bourgeois (ed.), *Une résidence des comtes d'Angoulême autour de l'an mil. Le* castrum *d'Andone (Villejoubert, Charente). Publication des fouilles d'André Debord (1971–1995)* (Caen: Publications du CRAHM, 2009), pp. 442–3.

10 R. Early, 'Château de Mayenne: les témoins archéologiques de l'évolution d'un centre de pouvoir entre le xe et le xiie s.', *CG*, 20 (2002), 247–61.

11 According to most scholars, the flanking tower, well known in Antiquity, 'semble avoir été oubliée très vite en Occident, où elle ne réapparut que plus tard': M. de Boüard, *Manuel d'archéologie médiévale* (Paris: Sedes, 1975), p. 120.

12 F. Blary, *Origine et développement d'une cité médiévale. Château-Thierry* (Amiens: Revue archéologique de Picardie, 2013), fig. 84 and 87. Despite these discoveries, flanking towers prior to the year 1000 remain uncommon, and this observation remains valid for the eastern part of the Carolingian and Ottonian realms. See, among others, P. Ettel, 'Frankish and Slavic fortifications in Germany from the seventh to the eleventh centuries', in J. Baker, S. Brookes and A. Reynolds (eds), *Landscapes of defence in early medieval Europe* (Turnhout: Brepols, 2013), pp. 261–4.

13 Bourgeois, *Le* castrum *d'Andone*, pp. 442–3.

14 F. Prodeo and L. Bourgeois (eds), *Les seigneurs du marais. La résidence fossoyée de La Mothe de Pineuilh (Gironde, X^e-XIIe s.)* (Caen: Presses universitaires de Caen, forthcoming).

15 In Saint-Denis, Peran or Andone, for example.

16 P. Racinet (ed.), *Le site castral et prioral de Boves du xe au xvie siècle. Bilan des recherches 1996–2000* (Amiens: *RAP*, 2002), pp. 36–8 and fig. 22.

17 Two ditches in Peran (Nicolardot and Guigon, 'le camp de Peran à Pledran'), three for La Truque de Maurélis, *AM* 2009, 270–2, etc.

18 M. Wyss, 'Plus d'un millénaire de techniques hydrauliques dans le *castellum* de Saint-Denis', in *Archéologie francilienne* (Paris: DRAC Île-de-France, 2018), pp. 133–40.
19 A diachronic analysis of these walled towns has been proposed by B. S. Bachrach, but it is based almost exclusively on texts: B. S. Bachrach, 'Imperial walled cities in the west and the early medieval *Nachleben*', in J. D. Tracy (ed.), *City walls. The urban enceinte in global perspective* (Cambridge: Cambridge University Press, 2000), pp. 192–218.
20 *The fourth book of the Chronicle of Fredegar with its continuations*, ed. J. M. Wallace-Hadrill, trans. O. Devillers and J. Meyers (Turnhout: Brepols, 2001), § 46.
21 H. Galinié, 'Fouilles archéologiques à Tours, 1980', *Bulletin de la Société archéologique de Touraine*, 39 (1980), 607–49 (637–9 and 641–5).
22 Flodoard, *Historia Remensis Ecclesia*, ed. J. Heller and G. Waitz, *MGH SS*, 13 (Hanover: Hahn, 1881), pp. 469 and 573.
23 J. Le Maho, 'Fortifications et déplacements de populations en France au temps des invasions normandes (IXe-Xe siècle)', *CG*, 22 (2006), 223–5.
24 L. Bourgeois, '*Castrum* et habitat des élites (France et ses abords, vers 880-vers 1000)', in D. Iogna-Prat, M. Lauwers, F. Mazel and I. Rosé (eds), *Cluny, les moines et la société au premier âge féodal* (Rennes: Presses universitaires de Rennes, 2013), pp. 471–94 (p. 474); S. Balcon-Berry, 'Autun. Étude sur l'enceinte réduite', *Bucema*, 13 (2009), 7–9.
25 P. Dupont (ed.), *Jeux de plans. Atlas archéologique* (Orléans: Service archéologique municipal, 2005), p. 22.
26 J. Catalo, 'Le Château narbonnais de Toulouse, porte monumentale antique transformée en forteresse', *Archéopages*, 19 (2007), 139–41.
27 *AM 2016*, pp. 266–7.
28 J. Trapp and S. Wagner (eds), *Atlas historique de Metz* (Metz: Éditions des Paraiges, 2013), p. 80.
29 F. Gama, *Document d'évaluation du patrimoine archéologique des villes de France. Verdun* (Tours: CNAU, 1997), pp. 33–5.
30 *La chronique de Nantes (570–1049)*, ed. R. Merlet (Paris: Picard, 1896), § XXVI.
31 L. Schneider, 'Entre Antiquité et haut Moyen Âge. Traditions et renouveau de l'habitat de hauteur dans la Gaule du Sud-Est', in M. Fixot (ed.), *Paul-Albert Février de l'Antiquité au Moyen Âge* (Aix-en-Provence: Publications de l'Université de Provence, 2004), pp. 173–200, pp. 36–7 and 48.
32 H. Gaillard and Y. Laborie, 'De la *magna porta* de la Cité de Périgueux à la résidence des Périgueux. Approche archéologique d'une reconversion architecturale (ive-xiie siècle)', in L. Bourgeois and C. Remy (eds), *Demeurer, défendre et paraître. Orientations récentes de l'archéologie des fortifications et des résidences aristocratiques médiévales entre Loire et Pyrénées* (Chauvigny: APC, 2014), pp. 401–23.
33 P. Joyeux (ed.), *Regards sur Orléans. Archéologie et histoire de la ville* (Orléans: Mairie d'Orléans, 2014), fig. 6–5.
34 Some monographies and regional syntheses in *Gallia*, 74:1 (2017).

35 L. Bourgeois, 'The fate of Late-Roman villas in Southern Gaul between the sixth and seventh centuries', in B. Effros and I. Moreira (eds), *The Oxford handbook of the Merovingian world* (Oxford: Oxford University Press, 2020), pp. 640–56.
36 A. Bayard, '"Prendre villes et places fortes, les ramener en son pouvoir selon le droit de guerre". La violence durant les campagnes d'Aquitaine (760–768)', *Hypothèses*, 2012 (Paris: Publications de la Sorbonne, 2013), pp. 301–13.
37 *Annales regni Francorum*, ed. F. Kurze and G. H. Pertz, *MGH SRG*, 6 (Hanover: Hahn, 1895), p. 85.
38 C. Gillmor, 'The logistics of fortified bridge building on the Seine under Charles the Bald', *Anglo-Norman Studies*, 11 (1989), 87–106; S. Coupland, 'The fortified bridges of Charles the Bald', *Journal of Medieval History*, 17 (1991), 1–12.
39 *Annales Bertianini*, ed. G. Waitz, *MGH SRG*, 5 (Hanover: Hahn, 1883), pp. 57 and 79.
40 *Annales Vedastini*, ed. B. de Simson, *MGH SRG*, 12 (Hanover: Hahn, 1909), pp. 40–82, here pp. 57–8.
41 Coupland, 'The fortified bridges', pp. 1–3.
42 H. Noizet, 'Le pont parisien de Charles le Chauve', *Mémoires de Paris et Île-de France*, 66 (2015), 5–37.
43 Synthesis of the written sources in J. Le Maho, 'Un grand ouvrage royal du ixe siècle: Le pont fortifié dit "de Pîtres" à Pont-de-l'Arche (Eure)', in É. Lalou, B. Lepeuple and J.-L. Roch (eds), *Des châteaux et des sources. Archéologie et histoire dans la Normandie médiévale* (Mont Saint-Aignan: PURH, 2008), pp. 143–58.
44 Le Maho, 'Le pont fortifié dit "de Pîtres"'.
45 Carpentier and Marcigny, 'Fort de Limaye'.
46 Le Maho, 'Le pont fortifié dit "de Pîtres"', pp. 154–5.
47 L. Bourgeois, 'La fortification des abbayes et des collégiales aux ixe-xe siècles. Quelques pistes de recherche', in J.-M. Duvosquel, P. Perin (eds), *Religion, quotidien et animaux au Moyen Âge. Études offertes à Alain Dierkens*, RBPH, 96–1/2 (Drukkerij: Groeninghe Uitgeverij, 2018), pp. 193–208.
48 I. Cartron, *Les pérégrinations de Saint-Philibert. Genèse d'un réseau monastique dans la société carolingienne* (Rennes: Presses universitaires de Rennes, 2009), pp. 32–5.
49 H. Noizet, *La fabrique de la ville. Espaces et sociétés à Tours (ixe-xiiie siècles)* (Paris: Publications de la Sorbonne, 2007), p. 100.
50 See C. L. H. Coulson, 'Fortresses and social responsibility in late Carolingian France', *Zeitschrift für Archäologie des Mittelalters*, 4 (1976), 29–36.
51 Saint-Denis, Compiègne and Limoges.
52 Folcuin, *Gesta abbatum lobiensium*, ed. and trans. J.-L. Wankenne and H. Berkans (Lobbes: Cercle de Recherches Archéologiques, 1993).
53 Noizet, *La fabrique de la ville*, pp. 97–119 and 193–212.
54 A. Chédeville, 'De la cité à la ville', in J. Le Goff (ed.), *Histoire de la France urbaine*, t. 2 (Paris: Le Seuil, 1980), p. 40.

55 *Recueil des actes d'Eudes, roi de France (888–898)*, ed. R.-H. Bautier (Paris: AIBL, 1967), n. 10.
56 H. R. Sennhauser, 'Klostermauern und Klostertürme', in H. R. Sennhauser (ed.), *Wohn- und Wirtschaftsbauten frühmittelalterlicher Klöster. Internationales Symposium 16.9–1.10.1995 in Zurzach und Müstair* (Zurich: Veröffentlichungen des Instituts für Denkmalpflege, 1996), pp. 195–218.
57 L. Bourgeois (ed.), *Les petites villes du Haut-Poitou de l'Antiquité au Moyen Âge. Formes et monuments*, vol. 2 (Chauvigny, APC, 2005), p. 75 and fig. 22.
58 Early, 'Château de Mayenne'.
59 Flodoard, *Annales*, ed. P. Lauer (Paris: Picard, 1906), pp. 24, 122–3 and 127.
60 F. Bonhomme, S. Guillin, R-P. Lehner and H. Mouillebouche, 'Trois châteaux bourguignons du Xe siècle datés par ^{14}C-AMS', *Chastels et maisons fortes*, III (Chagny: Centre de castellologie de Bourgogne, 2010), pp. 11–18.
61 Castelnau-Montratier, Lot; *AM*, 2009, pp. 270–2.
62 Aude; J.-P. Cazes, 'Le donjon du château de Saissac (Aude)', in L. Bourgeois and C. Remy (eds), *Demeurer, défendre et paraître. Orientations récentes de l'archéologie des fortifications et des résidences aristocratiques médiévales entre Loire et Pyrénées* (Chauvigny: APC, 2014), pp. 153–8.
63 Argelès-sur-Mer, Pyrénées-Orientales; A. Constant, 'Fouilles récentes au *castrum Vultrarıa* (Argelès-sur-Mer, Roussillon)', in R.Martí (ed.), *Fars de l'Islam* (Barcelona: Universitat Autónoma de Barcelona, 2008), pp. 39–55.
64 *AM*, 2017, p. 224 and 2018, p. 289.
65 Bourgeois, '*Castrum* et habitat des élites', pp. 479–80.
66 Maine-et-Loire; J. Mastrolorenzo, 'L'*aula* carolingienne de Doué-la-Fontaine. Nouvelles données', *Bulletin de liaison de l'AFAM*, 25 (2001), 58–66.
67 Nord; P. Demolon and É. Louis, 'Naissance d'une cité flamande. L'exemple de Douai', in P. Demolon, H. Galinié and F. Verhaeghe (eds), *Archéologie des villes dans le Nord-Ouest de l'Europe (viie-xiiie siècles)* (Douai: Société d'archéologie médiévale, 1994), pp. 47–58, here p. 55.
68 Eure; D. Pitte, 'Ivry-la-Bataille, Eure', in P. Mignot and J.-M. Poisson (eds), *Archéologie des résidences aristocratiques du xe siècle en* Francia Media (Namur: Agence wallone du patrimoine, forthcoming).
69 D. Mouton, *Mottes castrales en Provence. Les origines de la fortification privée au Moyen Âge* (Paris: Maison des Sciences de l'Homme, 2008) and D. Mouton (ed.), *La Moutte d'Allemagne-en-Provence: un* castrum *précoce du Moyen Âge provençal* (Paris: Errance – Aix-en-Provence: Centre Camille-Jullian, 2015).
70 Racinet, *Le site castral et prioral de Boves*, pp. 20–5.
71 A. Renoux, *Montfélix, un* castrum *comtal aux portes d'Epernay* (Caen: Presses universitaires de Caen, 2018), pp. 53–96.
72 Mouton, *Mottes castrales en Provence* and *La Moutte d'Allemagne-en-Provence*.
73 L. Ten Harkel, 'A Viking Age landscape of defense in the Low Countries? The Ringwalburgen in the Dutch province of Zeeland', in J. Baker, S. Brookes and A. Reynolds (eds), *Landscapes of defence in early medieval Europe* (Turnhout: Brepols, 2013), pp. 223–59.
74 D. Tyss, P. Deckers and B. Wouters, 'Circular, D-shaped and other fortifications in 9th and 10th century Flanders and Zeeland as markers of territorialisation

of power(s)', in N. Christie and H. Herold (eds), *Fortified settlements in early medieval Europe* (Oxford: Oxbow, 2016), pp. 175–91.
75 Prodeo and Bourgeois (eds), *Les seigneurs des marais*.
76 M. Petit (ed.), *L'habitat carolingien des Sureaux à la Grande-Paroisse (Seine-et-Marne). Une communauté villageoise à l'aube de l'an mil* (Nemours: Musée de Préhistoire d'Île-de-France, 2009), pp. 80–3.
77 T. Cornec, E. Barbier and S. Painsonneau, 'Saint-Projet-Saint-Constant, le Champ des Ronces', in *Bilan scientifique régional Poitou-Charentes 2009* (Poitiers: DRAC, 2010), pp. 44–7.
78 Thus, for the countryside around Laon or Reims, Flodoard already reported about thirty castles before 966, to which must be added the towns and fortified abbeys: M. Bur, *La formation du comté de Champagne (v. 950-v. 1150)* (Nancy: Université de Nancy II, 1977), p. 45.
79 A. Dierkens, 'Im Zentrum der karolingischen Macht im 8. Jahrhundert. Herstal, Jupille und Chèvremont', in F. Pohle (ed.), *Karl der Große. Charlemagne. Orte der Macht. Essays* (Dresden: Sandstein, 2014), pp. 210–17.
80 G. Fournier, 'Saint Géraud et son temps', *Revue de Haute-Auvergne*, 44 (1973), 342–52.
81 É. Louis, 'Les origines de Douai. Un réexamen', in A.-M. Flambard Héricher and J. Le Maho (eds), *Château, ville et pouvoir au Moyen Âge* (Caen: Publications du CRAHM, 2012), pp. 215–54.
82 L. Schneider and D. Garcia, *Carte archéologique de la Gaule, 34/1. Le Lodévois* (Paris: Académie des Inscriptions et Belles-Lettres, 1998), pp. 255–7.
83 S. Lebecq, B. Béthouart and L. Verslype (eds), *Quentovic. Environnement, Archéologie, Histoire* (Lille: Éditions du Conseil scientifique de l'Université Lille 3, 2010).
84 Le Maho, 'Fortifications et déplacements de populations', 228–30.

9

Gens Germana gente ferocior: Lombards and warfare between representation and reality

Stefano Gasparri

Velleius Paterculus, a historian from the time of Tiberius, wrote of the defeat of the Roman armies in Germany by peoples hitherto unknown, including the Lombards, who were 'the fiercest of the German peoples'. This terrifying description of the Lombards was supported by Tacitus who wrote: 'their scanty numbers are a distinction: though surrounded by a host of most powerful tribes, they protect themselves not by submission but by the peril of battles'.[1] The opinions of these Imperial Age Roman historians are apparently borne out by the Lombard saga in the two versions known to us: the *Origo gentis Langobardorum* and Paul the Deacon's *Historia Langobardorum*.[2] At the start of their migration, the Lombards received their name from the god Wotan in a ceremony that linked the assignment of their name to victory in war. In fact, the goddess Freya told her husband, 'as you have named them, you must also give them victory'. During the course of this ceremony, the Lombard women presented themselves to the god in the guise of warriors.[3] The saga continues with a long list of victorious battles that allowed the Lombards to prevail in the midst of hostile peoples; among their ranks there were even warriors known as 'cynocephali' (i.e. 'men with a dog's head'), whose description resembles that of the Scandinavian berserkers.[4] On the eve of the invasion of Italy, as the mythological tale makes way for historical events, the deeds of the young Alboin are described like those of a fearless warrior whose courage verges on recklessness: following his victory on the battlefield against the Gepids, he presented himself at the court of the king of the Gepids to claim the arms belonging to the king's son, whom Alboin himself has slain. Alboin had to do this in order to be received at the table of his own father, Audoin, because the passage to adulthood, at least for the members of the Lombard royal family, was marked by a warrior rite.[5]

In the saga there are other examples of heroic deeds, but these well-known episodes will suffice. They convey the image of a proud yet savage people, dedicated to war and violence, an image that historiography, especially Italian historiography, has long accepted.[6] However, it is hard to reconcile this powerful, warlike image with the wretched fate suffered by the Lombard kingdom at the hands of the Franks in the second half of the eighth century. The Franks descended into Italy on three separate occasions and each time the Lombards were defeated without putting up a fight. None of the sources mention any real battles fought by the Lombard kings to defend the Alpine barriers known as *clusae*, and we know that after the first clashes, they withdrew to Pavia to seek refuge behind its walls with their warriors.[7]

There are many reasons for this incongruity. The first and most fundamental reason is that the eighth-century Lombards were completely unlike the Lombards of the centuries prior to the invasion of Italy. Naturally, first-century Lombards were also very different from the sixth-century Lombards, but both groups were formed by barbarian peoples settled on the frontiers of the Roman Empire, all of whom engaged in continuous warfare, either against the empire or in alliance with it. All they had in common with the Lombards of Aistulf and Desiderius was their shared name, the meaning of which changed over time. In eighth-century Italy, the name 'Lombards' referred to the freemen of the Lombard kingdom who fought in its army when summoned by the king, a key aspect that I will return to later.[8] The second reason, no less important, concerns first of all the value to be given to the testimony of Velleius Paterculus and Tacitus, which is ethnographic and not properly historical; and then the character of the narrative of the saga, which was put in writing for the first time in Italy during the seventh century. The Lombards of the saga do not represent reality but are the ideal representation of the values of the aristocracy and of the Lombard royal court around which the kings in Italy sought to construct the identity of the Lombard people. The sagas, as we know, were texts of identity rather than narratives reflecting reality; this in no way diminishes their importance but rather shifts their meaning to a different level; in the case of the Lombard saga, its meaning lies in the proposition of an ideal model of militarisation of the society.[9]

In order to analyse the relationship between the reality of war in the Lombard kingdom and the values proposed to the aristocracy, I will begin by examining the phases of the history of the Lombard kingdom in which war played the greatest role. The first is the Lombard conquest of 568/9 and its consequences. Historians have always maintained that the conquest was destructive in nature and that it led to the end of Roman Italy. But the main documentary evidence for the massacres and destructions carried out by the Lombards amounts to no more than a single passage by Gregory of

Tours, and few passages by Gregory the Great, who, in the *Dialogi*, reports a post-eventum prophecy on the arrival of the Lombards, announced by thunder and lightning in the sky, and its tragic consequences: 'the cities have been depopulated, the castles destroyed, the churches burned ...'.[10]

In the eighth century, Paul the Deacon referred to Gregory of Tours and Gregory the Great's descriptions, melding them into a single account. We can also add two contemporary sources, although both are rather vague: a passage in the chronicle of the far-away John of Biclar, who refers only to the 'tragic war' of the Romans against the Lombards; and a reference by Marius of Avenches, whose description of the deaths from famine, sickness and war following the Lombards' arrival in Italy is so vague that it was quoted almost verbatim by Andreas of Bergamo three centuries later in reference to the conquest of Italy by Charlemagne.[11]

Overall, although the destruction caused by the Lombard conquest is well-attested by the written evidence, the sources are unreliable because they are largely based on rhetorical or more general affirmations, whereas the archaeological evidence does not show any significant traces of destruction. This should suffice to rule out any claims for massive devastation. Moreover, the Lombards' experience as Roman *foederati* in the Balkans makes it hard to imagine that their aggression would have exceeded the usual violence of armies in regard of civilian populations. In addition, it appears to have been such an easy invasion that it took place without a single battle being fought. The military conquest was probably also carried out with the connivance of the local Byzantine military commanders.[12]

Due to its ambiguous nature, the conquest was both slow and chaotic. The situation was one of endemic warfare that had a damaging impact both on the population and on the economy, and that dragged on until the first truce was agreed between the Lombards and the Byzantines around 600.[13] Unfortunately, no quantitative data is available. The most vivid images emerge from the letters written by Gregory the Great, who mentions cities in Tuscany governed by officials with barbarian names whose allegiances may have been either Byzantine or Lombard. In the duchy of Spoleto, the Lombard duke Ariulf acted like the leader of a *foederati* army whose salary was unpaid, maintaining himself by sacking the surrounding lands.[14]

This confused situation was aggravated by the fluid nature of the Lombard people, which was similar to that of the other unstructured barbarian military groups. At this point in time, the Lombards found themselves without a king for a decade (574–84) and with many of their leaders, the dukes (in particular the first dukes of Friuli), becoming imperial *foederati* from time to time. After the election of their new King Authari (584), followed five years later by Agilulf, the Lombards had to overcome two major military crises: the Frankish incursions into the area of Trento around 590 and the

Avar invasions in Friuli in 610. These two crises marked the end of the first period of Lombard domination, when the war had the greatest impact on the lives of the local peoples. It was during the incursions into the area of Trento that the Lombards obtained the only victories against the Franks remembered by the sources: but when the Lombards crossed the Alps, they suffered disastrous defeats.[15]

In the seventh century, in the hundred years or so between the reigns of Agilulf and Liutprand, although never far off, war did not play a key role in the formation and consolidation of Lombard society. In the space of an entire century we know of only three real battles being fought against external enemies: the Battle of Scoltenna between Rothari and the Byzantine exarch Isacius; the Battle of *Forinus* during the expedition of Emperor Constans II in the duchy of Benevento; and the Battle at *Flovius* between Duke Lupus of Friul and the Avars.[16] Three battles in the space of a century is very few. Of course, we must also consider the constant aristocratic struggle for royal power, which would certainly have involved some violent clashes. However, we should not allow ourselves to be misled by Paul the Deacon; most of the battles between contenders for royal power that he describes would have been mere skirmishes between armed factions. The only exception to this is possibly the Battle of Coronate between Cunincpert and Alahis, which was probably a confrontation on a larger scale.[17] The expeditions organised by Grimoald against the Byzantines, Franks or Avars were probably little more than border clashes, raids or reprisals more frequently resolved through cunning than through open battles.[18]

Within the kingdom, war was generally limited to small areas near the borders and was hardly a daily activity conditioning the evolution of Lombard society and its elites. However, the physiognomy of the dominant Lombard class was undeniably a warlike one, as Rothari's Edict of 643 makes clear. The Edict focuses on the freeman who was considered such by virtue of his warriorhood, establishing that any attack upon his personal freedom is punishable. Over thirty chapters of the edict deal with potential injuries to and mutilations of a freeman, laying down severe punishments; there are also punishments for anyone unseating a freeman from his horse or attacking a rival without warning, whether alone or at the head of a group of armed men.[19] Even if the testimony of a legal code is not easy to evaluate, it is clear that social relationships in Lombard society could become very violent, at least within the higher ranks. But we must bear in mind two things: the first is that to some extent the edict is describing the situation of the period before the Lombard occupation of Italy, given that it gives written form to many traditional regulations. The second is that the edict was drawn up in the seventh century, at a time when the king's authority had not yet acquired the weight that it would in the following century. In any case, the chapters of the edict already forbid the *faida*, or blood feuds, between family groups.[20]

The warrior-like character of the Lombard elite is also borne out by their grave-goods, which, during the seventh century, emphasise the warlike aspect of the individuals buried in the graves, especially in the so-called 'riders' graves' (*tombe dei cavalieri*): spurs, bridles, sometimes even saddles can be found along with belts and damascened swords, decorated shield bosses and perforated spearheads. Such richly furnished tombs are therefore generally associated with men clearly defined as warriors. But this practice is above all an affirmation of social status as an elite member of the kingdom, which was expressed using a military language that may not have always reflected the situation existing in reality. This practice related to weapon burials can also be found in other barbarian societies; for instance, most weapon burials in the Anglo-Saxon context studied by Heinrich Härke took place in times of relative peace, when the status of warrior was established by means of formal acts in the absence of continuous opportunities to prove one's worth on the battlefield.[21] Further proof of such reasoning, now consolidated in the archaeological literature, is the fact that weapons were also buried with individuals with physical problems, which would have prevented them from ever participating in a battle.[22] Thus, the primary purpose of this practice, which ended towards the end of the seventh century, was one of self-representation by the elites.

The only exception in Italy is Friuli. During the seventh and eighth centuries, the constant hostile presence of Slavs and Avars, clashes with the Byzantines, friction with the royal power and internal strife within the local elites all contributed to shaping Friulan society, which was the only duchy in Lombard Italy whose aristocracy consistently put warrior-like values into practice.

Friulan society is accurately depicted by Paul the Deacon, who describes several violent episodes typical of the eighth century. These episodes show that the aristocracy of the duchy of Friuli was clearly predisposed to armed violence. In particular, there was a marked propensity for competition linked to honour, both within the elite and between the elite and the duke or king. This explains the tragic massacre of Friulan warriors by the Slavs in the early years of the eighth century, which came about when Argait, a ducal officer or *sculdahis*, decided to challenge his duke Ferdulf who had previously accused him of cowardice. Argait's actions spurred the duke on to lead his men in a suicidal horseback attack against the enemy camp situated on a nearby hilltop: taken to an extreme, rivalry intended to augment or defend the challenger's honour led to the almost complete annihilation of the *nobilitas Foroiulanorum*.[23]

Honour is at the centre of another well-known episode. When Callistus, patriarch of Aquileia, removed the bishop of Cividale from office and took his place, believing that it was his right as patriarch to reside in the capital of the duchy, he was arrested by Pemmo, the duke of Friuli. However, King Liutprand intervened in favour of the patriarch and against the duke and his kinsmen, giving orders to have all of Pemmo's supporters arrested. Even though he had been pardoned along with his father and his brother Ratchis, Pemmo's other son, the future King Aistulf, could not bear the arrest of their other followers, considering it a blow to his honour, and attempted to attack the king with his sword. Only the swift intervention of his brother Ratchis prevented him from carrying out an action that would have certainly cost him his life.[24] Competition, agonism, exhibition of warrior-like values and behaviour are therefore characteristic of the eighth-century Friulan Lombard elite, which dominated over a strongly militarised frontier society

In his accounts, Paul, who was a Friulan, sought to emphasise the warlike character of Friuli's Lombard aristocracy. Although his history ends with the death of King Liutprand in 744, he then introduces the two subsequent kings – Ratchis and Aistulf – who were both Friulan like him and with whom he had personal ties. In addition to the aforementioned episode that took place at the court of Liutprand, Paul also narrates the brothers' youthful deeds in war. Ratchis is described fighting against the Slavs on the borders of the duchy, while both brothers participated in an expedition with Liutprand's army against the rebellious duchy of Spoleto, distinguishing themselves through their valour.[25]

Paul describes border skirmishes and internecine struggles within the kingdom; between the king and the dukes as well as within the aristocracy, as in the case of Ferdulf and Argait. But violent competition occasionally erupted within single families. One example comes from Tuscany wherein Walfrid, a rich landowner, founded the monastery dedicated to St Peter in Monteverdi in 754. A few years later, his son, the priest Gumfrid, fled from the monastery taking with him men and horses. Through this act, he refused to acknowledge the will of the founder, because he also took with him the original grant charter on which the rights of St Peter's were based, and which originally represented the family property.

Gumfrid was captured, sustaining serious injuries during the violent clash, and some years later became an exemplary abbot. The episode is described in the *Life of the Abbot Walfrid*, written towards the end of the eighth century by Andrew, Gumfrid's successor and third abbot of St Peter's, and considered a reliable document on the basis of its date and authorship.[26] Andrew's account reveals a situation of intra-family conflict characterised by the violence inherent to the Lombard aristocracy: the struggle for the control of the family property is transformed directly into an armed clash.

Gumfrid's rebellion takes place at a dramatic moment, during the reign of Desiderius, when competition within the Lombard aristocracy was at its height. The struggle to maintain an eminent position fits into a more widespread revision of family strategies: the aristocracy at the time was split into groups for and against Desiderius, and therefore for or against the Franks.[27] The story of Gumfrid's flight must be seen against this background of conflict.

Overall, the eighth century was a period in which war returned to the fore. Although exacerbated by the twenty years of severe political and military instability caused by the expeditions of Pippin and Charlemagne (754 and 756), it was originally triggered by the crisis affecting the Byzantine exarchate, which gave the Lombard kingdom the opportunity to expand. Liutprand took Emilia and even managed to occupy Ravenna for a period. The Byzantines then recaptured Ravenna, but this could not prevent the definitive fall of the Exarchate only a few years later (751) at the hands of Aistulf. The age of Liutprand probably marks the apex of the achievements of the Lombard military forces in the eighth century, revealed above all on the occasion of the expedition carried out against the Saracens in Provence at Pippin's request. This expedition – a triumph according to Paul the Deacon – concluded without a single blow being exchanged with the Saracens.[28]

Chapters 2 and 3 of the laws of Aistulf of 750, which coincide with the years of the definitive attack upon the Exarchate, establish the rules of mobilisation. It was the first time in the history of the kingdom that rules of this kind had been established, if we exclude a few partial provisions introduced by Liutprand.[29] Under the laws of Aistulf, freemen were summoned to serve in the army according to their wealth, defined in Chapter 2 as landed property. Chapter 3 also deals with mobilisation, in this case with regard to *negotiantes* or merchants. As the wealthiest men, landowners and merchants were the heavy cavalry, while the less rich formed the light cavalry and the poorest men were armed with shields, bows and arrows and fought in the infantry. This means that merchants in the eighth-century Lombard kingdom were important and numerous enough to be considered an autonomous group, on an equal footing with landowners, by the laws dealing with mobilisation in the army. Nothing of the kind is documented in any other early medieval kingdom.[30]

Only a few years earlier, Liutprand's laws referred to the freeman as *arimannus* or *exercitalis*. The same military terms appear in a number of judicial documents drawn up under the same king, where they refer to the majority of the free population. The freeman of the kingdom – *arimannus* or *exercitalis* – was a man who participated in assemblies and served in the royal army. This definition affirmed their status while establishing ties with the power of the king.[31] Such ties were essential for the king who required the support of the *exercitales* to rule and who, therefore, recognised their privileged status, setting their wergeld at a higher amount than the wergeld of freemen who could not become *exercitales* because they lacked the means to arm themselves.[32]

The situation I have just described shows that during the eighth century, just as war began to return dramatically to the fore, the social hierarchies within the Lombard kingdom underwent a reorganisation that was again military in nature but more clearly defined than in the past, consolidated by coherent written regulations.

What was the true importance of war in the kingdom's society, even in these bellicose years? By examining the wills of three men summoned to fight with the Lombard army we can gain a better idea of what happened outside the restricted circles of the military aristocracy. The first is the will of Bishop Walprand of Lucca who wrote that he intended to dispose of all of his property given that 'by order of King Aistulf I am bound for the army to depart with him'; it was the summer of 754 and Walprand is preparing to go and fight Pippin's Franks.[33] The second is the will of a man named Gaiprand, also from Lucca, who drew up this document 'because I have been summoned to leave for *Francia* with the army' and was therefore about to take part in an expedition heading for the Frankish kingdom.[34] The third will dates to 769, a period of great tension with Pope Stephen III, when the Pisan Domnolinus, who has been mobilised into the army like the other two men, decided to dispose of his goods 'because we are all unsure of the judgement of God', leaving them to Austricunda, 'my sweet sister'.[35] As Chris Wickham has pointed out, the writers of these three documents certainly would not have had a relationship with war like that of a professional soldier.[36] Similarly, nor would even the aforementioned 'strong citizens' described in a contemporary hymn, who took part in the expedition to Provence led by Liutprand.[37]

The Lombard army had no shortage of bellicose aristocrats resembling the ones filling the pages of Paul the Deacon's *History*, most of whom came from the Friulan aristocracy. However, the majority of the men summoned to participate in the army would have been like Domnolinus and Gaiprand, men for whom the war was just a sudden, dangerous interlude in anotherwise peaceful life. Obviously, it would be rash to reach too many conclusions on the basis of two or three documents, but this is undoubtedly the impression that they give.

A reflection is required at this point. Although an army formed of such recruits and led by Aistulf or Desiderius was capable of sacking the countryside around Rome and terrorising the popes from Zacharias to Hadrian I, it could never have held its ground in a battle with the Franks, who were used to fighting in 'seasonal wars' and in raids along the eastern borders of the kingdom. The drastic military inferiority of the warriors of Aistulf and Desiderius could also be explained by the fact that the Lombards had no armed clienteles comparable to Frankish vassals. However, the striking difference, not in the basic organisation of the army but in the experience of war, between the Lombards and the Franks in the army of Pippin and Charlemagne suffices in itself to explain the rapid defeat or even flight of the Lombards encountering the Franks at the alpine *clusae*.

The modest capacities of the Lombard army are also revealed in other episodes, such as the expulsion of Liutprand's warriors from Ravenna following an incursion of Venetian boats. Leaving aside all rhetoric about the future glory of the Venetian republic, this incursion would have involved at best a rather modest flotilla given that Venice would not have anything resembling a fleet for at least another century. Finally, the Lombard warriors who managed to enter Rome in 768 had the opportunity to take control of the city, yet according to the colourful account of the *Liber Pontificalis*, they were put to flight by a hastily assembled army.[38]

At the moment of the decisive fight against the Franks, the Lombard aristocracy, along with intermediate strata of Lombard society, lacked the hallmarks of a group of professional warriors. In the sixth-century age of Authari, the Lombards fought well against the Franks invading Trento, winning as well as losing battles; yet in 754, 756 and 774 they put up hardly any resistance. There would have also been political motives for this: we know, for example, that Desiderius did not have the undivided support of the Lombard aristocracy. But overwhelmingly the picture emerging of the Lombards in late eighth-century sources is one of extreme military weakness. The only exception is Friuli, which I have mentioned on numerous occasions, and which rebelled against Charlemagne.[39]

Events following Charlemagne's invasion suggest that Paul the Deacon's descriptions of Friuli and the belligerent behaviour of the local aristocracy were based in reality. Two different accounts of the Friuli revolt have reached us: one is contained in the Frankish Annals and one is by a ninth-century successor of Paul the Deacon, the aforementioned Andreas of Bergamo.[40] Although the two versions differ in many points, the substance of the facts is clear: in 776, Hrotgaud, the duke of Friuli, rebelled against Charlemagne and joined the other dukes of the Veneto in battle against the Franks, defending not only his duchy but the entire north-eastern corner of the kingdom – the Lombard *Austria* – from invasion. Hrotgaud was defeated and killed, and the revolt was violently put down. However, this story reveals that, on the eastern borderlands of the kingdom, the local aristocracy, tempered by their constant clashes with the Avars and Slavs, was not dissimilar to the Frankish army, albeit on a smaller scale. It also shows that the imbalance between the representation and reality of war in Lombard society overall may have been less marked among the highly militarised Lombard aristocracy of Friuli than in other areas of the kingdom far from the dangerous eastern frontier.

Notes

1. Velleius Paterculus, *Historia Romana* II, 26; Tacitus, *Germania* 40.
2. *Origo gentis Langobardorum*, ed. G. Waitz, *MGH*, *SRL*, I (Hanover: Hahnsche Buchhandlung, 1878), pp. 1–6, and Paulus Diaconus, *Historia Langobardorum*, ed. G. Waitz and L. Bethmann, *MGH*, *SRL*, I, pp. 1–24, pp. 47–62. For an evaluation of these texts, see W. Goffart, *The narrators of barbarian history. Jordanes, Gregory of Tours, Bede, and Paul the Deacon* (Princeton: Princeton University Press, 1988), pp. 329–431.
3. Paulus Diaconus, *Historia Langobardorum* I,8, p. 52.
4. *Ibid.*, I,11, p. 53.
5. *Ibid.*, I,23–4, pp. 61–2.
6. See for example: G. Pepe, *Il medioevo barbarico d'Italia* (Torino: Einaudi, 6th edn 1959), pp. 109–17; G. P. Bognetti, *L'età longobarda*, vo. I–IV (Milano: Giuffrè, 1966–8); P. Delogu, 'Il regno longobardo', in P. Delogu, A. Guillou and G. Ortalli (eds), *Storia d'Italia*, I (Torino: UTET, 1980), pp. 1–216, pp. 1–12.
7. L. Duchesne (ed.), *Le Liber pontificalis*, I (Paris: Thorin, 1886), p. 495; *Annales Regni Francorum*, ed. F. Kurze, *MGH*, *SRG*, 6 (Hanover: Hahnsche Buchhandlung,1895), pp. 36–7. The acts of bravery performed by Adelchi at the Chiuse of Val di Susa are just an invention of an eleventh-century monastic chronicle (*Cronaca di Novalesa*, ed. G. Alessio [(Torino: Einaudi, 1982], l. III, cc. 6–14, p. 143–61). Adelchi's only autonomous action during the war was to negotiate with the Franks for his escape in return for the delivery of the widow of Carloman, Gerberga, and his sons, in front of the city of Verona besieged by the Franks: Duchesne (ed.), *Le Liber pontificalis*, I, p. 496.
8. See below, notes 29 and 32.
9. W. Pohl, 'Gender and ethnicity in the early Middle Ages', in L. Brubaker and J. M. H. Smith (eds), *Gender in the early medieval world. East and west, 300–900* (Cambridge: Cambridge University Press, 2004) pp. 23–43; W. Pohl, 'Migration und Ethnogenesen der Langobarden aus Sicht der Schriftquellen', in J. Bemmann and M. Schmauder (eds), *Kulturwandel im Mitteleuropa. Langobarden – Awaren – Slawen* (Bonn: Habelt, 2008), pp. 1–9; F. Borri, 'Romans growing beards. Identity and historiography in seventh-century Italy', *Viator*, 45 (2014), 39–71.
10. Gregorius episcopus Turonensis, *Libri Historiarum X*, ed. B. Krusch, in *MGH*, *SRM*, I/1 (Hanover: Hahnsche Buchhandlung, 1951), IV,41, p. 174; Gregorii Magni *Dialogi*, ed. U. Moricca, *Fonti per la Storia d'Italia*, 24 (Roma: Istituto storico italiano per il medioevo, 1924), III,38, pp. 225–7.
11. Paulus Diaconus, *Historia Langobardorum*, II,32, pp. 90–1; Iohannes Biclarensis, *Chronica*, ed. T. Mommsen, *MGH*, *AA*, XI, *Chronica minora*, II (Berlin:

Weidmannsche Buchhandlung, 1894), p. 215: *Romani contra Longobardos in Italia lacrimabile bellum gerunt*. (578); Marius Aventicensis, *Chronica*, II, p. 238; Andrea Bergomatis, *Historia*, ed. G. Waitz, *MGH*, *SRL*, 4, pp. 224.

12 See the story of the commander of the Byzantine garrison of the Isola Comacina, Francio, who cooperated with the Lombards for more than twenty years: Paulus Diaconus, *Historia Langobardorum*, III,27, pp. 107–8, and S. Gasparri, 'Compétion ou collaboration? Les Lombards, les Romains et les évêques jusq'au milieu du VIIe siècle', in R. Le Jan, G. Bührer-Thierry and S. Gasparri (eds), *Coopétiton. Rivaliser, coopérer dans les sociétés du Haut Moyen Âge*, HAMA, 10 (Turnhout: Brepols, 2018), pp. 39–47 (Francio at p. 43).

13 Gregorius I papa *Registrum Epistolarum*, eds P. Ewald and L. M. Hartmann, *MGH*, *Epp*, II (Berlin: Weidmannsche Buchhandlung, 1891), IX,66, pp. 621–2 (end of 598); Paulus Diaconus, *Historia Langobardorum*, IV,28 (referred to years 604–5). On this truce, J. Jarnut, *Geschichte der Langobarden* (Kohlhammer: Stuttgart, 1982), p. 44.

14 Gregorius I papa *Registrum Epistolarum*, IX, 99 (599), X,13 (600), pp. 108, 247.

15 Paulus Diaconus, *Historia Langobardorum*, III,1, 3, 4 (the only Lombard victory beyond the Alps), 8, 9, 29, pp. 93–4, 96–7, 108. For the dukes of Friuli, see S. Gasparri, *I duchi longobardi*, Studi storici, 109 (Roma: Istituto storico italiano per il medio evo, 1978), pp. 65–6.

16 Paulus Diaconus, *Historia Langobardorum*, IV,45, V,9, 19–20, pp. 135, 148–9 and 151–2.

17 *Ibid.*, V,40–1, pp. 159–61.

18 *Ibid.*, V,21, p. 152. We can also mention the victory of Duke Wechtari against the Slavs (probably another little border clash): *ibid.*, V, 23, pp. 152–3.

19 The most important chapters of Rothari about the freeman are *Roth*. 30, 31, 32, 41, 42, 74: C. Azzara and S. Gasparri (eds), *Le leggi dei Longobardi. Storia, memoria e diritto di un popolo germanico* (Roma: Viella, 2005), pp. 22–7 and 30–1.

20 *Roth*. 45 and 74, *ibid.*, pp. 26–7 and 30–1.

21 C. La Rocca, 'L'archeologia e i Longobardi in Italia. Orientamenti, metodi, linee di ricerca', in S. Gasparri (ed.), *Il regno dei Longobardi in Italia. Archeologia, società e istituzioni* (Spoleto: CISAM, 2004), pp. 207–17; C. La Rocca, 'Rituali di famiglia. Pratiche funerarie nell'Italia longobarda', in F. Bougard, C. La Rocca and R. Le Jan (eds), *Sauver son âme et se perpétuer. Transmission du patrimoine et mémoire au Haut Moyen Âge* (Rome: Ecole Française de Rome, 2005), pp. 431–57; H. Härke, 'Swords, warrior graves and Anglo-Saxon warfare', *Current Archeology*, 16 (2004), 556–61.

22 A. A. Settia, 'Una "fara" in Collegno', in A. A. Settia (ed.), *Barbari e infedeli nell'alto medioevo italiano. Storia e miti storiografici* (Spoleto: CISAM, 2011), pp. 73–86, in part. pp. 83–6.

23 Paulus Diaconus, *Historia Langobardorum*, VI,24–6, pp. 172–4.

24 *Ibid.*, VI,51, pp. 182–3; see S. Gasparri, 'L'economia del dono. Scambio e competizione nell'Italia longobarda dell'VIII secolo', in C. Azzara, E. Orlando,

M. Pozza and A. Rizzi (eds), *Historiae. Scritti per Gherardo Ortalli*, Studi di Storia, 1 (Venezia: Edizioni Ca' Foscari, 2013), pp. 34–48.
25 *Ibid.*, VI,52 e 56, pp. 183–4 and 185.
26 H. Mierau, 'Edition und Übersetzung der Vita Walfredi', in K. Schmid (ed.), *Vita Walfredi und Kloster Monteverdi. Toskanisches Mönchtum zwischen langobardischer und fränkischer Herrschaft* (Tübingen: Max Niemeyer, 1991), pp. 1–18. On Walfrid's foundation, M. Costambeys, 'The transmission of tradition. Gregorian influence and innovation in eight-century Italian monasticism', in Y. Hen and M. Innes (eds), *The uses of the past in the early Middle Ages* (Cambridge: Cambridge University Press, 2000), pp. 78–101.
27 See S. Gasparri, *Italia longobarda. Il regno, i Franchi, il papato* (Rome: Laterza, 2012), pp. 121–6.
28 Paulus Diaconus, *Historia Langobardorum*, VI,54, pp. 183–4.
29 *Liut.* 83 and *Ahist.* 2–3, in Azzara and Gasparri, *Le leggi dei longobardi*, pp. 186–7, 280–1.
30 S. Gasparri, 'I mercanti nell'Italia longobarda e carolingia', in D. Chamboduc de Saint Pulgent and M. Dejoux (eds), *La fabrique des sociétés méditerranéennes. Le Moyen Âge de François Menant* (Paris: Éditions de la Sorbonne, 2018), pp. 37–47.
31 *Liut.* 44, *Notitia de actoribus regis*, 2–5, *Ratch.* 1–2, 4, *Ahist.* 4, in Azzara and Gasparri, *Le leggi dei longobardi*, pp. 164–7, 252–5, 260–3, 280–3.
32 *Liut.* 62, pp. 164–5.
33 *CDL*, I, ed. L. Schiaparelli, *Fonti per la storia d'Italia*, 62 (Roma: Istituto storico italiano per il medioevo, 1929), n. 114, pp. 334–6.
34 *CDL*, I, n. 117, pp. 353–5.
35 *CDL*, II, ed. L. Schiaparelli, *Fonti per la storia d'Italia*, 63 (Roma: Istituto storico italiano per il medioevo, 1933), n. 230, pp. 285–6.
36 C. Wickham, 'Aristocratic power in eight-century Lombard Italy', in A. C. Murray (ed.), *After Rome's fall. Narrators and sources of early medieval history. Essays presented to Walter Goffart* (University of Toronto Press: Toronto 1998), pp. 153–70.
37 *Versum de Mediolano civitate*, ed. E. Dümmler, in *MGH, Poetae Latini Aevi Carolini*, I (Berlin: Weidmannsche Buchhandlung 1881), pp. 24–6.
38 Paulus Diaconus, *Historia Langobardorum*, VI,54, pp. 183–4, and Duchesne (ed.), *Le Liber pontificalis*, I, pp. 469–70.
39 Gasparri, *Italia longobarda*, pp. 125–6.
40 *Annales Regni Francorum*, pp. 42–5; Andrea Bergomatis, *Historia*, in MGH, *SRL*, p. 224.

10

The blinkers of militarisation: Charles the Bald, Lothar I and the Vikings

Simon Coupland

By the Carolingian era, Frankish society had become profoundly militarised: all the criteria listed by Edward James in his seminal definition were demonstrably present.[1] There was no clear distinction between soldier and civilian, for the Frankish capitularies laid down that every freeman should serve in the host, in person; through pooling their resources to support others; or through payment of an army tax.[2] These men not only had the right to carry weapons, but were required to do so, with commanders providing arms for those who lacked them.[3] In the event of attack or invasion, even the poorest was obliged to defend their territory, and on occasion even the unfree.[4] Charles the Bald also ordered those free Franks too poor to join the army to construct fortifications, bridges and swamp crossings, and to guard forts and border regions.[5] As Bernard Bachrach notes, there is ample evidence for the 'militarization of the civilian population for local defense [sic]' under the Carolingians.[6]

The king was very definitely the commander-in-chief of the army, and military command was seen as an essential attribute of the monarchy.[7] Learning skill with weapons was part of the education of the young. In Ermold the Black's verse biography of Louis the Pious, the three-year-old Charles the Bald 'seizes his weapons, specially made for one of tender years' ('*arma aevo tenero tunc convenientia sumit*') and kills a doe which the huntsmen have brought back for him to dispatch.[8] The teenage William of Septimania was sent to form part of the king's guard in the early 840s,[9] and at a similar time Nithard described 'all the young men' ('*omni iuventute*') in the royal entourage taking part in simulated combat.[10] Count Eberhard of Friuli bequeathed to his sons swords, a helmet, body armour and leg guards, as well as a manuscript of Vegetius's *De re militari*.[11]

As for the place of warfare in Carolingian society, in the words of Tim Reuter, 'Carolingian and Ottonian societies were largely organized by war.

The political community, when it came together, was often called "the army" even when it was not functioning as one. And usually it did come together in order to function as one.'[12] This was hugely expensive, and Carolingian capitularies ensured that the cost of armament, equipment and provisions was met by the magnates, the freemen themselves, or through the payment of military taxes, the *heribannum* and *hostilitium*.[13] At the same time, warfare could be a major source of profit in the form of plunder or tribute, though it is important not to overstate its overall economic significance.[14]

Not only written texts but also contemporary images provide evidence of this militarisation. The painting of a Carolingian magnate on the wall of a church in Malles in Switzerland thus portrays him holding his sword,[15] while Charles the Bald and Lothar I are pictured in contemporary manuscripts flanked by armed bodyguards, one of them offering the king a sheathed sword.[16] Although it has been suggested that these were simply reproductions of earlier images, the sword hilts and belt mounts are unmistakeably Carolingian.[17]

One particularly significant development during the Carolingian period was the militarisation of the Church. Bishops and abbots stockpiled weapons and armour,[18] and certain monasteries contained workshops for shield-makers and swordsmiths.[19] Ecclesiastical magnates, like their secular counterparts, were required to pay military taxes, send properly equipped military contingents to join the host and potentially to lead them into battle, even though they, like all clergy, were forbidden from bearing arms.[20] Many of them consequently became victims of conflict: for example, at a battle against Pippin II of Aquitaine in 844, abbots Hugh and Richbod were killed, and Abbot Lupus of Ferrières was captured along with the bishops of Poitiers and Amiens.[21] Clergy went on campaign as chaplains, celebrating mass, hearing confession and carrying relics.[22] Bishops had armed retainers, such as those accompanying Bishop Hincmar of Laon to the synod of Douzy in 871.[23] The implications of this militarisation of the clergy, who were the principal chroniclers of the day, will become clear below.

This militarisation naturally also shaped perceptions of the monarchy. In his treatise on kingship, Archbishop Hincmar of Rheims told the king that his duties included 'defending the fatherland robustly and fairly against its enemies' ('*patriam fortiter et juste contra adversarios defendere*'), and studying the pursuit of war ('*hoc ergo studio regi praelium gerendum est*').[24] Although Notker's portrayal of Charlemagne leading the army as a ninth-century 'Iron Man', or Agnellus' depiction of an armed and armoured Charles the Bald after the Battle of Fontenoy, projected images of royal power and prestige rather than accurately reproducing contemporary events, they reflected the contemporary ideal of kingship.[25] The same is true of another of Notker's stories, in which Louis the German supposedly snapped in two a sword offered him by a Danish envoy, then bent another from hilt to tip 'like a withy' (*'in modum viminis'*).[26]

It is against this background that Charles the Bald, West Frankish king between 840 and 877, has come in for particular criticism, notably in relation to his defence against the Viking incursions. The Fulda annalist wrote caustically, 'He is more cowardly than a hare ... for his whole life long, wherever he had to face his opponents, he would either openly turn tail or secretly desert his troops' (*'est enim lepore timidior... omnibus enim diebus vitae suae, ubicumque necesse erat adversariis resistere, aut palam terga vertere aut clam militibus suis effugere solebat'*).[27] The Annals of Xanten were equally withering, describing Charles as 'suffering frequent onslaughts from the pagans, continually offering them tribute, and never emerging victorious in battle' (*'sepissime paganorum infestationem sustinens semperque eis censum opponens et numquam in bello victor existens'*).[28] It is true that these texts were written by Charles's rivals, the former in the East Frankish kingdom and the latter in Lotharingia, yet some West Frankish writers similarly criticised the king's lack of military prowess. Thus, when Charles paid tribute to a Viking army in 845, Bishop Hildegar of Meaux wrote that 'the strength and power of our leaders have turned to weakness', leading 'to ruin and destruction, confusion and shame' (*'principumque virtus ac potentia quam infirma... ad ruinam et ad interitum, ... ad confusionem et ignominiam'*).[29] And in the 860s, Ermentarius of Noirmoutier wrote, 'They ransom with tributes what they should defend with arms, and the kingdom of the Christians is ruined' (*'quod defendere debuerant armis, tributis redimunt, ac christianorum pessumdatur regnum'*).[30]

These negative judgements have shaped some modern historians' views of Charles's reign. For example, Donald Logan wrote: 'There was virtually no defence against the Vikings of this period: the only defence was self-defence; every man for himself',[31] while Philippe Contamine stated: 'In the military realm, it was nothing more than a simple facade, behind which remained only the shreds of power.'[32] The king's entry in the *Oxford encyclopedia of medieval warfare* is scathing:[33]

> Although one can see reconsideration and a sort of reestimation [sic] of Charles the Bald in the judgements of modern historians (for example, Janet Nelson)[34], one must be skeptical [sic] about the specific military abilities of this Carolingian ruler. Like others, he failed to stop the Norsemen and could not prevent them from plundering and ravaging his country.

It is the contention of this chapter that such criticisms are misguided, because the judgements were made from a militarised viewpoint rather than a reasoned assessment of the political and strategic effectiveness of Charles's actions. A re-examination of events will reveal that although there were significant weaknesses in West Frankish military power, Charles came up with imaginative, astute and effectual solutions to rid the kingdom of the Northmen. For the ecclesiastical chroniclers of Charles's reign, however, their strongly militarised mindset meant that anything other than victory on the battlefield represented weakness, even if the strategies adopted by Charles resulted in the removal of the Vikings. By failing to take this into account, some modern authors have judged the king unduly harshly. This is evident from the frequently unrecognised fact that the latter part of Charles's reign largely enjoyed peace and prosperity. It is also apparent from the criticism levelled by other contemporaries against Charles's brother Lothar I, ruler of the Middle kingdom between 840 and 855. He employed a different strategy against the Northmen, granting benefices to Viking leaders. This was equally successful and similarly vilified by certain churchmen. A reappraisal of these two reigns thus gives a fascinating insight into a significant limitation of militarisation; when those blinkers are removed, the achievements of these two Carolingian rulers are revealed in a more positive light.[35]

Looking first at Charles the Bald, it is important to note that he did in fact lead the West Frankish army into battle against the Vikings on several occasions,[36] and won at least three notable victories. He captured nine Danish ships on the Dordogne in 848, eight years later 'cut down [the Northmen] with great slaughter' in Normandy (*'maxima eos strage percussit'*),[37] and in 873 forced a Viking army occupying Angers to surrender and leave the kingdom.[38] The problem was, however, that, as King Carloman discovered after defeating the Northmen in 882, 'battle did nothing to subdue them' (*'nil eos haec pugna perdomuit'*).[39] They simply relocated to a safer area and regrouped. The movements of a Viking fleet led by Oskar in the early 850s provide a good illustration. Driven off the Seine by military defeat in 852, the Scandinavians travelled to the Loire instead. When forced to leave that river the following year, they raided in Brittany before returning to the Loire in the autumn.[40] Victory in battle was thus generally inconclusive. A further problem was that it was difficult to engage the Northmen in battle. They sought to avoid confrontation, remaining on the rivers where the Franks were unable to attack, or keeping to inaccessible areas (*'invia loca'*).[41] This was because at this stage the Scandinavians in Francia were after loot, not conquest.[42] On their ships and island bases, the Northmen were effectively impregnable, and Charles never attempted to attack them.[43] Two contemporaries did, and both attempts ended in abject failure. In 863, Lothar II's men refused to attack an island camp on the Rhine, and eight years later a local assault on an island in the Loire led to the Franks being repulsed with heavy losses.[44]

For Charles a further military concern was the fallibility or disloyalty of his magnates and their troops. The royal host consisted of contingents led by magnates, and during the turbulent years and conflicting loyalties of the 840s and 850s some aristocrats switched sides if they could see a potential advantage in doing so. In 858, for instance, Charles was besieging a Viking fleet on the Seine when Louis the German invaded the kingdom, whereupon many of Charles's magnates abandoned him and transferred their allegiance to Louis.[45] As John France noted, 'The raising of armies ... involved negotiation and discussion in the context of a whole web of political relationships. Between the military potential ... and military reality lay a political process of immense complication.'[46] Furthermore, the armies who faced the Vikings were often not the battle-hardened royal host. As noted above, every man had to turn out if the land were invaded,[47] and unlike those who served in the army, particularly the magnates who were schooled in warfare from their youth, the poorer Franks were neither militarily trained nor well equipped. This almost certainly accounts for several defeats suffered by Charles the Bald's forces.[48] Regino of Prüm vividly described what could happen when the Scandinavians faced an untrained local force: 'When the Northmen saw that this crowd of common people were not so much unarmed as bereft of any military training, they rushed upon them with a shout and cut them down in such a bloodbath that they seemed to be butchering dumb animals rather than people' ('*sed Nortmanni cernentes ignobile vulgus non tantum inerme, quantum disciplina militari nudatum, super eos cum clamore irruunt tantaque caede prosternunt, ut bruta animalia, non homines mactari viderentur*').[49]

Faced with the difficulty of attacking the Scandinavians and militarily driving them from the realm, what could Charles do? As the critics quoted above noted with disapproval, one strategy to which he resorted repeatedly, as I have discussed elsewhere, was the payment of tribute.[50] It is important to recognise that Charles was by no means alone in this: under Lothar I the Frisians gave tributes to Viking armies in 846 and 852, and Lothar II did the same in 864.[51] Similar payments were made by the Breton rulers Nominoë and Salomon, and across the Channel Alfred the Great paid tributes, which the Anglo-Saxon Chronicle described as 'making peace'.[52] At a local level, ransoms were paid by St Wandrille, Quentovic, Poitiers, St Stephen's in Paris, St Germain-des-Prés and St Denis.[53] Tribute payment should thus have been uncontroversial, so why did Charles the Bald come in for such criticism? The only other ruler to face similar opprobrium was Charles the Fat in 882.[54] He not only gave the Scandinavian chieftain Godfrid a tribute, however, but also a benefice in Frisia which, as we shall see, was an unacceptable strategy for some contemporaries.[55] What almost certainly made Charles the Bald's tributes different, and therefore the subject of censure, was his demand that the entire population contribute, including the clergy and ecclesiastical estates, rather than royal resources alone. In

877, the king also taxed church treasuries, leading the St Vaast annalist to complain that 'the churches are being plundered' ('*spoliantur ecclesiae*').[56] This echoes Ermentarius' earlier accusation against Charles, 'they ransom with tributes what they should defend with arms'.[57] It reflects a militarised Church which demanded a military solution while the king had opted for one which was pragmatic, political and economic. What this failed to appreciate, however, was that tribute payments were demonstrably more effective than victory in battle as a means of permanently removing Viking warbands. On every occasion when Charles paid tribute, the Northmen left shortly afterwards, with no suggestion from contemporaries that they returned. What was more, the tribute payments were economically affordable, both by the wealthy Frankish Church and by the West Frankish kingdom.[58]

One often underrated piece of evidence which highlights this is the introduction of a new coinage type in 864, known as the *Gratia dei rex* type after its obverse legend. Before 864, the monetary economy was in poor shape, with coins in circulation of a variety of types, frequently underweight and of poor quality silver.[59] After 864, virtually all Charles's mints struck coins of the same design, pure silver and good weight, while the old coinage and that of other rulers was swiftly and effectively removed from circulation.[60] Furthermore, a significantly larger number of mints struck this new coinage, to the same consistently high degree of design, weight and fineness.[61] This not only implies a high level of royal control and stability across the realm, but also a strong monetary economy in a financially prosperous kingdom, which had neither been ruined by the Viking invasions nor impoverished by the tribute payments.[62]

Tribute payment was not a desirable, satisfactory or lasting solution to the Scandinavian incursions, however. Fresh fleets kept coming from the north, all keen to take plunder and potentially also tribute. This required a solution that would expel the invaders and prevent new fleets from penetrating the rivers.

In 854, the Franks seemed to have found just such a tactic. The bishops of Orléans and Chartres stopped a fleet on the Loire by blocking the river with ships and lining the banks with soldiers (incidentally providing further evidence of clerical militarisation). As a result, the Scandinavians turned about and headed downstream.[63] Charles consequently adopted the same tactic when a fleet entered the Seine in 856. He apparently succeeded in containing the invaders throughout 857, and in July 858 tightened the screw by using ships to block the river as well.[64] Bishop Hildegar of Meaux, whose earlier criticism of Charles was quoted above,[65] commented admiringly that it was 'an amazing fleet, the like of which has never before been seen in our lands' ('*navigio mirabili ac numquam in nostris regnis simili viso*').[66] Charles was unable to drive home his advantage, however, because it was at this point that Louis the German invaded the kingdom, forcing Charles to abandon the siege.[67]

It was only in 862 that Charles managed to pursue the strategy to its conclusion, trapping a group of Vikings on the Marne by rebuilding a bridge at Isles-lès-Villenoy and stationing squadrons along both banks. With no East Frankish invasion to rescue them, the Northmen were forced to come to terms and left the kingdom shortly afterwards.[68] This was at last a defensive tactic which not only contained the invaders but also forced them to depart without the payment of tribute. In the years which followed, Charles therefore fortified bridges on the kingdom's two principal rivers, the Seine and the Loire, to provide a long-term defence of the realm.[69] In each case the king chose the bridge nearest the river mouth, at Pont-de-l'Arche on the Seine and Les Ponts-de-Cé on the Loire.[70]

This new strategy was considerably more effective than might be thought from the critical comments of contemporaries and historians cited earlier. Indeed, Charles's son-in-law Alfred very probably copied it in Wessex later in the century, for example on the River Lea in 895.[71] In the north of the kingdom, very little Viking activity was reported between 862 and 877. A fleet did enter the Seine in 865 and overwintered, in part because the fortifications at Pont de l'Arche had not been completed.[72] The king rapidly summoned the host and attempted to contain the Scandinavians on the river, but with only partial success. Seeing that a military solution was impossible, Charles agreed a tribute payment, and the Vikings put to sea once the four thousand pounds of silver had been handed over. Apart from the sacking of St Denis, remarkably little destruction was recorded.[73]

For the next ten years, the Seine remained free of longships. It was not until September 876, when the king was on campaign in the east following the death of Louis the German, that another Viking fleet entered the river. Charles, recently defeated at Andernach and preoccupied with internal politics, again gave the Scandinavians a tribute.[74] It was most likely this payment which led Hincmar to lament that 'for many years until now defence has had no place in this kingdom, but ransom and tribute have not only left people impoverished but also left once wealthy churches now stripped bare' (*usque modo jam ante pluros annos locum in isto regno defensio non habuit, sed redemptio et tributum et non solum pauperes homines, sed et ecclesias quondam divites jam evacuatas habent*').[75] Although this assessment has provided ammunition for critical historians,[76] the evidence set out here shows that it was pure hyperbole. Apart from the two short-lived and contained incursions on the Seine, Francia, Burgundy and northern Neustria enjoyed peace. At the same time, the new coinage type circulated freely and widely across the kingdom, with coins of the correct weight, good silver and a single design. This is clear evidence of royal control, political stability and economic prosperity. After a significant Frankish victory on the Charente in 865, the far south, too, was evidently free of Viking activity.[77] Only on the Loire did the Northmen remain a menace through the 860s, and it is clear from his actions that throughout his reign Charles regarded the Seine valley as a higher priority than the west. The turning point came in 873, when the king personally led the host to besiege the Viking army occupying Angers and forced them to leave the kingdom.[78] It was at this point that fortification construction began at Les Ponts-de-Cé, and over the next three years no Viking activity was recorded anywhere in West Francia.[79] Hincmar's portrayal of a realm left undefended and reduced to penury was thus without foundation. It reflected a militarised mindset which expected the king to drive out the Vikings by force rather than pay tributes which made financial demands on the Church.

Against this background, it is instructive to compare Charles's response to the Viking incursions to that of his brother Lothar I. The West Frankish kingdom was potentially a more attractive target for the Scandinavians because of its greater wealth in terms of towns, abbeys and commerce, and its longer coastline (only later did Viking warbands penetrate far inland). At the same time, Lothar's Frisian territory was equally vulnerable to attack from the sea, and the wealthy port of Dorestad was a prime target, even if it was already in decline.[80] Only twice is Lothar I known to have confronted the Scandinavians militarily, and neither event ended in victory. The first was ignominious: when the Northmen set fire to Dorestad in 846, the emperor is said to have looked on helplessly from the fortified palace walls of Nijmegen.[81] The second was in 852–53, when Lothar led his army to join his brother Charles in containing a Viking fleet on the Seine. Unable to attack the Scandinavians' island base, Charles paid a tribute, and Lothar and his men returned home.[82] A poem by Sedulius Scottus of Liège celebrates a great victory over the Northmen, but the date and location of the battle and the name of the Frankish commander are all unreported.[83] It probably refers to the battle won by Bishop Hartgar in Betuwe in 847 or 850 and described in another poem.[84] Behind Lothar's lack of military confrontation was a deliberate strategy, however; namely the granting of large tracts of Frisia, particularly the vulnerable western coast, to Scandinavian warlords in benefice. This practice, following a precedent established by his father and possibly grandfather as well, meant that Lothar gave responsibility for defending his Frisian coastline and rivers to Danes. As I have shown elsewhere, this approach was remarkably effective: the Viking warlord Rorik in particular appears to have deterred Scandinavian raids on Lothar's territory for over twenty years.[85] Like Charles the Bald's payment of tribute, however, this non-military strategy could come in for harsh clerical criticism.[86] Bishop Prudentius described it as 'an utterly detestable crime' ('*omni detestatione facinus*'), leading to Christians serving 'demon-worshippers' ('*daemonum cultoribus christiani populi deseruirent*').[87] There may have been a political angle to this complaint: Prudentius was loyal to Charles the Bald, like the lay magnate Nithard who voiced similar criticism.[88] The charge was nonetheless explicitly theological, just as in 882 when Charles the Fat was condemned as a modern King Ahab for granting a benefice to the Viking leader Godfrid.[89] Yet these criticisms ignore the fact that in each case the Danish warlord in question was baptised.[90] I believe that once again this is evidence of a militarised mindset which demanded defeat and expulsion rather than a pragmatic solution to the Scandinavian incursions, however effective it may have been.

To summarise, the Viking invaders were unlike any enemy the Franks had previously faced. Unassailable on their ships and island bases, uninterested in battle and undeterred by defeat, they forced Charles the Bald and his brother Lothar to come up with novel strategies to drive them from the kingdom. Charles offered military resistance where possible, but when it failed, paid tribute and built fortifications. This resulted in the great majority of his kingdom being peaceful and prosperous by the end of his reign. Lothar put Scandinavians in charge of his vulnerable Frisian coastline, again with considerable success. Yet the profound militarisation of Frankish society, and particularly the clergy who wrote most contemporary texts, meant that the effectiveness of these strategies was ignored or denied. When the blinkers of militarisation are removed, their merit can clearly be seen.

Notes

1 E. James, 'The militarisation of Roman society, 400–700', in A. N. Jørgensen and B. L. Clausen (eds), *Military aspects of Scandinavian society in a European perspective, AD 1–1300* (Copenhagen: The National Museum, 1997), pp. 19–24, at p. 19.

2 Among many discussions, see B. S. Bachrach, *Early Carolingian warfare. Prelude to empire* (Philadelphia: University of Pennsylvania Press, 2001), pp. 51–83; G. Halsall, *Warfare and society in the barbarian west, 450–900* (London: Routledge, 2003), pp. 71–81, 89–101; S. Coupland, 'The Carolingian army and the struggle against the Vikings', *Viator*, 35 (2004), 49–70, at 54–6.

3 S. Coupland, 'Carolingian arms and armor in the ninth century', *Viator*, 21 (1990), 29–50, at 30.

4 Coupland, 'The Carolingian army', pp. 52–4; T. Reuter, 'Plunder and tribute in the Carolingian empire', *Transactions of the Royal Historical Society*, 5:35 (1985), 75–94, at 89–91; T. Reuter, 'The end of Carolingian military expansion', in P. Godman and R. Collins (eds), *Charlemagne's heir. New perspectives on the reign of Louis the Pious* (Oxford: Oxford University Press, 1990), pp. 391–405, at pp. 399–400; W. Goffart, '"Defensio patriae" as a Carolingian military obligation',

Francia, 43 (2016), 21–39, who unfortunately misunderstood and therefore misrepresented my understanding of *lantweri*, which differs little from his.
5 Edict of Pîtres c. 27, ed. A. Boretius and V. Krause, *MGH, Capit.*, 2 (Hanover: Hahn, 1897), pp. 321–2. Coupland, 'The Carolingian army', pp. 55–6.
6 Bachrach, *Early Carolingian warfare*, p. 53.
7 Coupland, 'The Carolingian army', pp. 58–9; Halsall, *Warfare and society*, pp. 29–30.
8 Ermold the Black, *Carmen in honorem Hludowici* lines 2408–11, E. Faral (ed.), *Ermold le Noir: Poème sur Louis le Pieux et épitres au roi Pépin* (Paris: Les Belles Lettres, 1932, re-issued 1964), p. 184, trans. J. L. Nelson, *Charles the Bald* (London: Longman, 1992), pp. 79–80.
9 Dhuoda, *Liber Manualis* III,8: ed. P. Riché, *Dhuoda: Manuel pour mon fils* (Paris: Editions du Cerf, 1975), p. 166.
10 Nithard, *Historiarum libri IV* 3,6, ed. P. Lauer, *Nithard: Histoire des fils de Louis le Pieux* (Paris: Les Belles Lettres, 1926), pp. 110–12.
11 Coupland, 'Carolingian arms and armor', pp. 35, 38–9, 41, 45; T. Scharff, *Die Kämpfe der Herrscher und der Heiligen. Krieg und historische Erinnerung in der Karolingerzeit* (Darmstadt: Wissenschaftliche Buchgesellschaft, 2002), p. 29.
12 T. Reuter, 'Carolingian and Ottonian warfare', in M. Keen (ed.), *Medieval warfare. A history* (Oxford: Oxford University Press, 1999), pp. 13–35, at p. 13.
13 Halsall, *Warfare and society*, pp. 93, 95; Coupland, 'Carolingian arms and armor', p. 30; Coupland, 'The Carolingian army', pp. 54–5.
14 Reuter, 'Plunder and tribute', but see now D. Bachrach, 'Toward an appraisal of the wealth of the Ottonian kings of Germany, 919–1024', *Viator*, 44:2 (2013), 1–27.
15 M. Costambeys, M. Innes and S. MacLean, *The Carolingian world* (Cambridge: Cambridge University Press, 2011), p. 280.
16 J. Hubert, J. Porcher and W. F. Volbach, *L'empire carolingien* (Paris: Editions Gallimard, 1968), figs 129, 130, 133.
17 Coupland, 'Carolingian arms and armor', pp. 43–4, 46.
18 *Capitulare Bononiense* c. 10, ed. A. Boretius and V. Krause, *MGH, Capit.*, 1 (Hanover: Hahn, 1883), p. 167.
19 Coupland, 'Carolingian arms and armor', pp. 36 and 44.
20 Hincmar, *De fide Carolo regi servanda*, ed. J. P. Migne, *PL*, 125 (Paris: Sirou, 1852), cols 961–84, at col. 981; S. Coupland, 'The rod of God's wrath or the people of God's wrath? The Carolingians' theology of the Viking invasions', *Journal of Ecclesiastical History*, 42:4 (1991), 535–54, at 550.
21 *Annales Bertiniani* 844: F. Grat, J. Vielliard and S. Clémencet (eds), *Annales de Saint-Bertin* (Paris: Librairie C. Klincksieck, 1964), p. 47; *The Annals of St-Bertin*, trans. J. L. Nelson (Manchester: Manchester University Press, 1991), pp. 58–9.
22 Coupland, 'The rod of God's wrath', p. 550.
23 *Concilium Duziacense* 1: ed. Mansi 16, cols 569–688, at col. 662.
24 Hincmar, *De regis persona et regio ministerio* c. 2 and 8: ed. J. P. Migne, *PL*, 125, cols 833–56, at cols 835, 840.

25 Notker, *Gesta Karoli Magni* 2,17, ed. H. F. Haefele, *MGH, SRG NS*, 12 (Berlin: Weidmann, 1959; rev. 1962), pp. 83–84; Coupland, 'Carolingian arms and armor', p. 30; Agnellus, *Liber pontificalis ecclesiae Ravennatis* c. 174, ed. O. Holder-Egger, *MGH, SRL* (Hanover: Hahn, 1878), pp. 265–391, at p. 390.
26 Notker, *Gesta Karoli Magni* 2,18, ed. Haefele, pp. 88–9; E. J. Goldberg, *Struggle for empire. Kingship and conflict under Louis the German, 817–876* (Ithaca: Cornell University Press, 2006), p. 196.
27 *Annales Fuldenses* 875 and 877, ed. F. Kurze, *MGH, SRG* (Hanover: Hahn, 1891), pp. 85 and 90 (my translation), compare *The Annals of Fulda*, trans. T. Reuter (Manchester: Manchester University Press, 1992), pp. 77 and 83.
28 *Annales Xantenses* 869: *Annales Xantenses et Annales Vedastini*, ed. B. de Simson, *MGH, SRG* (Hanover: Hahn, 1909), p. 27.
29 Hildegarius, *Vita Faronis episcopi Meldensis* c. 122, ed. B. Krusch, *MGH, SRM*, 5 (Hanover: Hahn, 1910), pp. 171–203, at p. 200.
30 Ermentarius, *De translationibus et miraculis sancti Filiberti*, second preface: R. Poupardin (ed.), *Monuments de l'histoire des abbayes de Saint-Philibert* (Paris: Alphonse Picard et fils, 1905), p. 62.
31 F. D. Logan, *The Vikings in History* (London: HarperCollins, 1983), p. 118.
32 P. Contamine, *La Guerre au moyen âge* (Paris: Presses universitaires de France, 1980), p. 107 (my translation).
33 H.-H. Kortüm, 'Charles the Bald', in C. J. Rogers (ed.), *The Oxford encyclopedia of medieval warfare and military technology*, 3 vols (Oxford: Oxford University Press, 2010), vol. 1, pp. 365–6.
34 My name is cited with similar scepticism later in the entry.
35 This chapter draws on S. Coupland, 'Charles the Bald and the defence of the west Frankish kingdom against the Viking invasions, 840–877' (PhD dissertation, Cambridge University, 1987). See also Coupland, 'The Carolingian army'. Ferdinand Lot and Guy Halsall both recognised Charles's military abilities: F. Lot, *L'Art militaire et les armées au moyen âge en Europe et dans le proche Orient*, 2 vols (Paris: Payot, 1946), vol. 1, p. 107; Halsall, *Warfare and society*, pp. 99–101.
36 In addition to the next two notes, see *Annales Bertiniani* 852, 858, 862: ed. Grat, pp. 65, 78, 88, trans. Nelson pp. 75, 87, 98.
37 *Annales Fontanellenses* 848 and 855 [sic]: J. Laporte (ed.), 'Les premières annales de Fontanelle', *Mélanges de la Société de l'histoire de Normandie*, 15e série (Rouen and Paris, 1951), pp. 63–91, at pp. 81 and 91.
38 *Annales Bertiniani* 873, ed. Grat, pp. 192–6, trans. Nelson, pp. 183–5; Coupland, 'Charles the Bald', pp. 75–7.
39 *Annales Vedastini* 880, ed. de Simson, p. 53. Coupland, 'The Carolingian army', p. 67.
40 *Annales Fontanellenses* 851 [sic], ed. Laporte, p. 89; Coupland, 'Charles the Bald', pp. 37–41.
41 Coupland, 'The Carolingian army', p. 67, the quotation is from *Annales Vedastini* 891, ed. de Simson, p. 69.
42 A. d'Haenens, *Les Invasions normandes, une catastrophe?* (Paris: Flammarion, 1970), pp. 28–31; H. Zettel, *Das Bild der Normannen und der Normanneneinfälle*

43 Coupland, 'The Carolingian army', pp. 63–4.
44 *Annales Xantenses* 864 [sic], ed. de Simson, p. 21; *Annales Bertiniani* 871, ed. Grat, p. 181, trans. Nelson, p. 174. Coupland, 'The Carolingian army', p. 64.
45 *Libellus proclamationis adversus Wenilonem* c. 5, MGH, *Capit.*, 2, p. 451; Coupland, 'Charles the Bald', pp. 131–3.
46 J. France, 'The composition and raising of the armies of Charlemagne', *Journal of Medieval Military History*, 1 (2002), 61–82, at 70.
47 See p. 164 and note 4 above.
48 *Annales Bertiniani* 853, 866, ed. Grat, pp. 66, 125, trans. Nelson, pp. 75, 129–30; *Translatio sancti Germani Parisiensis* c. 12: *Analecta Bollandiana*, 2 (1883), p. 79.
49 Regino of Prüm, *Chronicon* 882, ed. F. Kurze, MGH, SRG (Hanover: Hahn, 1890), p. 118, trans. S. MacLean, *History and politics in late Carolingian and Ottonian Europe. The Chronicle of Regino of Prüm and Adalbert of Magdeburg* (Manchester: Manchester University Press, 2009), p. 185.
50 S. Coupland, 'The Frankish tribute payments to the Vikings and their consequences', *Francia*, 26:1 (1999), 57–75, reprinted in S. Coupland, *Carolingian coinage and the Vikings. Studies on power and trade in the 9th century* (Aldershot: Variorum, 2007).
51 *Annales Bertiniani* 846, 852 and 864, ed. Grat, pp. 51, 64 and 105, trans. Nelson, pp. 62, 74 and 112; S. Coupland, 'From poachers to gamekeepers. Scandinavian warlords and Carolingian kings', *Early Medieval Europe*, 7:1 (1998), 85–114, at 101–3, reprinted in Coupland, *Carolingian coinage*.
52 *Annales Bertiniani* 847, 869, ed. Grat, p. 54, 166, trans. Nelson, pp. 64, 163; S. D. Keynes and M. Lapidge, *Alfred the Great* (Harmondsworth: Penguin, 1983), p. 244.
53 St Wandrille: *Annales Fontanellenses* 841, ed. Laporte, p. 74; Quentovic (842), Poitiers (863), Paris, St Germain-des-Prés and St Denis (all 857): *Annales Bertiniani*, ed. Grat, pp. 42, 104, 75, trans. Nelson, pp. 53, 111 and 85.
54 *Annales Fuldenses* (A text) 882, ed. Kurze, pp. 98–9, trans. Reuter, *The Annals of Fulda*, p. 93.
55 Coupland, 'From poachers to gamekeepers', p. 109.
56 *Annales Vedastini* 877, cf. 884, ed. de Simson, pp. 41, 55. Coupland, 'Frankish tribute payments', pp. 65–8.
57 Ermentarius, *De translationibus* second preface: Poupardin (ed.), *Monuments de l'histoire*, p. 62.
58 Coupland, 'Frankish tribute payments', pp. 68, 72–5.
59 S. Coupland, 'The early coinage of Charles the Bald, 840–864', *Numismatic Chronicle*, 151 (1991), 121–58, reprinted in Coupland, *Carolingian coinage*.
60 G. Sarah, 'Charlemagne, Charles the Bald and the Karolus monogram coinage. A multi-disciplinary study', *Numismatic Chronicle*, 170 (2010), 227–86, at 232–3. The exception was Aquitaine, where the obverse bore the king's name +CARLVSREXFR.

61 Compare Coupland, 'The early coinage', p. 127 and D. M. Metcalf, 'A sketch of the currency in the time of Charles the Bald' in M. Gibson and J. L. Nelson (eds), *Charles the Bald. Court and kingdom* (Aldershot: Variorum, 2nd edn, 1990), pp. 65–97, at p. 87.
62 Coupland, 'Frankish tribute payments', pp. 72–3; Metcalf, 'A sketch of the currency', p. 88.
63 *Annales Bertiniani* 854, ed. Grat, p. 69, trans. Nelson, p. 79; Coupland, 'The Carolingian army', p. 64.
64 Coupland, 'The Carolingian army', p. 64.
65 See at note 29 above.
66 Hildegarius, *Vita Faronis* c. 125: ed. Krusch, p. 201.
67 *Libellus proclamationis adversus Wenilonem* c. 5, *MGH, Capit.*, 2, p. 451; Coupland, 'Charles the Bald', pp. 131–3.
68 S. Coupland, 'The fortified bridges of Charles the Bald', *Journal of Medieval History*, 17 (1991), 1–12, at 2–4.
69 *Ibid.*, pp. 4–10.
70 For the Loire, see Cassini de Thury sheet 98 (Angers): https://gallica.bnf.fr/ark:/12148/btv1b53095129z (accessed 16 January 2019).
71 J. M. Hassall and D. Hill, 'Pont de L'Arche. Frankish influence on the West Saxon burh?', *Archaeological Journal*, 127 (1970), 188–95.
72 Coupland, 'The fortified bridges', p. 6.
73 Coupland, 'Frankish tribute payments', pp. 62–8, Coupland, 'Charles the Bald', pp. 66–8 and 80–1.
74 Coupland, 'Frankish tribute payments', pp. 65–8.
75 Hincmar, *Ad Ludovicum balbum regem*, ed. J. P. Migne, *PL*, 125, cols. 983–90, at col. 988.
76 Kortüm, 'Charles the Bald', p. 366.
77 *Annales Bertiniani* 865, ed. Grat, p. 124, trans. Nelson, p. 128; Coupland, 'Charles the Bald', p. 68.
78 *Annales Bertiniani* 873, ed. Grat, pp. 192–6, trans. Nelson, pp. 183–5; Coupland, 'Charles the Bald', pp. 75–7.
79 Coupland, 'Charles the Bald', pp. 77–8.
80 S. Coupland, 'Boom and bust at ninth-century Dorestad', in A. Willemsen and H. Kik (eds), *Dorestad in an international framework. New research on centres of trade and coinage in Carolingian times* (Turnhout: Brepols, 2010), pp. 95–103.
81 *Annales Xantenses* 846, ed. de Simson, p. 15.
82 Coupland, 'From poachers to gamekeepers', pp. 94–5.
83 Sedulius Scottus, poem 45: J. Meyers (ed.), *Corpus Christianorum. Sedulius Scottus Carmina* (Turnhout: Brepols, 1991), pp. 80–2; trans. E. G. Doyle, *Sedulius Scottus, "On Christian rulers" and the poems* (Binghamton: Center for Medieval and Renaissance Studies, State University of New York, 1983), pp. 144–6. I am grateful to Elina Screen for this reference.
84 Sedulius, poem 8, ed. Meyers, pp. 21–2, trans. Doyle, pp. 109–10; W. Vogel, *Die Normannen und das fränkische Reich bis zur Gründung der Normandie (799-911)* (Heidelberg: Carl Winters Universitätbuchhandlung, 1906), p. 119.

85 Coupland, 'From poachers to gamekeepers', pp. 95–101.
86 Maria Schäpers, *Lothar I. (795–855) und das Frankenreich* (Vienna, Cologne and Weimar, 2018), pp. 646, 681–2.
87 *Annales Bertiniani* 841, ed. Grat, p. 39, trans. Nelson, p. 51.
88 Coupland, 'From poachers to gamekeepers', p. 92.
89 *Annales Fuldenses* (A text) 882, ed. Kurze, pp. 98–9, trans. Reuter, *The Annals of Fulda*, p. 93. The reference is to 1 Kings 20.
90 Coupland, 'From poachers to gamekeepers', pp. 92, 109.

PART III

ETHICS OF WAR

11

Manlike discipline and loyalty against the 'enemies of God': some observations on the militarised frontier society of eastern *Francia* around 600

Stefan Esders

If borders are to fulfil their primary functions properly – separating societies from one another, protecting a kingdom or an empire, and controlling transregional mobility – they must be conceived as spatial entities. A feature traceable in the late Roman period,[1] borders had to coordinate the various functions of a boundary within a spatial unit comprising fortresses, towns and fortified villages, as well as the supply and communications system of roads and waterways connecting them. Following the fall of the western empire, many late Roman fortifications were turned into 'nuclei of early medieval life'.[2] Their continued existence did not seem to depend too greatly on whether there was still a western Roman government in Ravenna. Now effectively decoupled from this government, local structures were able to fulfil important functions in establishing statehood as 'substructures' under new masters.

Austrasia, forming the eastern part of the Merovingian kingdoms, can to some extent be considered a frontier society. From the perspective of Metz, Austrasian capital since 565, what happened along the Rhine was no less an important issue than relations to the other Merovingian kingdoms situated in the more central regions of Gaul. But how would the kings at Metz conceive of the eastern frontier of Austrasia? Were there distinguishing – indeed demarcating – geographical, cultural, legal, ethnic or religious traits separating those groups that were directly placed under Frankish rule from those who were living further east and were not? To understand what became of the Roman border areas in the post-Roman era, 'militarisation' can be a potent tool in describing political and social change in a frontier society.

Three Austrasian central places around 600: Andernach, Maastricht and Cologne

The frontier regions of Austrasia comprised the territories of two provinces on the Rhine that were once part of the Roman Empire: *Germania superior* and *Germania inferior*. Their administration collapsed in the early fifth century. Nevertheless, important sites at these border areas remained settled under the Frankish rule that followed, even functioning as focal points in the region, as will be demonstrated for three towns in the Rhenish borderland.

Andernach was expanded into a fortress in late Antiquity and had served as the garrison for a legion (*legio Acincensis*) answerable to the *dux* of Mainz in the year 400.[3] The town had a granary (*horreum*), and its port functioned as an outpost for the Roman Rhine fleet.[4] Andernach came under the rule of the Rhine Franks after the end of the Mainz duchy, probably in the late fifth century. It was now included in the Frankish military organisation, which at that time was based in Cologne. Andernach then appears as a minting site in the sixth century, which suggests transregional economic and fiscal activities.[5] There is also evidence that Frankish kings stayed in a *villa regia*[6] located inside the fortress that had churches consecrated to St Geneviève of Paris and St Martin of Tours, two *patrocinia* that were directly associated with the Merovingian monarchy. In addition, numerous Merovingian fiscal estates have been verified in the vicinity of Andernach[7] that apparently go back to the Roman fiscal asset of *res privata*, suggesting the continuity of important ownership structures.[8] Several burial fields demonstrate the continuity of settlement for the Andernach fortress after the year 500. There was apparently no destruction here; even the continued use of the Rhine port of Andernach is currently under archaeological investigation.[9] In this respect, Andernach remained a border point on the Rhine. The Moselle river and the surviving road system nearby were important in connecting Metz to the border.[10] The Merovingian-era poet Venantius Fortunatus even described in a poem how, in the year 589, he and the Frankish King Childebert II travelled down the Moselle by ship from Metz to Andernach, where life pulsated in the royal palace.[11] Over forty Latin funerary inscriptions from the fifth to seventh centuries have been preserved from Andernach, most of them from the Frankish period.[12] We find, for example, a notary with the Roman name of *Amicatus*, from which we may be able to infer some continuity of late Roman administrative literacy.[13] The majority of the inscriptions are of Germanic names in Latinised form, however. They testify to a complex process of acculturation, such as a *Rainovaldus* from the side of the Rhine opposite Andernach who is said to have married a well-to-do Roman woman even though he himself was a barbarian.[14] As fate would have it, *invida mors* – 'envious Death' – came for him before his time.

Maastricht was also expanded into a fortress in late Antiquity. Founded as a trading post in Roman times at an important crossing over the Meuse (Maas) river, it is referred to in written material as a *vicus*.[15] Maastricht was located on an important supply road that connected Cologne, the province capital, with Cambrai and Amiens via Tongeren. Numerous fortresses were located here in late Antiquity,[16] making the town part of the defensive system on the Lower Rhine to secure the roads and also facilitate supply, since the fortress probably also housed a granary or *horreum*. Barbarian Laetians were stationed in neighbouring Tongeren in the fourth century – presumably Franks[17] – but the events of the fifth century made the fortified Maastricht more important; even the Bishop of Tongeren ultimately relocated to Maastricht.[18] In the case of Maastricht, too, there is proof of extensive Frankish fiscal estates in the area[19] that evidently trace back to former Roman fiscal estates. Such estates could be used in a wide variety of ways: they could be requisitioned for certain troops, as well as for servicing roads, which were considered public, or used for the salaries of public officials and others. Maastricht also had an important mint in the sixth century,[20] another parallel to Andernach. A minted gold coin of a one-third *solidus* (*tremissis*) recently offered for sale shows a Roman emperor in imperial regalia on the front. The other side has a cross and the Latinised Germanic name of the moneyer: *Rimoaldus*.[21] This mintage in particular provides an extraordinary wealth of information on the transformation of border spaces in the post-Roman era, as we observe in Merovingian Gaul and Germania a breathtakingly broad decentralisation of coin production. Whereas the number of minting sites throughout the Roman Empire had been reasonably straightforward, the Merovingian kingdom had 900 verified locations where between 500 and 750 coins were produced temporarily or long-term, many of them gold.[22] The proliferation of minting sites corresponded to a profound decentralisation of economic and fiscal structures: the coins were apparently produced in order to commute in-kind contributions into monetary payments.[23] Although a decline in quality and gold value cannot be denied, the high number of minting sites does not seem to suggest economic decline.[24]

In the late Roman era, the aforementioned town of Maastricht had been part of the province of *Germania inferior*, whose capital was Cologne.[25] Cologne also had secure and substantial continuity of settlement,[26] as well as appearing as a continuously operating minting site in the sixth and seventh centuries.[27] A grave inscription from as early as the late fourth century was constructed for a *centenarius* named Emeterius, who served here for over twenty-five years in a barbarian fighting force (*numerus*), the so-called *gentiles*.[28] In the fifth century, Cologne became the centre of a

Frankish ethnogenesis, which later led to the emergence of the so-called Ripuarians (literally 'shore soldiers') who are occasionally also referred to as 'Rhineland Franks'.[29] Cologne's status as an important political, military and religious centre likely played a role in Deutz, on the right bank of the Rhine, alongside its fleet and continuity of settlement.[30] Kings consistently resided in Cologne in the former governor's seat, the *praetorium*, which in the sixth century was designated the *aula regia*. Around 600, under kings Childebert II and Theudebert II, Cologne seems to have been the most important 'secondary residence' of the kings of the eastern Frankish kingdom, together with Reims and Metz.[31] Cologne was also a major bishopric: the ancient Roman province of *Germania inferior* lived on as a church province in the Cologne archdiocese.[32] The first Frank to become bishop was Ebergisil, around the year 590. He was apparently very close to the kingdom and took over important functions.[33]

King Childebert II's Decree of 596

Why have we concentrated on these three places in particular? There is an *ex post* argument to be made here. Specifically, an extensive decree has been preserved from the year 596, in which the Merovingian King Childebert II (575–96) sought to govern the affairs of the eastern Frankish kingdom.[34] Interestingly, the legislative act was preceded by three assemblies between the king and his army (his *leudes*, meaning 'people' or 'men', to whom we shall return later). At these gatherings, held exclusively in Andernach, Maastricht and Cologne, occurring on the not insignificant date of 1 March (as in the late Roman era, the first day of March was often used to elevate a new emperor or co-emperor and to announce the tax lists), and in the presence of the king's larger entourage and his *leudes*, standards were discussed, negotiated and adopted.[35] It was in Andernach, Maastricht and Cologne that troops of Frankish and other origins were assembled so that the Frankish king, in consensus with his military and clerical elite, could decree the legal standards of coexistence in this border area. On the other side of the Rhine they had to deal with more barbarians continually infringing on the border, mainly Frisians in the north and Saxons in the east. There were repeated attacks, sackings and worse. The Rhine border was more or less respected; its natural advantages were evident.

Childebert II and his advisers sought to revitalise concepts and elements of ancient border security. Their king decreed the validity of the new provisions with his military right of ban, to a degree reminiscent of the *imperium* of the Roman generals, which it probably drew upon.[36] The regulations devoted ample space to the prosecution of serious offenders and the maintenance of 'public order'. They stated that 'discipline should prevail among the whole people' (c. 7), with the leitmotif of *disciplina* appropriating Roman military vocabulary.³⁷ Several regulations (cc. 7 and 9–12) revolved around the *centena* or hundred, describing a smaller district headed by a centenary (*centenarius*), a military official empowered to summon adult freemen to judicial assemblies and recruit them for military service.³⁸ The Frankish *centena* developed out from the late Roman military organisation; the epitaph testifying to the *centenarius* from Cologne has already been referenced above. In the Merovingian period, the *centenarius* could use his mandate to persecute robbers and criminals who lacked a permanent residence; obviously a major cause of concern.³⁹ If a *centena* managed to apprehend a perpetrator, they were expected to exercise a kind of street justice, which was likewise modelled on Roman military law.⁴⁰

A second important objective of the king's decree concerned the crime of manslaughter and the *wergild* to be paid in a militarised border society. In Frankish law, it was customary when a person was killed to pay *wergild* to the person's relatives, a kind of monetary indemnity that effectively purchased their family's right to revenge. With the assent of his military elite, the king sought to limit this practice to unintentional homicides (cc. 5, 6 and 10). We may thus suspect some more complex legal reasoning behind this.

Most striking are the crimes of religion addressed in the decree, namely incest, bride kidnapping (*raptus*) and disregarding the Sunday rest. The decree called for exceptionally drastic punishment in all three cases. A person marrying his stepmother, for example, could face the death penalty, while other incestuous relationships drew a combination of secular and church punishments (penance), to be imposed by the local bishop (c. 2). Another provision calls a bride thief an 'enemy of God' (*inimicus Dei*) and therefore allows any person to persecute and kill the offender without additional proceedings – unless asylum is sought in the church (c. 4). Anyone defying the Sunday rest, for example by working, was subject to expensive fines (c. 14). Interestingly, these religious precepts that the Frankish king was now seeking to impress upon the people go back to legislative measures by the Roman Emperor Constantine and his successors.⁴¹ The regulations were an attempt to turn the external border into a civilising boundary as well, a religious boundary against the heathens: even if the Franks were not Romans, they strove to perpetuate the Roman Empire and its religious law within their territory.

Childebert's decree thus allows us a glimpse into how some late Roman structures became adapted, reshaped or to some extent even revived within the new political entity of Frankish Austrasia. The Frankish administration of public order grew out of late Roman provincial and military organisation. As in other regions of Frankish Gaul, the late Roman provincial order broke down and survived only in the ecclesiastical administration of dioceses and metropolitan sees. Against this background, it becomes clear why episcopal cities such as Cologne or Maastricht were important centres not just for the pastoral care of souls alone, as some of the regulations decreed by Childebert II envisage the imposition of ecclesiastical sanctions by bishops. While it is tempting to relate the envisaged imposition of drastic monetary sanctions such as the royal ban and the high payment of *wergilds* to the production of coins, a more detailed picture of the economy and society of this region can hardly be given based on the evidence produced by one law alone.

East Frankish society according to the seveneth-century Ripuarian Law-Code

A more comprehensive view can be given on the basis of the Ripuarian Law-Code,[42] which is certainly the most important document we have for society and political organisation in the east Frankish kingdom of Austrasia. Originally designed for the Rhineland in the area of the city of Cologne (*pagus Ribuarius*),[43] but extending its scope to other regions of the *regnum Austrasiae*, this law-code contains material that must have first been drafted in the sixth century and shows close resemblances to the Salic law-code, while other provisions clearly derive from the situation when the law-code was first drafted. A final redaction, on which the manuscript tradition depends, apparently took place under King Dagobert I, either when he became sub-king of Austrasia around 622, or on the occasion of appointing his underage son Sigibert III as sub-king of Austrasia in 633 or 634.[44]

The very term *Lex Ripuaria* suggests a very close connection to the emergence of the Ripuarians as a new ethnic group. The *Ripuarii* can be traced back to the late Roman *riparii*, parts of the limitan groups that had been stationed on the shores of the river Rhine and were to a large extent composed of people of barbarian origin in late Antiquity.[45] This functional group of 'river-soldiers' became the nucleus of a process of ethnic transformation. 'Ripuarian' became a term designating people of the Austrasian kingdom, in particular those living close to the Rhine, a mixed population composed of Franks, Alemans, Romans, Burgundians etc. who had migrated into the area around Cologne and beyond. A society characterised by military functions and values first becomes apparent from the *wergild* tariffs, whose heterogeneous character reveals a changing society that had to adjust its legal norms to military and political needs in order to enhance legal security within an ethnically mixed frontier society. The *wergild* tariffs are differentiated according to ethnic status (*L. Rib.* 40) and differed enormously, for if someone killed a foreigner (*advena*) of Frankish or of Aleman or Bavarian origin, he would have to pay 200 or 160 *solidi* to the relatives of the victim; if, however, the victim was a foreigner of Roman origin, a *wergild* of 100 *solidi* would have to be paid to buy from the victim's family their right to take revenge (*L. Rib.* 40, 1–4). These tariffs do not simply reflect social and ethnic differences, but we may also suspect some sort of 'ethnic engineering' behind such regulations.[46] In terms of ethnicity, the legal status of a person was defined through one's place of birth (*L. Rib.* 35, 1–4): for this reason, each person born in the Ripuarian *pagus* would be a *Ripuarius* or a *Ripuaria*, regardless of the ethnic identity of their parents. A political agenda apparently lay behind such rules. The society of the Ripuarian *pagus* witnessed immigration and an influx of people of differing ethnic status, who assimilated within one generation by accepting their children, if born in Ripuarian *pagus*, to become Ripuarians. The ethnic differences that appear so strong in the *wergild* tariffs thus applied to the migration generation alone, who were born elsewhere and thus had a different *natio* and were treated as foreigners (*advenae*) in the Rhineland. Why the Romans were treated so badly is another highly disputed matter, on which there is still no consensus.[47] It seems possible, however, that protecting the 'Germanic' groups by a higher *wergild* served to encourage these groups to migrate into the Ripuarian *pagus*, as their military capacities were undoubtedly much needed in this frontier society. At the same time, *wergild* tariffs for royal functionaries, higher clerics and persons who were *in verbo regis* and thus enjoyed special royal protection (*L. Rib.* 39, 3) sought to emphasise that the king and his advisers conceived them as belonging to the highest and most important functional elite of the kingdom. As the *wergild* tariffs amply demonstrate, the state withdrew to a large extent from the Roman idea that the ruler had to prosecute homicide indiscriminately.[48]

A number of regulations intend to define the legal sphere of kingship and specify the means of governance by which the king and his functionaries could intervene in local affairs. Particularly noteworthy is the title on the crime of infidelity towards the king (*L. Rib.* 72) that comprised two regulations: high treason was sanctioned with the death penalty to be inflicted upon the culprit and by confiscation of his property; as these two sanctions reveal, the model upon which this regulation was clearly built was the Roman *crimen maiestatis*; however, the legal justification for these sanctions was not rooted in Roman law anymore (which did not apply to most of the population in Austrasia), but in fact was the oath of fidelity sworn by the free and adult male population. In addition, the concept of infidelity also included the crimes of parricide and incest, which it punished with confiscation and exile. These crimes had also been most forcefully punishable under Roman law, but again, as it seems, the oath sworn to the ruler made it a norm to be observed by all members of Ripuarian society alike, be they Roman, Burgundian, Frank, etc. It seems as if the Roman idea of *ius publicum* with its multifold political, military and even religious implications became to a considerable extent absorbed by the concept of (in)fidelity. But it also illustrates that these norms were now becoming increasingly centred upon the person of the ruler, one could say 'personalised', as it was the image of the Christian king upon which normative expectations were now being projected. The oath of fidelity, to which we will return later, served as a sort of vehicle to arrange the legal transfer of Roman legal norms into a society which was not dominated by Romans anymore.[49]

It was on the basis of such regulations on infidelity and the authority of royal documents (*L. Rib.* 59) on which further provisions rested, which regulated the handling of royal authority by local royal officials such as the counts. When requesting the local population to perform military and other public services, the counts could use the royal ban of 60 *solidi* to threaten those who were not willing to attend the host with extremely high monetary fines. Although the ban was reduced for persons of lower social status, the ban as an instrument to delegate royal authority was clearly exercised without paying any respect to ethnic distinctions (*L. Rib.* 68, 1). It is obvious that such regulations were drafted to increase the capacities of defence and of warfare in this frontier society, but they also contain an element of fiscalising ban fines[50] which – along with *wergild* – should be kept in mind when speaking of the enormous minting of silver and gold coins in the eastern Frankish kingdom.

Finally, improving and protecting the legal position of the Christian church and fixing the status of ecclesiastical dependents is another important feature that pervades the Ripuarian law-code. The aforementioned *wergild* tariffs for clerics were dramatically lifted as 100, 200, 300, 600 and 900 *solidi* were payable for killing an ordinary cleric, a subdeacon, a deacon, a priest and a bishop respectively (*L. Rib.* 40, 5–9). In addition, it was church property and ecclesiastical dependents in particular that the code sought to protect. To a considerable extent, church property and dependents of churches were treated in analogy to fiscal property and fiscal dependents (*fiscalini*) (*L. Rib.* 61, 10–14), which apparently resulted from the fact that large parts of church property actually came into the hands of churches and monasteries through royal donation of property that once had belonged to the fisc. The famous general rule that the Church as an institution should live according to Roman law (*ecclesia vivit lege Romana*, *L. Rib.* 61, 1) sounds like a general privilege which was relevant in particular with regard to legal procedure and proof, allowing the Church to handle its cases without making its case through trial by combat and the like. Regulations on slaves who were manumitted in a church by use of tables and thus became *tabularii* (*L. Rib.* 61) clearly show a departure from the late Roman practice of *manumissio in ecclesia*, as now all freedmen who had been manumitted in a church came along with their offspring permanently under the patronage of the church in which their manumission had taken place. In the long term, this would cause the emergence of a legally distinct social group of *censuales* as ecclesiastical dependents of episcopal churches in particular.[51]

Fidelitas et leudesamio: Political, gendered and religious loyalty intertwined

While fidelity appears as a crucial concept in the Ripuarian law-code, a formulary contained in the collection of Marculf[52] that regulates the taking of the oath can be attributed to the establishment of the Austrasian sub-kingdom of Sigibert III, son of Dagobert I, in 633/4.[53] It should thus be read in conjunction with the Ripuarian law-code. Making the free male adult population of the kingdom swear fidelity to its rulers was a well-organised business involving several different actors operating on different local and legal levels. The formulary is addressed to a local count, who had to congregate and assemble all dwellers of his district (*pagenses*) who were obliged to swear in the relevant *civitates, vici et castella*. Taking the oath of loyalty presupposed, to some extent at least, central places that were in charge of holding the people living in the countryside accountable for public obligations. These places now became supervised by counts who combined military with civil and judicial functions, since in Austrasia there were larger *pagi* that often comprised several *civitates* and *vici*.[54] While the count, by using his power to command – the ban – had to coerce the people to attend the oath-taking at a fixed date, it was only a royal *missus* directed from the court who was allowed to accept the oath on behalf of the king. This also implies the existence of certain checks and balances to keep the power of an important local military official such as the count under control.

In fact, the whole administrative structure of the Frankish kingdom with its networks of dukes, counts, centurions and *decani* was conceived of as an extended military organisation.[55] Loyalty to the king was prevalent and constituted a principle that overrode ethnic distinctions.[56] Within the Austrasian militarised society the free adult male population was obliged to swear *fidelitas et leudesamio*, a characteristic double phrasing,[57] that specified fidelity as being the typical sort of loyalty of a man, a *leudis*. This would sound adequate for a militarised society, in which the very term *leudis* not only means 'man' but also '*wergild*'. One could translate the word-pair as the promise 'to be faithful to the king as a man should be', a forerunner of the Carolingian general oath of loyalty, according to which subjects swore to be faithful to Charlemagne, 'as a man according to law should be towards his lord' (*fidelem esse, sicut homo per drictum suo domino esse debet*).[58] The male-like behaviour clearly comprised military service and adherence to military virtues such as *disciplina*, but also obedience to royal commands such as the ban. And the idea of *wergild*, taking up the Latin term *vir*, while only in a secondary application extending this notion to women, is only the fitting expression of a fundamental transformation into a militarised society whose central concepts of political behaviour and virtues now appear to be 'male-centred'.

According to the formulary, the envoy sent by the king had to bring along relics on which the population should swear. This is an interesting illustration of the extent to which the Frankish kings were aware of the mutual interdependence of religious adherence and political loyalty.[59] In Andernach, the royal court introduced relics of St Geneviève, thereby transferring a crucial Merovingian saint from Paris into the less Christianised borderland, where religious practice was promoted so as to become intertwined with the very centres of Merovingian kingship. Moreover, one may also think here of the fact that the Merovingians propagated the cult of St Martin of Tours as their special royal patron, which they also did further east, as St Martin is often found as patron for fiscal properties.[60] We may thus assume that the saints' relics the *missi* brought to the communities for the oath-taking would remain at these places.

Conclusion

Building upon some late Roman 'hardware' – cities, fortifications and villages, along with roads and waterways – legal documents such as Childebert II's decree and the Ripuarian Law-Code can be interpreted as 'software' that was designed by kings and their lay and ecclesiastical advisers to frame the functioning of a frontier society, to organise its defence, to encourage immigration of military elites, to maintain public order and to Christianise it. Several features such as the *centena* structure, the functions of the counts and the use of the ban point to an extended military organisation. *Wergild*, indicating a man's worth, oath-bound political loyalty characterised as 'man-like fidelity' (*fidelitas et leudesamio*) and *disciplina* as a catchword of public order suggest that political discourse within this society changed significantly. It would be naive to assume that all of what the normative texts tell us was easily put into practice. However, these texts themselves formulated and maintained a certain level of expectation – and this in itself should be seen as a historical fact that was based upon manifold preconditions, and for this reason should not be dismissed.

Notes

1. B. Isaac, 'The meaning of the terms *limes* and *limitanei*', *Journal of Roman Studies*, 78 (1988), 125–47.
2. M. Konrad and C. Witschel (eds), *Römische Legionslager in den Rhein- und Donauprovinzen – Nuclei spätantik-frühmittelalterlichen Lebens?* (Munich: C.H. Beck, 2011); see also C. Later, M. Helmbrecht and U. Jecklin-Tischhauser (eds), *Infrastruktur und Distribution zwischen Antike und Mittelalter* (Hamburg: Dr. Kovač, 2015).
3. *Notitia dignitatum occ.* XLI,13 25: *Notitia dignitatum accedunt Notitia urbis Constantinopolitanae et Latercula provinciarum*, ed. O. Seeck (Berlin: Weidmann, 1876), pp. 213–14.
4. R. Scharf, *Der Dux Mogontiacensis und die Notitia Dignitatum. Eine Studie zur spätantiken Grenzverteidigung* (Berlin: De Gruyter, 2005), pp. 284–98; J. Oldenstein, 'Die spätrömischen Befestigungen zwischen Straßburg und Andernach im 4. und zu Beginn des 5. Jahrhunderts', in F. J. Felten (ed.), *Befestigungen und Burgen am Rhein* (Stuttgart: Franz Steiner, 2011), pp. 17–46.
5. C. Dietmar and M. Trier, *Colonia – Stadt der Franken. Köln vom 5. bis 10. Jahrhundert* (Cologne: Dumont, 2011), p. 108.
6. H. Ament, 'Andernach im frühen Mittelalter', in K. Schäfer (ed.), *Andernach im Frühmittelalter – Venantius Fortunatus* (Andernach: Stadtmuseum, 1988), pp. 3–16; L. Grünwald, 'Das Moselmündungsgebiet zwischen Spätantike und Frühmittelalter', *Berichte zur Archäologie an Mittelrhein und Mosel*, 5 (1997), 309–21; P. Dräger, 'Zwei Moselfahrten des Venantius Fortunatus (carmina 6,8 und 10,9)', *Kurtrierisches Jahrbuch*, 39 (1999), 67–88.
7. D. Flach, 'Königshof und Fiskus Andernach', in F.-J. Heyen (ed.), *Andernach. Geschichte einer Stadt* (Andernach: Stadtverwaltung, 1994), pp. 43–52.
8. On the question of continuities of this type, see E. Ewig, 'Waldorf am Vinxtbach. Römisch-fränkische Kontinuität auf dem Lande? Fakten und Fragen', *Rheinische Vierteljahrsblätter*, 59 (1995), 304–13.
9. E. Saal, 'Forschungen zum antiken Rheinhafen in Andernach', in H. Kennecke (ed.), *Der Rhein als europäische Verkehrsachse. Die Römerzeit* (Bonn: Vor- und Frühgeschichtliche Archäologie, Rheinische Friedrich-Wilhelms-Universität, 2014), pp. 63–77.
10. For the historical economic aspects of such continuities, see M. Windhausen, '*Angaria* und *scara* im Prümer Urbar: Transport- und Botendienste in einer frühmittelalterlichen Grundherrschaft im Kontext römischer Verkehrswege', *Beiträge zur Geschichte des Bitburger Landes*, 17 (2006), 4–30.
11. Venantius Fortunatus, *Carmen* X, 9 (*De navigio suo*), V. 63–82: *Venance Fortunat, Poèmes*, ed. and trans. M. Reydellet, vol. 3 (Livres IX–XI) (Paris: Les belles lettres, 2004), p. 130. See Saal, 'Forschungen zum antiken Rheinhafen'; D. Elmers,

'Archäologischer Kommentar zu dem Gedicht des Venantius Fortunatus über seine Moselreise', in K. Schäfer (ed.), *Andernach im Frühmittelalter – Venantius Fortunatus* (Andernach: Stadtmuseum, 1988), pp. 25–68; Dräger, 'Zwei Moselfahrten'.

12 W. Boppert, 'Die frühchristlichen Grabinschriften von Andernach', in K. Schäfer (ed.), *Andernach im Frühmittelalter – Venantius Fortunatus* (Andernach: Stadtmuseum, 1988), pp. 121–44; W. Schmitz, 'Die spätantik-frühmittelalterlichen Inschriften aus dem Moselgebiet', in T. Grünewald (ed.), *Germania inferior. Besiedlung, Gesellschaft und Wirtschaft an der Grenze der römisch-germanischen Welt* (Berlin: De Gruyter, 2001), pp. 261–305, at p. 262; A. Vogel, *Die merowingischen Funde aus Andernach (Kr. Mayen-Koblenz)* (Bonn: Habelt, 2006).

13 Vogel, *Die merowingische Funde aus Andernach*, no. 33 (late sixth or seventh c.): *Hic requies/cit in pace / santa nota/rius Amica/tus pluremis porrixit / dulceter ho/nore(m) meruit / tumulum in adri/a s(an)ctorum vixit / in secol(o) anno/rum XL obiit in / pace X [dies ante] Kalen/das Madias*. For the notariate see W. Bergmann, 'Fortleben des antiken Notariats im Frühmittelalter', in P.-J. Schuler (ed.), *Tradition und Gegenwart. Festschrift zum 175jährigen Bestehen eines badischen Notarstandes* (Karlsruhe: G. Braun, 1981), pp. 23–35.

14 CIL XIII, 7748 (7th c.?): *+ Hic requiescit in pa/ce Rainovaldus puer / amatus inter paren/tes [p]u(e)[ll](a)m nubelem pro/duxit in gentem in/veda mors astra(h)it / di secolum vixit quo/que annorum XXX[V], o/biit sub diae quod fa/cit Octuber dies undecim. Amen.*

15 T. A. S. M. Panhuysen, *Romeins Maastricht en zijn beelden. Corpus signorum imperii Romani. Corpus van de Romeinse beeldhouwkunst. Nederland, Germania inferior, Maastricht* (Maastricht: Van Gorcum, 1996).

16 R. Brulet, 'Das spätrömische Verteidigungssystem zwischen Mosel und Nordseeküste', in T. Bechert and W. J. H. Willems (eds), *Die römische Reichsgrenze von der Mosel bis zur Nordseeküste* (Stuttgart: Theiss, 1995), pp. 103–19, at pp. 111–13.

17 *Notitia dignitatum occ.* XLII, 43: *Notitia dignitatum*, ed. Seeck, p. 217.

18 M. Werner, *Der Lütticher Raum in frühkarolingischer Zeit. Untersuchungen zur Geschichte einer karolingischen Stammlandschaft* (Göttingen: Vandenhoeck & Ruprecht, 1980), pp. 228–340; F. Theuws, 'Maastricht as a center of power in the early Middle Ages', in M. de Jong and F. Theuws (eds), *Topographies of power in the early Middle Ages*, Transformation of the Roman World, 6 (Leiden: Brill, 2001), pp. 155–216, at pp. 160–78.

19 M. Van Rey, *Die Lütticher Gaue Condroz und Ardennen im Frühmittelalter. Untersuchungen zur Pfarrorganisation* (Bonn: L. Röhrscheid, 1977); Theuws, 'Maastricht as a center of power', pp. 182–5.

20 See A. de Belfort, *Description générale des monnaies mérovingiennes*, vol. 3 (Paris: Société Française de Numismatique, 1893), nos. 4438–45, pp. 308–9.

21 yorkcoins.com/me655__-_merovingian_kingdom,_%27national%27_gold_coinage,_austrasia,_maastricht_mint.htm (accessed 10 October 2019).

22 K. Dahmen, 'Zum Münzwesen des Merowingerreiches', in A. Greule, B. Kluge, J. Jarnut and M. Selig (eds), *Die merowingischen Monetarmünzen*

als interdisziplinär-mediaevistische Herausforderung (Paderborn: Wilhelm Fink, 2017), pp. 71–124.

23 J. Strothmann, 'Königsherrschaft oder nachantike Staatlichkeit? Merowingische Monetarmünzen als Quelle für die politische Ordnung des Frankenreiches', *Millennium. Jahrbuch zu Kultur und Geschichte des ersten Jahrtausends n. Chr.*, 5 (2008), 353–81.

24 See W. Bleiber, *Naturalwirtschaft und Ware-Geld-Beziehungen zwischen Somme und Loire während des 7. Jahrhunderts* (Berlin: Akademie-Verlag, 1981), p. 35.

25 W. Eck, *Köln in römischer Zeit. Geschichte einer Stadt im Rahmen des Imperium Romanum* (Cologne: Greven, 2004).

26 W. Eck, 'Köln im Übergang von der Antike zum Mittelalter', *Geschichte in Köln*, 54 (2007), 7–26.

27 J. F. Fischer, 'Geld und Geldwirtschaft in merowingischer Zeit in Köln', *Kölner Jahrbuch*, 35 (2002), 281–306; Dietmar and Trier, *Colonia*, pp. 76–7.

28 W. Schmitz, 'Die spätantiken und frühmittelalterlichen Grabinschriften in Köln (4.-7. Jahrhundert n. Chr.)', *Kölner Jahrbuch*, 28 (1995), 643–776, no. 4.

29 M. Springer, 'Riparii – Ribuarier – Rheinfranken nebst einigen Bemerkungen zum Geographen von Ravenna', in D. Geuenich (ed.), *Die Franken und die Alemannen bis zur 'Schlacht bei Zülpich' (496/97)*, RGA Ergänzungsbände, 19 (Berlin: De Gruyter, 1998), pp. 200–69.

30 M. Trier, 'Agripina Colonia und das Militärlager Divitia am Übergang von der Antike zum Mittelalter (400–700)', in M. Konrad and C. Witschel (eds), *Römische Legionslager in den Rhein- und Donauprovinzen – Nuclei spätantik-frühmittelalterlichen Lebens?* (Munich: C.H. Beck, 2011), pp. 175–96.

31 Dietmar and Trier, *Colonia*, p. 64.

32 F. W. Oediger, *Das Bistum Köln von den Anfängen bis zum Ende des 12. Jahrhunderts. Die Geschichte des Erzbistums Köln*, vol. 1 (Cologne: Bachem, 1991); H. Müller, 'Bischof Kunibert von Köln. Staatsmann im Übergang von der Merowinger- zur Karolingerzeit', *Zeitschrift für Kirchengeschichte*, 98 (1987), 167–205.

33 Gregory of Tours, *Liber historiarum X*, 15: *Gregorii episcopi Turonensis libri historiarum X*, ed. by B. Krusch and W. Levison, *MGH, SS rer. Mer.* I,1 (Hanover: Hahn, 2nd edn, 1951), p. 503. Dietmar and Trier, *Colonia*, p. 72.

34 *Decretio Childeberti II a. 596*: Capitularia regum Francorum 1, ed. A. Boretius (Hanover: Hahn, 1883) (henceforth quoted according to this edition), no. 7, pp. 15–17.

35 M. Springer, 'Jährliche Wiederkehr oder ganz anderes: Märzfeld oder Marsfeld?', in P. Dilg, G. Keil and D.-R. Moser (eds), *Rhythmus und Saisonalität* (Sigmaringen: Thorbecke, 1995), pp. 297–324.

36 See S. Esders, 'Treueidleistung und Rechtsveränderung im frühen Mittelalter', in S. Esders and C. Reinle (eds), *Rechtsveränderung im politischen und sozialen Kontext mittelalterlicher Rechtsvielfalt* (Münster: Lit, 2005), pp. 25–62, here pp. 50–9.

37 See, e.g., O. Stoll, '"Heeresdiziplin". Vom Einfluß Roms auf die Germanen', in O. Stoll, *Römisches Heer und Gesellschaft. Gesammelte Beiträge 1991–1999*

(Stuttgart: Franz Steiner, 2001), pp. 269–79; A. C. Murray, 'Pax et disciplina. Roman public law and the Merovingian state', in T. F. X. Noble (ed.), *Roman provinces to medieval kingdoms* (London: Routledge, 2006), pp. 376–88.

38 A. C. Murray, 'From Roman to Frankish Gaul. "Centenarii" and "centenae" in the administration of the Merovingian kingdom', *Traditio*, 44 (1988), 59–100; S. Esders, 'Amt und Bann. Weltliche Funktionsträger (*centenarii, vicarii*) als Teil ländlicher Gesellschaften im Karolingerreich', in T. Kohl, S. Patzold and B. Zeller (eds), *Kleine Welten. Ländliche Gesellschaften im Karolingerreich* (Ostfildern: Thorbecke, 2019), pp. 255–307.

39 J. Goebel, *Felony and misdemeanour. A study in the history of criminal procedure* (1937, repr. Philadelphia: University of Pennsylvania Press, 1976), pp. 65–77.

40 On the so-called *velox supplicium*, see C*Th.* VIII, 18, 11, 13, and 14: Theodosiani libri XVI, ed. T. Mommsen and P. M. Meyer (Berlin: Weidmann, 1905), vol. 1, pp. 347–8.

41 See, e.g., J. Evans-Grubbs, 'Abduction marriage in Antiquity. A law of Constantine (C. Th. IX, 24, 1) and its social context', *Journal of Roman Studies*, 79 (1989), 59–83; H. Siems, 'Zur Entwicklung des Kirchenasyls zwischen Spätantike und Mittelalter', in O. Behrends and M. Diesselhorst (eds), *Libertas. Grundrechtliche und rechtsstaatliche Gewährungen in Antike und Gegenwart* (Ebelsbach: Gremer, 1991), pp. 139–86; K. M. Girardet, 'Vom Sonnen-Tag zum Sonntag. Der *dies solis* in Gesetzgebung und Politik Konstantins des Großen', *Zeitschrift für antikes Christentum*, 11 (2007), 279–310.

42 *Lex Ribuaria*, ed. F. Beyerle and R. Buchner (Hanover: Hahn, 1954) (henceforth quoted according to this edition).

43 E. Ewig, 'Die *Civitas Ubiorum*, die *Francia Rhinensis* und das Land Ribuarien' (1954), in E. Ewig, *Spätantikes und fränkisches Gallien. Gesammelte Schriften (1952–1973)*, vol. 1 (Zurich/Munich: Artemis, 1976), pp. 472–503.

44 F. Beyerle, 'Zum Kleinreich Sigiberts III. und zur Datierung der Lex Ribuaria', *Rheinische Vierteljahrsblätter*, 21 (1956), 357–61. For more detailed discussion, see S. Esders, 'Lex Ribuaria', *Germanische Altertumskunde online* (forthcoming).

45 Springer, 'Riparii – Ribuarier – Rheinfranken'.

46 P. Wormald, 'The *leges barbarorum*. Law and ethnicity in the post-Roman west', in H.-W. Goetz, J. Jarnut and W. Pohl (eds), *Regna and gentes. The relationship between late antique and early medieval peoples and kingdoms in the transformation of the Roman world*, Transformation of the Roman World, 13 (Leiden: Brill, 2003), pp. 21–53, at pp. 31–2.

47 See most recently L. Bothe, 'From subordination to integration. Romans in Frankish law', in W. Pohl, C. Gantner, C. Grifoni and M. Pollheimer-Mohaupt (eds), *Transformations of Romanness. Early medieval regions and identities* (Berlin: De Gruyter, 2018), pp. 345–68.

48 For comparable developments in Bavaria, see S. Esders, 'Late Roman military law in the Bavarian Code', *clio@themis. Revue électronique d'histoire du droit*, 10 (2016) (La forge du droit. Naissance des identités juridiques en Europe, IVe–XIIIe siècles): cliothemis.com/IMG/pdf/3-_Esders-2.pdf (accessed 25 March 2020).

49 See S. Esders, 'Rechtliche Grundlagen frühmittelalterlicher Staatlichkeit. Der allgemeine Treueid' in W. Pohl (ed.), *Der frühmittelalterliche Staat. Europäische Perspektiven*, Forschungen zur Geschichte des Mittelalters, 16 (Vienna: Verlag der österreichischen Akademie der Wissenschaften, 2009), pp. 423–34.

50 See K. Bayerle, 'Einsatzfelder des weltlichen Bannes im Frühmittelalter', in H.-G. Hermann, H. Siems, T. Gutmann, M. Schmoeckel and J. Rückert (eds), *Von den leges barbarorum bis zum ius barbarum des Nationalsozialismus* (Cologne: Böhlau, 2008) pp. 13–34.

51 S. Esders, *Die Formierung der Zensualität. Zur kirchlichen Transformation des spätrömischen Patronatswesens im früheren Mittelalter* (Ostfildern: Thorbecke, 2010), pp. 50–61.

52 Marculf, *Formula* I, 40 (*Ut leudesamio promittantur rege*): Formulae Merovingici et Karolini aevi, ed. K. Zeumer (Hanover: Hahn, 1886), p. 68.

53 B. Krusch, 'Der Staatsstreich des fränkischen Hausmeiers Grimoald I.', in *Historische Aufsätze Karl Zeumer zum 60. Geburtstag als Festgabe* (Weimar: Böhlau, 1910), pp. 411–38, at pp. 414–15.

54 U. Nonn, *Pagus und Comitatus in Niederlothringen. Untersuchungen zur politischen Raumgliederung im früheren Mittelalter* (Bonn: Röhrscheid, 1983).

55 Murray, 'From Roman to Frankish Gaul', p. 73.

56 This is all the more remarkable as another formulary, Marculf I, 8 (*Carta de ducatu ed patriciate et comitatu*, ed. Zeumer, *MGH LL* Sect. V, pp. 47–8) asked the counts to pay respect to ethnic distinction in terms of law.

57 G. Dilcher, *Paarformeln in der Rechtssprache des frühen Mittelalters* (Darmstadt: Frotscher, 1961).

58 S. Esders, 'Fidelität und Rechtsvielfalt. Die *sicut*-Klausel der früh- und hochmittelalterlichen Eidformulare', in F. Bougard, D. Iogna-Prat and R. Le Jan (eds), *Hiérarchie et stratification sociale dans l'Occident médiéval (400–1100)* (Turnhout: Brepols, 2008) pp. 239–55.

59 S. Esders, '"Faithful believers". Oaths of allegiance in post-roman societies as evidence for eastern and western "visions of community"', in W. Pohl, C. Gantner and R. Payne (eds), *Visions of community in the post-Roman world. The west, Byzantium and the Islamic world, 300–1100* (Aldershot: Ashgate, 2012), pp. 357–74.

60 The cult of St Martin is often taken as evidence for a place once belonging to the fisc, see W. Metz, 'Adelsforst, Martinskirche und Urgautheorie. Bemkerkungen zur fränkischen Verfassungsgeschichte des 7. und 8. Jahrhunderts', in H. Beumann (ed.), *Historische Forschungen für Walter Schlesinger* (Cologne: Böhlau, 1974), pp. 75–85.

12

Swords in Christian hands: reflections on the emergence of the 'Schwertmission' in the early Middle Ages

Uta Heil

In which respects did Christianity, or some Christians, or the Christian Church, support a kind of militarisation in the early Middle Ages? One phenomenon could partially answer this question and exemplify this development, namely the so-called 'Schwertmission': the forced conversion to Christianity through the use of violence and the threat of war.[1] This is a new phenomenon of the early Middle Ages, as neither waging a missionary war nor organising mass baptism is known in late antique Christianity.[2] From the time of Constantine, however, it is taken for granted that the almighty God supports the good and orthodox Christian emperor in his campaigns and victories.[3] In addition, most Christians accepted that one could be a soldier and a good Christian at the same time, especially given that after Constantine the accompanying pagan rites lost their validity.[4] Nevertheless, waging war with the aim of converting the conquered to Christianity was a new phenomenon, such as occurred during Charlemagne's Saxon wars. What led to the idea of 'Schwertmission'?

Mauricius – mission by word

A good starting point is the story of Mauricius, a Christian soldier and the commander of a Roman legion at the beginning of the fourth century, for whom a *vita* has survived in two different versions, both dating to the beginning of the fifth century. Eucherius of Lyon, a monk and later bishop of Lyon († around 450), relates the story in his *Passio Agaunensium martyrum* (around 435) in the following way.[5]

The Emperor Maximianus was a cruel persecutor of Christians who used his military troops to track and kill Christians (*ad extinguendum Christianitatis nomen* [MGH SRM, 3, 33,12, ed. Krusch]). The soldiers of one among these legions, the so-called *Theban legion*, however, were venerated for their strength and bravery. This legion was composed of Christians: although they used their bravery to serve the emperor, they were ultimately devoted to Christ (*erga imperatorem fortitudine, erga Christum devotione certabant* [33,19f.]). When they were commanded to harass a multitude of Christians they dared, unlike the other soldiers, to refuse this task and declared that they would not obey commands of this kind. When Maximianus learned the reply of the *Theban legion*, he became so angry that he ordered every tenth person from that legion to be executed. According to Eucherius, the emperor hoped that the other members of the legion would be terrified to the extent that they would more easily yield to royal injunctions. Subsequently, he renewed his command and ordered the remaining soldiers to persecute the Christians (*ut reliqui in persecutionem Christianorum cogantur* [35,1f.]). However, the troops once again refused. At this point, the greatest encouragement to faith (*incitamentum maximum fidei* [35,15]) was given by Maurice, who was then *primicerius* of that legion. Together with the *campiductor/* drill master Exuperius and the *senator militum* Candidus, he encouraged his fellow soldiers by exhorting and advising them individually.[6] According to Eucherius, the soldiers together with Maurice composed the following letter to the emperor:

> We are your soldiers, O emperor, but God's servants, nevertheless, a fact that we freely confess. We owe military service to you, but our very existence to Him; from you we have received pay for our toil, but from Him we have received the origin of life. By no means can we follow an emperor in this, a command for us to deny God our Father, especially since our Father is your God and Father, whether you like it or not. Unless we are being forced on a path so destructive that we give (God) offence in this manner, we will still obey you as we have done hitherto; otherwise, we will obey Him rather than you. We offer our hands, which we think wrong to sully with the blood of innocents, against any enemy. Those right hands know how to fight against wicked enemies, not how to torture pious citizens. We remember to take arms for citizens rather than against citizens. We have always fought for justice, piety, and the welfare of the innocent. This has been the price of dangers hitherto faced. We have fought for faith; what faith will we keep with you at all, if we do not exhibit faith to our God? We swore oaths to God first, oaths to the king second; there is no need for you to trust us concerning the second, if we break the first. You order us to seek out Christians for punishment. You do not now have to seek out others on this charge, since you have us here confessing: 'We believe in God the Father, Maker of all and God His Son Jesus Christ.' We have seen our allies in toils and dangers being butchered with iron, and yet we neither wept nor grieved at the deaths of our most holy fellow soldiers and the murder of our brothers, but we praised and rejoiced in them, rather, since they had been deemed worthy to suffer for the Lord

their God. And this final necessity of life does not now force us into rebellion. That despair which is at its bravest amidst dangers has not even armed us against you, O emperor. Behold! We hold arms and do not resist, because we surely prefer to die rather than to live, and choose to perish as innocents rather than to live as criminals. If you ordain any further measure against us, give any further command, or direct any other measure, we are prepared to endure fire, torture, and steel. We confess that we are Christians and cannot persecute Christians.[7]

However, this pleading did not prevent the death of the soldiers: all of them were killed by the command of the emperor. Many historical implausibilities have led to the story being considered fictitious.[8] However, rather than merely questioning the historicity of the story, it appears more fruitful to look at Eucherius' depiction of a Christian soldier. According to him, Christian soldiers owed military service to the emperor, and would, in general, obey him. They would offer their forces against the enemy and take up arms to protect the empire's citizens but would not fight against them. They fought for justice, piety and the welfare of the innocent. Of course, Eucherius' depiction is of the ideal Christian soldier, written from the perspective of a just war theory as can be identified in the work of Augustine.[9] It was evidently taken for granted that a Christian man could be a soldier – Augustine even stated that an entirely Christian army would be the best army anyway.[10] Concurrently, the end of the fourth century marked the beginning of the Christianisation of the Roman army through laws issued by Theodosius I, especially after his defeat of the usurper Eugenius during the battle at the River Frigidus (394).[11] Clearly, this development shaped people's understanding of what a Christian soldier should be.[12] It was probably this context which led Eucherius of Lyon to record the martyr story the way he did. A sword in the hand of a Christian soldier correlates to the notion of just war, but Christians at arms were not meant to persecute other Christians, nor were they supposed to fight against innocent people – but rather protect them. However, this is in no respect related to a Christian mission by sword.

De conversione Saxonum – mission by sword

Eucherius' martyr story should be compared with a text written more than 300 years later, namely the poem *De conversione Saxonum*[13] attributed to either Angilbert of Saint-Riquier or Paulinus of Aquileia. It was written in 777 or shortly after the first Saxon conquest.[14] The *De conversione Saxonum* is a piece of political poetry and a panegyric on the triumph of Charlemagne, namely the conversion of the Saxons. In contrast to the *Royal Frankish Annals*, in which the Saxon's paganism and their baptism is only 'presented in the context of political submission' as a secondary issue, in the *De conversione Saxonum* the conversion and baptism of the Saxons is in the foreground and the central aim of the conquest.[15] According to Rabe, Charlemagne 'completes the work that Christ began';[16] it was he who brought the Saxons to the waters of the salvation-bearing baptism:

> This nation Charlemagne the prince, bravely girded with shining arms, crested with pointed helmets, helped by the wonderful strength of the eternal judge, he tamed through different destructions, through a thousand triumphs; and through blood-bearing shields, through spears of war, through the strength of virtues, through javelins smeared with gore, he crushed down and subjected it to himself with a shimmering sword. He dragged the forest-worshipping legions into the kingdoms of heaven …
>
> And afterwards poured over with the dew of salvation-bearing baptism, under the name of the Father and the Son and the dear Holy Breath, by which the only hope of our life stands firm; the Christ-worshipping rude ones, he sent to the stars of heaven; he anointed with chrism those washed by holy baptism, that they might already be able to rise above the smoky flames, and he led the new progeny of Christ into the great hall.[17]

This text describes what we may define as 'Schwertmission': Charlemagne as a Christian emperor is the agent or initiator; his main aim is Christianisation. The poem contemptuously describes the Saxons as pagans: 'sprung from depraved blood' (line 28: *pravo de sanguine creta*), 'a nation which long ago was placing filthy gifts at polluted temples … venerating the abominable cults of demons, and princes, gods, penates' (lines 30–34: *sordida pollutes quae pridem dona sacellis … et demonum cultus colla … suppliciter venerans proceresque, deosque, penates*).[18] However, according to the *Carmen*, Charlemagne brought these pagans to Christianity with divine help and with his weapons.

On the one hand, the *De conversione Saxonum* mentions 'barbaric rage attacking flowing marrows' (line 35: *barbarica rabie fluxas grassante medullas*) as the main cause of the war, likely referring to the Saxon retaliation in 774 for the Frankish invasion of 772/2. This evokes the impression that the campaign was justified as a defensive war against these Saxon attacks. On the other hand, however, the text gives an essential theological interpretation of these events. It stresses the importance of Christianisation to justify the conquest. According to *De conversione Saxonum*, Christ 'had come into the world for the sake of our salvation' (line 39: *ob causam nostrae in mundum venisse salutis*) – and Charlemagne now had 'led the new progeny of Christ into the great hall'. In addition, the time is portrayed as a qualified messianic time, as Charlemagne is reported to have finished the salvific deeds of Christ through his wars against the Saxons. Therefore, Charlemagne's 'sword, normally the instrument of death, becomes in his inspired hand the transmitter of life, soaked with sacred power ... his sword brings form out of chaos and life out of death' because, as *De conversione Saxonum* proclaims, Charlemagne, with his shimmering sword, dragged the forest-worshipping legions into the kingdom of heaven.[19]

Of course, this is an extreme and an enthusiastic panegyrical interpretation; other contemporary texts reveal different estimations. Alcuin, as is well known, displays particular reservations concerning these martial means for conversion,[20] although he is in full accord with the general idea of Christianisation as the goal of conquest.[21] In addition, current research mostly suggests that, indeed, the conquest of the Saxons only subsequently was interpreted as a missionary war with the aim to convert the Saxons to Christianity, as historians like Matthias Becher,[22] Ludger Körntgen[23] or Joachim Ehlers[24] have argued.

Nevertheless, the author of *De conversione Saxonum* had already composed this poem as a panegyric, praising the emperor for his deeds – influenced by biblical language, Christian millennialism, but also by Vergil's fourth Ecloge, as the editors have shown. Therefore, it is a mixture of Roman and Christian heritage, adjusted for the praise of the king and warrior Charlemagne, who is depicted as *salvator mundi* complementing the deeds of Christ.

Obviously, there is a huge difference between Eucherius of Lyon and this poem. What has happened during the intervening years? What is the background to these changes?[25]

Gregory the Great – mission by sword and by word

The writings of Gregory the Great (590–604) are of particular relevance.[26] Gregory is often referred to as an important supporter of militant missionary activities in modern secondary literature. Hans-Dietrich Kahl, for example, the author of an often-cited reference work, wrote:

> The marked general line of development, which shows the use of military means in mission work outside the Church as a post-ancient apparition, corresponds to the fact that Augustine is not yet crown witness for this problem ... The decisive step is also here connected with ... Gregory the Great ... Gregory did not give up his rejection of any immediate forced conversion. But this Church teacher, who for the following period was apparently to become much more decisive than Augustine, grasped another thought: it could be necessary to prepare the preaching of the gospel among pagan peoples outside the empire by their military subjugation, in whose protection then the peaceful proclamation of the Church could unhindered unfold.[27]

This estimation is confirmed by the reception of Gregory and his letters in the medieval decretal testimony.[28] Gregory's letter to Gennadius, the exarch of Africa (I,73), is particularly interesting in this respect. It demonstrates his conviction concerning the role and duties of rulers in the Roman Empire, God's holy commonwealth (*res publica*). Although living in a time when the Merovingians had risen to power in Gaul like the Visigoths in Spain, and although coming into contact with the emerging Anglo-Saxon kingdoms of England, Gregory nonetheless argues from the perspective of the late antique Christianised Roman Empire and was greatly influenced by the developments in Constantinople from the time of Justinian. His six years as papal *apocrisarius* in Constantinople between 579 and 586 also shaped these views. As Matthew del Santo writes:

> By the end of the sixth century, Justinian's conception of the role of the emperor had become an accepted element of the worldview of a wide section of Roman Christian society. Both the empire and the emperor were now defined as being expressly 'Christian', and were understood by contemporaries as imbued with a special purpose in God's merciful dispensation towards humankind. From this flowed the almost unquestioned authority of the emperor and his agents to intervene, where appropriate, the emperor enjoyed the right to count on the unfailing prayers which the latter offered before God for the prosperity of the Christian empire.[29]

This Christianised Rome theory and growing symbiosis of the Church and Empire form the background for Gregory's praise of Gennadius with the words quoted by Burchard and recorded in the *Decretum Gratiani*:

> For where does loquacious praise of your merits not spread, which would speak of wars you frequently rush into, not from a desire to pour out men's blood, but for the sake of extending the republic's domain, in which we see the worship of God, so that the name of Christ spreads in every direction through the subject nations, by preaching the Faith?[30]

The historical background was the ongoing rebellion of Mauretanian groups against which Gennadius had been appointed to lead campaigns by Emperor Tiberius II.[31] Interestingly, Gregory's remark is not a solitary one; rather, several equivalent passages exist.[32] According to Gregory, the emperor and his subordinate rulers had the duty to fight – with the help of the clergy – a double war, namely to 'resist adversaries to the Catholic Church in public wars, for the sake of Christian people, and bravely to fight ecclesiastical battles like a warrior of the Lord'. This quote comes from the other letter of Gregory to Gennadius and is referenced in the *Decretum Gratiani* as well.[33]

Therefore, the Cristina Ricci's conclusion in her study of 'Gregory's Missions to the Barbarians' must be amended. She writes that Gregory, 'in his relationships with the Lombards, Visigoths, Franks and Anglo-Saxons, did not pursue an ideological programme aimed at assimilation of non-Roman peoples into the political-religious sphere of the Roman-Byzantine Empire;

his programme was rather pastoral and his horizon universal'.[34] However, this appears to be a misleading anti-thesis: for Gregory, political assimilation and pastoral care represented two sides of the same coin. As Robert Markus states: 'Gregory adhered to the Byzantine representation of the Germanic nations as subject by divine providence to the universal Empire.'[35]

Gregory's letters to Sardinia are also important to understand the development of the concept of 'Schwertmission'.[36] Many of them deal with the pagans on the island, the so-called *Barbaricini*. In the spring of 594, Gregory sent his fellow bishop Felix and the monk Cyriacus to Sardinia, marking Gregory's first missionary activity and a kind of forerunner of his missionary plan for England. In one letter (IV,23), he advises the nobles and landowners in Sardinia to restrain the peasants (*rusticos*) on their estates from idolatry and argues that the end of the world and judgement are at hand. In a letter to Januarius, the bishop of Cagliari (IV,26), he complains about peasants persisting in paganism and recommends drastic measures, namely: if a peasant is found with such perfidy and obstinacy that he does not consent to come to God, he must be crushed with such heavy burden of tax, that he is forced to seek righteousness quickly through the very penalty of taxation.[37]

In an additional letter to the duke Hospiton of the *Barbaricini*, who seems to have converted at an earlier date, Gregory advises the duke to 'prove his faith with good acts', namely, 'to offer to Christ what is in your power': he should gather 'as many as you can, and have them baptised, warning them to love eternal life'. As before, the *Barbaricini* 'live like senseless animals ... worshipping sticks and stones' – as Gregory describes their paganism in blatant terms.[38] If, however, the duke could not achieve this, he was at least to support the missionary activities of Felix and Cyriacus. As Jeffrey Richards writes: 'Just at the time when Felix and Cyriacus arrived in Sardinia, the military commander of the empire, Zabardas, had brought the Barbaricini a severe defeat and had insisted – perhaps at the suggestion of the papal representatives – that conversion to the Christian faith be included in the establishment of the conditions of peace.'[39] Therefore, in another letter, Gregory praises the duke Zabardas of Sardinia for his support of his missionaries and for 'making peace with the *Barbaricini*, on the condition that you bring the same *Barbaricini* to the service of Christ'.[40] Later, in 599, he advises Januarius of Cagliari to arrest those unwilling to better themselves and repent, and, 'if they are slaves, to beat them with lashes and torments, by which they might achieve purification'.[41]

In sum, these letters show the same ecclesiastical claims and imperially driven missionary activities as can be seen in Gregory's letter to Gennadius in Africa. It is noteworthy that Gregory did not differentiate between pagans, heretics and schismatics, as has sometimes been stated.[42] As already mentioned, Gregory's desire to Christianise the pagans or correct the error of heretics and schismatics was, in addition, the result of his conviction that the end of the world was fast approaching.[43] This belief thereby led to his missionary activities, because the universal growth of the Christian community, even at the furthest reaches of the Earth (where e.g. the Anglo-Saxons lived), was the next step in God's salvation history. This was probably the background for the passages mentioned above, which show Gregory losing patience and demanding sustained threats against pagans and heretics.

Interestingly, Gregory also states that conversion by force and baptism under constraint would be useless unless accompanied by preaching: 'For when anyone approaches the baptismal font not due to the sweetness of preaching but under constraint, he returns to his former superstition from where he seemed to be reborn, and dies in a worse state.'[44] But this is just one – and often quoted – passage in the many letters of Gregory. And a close look at the text reveals that Gregory did not criticise the use of force in itself, but rather the use of force alone. Obviously, he was convinced that preaching was as compelling and persuasive as secular violence.

Comparison

Gregory's thoughts could be summarised as 'mission by sword and word'. The inherited Christianised Rome theory, the impact of Justinian's empire and the expectation of the fast-approaching end of the world created the background for his many commands for imperial governors and clerics to compel pagans and heretics to abandon their errors. In contrast to the *Carmen de conversione Saxonum*, Burchard of Worms, and the *Decretum Gratiani*, Gregory's horizon was the Roman Empire, considered as having been granted by God a special role in salvation history. This perspective is also apparent in the previously cited quotation from Gregory's letter to Gennadius.[45] Interestingly, the reception of Vergil in the *Carmen* also demonstrates the presence of a Christianised Rome theory.

In contrast to the *Carmen de conversion Saxonum*, however, Gregory argues for cooperation of Church and Empire, of imperial force and ecclesiastical preaching, of sword *and* word. This difference is obviously also the result of the genre, as the *Carmen* was written to praise the Emperor Charlemagne; Gregory, however, wrote letters of advice to clerics and rulers. However, other aspects are similar: the possibility of using military force as a 'convincing' corrective measure, the apocalyptic estimation that the end of the world was fast approaching, and the heritage of a Christianised Rome theology.

It is impossible to decide whether the ideas of Gregory and the *Carmen de conversione Saxonum* promoted a growing militarisation of society in the Early Middle Ages or if one has to describe it the other way around: that a growing militarisation led to new ideas about Christianisation rising out of the heritage of Christianised Rome theology. However, Gregory's heritage is indeed decisive as the reception of his letters in the *Decretum Gratiani* demonstrate.[46]

Notes

1. H. Kamp and M. Kroker (eds), *Schwertmission: Gewalt und Christianisierung im Mittelalter* (Paderborn: Ferdinand Schöningh, 2013); J. Beestermöller (ed.), *Friedensethik im frühen Mittelalter: Theologie zwischen Kritik und Legitimation von Gewalt* (Münster: Aschendorff, 2014); H.-W. Goetz, *Die Wahrnehmung anderer Religionen und christlich-abendländisches Selbstverständnis im frühen und hohen Mittelalter (5.-12. Jahrhundert)*, 2 vols (Berlin: Akademie Verlag, 2013), esp. pp. 31–232 of vol. 1, about the perception of the pagans. Compare, in general, H.-D. Kahl, 'Die ersten Jahrhunderte des missionsgeschichtlichen Mittelalters. Bausteine für eine Phänomenologie bis ca. 1050', in K. Schäferdiek (ed.), *Die Kirche des früheren Mittelalters,* Kirchengeschichte als Missionsgeschichte, 2 (Munich: Chr. Kaiser Verlag, 1978), pp. 11–76, here pp. 42–70.
2. On baptism in late Antiquity see the thorough articles in D. Hellhom, T. Vegge, O. Norderval and C. Hellholm (eds), *Absolution, initiation, and baptism. Late Antiquity, early Judaism, and early Christianity*, Beihefte zur Zeitschrift für die neutestamentliche Wissenschaft, 176 (Berlin: De Gruyter, 2011), and A. Fürst, *Die Liturgie der Alten Kirche. Geschichte und Liturgie* (Münster: Aschendorff, 2008).
3. K. Ehling and G. Weber (eds), *Konstantin der Große: Zwischen Sol und Christus* (Mainz: Philip von Zabern, 2011); compare the statement of Ambrose of Milan in his *De fide ad Gratianum* 1, prologus 1,3 (Fontes Christiani 47/1, 140,2 ed. C. Markschies): *nosti enim fide magis imperatoris quam virtute militum quaeri solere victoriam.* / 'You know namely that one is used to win the war more through the faith of the emperor than through the bravery of the soldiers' – of course the orthodox faith Ambrose is demonstrating in his books *De fide.*
4. On Christians as soldiers: H. C. Brennecke, '"An fidelis ad militiam converti possit"? [Tertullian, de idololatria 19,1]: Frühchristliches Bekenntnis und Militärdienst im Widerspruch?', in U. Heil, A. von Stockhausen and J. Ulrich (eds), *Ecclesia est in re publica: Studien zur Kirchen- und Theologiegeschichte im Kontext des Imperium Romanum*, Arbeiten zur Kirchengeschichte, 100 (Berlin: De Gruyter, 2007), pp. 179–232; M. Clauss, '"Gebt dem Kaiser, was des Kaisers ist!". Bemerkungen zur Rolle der Christen im römischen Heer', in P. Kneissel and V. Losemann (eds), *Imperium Romanum. Studien zu Geschichte und Rezeption* ([FS Karl Christ] Stuttgart: Franz Steiner Verlag, 1998), pp. 93–104; A. von Harnack, *Militia Christi. Die christliche Religion und der Soldatenstand in den ersten drei Jahrhunderten* (Tübingen: Mohr [Paul Siebeck], 1905); J. Helgeland,

'Christians and the Roman army from Marcus Aurelius to Constantine', in W. Haase (ed.), *Aufstieg und Niedergang der römischen Welt* II,23,1 (Berlin: De Gruyter, 1979), pp. 724–834; B. Stoll, *De Virtute in Virtutem. Zur Auslegungs- und Wirkungsgeschichte der Bergpredigt in Kommentaren, Predigten und hagiographischer Literatur von der Merowingerzeit bis um 1200*, Beiträge zur Geschichte der biblischen Exegese, 30 (Tübingen: Mohr Siebeck, 1988). See also the literature in note 9.

5 Critical Edition: Eucherius of Lyon, *Passio Acaunensium martyrum*, ed. B. Krusch, *MGH, SRM,* 3 (Hanover: Hahn, 1896), pp. 32–41. There exists a second anonymous vita (E. Chevalley, 'La Passion anonyme de saint Maurice d'Agaune. Édition critique', *Vallesia,* 45 [1990], 37–120) which situates the persecution of the Christian soldiers within a war against the Bagauds.

6 These terms hint at leading positions in the legion to stress the importance of Maurice; compare H. Bellen, 'Der primicerius Mauricius. Ein Beitrag zum Thebäerproblem', *Historia,* 10 (1961), 238–47; M. F. Schwarze, *Römische Militärgeschichte. Vol. 2: Studien zur römischen Armee und ihrer Organisation im sechsten Jahrhundert n. Chr.* (Norderstedt: Books on Demand, 2017), pp. 236–38.

7 Eucherius of Lyon, *Passo Acaunensium martyrum* 9 (ed. Krusch, 36,5–37,5): *Milites sumus, imperator, tui, sed tamen servi, quod libere confitemur, Dei. Tibi militiam debemus, illi innocentiam; a te stipendium laboris accepimus, ab illo vitae exordium sumpsimus. Sequi imperatorem in hoc nequaquam possumus, ut auctorem negemus Deum, utique auctorem nostrum, Deum auctorem, velis nolis, tuum. Si non in tam funesta conpellimur, ut hunc offendamus, tibi, ut fecimus hactenus, adhuc parebimus; si aliter, illi parebimus potius, quam tibi. Offerimus nostras in quemlibet hostem manus, quas sanguine innocentium cruentare nefas ducimus. Dexterae istae pugnare adversum impios adque inimicos sciunt, laniare pios et cives nesciunt. Meminimus, nos pro civibus potius, quam adversus cives arma sumpsisse. Pugnavimus semper pro iustitia, pro pietate, pro innocentium salute. Haec fuerunt hactenus nobis pretia periculorum. Pugnavimus pro fide; quam quo pacto conservabimus tibi, si hanc Deo nostro non exhibemus? Iuravimus primum in sacramenta divina, iuravimus deinde in sacramenta regia; nihil nobis de secundis credas necesse est, si prima perrumpimus. Christianos ad poenam per nos requiri iubes. Iam tibi ex hoc alii requirendi non sunt, habes hic a nos confitentes: „Deum patrem auctorem omnium et filium eius Iesum Christum deum credimus". Vidimus laborum periculorumque nostrorum socios, nobis quoque sanguine aspersis, trucidari ferro, et tamen sanctissimorum conmilitonum mortes et fratrum funera non flevimus, non doluimus, sed potius laudavimus et gaudio prosecuti sumus, quia digni habiti essent pati pro domino Deo eorum. Et nunc non nos vel haec ultimae vitae necessitas in rebellionem coegit, non nos adversum te, imperator, armavit ipsa saltim, quae fortissima est in periculis, desperatio. Tenemus, ecce! arma et non resistimus, quia mori quam occidere satis malumus, et innocentes interire, quam noxii vivere praeoptamus. Si quid in nos ultra statueris, si quid adhuc iusseris, si quid admoveris, ignes, tormenta, ferrum subire parati sumus. Christianos nos fatemur, persequi christianos non*

possumus. English translation, slightly altered, by D. Woods, *St. Maurice and the Theban Legion. The Passion of St. Maurice and the Theban Legion*, ucc.ie/archive/milmart/BHL5740.html (accessed 26 January 2019).
8 On Mauritius, compare D. van Berchem, *Le martyre de la Légion Thébaine. Essai sur la formation d'une légende* (Basel: Reinhardt, 1956); B. Näf, *Städte und ihre Märtyrer. Der Kult der Thebäischen Legion* (Fribourg: Academic Press, 2011); D. O'Reilly, *Lost legion rediscovered. The mystery of the Theban Legion* (Barnsley: Pen & Sword Books, 2011); O. Wermelinger (ed.), *Mauritius und die Thebäische Legion* (Fribourg: Academic Press, 2005).
9 Relevant are Aug., *De civitate Dei* V,19; XIX,7; XIX 12f. (*CCSL*, 47–48, ed. B. Dombart and A. Kalb); *ep*. 93; 138; 189; 229 (CSEL, 34; 44; 57, ed. A. Goldbacher); *Contra Faustum* XXII,70–9 (CSEL, 25, ed. J. Zycha); *Quaestiones in Heptateuchum* VI,10 (*CCSL*, 33, eds J. Fraipont and D. de Bruyne). Compare the quotations of Augustine in *Decretum Gratianum*, second part, causa 23, quaestio 1 and 2 (*Decretum magistri Gratiani*, Corpus iuris canonici, 1), Leipzig 1879: digital https://geschichte.digitale-sammlungen.de/decretum-gratiani/online/angebot (accessed 13 September 2019); C. Baumgartner, 'War', in K. Pollmann and W. Otten (eds), *Oxford guide to the historical reception of Augustine*, 3 (Oxford: Oxford University Press, 2013), pp. 1889–95; J. Brachtendorf, 'Augustinus Friedensethik und Friedenspolitik', in A. Holzem (ed.), *Krieg und Christentum. Religiöse Gewalttheorien in der Kriegserfahrung des Westens* (Paderborn: Ferdinand Schöningh, 2009), pp. 234–53; R. Kany, 'Bella pacata sunt. Von der mittelalterlichen und neuzeitlichen Umdeutung der augustinischen Friedenslehre zu einer Legitimation des Krieges', in F. Sedlmeier and T. Hausmanninger (eds), *Inquire Pacem. Beiträge zu einer Theologie des Friedens* (Augsburg: Sankt Ulrich Verlag, 2004), pp. 106–23; R. Schulz, 'Augustinus und der Krieg', in *Millennium. Jahrbuch zu Kultur und Geschichte des ersten Jahrtausends n. Chr.*, 4 (2008), 93–110; see also the literature in note 4. Augustine of course takes up ideas developed by Cicero.
10 Compare Augustine, *ep*. 138,14 (ed. A. Goldbacher, *S. Augustini Epistulae* [CSEL, 44], Vienna: Verlag der Österreichischen Akademie der Wissenschaften, 1904, p. 140,8–15). Also Tertullian, *Apologeticum* 37,4; 42,3 (*CCSL* 1, ed. E. Dekkers): Christians are in the army and therefore faithful citizens; synod at Arles 314, can. 3 (*CCSL* 148, ed. C. Munier): Christians must not desert the army even at peace times; Eusebius, *h.e.* VIII,4 (GCS NF 6, ed. E. Schwartz, T. Mommsen and F. Winkelmann): Diocletian purges the army from Christians.
11 *CTh* XVI,5,29; XVI,5,42 against heretics, and *CTh* XVI,10,21 against heathens in the army.
12 Compare also Ambrose, *De fide ad Gratianum* II,16 (Fontes Christiani, 47/2, ed. C. Markschies) and *De officiis* I,27; 29; 35 (*CCSL*, 15, ed. M. Testard): on faith and justice in war – Ambrose accepts Christians as soldiers in wars; John Chrysostom, *ep*. 213; 218 (PG 52, 729–732) and Sozomenos, *Historia ecclesiastica* I,8,10f. (GCS, NF 4, ed. G. C. Hansen) on military chaplaincy. However, soldiers are not allowed to become clerics (synods of Rome in 386,

can. 3; Toledo in 400, can 8; Chalcedon in 451, can 7). For further information, see the literature in note 4.
13 Edition: *MGH Poeta* I, ed. E. Dümmler (Berlin: Weidmann, 1881), p. 380f.
14 S. A. Rabe, *Faith, art, and politics at Saint-Riquier. A symbolic vision of Angilbert* (Philadelphia: University of Pennsylvania Press, 1995) – she analyses this poem in ch. 3: 'Dogmatibus Clarus, Principibus Sotius. Angilbert of Saint-Requier', pp. 52–84. Dieter Schaller votes for Paulinus of Aquileia as the author of this poem: D. Schaller, 'Der Dichter des *Carmen de conversione Saxonum*', in G. Bernt, F. Rädle and G. Silagi (eds), *Tradition und Wertung* (Sigmaringen: Jan Thorbecke, 1989), pp. 27–45, reprint in D. Schaller, *Studien zur lateinischen Dichtung des Frühmittelalters* (Stuttgart: Hiersemann, 1995), pp. 313–31; see also D. Schaller, 'Karl der Große im Licht zeitgenössischer politischer Dichtung', in P. Butzer, M. Kerner and W. Oberschelp (eds), *Charlemagne and his heritage* (Turnhout: Brepols, 1997), pp. 194–211; C. Ratkowitsch, 'Das Karlsbild in der lateinischen Großdichtung des Mittelalters', in B. Bastert (ed.), *Karl der Große in den europäischen Literaturen des Mittelalters. Konstruktion eines Mythos* (Tübingen: Max Niemeyer Verlag, 2004), pp. 1–16. Angilbert grew up at the court of Pippin and was a member of Charlemagne's palace chapel, in a relationship with Charles's daughter Berta and in 789 was appointed as abbot of the monastery Saint-Riquier near Amiens. However, Paulinus of Aquileia seems to be the better candidate for this poem, especially in comparison with another poem of Paulinus which was discovered in 1995: D. Schaller, 'Ein Ostercanticum des Paulinus von Aquileia für Karl den Großen. Erstedition und Kommentar', in D. Schaller, *Studien zur lateinischen Dichtung des Frühmittelalters* (Stuttgart: Hiersemann, 1995), pp. 361–98. See also K. Hauck, *Karolingische Taufpfalzen im Spiegel hofnaher Dichtung. Überlegungen zur Ausmalung von Pfalzkirchen, Pfalzen und Reichsklöstern* (Göttingen: Vandenhoeck & Ruprecht, 1985).
15 Rabe, *Faith* (note 14), p. 61. On the Saxon wars in general, see the literature in notes 22–24.
16 Rabe, *Faith* (note 14), p. 67.
17 *Carmen de conversione Saxonum*, ed. E. Dümmler, *MGH Poeta*, I (Berlin: Weidmann, 1881), p. 381–2, lines 40–7 and 56–62: *Hanc Carolus princeps gentem fulgentibus armis / Fortiter adcinctus, galeis cristatus acutis / Arbitri aeterni mira virtute iuvatus / Per varios casus 1 domuit, per mille triumphos / Perque cruoriferos umbos, per tela duelli / Per vim virtutum, per spicula lita cruore / Contrivit, sibimet gladio vibrante subegit / Traxit silviculas ad caeli regna phalanges ...; Postque salutiferi perfusos rore lavacri / Sub patris et geniti, sancti sub flaminis almi / Nomine, quo nostrae constat spes unica vitae / Christicolasque rudes ad caeli sidera misit / Chrismatibus sacro inunxit baptismate lotos / Quo iam fumiferas valeant transcendere flammas / Progeniemque novam Christi perduxit in aulam.* English translation by Rabe, *Faith*, pp. 64–5.
18 Rabe, *Faith*, p. 64.
19 *Ibid.*, p. 68.
20 Compare Alcuin, *ep.* 107 (see the extracts in S. Allott, *Alcuin of York – his life and letters* [York: William Sessons, 1974], *ep.* 59 on pp. 75–6) to Arno of

Salzburg on the necessity of preaching instead of demanding tithes; *ep.* 110 to Charlemagne (in Allott, *ep.* 56 on pp. 72–4) that preaching must come first, namely on the immortality of soul and future life, on eternal punishment and sins and on the Trinity and the full creed, and only afterwards baptism; *ep.* 111 to Charlemagne (in Allott, *ep.* 57 on p. 74) on the necessary voluntary conversion and baptism (*MGH Epp.* IV 2, 160,19f. ed. Dümmler): *Fides quoque, sicut sanctus ait Augustinus, res est voluntaria, non necessaria* (with reference to Augustine, *ep.* 217).

21 Compare Alcuin, *ep.* 6 on the Saxons, Danes, Slavs, Huns (= Avars; in Allott, *ep.* 55 on pp. 71–2); *ep.* 99 (*MGH Epp.* IV 2, 143, 23 ed. Dümmler; in Allott, *ep.* 58 on pp. 74–5) to Paulinus of Aquileia on the Avars: *subiectionem pacificam et christianitatis fidem promittentes*.

22 M. Becher, 'Der Prediger mit eiserner Zunge. Die Unterwerfung und Christianisierung der Sachsen durch Karl den Großen', in H. Kamp and M. Kroker (eds), *Schwertmission. Gewalt und Christianisierung im Mittelalter* (Paderborn: Ferdinand Schöningh, 2013), pp. 23–52.

23 L. Körntgen, 'Heidenkrieg und Bistumsgründung. Glaubensverbreitung als Herrscheraufgabe bei Karolingern und Ottonen', in A. Holzem (ed.), *Krieg und Christentum. Religiöse Gewalttheorien in der Kriegserfahrung des Westens* (Paderborn: Ferdinand Schöningh, 2009), pp. 281–304.

24 J. Ehlers, 'Die Sachsenmission als heilsgeschichtliches Ereignis', in F. J. Felten and N. Jaspert (eds), *Vita Religiosa im Mittelalter* (Berlin: Duncker & Humblot, 1999), pp. 37–53; J. Ehlers, *Die Integration Sachsens in das fränkische Reich* (Göttingen: Vandenhoeck & Ruprecht, 2014).

25 Further related aspects should be taken into consideration but go far beyond a short chapter: the role and importance of Christian mission in general (which was no central aspect in late Antiquity); Christian ideas about conversion, baptism and catechism (What makes a Christian? Is baptism more important than catechism?); Christian thoughts about war (see above notes 4 and 9); Christian thoughts about a Christian emperor or king and his duties, and Christian ideas about measures against paganism, heretics and apostasy.

26 In addition, it was this pope who initiated new missionary activities among the Anglo-Saxons (note 46). On Gregory, compare B. Neil and M. Dal Santo (eds), *Companion to Gregory the Great* (Leiden: Brill, 2013). See also the literature in notes 29, 34 and 36.

27 Translated from original, Kahl, 'Die ersten Jahrhunderte', pp. 62–64.

28 Burchard of Worms, *Decretorum libri* XX (*PL* 140, 537–1058) presents in c. 15 of *De laicis* some paragraphs about rulers as kings and emperors (§ 10–44) which contain some quotations from Gregory's letters (*PG* 140, 896–900), namely to Gennadius, exarch of Ravenna (I,73), to Brunhild (XI,46), to Theoderich of the Franks (XI,47), and to Asclepiodorus (XI,43). This was obviously inspiration for the compiler of the *Decretum Gratiani*, which contains the same quotations of the letter to Gennadius, as well as a quotation from a second letter to this Gennadius (I,72) and from another letter to Brunhild (VIII,4), in the famous chapter on 'just war' (second part, causa 23; see note 9) – all in the context

of the related question (q. 4): *An vindicta sit inferenda?* Letters of Gregory are edited by D. Norberg (*CCSL*, 140 and 140A; Turnhout: Brepols, 1982); an English translation: J. R. C. Martyn, *The Letters of Gregory the Great. Translated with introduction and notes* (Rome: Pontifical Institute of Medieval Studies, 2004).

29 M. Dal Santo, 'Gregory the Great, the empire and the emperor', in B. Neil and M. Dal Santo (eds), *Companion to Gregory the Great* (Leiden: Brill, 2013), pp. 57–81, here p. 68; compare also R. Markus, *Gregory the Great and his world* (Cambridge: Cambridge University Press, 1997), ch. 6: *Christiana respublica*.

30 Gregory, *ep.* I,73 (*CCSL*, 140, 81,8–82,2 ed. Norberg): *Vbi enim meritorum uestrorum loquax non discurrit opinio, quae et bella uos frequenter appetere non desiderio fundendi sanguinis sed dilatandae causa rei publicae, in qua deum coli conspicimus, loqueretur, quatenus christi nomen per subditas gentes fidei praedicatione circumquaque discurreret.* Compare above note 28.

31 D. L. Wilhite, *Ancient African Christianity. An introduction to a unique context and tradition* (London: Routledge, 2017), pp. 301–8; J. Patout Burns and R. M. Jensen (eds), *Christianity in Roman Africa: The development of its practices and beliefs* (Grand Rapids: W. B. Eerdmans, 2014), pp. 80–2.

32 Compare Gregory, *ep.* I,59 to Gennadius; *ep.* VII,5 (*CCSL*, 140, 452.163–6, ed. Norberg) to Patriarch Cyriacus of Constantinople: priests must pray for the emperor, *ut omnipotens deus eorum pedibus barbaras nationes subiciat, longa eis et felicia tempora concedat, quatenus per christianum imperium ea quae in christo est fides regnet.*

33 Gregory, *ep.* I,72 (*CCSL*, 140, 80,5–8 ed. Norberg): *... cum et forensibus bellis aduersariis catholicae ecclesiae pro christiano populo uehementer obsistitis, et ecclesiastica proelia sicut bellatores domini fortiter dimicatis.* He later mentioned that the Donatists in north Africa as well as those bishops who resisted the condemnation of the so-called Three Chapters were heretics and schismatics.

34 C. Ricci, 'Gregory's mission to the barbarians', in B. Neil and M. Dal Santo (eds), *Companion to Gregory the Great* (Leiden: Brill, 2013), pp. 29–56, here pp. 55–6.

35 Markus, *Gregory*, p. 164.

36 Compare J. Richards, *Gregor der Große. Sein Leben – seine Zeit* (Graz: Styria, 1983), pp. 241–4.

37 Gregory, *ep.* IV,26 (*CCSL*, 140, 245,19–22 ed. Norberg).

38 Gregory, *ep.* IV,27 (*CCSL*, 140, 246,2–10 ed. Norberg). See also *ep.* V,38.

39 Richards, *Gregor der Große*, p. 243: 'Eben zu dem Zeitpunkt, als Felix und Cyriacus in Sardinien eintrafen, hatte der militärische Reichsbefehlshaber Zabardas den Barbaricini eine schwere Niederlage beigebracht und bei der Festlegung der Friedensbedingungen darauf bestanden – vielleicht auf Vorschlag der päpstlichen Bevollmächtigten –, dass die Bekehrung zum christlichen Glauben mit eingeschlossen sei.'

40 Gregory, *ep.* IV,25 (*CCSL*, 140, 244,7–8, ed. Norberg): *... quod eo pacto cum barbaricinis facere pacem disponitis, ut eosdem barbaricinos ad christi seruitium adducatis.*

41 Gregory, *ep.* IX,205 (*CCSL*, 140A, 764,29–37, ed. Norberg): *Quos tamen emendare se a talibus atque corrigere nolle reppereris, feruenti comprehendere zelo te uolumus et, siquidem serui sunt, uerberibus cruciatibus que quibus ad emendationem peruenire ualeant, castigare.* See also Gregory, *ep.* XI,12 (congratulation to Spesindeo in converting and baptizing many natives and provincials). Also *ep.* VIII,19 to Agnellus of Terracina about paganism; *ep.* XI,37 to King Aethelbert on destroying pagan temples and persecuting idolatry. See also above note 28.

42 Kahl, 'Die ersten Jahrhunderte', but compare Markus, *Gregory*, p. 81: he 'did not make a sharp distinction'.

43 On this see the contribution of A. Fürst, 'Christliche Friedensethik von Augustinus bis Gregor dem Großen – Religion, Politik und Krieg am Ende der Antike', in G. Beestermöller (ed.), *Friedensethik im frühen Mittelalter: Theologie zwischen Kritik und Legitimation von Gewalt* (Münster: Aschendorff, 2014), pp. 19–52, here pp. 39–44 (although he is not dealing with Gregory's missionary activities); Markus, *Gregory*, pp. 51–67; L. E. von Padberg, *Mission und Christianisierung. Formen und Folgen bei Angelsachsen und Franken im 7. und 8. Jahrhundert* (Stuttgart: Franz Steiner, 1995), pp. 42–6.

44 Gregory, *ep.* I,45 about conversion of Jews in Gaul (*CCSL*, 140, 59,18–20, ed. Norberg): *Dum enim quispiam ad baptismatis fontem non praedicationis suauitate sed necessitate peruenerit, ad pristinam superstitionem remeans inde deterius moritur, unde renatus esse uidebatur.*

45 See note 30.

46 On the wide reception of Gregory among the Anglo-Saxons (Bede) and also the Carolingians, compare C. J. Mews and C. Renkin, 'The legacy of Gregory the Great in the Latin west', in B. Neil and M. J. Dal Santo (eds), *Companion to Gregory the Great* (Leiden: Brill, 2013), pp. 315–41; see also *CCSL*, 140, pp. V–XII on the manuscripts and letter collections. Interestingly the passages quoted above were not taken from those letters which do deal with Gregory's famous initiative to send missionaries to the Anglo-Saxons, where we can detect different estimations on missionary methods. See R. A. Markus, 'Gregory the Great and a papal missionary strategy', in G. J. Cuming (ed.), *The mission of the Church and the propagation of the faith* (Cambridge: Cambridge University Press, 1970), pp. 29–38, about Gregory changing his attitude in the context of his Anglo-Saxon missionary activities. Perhaps this formed the background for Alcuin's critique (see above note 20).

13

'Holy wars'? 'Religious wars'? The perception of religious motives of warfare against non-Christian enemies in ninth-century chronicles

Hans-Werner Goetz

To discuss the perception and comprehension of war and 'the military' within the aims of the current volume, the Christianisation of warfare is an important factor. As a small contribution within this larger frame, I have chosen a very specific theme that nevertheless seems to be typically medieval: the religious (or religiously motivated) war in Carolingian times as it was perceived by contemporary chroniclers of the ninth century (whose convictions need not, of course, be identical with those who waged these wars). My general question, therefore, is: are early medieval wars perceived as 'religious wars'? While we possess a huge number of studies on medieval wars and warfare, including its religious aspects, it may seem astonishing that this question, as far as a concrete religious legitimisation of wars is concerned, has been widely neglected or is discussed controversially.

Some terminological and methodological explications are necessary in advance. In early medieval Christianised society, religious ideas and acts of piety were widespread in all spheres of life, including warfare, in a mutual process: a Christianisation of warfare as well as a militarisation of religious thinking. The 'militarisation of the Church'[1] results necessarily from the Christianisation of the pagan realms (beginning as early as with the late antique Roman Empire and continued in the successor states), a process which inevitably also extends to early medieval warfare. There can be no doubt, as Laury Sarti has shown, that medieval wars could be approved by the Church as early as in Merovingian times,[2] that war, as Thomas Scharff has analysed before, was further Christianised in the Carolingian era[3] and, following the comprehensive study of David Bachrach, in Ottonian times.[4] Bishops and clerics participated in wars and battles,[5] God was expected to intervene in battles and Christ and the saints served as 'assistants in battles'.[6] Consequently, prayers and sacral rites accompanied wars[7] to implore God for help, and the outcomes of battles were interpreted as judgements of

God (or ordeals),[8] while defeats or hostile attacks were perceived as a punishment of sins.[9] All this has been frequently emphasised in pertinent studies and can be assumed to be well known.

Comparisons of contemporary wars with those of the Israelites in the Old Testament,[10] the metaphorical application of a martial terminology to monks and saints who are frequently even comprehended as 'warriors of Christ' ('milites Christi')[11] in religious texts, the veneration of military saints (such as Victor or Maurice),[12] or the comprehension of Christian life as such and particularly monastic life as a constant fight against the devil further complete this picture and contribute to a 'Christianisation of war'[13] and a 'militarisation of "the Holy"'.[14] Other studies have expressly emphasised a close relation between Christianity and violence.[15] All this is *not* an expression of a developing 'military society', but of one already established and integrated into Christian rule. It shows that medieval wars were constantly religiously 'undergirded' or 'piously waged'. Decidedly exaggerating this fact, Notker Balbulus lets Charlemagne, on his way to the conquest of Pavia, command the erection of a complete small stone church, decorated with pictures, within a few hours.[16]

It seems small wonder that 'Holy War' has become a current expression for medieval warfare[17] as early as in the early Middle Ages (as for the early 'Reconquista' by Alexander Bronisch),[18] although the term is more often restricted to the times of the Crusades and beyond.[19] However, here we face a great terminological problem, because in medieval nomenclature no conceptual equivalent for a 'holy (or sacred) war' ('bellum sacrum' or 'bellum sanctum') exists,[20] while a 'bellum iustum' is more or less a precondition of each medieval war,[21] but not necessarily religiously motivated.

These circumstances call for a more specific definition of the term: 'Holy war' is a modern artificial term, dependent on the respective definition, but used far from unequivocally.[22] How, then, can it be defined? When Carl Erdmann, in his fundamental study on the concept of the Crusades, conceives a 'holy war' as 'each war that is regarded as a religious action or as being related somehow else to religion',[23] there would be no medieval war that was *not* 'holy' (as Erdmann himself realises[24] in order to distinguish the Crusades as a completely different dimension).[25] However, Bronisch's definition of a 'holy war' as a war that is ordered by God out of divine providence, according to the examples of the Old Testament,[26] is equally problematic, because we can hardly find any medieval war where this is explicitly confirmed. When, in contrast, Helen Nicholson thinks that '"Holy war", in Christian terms, was war against the enemies of Christendom',[27] every war against non-Christians would be 'holy' (which is not the impression we get from our sources). In medieval terms, every war seems somehow religious, but almost none is 'holy'.

Religious allusions are characteristic of every war including wars among Christians which may be perceived as being 'just', but cannot be fought for the sake of faith. When Nithard, a partisan of Charles the Bald and far from being impartial, reports on the civil war between the sons of Louis the Pious, he lets Charles's followers reassure their king that he could rely on their and God's aid, because his cause was just;[28] before the battle, Charles went to Saint-Denis to implore God's help.[29] Later, he and Louis sent envoys who should con*jure* Lothar to remember the Almighty God and give peace to his brothers and the whole Church; otherwise, with their activities being just, they could rely on God's assistance.[30] When this turned out to be of no avail, they were ready to fight 'against their will' and challenged Lothar to face up to 'the judgement of the Almighty God'.[31] After their victory, the bishops of the victorious party hastened to confirm that the allies had fought exclusively for justice and equity which, as they thought, was manifestly confirmed by God's judgement; thus everyone involved was God's innocent instrument.[32] According to the Annals of Fulda, the three brothers even deliberately began the battle (of Fontenay) in order to seek God's judgement therein.[33] Certainly, this fratricidal war was a particularly delicate affair that had to be specifically legitimised. Nevertheless, it is remarkable that a justification of the just party was effected by all religious arguments that were possible, although it was clearly *not* a fight for one's faith.

When, some thirty years later, Charles the Bald attacked the realm of his nephew Louis the Younger, the young king, according to the Annals of Fulda, similarly admonished his uncle to keep peace, since it was forbidden to wage war even against foreign peoples unless they had refused peace, and he reminded him of their kinship and his inheritance, and of his promises on oath to his father, and warned him against the inherent danger for the Christian people: God granted victory independently of the dimension of the armies.[34] The chronicler comments on Louis's victory with the words: 'Without any doubt this battle against Charles has been fought from heaven.'[35] Religious allusions in these two examples show clearly (and many more would confirm this impression) that in Carolingian times every war – even those between relatives – was perceived under religious auspices and that wars were interpreted according to religious criteria, thus demonstrating a Christianisation of warfare as a whole.

However, precisely because this applies to every war it still does not make it a 'religious war'. Such a classification calls for a subtler definition and should be restricted to wars with explicitly religious motives:[36] to wars that are led for the sake of one's own faith.[37] At least this is what I shall understand by this term in this chapter, in order to avoid confusion. In this sense, however, wars against other Christians can be considered to be just and rely on God's help, but they can never be waged for the sake of faith. Consequently a 'religious war' can be led exclusively against enemies of a different faith (who, in medieval terms, are not merely non-Christians, but 'unbelievers', *infideles*). Constant hostile attitudes towards such 'unbelievers' provide a fertile breeding ground for wars against them in a Christian society. Nevertheless, since the motive is decisive, not every war against members of other religions is necessarily perceived as a 'religious war' either. Ninth-century chroniclers (and warriors) are well aware of their enemies being non-Christians, but often enough this is not particularly emphasised, and it usually does not represent the reason for a war. Thus, to be classified as a 'religious war' three preconditions should be fulfilled: they should be described, interpreted and justified by religious elements, directed towards non-Christians, *and* have religious motives. Consequently, my initial question ought to be refined: (how far) are wars against non-Christians in the ninth century perceived as 'religious wars' waged for the sake of faith; that is, in a wider spectrum, is Christianity a reason for warfare?

In the following, I shall briefly recall the very different assessments in current research concerning religious motives, on the basis of Charlemagne's Saxon and Hispanic wars, and subsequently ask whether medieval authors of the Carolingian period emphasised and perceived such religious motives (while they certainly perceived religious features), through two examples: the defensive warfare against Viking attacks in Carolingian chronicles and the (defensive and aggressive) wars in northern Spain in the Asturian chronicles.

For a long time, Charlemagne's Saxon campaigns have been regarded as religious wars (and were indubitably interpreted this way in retrospect even by Saxon authors, such as Widukind of Corvey). Recently, however, such a classification has been contested, because the oldest, more or less contemporary source, the Frankish Royal Annals, does not mention such a motive during the first years of warfare.[38] Nevertheless, Charlemagne's very first attack resulted in the destruction of the pagan sacred site at the *Eresburg*,[39] and there can be no doubt that the conversion of the Saxons and the Christianisation of Saxony soon became a primary goal in the course of political conquest.

Conversely, in a recent article from 2016,[40] Samuel Ottewil-Soulsby still pre-assumes that Charlemagne's wars were religiously motivated and he attempts to demonstrate that his Spanish campaign against the Saracens (the only case for which no religious motives have been claimed)[41] has equally to be interpreted as religious warfare, rightly defined by himself as a war where 'one of the major stated or implied aims of the parties involved is the protection and propagation of their faith'.[42] However, his five arguments are not convincing from the point of view of medieval perceptions: the fact that the Saracens are recognised and judged as non-Christians[43] is a precondition of a religious war, but does not testify to religious motives; the fact that Pope Hadrian I, in his letter to Charlemagne, compares the Spanish campaign with the destruction of the Egyptian Pharaoh in the Red Sea,[44] confers an exegetical interpretation and relevance to the episode, but it does not say anything about the motives nor does it necessarily describe Charlemagne's own motives;[45] furthermore, it is applicable (and applied) to every war.[46] The same applies even more to a war liturgy:[47] people prayed to God for assistance before every war.[48] Similarly, the granting of charters and donations to individual followers[49] is a completely normal procedure and not at all a proof of a religious war. In any case, Charlemagne does not merely become a defender of faith because the Saracens are the enemies of the Christians.[50] None of the proffered arguments is convincing and the conclusion 'that from the early 780s Charlemagne portrayed his wars in Spain as in aid of protecting Christians against a common non-Christian enemy' and that 'religion was an important factor',[51] is by no means conclusive. These arguments testify to religious interpretations, but not to a religious war as Ottewill-Soulsby himself defines it. Moreover, Charlemagne occupied the Saracen town of Zaragoza/Saragossa and took hostages, whereas he destroyed the (Christian) Basque town of Pamplona completely![52] Thus, in this case, his actions against rebelling Christians seem to be even harsher than against the non-Christian Saracens. Religious motives of the campaigns against the Muslims certainly cannot be excluded, but they must by no means be *a priori* assumed.

What do the sources really reveal? My first case study is the Christian defence against the attacks of the pagan Vikings in the ninth century where we find greatly diverging perceptions. If we look to the *Annales Vedastini*, the Vikings are merely called *Nortmanni* throughout and are simply (very cruel) enemies whose attacks had to be repelled. They are never even classified as pagans (although the authors, of course, knew this fact).[53] In contrast, the *Annales Xantenses* lay clear emphasis on the religious difference. In the very first encounter 'pagans raided the Christians in many places',[54] and henceforth the Vikings are classified as *gentiles*[55] or *pagani*[56] who afflicted the Christians: 'Paganity habitually inflicted damage on Christianity from the north';[57] in this sentence, the collective nouns (*gentilitas*, *Christianitas*) make a single attack even resemble a *kind* of 'clash of religions'. The *Annals of Fulda*, in their earlier parts, again, report frequently on Viking raids without religious allusions. It is not until 854 that the author interprets the quarrel within the Danish royal family that nearly extinguished all its members as God's revenge for the sacrileges against his saints.[58] We have to wait nearly a further twenty years until 873 for the next pertinent report when the inhabitants of sites in the county of Albdag refused to pay tribute to the Viking leader Hruodolf and his men who threatened to kill them all, 'ignorant of the revenge from heaven that was to pursue him', while the Christians defended themselves 'by invoking the name of God who had liberated them frequently from their enemies'.[59] An allegedly clear sign of religious motives is the speech with which King Arnulf addressed his army before the battle against the marauding Vikings at the river Dyle in 891: the king referred to 'those who worship God' (thus separating the Christians from the pagan Vikings) 'who had always been invincible while defending their country under God's grace', and he recalled how those enemies, raging in a most pagan manner, had shed the pious blood of their 'parents', destroyed God's churches in their country and killed His high-ranking priests.[60] The Frankish victory is interpreted accordingly: 'By God's assisting grace the victory fell to the Christians.'[61] Thus, Arnulf interprets the pending battle as a fight for God to avenge the destruction of churches and priests *as well as* for their country and their ancestors whose bloodshed should be avenged. Political and religious motives intertwine in his argument. This is indeed a fight for God and faith, although not necessarily a 'holy war' against pagans, but concentrating on concrete, defensive reasons. Thus, chroniclers (sometimes) refer to religious motives as well as religious aid (by God), together with political motives, particularly to incite a spirit of defence against the furiously attacking pagans, but they are not really represented much differently from reports on wars between Christians. It is still confidence in God and divine aid that led to victories and Christian sins that prevented them.

My second case study is based on the so-called *Chronicles of Alfonso III* of Asturia and their reports on military encounters with the Saracens.[62] According to Bronisch, the early 'Reconquista' is a 'holy war' in the sense that it was ordered and led by God.[63] Again, however, allusions to faith remain scarce (and are mostly concealed in biblical verses or comparisons) with most encounters recorded in political rather than religious terms. When, in the very beginning, the defeat of the Visigothic King Roderick by the invading Arabs is interpreted as a divine punishment for abandoning God,[64] this would be the precise opposite of a 'religious war' fought for one's faith.[65] Following on from that, the chroniclers frequently report on victories over the 'Chaldaeans' without explicitly mentioning their faith (which, however, is more or less inherent in this term).[66] Often enough, the Muslims were the aggressors.[67] Where the Asturians penetrated Islamic territories it seems conspicuous that even after their victories they quickly returned to their own countries:[68] obviously conquest was not their aim (or within their capabilities).[69] The Asturian kings even received Muslim refugees (and if they were fought, this was not the result of their faith but rather of their repeated rebellions).[70] Moreover, there were times of negotiations and peace.[71] It is equally noticeable that by *Spania* all the authors throughout do not mean their own *patria* (Asturias), but the Islamic territory.[72]

Where faith is concerned, we find these rather traditional allusions. Sometimes (but not often) the 'Christians' are adversaries of the Saracens or Chaldaeans,[73] making it clear that the authors are well aware of the religious difference without emphasising it. It seems more remarkable that the victories of the Asturians are achieved by God's help,[74] although, again, as emphasised above, this would also be possible in any other war. The only clearer allusion is the well-known episode concerning Pelayo, the founder of the Asturian kingdom in the Pyrenees, and the following Battle of Cavadonga more than a century and a half before the chronicle was written.[75] In the famous (fictitious) dialogue between Pelayo and the first known Mozarab bishop, Oppa, handed down only in the Versio Rotensis, it is ironically the bishop who pleads for subjection under the Saracens, whereas the king wants to fight for liberty, recalling the biblical verse[76] that God lets the church grow large again from a mustard seed[77] (that is, relying on His help against a superior enemy).[78] Pinning all his hope on Christ, the king prophesies that his small mountain might be the starting point for the welfare of Spain and the recuperation of the army of the Visigothic people, as a fulfilment of David's prophecy through Pelayo's people.[79] The *Chronicle of Albelda*, although omitting the dialogue between Pelayo and Oppa, goes one step further by interpreting the death of the Saracen leader Munnuza in this battle as the liberation of the Christian people: '*Sicque ex tunc reddita est libertas populo Xp(ist)iano.*'[80] Obviously, Pelayo's victory is stylised as a defence of Christianity and a model for the future.

For the moment, Pelayo's victories achieved no more than securing the small Christian country, although the prophecies may use a past fiction in order to summon the present (the age of Alfonso III) to a reconquest of Islamic Spain. However, first, such a concept is *not* pursued like a red thread through the whole chronicle; second, there are no direct indications of a religious war under Pelayo's successors up to Alfonso III.[81] In a poem about the king, his campaigns against Basques and Arabs are mentioned in the same breath, but here his victories are labelled *sacra uictoria* through Christ's help.[82] Third, nevertheless, even these campaigns against non-Christian enemies resemble political rather than religious wars: the authors do not lay special emphasis on the difference in religion, let alone religious motives. Thus, it may be significant that the most distinct indication of religion is retrospective and refers back to the very beginnings of the Asturian kingdoms. However, even if the prophecies are a plea to the present to reconquer the whole country (and note: the *country*!) from the Saracens, this resembles a political reconquest rather than a religious one that is at the most implied by the evident fact that it is a fight against unbelievers.

This seems different in the so-called *Prophetical Chronicle*[83] which embeds the prophecy in the fulfilment of the Old Testament: it begins with an alleged quotation of the prophet Ezekiel who called on the Israelites to turn against Ishmael (while identifying Gog with the Goths),[84] and it predicts that the audaciousness of the enemies will be completely destroyed within 170 years, returning peace to the Church, and hopes that Alfonso (III) will reign over all of Spain.[85] At the end, the author expects revenge on the Saracens the very next year to liberate the children of God from the power of the devil and the yoke of the Ishmaelites.[86] This is not yet a 'holy war', but nevertheless a prophecy directed against the Saracens by applying a prophecy from the Old Testament to their imminent destruction. However, it is small wonder that this chronicle was not continued.

From the perspective of the Christianisation of warfare under the specific aspect of 'religious wars', 'militarisation' resembles not so much (as with James and Sarti) a lack of differentiation between the military and the civil,[87] but rather a lack of differentiation between religion and politics in warfare. Moreover, regarding the religious connotations of early medieval wars, first, we have to distinguish sharply between religious activities in and religious interpretations of these wars on the one hand and genuine 'religious wars' as being motivated by faith on the other, that is, whether faith is (or is perceived as) the decisive motive of a war, an aspect that seems to have been widely neglected by former research. There can be no doubt that Carolingian chroniclers perceived warfare from a political as well as a religious perspective – and it would be anachronistic to contrast both aspects as mutually exclusive. Religious allusions, actions and interpretations permeate the pertinent reports (and certainly also warfare itself) throughout. Thus, a Christian 'religionisation' of warfare cannot be overlooked. However, such religious characterisations can refer to every (Christian) war. They are particularly applied where a thorough legitimation seems necessary. Nevertheless, they are seldom predominant and almost always intermingled with political motives.

Second, the authors thus do not make any difference between wars against Christians and those against unbelievers as far as their religious allusions and interpretations are concerned, and they could not even have expressed such a distinction terminologically: 'religious war' and 'holy war' are modern, not medieval classifications, although every war is conducted under religious auspices.

Finally, not every war against 'unbelievers' is stylised as a 'religious war' either. In fact, religious motives in the sense of fighting for the sake of faith occur but are very rare and refer to cases of defence rather than conquest. 'Religious war' (in this sense) is not something beyond early medieval imagination (and, in any case, not an invention of the Crusade era, which rather seems to be a consequence of such ideas), but it is far from being predominant.

It is self-evident that my few examples should be reappraised by an overall enquiry into this theme. So far, it seems that wars are perceived (and conducted) throughout under religious perspectives. If militarisation applies to society as a whole,[88] in a Christian society war is being (and has to be) 'Christianised'. Nevertheless, however unquestionable Christianisation of warfare was in Carolingian times, this does not go to the extent of perceiving all wars, particularly against non-Christians, as 'religious wars' on principle in the sense of being waged for the sake of faith.

Notes

This chapter is based on another paper given at the *51. Deutsche Historikertag* (Hamburg, September 2016), where I concentrated on the discussion of the term and the religious background while the case studies on a historiographical perception of religious wars ranged in a wider chronological frame from Gregory of Tours until the First Crusade. This paper has been published under the title '"Glaubenskriege"? Die Kriege der Christen gegen Andersgläubige in der früh- und hochmittelalterlichen Wahrnehmung', *Frühmittelalterliche Studien* 53 (2019), 67–114. In contrast, the present chapter, according to this volume, is focused on the relevance of religious motives for military wars.

1 Thus F. Prinz, *Klerus und Krieg im früheren Mittelalter. Untersuchungen zur Rolle der Kirche beim Aufbau der Königsherrschaft*, Monographien zur Geschichte des Mittelalters, 2 (Stuttgart: Hiersemann, 1971), p. 197.
2 L. Sarti, *Perceiving war and the military in early Christian Gaul (ca. 400–700 A.D.)*, Brill's Series on the Early Middle Ages, 22 (Leiden: Brill, 2013), particularly ch. 6, pp. 315–57.
3 T. Scharff, *Die Kämpfe der Herrscher und der Heiligen. Krieg und historische Erinnerung in der Karolingerzeit*, Symbolische Kommunikation in der Vormoderne. Studien zur Geschichte, Literatur und Kunst (Darmstadt: Wissenschaftliche Buchgesellschaft, 2002), who embeds the theme in the wider perspective of war in general.
4 D. S. Bachrach, *Religion and the conduct of war, c. 300–1215*, Warfare in History (Woodbridge: Boydell, 2003).
5 Compare Prinz, *Klerus und Krieg*; L. Auer, 'Der Kriegsdienst des Klerus unter den sächsischen Kaisern', *Mitteilungen des Instituts für Österreichische Geschichtsforschung*, 79 (1971), 316–407, and *ibid.*, 80 (1972), 48–70; for later periods, see T. Reuter, '*Episcopi cum sua militia*. The prelate as warrior in the early Staufer era', in T. Reuter (ed.), *Warriors and churchmen in the high Middle Ages. Essays presented to Karl Leyser* (London: Hambledon, 1992), pp. 79–94; E.-D. Hehl, *Kirche und Krieg im 12. Jahrhundert. Studien zu kanonischem Recht und politischer Wirklichkeit*, Monographien zur Geschichte des Mittelalters, 19 (Stuttgart: Hiersemann 1980); T. Haas, *Geistliche als Kreuzfahrer. Der Klerus im*

Konflikt zwischen Orient und Okzident 1095–1221, Heidelberg Transcultural Studies, 3 (Heidelberg: Winter 2012).

6 Compare F. Graus, 'Der Heilige als Schlachtenhelfer – Zur Nationalisierung einer Wundererzählung in der mittelalterlichen Chronistik', in K.-U. Jäschke and R. Wenskus (eds), *Festschrift für Helmut Beumann zum 65. Geburtstag* (Sigmaringen: Thorbecke, 1977), pp. 330–48; Scharff, *Kämpfe der Herrscher*, pp. 175–8.

7 See Bachrach, *Religion and the conduct of war*.

8 Compare R. Schieffer, 'Iudicium Dei. Kriege als Gottesurteile', in K. Schreiner (ed., with the collaboration of E. Müller-Luckner), *Heilige Kriege. Religiöse Begründungen militärischer Gewaltanwendung. Judentum, Christentum und Islam im Vergleich*, Schriften des Historischen Kollegs. Kolloquien, 78 (Munich: Oldenbourg, 2008), pp. 219–28.

9 See M. Clauss, *Kriegsniederlagen im Mittelalter. Darstellung – Deutung – Bewältigung*, Krieg in der Geschichte, 54 (Paderborn: Schöningh, 2010), particularly pp. 187–213.

10 See A. P. Bronisch, *Reconquista und Heiliger Krieg. Die Deutung des Krieges im christlichen Spanien von den Westgoten bis ins frühe 12. Jahrhundert*, Spanische Forschungen der Görresgesellschaft. Zweite Reihe, 35 (Münster: Aschendorff 1998), pp. 224–6.

11 Compare Scharff, *Kämpfe der Herrscher*, pp. 33–6; Sarti, *Perceiving war*, pp. 330–40; for the High Middle Ages, K. A. Smith, *War and the making of medieval monastic culture*, Studies in the History of Medieval Religion, 37 (Woodbridge: Boydell 2011). Compare also A. von Harnack, *Militia Christi. Die christliche Religion und der Soldatenstand in den ersten drei Jahrhunderten* (Tübingen: Mohr, 1905; repr. Darmstadt: Wissenschaftliche Buchgesellschaft, 1963).

12 Compare Sarti, *Perceiving war*, pp. 335–40; for the High Middle Ages, E. Dehoux, *Saints guerriers. Georges, Guillaume, Maurice et Michel dans la France médiévale (XIe-XIIIe siècle)*, Histoire (Rennes: Presses universitaires, 2014).

13 Thus T. Scharff, 'Karolingerzeitliche Vorstellungen vom Krieg vor dem Hintergrund der romanisch-germanischen Kultursynthese', in D. Hägermann, W. Haubrichs and J. Jarnut (eds, with the collaboration of C. Giefers), *Akkulturation. Probleme einer germanisch-romanischen Kultursynthese in Spätantike und frühem Mittelalter*, RGA Ergänzungsbände, 41 (Berlin: De Gruyter, 2004), pp. 473–90, here pp. 477–9.

14 Thus *ibid.*, pp. 479–85.

15 Compare A. Holzem (ed.), *Krieg und Christentum. Religiöse Gewalttheorien in der Kriegserfahrung des Westens*, Krieg in der Geschichte, 50 (Paderborn: Schöningh, 2009); G. Althoff, *'Selig sind, die Verfolgung ausüben'. Päpste und Gewalt im Hochmittelalter* (Darmstadt: Wissenschaftliche Buchgesellschaft, 2013); most recently Ph. Buc, *Holy war, martyrdom, and terror. Christianity, violence, and the west, ca. 70 C.E. to the Iraq War* (Philadelphia: University of Pennsylvania Press, 2015); Ph. Buc, 'Crusade and eschatology. Holy War fostered and inhibited', *Mitteilungen des Instituts für Österreichische Geschichtsforschung*, 125 (2017),

304–39. Differently, A. Angenendt, *Toleranz und Gewalt. Das Christentum zwischen Bibel und Schwert* (fifth edn, Münster: Aschendorff, 2009).

16 Notker Balbulus, *Gesta Karoli Magni*, 14, ed. H. F. Haefele, *MGH SRG, n.s.*, 12 (Munich: MGH, second edn, 1980), pp. 84f.

17 Compare T. P. Murphy (ed.), *The Holy War* (Columbus: Ohio State University Press, 1976); Bronisch, *Reconquista and Heiliger Krieg*; Schreiner (Ed.), *Heilige Kriege*; recently B. Gübele, *Deus vult, Deus vult. Der christliche heilige Krieg im Früh- und Hochmittelalter*, Mittelalter-Forschungen, 54 (Ostfildern: Thorbecke, 2018).

18 Bronisch, *Reconquista and Heiliger Krieg*. Bronisch's use of the term has not remained without contradiction; compare P. Henriet, 'L'idéologie de guerre sainte dans le haut Moyen Âge hispanique', *Francia*, 29 (2002), 171–220, and the counterplea of A. P. Bronisch, '"Reconquista und Heiliger Krieg". Eine kurze Entgegnung auf eine Kritik von Patrick Henriet', *ibid.*, 31 (2004), pp. 199–206.

19 Thus already C. Erdmann, *Die Entstehung des Kreuzzugsgedankens*, Forschungen zur Kirchen- und Geistesgeschichte, 6 (Stuttgart: Kohlhammer, 1935; repr. Darmstadt: Wissenschaftliche Buchgesellschaft, 1974); see also H. E. J. Cowdrey, 'The genesis of the crusades. The springs of western ideas of Holy War', in Murphy (ed.), *Holy War*, pp. 9–32. J. Phillips entitles his *A modern history of the crusades* (London: Randam House, 2009), *Holy warriors*, but leaves this title unexplained.

20 For the few references that all point in different directions (and not to a 'religious war'), compare E.-D. Hehl, 'Heiliger Krieg – eine Schimäre? Überlegungen zur Kanonistik und Politik des 12. und 13. Jahrhunderts', in Holzem (ed.), *Krieg und Christentum*, pp. 323–40, here p. 324; Goetz, 'Glaubenskriege', p. 76.

21 Compare Russell, for high medieval canon law and theology, Semmler for the early Middle Ages.

22 See Bronisch, *Reconquista*, pp. 220f. Comprehensively discussing former definitions: Gübele, *Deus vult*, pp. 13–23.

23 Erdmann, *Entstehung*, p. 1: 'heiliger Krieg ... ist jeder Krieg ... der als religiöse Handlung aufgefaßt oder sonst zur Religion in eine direkte Beziehung gesetzt wird'.

24 *Ibid.*: 'Auf dieser Stufe gibt es keinen Unterschied zwischen heiligem und profanem Krieg, vielmehr ist jeder Krieg als solcher heilig, da er eine Handlung des Volkes und das Volksganze Träger der Religion ist.'

25 *Ibid.*, p. 26.

26 Bronisch, *Reconquista*, p. 226. Similarly, H.-H. Kortüm, *Kriege und Krieger, 500–1500* (Stuttgart: Kohlhammer, 2010), pp. 109f: a war is holy 'if God wants it' (obviously thinking of the Crusade sermon of Pope Urban II).

27 H. Nicholson, *Medieval warfare. Theory and practice of war in Europe 300–1500* (Basingstoke: Palgrave Macmillan, 2004), p. 26.

28 Nithard, *Historiae*, II,5, ed. E. Müller, *MGH SRG*, 44 (Hanover: Weidmann, 1907), p. 19: '*sin aliter, fretus iusticia ac per hoc auxilio divino suorumque fidelium et, quicquid regni pater suus amborumque fidelium consensu illi dederat, obtinere omni virtute non neglegat*'.

29 *Ibid.*, II,6, p. 20. Envoys from Aquitania who arrived one day before Easter, bringing gold, gems and a crown, were interpreted as being led '*nutu divino*' (*ibid.*, II,8, p. 22).
30 *Ibid.*, II,9, p. 24: '*insuper obsecrent, ut memor sit Dei omnipotentis et concedat pacem fratribus suis universeque ecclesiae Dei. ... sin aliter, aiebant se divino ex munere suffragium absque dubio sperare posse, si omne quod iustum est vellent.*' The same conjuration was repeated before the Battle of Fontenay (*ibid.*, II,10, pp. 25f).
31 *Ibid.*, p. 27: '*aut nosset illos in crastinum ... ad omnipotentis Dei iudicium, quod illis absque illorum voluntate mandaverat, esse venturos*'.
32 *Ibid.*, III,1, p. 28: '*Quam ob rem unanimes ad concilium omnes episcopi confluunt, inventumque in conventu publico est, quod pro sola iusticia et aequitate decertaverint et hoc Dei iuditio manifestum effectum sit ac per hoc inmunis omnis Dei minister in hoc negotio haberi.*'
33 *Annales Fuldenses*, a. 841, ed. F. Kurze, *MGH SRG*, 7 (Hanover: Hahn, 1891), p. 32: '*ferro decernendum et Dei iudicio causam examinandam decreverunt*'.
34 *Ibid.*, a. 876, p. 87: '"*Cur ascendisti ad bellandum contra me? quandoquidem nec exteris gentibus bellum est (antiquo populo penitus) inferre praeceptum, nisi pacem oblatam respuerint. Revertere, quaeso, pacifice in regnum tuum et esto contentus gloriae tuae et noli regnum nobis a genitore nostro iure haereditario derelictum more tyrannico invadere et iura propinquitatis, quae inter nos naturaliter existunt, huiuscemodi factionibus violare. Memento etiam sacramentorum (tuorum), quae patri meo non semel neque bis praestitisti; simulque considera periculum christianae plebis, si in hac pertinacia irrevocabiliter persistere volueris. Esto, forsitan confidis in multitudine exercitus tui, quem de diversis locis conduxisti, et ideo te bella movere delectat. Quare ergo non cogitas, quia 'apud Deum impossibile non est liberare in multis et in paucis'* (1. Macc 3,18)? *Refrena igitur animum tuum ab huiuscemodi appetitu, quoniam ea, quae te peragere arbitraris, qualem exitum habeant, penitus ignoras*"'.
35 *Ibid.*, p. 89: '*In hoc certamine contra Karolum procul dubio caelitus dimicatum est.*'
36 Compare J. Burkhardt, 'Religionskrieg', *Theologische Realenzyklopädie*, 28 (1997), 681–7, who defines a 'religious war' as a war where religion has any impact on the character of warfare or on the motives of the participants. Since the first criterion applies to every war, the motives actually are the decisive element; see also F. W. Graf, 'Sakralisierung von Kriegen. Begriffs- und problemgeschichtliche Erwägungen', in Schreiner, *Heilige*, pp. 1–30, particularly pp. 13–23.
37 While a historian of Early Modern Europe, K. Repgen, 'Was ist ein Religionskrieg?' *Zeitschrift für Kirchengeschichte*, 97 (1986), 334–49, denies the existence of religious wars in this sense in the Middle Ages, another historian of that period, M. Pohlig, 'Religiöse Gewalt? Begriffliche Überlegungen an Beispielen des konfessionellen Zeitalters', *Saeculum*, 65 (2015), 115–34, here 124–9, defines the term using five criteria, of which four would apply very well to the Middle Ages: the conviction that one's own religion is the only true faith, the fact that religion

38 Compare M. Becher, 'Der Prediger mit eiserner Zunge. Die Unterwerfung und Christianisierung der Sachsen durch Karl den Großen', in H. Kamp and M. Kroker (eds), *Schwertmission. Gewalt und Christianisierung im Mittelalter* (Paderborn: Schöningh, 2013), pp. 23–52; W. Hartmann, 'Heidenkrieg bei Karl dem Großen?' in G. Beestermöller (ed.), *Friedensethik im frühen Mittelalter. Theologie zwischen Kritik und Legitimation von Gewalt*, Studien zur Friedensethik, 46 (Baden-Baden: Nomos, 2014), pp. 149–74.
39 See B. S. Bachrach, *Charlemagne's early campaigns (768–777). A diplomatic and military analysis*, History of Warfare, 82 (Leiden: Brill, 2013), pp. 230–9.
40 S. Ottewill-Soulsby, '"Those same cursed Saracens". Charlemagne's campaigns in the Iberian Peninsula as religious warfare', *Journal of Medieval History*, 42 (2016), 405–28.
41 Compare A. T. Hack, 'Karl der Große, Hadrian I. und die Muslime in Spanien. Weshalb man einen Krieg führt und wie man ihn legitimiert', in W. Hartmann and K. Herbers (eds), *Die Faszination der Papstgeschichte. Neue Zugänge zum frühen und hohen Mittelalter*, Forschungen zur Kaiser- und Papstgeschichte des Mittelalters. Beihefte zu J. F. Böhmer, Regesta imperii, 28 (Cologne: Böhlau, 2008), pp. 29–54, who pleads for a war of conquest; K. Herbers, *Europa. Christen und Muslime in Kontakt und Konfrontation. Italien und Spanien im langen 9. Jahrhundert*, Abhandlungen der Geistes- und sozialwissenschaftlichen Klasse 2016, 2 (Mainz: Akademie der Wissenschaften und der Literatur Mainz, 2016), p. 24.
42 Ottewill-Soulsby, 'Those same cursed Saracens', p. 406. Such a motive is expressed, again in retrospect, by the so-called Astronomus, *Vita Hludowici imperatoris*, 1, ed. E. Tremp, *MGH SRG*, 64 (Hanover: Hahn, 1995), p. 286, who claims that Charlemagne wished to help the Church that was oppressed by the pagans, since it was his intention to lead all enemies of the Christian name in whatever way to the acknowledgment of the truth (*ibid.*, p. 284).
43 Ottewill-Soulsby, 'Those same cursed Saracens', pp. 407–12. Compare *ibid.*, p. 412, in a kind of 'negative' argumentation: 'Charlemagne did not need to conceive of Islam as a faith in order to wage holy war upon its adherents.'
44 *Ibid.*, pp. 414–16.
45 If Charlemagne considers the campaign defensive warfare, this is testified to only by the papal letter of response. According to Hack, 'Karl der Große', pp. 35f and 54, this is in contrast to the facts, the more so as the so-called *Annals of Einhard* represent Charlemagne's campaigns as a war of aggression (*ibid.*, pp. 33–5).
46 Compare, for example, *Vita Athanasii episcopi Neapolitani*, 7, ed. G. Waitz, *MGH SRL* (Hanover: Hahn 1878), p. 446, concerning the defence of the Saracens by the Emperor Louis II: '*Sed Deus, qui subvertit Pharaonem, confregit et illorum superbiam et in fugam versi sunt.*'

47 Ottewill-Soulsby, 'Those same cursed Saracens', pp. 416–19.
48 Compare Charlemagne's letter to his wife Fastrada during the war against the Avars (Alcuin, *Epistulae*, ep. 20, ed. E. Dümmler, *MGH Epp.* 4 (Berlin: Weidmann, 1895, pp. 528f).
49 Ottewill-Soulsby, 'Those same cursed Saracens', pp. 419–21. Some of the recipients bear Arabic names which, according to Ottewill-Soulsby, is a misconception of the scribes. However, Charles may have rewarded Saracen (or Mozarab) allies by these donations, which would be a convincing argument against a religious war.
50 Thus *ibid.*, p. 419.
51 *Ibid.*, p. 421. Charlemagne himself considered heretical schisms, as Ottewill-Soulsby (*ibid.*, pp. 424f) himself observes, more serious than threats from outside.
52 Compare *Annales regni Francorum*, a. 778, p. 50.
53 Their paganism is expressed only indirectly by contrasting them with the Christians; for example, when the Vikings 'slaughtered' the Christian people (*Annales Vedastini*, a. 880, ed. B. von Simson, *MGH SRG*, 12 (Hanover: Hahn, 1909), p. 48: '*die noctuque non cessant aecclesias igne cremari populumque Christianum iugulari*') or when 'they did not cease to capture and kill the Christian people' (*ibid.*, a. 884, p. 54: '*Nortmanni vero non cessant captivari atque interfici populum Christianum*') who 'were plundered to destruction' (*ibid.*, p. 55: '*videntes populum Christianum usque ad internitationem devastari*'), or when the Christians fought bravely and victoriously against them (*ibid.*, a. 885, p. 59). The death of margrave Henry delighted the Danes and pained the Christians (*ibid.*, a. 886, p. 61). It is only by such indirect expressions that the religious difference shines through the text.
54 *Annales Xantenses*, a. 845, p. 14: '*Eodem anno multis in locis gentiles Christianos invaserunt.*'
55 *Ibid.*, p. 15 (three times, also: '*cum omni populo gentilium*'); a. 848, p. 16 ('*et gentiles Christianis, ut consueverant, nocuerunt*').
56 *Ibid.*, a. 862, p. 20 ('*et desolatio paganorum per regna nostra*'); a. 864, p. 20 ('*pagani sepe iam dicti aecclesiam undique vastantes*'); a. 867, p. 25 ('*bellum inter Gallos et paganos geritur in Gallia*'); a. 869, p. 27 ('*sepissime paganorum infestationem sustinens*'). While the first part of the annals (or the first author) exclusively uses the term '*gentiles*', the second equally exclusively applies the term '*pagani*', both being obviously synonymous expressions used here by different authors.
57 *Ibid.*, a. 849, pp. 16f: '*Gentilitas vero consueto ab aquilone Christianitatem nocuit.*'
58 *Annales Fuldenses*, a. 854, p. 45: '*Domino sanctorum suorum iniurias ulciscente et adversariis digna factis retribuente.*'
59 *Ibid.*, a. 873, p. 80: (Hruodolfus) '*ille vehementer iratus iuravit prae superbia se cunctis maribus occisis mulieres et parvulos cum omni substantia (eorum) in captivitatem esse ducturum, ignarus vindictae, quae eum de caelo erat secutura. ... Illi autem Dominum invocantes, qui eos saepius ab hostibus liberaverat, hosti infestissimo armati occurrerunt.*' In the continuation of the Vienna manuscript,

The perception of religious motives of warfare 225

God revenged their deeds in the way they deserved, and the author distinguishes 'the Christians' from 'Nordmanni' (*ibid.*, a. 884, p. 101). When one of their mightiest leaders, Geoffrey ('Gotafrid'), became a Christian, this necessarily alludes to the fact that he had been a pagan before (*ibid.*, a. 885, p. 102); he broke his oath but could not accomplish his plans to subdue the different places along the River Rhine under his power, 'because God denied it' ('*Deo renuente*': *ibid.*, p. 102). Later on, the Frisians came to the rescue of the fleeing Saxons, 'as if they had been sent by God' ('*quasi a Domino destinati*': *ibid.*).

60 *Ibid.* (Continuatio Ratisbonensis), a. 891, p. 120: '*Viri, Deum recolentes et semper sub Dei gratia patriam tuendo fuistis invincibiles; inspirate animis, si ab inimicis quandoquidem more paganissimo furentibus pium sanguinem parentum vestrorum effusum vindicari recolitis et sacra sub honore sanctorum creatoris vestri templa eversa iam in patria vestra cernitis, ministros eciam Dei summo gradu consistentes prostratos videtis.*'

61 *Ibid.*: '*sed non in diu subveniente gratia Dei victoria ad christianos concessit*'. Similar arguments can be found in Regino of Prüm, *Chronicon*, a. 882, ed. F. Kurze, *MGH SRG*, 50 (Hanover: Hahn, 1890).

62 Four different versions, all from the end of the ninth century, have survived: The *Chronicon Albeldense* from 883, probably briefly afterwards the *Cronica Adefonsi III* in two versions, the *Versio Rotensis* and the *Versio ad Sebastianum*, and the (dependent) *Cronica Profetica*, although the problem of whether the *Prophetical Chronicle* is an independent version has been much discussed, but not sufficiently resolved. In any case, this version has significant changes against the *Chronicon Albeldense*. There are several modern editions of these chronicles (with only slight textual differences, but unfortunately with different numbering of the chapters). I follow the older standard edition by J. Gil Fernandez, *Cronicas Asturianas*, Universidad de Oviedo. Publicaciones del departamento de historia medieval, 11 (Oviedo: Servicio de Publicaciones, Universidad de Oviedo, Departamento de Historia Medieval, Departamento de Filología Clásica, 1985), adding in brackets the corresponding chapters and pages according to Y. Bonnaz' edition, *Chroniques asturiennes*, Sources d'histoire médiévale (Paris: Éditions du Centre National de la Recherche Scientifique, 1987), who adapts spelling and grammar to 'normal' Latin, thus making it easier to understand the text, while the Iberian peculiarities are obscured. Gil's new edition in CCL 65 was not yet available when this chapter was submitted.

63 Bronisch, *Reconquista*, p. 226; for the 'Reconquista' as 'holy war': *ibid.*, pp. 230–4; for an extensive interpretation of the Asturian chronicles in this sense, compare *ibid.*, pp. 124–56. Nevertheless, I find it difficult to confirm that, according to these chronicles, it 'was the most pious task of a Christian king to fight the Chaldaeans', that the kings 'were enveloped in an aura of holiness', or 'the aim of the battle was the ultimate expulsion of the invaders' (*ibid.*, p. 231). Bronisch has to admit himself that the sources do not explicitly emphasise such an interpretation, often being exclusively based on mere allusions to biblical verses.

64 *Chronica Adefonsi. Versio Rotensis*, 7, pp. 120/122 (ed. Bonnaz, 5,2, p. 37): '*Et quia derelinquerunt Dominum ne seruirent ei in iustitia et ueritatem derelicti*

sunt a Domino, ne auitarent terram desiderauilem.' Such a characterisation is missing in the *Versio Ad Sebastianum.*

65 According to the *Versio Ad Sebastianum* it was even Witiza's sons who had called the Saracens for help, thus making it clear that this purely political motive was far from being a religious one; *ibid., Versio Ad Sebastianum*, 6, p. 121 (5, p. 37): '*Sed ipsi qui patrie excidium intulerunt, simul cum gente Sarracenorum gladio perierunt.*'

66 Compare *Chronica Adefonsi. Versio Rotensis* 16, p. 134 (9, p. 47), concerning King Fruela ('Uictorias multas fecit'); similarly, *Chronicon Albeldense*, 4, p. 174 (39, p. 24). The *Versio Ad Sebastianum*, 16, p. 135 (9, p. 47), adds: '*uictorias multas egit aduersus hostem Cordubensium*'. Compare *Chronica Adefonsi. Versio Rotensis*, 16, p. 134 (9, p. 47): '*Cum hostem Cordubense in locum Pontubio prouintia Gallecie prelium gessit, ibique LIIII^{or} milia Caldeorum interfecit*', Ibid., 25, p. 144 (16,1, p. 55), concerning King Ordoño: '*Cum Caldeis sepissime prelia habuit et semper triumfator extitit*'; similarly *Ad Sebastianum*, 25, p. 147 (16,1, p. 55): '*Aduersus Caldeos sepissime preliatus est et triumphabit*'; Chron. Albeldense, 11, p. 175 (46, p. 25): '*Super Sarracenos uictor sepius exstitit*'.

67 Compare *Chronica Adefonsi*, 21, pp. 138/139 (14,1, p. 509), both versions, concerning the era of King Alfonso II.

68 Compare *Chronica Adefonsi. Versio Rotensis*, 23, p. 142 (15,1, p. 54), concerning King Ramiro I: '*Ciuitatem Ispalim sunt ingressi ibique magna agmina Caldeorum partim gladio, partim igni sunt deleti*'; after one year they returned (similarly *Versio Ad Sebastianum, ibid.*, p. 143). *Ibid.*, 26, p. 148 (16,2, p. 57), concerning King Ordoño: '*et cum magna uictoria ad propria reppedauit*'.

69 According to the *Chronicon Albeldense*, 11, p. 175 (46, p. 25), only Ordoño expanded his realm: '*Iste Xp(ist)ianorum regnum cum Dei iubamine ampliauit*'.

70 Compare *Chronica Adefonsi, ibid.*, 22, pp. 140/142 (14,2, p. 52), both versions, concerning Mahamuth.

71 Compare *Chronica Adefonsi. Versio Rotensis*, 17, p. 136 (10, p. 48), concerning King Aurelio: '*Cum Caldeis pacem abuit*' (*Ad Sebastianum*, 17, *ibid.*, p. 137: '*Prelia nulla exercuit, quia cum Arabes pacem habuit*'). *Ibid.*, 18, p. 136/137 (11, p. 49), both versions, concerning King Silo: '*Cum Ismaelites pacem habuit.*'

72 Compare, for example, *Chronicon Albeldense*, 6, p. 174 (41, p. 24), concerning King Silo: '*Cum Spania ob causam matris pacem habuit*'; *ibid.*, 12, p. 177 (47,4, p. 27), concerning King Alfonso III: '*Postea rex noster Sarracenis inferens bellum, exercitum mobit et in Spaniam intrauit*'; *Chronica Adefonsi. Versio Rotensis*, 25, p. 144 (16,1, p. 55), concerning King Ordoño: '*populo partim ex suis, partim ex Spania aduenientibus impleuit*'.

73 Compare *ibid.*, 13, p. 132 (8,1, p. 45): '*omnes quoque Arabes gladio interficiens, Xp(ist)ianos autem secum ad patriam ducens*'. Similarly, *Versio Ad Sebastianum, ibid.*, p. 133 (p. 46): '*omnes quoque Arabes occupatores supra dictarum ciuitatum interficiens, Xp(ist)ianos secum ad patriam duxit*'.

74 Compare *ibid., Versio Rotensis*, 24, p. 144 (15,2, p. 55), concerning two victories of Ramiro I over the Saracens: '*Cum Sarrazenis uis prelium gessit, sed obitulante Deo uictor semper extitit*'. Similarly, *ibid.*, 25, p. 144 (16,1, p. 55), concerning

Ordoño's campaign against the Basques: '*statim ex alia parte hostes Sarrazenorum aduersus eum superuenit; sed Deo fabente Caldeos in fugam uertit et Uascones proprio iure recepit*'. The *Versio Ad Sebastianum* even lacks the reference to God in both cases.

75 *Chronica Adefonsi. Versio Rotensis*, 9, pp. 124/126 (6,2 f, pp. 41–4).
76 Compare Matthew 13,31 (or else Mark 4,31 and Luke 13,19), however, in a very loose interpretation. Bronisch, *Reconquista* p. 139, underlines the frequent biblical allusions in this chronicle.
77 *Chronica Adefonsi. Versio Rotensis*, 9, p. 126 (6,2, pp. 41f): '"*Non legisti in scripturis diuinis quia eclesia Domini ad granum sinapis deuenitur et inde rursus per Domini misericordia in magis erigitur? ... Et nunc ex eo fidens in misericordia Iesu Xp(ist)i hanc multitudinem despicio et minime pertimesco [prelium].*"' (According to Gil's edition, *prelium* belongs to the next sentence.)
78 Accordingly, the victory of Covadonga was achieved by God's help for the minority: *ibid.*, 10, p. 128 (6,3, p. 42): '*Sed in hoc non defuisse Domini magnalia. ... Et quia Dominus non dinumerat astas, set cui uult porrigit palmas.*' The many slaughtered Saracens remind the author of the ruin of the Old Testamental Egyptians in the Red Sea. He ends with thanksgiving towards God, *ibid.*, 11, p. 130 (6,4, p. 44): '*Sit nomen Domini benedictum, qui confortat in se credentes et dextruit inprouas gentes.*'
79 *Ibid.*, 9, p. 126 (6,2, pp. 41f): '*Spes nostra Xp(istu)s est, quod per istum modicum monticulum quem conspicis sit Spanie salus et Gotorum gentis exercitus reparatus. Confido enim quod promissio Domini impleatur in nobis quod dictum est per David.*' In the version *Ad Sebastianum*, *ibid.*, p. 127 (p. 41), the text is almost identical in the last part, but is preceded by more general words (comparing the fate of the Church with the waxing and waning moon): '*Sed tu non nosti quia ecclesia Domini lune conparatur, que et defectum patitur et rursus per tempus ad pristinam plenitudinem reuertitur? Confidimus enim in Domini misericordia quod ab isto modico monticulo quem conspicis sit Yspanie salus et Gotorum gentis exercitus reparatus.*' At least in this context the Saracens are (only once!) characterised as pagans, *ibid.*, p. 127 (p. 42): '*Unde hanc multitudinem paganorum spernimus et minime pertimescimus.*'
80 *Chronicon Albeldense*, 1, p. 173 (36, p. 23).
81 Again, the Saracens are the aggressors; compare *ibid.*, 12, p. 176 (47,2, p. 26): '*Ismahelitica ostis ad Legionem* [León] *uenit, duce Almundar filio de Abderrhaman rege, fratre de Mahomat Cordouense rege*' (repelled by Alfonso). Afterwards several towns '*a christianis populantur*' (*ibid.*). A further attack is equally put to rout: *ibid.*, p. 177 (47,3, p. 26): '*Ipsisque diebus sub era DCCCCXVI Almundar filius regis Mahomat atque duce Iben Ganim cum oste Sarracenorum ex Cordoua Asturicam atque Legionem uenit.*' Three years of peace with Abuhalit followed. After that, Alfonso invaded Muslim territory and even crossed over the River Tajo, as the first Asturian king ever, as the author emphasises, but again was (or had to be) content with his victory and returned to his royal seat, *ibid.*, p. 177 (47,4, p. 27): '*Postea rex noster Sarracenis inferens bellum, exercitum mobit et Spaniam intrauit, sub era DCCCCXVIIII*' (across the River Tajo towards

the region of Mérida and across the River Guadiana towards Ojíferos): '*quod nullus ante eum princeps adire temtauit. Sed et hic quidem glorioso ex inimicis triumfhauit euentu ... Sicque inde cum principe nostro atque uictoria sedem reuertitur regiam.*'

82 Ed. Bonnaz 47,6, pp. 27f (the verses are not in Gil's edition): '*Clarus in Astures, fortis in Vascones/ Vlciscens Arabes et protegens ciues:/ Cui principi sacra sit uictoria data;/ Christo duce iuuatus, semper clarificatus,/ Polleat uictor saeculo, fulgeat ipse caelo;/ Deditus his triumpho, praeditus ibi regno.*' Nevertheless, the following activities show no difference to the former ones, *ibid.*, 13, p. 178 (47,7, p. 28); *ibid.*, p. 180 (47,10, p. 30). The chronicle ends with an Asturian legation to Córdoba.

83 *Cronica profética*, ed. Bonnaz, *Chroniques asturiennes*, pp. 2–9.

84 *Ibid.*, 1, p. 2: '*Factum est uerbum Domini ad Ezechiel dicens. Fili hominis, pone faciem tuam contra Ismael et loquere ad eos dicens: "Fortissimum gentibus dedi te, multiplicaui te, corroboraui te et posui in dextera tua gladium et in sinistra tua sagittas ut conteras gentes."*' In the Old Testament, Ezechiel encourages the 'fili hominis' to turn against 'the daughters of their own people', take 'the way to the south', towards Jerusalem, against the sons of Ammon, Sidon, the Pharaoh, but never against Ishmael.

85 *Ibid.*, 2,2, p. 3: '*Spes nostra Christus est: quod completis proximiori tempora CLXX annis, inimicorum audacia ad nicilum redigatur et pax Christi Ecclesiae Sanctae reddatur. ... hic princeps noster, gloriosus domnus Adefonsus, proximiori tempore in omni Spania praedicetur regnaturus.*' The author adds a genealogy from Abraham and Israel to Mohammed and further to the Ummayad caliph Mohammed as well as a 'biography' of the prophet and the Arab conquest of Spain.

86 *Ibid.*, 8, p. 9: '*Remanent usque ad diem Sancti Martini III idus nouembris, menses VII, et erunt completi anni CLXVIIII, et incipiet annus centesimus septuagesimus quo, dum Sarraceni complerint, secundum praedictum Ezechielis prophetae superius adnotatum, expectabitur ultio inimicorum aduenire et salus christianorum adesse. Quod praestet omnipotens Deus ut, sicut filii eius Domni nostri Iesu Christi cruore uniuersum mundum dignatus est a potestate diaboli redimere, ita, proximiori tempore, Ecclesiam suam iubeat ab Ismaelitarum iugo eripere.*'

87 Compare James Chapter 15, in this volume, p. 253 below; the Introduction to this volume, pp. 10 and 14 above, referring to James.

88 Thus, the Introduction to this volume, pp. 7 and 16 above.

PART IV

PERCEPTIONS OF THE WARRIOR

14

Change of habit equals change of values? Burials of 'military men' between 300 and 500

Benjamin Hamm

In the last centuries of the Roman Empire, the burial habits[1] of military men changed fundamentally. Men in imperial service buried in the middle of the fourth century at Scorton (England) were only marked as military men by their belts and *fibulae*.[2] Such burials with militaristic habit form at best a very small minority in the funerary landscape of the fourth and early fifth centuries.[3] By the end of the fifth century, burial habits of military men had undergone a paradigm shift. In contrast to the fourth-century burials, the proportion of graves with military content increased considerably (see Figure 14.2).

Burials of heavily armed men, like grave 59 from Jülich (Germany), became normative in the post-Roman cemeteries and mark a shift to martiality in the expression of graves.[4] Weapons became highly prominent, and rather than erecting monuments or gravestones, burying communities spent their energy creating more intimate tableaus that were viewed only by those who attended the funerals. During the last decades of the fifth century, all over the former western empire, the importance of weapons as grave-goods had increased to such an extent that almost every second male burial in the developing row-grave cemeteries contained some form of weapon.[5] It is the purpose of this chapter to investigate these changes in the burial rites of military men in cemeteries located in the western provinces of the later Roman Empire between 300 and 500 (see Figure 14.1). Throughout this two-hundred-year period, different strategies were employed to express martial values, military affiliation and masculinity in burial rites. Therefore, the meaning and combination of weapons, clothing and the design of the grave within the funerary rites varies considerably between different sites and throughout the time period under consideration. Do these changed habits also reflect a change in the values of post-Roman burial communities?

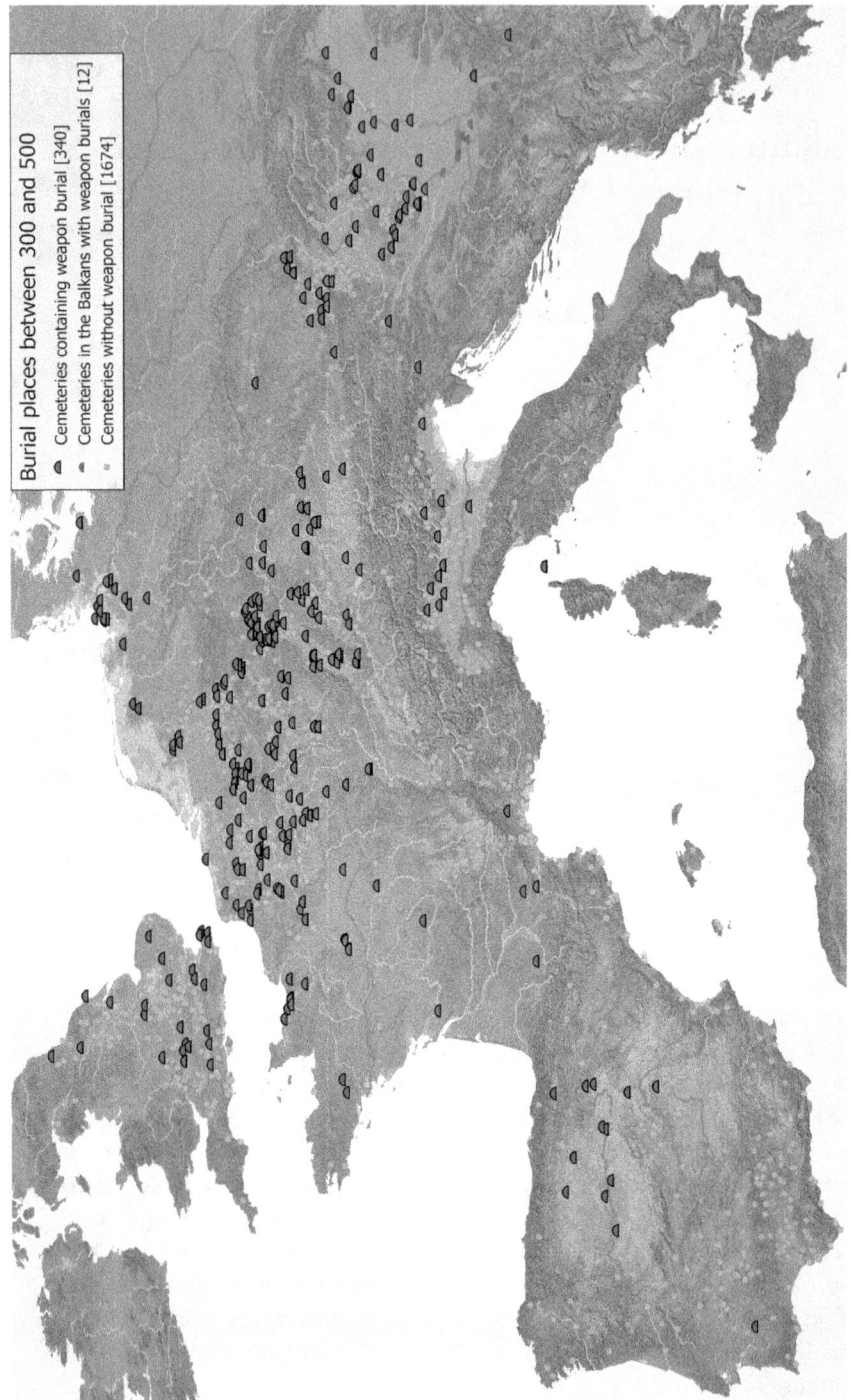

Figure 14.1 Cemeteries of the time between 300 and 500. Based on the author's research of 2014 cemeteries examined. In 340 necropolises one or more burial containing weaponry were detected. These concentrate foremost along the frontiers of the late Roman Empire but can also be found in central provinces in the Iberian Peninsula, northern Italy and the Balkans

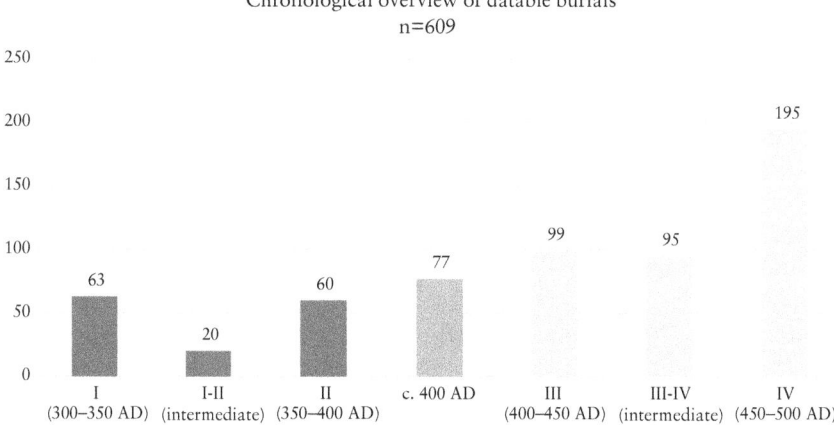

Figure 14.2 The diagram gives an impression of the chronological development of weapon-burials in the time between 300 and 500

Before considering the burials in depth, there are some issues that deserve consideration. First, a broad variety of socially or legally defined groups, such as regular soldiers, veterans or *foederati*, had the notion of an exclusive identity as active fighting men. Their affiliation with the armed services and their tendencies towards violent behaviour as part of their professional duties, which also might corrupt their civil lives, often separated these groups from other parts of society. A specific burial practice, including weaponry and military attire, offered a way to distinguish their status and communicate military affiliation even in death. To further complicate the situation, late antique written sources provide additional evidence of other groups without direct connections to the army, such as members of local aristocracy or armed private retinues like *bucellarii*, who, as actors competent in military violence outside the regular army, were also likely to utilise militaristic symbols and dress when designing their graves.[6] Excavation evidence seldom provides information about these specific individual identities and it is hard to decide based only on the archaeological evidence whether a buried person was being fashioned as a professional soldier, i.e. a warrior in the service of a local warlord, or a civilian with an enthusiasm for military symbols. Some individuals who were buried with weapons may have adopted manifold roles during their lifetime. In the following, therefore, the term 'military men' will be used to denote a general concept that incorporates all social identities with a military affiliation that are represented in burials, without using restrictive categories such as 'soldier' or 'warrior', which from an anthropological point of view are based on a fixed definition and associated qualities.[7]

To define a single burial as that of a 'military man', one must first look at the grave itself and its contents. Weaponry of differing quality and quantity, as well as dress elements defined as part of an official military costume (*habitus militaris*), such as crossbow-brooches or specific belts, can indicate a military man's burial. Exterior designs, like gravestones that depict the departed in military attire or bear inscriptions referencing aspects of a military career, suggest the intended communication of the military context of the tomb. The wider archaeological context of burials and cemeteries can additionally imply a militaristic background for the buried; for example, by considering whether the graves are located in proximity to military structures like fortifications, *castella* or hill forts.[8] The choice of a burial site close to military installations was additionally of symbolic significance. As long as the Roman legions were intact, it was important and prestigious for military personnel to communicate this affiliation beyond death by choosing a burial site close to such structures. Indeed, even after the political end of the empire in the west, the control of a Roman military complex was still of great importance for the local elites. With the burial of a potential ancestor in the environment of a Roman fortification, the burying community could make several statements: first, such a burial context highlighted the military role of the deceased. Second, the deceased and his potential successors could be portrayed in the tradition of imperial rule and thus tasks such as maintaining public order or protecting the local population from external threats by their military strength could be assumed. Finally, the burial at a strategically important location specifically chosen for fortification underscored the claim to the surrounding area.[9]

However, it is not always possibly to identify the burial of a 'military man' based on the above-mentioned criteria, as certain factors influence the value of information relating to individual grave findings. Natural preservation conditions and intentional grave opening in historical times or differing qualities of excavation and preservation methods used by archaeologists additionally impact on the burial itself and the objects therein. Furthermore, building activity and agricultural use over the centuries, in combination with only selective excavations, impacts the surface grave design and topographical aspects of the cemeteries. Such a combination of factors often makes it hard to draw specific conclusions relating to the grave and the landscape. Despite these limitations, archaeology and its findings open a new and important bottom-up perspective for research. In other words, they reveal local developments in late- and post-Roman societies from the perspective of burial communities often neglected by ancient authors.

For such fundamental changes – as mentioned above – to take place in the burial traditions of late Roman provincial societies, there must have existed a great acceptance of militaristic values and, in turn, their representation in burials. This raises a number of questions. What did military graves look like before weapons began to dominate the inventories? What role did the political stability of the struggling Roman Empire play in the design and the intended statement of graves? Do these late antique graves mark a starting point of a phenomenon of mass militarisation, which affected parts of society formerly separated and uninvolved from military matters? Does such a rise of openly demonstrated militaristic attitudes within the burial processes prove the militarisation of post-Roman societies and their attitude to military values – or simply indicate a change of media in a society that was already militarised?[10]

Academic research has also recognised changes to late antique military burial and offered a variety of differing theses for interpretation, focusing particularly on the presence of weaponry.[11] Traditionalist German-speaking scholars tend to view military habit in burials as an impact of incoming Germanic groups who announced their ethnic identity and privileged military status, earned by serving as *laeti* or *foederati* in the Roman army.[12] This popular thesis neglects imperial traditions of military burial, as well as the formal integration of 'Germanic' and other native troops into the administrative structures of the empire which depended on imperial funds for their subsistence.[13] Furthermore, it should be noted that these burials were a statement of social identity, indicating membership of a separate military class composed of different cultural influences that formed in the militarised zone of the imperial frontiers, and not as a statement of one specific ethnic identity.[14]

In the early 2000s and 2010s, there was an altering of the perceptions of military habit in late-Roman burial in academic debate. While questions of ethnic identity and narratives of barbarian invasion became controversial, debates focused on the problem of burying communities adapting to multiple influences of social and political change, memory and post-mortem identities.[15] On the example of northern Gaul, Frans Theuws postulated that fourth-century weapon-graves, most commonly containing axes and lances, did not indicate conquering warriors but rather a centrally organised process of recultivation. This included the repopulation of deserted areas beyond the militarised frontier zones during the late third and fourth centuries by settlers of different origins. By burying their ancestors with their tools in formally ownerless, uncultivated land, these newcomers claimed possession of that land and expressed their will to remain outside the traditional bonds of *dominus* and client.[16] Other approaches focus on richly furnished burials of the late fourth and fifth centuries that contain (full) sets of war gear, comprised of a sword, shield and lance as well as other potential tools of war, such as axes and arrowheads, as indicators of social stress in times of crisis. These burials were part of a ritualised communication of competition between privileged social groups struggling for local influence in a failing empire, and a proclamation of a new elite lifestyle idealising a life of fighting and feasting. By repeating the rites, post-Roman burial communities created images of weapon-bearing men memorialised as martial, and thus protective, ancestors.[17]

After these introductory remarks, the following section will focus on the classical military burials of the fourth and early fifth centuries, before discussing the subsequent profound changes in burial culture in the course of the fifth century and their possible implications for a militarisation of post-Roman society.

Military graves of the long fourth century: barely armed men in burial

Most burials of military men during the fourth century do not reveal a martial identity until closely examined, and were far from the homogeneous group prescribed by traditional archaeological thinking that all too often deduced the identity of the buried person as a non-Roman military man based on a single potential weapon, such as an axe. Consequently, it is important that late antique graves containing weapons should not be regarded as a homogeneous find group, but rather be divided in the following discussion into different categories on the basis of their dating and equipment. Civilian objects, like glass and ceramic vessels, were mostly the products of provincial workshops and dominated the grave inventories in all fourth-century cemeteries, whilst weapons were only rarely part of the burial equipment. Some factors may have regulated both the furnishing of a burial and the selection of the objects placed inside, which also influences the archaeological evidence. For example, did legislation on weapon ownership limit the presence of arms in the funeral context? Did expected normative behaviour, such as gift-giving to the deceased in the process of burial rites, influence the combination of grave-goods?[18] By repeating funeral rites, burying communities negotiated and ensured normative frameworks at every funeral.

The greater part of the so-called 'weapon-graves' during late Antiquity, especially dating to the fourth century, held an axe, lance or arrows as the only weapon (see Figure 14.3). A mere 20 per cent of the 742 fourth- and fifth-century burials in this study contained sword and shield – which could only be used for military purposes and were rare before the mid-fifth century. In the traditional view, the presence of an axe in the burial was enough to define the buried man as a warrior.[19] But these possible weapons were more likely used as everyday tools for cutting wood, carpentry or the clearing of forested land for agriculture. For example, we can identify a spotty pattern

Burials of 'military men' between 300 and 500 237

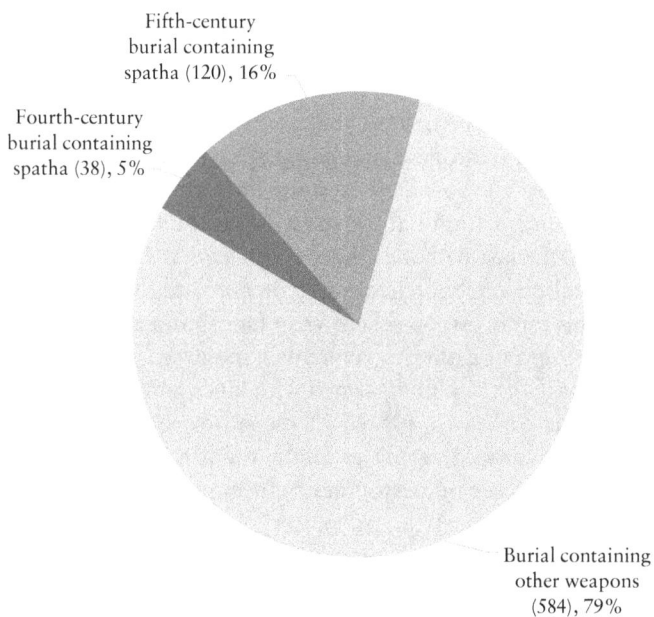

Figure 14.3 Share of graves with spatha within the weapons inventory of the observation period

of distribution of potential 'weapon' burials in late third- and fourth-century archaeological records from several regions of northern Gaul. Cemeteries from central Meuse area, upper Somme Valley, the modern French departments Pas de Calais and Nord and the Marne/Aisne region give evidence of burials containing axes and/or lances as the only 'weaponry'. All these regions have a rather indirect association with the military zones of the Rhine frontier as agricultural hinterland. Consequently, fourth-century burials containing ambiguous objects like axes do not indicate militarised identities, and instead contain everyday tools which intended to show the deceased as a cultivator rather than as a fighting man.[20] Along the Rhine and Danube frontiers, where a strong military presence could be expected, the fourth-century cemeteries show a similar pattern, with only a few burials containing weapons. So, if members of the regular military would have displayed their military identity by placing weapons in burial, we should expect a greater number of items that were only useful in a military context and their widespread distribution. Therefore, we must assume that fourth-century military men used other techniques to demonstrate their role as soldiers of the empire in burial.

During the fourth and early fifth century, the quantity of spears and lances in the burial context is second only to axes. Beyond a military interpretation, the lance and spear were prominent tools for hunting and representative of status. Imperial iconography of the fourth and early fifth century on portable media such as coins, silver tableware and ivory diptychs show the emperor or high officials carrying and using lances as symbols of power.[21] On contemporary gravestones, lances and spears are more prominent than any other weapons. The so-called 'Testament of the Lingon', an inscription on a burial monument found at Langres (France) dating to the late second century, refers to the last will of a citizen of the *civitas Lingonum*. It produces a list of personal objects which were to be cremated with the deceased or placed within his tomb. Among these were lances and a *gladius* not used for a military purpose, but rather to remember the deceased as an enthusiastic hunter.[22] The image of the hunter, armed with lance and spear, was a favourite in late Roman art. Mosaics placed in reception rooms in villas, like the 'Great Hunt' at Piazza Armerina in Sicily, point to the importance of this pastime to the late Roman aristocracy.[23] In burials, hunters' deeds can be seen carved on glass vessels or on pottery.[24] To complete the image of a passionate hunter, the tools of this craft, lances and spears, could easily be a part of a richly furnished burial. In the burial context, these objects can point to aristocratic ideals such as manliness, courage or the deceased's skills with weapons. All these values were very important for military men but were not reserved to them exclusively. They were also appropriate for an aristocrat who wished to demonstrate his noblesse and his claims to landownership by being depicted as hunting on horseback on his own estate.

Evidence based on the *Notitia Dignitatum* suggests that the soldiers' weapons were state property provided by imperial workshops.[25] After their active service, soldiers had several options, of which the gift to the grave was only one.[26] They could or had to return the weapons, sell them or deposit them in sanctuaries. This could be another reason for the small number of weapons in fourth-century burials. However, weapons were not the only medium available for communicating military values and affiliations in the burial context. Clothing components show unique features and can therefore be regarded as personal property of the soldiers, making them available for burial equipment. Dress accessories like crossbow-brooches and richly furnished belt-sets, often made of chip-carved bronze that was sometimes gilded or silvered, as well as specific military footwear like the nailed *caligae*-boots, were available for funerary rites. Under normal circumstances, only the clothing's metal components are preserved and allow only a glimpse of the textiles and colours used for military clothing such as tunics and *sagis*. High-quality textile (wool, cotton or silk) and flamboyant colours (purple or bright red) may also have influenced the burial rite, but our record seldom gives that information. Placing such dress-elements in the graves – as if worn in life or placed in proximity to the body – could hint to the deceased's imperial connection as soldier or official during the fourth century.[27] Up to the first decades of the fifth century, dress was an accepted option by which soldiers could distinguish themselves from other social groups in burial, and can be traced in Britannia as well as in the eastern provinces of the empire.[28] Sites like Scorton (England), Zwentendorf (Austria) and Esztergom (Hungary) provide archaeological evidence for military structures and nearby cemeteries which produce a great number of burials with military dress accessories.[29] By contrast, most of the fourth-century cemeteries that were close to military sites include only a small number of burials that contain weapons. Openly displayed in burial rites, these dress accessories were sufficiently indicative of the deceased's membership to a weapon-bearing class to connect them to a community of professional military men. For future research, it is conceivable to regard the presence in graves of official clothing as an indicator of the stability of the empire. So long as the imperial structures were intact, and the official character of these objects were understood as demonstrating an imperial affiliation that guarantied prestige and material advantages such as wages and land-use rights, brooches and belt-sets were placed into graves as an 'official' way to identify military men in imperial service.

Erecting a grave monument on which the buried person was idealistically depicted with all the external indicators of his social status could be an additional, or possibly alternative, way to represent the deceased as a military man.[30] Detailed images of armed men were carved on durable materials like stone or marble or were painted inside burial chambers. A gravestone from Longeau (France) gives an impression of this late Roman tradition (see Figure 14.4). Typical for this form of tomb monument are depictions which show the deceased arrayed in military dress and accompanied by important objects linked to the military sphere; for example, his weapons. The presence of real weapons inside the grave itself was not essential. Epigraphic evidence can deliver a further biographical background for the deceased. An inscription found in Budapest, in which the deceased claimed to be a Frank by birth and in private life, but also a *miles romanus* in service of the empire, demonstrates that late antique individuals had multiple identities in their lifecycle without any hint of conflicting loyalties.[31]

The central aim of these tombstones and rare paintings in catacombs was to show the deceased in all the splendour of his military world and to create a place where relatives and companions could remember the deceased for years to come. By means of colour, further accents could be set and the typical military clothing of individual units shown.[32] Through such methods, the deceased was depicted as part of the empire and its professional army. Furthermore, because both institutions claimed perpetuity, so did the memorial. Unfortunately, in many cases, the gravestones are not found *in situ* and

Figure 14.4 Late Roman burial scene with gravestone, which is inspired by finds from Aquileia and Longeau

made contextualisation with a specific burial impossible. Objects deposited as grave-goods, such as weapons and clothing components, are only visible in the moment of the burial itself, or a short time before the actual funeral, if the deceased was laid out with all his funeral equipment by the burial community. Only the audience that was present at the entombment saw these objects, and only they could understand the messages communicated through these objects. This limits the communication framework to a locally present group at the moment of the burial. In contrast, by communicating through images on gravestones, a larger audience could be addressed. Long-term visibility was guaranteed to an audience not present at the funeral, as well as to passers-by, and in addition the tombstone created a place for commemoration. This effect was increased by placing the cemeteries near frequented roads. In this way the communication framework was increased, both spatially and temporally.

Early fifth century – continuity and change in the peripheries

At the beginning of the fifth century, however, it became apparent that these traditional habits were no longer sufficient to portray the deceased as military men. Around 400, significant changes occurred in the grave furnishings of military men. In small necropolises, often containing less than 50 graves, a new type of burial appeared which pointed directly to military aspects by combining elements of the imperial *habitus militaris* with *spathae* or complete sets of weaponry. Examples from Kemathen, Liebenau and Frankfurt-Praunheim, all sites located in Germany, represent two aspects of the image of a military man of status for the burial community.[33] These graves were equipped with sets of weaponry that always included a sword and shield. In the cases of Frankfurt and Kemathen, the interred individual was equipped with a belt-set, and in contrast to fourth-century burials, with *spatha* and shield. At Liebenau, the grave included a belt-set and, in addition to sword and shield, a spear and a set of seven arrowheads.

The deposition of these weapons in the context of burial may signify a change concerning weapon ownership. While weapons were state property in times of an intact Roman army, an increased use of weapons in the burial equipment seems to indicate that the armament was now the personal property of the interred or his community. It can be assumed that the deceased or those close to him could dispose of the weapons or regarded them as inalienable personal or collective possessions that were essential for the deceased. Thus, a first step towards the militarisation of late antique societies is made tangible by an increasing proliferation of weapons in private hands. Furthermore, all these burials mentioned above contain elaborate belt-sets, chip-carved with animal-headed buckles and rich fittings. This attire illustrates the affiliation of the deceased to imperial institutions and formulates a last reminder of the privileges and prestige gained by imperial service. Ceramics produced according to models of provincial workshops point to economic links between the burial community and a still intact, but more locally focused, imperial trading network.[34] This suggests that the empire's influence on its peripheries was still sufficiently strong to be recognised by the local population and considered important.

Gravestones, a traditional custom of representation of martial values, were missing in these burials. It seems that with a failing empire, the tradition of long-term memorialisation vanished. Therefore, we should interpret the burials of the mid- and late-fifth century as locally focused affairs, only addressing the audience present at the funeral. There are still inscriptions in burial sites in urban centres like Cologne or Trier during early medieval times, but in rural cemeteries this habit disappears. However, due to the nature of the archaeological evidence, we cannot rule out the possibility that the graves of this period contained any form of tomb monument. Wooden grave markings were also a conceivable option, such as those that have survived under better preservation conditions from the late antique necropolis of the Pauline monastery in Thebes (Deir el-Bachît, Egypt).[35] The construction of burial mounds and earthworks are also documented, but are subject to the aggressive transformation of the landscape in the intervening 1500 years through agricultural and construction activity. In most cases, only sparse remains of this post-Roman burial architecture are preserved.

To address these rural communities, weaponry as media became popular as a central object in burial rite. On the other hand, individual military abilities became a crucial factor for structures of power on the peripheries of a failing empire.[36] The open communication of military preparedness and aspects of a martial life during the lifetime of the deceased were the central statement of these burials. Military retinues or even access to former imperial military structures were likely essential for new claims to local power.[37] It is tempting to see the richly endowed 'weapon graves' as an indication of new post-Roman elite. Based on archaeological findings, i.e. rich burials containing weapons like Landifay in northern France, Charles R. Whittaker argues that local elites in the peripheral regions of the empire developed from being civilian-focused during the fourth century, to being 'warlords' in the course of the fifth century. Further research may reveal information concerning the pattern of local distribution of such post-Roman petty 'warlords', who were in most cases no more than the richest landowner in their communities.[38] The combination of land ownership and military service for the empire gave this heterogeneous group of provincial aristocracy, native army commanders and upstarts the opportunity to offer military solutions at the local level in the event that imperial institutions failed. Their economic resources enabled them to recruit armed followers and thus control their local environment. This was a key development towards military-based local rule as described by Whittaker. Thus, these graves represent an experiment in establishing a new medium of self-representation. Whether the warlords themselves or their armed followers were buried in these burials, who received a prominent position through military service and proximity to the warlord cannot always be clearly distinguished.

New ways to show military membership – burials dominated by war-gear

Up to the last decades of the fifth century, subtle approaches to communicate military aspects within burials were replaced by more manifest appeals. In most areas of the west, an official framework which limited military activity to a legally defined social group of regular soldiers was gone for good. Imperial institutions were no longer regimented or exemplary. 'Imperial' ambitions, and in turn a wider space of communication, were not relevant for most of those buried around 500. Objects of the *habitus militaris* which had served as a supra-regional, empire-wide mode of communication disappeared completely from burial evidence. The disappearance of imperial institutions made the display of their symbols in the context of graves superfluous, because fibulae and belts promised neither prestige nor material gain. Perhaps for this reason, too, belts and fibulae were 'disposed of' in the grave. The loss of an imperial stage as an arena for action also changed the audiences addressed by a military-style burial. The spectators of burials were primarily the communities using the same cemeteries. Only those present during the burial could view the body and the gifts that were placed in the grave.

Weaponry became the most important object of male grave furniture. Apart from personal objects, such as toilet bag items like combs or tweezers or individual drinking vessels, objects associated with civilian life became less important than weapons. In the early occupancy periods of the so-called '*Reihengräberfelder*', only one or two male individuals per cemetery and phase stand out from the already small group of richly endowed graves by emphasising their military potential with complete weapon-sets. For example, two burials found at Gültlingen in south-west Germany and the prominent late fifth-century burial of a certain Childerich at Tournai (Belgium) use full sets of war-gear to create an image of the deceased as a 'military man' and may hint at a professional attitude towards warfare.[39] Complete armament and the increased presence of a sword, a shield and a lance in the graves show an increased significance of military performance in the elite lifestyle at the end of the fifth century. Apart from economic prosperity, the status of local magnates depended on their military capacity as 'warlords' and their ability to regulate the potential for military violence within their small sphere of influence. By presenting the local community with an ancestor equipped with full weaponry as a symbol of power during the burial, a statement is made about the strength of the deceased that reinforced claims to status.

Nevertheless, it seems odd to conclude that post-Roman society was militarised because of a small number of richly furnished burials. These burials are attractive objects of study due to the large amount of gold and manly accessories they contain, such as ornate sword-belts and other weaponry, giving these rural cemeteries a pinch of royal glamour. But post-Roman militarisation is not only an elite phenomenon. It took place elsewhere and should be considered from a bottom-up perspective. Without the economic potential to raise and maintain standing troops from their domains, when it came to military matters local magnates were required to mobilise their immediate environment. Around 500, another group of weapon-bearing men found their last rest in proximity to the heavily armed 'warlord' burials. This development can be seen both in early medieval burial sites on the Continent and in Britain. The cemetery in Bulles in northern France provides a good example of this development. During the earliest phase of occupation in the late fifth and early sixth centuries, this site provided six burials which René Legoux, owing to the presence of *spatha* or sword-belts in these graves, classified as 'chef de militaire'. In contrast, Legoux paid less attention to a further nineteen burials that were equipped with various combinations of lances, axes and arrowheads.[40] However, in my opinion, these simply furnished graves, which contain few objects other than spears, shields and knives, are more important for evidencing a militarisation of late Antiquity and early medieval societies. Particularly noteworthy is a significant increase in the number of shields placed in less well-equipped burials. Among the graves of the fourth century included in this study, only 5 per cent contained a shield and, even at the beginning of the fifth century, shields only appeared in prominent burials. By contrast, of the 246 graves dated to the period around 500, 86 contained a shield as part of the weapons equipment, which corresponds to a share of 35 per cent. This considerable increase in simple but affordable weapons as the primary, and often only, objects in the grave indicates that a large proportion of the population in the former provinces of the western empire now adopted expressions of military activity in the burial context. Basic weapons in burial sites imply military potential and an obligation of military service from the deceased. As for fourth-century graves, grave-goods in these less elaborate burials refer to personal everyday equipment of the deceased and not to their role as free men or 'Germanic warrior[s]' as stated by traditionalists.[41] Participation in armed conflict, given freely or forced, became an open concept in which large parts of the population were involved. For a large proportion of those buried, however, it is likely that military activity was a significant part of their lives. In addition to their actual activities as farmers or artisans, the number of war missions of these potential fighters may have been limited to a few occasions in their lifetime. Nevertheless, the availability of broad strata of societies for military service was not limited to the elite or a separate group of professional arms bearers. As such, these graves of would-be fighters mark the militarisation of post-Roman societies, for they fulfil an essential criterion that Edward James set out to define a militarised society.[42] A clear separation between the military and civil society, regardless of the frequency of an individual's military activity during his lifetime, is no longer possible, at least within the cemeteries. Called in for military service by their local warlord in life, the burials of these men illustrate a high degree of military potential and an adaptation of military habit in burial. It can be assumed that it was important for the funeral rite to emphasise the image of the deceased as a fighter through weapons. However, for the majority of those buried with weapons, warfare was a seasonal activity. This stands in clear contrast to the military disputes of the late imperial period, which were carried out by contingents of paid, centrally organised and equipped full-time soldiers. Therefore, the burial communities seem to deny these part-time fighters a military burial with expensive full war-gear for economic reasons or the necessity for future generations to continue the use the armaments. Only a few individuals used complete weaponry in the grave context. This suggests that such a privilege was reserved for the few full-time military men, like local warlords and their armed retinues, whose central role within post-Roman societies was to form the professional core of the local forces. They functioned as leaders and champions in times of war and ensured public order in their environment in times of peace. Whether these were the wealthiest members, who tried to underpin their position within the community by means of the valuable weapons in the grave of their deceased kinsmen, or whether the most capable fighters were distinguished by panoply of weapons, can only be assumed from the archaeological findings.

Conclusion

During late Antiquity, there were social groups that wished to represent their military values. Therefore, a rise of militaristic attitudes in burial does not indicate a change in the contemporary mind-set due to the influence of newcomers, nor the simplistic postulation of a 'barbarisation' of the Roman army during the fourth and fifth centuries. Archaeological records reveal different habits with which to display the martial skills of the deceased, or to show that they belonged to a community of fighting men. A broad variety of media existed for the deceased and his environment to indicate a militaristic way of life and allow them to conserve this image in burial. The foregoing analysis leads to the following conclusion that includes an educated guess for different types of militaristic burials.

The graves that contain martial tools dated between 300 and 500 should be read as a normative statement of the martial prowess of the deceased; their social environment wanted them to be remembered as weapon-bearers and protectors in burial. By appropriately burying the honoured ancestor, descendants were able to claim status and privileges that were earned by the military charisma of their forebears. During the fourth and early fifth centuries, in times of an intact imperial army and administration, an established code of regulations and traditions directed how military values were to be presented. This burial-type marked an indirect approach which communicated the image of the deceased as a military man by using objects and symbols that were recognised across the empire. Gravestones, inscriptions and uniform objects of a *habitus militaris* were placed in the burial as adequate media to communicate military aspects. Weapons were seldom part of fourth-century grave furniture and were not yet central indicators that expressed the status of a 'military man'.

With the fall of the Roman Empire and its institutions beginning in the early fifth century, different and more direct channels of communication had to be utilised and military values were expressed through new forms of transmission. At first, older strategies were kept alive. Military clothing, first and foremost chip-carved belt-sets, remained a medium that showed military prowess and affiliation to the imperial world. Especially at the peripheries of the empire, a type of burial equipped with a combination of belt-sets and full war-gear emerged. Weapons became the central objects of grave furniture, pointing directly to the social role of the deceased as fighters and local magnates. In addition to the memory of the high status of the deceased, the burying community could claim prestige from its connection to the departed through a correctly conducted burial. Durable monuments like gravestones became rare, indicating that a more local audience was present at the moment of burial. Therefore, a second type of burial can be detected in the first half of the fifth century: it combined subtle aspects of dress with the brute force of full sets of weapons. But the limited number of such burials do not tell a story of mass-militarisation during the first half of the fifth century.

The political end of the Roman Empire brings the final step in this evolution of burial rites. By the second half of the fifth century, established forms of communication and regulations were gone for good. After a transformation of administration and the army, the west was now dominated by a system which allowed for more local policy rather than an empire-wide administrative framework. This process of localisation included an adaptation to the new perspectives of social life. Showing the insignia of the imperial army in burial was mere nostalgia. At this time, objects of the *habitus militaris* disappear completely or become curiosities. Martial capacity was one crucial factor in the conflict of influence in the post-Roman world. Heavy arms and elaborated swords became 'a kind of mirror for [military] men'.[43] It is hard to tell whether the men who were buried fully armed were the new elite or professionals of inferior rank forming armed retinues. Certainly, there existed social groups that had a professional relationship to military violence and armed conflict even after the end of the empire. However, this does not mean that a mass-militarisation took place during the last decades of the fifth century. Burials of fully armed military men were still rare in the funerary landscape of the post-Roman west, with just one or two individuals being buried with weapons per generation. However, with the end of a regular (imperial) army, the circle of persons needed and potentially available for armed service expanded. Warfare became a locally focused affair where a growing number of people were involved. Bearing arms was no longer restricted to a closed social group of professionals. Every male individual of free legal status became potentially part of armed deployments and gained a further social role: that of a military man. Burial evidence illustrates this availability to armed service, but if there was gain or glory in it for all members of society, archaeology alone cannot tell.

Notes

1 In this context, the term 'habit' describes the set of customs that influenced the design and furnishings of these burials, in contrast to the usual usage that focuses on the clothing and the external appearance of an individual.
2 H. Eckardt, G. Müldner and G. Speed, 'The late Roman field army in northern Britain? Mobility, material culture and multi-isotope analysis at Scorton (N Yorks.)', *Britannia*, 46 (2015), 191–223.
3 Estimations for military burials in late Roman northern Gaul show 1 to 4 per cent of total burials. H.-W. Böhme, 'Gallische Höhensiedlungen und germanische Söldner im 4./5. Jahrhundert', in H. Steuer and V. Bierbrauer (eds), *Höhensiedlungen zwischen Antike und Mittelalter von den Ardennen bis zur Adria*, RGA Ergänzungsbände, 58 (Berlin: Walter de Gruyter, 2008), pp. 71–103, at p. 96.
4 H. Pöppelmann, *Das spätantik-frühmittelalterliche Gräberfeld von Jülich, Kr. Düren*, Bonner Beiträge zur vor- und frühgeschichtlichen Archäologie, 11 (Bonn: Rheinische Friedrich-Wilhelms-Universität, 2010), pp. 363, pl. 20–1.
5 F. Siegmund, 'Kleidung und Bewaffnung der Männer im östlichen Frankenreich', in Reiss-Museum Mannheim (ed.), *Die Franken, Wegbereiter Europas* (Mainz: von Zabern, 1996), pp. 691–706; at p. 700.
6 J. H. G. W. Liebeschuetz, 'Generals, federates and bucellarii in the Roman armies around AD 400', in Ph. Freeman and D. Kennedy (eds), *The defence*

of the Roman and Byzantine east 2 (Oxford: BAR Int. Ser. 297), pp. 463–74; N. Lenski, 'Harnessing violence. Armed forces as manpower in the late roman countryside', *Journal of Late Antiquity*, 6:2 (2013), 233–50, at 243–7. R. Collins, 'Late roman frontier communities in northern Britain. A theoretical context for the 'end' of Hadrian's Wall', in B. Croxford, H. Goodchild, J. Lucas and N. Ray (eds) *TRAC 2005: Proceedings of the fifteenth annual theoretical Roman archaeology conference* (Oxford: Oxbow Books, 2006), pp. 1–11; at pp. 6–7.

7 L. Jørgensen, 'The "Warriors, soldiers and conscripts" of the anthropology in late Roman and Migration period archaeology', in B. Storgaard (ed.), *Military aspects of the aristocracy in babaricum in the Roman and early migration periods* (Copenhagen: The National Museum, 1999), pp. 9–19, at pp. 9–11.

8 J.-P. Lémant, *Le cimetière et la fortification du bas-empire de Vireux-Molhain, Dép. Ardennes* (Bonn: Habelt, 1985); J. Mertens and L. van Impe, *Het laat-romeins grafveld van Oudenburg*, Archaelogica Belgica, 135 (Brussel: Nationale Dienst voor Opgravingen, 1971); A. Gorbach, *Das spätantike Gräberfeld-West von Zwentendorf–Asturis* (St. Pölten: Landessammlungen Niederösterreich, 2016), p. 9, fig. 2.

9 R. Collins, 'Soldiers to warriors. Renegotiating the Roman frontier in the fifth century', in F. Hunter and K. Painter (eds), *Late Roman silver* (Edinburgh: Society of Antiquaries of Scotland, 2013), pp. 29–44; at p. 39.

10 E. James, 'The militarisation of Roman society, 400–700', in A. Nørgård Jørgensen and B. L. Clausen (eds), *Military aspects of Scandinavian society in a European perspective, AD 1–1300* (Copenhagen: The National Museum of Denmark, 1997), pp. 19–24. L. Sarti, *Perceiving war and the military in early Christian Gaul (ca. 400–700 A.D.)*, Brill's Series on the Early Middle Ages, 22 (Leiden: Brill, 2013), p. 174; p. 249.

11 For a comprehensive overview, see: B. Effros, 'A century of remembrance and amnesia in the excavation, display and interpretation of early medieval burial artefacts', in J. Jarnut and M. Wemhoff (eds), *Erinnerungskultur und Bestattungsritual* (Munich: Fink, 2003), pp. 75–96; H. Fehr, *Germanen und Romanen im Merowingerreich. Frühgeschichtliche Archäologie zwischen Wissenschaft und Zeitgeschehen*, RGA Ergänzungsbände, 68 (Berlin: De Gruyter, 2010), pp. 177–652, pp. 750–63.

12 H.-W. Böhme, *Germanische Grabfunde des 4. bis 5. Jahrhunderts zwischen unterer Elbe und Loire* (Munich: C. H. Beck, 1974), pp. 2–3; pp. 174–94. M. Martin, 'Ethnic identities as constructions in archaeology (?). The case of the Thuringi', in J. Fries-Knoblach, H. Steuer and J. Hines (eds), *The Baiuvarii and Thuringi. An ethnographic perspective* (Woodbridge: Boydell Press, 2014), pp. 243–70, at p. 244; R. Gottschalk, *Spätrömische Gräber im Umland von Köln* (Darmstadt: Philip von Zabern, 2015), p. 256.

13 A. Márton, 'Roman burial with a weapon from the Bécsi road cemetery (Aquincum-Budapest)', *Communicationes archaeologicae Hungariae*, 2002, pp. 117–52. J. Nicolay, *Armed Batavians. Use and significance of weaponry and horse gear from non-military contexts in the Rhine Delta (50 BC to AD 450)* (Amsterdam: Amsterdam University Press, 2007), pp. 199–207; Z. Mráv,

'Graves of auxilliary soldiers and veterans from the first century AD in the northern part of Pannonia', in: M. Sanader, A. Rendić-Miočević, D. Tončinić and I. Radman-Livaja (eds), *Weapons and military in a funerary context. Proceedings of the 17th Roman Military Equipment Conference* (Zagreb, 24–27 May 2010) (Zagreb: Filozofskog Fakulteta Sveučilišta u Zagrebu, 2013), pp. 87–116; C. R. Whittaker, *Frontiers of the Roman empire. A social and economic study* (Baltimore: Johns Hopkins University Press, 1994), pp. 224–5; H. Elton, *Warfare in Roman Europe, AD 350–425* (Oxford: Clarendon Press, 1996), pp. 134–54; G. Halsall, *Barbarian migrations and the Roman west, 376–568* (Cambridge: Cambridge University Press, 2007), pp. 101–10. C. Delaplace, 'The so-called "Conquest of the Auvergne" (469–75) in the history of the Visigothic kingdom. Relations between the Roman elites of southern Gaul, the central imperial power in Rome and the military authority of the federates on the periphery', in D. Brakke, D. Deliyannis and E. Watts (eds), *Shifting cultural frontiers in late Antiquity* (Farnham: Ashgate, 2012), pp. 271–81, at pp. 280–1.

14 E. Swift, 'Constructing roman identities in late Antiquity? Material culture on the western frontier', in W. Bowden, A. Gutteridge and C. Machado (eds), *Social and political life in late Antiquity* (Leiden: Brill 2006), pp. 97–111; at pp. 100–6. L. Sarti, 'Die spätantike Militärpräsenz und die Entstehung einer militarisierten "Grenzgesellschaft" in der nordwesteuropäischen *limes*-Region' in C. Rass (ed.), *Militärische Migration vom Altertum bis zur Gegenwart*, Studien zur Historischen Migrationsforschung, 30 (Paderborn: Schöningh, 2016), pp. 43–56, at p. 50.

15 H. Fehr, 'Germanische Einwanderung oder kulturelle Neuorientierung? Zu den Anfängen des Reihengräberhorizontes', in S. Brather (ed.), *Zwischen Spätantike und Frühmittelalter*, RGA Ergänzungsbände, 57 (Berlin: De Gruyter, 2008), pp. 67–102, at pp. 87–9 and pp. 96–102; J. Kleemann, 'Hospes. Archäologische Aspekte zur Integration von Barbaren in das römische Imperium. Eine vergleichende Betrachtung zur Beigabensitte in gallischen und pannonischen Provinzen', in T. Vida (ed.), *The frontier world – Romans, barbarians and military culture* (Budapest: Eötvös Loránd University, 2015), pp. 499–516; St. Heeren and N. Roymans, 'Contextualising ethnicity and the rhetoric of burial rites in late antique northern Gaul. The evidence from settlements and precious metal circulation', in M. Kars (ed.), *Rural riches and royal rags? Studies on medieval and modern archaeology presented to Frans Theuws* (Zwolle: SPA-Uitgevers, 2018), pp. 8–14, at pp. 12–14.

16 F. Theuws, 'Grave goods, ethnicity, and the rhetoric of burial rites in late antique northern Gaul', in T. Derks and N. Roymans (eds), *Ethnic constructs in Antiquity. The role of power and tradition* (Amsterdam: University Press, 2009), pp. 283–320, at pp. 301–11.

17 G. Halsall, 'Archaeology and the late roman frontier in northern Gaul. The so-called "Föderatengräber" reconsidered', in W. Pohl and H. Reimitz (eds), *Grenze und Differenz im frühen Mittelalter* (Vienna: Verlag der österreichischen Akademie der Wissenschaften, 2000), pp. 167–80, at p. 180; F. Theuws and M. Alkemade, 'A kind of mirror for men. Sword depositions in late antique northern Gaul', in F. Theuws (ed.), *Rituals of power: From late Antiquity to*

the early Middle Ages, Transformation of the Roman World, 8 (Leiden: Brill, 2000), pp. 401–76, at pp. 461–70.
18 H. Härke, 'Grave goods in early medieval burials. Messages and meanings', *Mortality*, 19:1 (2014), 1–21.
19 Böhme, *Germanische Grabfunde des 4. bis 5. Jahrhunderts zwischen unterer Elbe und Loire*, p. 104.
20 Nicolay, *Armed Batavians*, p. 258; F. Theuws, '"terra non est" – Zentralsiedlungen der Völkerwanderungszeit im Maas-Rhein-Gebiet', in H. Steuer and V. Bierbrauer (eds), *Höhensiedlungen zwischen Antike und Mittelalter von den Ardennen bis zur Adria* (Berlin: Walter de Gruyter, 2008), pp. 765–93, at pp. 769–70.
21 W. F. Volbach, *Elfenbeinarbeiten der Spätantike und des frühen Mittelalters* (Mainz: von Zabern, 1976), pp. 55–6, table 35; Y. Rivière, 'The Medallion of Arras', in J.-J. Aillagon (ed.), *Rome and the barbarians. The birth of a new world*, Catalogue exibition by Palazzo Grassi, Venice 2008 (London: Thames and Hudson, 2008), pp. 194–5, Y. Rivière, 'Die Stabilisierung des Römischen Reiches. Von den Tetrarchen zu Konstantin', in Kunst- und Ausstellungshalle der Bundesrepublik Deutschland GmbH (ed.), *Rom und die Barbaren. Europa zur Zeit der Völkerwanderung*. Catalogue exibition Kunst- und Ausstellungshalle der Bundesrepublik Bonn, 22.08.-07.12.2008 (Bonn and Munich: Hirmer 2008), pp. 117–24, Cat.-No. 742.
22 CIL XIII, 5708, 2, lines 22–5: '*Volo autem omne instrumentum meum, quod ad venandum et aucupandum paravi, mecum cremari cum lanceis, glad[i]i[s], cultris, retibus, plagis, laqueis, [k]alamis, tabernaculis, formidinibus, balnearibus, lecticis…*': P. Sage, 'Le testament du Lingon. Remarques sur le texte et sur son interpretation', in Y. Le Bohec (ed.), *Le Testament du Lingon* (Lyon: De Boccard, 1991), pp. 17–40, p. 21.
23 Piazza Armerina: K. M. D. Dunbabin, *Mosaics of the Greek and Roman world* (Cambridge: Cambridge University Press, 1999), pp. 130–43, figures 137; 142; 143; 145.
24 For example, a glass bowl showing a riding huntsman fighting a lion was found in an incineration burial excavated in 1950 at Nettersheim in the Rhineland (GER). See Gottschalk, *Spätrömische Gräber im Umland von Köln*, p. 368 pl. 136.
25 Y. Le Bohec, *Das römische Heer der Späten Kaiserzeit* (Stuttgart: Steiner, 2010), p. 131.
26 Nicolay, *Armed Batavians*, pp. 166–71; pp. 173–206.
27 V. van Thienen and S. Lycke, 'From commodity to singularity. The production of crossbow brooches and the rise of the Late Roman military elite', *Journal of Archaeological Science*, 82 (2017), 50–61, fig. 1, Swift 'Constructing roman identities', pp. 102–6. M. Gagnol, 'Le petit mobilier issu d'une nécropole de L'Antiquité tardive à Savasse (Drôme)', in S. Raux, I. Bertrand and M. Feugère (eds), *Actualité de la recherche sur les mobiliers non céramique de l'Antiquité et du haut Moyen Âge* (F, Rhône), 18–20 octobre 2012, Monographie Instrumentum, 51 (Montagnac: Éditions Monique Mergoil, 2015), pp. 269–90, at pp. 283–5; F. Pérez Rodríguez-Aragón and M. Barril Vicente, 'El cementerio tardorromano

de Aguilar de Anguita y la problemática de las necrópolis con ajuares "tipo Simancas-San Miguel de Arroyo"', *Sautuola*, XVI/XVII (2010–12), 215–37, at p. 225.
28 E. Swift, *Regionality in dress accessories in the late Roman west* (Montagnac: Éditions Monique Mergoil, 2000), pp. 88, pp. 185–204, pp. 230–3; Ch. Eger, *Spätantikes Kleidungszubehör aus Nordafrika I. Trägerkreis, Mobilität und Ethnos im Spiegel der Funde der spätesten römischen Kaiserzeit und der vandalischen Zeit* (Wiesbaden: Reichert, 2012), pp. 118–59.
29 H. Eckardt et al., 'The late Roman field army in northern Britain', pp. 196–207; Gorbach, *Das spätantike Gräberfeld-West von Zwentendorf–Asturis*, pp. 20–33; M. Kelemen, 'Solva. Esztergom későrómai temetői/ Die spätrömischen Gräberfelder von Esztergom', *Libelli Archaeologici Ser. Nov. No. III* (Budapest: Magyar Nemezeti Múzeum, 2008), pp. 202–4; p. 209, Tàb. 57; 70.
30 G. Lettich, *Itinerari epigrafici aquileiesi. Guida alle epigrafi esposte nel Museo Archeologico Nazionale di Aquileia* (Trieste: Editreg SRL, 2003), pp. 97–8, nn. 108; 100, nn. 113; 103, nn. 119.
31 ILS 2814, *Francus ego civis, Romanus miles in armis egregia virtute tulinello mea dextera simper...*
32 M. Jelusić, 'Zu einem Schildzeichen der Notitia Dignitatum. Neubewertung einer Grabmalerei mit der Darstellung des spätantiken Soldaten Flavius Maximianus aus der Villa Maria-Katakombe in Syrakus (Reg. Siciliana, I)', *Archäologisches Korrespondenzblatt*, 47:4 (2017), 513–32, at 516–18, fig. 3;4.
33 Th. Fischer, 'Mutmaßliche und gesicherte germanische Kammergräber des 3. bis 5. Jahrhunderts n. Chr. aus dem Vorland des ostraetischen Limes (Berching-Pollanten, Kemathen, Ifersdorf)', in A. Abegg-Wigg and N. Lau (eds), *Kammergräber im Barbaricum – Zu Einflüssen und Übergangsphänomenen von der vorrömischen Eisenzeit bis in die Völkerwanderungszeit*, Schriften des Archäologischen Landesmuseums Ergänzungsreihe, 9 (Neumünster: Wachholtz, 2014), pp. 271–308, at pp. 299–301, fig. 15–21. B. Steidl, *Die Wetterau vom 3. bis 5. Jahrhundert n. Chr.* (Wiesbaden: Landesamt für Denkmalpflege Hessen, 2000), pp. 233–5, pl. 50–4. E. Cosack and H.-J. Häßler, *Das sächsische Gräberfeld bei Liebenau, Kr. Nienburg (Weser)* (Berlin: Mann, 1982), pp. 28–9, pl. 5–8; C. Miks, *Studien zur römischen Schwertbewaffnung in der Kaiserzeit* (Rahden: VML, 2007), pp. 652–3, no. A 424, pl. 133; 277; 285.
34 P. van Ossel, 'Rural impoverishment in northern Gaul at the end of Antiquity. The contribution of Archaeology', in W. Bowden, A. Gutteridge and C. Machado (eds), *Social and political life in late Antiquity* (Leiden: Brill 2006), pp. 533–65, at pp. 559–61; M. Whittow, 'How much trade was local, regional and interregional? A comparative perspective on the late antique economy', in L. Lavan (ed.), *Local economies? Production and exchange of inland regions in late Antiquity* (Leiden: Brill, 2013), pp. 133–65, at pp. 158–60.
35 I. Eichner, 'Death and burial in the monastery of St. Paulos at Western Thebes, Upper Egypt', in Ch. Eger and M. Mackensen (eds), *Death and burial in the Near East from Roman to Islamic times. Research in Syria, Lebanon, Jordan and Egypt* (Wiesbaden: Reichert Verlag, 2018), pp. 227–42, at pp. 237–8.

36 D. H. Miller, 'Frontier societies and the transition between late Antiquity and early Middle Ages', in R. Mathisen and H. Sivan (eds), *Shifting frontiers in late Antiquity* (Aldershot: Variorum, 1996), pp. 158–71, at pp. 166–7, pp. 169–71.
37 Collins, 'Late roman frontier communities in northern Britain', pp. 2–3.
38 Whittaker, *Frontiers of the Roman Empire*, pp. 233–40, fig. 49, pp. 243–78.
39 D. Quast, *Die merowingerzeitlichen Grabfunde aus Gültlingen (Stadt Wildberg, Kr. Calw)* (Stuttgart: Konrad Theiss, 1993), pp. 20–60; D. Quast, 'Die Grabbeigaben – Ein kommentierter Fundkatalog', in D. Quast (ed.), *Das Grab des fränkischen Königs Childerich in Tournai und die Anastasis Childerici von Jean-Jacques Chifflet aus dem Jahre 1655* (Mainz: Verlag des Römisch-Germanischen Zentralmuseums, 2015), pp. 165–208, pl. 20–2.
40 R. Legoux, *La nécropole mérovingienne de Bulles (Oise)* (Saint-Germain-en-Laye: Association Française d'Archéologie Mérovingienne, 2011), pp. 63–74, fig. 96. For further examples, see V. I. Evison, *Anglo-Saxon cemetery at Alton, Hampshire*, Hampshire Field Club and Archaeological Society: Monograph, 4 (Gloucester: Alan Sutton Publishing, 1988), pp. 5–7, fig. 36 and 45.
41 Gottschalk, *Spätrömische Gräber im Umland von Köln*, p. 242.
42 James, 'The militarisation of Roman society', p. 19.
43 Theuws and Alkemade, 'A kind of mirror for men', at p. 454 and pp. 464–70.

15

Warlike and heroic virtues in the post-Roman world

Edward James

In the proceedings of a conference that took place in Copenhagen in 1996, I proposed a definition of militarisation:

> By a militarised society I mean a society in which there is no clear distinction between soldier and civilian, nor between military officer and government official; where the head of state is also commander-in-chief of the army; where all adult free men have the right to carry weapons; where a certain group or class of people (normally the aristocracy) is expected, by reason of birth, to participate in the army; where the education of the young thus often involves a military element; where the symbolism of warfare and weaponry is prominent in official and private life, and the warlike and heroic virtues are glorified; and where warfare is a predominant government expenditure and/or a major source of economic profit.[1]

There are all sorts of untested problems with this definition, and this chapter deals with one of them: the assumption that in a 'militarised society' 'the warlike and heroic virtues are glorified'.

At first sight that assumption seems uncontroversial. After all, the fifth and sixth centuries are 'the Heroic Age'.[2] Right through the Middle Ages, tales were told of the heroes of these centuries. The fifth and sixth centuries are the chronological home of the British hero Arthur, of course; but also of Irish heroes such as Niall of the Nine Hostages, and Germanic heroes such as Theodoric of Verona (Dietrich von Bern), and many others. In the Icelandic *Saga of the Volsungs* we meet some of them, in heavy disguise: Gundahar of the Burgundians appears as Gunnar, Attila of the Huns as Atli, and Eormanric of the Goths as Jormanrek; and the doomed Frankish royal couple Sigibert (assassinated 575) and Brunechild (pulled apart by wild horses in 613) may have been partially responsible for the equally doomed Sigurd the Volsung, the dragonslayer, and Brynhild, the warrior-maiden. The Anglo-Saxon poem *Beowulf*, memorialising the great deeds of the sixth-century Swedish hero Beowulf – the only other dragon-slayer in early medieval literature apart from Sigurd[3] – mentions the Volsung hero, though it ascribes the dragon-slaying to Sigurd's father Sigmund, Sigemund Waelsing.

The trouble with all these great heroes of the fifth and sixth centuries is that, although we know from contemporary sources that many of them existed (though we can never be sure about Arthur and Beowulf), what we know of their heroism comes from very much later sources. There is nothing about Arthur until the ninth century or later. The sole *Beowulf* manuscript is from the eleventh century, and how can we be sure that the poet lived very much earlier than that? To what extent was the picture provided by the undoubtedly Christian poet, of Beowulf, 'the mildest of men and most kindly, most gentle to his people and most eager for praise', as the closing words of the poem have it, an attempt to remember the pagan hero as someone a much later Christian could admire? Many of our Germanic heroes were preserved in the memory of Icelandic bards and story-tellers – or created with their imaginative art – and written down sometime after 1200. To what extent was early medieval heroism rewritten in the light of later realities? A much-quoted study of the literary motif of the loyal retainer preferring to die with his king rather than surrender suggests that, since it does not surface in the sources between Tacitus in the first century AD and *The Battle of Maldon* poem of the eleventh century, it may in *Maldon* be more a reflection of the burgeoning knightly values of the eleventh century than a harking back to the imagined Germanic values of the Heroic Age.[4]

Three years before the Copenhagen conference there was a conference in Rome on the Germanic hero: the proceedings were published in 1995, although I had not seen a copy myself in 1996. In those proceedings, Walter Goffart argued that heroism in the early Frankish period was conspicuous by its absence.[5] Some years later he published an update to this paper, in a volume of essays about Gregory of Tours, and was there able to answer Ute Schwabe, an early critic of his Rome paper.[6] As far as I have been able to discover, there has been relatively little comment on Goffart's ideas, apart from in several places in Laury Sarti's 2013 book;[7] certainly there has been no sustained comment. Since much of Goffart's 1993 paper appears, sometimes elaborated and sometimes unaltered, in the 2002 version, I shall engage with that later version.

Goffart's main problem with earlier scholarship, above all literary scholarship, is its frequent assumption that because the personnel of early heroic poems in Germanic languages lived in the fifth and sixth century, the poems must date to that period, even if they were not written down then. He quotes Alfred Ebenbauer to the effect 'daß die klassische Zeit des germanischen Heldenlieds der Völkerwanderung ist' and that 'es … nicht Vorzeitkunde

[ist], sondern ... heroische Gegenwart [schildert]'.[8] The Heroic Age is not just the age in which most of the heroes of Germanic literature lived, but the age in which the poems entered the oral tradition, to be written down for the first time several centuries later. As Goffart sums up, 'this conception cannot be disproved, but neither can it be corroborated'.[9]

Goffart's subsequent discussion, therefore, is concerned not with the vernacular poetry of the northern Germanic-speakers, but with Latin literature, and mostly with Latin historiography. 'The fullness of his narrative makes Gregory [of Tours] my main spokesman for the absence of heroism' (p. 370). In Gregory we find literature, not real life, he notes. And, as he says, 'any author worth his salt' (p. 370) can make some ordinary fighting into epic combat or reduce gallant action into boring routine. Gregory's tactic is to aim for the latter, to 'puff down' (p. 370). Goffart shows Gregory's technique in relation to a number of military encounters which he could have treated in heroic fashion, but did not: the survival of Clovis in battle against the Visigoths (saved by his cuirass) (*Hist.* 2.37); Ursio, defending himself against overwhelming odds until he was exhausted and then killed (*Hist.* 9.12);[10] Eberulf, dying in similar circumstances (*Hist.* 7.29); and, in battle, the deaths of King Chlodomer (*Hist.* 3.6) and Duke Desiderius (*Hist.* 8.45). Goffart concludes: 'Gregory's narrative is full of military incompetence and debacles. He gives a negative impression of war, as an activity in which no one is heroic' (pp. 373–4).

Later Frankish historians came closer to the heroic mode than Gregory did. Fredegar, in the mid-seventh century, approaches the heroic in his picture of Theodoric of Italy (the later heroic figure of Dietrich von Bern) and in his account of the Emperor Heraclius. The *Liber Historiae Francorum*, in the mid eighth century, contains 'one long battle scene authentically suggestive of heroic narrative, and unparalleled in Gregory of Tours or Fredegar' (378–9): it is the story of Chlothar II (d. 629) engaging Bertoald, the leader of the Saxons, in single combat on the banks of the River Weser. This tale is set 'after a long interval in which heroic traits are virtually invisible in literature' (p. 379). When we get to the Carolingian era, we have Paul the Deacon's *Historia Langobardorum*, 'a work rich in heroic touches' (p. 380), and the earliest traces of vernacular heroic literature: 'in the age of Charlemagne, heroes were back' (p. 380).

Goffart ends his discussion of Gregory with the anecdote from *Hist.* 5.25, about the attempted arrest by Dragolen of the repeat offender Guntram Boso. The latter reminds Dragolen of his oath to give him free passage and offers to surrender all his possessions in return for such passage. Dragolen refuses and charges; he is unhorsed by Guntram Boso and is killed. Goffart notes that for Gregory this is an edifying story: we have already seen Dragolen as someone who does not keep his word, and thus 'he is tagged for divine retribution'. Guntram Boso, on the other hand, invoked the name of the great St Martin. It leads Goffart into his concluding section, arguing that the Christian church was responsible for the eclipse of heroism – or, one should say, of secular forms of heroism. The heroism of the martyr and the holy man was acceptable, and those kings who were admired were Tiberius (in Gregory), whose Christian charity was immense, or Oswald (in Bede), who prayed before battle rather than doing whatever pre-Christian Anglo-Saxon kings had done before battle. Goffart notes Patrick Wormald's classic article on the conversion of the Anglo-Saxon aristocracy, in which Wormald argued that although the Church tried to change the ethos of warrior society, they largely failed: 'pre-Christian heroism and martial values lived on triumphant in England' (p. 385).[11] But he does not accept Wormald's idea that Latin/Christian and vernacular/traditional cultures lived side by side with relatively little communication between the two. Even if this was true in England, Goffart suggests, it was very different on the Continent: there was no 'vast zone of silence' (Wormald, p. 35) separating historians like Gregory and Fredegar from the warrior class, although one might note that Bede's *Letter to Egbert* actually suggests that Bede was perfectly well acquainted with the problems of the Anglo-Saxon aristocracy, even if he largely concealed this knowledge when we wrote the *Historia Ecclesiastica Gentis Anglorum*. But Goffart ends by saying that even in England 'the heroic mode' may be a later development, and not present ever since the period of the English invasions and settlement. There was no reason why there might not have been 'intermittent occurrences of bravery, self-sacrifice, and other manifestations of heroic conduct' in early Francia. 'The one certainty, however, is that contemporary authors do not trumpet such incidents: there was no heroic literature' (p. 387).

There is a postscript at the end of Goffart's 2002 article, in which he discusses Ute Schwabe's criticism of the earlier version of his paper.[12] Schwabe, like Wormald and like her peers in the community of scholars devoted to the study of early Germanic literatures, believes that there existed twin cultures of memory-keeping: a literate Latin culture, largely adhering to classical ideas of literary genres, and an oral culture, which only wrote down its stories and traditions several centuries after the Migration Period. Goffart does not accept the possibility that these two cultures did not speak to each other. And given the frequent political and cultural ruptures that took place among the Germanic peoples in the fifth and sixth centuries, it is reasonable to think that there were ruptures of historical memory as well. He ends with noting that there are other ways of dealing with the material, such as the challenging one recently published, he writes, in *The Cambridge companion to English literature* (p. 393).

This is a reference to Roberta Frank's chapter on 'Germanic legend in Old English literature'.[13] As she says, early Germanic tradition in England survives in just five Old English poems, all surviving only in single manuscripts from the last generations of Anglo-Saxon England. *Beowulf* is, famously, about a Swedish hero active in Denmark and later in Sweden. They are all 'Germanic' heroes, although we may doubt that early Anglo-Saxons, uneducated as they were in the ways of nineteenth-century Germanist studies, were necessarily aware of the fact. It is perhaps only in later Anglo-Saxon England that Germanic legend became something 'people had to know, like chess, claret or cricket, if they wanted to be thought cultured' (p. 97). Clearly what survives is a fragment of what may have been an enormous mass of heroic poetry – 'Each name or episode in *Widsith*, *Deor* and *Beowulf* may be regarded as an allusion to another poem' (p. 101); nevertheless 'it is impossible to know how much more (or less) the Anglo-Saxons knew of Germanic legend than we do' (p. 103).

Goffart is right that there is not a great deal of evidence from the earliest Middle Ages for the existence of a vernacular heroic literature. There are some hints, however.[14] Jordanes said that the Goths sang songs of their heroes in early times, and that when the Visigoths found Theodorid dead on the battlefield, having defended Gaul against Attila, they 'honoured him with songs'. Venantius Fortunatus, in a poem addressed to Duke Lupus, said that the barbarians [that is, the Franks] praised his bravery and deeds of arms with the harp, just as the Roman praised his learning and justice with the lyre.[15] In the Carolingian period, Paul the Deacon and Poeta Saxo both noted that the deeds of sixth-century kings had been, or indeed still were, celebrated in song.[16] None of these sources are without their problems, and even the accumulation of such sources does not prove a case. But, unlike Goffart, I do not feel that proving the existence of a body of vernacular heroic literature in the earliest Middle Ages is essential to the rehabilitation of the idea that an heroic ethos may have existed in that period. The absence of evidence for martial heroism is in fact an aspect of the problem with our sources, which on the whole do not provide us with details of warfare. That, wrote Guy Halsall, 'is one of the most intriguing aspects of the study of war in this period';[17] and, moreover, it is 'utterly intractable'.[18]

Indeed, we know very clearly that a heroic ethos did exist in the sixth century, thanks to Gregory's near-contemporary Prokopios, who wrote far more extensively on warfare than any other sixth-century writer. Even though he came from a different, Greek-speaking, culture, he shows that enthusiastic admiration for the warlike virtues was active in at least one part of the sixth-century world.[19] Martial heroism is described in essentially four different contexts: general praise of individuals where their military virtues are emphasised;[20] descriptions of individuals performing heroic acts in battle;[21] general heroic behaviour by more than one individual (including an entire unit of the army) in a battle;[22] and finally descriptions of occasions where a soldier offers single combat before the formal start of a battle.[23] At least twice 'valour' in the contemporary situation is mentioned in hyperbolic terms (the word being translated by 'valour' is the Greek *arete*). The men that surrounded and protected Belisarios 'made a display of valor such, I imagine, as has never been shown by any man in the world to this day' (*Wars* 5.18.12, p. 294); 'There a battle took place and a display of valor by both Romans and Persians such as I at least believe has never once been seen in these times' (*Wars* 8.11.41, p. 486). A further comparison of the heroes of the present and those of the past comes in one of the last battles against the Goths: 'And now I come to describe a battle of great note and the virtue of a man inferior, I think, to none of the heroes of legend, namely, which Theia displayed in the present battle' (*Wars* 8.35.20, p. 542). It is worth noting that throughout Prokopios gives credit to heroic deeds regardless of which side the hero was on: Romans, Persians and Goths all receive praise.

One passage is worth quoting in full, even if it is not technically a deed of heroism. It is an astonishing and unique (for this period) record of the significance of display, both in terms of apparel but also of personal military skills. It describes Totila, king of the Goths, before the Battle of Taginae or Busta Gallorum, in 552.

> First of all, he was not reluctant to make an exhibition to the enemy of what kind of man he was. The armor in which he was clad was abundantly plated with gold, and the ample adornments that hung from his cheek-plates as well as from his helmet and spear were not only of purple but in other respects befitting a king marvellous in abundance. And he himself, sitting upon a very large horse, began to perform the dance under arm skilfully between the armies. For he wheeled his horse around in a circle and then turned again to the other aside, and so made him run round and round. As he rode he hurled his javelin into the air and caught it again as it quivered above him, then passed it rapidly from hand to hand, shifting it with consummate skill, and he gloried in his practice of the art, falling back on his shoulders, spreading his legs and leaning from side to side, like one who has been instructed with precision in the art of dancing from childhood. By these tactics he wore away the whole early part of the day. (*Wars* 8.31.18–21, pp. 533–4)

Procopios makes it clear that this display was not customary: indeed, Totila was successfully using delaying tactics, because he was waiting for an additional two thousand Gothic soldiers to arrive and take up position. It availed him little; the Goths lost the battle and Totila lost his life. We have nothing like this from a contemporary Latin writer: but, then, we have no contemporary Latin writers working within the secular pre-Christian tradition of historiography, as Prokopios was.

The most sustained critique of Goffart's theory can be found in Sarti's book *Perceiving war*. She points out first of all that there are fifth-century sources which contain heroic elements. Sidonius writes to his brother-in-law Ecdicius about his deeds, including how 'with a following of barely eighteen mounted comrades you made your way through several thousands of Goths not merely in the middle of the day, but in the middle of an open plain – an achievement such as posterity will scarcely credit'.[24] He lists further military achievements, and describes the adulation Ecdicius had received from the people of Clermont.[25] (Gregory oddly reduces the eighteen men to ten when he describes the same incident at *Hist.* 2.24.) Also from fifth-century Gaul is Merobaudes' panegyric for Aëtius, which Sarti calls 'the most open commendation for martial abilities to be found in the written sources composed in Gaul between the fifth and seventh centuries';[26] while Gregory's own description of Aëtius (*Hist.* 2.8) is 'the most detailed description of a non-royal military man found in Merovingian sources'.[27] On the other hand, the most significant Latin writer in sixth-century Gaul – Venantius Fortunatus – has no more emphasis on martial prowess than Gregory. His panegyric to Chilperic mentions the king's martial virtues, but only in passing. Only the poems dedicated to the *domesticus* Conda and the *dux* Lupus draw attention to military virtues and actions, although in the former, while mentioning how Conda's sons died in battle, Fortunatus comes out with the conventional line 'those who fight for glory live forever'.[28]

An interesting comparison is to be made in the case of Mummolus. Fortunatus' poem dedicated to him does not mention his military abilities, except by 'jokingly comparing the banquet at the centre of his poem to a magnificent battle fought in his stomach'.[29] Yet according to Gregory, Mummolus was the leading non-royal Frankish general of the sixth century. Gregory indeed seems at times to be on the verge of describing him in heroic terms; he certainly describes him as 'always victorious' and says that the Lombard leaders were 'all terrified by the prowess of Mummolus'.[30] As Sarti points out,[31] Gregory offers no negative comments on Mummolus. But although it would have been easy to cast Mummolus in a heroic light, Gregory does not do so. His death came about as a result of betrayal by his former ally Leudegisel; he was run through by the lances of Leudegisel's men.[32]

Sarti argues that in the case of Mummolus, as in the cases of Munderic and Ursio, Gregory does not give us a picture of heroism. But, she says, he does show us 'heroic moments': events that could well have been initially couched in heroic mode, and indeed had perhaps come to Gregory in heroic form.[33] Munderic was an early sixth-century pretender, who had to retreat into a fortress when King Theuderic advanced toward him with a much larger army. Theuderic besieged the fortress. Munderic said to his men, and this is reported by Gregory: '"Let us stand firm, and fight to the death together, for we must never submit to our enemies."'[34] In the end, Theuderic's man Aregisel is sent to Munderic with a false promise of safe conduct; and even does so on an altar. When Aregisel leaves the fortress, holding Munderic's hand, he gives a sign to his men to kill Munderic. But Munderic realises what is happening and thrusts a javelin through Aregisel's back. 'Munderic then drew his sword and with his own men around him slew one after another of the enemy troops. As long as there was breath in his body he continued to cut down every man within his reach.'[35] He was killed in the end, of course. The death of Ursio, who had conspired against Childebert II, was similar. Childebert's men surrounded the church in which Ursio and his men had taken refuge. They started to set it on fire. Ursio took his sword and left the church. 'He killed so many of the besiegers that of all those that came within range of him not one was left alive. Trudulf, Count of the Royal Palace, died in this skirmish, and many of his troops were killed.'[36] In the end, Ursio betrayed that he was tired by breathing hard, was rushed, and killed. For Goffart, Munderic and Ursio were 'merely human in their fighting and bound to succumb when their strength gave out'. For Ursio in particular 'Gregory does not invite admiration'; 'The detail about labored breath brings him down to our level and undercuts any heroic aura.'[37] One may doubt Goffart's assumption that a hero has to be superhuman. But more to the point is that although Gregory does not express admiration of these men, we may imagine that others – including those who passed the stories on to Gregory – might well have done. Sarti concludes that it seems 'highly likely' that these stories had come to Gregory in heroic mode, and that Gregory adjusted them to suit his own purposes.[38]

To understand what those purposes might be, we may turn to an exceptionally important study of four early medieval historians published now over thirty years ago in 1988, by the same Walter Goffart.[39] Goffart divides Gregory's works into two categories (which Gregory did not quite do himself at *Hist.* 10.31): ten books of *Histories* (*Historiae*) and eight books of *Wonders* (*Miracula*). In terms of his narrative treatment, the two works have much in common, and 'saints and miracles are no strangers to the *Histories*' (*Narrators*, p. 152). 'The main difference is that the *Wonders* is an account of unrelieved good news: the bountifulness of divine gifts, the proximity of the holy, and its ready accessibility to men' (pp. 152–3). The *Wonders* are about *virtutes*; the *Histories* are about *strages gentium*, 'the slaughter of peoples', and *miserorum excidia*, 'the downfall of worthless men'. Goffart identifies the predominant mode in the *Histories* as irony, and Gregory uses that weapon to cast most activities of the secular world – Goffart lists warfare, political manoeuvrings, administration of justice, rebellion, adultery, rape and murder (p. 181) – in a dark and frequently condemnatory light.

He is able to do that in part because he selects and shapes facts to his purpose, and in part because he suppresses them.[40] Contemporaries were even better able to appreciate Gregory than we are. Apart from being given 'a jolting lesson in Christian values', 'the first thing they were to understand about profane *gesta praesentia* was that, almost without exception, they were crimes and follies expressive of empty and futile cravings' (p. 230). The celebration of any martial heroism would be totally out of place in Gregory's scheme.

There were heroes in Gregory's work, however. They were, almost without exception, martyrs or holy men (and a few women). It was largely a male thing: there is one woman among the twenty-three 'Fathers' whose lives are celebrated in Gregory's *Life of the Fathers*, but the woman, Monegundis, was there in part because she fought 'with a virile strength'.[41] Sometimes this is heroism that the modern world would recognise. There was the priest Cato, whose ecclesiastical ambitions were greeted by Gregory with scorn, but who stayed in Clermont during the plague and 'with great courage' said Mass until his death. 'This priest was a person of great humanity and devoted to the poor. He was a proud man, it is true, but what he did at this moment excused everything.'[42] But all martyrs and confessors were heroes, in their fight against persecutors and the wiles of the world, but above all against the wiles of the Devil and his temptations. These were Gregory's heroes: these were the role-models Gregory was placing before his contemporaries.

As Conrad Leyser has pointed out in his article on nocturnal emission (a perennial problem for the would-be celibate and ascetic), the 'rise of ascetic masculinity' in the early Middle Ages was not 'an introverted discourse of sexual anxiety', but part of 'a fiercely competitive culture of public power'.[43] The fifth and sixth centuries may have been the Heroic Age of the warrior in the minds of H. M. Chadwick and others; they were also the centuries when ascetics began to chip heroically away at the ideals of traditional heroism, and of traditional masculine values as a whole, to set up their own counter-culture of heroic asceticism. The creation of an alternative heroic ethos based on Christian values, of course, implies the existence of a secular concept of heroism.

Think for a moment of the life of a traditional hero, even if it is that of an imagined hero of later epic, romance or saga. His worth is recognised above all in battle, in his courage and fortitude: in short, his ability to kill people. He has pride in his birth, and in his ability to produce children, and in his own honour and that of his family. His boastfulness about his achievements is celebrated, the more so if it is done artistically and extravagantly. He is generous to his men; which means, among other things, having frequent feasts and celebrating their community by drinking with them. He has obligations to his men and to his people; his role is to protect them from their enemies. These values are above all seen as expressions of masculinity.

The life of a good ascetic Christian is almost diametrically opposed. The ascetic rejects bloodshed, and even those emotions that lead to bloodshed, particularly anger. The ascetic rejects his family, and if he left property to the church hedged it around with legal protections in order to stop his family claiming back what they no doubt seriously believed was theirs. The ascetic rejected public obligations and public office, despite the desperation with which late Roman authorities tried to enforce those obligations. The ascetic rejected boastfulness and pride, and the luxuries and pleasures of the world, particularly those involved in gluttony and fornication. So, the true hero in the new Christian world was the ascetic, who fought the temptations of the devil and his minions, who are literally all around us. A discerning saint could see these demons; but any ascetic ought to recognise the temptations that they sow among men and women, and ought to devote himself to a life of heroic struggle against them. The true Christian hero is marked out by struggle, therefore; he gains his heroism by struggle just as the military hero does, except that his struggle is against the Devil and not in alliance with him. An ascetic who achieves freedom from, say, lechery without struggle, merely because he has little passion, is not a true hero. Indeed, he is like the eunuch, says John Cassian: 'it is one thing to attain to peace by passive good fortune, and another to be worthy of a triumph thanks to one's glorious virtues [*virtutes*]'.[44] To be a proper ascetic you need to be a spiritual warrior: to have won your masculinity and heroism as a secular warrior did – by bravery, persistence and struggle.

Cassian and others in the fifth century thus postulated a different type of *vir* and a different type of *virtus* or manliness from that described by secular writers such as Ammianus Marcellinus; but it is in some ways not very different. After all, self-control was the first of the *virtutes* that Ammianus had found in Julian. A Stoic refusal to allow the passions to surface had long been admired among Romans; the dangers of giving in to sexual passion, indeed the desirability of avoiding sexual relations altogether, was something that was stressed by Roman moralists, but also by Roman doctors – Julian's own doctor Oribasius was a supporter of total abstinence as a route to health.[45] And Christian moralists had not dropped some of the crucial aspects of *virtus*: above all, courage in the face of adversity. The language of manliness was merely given a new twist, in a spiritual direction. Ascetics were soldiers of Christ, or they were athletes of Christ, and they were even claimed to be *more* manly than those in the lay world. St Jerome said that marriage made a man effeminate and noted that 'no soldier marches into battle with a wife'.[46] It was even argued that accepting orders from a superior in the outside world was unmanly; but obedience to an abbot was liberating, because it led to salvation. The greatest virtue was humility, and he who was most humble had the most authority: thus, at the end of the sixth century, Pope Gregory would assert his superiority by declaring himself 'the slave of the slaves of God'. The danger was, of course, that truly humble people – the poor – would gain authority from their humility; but this was a danger Jerome had recognised and dismissed: men raised from poverty or low social position would be grasping and eager for power; only superior men could be humble.[47]

It was not necessary for Gregory of Tours to have read widely in the literature of asceticism for him to have grasped all this. By the sixth century, such ideas were all pervasive. The absence of secular heroic values from Gregory's writings tell us nothing about the presence or absence of secular heroic values in Gregory's world. The reason why Gregory was so consistent in his hostility to the glamour of warfare was that admiration of secular heroism was all too prevalent in the world in which he lived. As Goffart rightly says (p. 386), Gregory took 'a sustained interest in the lay aristocracy'; there was no 'vast zone of silence' separating him from the Frankish warrior class. But that does not mean that he was at all sympathetic to their values and behaviour.

Notes

1 E. James, 'The militarisation of Roman society, 400–700', in A. N. Jørgensen and B. L. Clausen (eds), *Military aspects of Scandinavian society in a European perspective, AD 1–1300* (Copenhagen: National Museum, 1997), pp. 19–24, at p. 19.
2 Echoing H. M. Chadwick, *The heroic age* (Cambridge: Cambridge University Press, 1912); J. de Vries, *Heroic song and heroic legend* (Oxford: Oxford University Press, 1963) has also been influential.
3 Though see C. Rauer, *Beowulf and the dragon. Parallels and analogues* (Woodbridge: Boydell and Brewer, 2000).
4 R. Frank, 'The ideal of men dying with their lord in *The Battle of Maldon*. Anachronism or Nouvelle Vague?', in I. Wood and N. Lund (eds), *People and places in northern Europe, 500–1600* (Woodbridge: Boydell and Brewer, 1991), pp. 95–106.
5 W. Goffart, 'Conspicuous by absence. Heroism in the early Frankish era (6th-7th cent.)', in T. Pároli (ed.), *La funzione dell'eroe germanici. Storicità, metafora, paradigma* (Rome: Il calamo, 1995), pp. 41–56.
6 W. Goffart, 'Conspicuously absent. Martial heroism in the *Histories* of Gregory of Tours and its likes', in K. Mitchell and I. N. Wood (eds), *The world of Gregory of Tours* (Leiden: Brill, 2002), pp. 365–93.

7 L. Sarti, *Perceiving war and the military in early Christian Gaul (ca. 400–700 A.D.)*, Brill's Series on the Early Middle Ages, 22 (Leiden: Brill, 2013), esp. pp. 112–18.
8 A. Ebenbauer, 'Heldenlied und "historisches Lied" im Frühmittelalter und davor', in H. Beck (ed.), *Heldensage und Heldendichtung im Germanischen*, RGA Ergänzungsbände, 2 (Berlin: De Gruyter, 1988), pp. 15–34, at p. 30 and p. 28.
9 Goffart, 'Conspicuously absent', p. 368. All subsequent page references to Goffart's article will be in the text.
10 Not *Hist.* 1.12, as Goffart's footnote says.
11 P. Wormald, 'Bede, *Beowulf* and the conversion of the Anglo-Saxon aristocracy', in R. T. Farrell (ed.), *Bede and Anglo-Saxon England*, British Archaeological Reports, British Series, 46 (Oxford: BAR, 1978), pp. 32–95.
12 Goffart, 'Conspicuously absent', pp. 387–93; U. Schwabe, 'Kritische Bemerkungen zu einer Sammlung von Vorträgen über den "germanischen Helden"' *Amsterdamer Beiträge zur älteren Germanistik*, 46 (1996), 189–215, esp. 196–8.
13 In M. Godden and M. Lapidge (eds), *The Cambridge companion to Old English literature* (Cambridge: Cambridge University Press, 1991), pp. 88–106.
14 The evidence has been collected and discussed in H. Moisl, *Lordship and tradition in barbarian Europe*, Studies in Classics, 10 (Lewiston: Edwin Mellen, 1999). Moisl at one point comments plaintively 'why Goffart is so hostile to historical tradition is not entirely clear' (p. 36).
15 Cited with commentary by Moisl, *Lordship and tradition*, pp. 31–2, 33, and 57 (Jordanes, *Getica*, 28, 214; Fortunatus, Carm. 7.8, ll. 60–71). Other references to heroic songs may be found in Merobaudes, Paneg. 2, ll. 186–8; Sidonius Carm. 5, ll 206–7; Fortunatus Carm. 1. pref 5; Fortunatus Carm. 7.7, ll. 49–50 and 54; Fortunatus Carm. 7.10, ll. 1–6; and the barbara et antiquissima carmina mentioned in Einhard, *Vita Karoli Magni* 2-15, ed. O. Holder-Egger, MGH SRG, 25 (Hanover: Hahnsche Buchhandlung, 1911).
16 Moisl, *Lordship and tradition*, pp. 43 and 55.
17 G. Halsall, *Warfare and society in the barbarian west, 450–900* (London: Routledge, 2003), p. 2.
18 *Ibid.*, p. 6.
19 My page references relate to *Prokopios. The wars of Justinian*, trans. H. B. Dewing and A. Kaldellis (Indianapolis: Hackett, 2014).
20 *Wars* 1.11.5 (p. 24); 4.10.4 (p. 210); 7.1.4–22 (pp. 383–4) (Belisarios); 8.11.16 (Totila's display) (pp. 533–4).
21 *Wars* 1.18.38 (p. 48); 3.19.15 (p. 182); 5.18.4–15 (pp. 293–4); 5.18.33 (p. 295); 7.28.15 (p. 435); 8.11.40, 48 (p. 486); 8.11.57 (p. 487); 8.29.22–28 (pp. 529–30); 8.35.20 (p. 542).
22 *Wars* 1.14.39 (p. 36); 5.15.4–15 (pp. 293–4); 7.24.15 (p. 428); 7.24.24 (p. 429); 7.36.18–23 (p. 453); 8.11.41 (p. 486); 8.29.22 (p. 529).
23 *Wars* 1.13.31–38 (p. 33); 7.5.21 (p. 391); 8.31.11–16 (p. 533)
24 *Ep.* 3.3: *Sidonius. Letters III-IX*, trans. W. B. Anderson (Cambridge, MA: Harvard University Press, 1965), pp. 14–15.

25 See Sarti, *Perceiving war*, pp. 109–10.
26 *Ibid.*, p. 104.
27 *Ibid.*, p. 107.
28 *Carm.* 7.16, line 52: discussed in Sarti, *Perceiving war*, pp. 114–15.
29 *Carm* 7.14, lines 35.6; quoting Sarti, *Perceiving war*, p. 115.
30 *Hist.* 4.45, 4.44; trans. L. Thorpe, *Gregory of Tours. History of the Franks* (Harmondsworth: Penguin, 1974), p. 241.
31 Sarti, *Perceiving war*, p. 112.
32 *Hist.* 7.39.
33 Sarti, *Perceiving war*, p. 112.
34 *Hist.* 3.14; Thorpe, p. 174.
35 *Hist* 3.14; Thorpe, p. 175.
36 *Hist.* 9.12; Thorpe, p. 495.
37 Goffart, 'Conspicuously absent', p. 371.
38 Sarti, *Perceiving war*, p. 113.
39 W. Goffart, *The narrators of barbarian history. Jordanes, Gregory of Tours, Bede, and Paul the Deacon* (Princeton: Princeton University Press, 1988).
40 Goffart discusses Gregory's distortion of the facts in the context of Avitus' conversion of the Jews of Clermont, pp. 163–4.
41 *Life of the fathers* 19, Preface: trans. E. James, *Gregory of Tours. Life of the fathers*, 2nd edn (Liverpool: Liverpool University Press, 1991), p. 118.
42 *Hist.* 4.31: trans. Thorpe, p. 226.
43 C. Leyser, 'Masculinity in flux. Nocturnal emission and the limits of celibacy in the early middle Ages', in D. M. Hadley (ed.), *Masculinity in medieval Europe* (London: Longman, 1999), pp. 103–20, at p. 105.
44 John Cassian, *Conlationes*, 22.3, quoted in M. Kuefler, *The manly eunuch. Masculinity, gender ambiguity, and Christian ideology in late Antiquity* (Chicago: University of Chicago Press, 2001), p. 81.
45 Kuefler, *Manly eunuch*, pp. 79–80.
46 Jerome, *Adv. Jovinian* I.28 and *Epist* 22.21; cited by Kuefler, *Manly eunuch*, p. 181.
47 *Ibid.*, p. 155.

16

Military equipment in late antique and early medieval female burial evidence: a reflection of 'militarisation'?

Susanne Brather-Walter

Merovingian period 'row-grave cemeteries' show a variety of burial furnishings. Men were equipped with belts and weapons, women with dress accessories and jewellery. Furthermore, graves contained 'non-gendered' objects such as vessels or furniture. Grave-goods assemblage additionally varied based on the age of the deceased, the location of their burial, and the point of time at which they had been buried.

When weapons (sword, lance, bow and arrow, shield) and equestrian equipment (spurs, stirrups and saddle) are found only in male graves, a relatively strict gender separation must be postulated: no female burials contain weapons and no male burials contain jewellery. But there are exceptions. Occasionally, parts of military equipment have been discovered in early medieval female graves and sometimes female objects were found in male burials. What conclusions may be drawn from these findings?

To explain this phenomenon, modern research has resorted to concepts like that of 'Amazons' when interpreting a female burial equipped with weapons.[1] A skeleton of a triple burial of armed individuals from Niederstotzingen (south-western Germany) excavated in 1962[2] and dating to the early seventh century has been of particular interest. As one of the three individuals was considered female, she was interpreted as an 'Amazon following the antique literary *topos*'. Such an interpretation, if accepted, would imply that the deceased was a heavily armed women acting like a man.[3] Recent genetic analyses, however, have refuted this assumption and proven that all three individuals were male.[4] Another common approach is to speak of 'iron ladies' by referring to the unflattering nickname of the former British prime minister Margaret Thatcher (1925–2013).[5] These interpretations appear to be unsatisfying, however. On the one hand, they appear quite straightforward as they focus on one single observation: the occurrence of weaponry in female burials. On the other hand, the wider context of these findings is not taken into consideration. Questions that often lack further consideration include the exact types of 'weapons' deposed in female graves, the accompanying grave-goods and the overall circumstances of the burial.

Anyone looking for examples of female burials with military equipment would expect to be confronted with a consistent phenomenon. However, an in-depth search would quickly reveal that weapons and other military equipment in women's graves varies in several aspects. The aim of the following chapter is to present a short survey of the relevant evidence.

Before we start, an important observation should be made: the appearance of weapons in female graves raises the question about the meaning of this phenomenon. Should we interpret this as a transfer from the male into the female sphere? If so, does this also imply the transmission of male/masculine ideals? Alternatively, a transformation of the 'original' male signification attributed to weapons deposed in burials would be conceivable, implying the introduction of a new aspect of female representation; for example, as symbols of protection.

Returning to the range of military objects found in female graves, six categories may be distinguished that can divided into two main groups:

A. Weapons in female graves:
   1. weapons *'en miniature'*,
   2. fragments of defensive armour and horse gear,
   3. parts of harness, military belt-buckles and strap ends.
B. Pictorial representations of warriors on portable media:
   4. scenes of warriors on brooches or other accessories,
   5. the motif of the horseman with lance on ornamental discs,
   6. simplified scenes of warriors on brooches or other accessories.

Weapons *'en miniature'* in bronze or silver – swords, shields, axes and hammers

Weapons *'en miniature'*[6] are often associated with chains or necklaces. The late third-century grave of Hassleben (Germany) may serve as an example, wherein the necklace consisted of many beads in the shape of small axes made of gold and silver.[7] Such pendants have been discovered between northern Germany and the Carpathian Basin. Most of them belong to the third and fourth centuries and have been found both within and outside the Roman Empire. Most famous is the golden chain of Szilágy-Somlyó (Șimleu Silvaniei, Romania)[8] dated to the first half of the fifth century. A multitude of pendants are attached to this chain, including objects of everyday life (knife, scissors, axe, hammer, spade, key), magic symbols (wine leaves, cairngorm globe), and weapons (sword, shield). The reconstruction of the chain suggests that the most likely way of wearing it would be as an ornament carried around either an individual's hips or neck. The chain may have served as a model for Merovingian girdle hangers, but its contemporary character or function remains unclear.

Miniature weapons were also discovered in a later-sixth century grave near Sontheim/Brenz (south-western Germany).[9] This burial contained some weapons that were just a few centimetres in length: a small knife, a shield and a sword deposited on the chest of the woman. Such late finds remain much more limited in number than their precursors, however. Archaeology has mainly interpreted these pendants as amulets, *phylakteria*, talismans or magic symbols of supernatural power, according to concepts of apotropaic agency. These supposedly 'magic' objects are often related to paganism, but this appears to be a misleading interpretation. Although 'magic' may be related to different religious ideas, there is no indication clearly associating these objects with non-Christian concepts or rituals. As such, there is no reason to assume that magical objects did not also have a place within a Christian milieu.

One type of object within the mentioned category has been consistently considered as a pagan symbol: the 'Thor's hammer' and the 'Donar's mace amulet' made of bone[10] and decorated with engraved lines and stamped circular eyes. Although it is mainly found in male graves, some have been discovered in female burials. Although Scandinavian influences have been suggested, drawing on references to the much later Saga literature, the objects themselves do not provide any indication confirming the supposed meaning. While the so-called 'Thor's hammer' gradually disappeared from the late fourth and until the fifth century in the territory of the later Merovingian kingdoms, it reappeared during the tenth century in southern Scandinavia, presumably as a reaction to the Christian cross.[11] Meanwhile, the 'Donar's mace amulets' continued to be used until the late sixth century as pendants on girdle hangers.

Another example may be related to 'exchanges' taking place between the male and the female sphere – different in subject but similar in symbolic meaning. Polyhedral crystal beads attached to swords are considered to have been used by men as 'magic beads', while related to women the same objects are interpreted as pendants that were attached to their belts (*Gürtelgehänge*). As these objects were obviously used simultaneously by both genders, no chronological development from men to women or vice versa may be postulated. Nonetheless, a gendered difference may be observed: the promise of victory for warriors and health for women.

Fragments of defensive armour and horse gear

Rings as part of chain armour

These meshed rings were originally parts of chainmail, whether in the form of body armour or the neck guard of a helmet. Only small parts of the armour were used, including around a dozen rings. In Ukraine, an early female grave has been discovered containing such a ring-mesh talisman/amulet that is dated to the decades around 300.[12] In the early Middle Ages, these objects were fixed as pendants on female belts known as *Gürtelgehänge*; i.e. belts with an arrangement of strings hanging down with a large number of objects either used as practical tools, talismans or apotropaic objects. In the west, the earliest examples of this type of talisman occur around 400 in female burials.[13] Generally speaking, however, this type of amulet is largely known from female graves dating to the fifth and sixth centuries, with a distribution extending from northern France up to the middle Danube. Thus, these amulets (see Figure 16.1) and related burial tradition had a long history, even if their specific origins remain difficult to explain.

It remains unclear how these components of armour were transformed into talismans. Had they simply been collected by chance as 'anonymous' objects; or were they intentionally taken from a specific man's armour, indicating a special individual relationship? It is also possible that these items did not possess such a symbolic meaning. For example, ring meshes might have been used pragmatically as metal sponges to clean metal cooking utensils. Nevertheless, it is hard to imagine that these ring meshes were made specifically for domestic needs. It appears more convincing to argue that they were deposed in female burials for symbolic, emotional or ritual purposes.

Lamellar armour

A few female graves of the Avar period[14] contain fragments of lamellar armour. They represent small components from defensive armour. Although these burials belong to the late sixth to the early ninth centuries, i.e. a later period, as well as to another region (Pannonia), the assumption that these fragments were protective amulets appears likely in this context.

Parts of lances

Decorated rivet plates were originally used as washers for rivets, which attached lance heads at their shaft. They were later used as pendants on

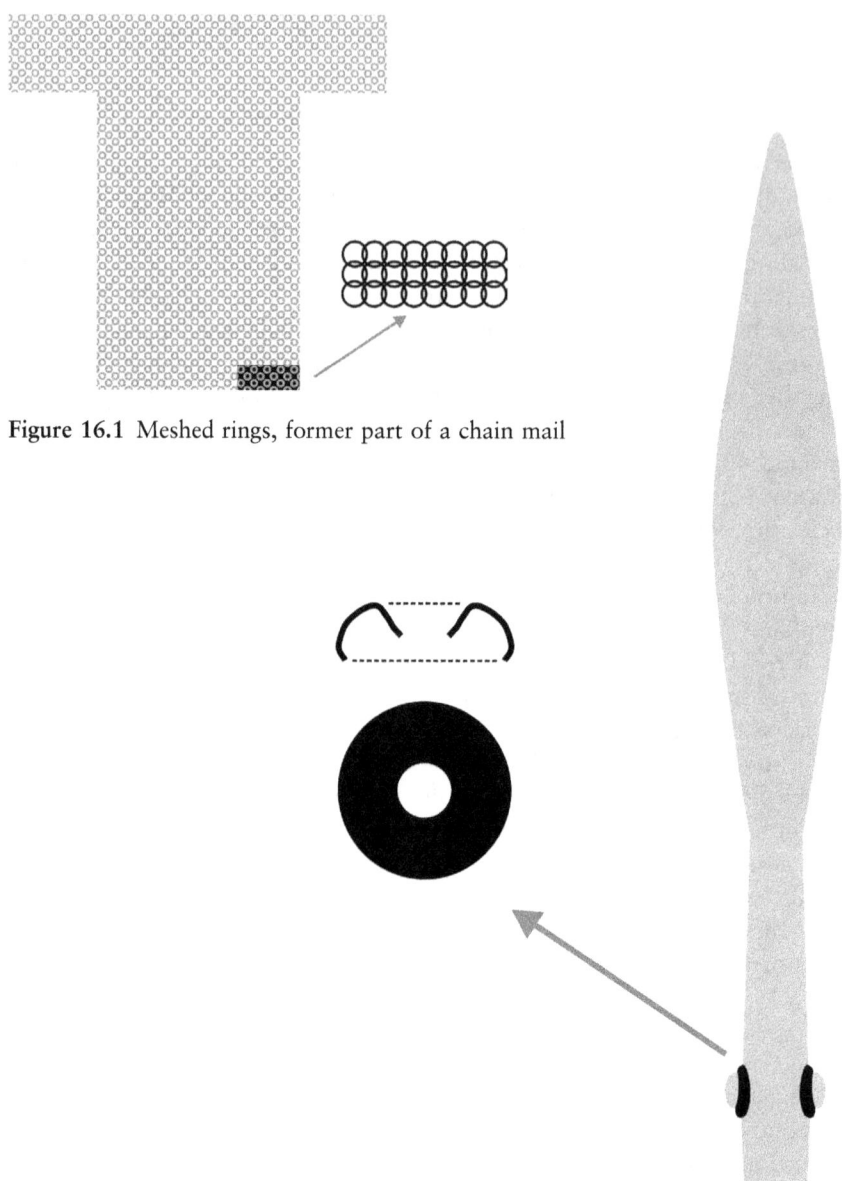

Figure 16.1 Meshed rings, former part of a chain mail

Figure 16.2 Washer, former part of a lance head

necklaces, as attested in two seventh-century female burials from Lauchheim (see Figure 16.2).[15] Again, two interpretations are possible: the washers may have been symbols of protection or power, but it is also conceivable that they were used as profane decorative items.

Horse gear

Depending on the definition of 'weaponry', components of horse gear can also be considered. Horse gear and horse burials were mostly combined with a set of weapons in the adjoining male grave, a connection that suggests a military context of riding. From a general perspective, this equipment is connected to the male sphere.

Parts of the horse harness, such as *phalerae* – i.e. ornamented discs – were reused as a brooch in female grave no. 4 near Schwenningen (Germany).[16] Nearly identical discs have been discovered in the so-called 'Chiefs' Graves' of Apahida (Romania).[17] Another female burial, grave no. 2 of the graveyard at Lauffen (Germany),[18] contained a piece of an original saddle decoration plate, which was reused as a pendant or amulet.

In Lauchheim, snaffles were discovered in some female graves, most of which date to the seventh century. It appears that they were used as substitutes for chain links on hangers. Any interpretation should consider a possible pragmatic function in the sense of a 'misappropriation' of their original function by substituting missing elements of a chain. This seems more likely than their interpretation in the context of a specific symbolic meaning; for example, in reference to a military context.

There is, nevertheless, a noticeable trend over time. In the seventh century, material related to equestrian warriors was notably frequent in burials, suggesting that these were considered particularly important at that time. It is possible that the snaffles found in female graves had a comparable function, even though they were no longer in use as horse harnesses since they had become parts of female dress accessories.

Military belt fittings and military insignia

Burials of the fifth century mainly contain many elements of Roman late antique elite status representation – folding chairs, bronze vessels or silver spoons. Prestigious objects occur in the graves of men as well as in those of women.[19] Along the Upper Rhine, for example, there are a number of such richly equipped female burials.[20] These objects represent the new military elite, created by the 'transformation of the Roman world' and opposed to the traditional Roman elite,[21] and these valuable grave-goods may be interpreted as status symbols. They belong to burials of both genders insofar as they are not gender specific.

Military belts

Surprisingly, military belts or parts of them can also be found in some female graves. Such burials occur along the periphery of the former Roman

Empire, according to the newly developed burial rite in these areas.[22] The female burial 363 of Schleitheim-Hebsack (Switzerland),[23] for example, contained a complete *cingulum* instead of a mere few individual pieces. Did this woman wear the *cingulum* during her lifetime, or was it simply placed upon her body for the funeral in order to represent social rank and power?

In many cases, pieces of 'military belt-sets' have been found in female graves (Figure 16.3). What did they represent, and why did women resort to wearing men's belts? Perhaps they could represent women associated with the military men of that period, or that something has shifted from the men to the women. On the one hand, one could argue that these were worn on a purely pragmatic basis, since there were no specific female belts. On the other hand, a certain social prestige could be supposed to have been expressed symbolically through these belts, perhaps referring to the men of these women.

Furthermore, one could see these belts as a copy of a Mediterranean fashion, involving the provision of a large decorative belt.[24] Is it possible to imagine that some women received the discarded kit of men? Answering this question would require the extensive study and verification of the extent to which these buckles were still used for their functional purpose. It is also be possible that these buckles were given to women solely in the context of burial – in order to emphasise their social role or that of their families.

This is supported by the fact that the belts and their components, as well as the state of their preservation, vary widely. For the majority, it is only the buckles themselves which are found in female graves; occasionally they are still combined with strap-ends.[25] The complete *cingulum* from Schleitheim-Hebsack remains an absolute exception.

Military insignia ('Zwiebelknopffibeln')

In this respect, the so-called '*Zwiebelknopffibeln*' (crossbow-brooches) represent another interesting group of military objects. In Roman times, they were regarded as military as well as civilian insignia, and they were awarded to high-ranking officers.[26] Such insignia occasionally appear in female burials, where they have been used instead of brooches. The female grave 16 of Basel-Gotterbarmweg (Switzerland)[27] may serve as an example. The burial dates back to the fifth century.

Did this fibula serve symbolically as a status symbol? Or did it practically substitute a bow brooch as the 'regular' dress fastener? At the moment, it is unclear whether this was a singular case or was more frequently documented. Was the primary meaning of the brooch as characterising late antique high officials still recognised? Or was it forgotten already, and recognised only as an exotic ornament?

Military equipment female burial evidence 273

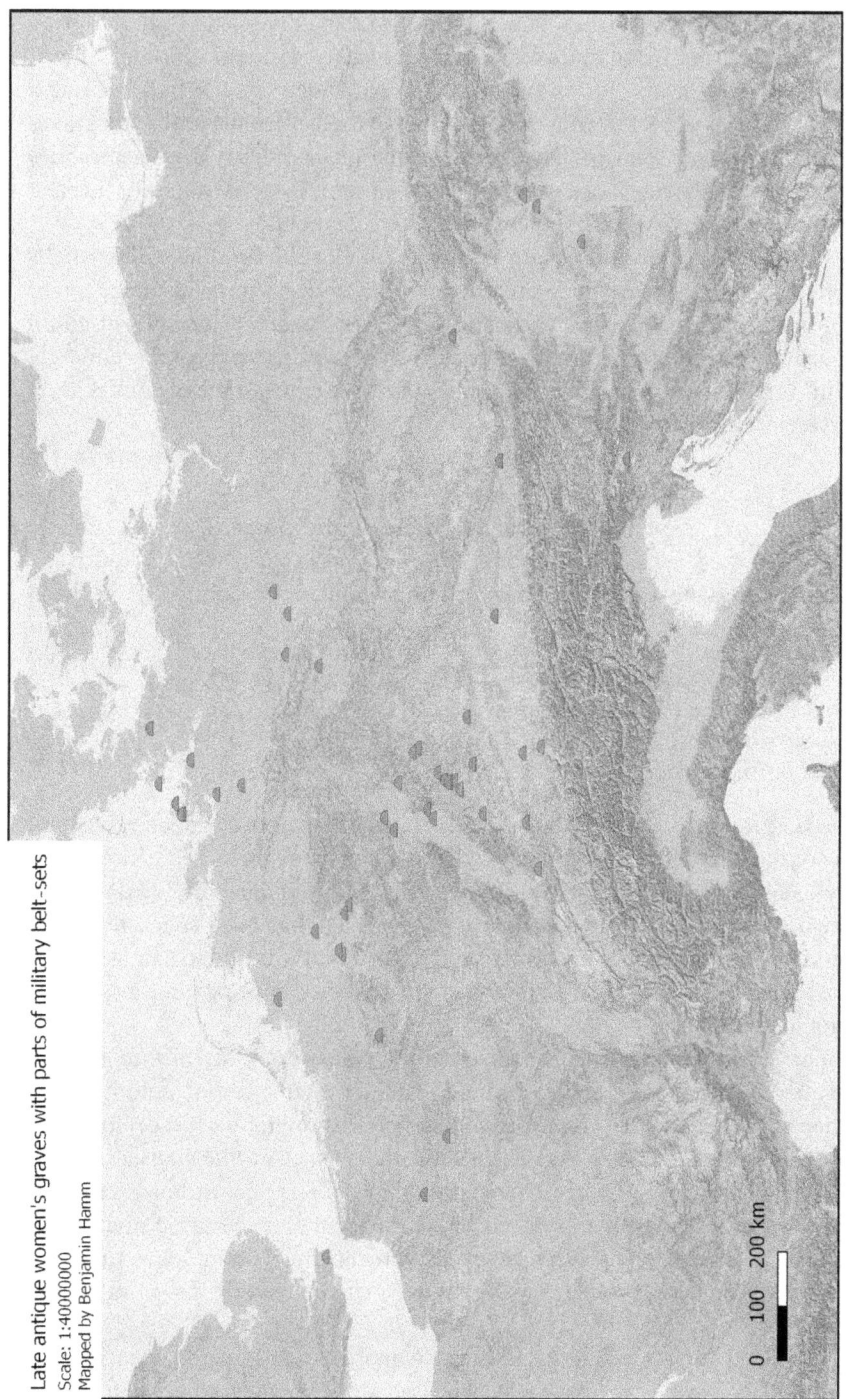

Figure 16.3 The distribution of late antique female graves with military belts

In general, bow brooches, which were common in women's fashion during the later fifth and the sixth centuries, derived from them typologically. If so, this would mean that an original military badge of rank had become a common accessory of female dress. At the very least, female and male graves were not contemporary in this respect. Former male military dress accessories appeared in female burials as 'antiques', often some decades or even a century later than when they had been used by men.

Again, two suggestions might be made. One could say that military belts in female graves, sometimes present together with military insignia, might be interpreted as a kind of 'masculinisation' of female fashion. Or it could be argued these actually 'masculine' attributes in the female sphere merely symbolise affiliation to a higher social class. We have no means of deciding between these two options.

Scenes of warriors, victory and power

Summarising the evidence, four different images of fighting have been described:

- the 'confrontation' of two fighting warriors,
- a rider's victory over an infantryman,
- warriors on parade,
- shooting archers.

The first image is applied to the head-plates of two bow-brooches, at least one of them in a funerary context.[28] The brooch from grave 85 at Kirchheim/Teck (south-western Germany) shows – in a reduced and simplified manner – two men, face-to-face. Traditionally, the image has been suggested to be a combat scene. But it has recently been argued that it is, in fact, an 'acclamation' scene – with both warriors coming together approaching a lance or some other item.[29]

The second subject also has a tradition going back at least to Roman times; one need only think of the so-called 'Jupiter-Giant' columns and other images. In our context, the same scene is shown on a decorated plate disc in a female burial of the early seventh century, in Pliezhausen (south-western Germany).[30] Once produced as a *phalera* as part of horse gear, the piece was subsequently reworked into a brooch. But the same image also appears contemporarily on military equipment – for example, in the form of *appliqué* on a press-plate on a helmet in male grave 8 from Valsgärde (Sweden).[31]

The third topic – parading infantry warriors with lowered spears – can be found, for instance, on a pair of pressed-sheet metal strap-ends in female grave 209 from Rain (Bavaria).³² It belongs to the first half of the seventh century. Once again, the same pictorial representation is found on a pressplate on a helmet in male grave 7 from Valsgärde.³³

The fourth and last picture deals with shooting archers. As one example, these archers are shown kneeling opposite each other on two discs connected by a loop. They came to light in female grave 144 from Mödling (Austria),³⁴ and they probably served as the fasteners of a cape or something similar.

Interestingly, identical pictorial scenes appear with men and women. In male burials, these warrior figures are attached to helmets or shields, while in female burials they decorate dress accessories like bow brooches. How these similar images and different contexts relate to one another has not thus far been argued.

It has been often suggested that the images represent specific narratives which were told and understood by contemporaries. Saying this, the question arises of its precise content. What content was transmitted by these pictures? Were they heroic legends and myths? Is it a pictorial language of its own in a world that was still largely without writing?³⁵

But we have to be very cautious and cannot simply connect these images directly to the Saga literature, because of the geographic and chronological gap. Some of the objects, especially the fibulae depicting such scenes, may refer to Scandinavia, but it remains questionable to what extent the wearers were interested in the specific content of the pictures. Looking at the antique prototypes, we could suggest that the images remained 'powerful' on a more general level.³⁶

Again, should we expect to find a transformation from the male sphere to the female one? At least we see the appearance of such images on 'male' defensive armour as well as on 'female' dress accessories. We find here that there is no chronological difference, but rather contemporaneous similar pictures for both men and women.

The 'horseman with a lance'

In the late sixth and throughout the seventh centuries, the 'horseman with a lance' was a common pictorial representation. This subject can be found on a few ornamented discs, such as female dress accessories, especially in south-western Germany and Switzerland.³⁷ Such discs were components of the so-called 'girdle hanger', which was worn along the left side of the female body, and was completed by the discs at the lower end.

Such objects were distributed over a larger area, mainly northern Gaul (Figure 16.4). In a general sense, they represent a victorious, powerful riding warrior. Snakes or other dangerous creatures below the horse are missing,

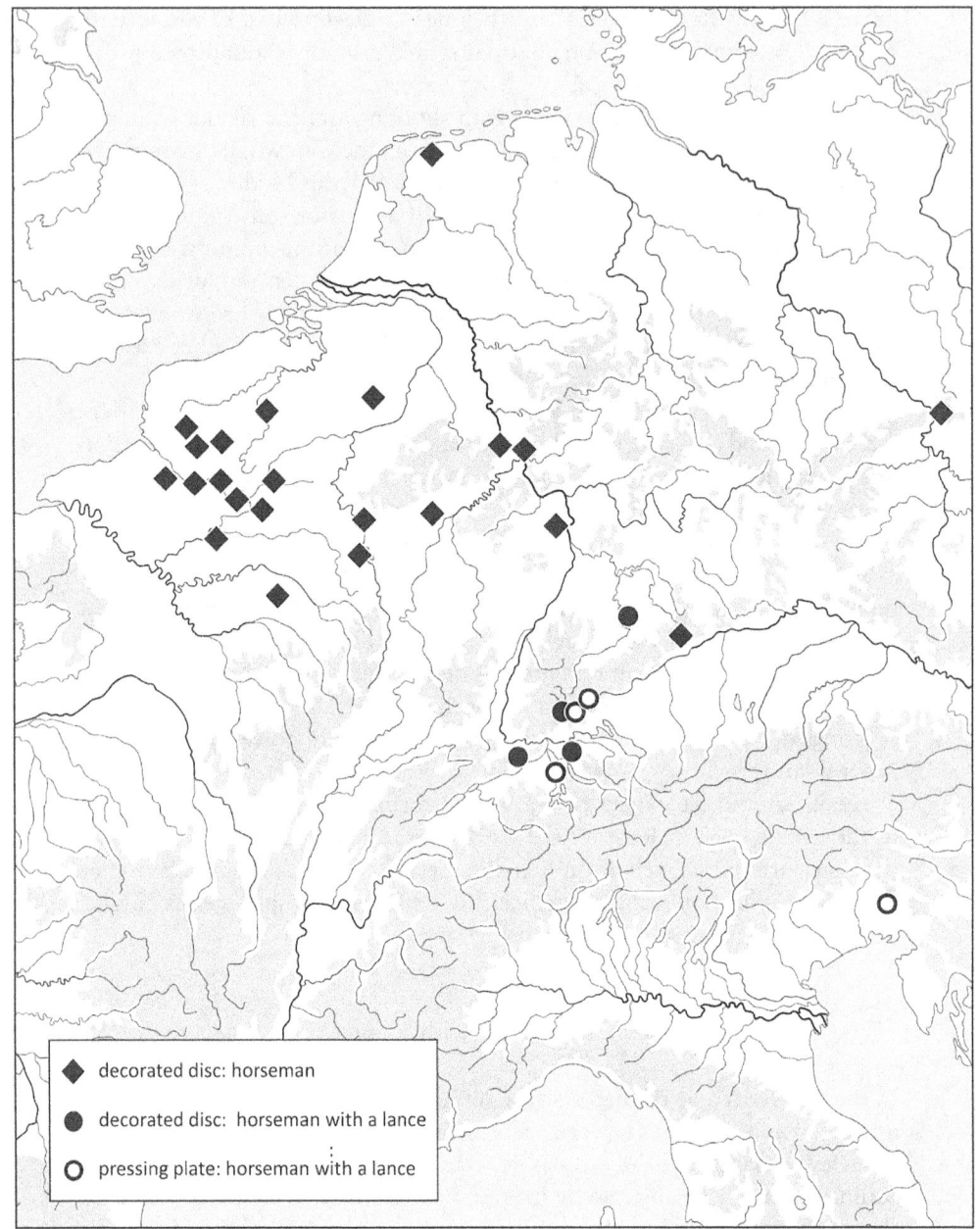

Figure 16.4 The distribution of seventh-century decorated discs with 'horseman with a lance'

which may have represented 'evil' and demonstrated victory over it. This image is adapted to Christian scenes, but with our objects there is no explicit Christian connotation.

At the same time, the image is found attached to horse-gear *phalerae* in male burials, for example in Hüfingen and Nendingen (south-western Germany);[38] both graves date to the early seventh century. In the case of Hüfingen, three *phalerae* result in a set: two riders, one seen from the left and the other one from the right, flank the virgin with the child in the centre. This image is clearly Christian and refers back to a Byzantine motif.[39]

Were the buried dead, equipped with such horse-riding equipment, portrayed as *milites Christi*?[40] I would say so, because the parallel of the rider image and the horse mount in the grave is apparent and intended. In this respect, the objects again would have been provided with a protective symbolism, however much in connection with Christian belief. Therefore, the riders depicted have to be understood as patron saints.

Fading images

Brooches of the later sixth century sometimes present figures which can barely be separated from pure ornamentation. By comparing them to accurate pictures, they can be identified and understood as warriors albeit in very much a simplified manner. Such a scene decorates the head plate of a bow-brooch from Lingotto in Italy, where two warriors are shown squeezed into a semi-circular frame. The brooch belongs to the time around 600.

In a women's grave in Nocera Umbra in Italy, as well as from two female burials in Southern Germany, fibulae have been found, which may be copies or imitations of the Lingotto[41] fibula. While the representation on the Nocera Umbra brooch[42] is still reasonably recognisable, the scene on the head-plate of the brooches from Staubing[43] and Selzen[44] can barely be reconstructed. The former figurative illustration has been simplified into an ornament.

A decorative metal sheet of a helmet from male grave XIV in Vendel (Sweden)[45] shows a very similar scene, which is dated to the first half of the seventh century. We see two warriors, standing in front of each other; both have a shield in their left hand and a sword in their right – not necessarily the depiction of a fight, but perhaps an acclamation scene. Astonishingly, this image has been found in northern Italy as well as in Scandinavia – the motif thus became popular over large distances.

The scene of two warriors could be associated with male as well as with female objects. What does it mean? Do we observe the regression of 'military' representation into the female sphere? Apparently, this was not the case – this phenomenon was simply the result of the time that had elapsed. In many parts of the Merovingian kingdoms, the production and use of fibulae had already come to an end. Therefore, brooches from Italy were continuously copied. As a result, not only did the production technique simplify, but the forms of image also became more abstract – the image originally depicting two warriors changed into a no longer decipherable picture, almost reduced to mere decoration. In this context, the depiction itself no longer played a role, but rather the bow-brooch did so as a symbol of prestige or status.

Conclusion

This examination makes it apparent that military objects or images in female graves represent a complex and dynamic set of phenomena. The general tendency of these objects can be summarised as follows:

1. Military equipment in female graves is not just one archaeological categorisation, but includes a variety of objects and images which relate in some way to the male sphere.
2. Since the third century, weapons *en miniature* and components of armour appear in female graves; from the sixth century onwards, images of warriors are found instead.
3. Therefore, the interpretation oscillates: amulets and the representation of status through weapons seem to be replaced by images which convey narrative and reflect Christian belief.

To conclude, it appears that the archaeological evidence does not document militarisation. Some male attributes and images seem to have been included into the female representation. The purpose behind this procedure, however, is a question that would require another chapter. However, it appears that implying a general process of 'militarisation' from the evidence discussed here would be an exaggeration, as the female burials do not contain any military *habitus*. However, the following aspects become apparent:

1. Weapons *en miniature* can be interpreted as apotropaic talismans, as they are small fragments of 'real' defensive weapons. These objects thus may have served to provide protection and integrity.
2. Furthermore, these objects can be considered as symbols of power. Thus, they could have expressed belonging to powerful groups or claiming their support. The social status of the buried women was defined by their respective family.[46]
3. Male garments have sometimes found in female graves and were perhaps used by women. This may indicate that although there was no female 'emancipation' or 'equal status' of women, women were somewhat appreciated.

4. In the early Middle Ages, miniature weapons or fragments of real weapons were replaced by figurative images which appear to refer to powerful or victorious warriors, comparable to antique pictorial scenes and narratives.
5. As a consequence of Christianisation, these 'military' or 'male' symbols changed into representative equestrian saints. What is important here is that these pictures have been discovered as part of both female and male attire, including decorated discs in female and helmets in male burials.

Notes

I am thankful to Mischa Meier, Steffen Patzold, Sebastian Schmidt-Hofner and the Deutsche Forschungsgemeinschaft Center for Advanced Studies 2496, 'Migration and Mobility in Late Antiquity and the Early Middle Ages', in Tübingen, for hosting me as a fellow.

1 J. Wahl, G. Cipollini, V. Coia, M. Francken, K. Harvati-Papatheodorou, M.-R. Kim, F. Maixner, N. O'Sullivan, T. Douglas Price, D. Quast, N. Speith and A. Zink, 'Neue Erkenntnisse zur frühmittelalterlichen Separatgrablege von Niederstotzingen, Kreis Heidenheim', *Fundberichte aus Baden-Württemberg*, 34:2 (Stuttgart: Theiss, 2014), pp. 341–90.
2 P. Paulsen, *Alamannische Adelsgräber von Niederstotzingen* (Kreis Heidenheim). Veröffentlichungen des Staatlichen Amtes für Denkmalpflege in Stuttgart. Vol. A 12 (Stuttgart: Müller & Gräff, 1967).
3 There is a regulation in the *Lex Baiuvaria* which applies a male *wergild* to a woman if she behaves like a man: *Lex Baiuvariorum* 3.29. – Compare K. A. Eckhardt (ed.), *Die Gesetze des Karolingerreiches 714–911*. Vol. 2: *Alemannen und Bayern* (Germanenrechte, 2) (Weimar: Boehlau, 1934), p. 108.
4 N. O'Sullivan, C. Post, V. Coia, V.J. Schuenemann, T. D. Price, J. Wahl, R. Pinhasi, A. Zink, J. Krause and F. Maixner, 'Ancient genome-wide analyses infer kinship structure in an Early Medieval Alemannic graveyard', *Science Advances*, 4 (9) (2018): eaao1226; DOI: 10.1126/sciadv.aao1262.
5 B. Hamm, 'Amazonen und Iron Ladies? Überlegungen zu spätantiken Militärgürteln in Frauengräbern Mitteleuropas (300–500 n. Chr.)', in A. Wieczorek and K. Wirth (eds), *Von Hammaburg bis Herimundesheim*. Festschrift für Ursula Koch. Mannheimer Geschichtsblätter, Sonderveröffentlichung, 11 (Ubstadt-Weiher: Verlag Regionalkultur, 2018), pp. 51–66.
6 A general overview can be found in I. Beilke-Voigt, *Frühgeschichtliche Miniaturobjekte mit Amulettcharakter zwischen Britischen Inseln und Schwarzem Meer*. Universitätsforschungen zur Prähistorischen Archäologie, 55 (Bonn: Habelt, 1998).
7 S. Dušek, s. v. 'Haßleben', in *RGA*, 14 (Berlin: de Gruyter, 1999), pp. 41–3; E. Droberjar, 'Neue Erkenntnisse zu den Fürstengräbern der Gruppe Hassleben

Leuna Gommern in Böhmen', *Přehled výzkumů*, 48 (2007), pp. 93–103; H. Beck and H. Jahnkuhn, s. v. 'Axtkult', in: *RGA*, 1 (Berlin: de Gruyter, 1973), pp. 562–8.

8 M. Martin, 'Die goldene Kette von Szilágy-Somlyó und das frühmittelalterliche Amulettgehänge der westgermanischen Frauentracht', in U. von Freeden and A. Wieczorek (eds), *Perlen. Archäologie, Techniken, Analysen*. Kolloquien zur Vor- und Frühgeschichte, 1 (Bonn: Habelt, 1997), pp. 349–72; T. Capelle, *Die Miniaturenkette von Szilágysomlyó (Şimleul Silvaniei)*. Universitätsforschungen zur prähistorischen Archäologie, 22 (Bonn: Habelt, 1994).

9 Grave 187: Chr. Neuffer-Müller, *Ein Reihengräberfeld in Sontheim an der Brenz (Kreis Heidenheim)*. Veröffentlichungen des Staatlichen Amtes für Denkmalpflege, A/11 (Stuttgart: Silberburg, 1966), pl. 28C, 3–5.

10 J. Werner, 'Herkuleskeulen und Donar-Amulett', *Jahrbuch des Römisch-Germanischen Zentralmuseums Mainz*, 11 (1964), pp. 176–97.

11 J. Staecker, *Rex regum et dominus dominorum. Die wikingerzeitlichen Kreuz- und Kruzifixanhänger als Ausdruck der Mission in Altdänemark und Schweden*. Lund Studies in Medieval Archaeology, 23 (Stockholm: Almqvist & Wiksell International, 1999).

12 B. Haas-Gebhard, *Unterhaching. Eine Grabgruppe um 500 n. Chr. bei München*. Abhandlungen und Bestandskataloge der Archäologischen Staatssammlung, 1 (Munich: Archäologische Staatssammlung, 2013), p. 101.

13 For example, the female grave 1 of Mengen, Löchleacker: Ch. Bücker, *Frühe Alamannen im Breisgau. Archäologie und Geschichte*. Freiburger Forschungen zum ersten Jahrtausend in Südwestdeutschland, 9 (Sigmaringen: Thorbecke, 1999), pl. 1,8.

14 For example, in tombs of the graveyard of Alattyán: I. Kovrig, *Das awarenzeitliche Gräberfeld von Alattyán*. Archaeologica Hungarica, 40 (Budapest: Akad. Kiadó, 1963), p. 118.

15 Grave 290, e.g.: B. Höke, F. Gauß, Chr. Peek and J. Stelzner, *Lauchheim II.1. Katalog der Gräber 1–300*. Forschungen und Berichte zur Archäologie in Baden-Württemberg, 9 (Wiesbaden: Dr. Ludwig Reichert Verlag, 2018), pp. 363–4, and https://doi.org/10.11588/data/SJB7RU.

16 H. Steuer, 'Krieger und Bauern – Bauernkrieger. Die gesellschaftliche Ordnung der Alamannen', in *Die Alamannen* (Stuttgart: Theiss, 1997), pp. 275–87, here p. 279 fig. 300.

17 Apahida: A. Wieczorek and P. Périn (eds), *Das Gold der Barbarenfürsten. Schätze aus Prunkgräbern des 5. Jahrhunderts zwischen Kaukasus und Gallien* (Stuttgart: Theiss, 2001), pp. 147–55, here p. 150 fig. 4.8.4.2., p. 152 fig. 4.8.24.

18 Lauffen: H. Schach-Dörges, 'Zusammengespülte und vermengte Menschen. Suebische Kriegerverbünde werden sesshaft', in *Die Alamannen* (Stuttgart: Theiss, 1997), pp. 79–102, here p. 90 fig. 72.

19 Compare Wieczorek and Périn, *Das Gold der Barbarenfürsten*.

20 S. Brather-Walter and S. Brather, '"Rich" women along the Upper Rhine. An extraordinary group of single female burials ca. 450–500 AD', in M. Kars, R. van Oosten and M. A. Roxburgh (eds), *Rural riches and royal rags? Studies on Medieval and Modern Archaeology, Presented to Frans Theuws* (Zwolle: SPA-Uitgevers, 2018), pp. 86–8.

21 Ph. von Rummel, *Habitus barbarus. Kleidung und Repräsentation spätantiker Eliten im 4. und 5. Jahrhundert*. RGA Ergänzungsbände, 55 (Berlin: de Gruyter, 2007).
22 Finally listed by Hamm: B. Hamm, 'Amazonen und Iron Ladies', pp. 54–6.
23 A. Burzler, M. Höneisen, J. Leicht and B. Ruckstuhl, *Das frühmittelalterliche Schleitheim. Siedlung, Gräberfeld und Kirche*. Schaffhauser Archäologie, 5 (Schaffhausen: Baudepartement des Kantons Schaffhausen, Kantonsarchäologie, 2002), p. 247, pl. 26.
24 M. Martin, 'Zur frühmittelalterlichen Gürteltracht der Frau in der Burgundia, Francia und Aquitania', in G. Donnay (ed.), *Actes du colloque sur "L'art des invasions en Hongrie et en Wallonie"*. Musée royale de Mariemont, Monographies, 6 (Morlanwelz: Musée Royal de Mariemont, 1991), pp. 31–84.
25 For example, Lauffen; Schleitheim-Hebsack.
26 H. Steuer, s. v. 'Zwiebelknopffibel' in: *RGA*, 34 (Berlin: de Gruyter, 2007), pp. 605–23.
27 E. Vogt, 'Das alamannische Gräberfeld am alten Gotterbarmweg in Basel', *Anzeiger für Schweizerische Altertumskunde NF.*, 32 (1930), 145–64.
28 One brooch was found in the female grave 85 of the cemetery of Kirchheim/Teck: G. Haseloff, *Die germanische Tierornamentik der Völkerwanderungszeit. Studien zu Salin's Stil I*. Forschungen zur Vorgeschichte, 17:1 (Berlin: de Gruyter, 1981; reprint 2015), pp. 288–93, especially p. 292 fig. 193a–b. – Another of this type is displayed in the Museum of Frankfurt/Main but without context: H. Roth and E. Wamers (eds), *Hessen im Frühmittelalter. Archäologie und Kunst* (Sigmaringen: Thorbecke, 1984), p. 117; p. 118 fig.
29 Compare S. MacCormack, *Art and ceremony in late Anqituity* (Berkeley: University of California Press, 1981); J. Elsner, *Imperial Rome and Christian triumph. The art of the Roman Empire AD 100–450* (Oxford: Oxford University Press, 1998).
30 K. Böhner and D. Quast, 'Die merowingerzeitlichen Grabfunde aus Pliezhausen, Kr. Reutlingen', *Fundberichte aus Baden-Württemberg*, 19:1 (Stuttgart: Theiss, 1994), pp. 383–419.
31 G. Arwidsson, 'Valsgärde', in J. P. Lamm and H.-Ä. Nordström (eds), *Vendel period Studies*. Statens Historiska Museum, 2 (Stockholm: Statens historiska museum, 1983), pp. 71–82, here p. 78 fig. 3a.
32 S. Zintl and M. Blana, 'Krieger auf dem Weg ins Depot. Merowingerzeitliche Riemenzungen mit figürlicher Darstellung aus Rain', *Das archäologische Jahr in Bayern, 2016* (Darmstadt: Wissenschaftliche Buchgesellschaft, 2017), pp. 106–8.
33 Valsgärde: G. Arwidsson, *Die Gräberfunde von Valsgärde*. Vol. 2: *Valsgärde 8*. Acta Musei Antiquitatum Septentrionalium Regiae Universitatis Upsaliensis/Museum för Nordiska Fornsaker, 4 (Uppsala: Almqvist & Wiksell, 1954), p. 120 fig. 79.
34 F. Daim (ed.), *Hunnen und Awaren. Reitervölker aus dem Osten*. Katalog der Burgenländischen Landesausstellung im Schloß Halbturn (Eisenstadt: Burgenländische Landesregierung, 1996), p. 354, Object-Nr. 5.283.
35 On the same subject, J. M. Harland, *Memories of migration the anglo saxon burial costume of the fifth century*. Antiquity, 2019: https://doi.org/10.15184/aqy.2019.60, pp. 1–16, here pp. 3–10.

36 Compare M. Helmbrecht, *Wirkmächtige Kommunikationsmedien. Menschenbilder der Vendel- und Wikingerzeit und ihre Kontexte*. Acta Archaeologica Lundensia, 4:30 (Lund: Lunds Univ., 2011).
37 For example, in Bräunlingen, Oberesslingen, Bubendorf and Neftenbach: S. Brather-Walter, 'Das "Reiterle" von Oberesslingen. Das Motiv des Lanzenreiters im 7. Jahrhundert und sein Kontext', *Esslinger Studien*, 47, 2009/10 (2013), 9–23, here 17 fig. 5.
38 Hüfingen and Nendingen: G. Fingerlin, 'Die ältesten christlichen Bilder der Alamannia. Zur Herkunft und Ikonographie der drei silbernen Phalerae aus dem Kammergrab von der ‚Gierhalde' in Hüfingen, dem Hauptort der frühmittelalterlichen Baar', in V. Huth and R. J. Regnath (eds), *Die Baar als Königslandschaft*. Veröffentlichung des Alemannischen Instituts, 77 (Ostfildern: Thorbecke, 2010), pp. 25–46.
39 R. Warland, 'Byzanz und die Alemannia. Zu den frühbyzantinischen Vorlagen der Hüfinger Scheiben', *Jahrbuch für Antike und Christentum*, 55 (2014), 132–9.
40 S. Brather, 'Christliche Reiter – milites Christi? Grabausstattungen des 7. Jahrhunderts und ihre Symbolik', in R. Haensch and P. von Rummel (eds), *Religiöse Identitäten und reale Lebenswelten in der Spätantike* (forthcoming).
41 Lingotto: H. Kühn, *Die germanischen Bügelfibeln der Völkerwanderungszeit aus Süddeutschland* (Graz: Akademische Druck- u. Verl.-Anst., 1974), pl. 328.96, 26.
42 Nocera Umbra: Kühn, *Die germanischen Bügelfibeln*, pl. 327.96, 23.
43 Staubing: Th. Fischer, *Das bajuwarische Reihengräberfeld von Staubing*. Studien zur Frühgeschichte im bayerischen Donauraum. Kataloge der Prähistorischen Staatssammlung, 26 (Kallmünz/Opf.: Lassleben, 1993), pl. 31,6.
44 Selzen: Kühn, *Die germanischen Bügelfibeln*, pl. 305.29, 5.
45 H. K. Stolpe and T. A. J. Arne, *Graffältet vid Vendel*. Monografiserien. Kungliga Vitterhets Historie och Antikvitets Akademien, 3 (Stockholm: Beckman, 1912), pl. XLI, 3.
46 There was no specific 'female elite', as is argued by D. Quast (ed.), *Weibliche Eliten in der Frühgeschichte*. Römisch-Germanisches Zentralmuseum Mainz, Tagungen, 10 (Mainz: Verlag des Römisch-Germanischen Zentralmuseums, 2011).

17

The construction of the enemy in pre-Viking England

Ellora Bennett

There is no doubt that the arrival of the Vikings altered the nature of warfare in early medieval Britain. It is the traditional conclusion that these sea-borne raiders, with a reputation for bloodlust and ruthlessness, did not conform to the language of warfare understood by the Anglo-Saxons[1] and as such were able to tear through all resistance until only Wessex, under the direction of Alfred the Great, remained.[2] By his death in 899, Alfred left to his successors the military, administrative and financial resources required to capitalise on his accomplishments and reconquer land taken by the Vikings.[3] It is therefore unsurprising that examinations of early medieval and pre-Conquest English warfare generally begin around 800.[4] Not only do the Vikings offer an enemy against which the Anglo-Saxon mettle could be tested, but the available source material vastly increased in both quality and quantity from the ninth century.[5] The overall result is that warfare conducted between the *adventus Saxonum* in the fifth century and *c*. 800 is glossed over, generalised or ignored altogether.

It is the purpose of this chapter to go a little way to filling this gap by posing two questions: who were the enemies of the Anglo-Saxons before the Vikings?[6] And how were they constructed in the available sources? By considering who fought against (or alongside) the pre-Viking Anglo-Saxons, it is possible to note a few key issues related to early medieval warfare and the larger concept of militarisation. As stated in this volume's Introduction, a society at war did not necessarily equate to a militarised society. However, considerations of how the Anglo-Saxons perceived their enemies and themselves in relation to that 'other' reveals how conceptual elements of the phenomenon are transferred to, and found embedded within, the written sources. This is an important approach because not only structures experienced militarisation, but also the mentalities of those whose world experiences were shaped by warfare – in this case, the mentalities of those who authored the written sources of pre-Viking England. Thus, considering the construction of the enemy reveals how militarisation impacted on contemporary mentalities by considering its influence on the creation of identities in relation to war.

Before the late ninth or early tenth century, the concept of a universal 'Englishness' did not exist. The island of Britain was a patchwork of separate entities, later kingdoms, whose leaders traced their lineage to varying continental and northern European mythological ancestors, including the pagan war god Woden.[7] Traditional narratives, based on Bede's eighth-century *Historia Ecclesiastica gentis Anglorum* (hereafter *HE*), state that those in the south were of primarily Saxon and Jutish descent whilst those of the north and midlands consisted of Anglian peoples.[8] The accuracy of Bede's claims have long been scrutinised but there were undoubtedly significant differences between communities across late antique and early medieval England. The southern kingdom of Kent had strong economic and political ties to Francia, for instance, while the northern kingdom of Northumbria (itself an amalgam of Bernicia, Deira, and several Celtic kingdoms)[9] was more closely connected to the Picts and Scots.[10] The kingdoms of Mercia and Wessex rubbed shoulders with the British peoples who dwelt in the west of the island. It is notable, for example, that the nomenclature of the early West Saxon dynasty indicates a close British connection, and the Mercians are called thus because they were 'dwellers on the march' between British and other territories.[11] It must therefore be acknowledged that references to the 'Anglo-Saxons' reflect a traditional and convenient terminology for an array of peoples who perceived themselves to have Germanic origins who later become 'English'.[12]

Clearly, the Anglo-Saxons were not a singular unit, and different kingdoms exhibited cultural idiosyncrasies. In theory, the arrival of Christianity united these disparate peoples under a single banner; yet by the mid seventh century, there remained considerable variations in custom and the Church lacked an overarching organisational structure, not to mention that until 655 the kingdom of Mercia remained aggressively pagan.[13] However, a different story is told by Bede in his *HE*. Herein is presented an image of 'Englishness' when few others would have recognised such a notion. In his view, Christianity was indeed a unifying force that formed the foundation of the *gens Anglorum*.[14] Bede also stated that the *gens* shared a common language – English – that was distinct from the non-Germanic tongues of the natives (British, Scottish and Pictish) with Latin 'in general use among them all'.[15] The *gens* were also at points politically linked, as on several occasions a single king held *imperium* over all others, although the precise nature this office and its impact on the creation of an overall 'Englishness' has been much debated.[16]

Against this concept of 'Englishness' were Bede's vitriolic views of the British. To Bede, their shortcomings were numerous: the British Church did not abide by the Roman calculation for Easter, had not made enough effort to convert the Anglo-Saxons after the *adventus Saxonum*, and had disdained Augustine, the spearhead of the English conversion.[17] Unsurprisingly, these shortcomings heavily influenced how Bede represented the British in relation to the Anglo-Saxons, as shall be demonstrated below.

It is also worth noting that the *Anglo-Saxon Chronicle* (hereafter ASC),[18] another essential narrative source for the pre-Viking period, was likely compiled at the court of Alfred the Great himself and as such recounts the events of the foregoing centuries within the framework of West Saxon ascendancy and the development of the houses of Cerdic and Ecgberht, Alfred's eminent grandfather.[19] Essentially, the extent to which the Anglo-Saxon source material constructed the enemy in opposition to 'self' was linked to the intentions and bias that shaped its initial composition.

Othering, outgroups and the enemy

Constructing an enemy relates to two entwined concepts: othering and the formation of ingroup and outgroup categories. First, othering is the process by which the 'self' shapes the identity of an encountered group or individual on perceived differences between the parties, often connected to notions of self-superiority versus other-inferiority, or radical alienisation.[20] Although an infinitely complex social theory, it is sufficient for the following investigation to highlight that the sense of 'self' versus 'other' is often elicited when two different individuals (individual me-versus-you) or groups (social us-versus-them) come into contact.[21] In turn, othering is strongly linked to the second concept: that of ingroup/outgroup formation. Group membership is the cornerstone of social identity, with the need to belong being a fundamental element of human nature.[22] Generally speaking, the ingroup is seen as possessing superior characteristics whilst those of the outgroup are deemed inferior; a result of the group being 'othered'. In practical terms this requires the construction of distinct boundaries based on either real or perceived differences. Ethnicity, language or religious affiliation could delineate social or political groupings, and might additionally be accompanied by visual or audio cues that allowed members of the ingroup to immediately recognise the outgroup.[23] Note Bede's assertion that four distinct languages were spoken in Britain, with all those of 'Germanic' descent speaking 'English'. Speaking a different tongue was thus a clear sign of outgroup status.

That the outgroup should be so easily identified based on such criteria hints at an underlying process that reduces the outgroup to a homogenous stereotype. This is based on the notion that the outgroup has some natural, innate or biological penchant towards characteristics deemed inferior by the ingroup, making these perceptions particularly durable.[24] Yet the outgroup 'other' is not *inherently* the enemy; rather, it is a concept against which ingroup unity can be forged. However, the outgroup can easily be framed as the enemy when the ingroup feel sufficiently threatened by the outgroup's alien (and therefore potentially hostile) nature.[25]

The *Oxford living dictionaries* defines 'enemy' thus: 'a person who is actively opposed or hostile to someone or something, [or a] hostile nation or its armed forces, especially in time of war'.[26] If to this one adds the dimension of being the object of hostility, the 'enemy' is revealed to be in close conceptual proximity to the outgroup or other. It could be argued that the enemy, as it is represented in the historical sources, is the 'activated' other; the threat posed by the outgroup's dissimilitude and purported inferiority is encapsulated as an active and opposing force against which the ingroup could prove their worth. Finally, it is important to recognise that the enemy as 'activated' other need not have been an *active* adversary. As will be demonstrated in the following discussion, a group's status as the 'enemy' could amount to little more than being the *object* of the ingroup's hostilities, and it is in these cases that the clear lines between 'protagonists' and 'antagonists' could blur depending on the source's perspective.

The pre-Viking enemies of the Anglo-Saxons

According to the written sources, the peoples of pre-Viking England fought against three basic categories of enemy: 'non-Anglo-Saxons' (British/Welsh, Picts and Scots), 'Anglo-Saxons' (competing polities such as kingdoms), and internal or dynastic enemies. Conflicts with the former two groups can be categorised as *folcgefeoht* ('folk-battle'), war that is fought between the 'forces of one people and those of another', the *publicum bellum* of the *Penitential of Theodore*.[27] On the other hand, the latter group represents instances of what Isidore of Seville described as 'more than civil' war, 'where not only fellow-citizens, but also kinfolk fight'.[28] These instances of internal violence rarely entailed clear battles identifiable in the laconic sources – the saga-like episode between King Cynewulf and Ætheling Cyneheard of Wessex being a notable exception.[29] In the interest of brevity, this chapter will focus on the enemy as constructed in instances of *folcgefeoht*; first against a number of 'non-Anglo-Saxon' enemies, and second in respect to the prolonged conflict between Mercia and Northumbria.

By collating instances of warfare in the *ASC* and Bede's *HE*, it appears that most common foe of the pre-Viking Anglo-Saxons were natives of the British Isles, primarily the British (often referred to as 'Welsh'), Picts, Scots and occasionally the Irish.[30] The early annals of the *ASC* erupt with warfare the moment the Anglo-Saxons enter the record in 449. These annals are of interest as the Anglo-Saxons themselves begin as the 'other' to the native British, not only in origin (having arrived on ships) but in behaviour. According to Bede's narrative, the British people were beset on all sides by the Irish and Picts who took the opportunity to ravage the island in the wake of the Roman withdrawal. This led a certain Vortigern to invite Anglian and/or Saxon warriors to settle in exchange for their protection.[31] However, Bede, drawing on the writings of sixth-century monk Gildas, immediately highlights the duplicity of the newcomers; he believed that their true intentions were not to protect the British but to conquer them, which they did with gusto after breaking their agreement and temporarily aligning with the Picts.[32] In the view of Bede's eighth-century audience, breaking an agreement was a particularly damning act of anti-heroic behaviour in a culture that so highly valued oath-swearing and bonds of loyalty. Furthermore, Bede's rhetoric expounds on the intensity of violence employed by the invaders, stating that 'there was no one left to bury those who had died a cruel death', and refers to the Saxons as the 'enemy' (*hostilis exercitus*).[33] Whether this reflected the reality of the Anglo-Saxon migration, the idea that the process involved intense violence remained current into the tenth century, when the Battle of Brunanburh (937) was commemorated in alliterative verse, stating that 'never yet in this island was there a greater slaughter of people felled by the sword's edges ... since Angles and Saxons came here from the east ... overcame the Welsh, seized the country'.[34] The intensity of violence and their duplicitous nature creates an image of the early Anglo-Saxon peoples as distilling the danger and disorder of the unknown, permeating their image with threatening otherness. However, this construction is tempered by the depiction of the British themselves that resulted from his own disdain and the narrative provided by Gildas. Gildas othered the Saxons by comparing them to lions and expounding on their hatefulness, yet the British were not underserving, corrupted as they were by sloth and tyranny.[35] Bede assures his readers that 'the fire kindled at the hands of the heathen executed the just vengeance of God on the nation for its crimes'.[36] Despite this, Bede referred to the Saxons as the 'enemy' and attributed the British victory at Mount Badon (*c.* 500) to divine intervention.[37] Evidently, the image of British 'victims' and Saxon 'enemies' was negotiated and renegotiated as the narrative required.

The annals of the *ASC* that follow the arrival of the 'three tribes of Germany' quickly develop formulaic phrases and patterns that demonstrate clearly constructed enemy groups:

> 455. Here Hengest and Horsa fought against Vortigern the king in a place that is called Aylesford ...

457. Here Hengest and Æsc fought against the Britons in the place which is called Crayford, and there killed 4,000 men ...

465. Here Hengest and Æsc fought against the Welsh near Wipped's Creek, and there killed 12 chieftains ...[38]

In these annals, the quasi-mythic progenitors of Kent are given individual constructions, but the enemies are described as a collective group with the location of the encounter taking precedence over meaningful descriptions of the enemy. The entry for 465 highlights the intersection of these concerns, stating that out of the twelve 'chieftains' killed at Wipped's Creek (*Wippedesfleot*), one was named 'Wipped'.[39] Evidently this detail reflects a remnant of a narrative attempt to explain the creek's name and is entwined with the *Chronicler's* understanding of these quasi-mythical years and events, creating a generally faceless enemy but one that could nonetheless be identified within the landscape.

The annalistic format of the *ASC* reinforces the faceless otherness of the early 'non-Anglo-Saxon' enemy, threatening only as objects of the Anglo-Saxon protagonists' hostility. This impression is edified by the instances of British flight: in 457 they 'abandoned the land of Kent and fled in great terror to the stronghold of London' and 'fled from the English like fire' in 473, the latter reminiscent of Bede's comments concerning God's punishment of the British.[40] It is the Anglo-Saxons themselves who invoke threat, but the connotations are not negative. Rather, their violence behaviour highlights their superiority and overall destiny. Such moments reveal the militarised mindset of the chronicler, as it is with the successful conduct of warfare that the Anglo-Saxons prove themselves to be of worth. The 'non-Anglo-Saxon' enemy in the early annals of the *ASC* was a construction against which the Anglo-Saxons, particularly the West Saxons, could measure their martial superiority. The 'timeless' image of successful warrior kingship edified the dynastic identity of the ninth-century West Saxons under whose auspices the *ASC* was compiled.[41] Indeed, the accession of a new king was often accompanied by a general statement that he 'constantly made war' against a 'non-Anglo-Saxon' group – a clear indicator that he was a good or worthy king.[42]

Turning from West Saxon military encounters, the *ASC* records that in 547 Ida, 'from whom originated the royal family of Northumbria', acceded to the throne. However, it is not until 603 that the *ASC* records an instance of warfare beyond the Humber, when Aedan, king of the Scots, fought against the Northumbrian King Æthelfrith (r. 592–616).[43] Bede stated that Aedan, 'king of the Irish living in Britain,' gathered 'an immensely strong army' to challenge King Æthelfrith. Despite his paganism, Æthelfrith was one of Bede's most highly praised warrior-kings; Bede compared him to

Saul and detailed his extensive ravaging and subjugation of British lands, which he apparently did 'more extensively than any other English ruler'.[44] Thus, the clash between Æthelfrith and Aedan was between two hitherto successful warrior kings, and despite the death of Æthelfrith's brother Theobald, the Northumbrians won a lasting victory. In Bede's narrative there was no doubt about this outcome. His perception of kingship was based on Old Testament models in which military prowess was essential to expanding a ruler's influence and thus the land's overall prosperity. Moreover, just as Saul had done for David, Æthelfrith later made way for Edwin, the first Christian king of the Northumbrians.[45] Here, Aedan's forces fulfilled the role of 'activated' other; an enemy force whose defeat proved the strength of 'English' (more specifically, Northumbrian) Christian destiny.

Æthelfrith's victory at the Battle of Chester (615/616) follows a similar logic. Here, Æthelfrith was victorious against the British at the former Roman legionary fortress.[46] Bede presents a narrative that the British defeat was the culmination of an earlier prophecy of Augustine: if the British Church did not aid him in his mission, they would die at the hands of 'their enemies', i.e. the 'English'.[47] Bede's account of the battle reinforces this, beginning with a statement that Æthelfrith's forces 'made a great slaughter of that nation of heretics'.[48] Before battle was joined, the pagan Æthelfrith enquired as to the function of a large group of British priests who had gathered to pray. These priests, Bede relates, stood apart from the soldiers 'in a safer place' and were guarded by a certain Brocmail.[49] Once the king discovered they were praying 'to their God against us', he ordered the priests to be the first attacked. Thus 1,200 men 'who had come to pray' were killed by Æthelfrith's forces, and Brocmail abandoned his duty and fled as one of only fifty survivors. First, the priests elicit threat by praying to God *against* the Anglo-Saxon protagonist, and second Brocmail, standing as proxy for the British forces overall, acts in a way wholly inimical to ingroup standards of behaviour. In effect these elements combined to create an enemy that engineered its own defeat, exonerating the viciousness of Æthelfrith's barbarian forces.

However, not all Bede's kings enjoyed Æthelfrith's reputation. King Ecgfrith of Northumbria (r. 670–85) was a similarly war-like king, with the advantage of being Christian, yet his inability to heed the advice of Churchmen proved to be his doom. This played out in dramatic fashion when he was killed fighting the Picts at the Battle of Nechtansmere (685). This event is an exceptional instance of a king being slain by a 'non-Anglo-Saxon' enemy before the arrival of the Vikings. Ecgfrith's death was additionally impactful as he left no clear heir, leading to his half-brother Aldfrith taking the throne. According to Bede's *Life of Cuthbert*, Aldfrith had 'willingly exiled' himself to Ireland for his 'love of learning', making it all the more interesting that in the *HE* Ecgfrith's demise at Nechtansmere was presented as the direct consequence of sending an army to Ireland the previous year.[50] A Northumbrian force led by Ealdorman Berht had attacked Irish churches and monasteries, devastating 'a harmless race that had always been most friendly to the English'.[51] The motivation for this attack is unclear. It is possible Ecgfrith sought to eliminate residual threats from earlier campaigns, or perhaps he intended to dispose of his half-brother.[52] Whatever the case, Bede stated that the Irish implored God's aid and 'justly cursed' those who assailed them, directly leading to Ecgfrith's defeat at Nechtansmere.[53] Notably, Bede wrote that Bishop Egbert and St Cuthbert, both of whom had strong connections to the Irish Church, had advised Ecgfrith against his 684 Irish expedition and the 685 Pictish raid.[54] Bede held the Irish Church in esteem as it played a key role in his narrative of Northumbria's Christianisation.[55] Again, the Anglo-Saxon protagonists are presented as the threatening or inferior party. However, that sense of disjunction is not between Ecgfrith's forces and the Irish, but between Northumbria's temporal leader and the kingdom's spiritual elite. Through Bede's narrative, this conflict is played out in Ecgfrith's military engagements, wherein the king's behaviour reflects his irresponsibility in rejecting the Churchmen's counsel.

Ecgfrith is described as ravaging the Picts with 'brutal and ferocious cruelty', language strikingly similar to when the British (Christian) prince Caedwalla ravaged Northumbria with 'bestial cruelty' in 633.[56] According to the *HE*, at the Battle of Nechtansmere the Picts feigned flight and lured Ecgfrith into a narrow pass.[57] The king fell for a ruse that decimated his forces and resulted in his own death: a fitting end for a foolish king. Similarly to the early sections of the *ASC*, the Picts remain a faceless, heterogenous enemy lacking a named leader as opposed to Æthelfrith's defeat of King Aedan and his forces.[58] Finally, Bede expounds on the defeat's consequences: the Picts recovered lands previously under the Northumbrian hegemony and the Irish in Britain (the Dál Riata) were once again independent. The English were killed, enslaved or driven out. The enemy did to them what the Northumbrians, with God on their side, should have done to the enemy.[59]

The above discussion shows that the Irish, British and Scots were often depicted as a mostly homogenous enemy against which the Anglo-Saxon protagonists tested their strength and furthered the 'destiny' of their ingroup, expressing the inherent manifestation of a militarised mindset; for the early West Saxons, this was the ascendancy of the House of Cerdic, whilst Bede's Northumbrian kings fought for the expansion of Christianity. In the latter case, the pagan Æthelfrith was able to kill Christians because his kingship was essential to Bede's overall narrative. Once Christianity had been largely established in early medieval England, it was an essential characteristic of the ingroup and superseded the notion of a common 'Germanic' background.[60]

Penda and the Mercian enemy

The exact date Penda came to the throne is unknown, but by his death in 655, he had killed four kings in battle and had driven a fifth into exile.[61] Penda's career began in 633 with the defeat of King Edwin of Northumbria at Hatfield Chase, wherein the Mercian king supported the British King Cædwalla in his rebellion against Edwin.[62] Bede stated that Penda was a 'most energetic member of the royal house of Mercia' (*viro strenuissimo de de regio genere Merciorum*) and a pagan alongside the Mercian people.[63] In the wake of King Edwin's defeat, Cædwalla and Penda ravaged Northumbria, and it appears that for a year the kingdom was dominated by this British–Mercian alliance.[64] During this time, Penda attempted to burn down the royal seat of Bamburgh after unsuccessful attempts to capture it. However, Bede reports that the fortress was saved by a miracle performed by Bishop Aiden, who specifically drew God's attention to Penda's 'evil' doing. The flames changed direction, injuring and terrifying the Mercian forces.[65] Once again, the symbology of fire was employed to stress the righteousness of the victorious forces whilst the enemy that fled before it embodied its total negation. Penda's paganism ensured a symbolic moral distance between the Mercian and Northumbrian forces, maintaining the image of Penda as the distinct other.

Penda was not only othered through his behaviour, he also belonged to an outgroup that transcended his paganism: his ally Cædwalla was a British Christian but more akin to the 'heathen' through his 'barbarous' actions.[66] Thus, Penda is presented as the antithesis of a just Anglo-Saxon warrior king. As a pagan, God did not guide his actions (unlike the Northumbrian heathen king Æthelfrith), and his association with the heretic King Caedwalla only served to bolster Penda's dangerous image. Indeed, Bede makes it clear that Penda did not abide by the same social rules as the Northumbrians. At the Battle of Hatfield Chase, Edwin's son Eadfrith was 'compelled to desert to King Penda' by whom he was afterwards murdered 'in spite of an oath'.[67] Oath-swearing was essential to peace-making and often went hand in hand with the exchange of hostages, which might reveal the truth of Eadfrith's relationship with Penda.[68] Whatever the case, Penda broke an agreement that should have been binding. Not unlike the auxiliaries who turned against their British employers, and Brocmail, who fled at the Battle of Chester, Penda's unjust killing of Eadfrith proved his otherness through anti-heroic behaviour deplored by those who set the ingroup standards.

At the Battle of Winwæd in 655, Penda was defeated by Oswiu, the brother of Oswald whom Penda had previously killed at *Maserfelth* in 642.[69] Bede stated that Winwæd was the culmination of Penda's incessant raiding of Northumbrian territory. Refusing to make peace, Penda led the 'barbarous and evil enemy' against Oswiu's small force intent on destroying the 'whole people' of Northumbria. Such rhetoric arises from the Old Testament-lens through which Bede viewed Northumbria's narrative of Christianisation, in which Penda and the Mercians took on the role of the Philistines, and Oswiu that of King David.[70] Indeed against Oswiu's small force, Penda commanded 'thirty legions' drawn from his allies, likely including a British contingent under King Cadafael of Gwynedd and other *duces* of excellent repute in war.[71] To further stack the odds against Oswiu, Bede stated that the Oswiu's own nephew Oethelwald fought on Penda's behalf and led a Mercian contingent, but he withdrew from the fighting to await the battle's conclusion. Oswiu's small force, with God on their side, gained the victory and killed Penda and almost all his allies.

According to a Latin poem written by Alcuin of York the following century, Penda proved his inferiority by attempting to flee the field but was cut down 'by the victor's sword'.[72] Practically speaking, Penda's attempt to abandon the field reflects the logical way by which a warband's leader, and in turn the warband itself, avoided complete destruction.[73] Yet it was in flight that Penda was killed rather on the field where he should have remained resolute. Penda's actions thus contrasted with Oswiu's boldness as he entered the battle. This contrast is echoed elsewhere in the poem. For instance, King Oswiu protected his followers with the 'weapons of Christ', but the enemy 'forgot' the battle and 'abandoned all its weapons' when overcome by fear.[74] The Mercians and their allies failed to fulfil their role as warriors bound to the field through the obligation of loyalty, and so abandoned the duties that underlay the Anglo-Saxon heroic ethos that applied to pagan and Christian alike.[75]

So closely was Mercian identity connected with Penda's paganism that on his death in 655, the *ASC* records simply that 'Penda perished, and the Mercians became Christians'.[76] Yet the legacy of Penda and this idea of Mercian otherness was far-reaching. The *Life of Wilfrid* stated that Wulfhere, Penda's son and successor, was not merely intent on war against the Northumbrians but on their enslavement. Wulfhere may have been a Christian, but the insistence that 'his designs were not inspired by God' clearly showed that the work's author considered Wulfhere to be cut from the same cloth as his father.[77] Decades of Mercian aggression and military expansion meant that for those who encountered them, the Mercians represented a significant enemy. The Northumbrian sources thus constructed a hostile image of the Mercians by emphasising their pagan otherness, which was associated with inherent behaviours deemed inferior by the ingroup. Undoubtedly, the

Mercians represented an ambitious and dangerous enemy to the other kingdoms, but so long as Mercian sources are lacking, this construction can only be viewed from the outside through the moral lens of Bede and other Christian (particularly Northumbrian) writers.

Conclusion

What this brief discussion of the pre-Viking enemy has shown is that images of the ingroup and outgroup are often far more blurred than one might have expected, one result of the process of militarisation that shaped ideas of identity in relation to military victory. Either party could be constructed with elements of the other, depending on the political or religious context of the encounter. Notably, the 'non-Anglo-Saxon' enemy was shaped relative to their narrative purpose. The Welsh and Britons of the *ASC*'s early annals offered an enemy against which the budding West Saxon dynasty could establish their military superiority and thus their dynastic destiny. Similarly, the Picts and Scots served to test the military might and wisdom of the Northumbrian kings. When a king acted foolishly, as Ecgfrith did in 684–85, he took on elements of the other; but when kings acted justly and in the interests of Bede's overall narrative, even the pagan King Æthelfrith could deliver divine justice. Importantly, in this latter case the enemy was the British Church whose presentation was coloured by Bede's animosity. At the Battle of Chester, this was distilled into the character of Brocmail who shirked his duty to protect the priests and fled, ensuring their destruction and further revealing their inferiority. This process of othering based on displaying the enemy's inferior behaviour or characteristics carried over to other groups. Not only a significant enemy, the Mercians under Penda represented an antithesis of good Christian kingship. Anti-heroic behaviour, such as the breaking of oaths, further reinforced their otherness.

This brief exploration has shown that the construction of the enemy in pre-Viking England was rooted in ingroup introspection, concerned with the entanglement of Christian morality, the warrior ethic and the exercise of military supremacy. Yet, importantly, it is the mentalities of the later writers, rather than those who experienced the events, that are revealed. This suggests that the values expected of militarised societies, such as 'heroic' behaviours and success in battle, continued to be of concern to those who lived long after the transition from late antique to early medieval Britain. These concerns permeated the creation and negotiation of group identities and the delineation of ingroup/outgroup behavioural standards. Thus, this chapter has gone a little way to addressing who engaged in warfare before the arrival of the Vikings, and, furthermore, reveals the mindsets of those writers whose lives were militarised not by their direct participation in warfare, but by warfare's ubiquitous influence on constructing and negotiating contemporary identities.

Notes

1 As stated in this volume's Introduction, the terms 'Anglo-Saxon' and 'Anglo-Saxons' are increasingly recognised as problematic. In the following discussion, 'Anglo-Saxon' in reference to periodisation has been replaced with the paradigm proposed by Susan Oosthuizen in *The emergence of the English* (York: ARC Humanities Press, 2019): 'Late antique' for 400–600 (traditionally termed 'early Anglo-Saxon') and 'early medieval' for 600–850 (traditionally 'middle Anglo-Saxon'). It is more difficult to find alternative terminology for 'Anglo-Saxon' as a descriptor of people, culture or artefacts, etc. This is because there is no clear evidence for the name these people gave themselves, and alternatives such as 'Englisc' or 'Angelcynn' pose their own significant problems. 'Anglo-Saxon' is therefore used as a descriptor but with the recognition that a more appropriate term may later come into use. See S. Reynolds, 'What do we mean by "Anglo-Saxon" and "Anglo-Saxons"?', *Journal of British Studies*, 24 (1985), 395–414.
2 G. Halsall, 'Playing by whose rules? A further look at Viking atrocity in the ninth century', *Medieval History*, 2 (1992), pp. 3–12; R. Lavelle, *Alfred's wars. Sources and interpretation of Anglo-Saxon warfare in the Viking Age* (Woodbridge: Boydell and Brewer, 2010), pp. 32–46. See also Lavelle's Chapter 5, this volume.
3 On Alfred's accomplishments, see R. Abels, *Alfred the Great. War, kingship and culture in Anglo-Saxon England* (London: Routledge, 1998).
4 For example P. Hill, *The Anglo-Saxons at war 800–1066* (Barnsley: Pen and Sword, 2012).
5 This is partially due to the 'Alfredian' translation programme, itself a much-debated topic. See M. Godden, 'Did King Alfred write anything?', *Medium Ævum*, 76 (2007), 1–23; J. Bately, 'Did King Alfred actually translate anything? The integrity of the Alfredian Canon revisited', *Medium Ævum*, 78 (2009), 189–215.
6 For the purposes of this chapter, I am using the date 800 as a convenient end-date of the 'pre-Viking' period in England.
7 This issue has its own vast historiographic tradition. For example: C. R. Davis, 'Cultural assimilation in the Anglo-Saxon royal genealogies', *Anglo-Saxon England*, 21 (1992), 23–36; D. N. Dumville, 'Kingship, genealogies and regnal lists', in I. Wood and P. H Sawyer (eds), *Early medieval kingship* (Leeds: University of Leeds, 1977), pp. 72–104.
8 *HE* I.15. English translation used is *The Ecclesiastical History of the English People*, eds R. Collins and J. McClure (Oxford: Oxford University Press, 2008). Latin is *Historia Ecclesiastica Gentis Anglorum*, eds B. Colgrave and R. A. B. Mynors (Oxford: Clarendon Press, 1969). References are to book and chapter.
9 *Ibid.*, p. 74.

10 B. Yorke, *Kings and kingdoms of early Anglo-Saxon England* (Seaby: London, 1990), pp. 39–43.
11 *Ibid.*, pp. 138–9 and 102.
12 See above, note 1. B. Ward-Perkins, 'Why did the Anglo-Saxons not become more British?', *The English Historical Review*, 115 (2000), 513–33, at 513. Susan Oosthuizen breaks down the traditional narrative of a Germanic migration or invasion, favouring instead a process of internal development and a shift of cultural influences from the Mediterranean to the North Sea sphere. Oosthuizen, *The emergence of the English*.
13 B. Yorke, *The Anglo-Saxons* (Stroud: Sutton, 1999), p. 34; J. Campbell (ed.), *The Anglo-Saxons* (London: Penguin, 1991), p. 46.
14 S. Foot, 'The making of the *Angelcynn*. English identity before the Norman Conquest', *Transactions of the Royal Historical Society*, 6 (1996), 25–49, at 38–9.
15 *HE* I.1.
16 *HE* II.5; S. Fanning, 'Bede, imperium, and the Bretwaldas', *Speculum*, 66 (1991), 1–26. See P. Wormald, 'Bede, the Bretwaldas and the origins of the Gens Anglorum', in P. Wormald, D. Bullough, and R. Collins (eds), *Ideal and reality in Frankish and Anglo-Saxon society. Studies presented to J. M. Wallace-Hadrill* (Oxford: Blackwell, 1983), pp. 99–129; B. Yorke, 'The Bretwaldas and the origins of overlordship in Anglo-Saxon England', in S. Baxter, C. E. Karkov, J. L. Nelson and D. Pelteret (eds), *Early medieval studies in memory of Patrick Wormald* (Aldershot: Routledge, 2009), pp. 81–95.
17 *HE* I.22, II.2.
18 English translation used is M. Swanton (ed.), *The Anglo-Saxon Chronicles* (London: Phoenix Press, 2000). References to the Old English text are to J. Bately and D. N. Dumville (eds), *The Anglo-Saxon Chronicle. A collaborative edition,* Volume 3 MS. A (Cambridge: D. S. Brewer, 1986); S. Irvine (ed.), *The Anglo-Saxon Chronicle. A collaborate edition*, Volume 7 MS. E (Cambridge: D. S. Brewer, 2004).
19 See B. Yorke, 'The representations of early West Saxon history in the Anglo-Saxon Chronicle', in A. Jorgensen (ed.) *Reading the Anglo-Saxon Chronicle. Language, literature, history* (Turnhout: Brepols, 2010), pp. 141–60; T. A. Bredehoft, *Textual histories. Readings in the Anglo-Saxon Chronicle* (Toronto: University of Toronto Press, 2001); N. P. Brooks, 'Why is the Anglo-Saxon Chronicle about kings?', *Anglo-Saxon England*, 39 (2010), 43–70; N. Brooks, '"Anglo-Saxon Chronicle(s)" or "Old English royal annals"?', in J. L. Nelson, S. Reynolds and S. M. Johns (eds), *Gender and historiography. Studies in the earlier Middle Ages in honour of Pauline Stafford* (Liverpool: School of Advanced Study, University of London, Institute of Historical Research, 2012), pp. 35–48.
20 L. Brons, 'Othering, an analysis', *Transcience*, 6 (2015), 69–90.
21 *Ibid.*, 72.
22 M. J. Bernstein, 'Ingroups and outgroups', in J. Stone, R. M. Dennis, P. S. Rizova, A. D. Smith and X. Hou (eds), *The Wiley Blackwell encyclopedia of race, ethnicity, and nationalism* (Malden: Wiley-Blackwell, 2016), pp. 1–3, p. 1;

R. F. Baumeister and M. R. Leary, 'The need to belong. Desire for interpersonal attachments as a fundamental human motivation', *Psychological Bulletin*, 117 (1995), 497–529.

23 Bernstein, 'Ingroups and outgroups', p. 2. See also G. Halsall, 'Otherness and identity in the Merovingian cemetery', in J. L. Quiroga, M. Kazanski and V. Ivanišević (eds), *Entangled identities and otherness in late antique and early medieval Europe* (Oxford: BAR International Series 2852, 2017), pp. 189–98.

24 *Ibid.*, p. 2. On the idea that information about the outgroup is processed in an over-simplified manner, see Baumeister and Leary, 'The need to belong', p. 504.

25 This idea is discussed in L. Campos Pérez, 'Representing the enemy. The iconography of the other in history schoolbooks during the first years of Franco's regime', *Contributions to the History of Concepts*, 5 (2009), 140–61, here 141–2.

26 en.oxforddictionaries.com/definition/enemy (accessed 27 March 2019).

27 *BT*, 'folc-gefeoht'. J. T. McNeill and H. M. Gamer, *Medieval handbooks of penance. A transaltion of the principle Libri Poenitentiales*, reprint (New York: Columbia University Press, 1990), p. 187.

28 S. A. Barney, W. J. Lewis, J. A. Beach and O. Berghof (eds), *The etymologies of Isidore of Seville* (Cambridge: Cambridge University Press, 2006), p. 359.

29 *ASC* 755 [757]. See F. Leneghan, 'Royal wisdom and the Alfredian context of Cynewulf and Cyneheard', *Anglo-Saxon England*, 39 (2011), 71–104; B. Yorke, 'The representations of early West Saxon history in the Anglo-Saxon Chronicle', in A. Jorgensen (ed.), *Reading the Anglo-Saxon Chronicle. Language, literature, history* (Turnhout, 2010), pp. 141–160, here p. 144.

30 The Irish who dwelt in Ireland, and the Irish that dwelt in Britain, e.g. the kingdom of Dál Raita. See A. P. Smyth, *Warlords and holy men. Scotland AD 80–1000* (London: Edward Arnold, 1984), p. 79.

31 *HE* I.12–15. P. Sims-Williams, 'The settlement of England in Bede and the chronicle', *Anglo-Saxon England*, 12 (1983), 1–41, here 5.

32 *HE* I.15.

33 *HE* I.15, '*nec erat, qui crudeliter interemtos sepulturae traderet*'.

34 *ASC* 937. On Anglo-Saxon immigration models, see M. G. Thomas, M. P. H. Stumpf and H. Härke, 'Evidence for an apartheid-like social structure in early Anglo-Saxon England', *Proceedings of the Royal Society*, 273 (2006), 2651–7; J. E. Pattison, 'Is it necessary to assume an apartheid-like social structure in early Anglo-Saxon England?', *Proceedings of the Royal Society*, 275 (2008), 2423–9.

35 On Gildas' representation of the 'British' in relation to the 'Saxons', see J. M. Harland, 'Rethinking ethnicity and "otherness" in early Anglo-Saxon England', *Medieval Worlds*, 5 (2017), 113–42.

36 *HE* I.15, '*accensus manibus paganorum ignis, iustas de sceleribus populi Dei ultiones expetiit*'.

37 *HE* I.16. The precise date of the battle is unknown. G. Halsall, *Worlds of Arthur. Facts and fiction in the Dark Ages* (Oxford: Oxford University Press, 2013), p. 17.

38 *ASC* 455, 457, 465.
39 On the other hand, MS F states that Wipped was a member of Hengest's party and not one of the chieftains. Swanton, *The Anglo-Saxon Chronicles*, p. 15 n. 18.
40 *HE* I.15.
41 Yorke, *Kings and kingdoms of early Anglo-Saxon England*, pp. 128–30.
42 For example, the accession of Ceolwulf: '... he continually strove either against the Angle race, or against the Welsh, or against the Picts, or against the Scots'. *ASC* 597. Yorke, *Kings and kingdoms*, pp. 16–17.
43 *ASC* 547, 603.
44 *HE* I.34.
45 J. McClure, 'Bede's Old Testament kings', in P. Wormald, D. Bullough, and R. Collins (eds), *Ideal and reality in Frankish and Anglo-Saxon society* (Oxford: Blackwell, 1983), pp. 76–98, p. 87.
46 *HE* II.2. The *ASC* records the battle under the year 606 (MS A) and 605 (MS E).
47 S. Davies, 'The Battle of Chester and warfare in post-Roman Britain', *History*, 95 (2010), 143–58, here 145. *HE* II.2.
48 *HE* II.2, 'maximam gentis perfidae stragem'.
49 *HE* II.2.
50 B. Colgrave (ed.), *Two Lives of Saint Cuthbert. A Life by an anonymous monk of Lindesfarne and Bede's prose Life* (Cambridge: Cambridge University Press, 1940), pp. 236–7, *HE* IV.26.
51 *HE* IV.26, '*uastauit misere gentem innoxiam, et nationi Anglorum semper amicissimam*'. The event was significant enough to be recorded in the *Annals of Ulster*. *AU*, 684.
52 Smyth, *Warlords and holy men*, p. 26.
53 *HE* IV.26.
54 *HE* IV.26, III.4; D. H. Farmer (ed.) and J. F. Webb (trans.), *The age of Bede* (London: Penguin Books 2004), p. 15.
55 R. Meens, 'A background to Augustine's mission to Anglo-Saxon England', *Anglo-Saxon England*, 23 (1994), 5–17.
56 Colgrave, *Two Lives of Saint Cuthbert*, pp. 242–43, *HE* II.20. Both descriptions contain the noun *atrocitas*.
57 *HE* IV.26.
58 'Non-Anglo-Saxon' sources record the leader of the Picts as King Bridei son of Brile. L. Alcock, 'The site of the "Battle of Dunnichen"', *The Scottish Historical Review*, 75 (1996), 130–42; Smyth, *Warlords and holy men*, p. 66.
59 *HE* IV.26.
60 On the conversion of the Anglo-Saxons to Christianity, see Campbell, *The Anglo-Saxons*, pp. 45–53.
61 Penda defeated Edwin of Northumbria in 633 (*HE* II.20), Sigeberht (formerly king) and Ecgric of East Anglia (*HE* III.18), and Oswald of Northumbria in 642 (*HE* III.9). He 'drove out' Cenwalh of Wessex in 645 (*ASC* 645, *HE* III.7).
62 *HE* II.20.

63 *Ibid.*
64 *HE* III.1, T. M. Charles-Edwards, 'Wales and Mercia, 613–918', in M. P. Brown and C. A. Farr (eds), *Mercia. An Anglo-Saxon kingdom in Europe* (Leicester: Leicester University Press, 2001), pp. 89–105, here p. 92.
65 *HE* III.16.
66 *HE* II.20.
67 *Ibid.*
68 Lavelle, *Alfred's wars*, p. 325; R. Lavelle, 'The use and abuse of hostages in later Anglo-Saxon England', *Early Medieval Europe*, 14 (2006), 269–96; A. J. Kosto, 'Hostages in the Carolingian world (714–840)', *Early Medieval Europe*, 11 (2002), 123–47.
69 *HE* III.24, III.9. *ASC* MS E s.a. 654 states that the battle was fought at *Winwidfeld*, unidentified.
70 McClure, 'Bede's Old Testament kings', pp. 88–91.
71 Charles-Edwards, 'Wales and Mercia', p. 93.
72 P. Godman (ed.), Alcuin, *The bishops, kings, and saints of York* (Oxford: Clarendon Press, 1982), pp. 46–7.
73 R. Abels, '"Cowardice" and duty in Anglo-Saxon England', *Journal of Medieval Military History*, 4 (2006), 29–49.
74 Godman, *The bishops, kings, and saints of York*, pp. 46–7.
75 Abels, 'Cowardice', pp. 44–5.
76 *ASC* 655.
77 B. Colgrave (ed.), *The Life of Wilfrid by Eddius Stephanus*, revised edn (Cambridge: Cambridge University Press, 2010), pp. 42–3.

18

Warriors and warlike kings in the *Gesta Karoli* of Notker the Stammerer

Thomas Wittkamp

Notker the Stammerer, a learned monk of St Gall, between 885 and 887 completed his *Gesta Karoli Magni* (Deeds of Charlemagne), a collection of tales about Charlemagne written on behalf of Emperor Charles the Fat.[1] Until the middle of the twentieth century, many historians disdained Notker's *Gesta* due to the anecdotal and unhistorical character of many of its tales,[2] and it has been only gradually rehabilitated since the 1940s. Scholars have demonstrated, for example, that the *Gesta* cannot be properly understood without uncovering Notker's literary references, narrative intentions and, not least, his humour.[3] Meanwhile, although historians no longer use the *Gesta* as a historical source for the age of Charlemagne, they continue to resort to it to understand the mindset of Notker and his ninth-century contemporaries.[4] More recently, Eric J. Goldberg stated that the tales of the *Gesta* contributed to a warlike style of representation at the courts of King Louis the German and his successors in late ninth-century East Francia.[5] Thus, the mentioned shift towards a history of perceptions should also allow analysis of the *Gesta* in terms of early medieval militarisation as defined by Edward James in 1997.[6] But did Notker's *Gesta* really contribute to a distinct warrior-identity and does it really provide evidence of early medieval militarisation in East Francia? To answer these questions, the present chapter will analyse the significance of the military by focusing on three warrior narrations taking place in the framework of Charlemagne's Saxon wars and a tale about the giant Alemannic warrior-hero Eishere, whose physical size and deeds are meant to embody the perfect warrior. The chapter will conclude with a discussion of the military representation of the Carolingian rulers in order to better understand the political intentions behind Notker's narrations.

The significance of the military in the *Gesta Karoli*

At first glance, the *Gesta Karoli* appear to provide much information about the military. Notker explicitly devoted the second book of his *Gesta* to 'the wars of the most vigorous Charlemagne' (*de bellicis rebus acerrimi Karoli*).[7] Obviously, the author considered the description of the lifestyle of warriors indispensable for a biography about Charlemagne as his narrations about warriors and warlike kings may have been adapted to his courtly audience.[8] Furthermore, Notker shows great interest in the details of ninth-century warfare and weaponry. In his second book, for example, he provides one of the most detailed descriptions of armour known from the ninth century.[9] Notker's interest in military details was not exceptional. The *Golden Psalter of St. Gall*, with its sophisticated military illustrations, proves that his fellow monks must have been well-informed about contemporary military equipment and tactics.[10] Notker explains that the narrations contained in his second book are based on first-hand reports from the battlefield provided by his foster-father Adalbert, a veteran of Charlemagne's campaigns against the Avars, Saxons and Slavs. The author begins his account of the wars of Charlemagne in the form of a dialogue with his foster-father describing the nine rings of the Avars, i.e. concentric circles of fortifications which are meant to have protected the Avar homeland. As the description does indeed correspond to archaeological evidence related to early medieval east European fortifications, it appears that Notker was an attentive listener and that he was interested in such military detail.[11]

Nonetheless, unlike his foster-father and the audience he addresses, Notker does not seem to have actually liked stories about the military. Notker explains that as a young boy he only reluctantly listened to the narrations of his foster-father and had to be forced to do so, thus exposing his attitude towards the military. This statement should not be given too much credence, however, given the likelihood that Notker said so only to underline his early determination to become a monk.[12] Thus, his autobiographical retrospection attests that the *Gesta* were written from a monastic perspective. Notker's work was inevitably compared to the earlier biography of Charlemagne written by the layman Einhard, which largely focused on wars and conquests. However, and unlike Einhard, Notker begins his *Gesta* with narrations that highlight the importance of learning.[13] In his first book, the author focuses on liturgical and ecclesiastical affairs, whereas military matters are set aside for the second book. Still, this second book mostly deals with diplomacy and court ritual, i.e. not with the actual practice of warfare. The description of the Avar rings, for example, is followed by just a short narrative on the Saxon wars, which is followed by prolonged reports of the reception of

Persian, Byzantine and Viking legations and an account of conspiracies directed against Charlemagne.[14]

Notker's references to the military mostly serve non-military narrative purposes. He uses his description of the arrival in 773 of Charlemagne's army at the gates of the city of Pavia, for example, to stress the significance of teaching Latin grammar. When he describes Charlemagne's armour, Notker inserts a full declension of the singular of *ferrum* (iron).[15] It appears likely that he did so in order to convince his aristocratic audience of the importance of learning and literacy. Learning is also crucial in Nothker's narrative about the forced instruction by his illiterate foster-father, as here he combines the military sphere of his illiterate foster-father and his aristocratic audience with the learned world of the monks of St Gall.

Notker also points to the literary background of his work. His description of the nine Avar rings, for example, is not merely a simple repetition of Adalbert's war memories. Rather, Notker's nine rings can be traced back to the nine bends of the mythical underworld River Styx in Virgil's *Aeneid*, a work Notker quotes liberally in several chapters of his *Gesta*.[16] The monk refers to the number of the rings to point their literary origin out to his learned readers. That indicates that, despite the similarities to archaeological findings in eastern Europe, he was obviously more interested in relating the rings to Virgil's *Aeneid* than in providing an accurate account of the Avar fortifications. So, even if his description of the Avar rings is in line with reality, it is rather fictional or literary in origin. In conclusion, any analysis of Notker's narrations about warriors and warlike kings has to take account of his literary references and narrative intentions.

Warriors of the Saxon wars

As mentioned above, Notker begins his second book with three short narratives about fighting men that are set in Charlemagne's Saxon wars. He starts with a narration about two followers (*privati homines*) of a man named Kerold proving their military skills by forming a *testudo*-formation (a roof of shields) in order to be able to 'most vigorously' (*acerrime*) destroy the walls of a well-fortified Saxon settlement. Charlemagne, who had personally observed their efforts, made one of them a prefect stationed between the Rhine and the Italian Alps and he bestowed land on the other.[17]

A closer look at Notker's narration also provides insight into ninth-century military virtues. The use of the Latin word *acerrime*, the superlative of the adverb *acriter*, which may be translated as 'eagerly', 'energetically', 'vigorously', 'keenly' or 'fiercely', is significant. It refers to characteristic traits and virtues such as vigour, resolution, zeal, alacrity and commitment. In the *Gesta*, Notker uses this term to emphasise such qualities by making them an integral part of his narrations about warriors and warlike kings. For example, the superlative of the corresponding adjective is used in his characterisation of the 'most vigorous Charlemagne' (*acerrimus Karolus*).[18]

The description of the aforementioned traits is not limited to the words *acer* and *acriter*. In his description of the siege of Pavia, for example, Notker stresses that Charlemagne's 'palace guard knew no rest' (*scola vacationis semper ignara*) as they helped to build a chapel in front of the gates of Pavia even during the siege. The monk interpreted the construction of the chapel as an example of the industriousness (*industria*) of Charlemagne, who had ordered his craftsmen to do so in order to avoid idleness. Notker emphasises the significance of this quality by stressing at two further occasions that the 'most energetic' (*exercitatissimus*) Charlemagne despised idleness.[19] The *Gesta* is not the only Carolingian source to accentuate the industriousness of warriors or kings, suggesting that vigour and commitment were considered key qualities in late Carolingian warrior culture. Regino of Prum, for example, a contemporary of Notker, regularly employed the terms *strennuus* (strenuous) and *industrius* (industrious) in his chronicle to characterise distinguished military commanders and kings.[20] Notker was familiar with these terms, as he combined them in another narration describing a 'very strenuous and industrious' (*valde strennuus et industrius*) vassal of a bishop named Recho who was not appropriately rewarded by his master: for a long time, the vassal strove for the bishop's gratitude, although in vain, and he only won the affections of his episcopal lord when he feigned a miracle in the latter's name.[21] Although the tale of the bishop's vassal is not set in a military context, this narration may be compared to the Kerold tale.

Unlike the episcopal vassal, Kerold's two followers received their reward for the destruction of the walls of the Saxon settlement on the spot. The mention of immediate reward fits the general tone of the *Gesta*, as Notker tends to propagandise the idea of meritocracy, i.e. a society wherein individuals are rewarded and appointed to public offices not due to their social rank but due to their efforts, talents and achievements. In numerous chapters of his first book, he stresses that Charlemagne nominated his candidates for bishoprics by taking into account their respective talents.[22] In his narration about the two followers of Kerold, Notker combined the glorification of particular military virtues, notably vigour and industriousness, with a merit-based reward. Thus, he transferred his idea of meritocracy from his narrations about the appointment of bishops to the military sphere. This assumption is supported by further examples added by Notker to make the same point.

Following the Kerold tale, for example, Notker refers to the sons of two dukes who showed far less vigour than the mentioned followers. The ducal sons failed to guard Charlemagne's tent at night because they were drunk and fell asleep. Charlemagne, who according to his habit was always awake at night, noticed the sleeping youths when walking around the camp, but returned unheeded to his tent. In the morning, Charlemagne summoned the nobles of his army and asked them what kind of judgement a man would deserve who handed over the leader of the Franks to the enemy. Whereupon the assembled nobles, not knowing what had happened the night before, sentenced the hypothetical man to death. Charlemagne, however, only publicly reprimanded the ducal sons with harsh words and dismissed them unharmed.[23]

Although the dukes' sons should have faced the death penalty, they got off lightly. Charlemagne obviously did not intend to impose a more severe punishment than this public dressing down, a decision that might have been taken in consideration of their fathers' status as highest-ranking military officers. Although the assembled nobles had suggested the death penalty, Charlemagne preferred to temper justice with mercy. Maybe the monarch wanted to avoid the indignation of his nobles. On the other hand, being trusted as the guard of Charlemagne's tent certainly was considered an honour, a task that was probably entrusted to the two youths in consideration of their noble origin. Thus, Charlemagne's reprehension and disclosure of their negligence in front of the assembled nobles dishonoured them, a public humiliation that in a society based on rank and honour was often accompanied by the loss of the king's or lords' favour. In consequence of such a dishonouring, the person concerned could be passed over when it came to appointments to public office and he could be faced with the deprivation of his offices and privileges. Moreover, since the boys' fathers were high military officers, it appears likely that they were present at the camp and that their sons had to face the anger and humiliation of their fathers as well.

The narrative about the ducal youth is addressed to the Carolingian nobility as a whole. Charlemagne had lured his nobles into a trap and made them unknowingly impose the death penalty on their peers. In so doing, Charlemagne doubtless took his nobles by surprise, making them admonish their peers involuntarily, and they must have then realised that they too might have to face severe consequences if they were ever caught neglecting their duties. Thus, by referring to the judgement of the assembled nobles, Notker reminded his readers that a high rank also demanded an equivalent praiseworthy performance. On that basis, the carelessness of the dukes' sons was even more embarrassing, because it was in blatant contrast to the vigilance of Charlemagne. What is more, given that the king did not consider himself too important to walk around the camp at night, there were no excuses to be made by arguing that standing guard was a negligible task or could be left to the rank and file. To counter such arguments, Notker included numerous narrations in his *Gesta* in which Carolingian kings reprimanded aristocrats or bishops due to malfeasance and failure.[24] All in all, Notker established an inverse interdependence between rank and – in this context military – performance, by stressing that performance is first and foremost demanded from the elite.

The inverse interdependence between rank and performance, which the narration of the dukes' sons stands for, is turned upside down in the last and most interesting of Notker's three short warrior narratives. It relates to two bastards from the city of Colmar who were raised in a *genicium*, a house where women worked together as sewers providing employment and lodging for unmarried mothers and their illegitimate children. In any case, Notker's reference to the *genicium* seems to point to the inferior origin of the two bastards.[25] Still, the two bastards are said to have proved their worth during the Saxon war. Charlemagne, who had observed their military efforts, summoned them and asked them where they came from. After he had learned about their humble beginnings, he offered them the opportunity to serve him as servants of the chamber. Hiding their disappointment, the bastards agreed, but when the king fell asleep, they secretly left and went to the Saxon camp to start a fight. Notker concludes that the two bastards preferred 'rather to wash away the disgrace of servitude with their own blood and the blood of enemies' than to serve Charlemagne as attendants of the chamber.[26]

Remarkably, Notker did not disapprove of the bastards' deed, even though they were disobedient to Charlemagne. Maybe he refrained from condemning their deed because they had already paid for their disobedience with their blood, but maybe he also considered their actions acceptable, if not praiseworthy. In comparison to the previous narrative, it appears that Notker deemed the boys' actions no worse than the failure of the ducal sons. Indeed, the bastards' reckless procedure contrasts sharply with the irresponsible sleep of the dukes' sons: irrespective of their ignoble origin, they far surpassed the dukes' sons in courage, commitment and ambition, as they distinguished themselves in war and strove to rid themselves of their ignoble origin. The dukes' sons, in contrast, neglected a privilege with which they had been honoured by birth. One could add that the bastards even managed to evade the king's attention, who was usually awake at night. And in addition, they rejected the best offer they would ever get. Given their inferior origin, born out of wedlock and raised in a *genicium*, the position of attendant of the chamber was a great opportunity. Although they probably dined after the elite and the warriors among the other servants and worked together with women, some narratives contained in the *Gesta* demonstrate that the servants of the chamber ranked among the most influential courtiers, because they worked very close to the king and could even control access to him.[27] The bastards' reluctance to accept Charlemagne's offer may be explained by the non-military and constrained character of the position offered. The office of attendant of the chamber contrasts strongly with the military ambitions the bastards had previously shown and would not necessarily have helped them to finally overcome their inferior origin. Here, military activity seems indispensable for advancement in social rank. Thus, the narration of the two bastards may be the most convincing evidence for early medieval militarisation in the *Gesta* given that the bastards strove for military glory at all costs. They tried to free themselves of the 'disgrace of servitude', even if that meant that they had to reject the generous offer of a civil office and pay for this rejection with their blood.

To summarise, in his three warrior narrations Notker defines key virtues of late ninth century warriors: commitment, vigour and performance were the most important and indispensable, while negligence and idleness were to be condemned. He holds up these particular virtues and vices in order to promote his concept of meritocracy. Moreover, Notker combines the merit principle with the different social positions of the protagonists. Their rank varies from middle (the two followers of Kerold) through very high (the sons of the two dukes) to very low (the bastards from Colmar). The lower their social origin, the more the protagonists may achieve by means of military service. The higher their status, the more is demanded of them and the more they are embarrassed or shamed if they fail or neglect their duties. In the end, however, advancement and decline in social rank by means of military performance were limited according to the protagonist's social origin.

Eishere

Apart from social rank, Notker accentuates a warrior's territorial origin. It is noteworthy that the author in particular attributed military skills to characters of Alemannic origin. The author obviously favoured his fellow countrymen.[28] For instance, the mentioned two bastards came from the city of Colmar, which in the early Middle Ages was part of the territory of Alemannia; while Kerold, the lord of the mentioned *privati homines*, was a brother of the Alemannic wife of Charlemagne named Hildegard. In contrast, the negligent ducal sons are not associated with any Alemannic origin. Thus, it appears that Notker aimed to create a formidable Alemannic warrior identity.

This assumption is supported by the narrative about the Alemannic war-hero Eishere. It is part of a long chapter about rebellions and conspiracies against Charlemagne. Apart from Notker's foster-father, Adalbert, Eishere is the sole warrior whose name is mentioned in the *Gesta*. The name is particularly suited to its owner: the Old High German word *eis* or *egis* refers to horror or terror, especially when related to supernatural creatures, while *here* is derived from the Germanic word *heri* ('army' or 'warrior').[29] Notker himself relates the name to Eishere's outstanding contribution to Charlemagne's terrible or awe-inspiring army (*magna pars terribilis exercitus*), which Eishere accompanied during the Slavic wars. In this context, Notker notably accentuated the extraordinarily tall figure of Eishere and he compares him with the descendants of the biblical Anak, who were well-known for their phenomenal size. Thus, Eishere must have been a physical giant. The enormous size of his body must have been an important contribution to Charlemagne's army as his physical appearance is likely to have helped to spread terror among the enemy. This is well reflected in Eishere's deeds: Notker claims that after invoking Saint Gallus, Eishere was able to pull his enormous but intractable horse across the fast-running River Thur at high tide. The author adds that his fellow countryman also mowed down the Slavic enemies like grass and that Eishere himself declared that he usually impaled up to nine of the enemy warriors on his spear in the manner of a bird catcher.[30]

But why did Notker tell the tale of the giant warrior Eishere in the first place? Was it only out of pride that such a formidable warrior stemmed from his own homeland near Thurgau (northern Switzerland), which is in close proximity to St Gall? A closer inspection of the narrative's context suggests, instead, that Notker's insertion of the Eishere tale was mainly motivated by worries he had about current political threats. It appears that the physical giant Eishere is related to some mysterious giants (*gigantes*) which Notker had introduced at the very beginning of his chapter about rebellions and conspiracies against Charlemagne. According to the *Gesta*, giants like Eishere descended from biblical ancestors but were far more dangerous than Eishere. Notker explicitly warns Charles the Fat that these *gigantes* had stood ready to usurp the kingdom since the days of his grandfather, Emperor Louis the Pious, and advised Charles to ally with the *mediocres* (the men of medium rank) who in the past had prevented every usurpation by the *gigantes*.[31]

Modern scholars have suggested that Notker's *gigantes* represent the descendants of the female lineages of the Carolingian dynasty, including personalities like Boso of Provence. At the end of the ninth century, these powerful magnates threatened to usurp kingship and overthrow the male line of Carolingian succession.[32] Eishere, on the other hand, being the owner of a warhorse and a professional warrior, seems to represent the *mediocres* who at the beginning of Notker's chapter thwarted the usurpations of these *gigantes*. Although Eishere was no political giant, his fellow countrymen must have been impressed when told that the enemy Slavs were no match for him. Moreover, Notker appears to stress that Eishere's strength and size act as a deterrent to any usurpers as they would have to fear a real giant if they dared to threaten the Carolingian succession. Thus, Notker contrasts the physical giant Eishere with his symbolic political *gigantes*. But although both Eishere and the *gigantes* were related to biblical giants, only Eishere displays the strength and size Notker's audience would have expected from a true giant.

Eishere's contribution to Charlemagne's army far exceeded that of the powerful magnates. This was not only due to his intimidating appearance and size but also his words and deeds. The taming of his enormous warhorse and his disrespect for his Slavic enemies, as well as the fact that he found it very easy to defeat the Slavs, make him a perfect conqueror of barbarians.[33] Only a few lines before Notker starts reporting on Eishere, he claims that Charlemagne had complained about having to campaign in person against the barbarian peoples, though his commanders should have been able to fight the barbarians on their own. Thus, Eishere unintentionally demonstrates the military performance and commitment that Charlemagne had in vain demanded from his commanders. The fact that a man of medium rank surpassed Charlemagne's commanders in both physical size and military skill undoubtedly contributed to Notker's promotion of meritocracy. What is more, Eishere as a man of medium rank also surpassed the same commanders in terms of political reliability. Consequently, Notker in his narrative about Eishere suggests that a man like Eishere could replace the powerful magnates because they do not even perform those military tasks Charlemagne had assigned to them, not to mention their lacking political reliability. Thus, Notker stresses that meritocracy in the military could also be applied to politics.

Warlike kings

The Eishere tale highlights the limits of the military activity of the Carolingian rulers. It shows that even Charlemagne had to resort to able and loyal commanders who campaigned on his behalf. However, Notker's *Gesta* also portray Carolingian rulers as army commanders and they repeatedly emphasise their martial qualities and military skills. Still, Notker in his representations of kings and emperors has a preference for the machinations of diplomacy and the splendour of court ritual, the hardships of warfare and the horror of battles only being of secondary importance. This restriction may be due to the fact that Carolingian kings did not risk their own lives in battle, which meant that Notker had to glorify their military skills in a non-combatant context. In consequence, the kings had to face their enemies in court ritual, by demonstrations of physical strength, and sometimes they were even beaten by regal luck.

In a short narrative, for example, Notker recounts how Pepin the Short killed a lion and a bull with only one blow of his sword. Prior to this, Pepin had found himself in a situation where he had to break off his campaign in Italy in respect of the current diplomatic relations with the Romans and Byzantines. His political precaution undermined his royal authority, however, as his retreat could be construed as evidence of military weakness. That is why, according to Notker, he decided to set a lion on a bull and kill the two fighting beasts, thus impressing his nobles with an exploit they did not dare to perform. By this demonstration of courage and power, Pepin could make up for his retreat in Italy and silence his critics.[34] Thus, the tale highlights Pepin's military skills and at the same time justifies a military retreat.

Charlemagne, according to Notker, also preferred non-violent means of assertion, as is suggested by the mentioned siege of the city of Pavia. Instead of taking the city by force or famishing, he ordered his craftsmen and soldiers to raise a chapel in front of the gates. The inhabitants of Pavia, according to the *Gesta*, were so impressed by both Charlemagne's industriousness and fearsome army, that the Carolingian king was able to conquer the city without bloodshed. This is noteworthy as it is due to Notker's description of Charlemagne's iron-armoured army that modern scholars until now have characterised the king's arrival at the gates of Pavia as the culmination of the martial representation of Carolingian kingship in the *Gesta*.[35]

Given the Viking threat of the early 880s, it is also notable that Notker did not insert any mention of a military confrontation of Charlemagne or his grandson Louis the German. The *Gesta* claim that the Vikings took flight as soon as they spotted Charlemagne near an unnamed coastal city of southern Gaul. Another chapter mentions a campaign against invading Vikings that failed due to an epidemic, whereas the Viking King Godfrid is said to have been killed by his own son before Charlemagne could attack him.[36] Referring to Louis the German, Notker claims that no campaign was required as the Viking kings voluntarily sent their swords as a symbol of their subjugation, together with a tribute in gold and silver. Louis the German, however, reportedly disdained the precious metal and only accepted the weapons offered. Notker adds that the Vikings were impressed by Louis' preference for iron, which Louis had shown since his adolescence, and wished their own kings would do the same. Louis the German took the Viking swords and bent their blades to the hilt in a performance of his extraordinary strength. The breaking blades aroused great admiration among the Vikings, who now also offered their own swords to Louis, assuming that their blades would be too strong for him. To avoid any suspicion of an assassination attempt, the Vikings handed over their swords hilt first. Notker explains that in this way, however, they unintentionally acted like unfree servants and thus ritually confirmed their subjugation. In the end, Louis the German thus did not subdue the Vikings by force, but demonstrated his superiority as a warrior king by displaying his preference for iron and his extraordinary strength.[37]

Louis the Pious, Louis the German's father, did not have to subdue the Vikings by force. According to Notker, he benefited from the terror that his father Charlemagne had spread among the Viking invaders who still paid their tributes. In the *Gesta*, Louis the Pious repeatedly baptises large numbers of Vikings who reportedly exploit the sacrament of baptism to receive gifts from their godfathers as often as possible. Notker adds that, while the Franks were already running out of white garments, one older Viking complained to the emperor that the linen sack he had received after his twentieth baptism was not suitable for warriors but only for swineherds.[38] Although this narration appears to mock the Viking candidates for baptism, who obviously did not understand the symbolic meaning of this gift, modern scholars have argued that Notker also used this narrative to criticise Charles the Fat's naivety in the face of the Viking audacity and greed.[39] The narration ends with Notker's complaint that he wished 'one should only find this [i.e. disrespect for baptism] among pagans, and not so often even among those who are called Christians'.[40] This means that the narrative is explicitly turned against those Christians who did not sufficiently honour the sacrament of baptism. This can only refer to the political opponents of Charles the Fat, who had denounced the baptism of the Viking leader Godfrid together with the peace treaty concluded in 882 due to their animosity towards Charles the Fat and the known unreliability of the Vikings.[41] Contrary to the interpretation of most modern scholars, Notker's intention was neither to mock the Vikings nor to criticise Charles the Fat, but to attack the latter's critics. With his complaint, the author accused the latter of nothing less than blasphemy, sacrilege or maybe even apostasy, as those Christians who did not honour baptism were considered worse than pagans. This accusation was meant to justify the mentioned peace treaty which had resulted from Charles the Fat's decision in 882 to break off his siege of the Viking camp due to an epidemic. Given the analogy between Charles the Fat's campaign in 882 and a previous campaign by Charlemagne mentioned in the *Gesta*, which both had to be discontinued due to epidemics, it seems possible that the narration about Charlemagne's campaign was included in the *Gesta* to justify the highly controversial peace agreement of 882. Considering that no other Carolingian king in the *Gesta* triumphed over the Vikings by force, it appears likely that all Notker's narrations about non-violent encounters with the Vikings served this same purpose. If Charlemagne and his successors found non-violent means to subdue the Vikings, it could not be considered dishonourable if Charles the Fat chose to make peace with the Vikings after a bloodless end to the fighting.

Despite his warlike representations of the Carolingian rulers, Notker appears to promote a concept of peaceful kingship. Although Pepin, Charlemagne and Louis the German are presented as warlike kings in the *Gesta*, they do not partake in battle themselves. Rather, they triumph away from the battlefield, proving their strength and industriousness in non-violent situations. Farthest away from the battlefield is the Emperor Louis the Pious, who is not represented as a warlike king but as patiently baptising the Vikings, comparable to what Charles the Fat reportedly did in 882. This and the analogies between Charles the Fat and the non-violent triumphs of the Carolingian kings mentioned in the *Gesta* suggest that there is more behind Notker's stories than the aim to represent their martial qualities away from the battlefield. For example, Notker might have tried to suggest to Charles the Fat that he imitate his grandfather by establishing a peaceable style of royal representation.

Conclusion

How do Notker's representations of non-violent Carolingian kings fit the concept of early medieval militarisation? As far as we can see, Notker did not specifically accentuate the military, although he had detailed knowledge of armour, tactics and fortifications. Instead, it seems that Notker made use of military contexts to transmit intellectual and political messages to his audience. His narratives and the military virtues he praises are in line with his promotion of meritocracy. Notker deliberately established an inverse interdependence between military performance and social rank in order to exemplify his concept of meritocracy. Thus, the *Gesta* characterises military performance as crucial to social advancement, even though the latter is limited by social origin. The fact that Notker on several occasions links military skills to characteristics of Alemanic origin demonstrates that military exploits were desirable. Concurrently, his portrayals of giant warriors and extraordinarily strong kings address political problems like the unreliability of powerful magnates and the precariousness of royal authority following a military retreat. Notker's tales about warlike kings, on the other hand, may have served to support the idea of peaceful kingship. Still, the need to stress the effectiveness of peaceful kingship postulates the wide recognition of the warlike king as a model in Carolingian society. Notker obviously was well aware of his warlike audience at the court of Charles the Fat, which he needed in order to transmit his ideas about meritocracy and peaceful kingship.

Notes

1 Notker der Stammler, *Taten Kaiser Karls des Großen* I,18, ed. H. F. Haefele, *MGH SRG, NS*, 12 (Berlin: Weidmannsche Buchhandlung, 1959), p. 22. S. MacLean, *Kingship and politics in the late ninth century: Charles the Fat and the end of the Carolingian empire* (Cambridge: Cambridge University Press, 2003), pp. 201–6.
2 L. Halphen, 'Le Moine de Saint-Gall (Études critiques sur l'histoire de Charlemagne, IV)', *Revue Historique*, 128 (1918), 260–98. Compare T. Siegrist, *Herrscherbild und Weltsicht bei Notker Balbulus: Untersuchungen zu den Gesta Karoli* (Zurich: Peter Lang, 1963), pp. 7–16, 33–9.
3 Siegrist, *Herrscherbild*, p. 22. D. Ganz, 'Humour as history in Notker's Gesta Karoli Magni', in E. B. King, J. T. Schaefer and W. B. Wadley (eds), *Monks, nuns, and friars in medieval society* (Sewanee: Press of the University of the South, 1989), pp. 171–83, at p. 182. W. Berschin, *Biographie und Epochenstil im lateinischen Mittelalter. Vol. 3: Karolingische Biographie 750–920 n. Chr.* (Stuttgart: Hiersemann, 1991), p. 400. M. J. Innes, 'Memory, orality and literacy in an early medieval society', *Past and Present*, 158 (1998), 3–36, 13–14, 19. P. J. E. Kershaw, 'Laughter after Babel's fall. Misunderstanding and miscommunication in the ninth-century west', in: G. Halsall (ed.), *Humour, history and politics in late Antiquity and the early Middle Ages* (Cambridge: Cambridge University Press, 2002), pp. 179–202, at pp. 180, 191–9.
4 Siegrist, *Herrscherbild*, pp. 14–16 and 146. H. Löwe, 'Das Karlsbuch Notkers von St. Gallen und sein zeitgeschichtlicher Hintergrund', *Schweizerische Zeitschrift für Geschichte*, 20 (1970), 269–302, here 279, 302. H.-W. Goetz, *Strukturen der spätkarolingischen Epoche im Spiegel der Vorstellungen eines zeitgenössischen Mönchs. Eine Interpretation der Gesta Karoli Notkers von St. Gallen* (Bonn: Habelt, 1981), pp. 2–6, 21, 37, 114–15. MacLean, *Kingship*, pp. 199–229.
5 E. J. Goldberg, 'More devoted to the equipment of battle than the splendor of banquets. Frontier kingship, martial ritual, and early knighthood at the court of Louis the German', *Viator*, 30 (1999), 41–78, here 46–59, 71.
6 E. James, 'The militarisation of Roman society 400–700', in A. Nørgård Jørgensen and B. L. Clausen (eds), *Military aspects of Scandinavian society in a European perspective AD 1–1300* (Copenhagen: National Museum, 1997), pp. 19–24.
7 Notker, *Taten* II.*praefatio*, p. 48.
8 MacLean, *Kingship*, pp. 200–4, 213, 216–18, 227–9.
9 Notker, *Taten* II.17, pp. 83–4.
10 Ganz, *Humour*, p. 180. Goldberg, *Frontier kingship*, p. 47.
11 Notker, *Taten* II.*praefatio*, p. 48; II,1, p. 49–51. Compare the contribution by M. Hardt in E. Bennett, 'Tagungsbericht. Military Organisation and Society

in the post-Roman World, 15.08.2016 – 16.08.2016 Berlin', *H-Soz-Kult*, 19. December 2016, hsozkult.de/conferencereport/id/tagungsberichte-6886 (accessed 10 February 2019).
12 Notker, *Taten* II.*praefatio*, p. 48.
13 Ganz, *Humour*, pp. 171–8. Notker, *Taten* I.1–3, pp. 1–5. Compare Einhard, *Vita Karoli Magni* 2–15, ed. O. Holder-Egger, *MGH SRG*, 25 (Hanover: Hahnsche Buchhandlung, 1911), p. 4–18.
14 Notker, *Taten* II.5–9, II.12, II.18, II.19, pp. 53–65, 70–4, 88–90.
15 M. Fuhrmann and G. Fink, 'Erwartungshorizont und Lesersteuerung. Drei Beispiele aus Notkers Gesta Karoli', *Der Altsprachliche Unterricht*, 23,3 (1980), 41–52, at p. 47.
16 Halphen, *Le Moine*, p. 291 with notes 2 and 3.
17 Notker *Taten* II.2, p. 51.
18 Notker *Taten* II.*praefatio*, p. 48.
19 Notker *Taten* II.17, pp. 83, 85–6.
20 Regino abbas Prumiensis, *Chronicon cum continuatione Treverensi*, ed. F. Kurze, *MGH SRG*, 50 (Hanover: Hahnsche Buchhandlung, 1890), pp. 78 (a. 860), 79 (a. 861), 91 (a. 866), 93 (a. 867), 114 (a. 879), 120 (a. 883), 123 (a. 885), 126 (a. 887), 130 (a. 888), 140 (a. 892).
21 Notker, *Taten* I.20, pp. 26–7.
22 Notker, *Taten* I.3–9, pp. 4–12. Goetz, *Strukturen*, pp. 20, 38, 95.
23 Notker, *Taten* II.3, p. 52.
24 Notker, *Taten* I.3, pp. 4–5; I,11–12, p. 16; I,16–19, pp. 19–25; I,34, pp. 46–8; II,17, pp. 86–8. Compare Löwe, *Karlsbuch*, p. 284. Goetz, *Strukturen*, p. 95.
25 O. Salten, *Vasallität und Benefizialwesen im 9. Jahrhundert. Studien zur Entwicklung personaler und dinglicher Beziehungen im frühen Mittelalter* (Hildesheim: Franzbecker, 2013), pp. 52–3, 171. Compare Löwe, *Das Karlsbuch*, p. 284 note no. 63. Goetz, *Strukturen*, p. 19–20.
26 Notker, *Taten* II.4, p. 52.
27 Notker, *Taten* II.6, pp. 56; II.12, p. 72.
28 Goetz, *Strukturen*, pp. 13–15.
29 Art. 'egislîh, adj.' and 'heri, st. n.', *Althochdeutsches Wörterbuch, Sächsische Akademie der Wissenschaften zu Leipzig*, awb.saw-leipzig.de (accessed 25 September 2019).
30 Notker, *Taten* II.12, pp. 74–5.
31 *Ibid.*, pp. 70–1.
32 MacLean, *Kingship*, pp. 220–2. Löwe, *Karlsbuch*, pp. 229–302. Goetz, *Strukturen*, pp. 29 note no. 87, 37.
33 Goldberg, *Frontier kingship*, pp. 46, 50. Kershaw, *Laughter*, p. 180.
34 Notker, *Taten* II.15, pp. 78–80.
35 Notker, *Taten* II.17, pp. 82–5. Berschin, *Biographie*, pp. 398–9. Innes, *Memory*, p. 27. Goetz, *Strukturen*, p. 33–4.
36 Notker, *Taten* II.13, pp. 75–6; II,14, p. 77.
37 Notker, *Taten* II.18, pp. 88–9. Goldberg, *Frontier kingship*, pp. 44–59.
38 Notker, *Taten* II.19, pp. 89–90.

39 Kershaw, *Laughter*, pp. 195–7. Löwe, *Karlsbuch*, pp. 287–9, 292–3. Goetz, *Strukturen*, p. 33. MacLean, *Kingship*, pp. 206–15 and pp. 226–9.
40 Notker, *Taten* II.19, p. 90: *Quod utinam apud gentiles tantum et non etiam inter eos, qui Christi nomine censentur, sepius inveniretur!*
41 *Annales Fuldenses* a. 882, ed. F. Kurze, *MGH SRG*, 7 (Hanover: Hahnsche Buchhandlung, 1891), pp. 98–9. H. Keller, 'Zum Sturz Karls III.', in E. Hlawitschka (ed.), *Königswahl und Thronfolge in fränkisch-karolingischer Zeit* (Darmstadt: Wissenschaftliche Buchgesellschaft, 1975), pp. 432–94.

19

Early medieval 'warrior' images and the concept of *Gefolgschaft*

Michel Summer

In his 1936 lecture on the Old English poem *Beowulf*, J. R. R. Tolkien criticised the fact that researchers have treated the poem as a historical document and that they expressed 'disappointment at the discovery that it was itself and not something that the scholar would have liked better – for example, a heathen heroic lay, a history of Sweden, a manual of Germanic antiquities, or a Nordic *Summa Theologica*'.[1] As Tolkien points out, the 'illusion of historical truth' created by the poem has prompted scholars to use it as a 'quarry' in the search for historical facts.[2] This observation also applies to archaeological studies. Tolkien delivered his paper only three years before the discovery of the seventh-century burials on the site of Sutton Hoo in Suffolk (England). The most prominent find to emerge from the excavations is the helmet from Mound 1. The iron crest that runs along the top of the cap and the boar heads decorating the eyebrows of the face mask are all features of helmets mentioned in *Beowulf*.[3]

Within the poem, helmets, armour and swords are used as gifts and grave-goods. The poet presents these items as playing a pivotal role in the establishment and the perpetuation of the ties that existed between a military leader and his warriors.[4] Although their authors were Christian and chronologically removed from the periods they described, texts such as *Beowulf* or the sagas written in Old Norse are used by historians and archaeologists to reconstruct the use and symbolic meaning of artefacts such as the Sutton Hoo helmet.[5] This especially concerns the images on the bronze-foils (*Pressbleche*) that had originally been attached to the cap of the helmet. Among the decorative panels, which were embossed using die-plates, two motifs of figures carrying weapons occur.[6] Across western Europe, foils and die-plates with similar images dating between the second half of the sixth and the late seventh centuries survive.[7]

'Warrior' images and the concept of Gefolgschaft 315

In conjunction with the emphasis of certain written sources, such as Old English and Old Norse poems, on heroic warfare, these images have been identified as the representations of 'warriors' and as a key to the understanding of early medieval military organisation.[8] Retinues, upheld by the mechanisms of honour and gift-giving, apparently formed the basis of armies in post-Roman Britain, the Merovingian kingdoms and Scandinavia.[9] 'Warrior' images, such as those known from Sutton Hoo, are used to support this view as they seem to reflect the visibility and the importance of weapons and military values within their respective societies.[10] This chapter reassesses this notion by examining the traditional interpretation, prevailing especially in German-speaking archaeology, whereby the images known from early medieval embossed foils reflect the establishment of a 'Germanic' military culture prevalent after the fall of the western Roman Empire. Focusing on the concept of Gefolgschaft, created in the nineteenth century by German historians to denote the military retinue, this brief study analyses how the idea of a specifically Germanic military institution, developed from the written sources, has influenced archaeological research on the 'warrior' images. By disentangling their archaeological context and the historical framework according to which they have traditionally been studied, the extent to which the images testify to the development of 'militarised' societies in the sixth and seventh centuries is reconsidered. The discussion is restricted to the criteria in Edward James' definition of a militarised society, whereby in such a society 'the symbolism of warfare and weaponry is prominent in official and private life, and ... warlike and heroic virtues are glorified'.[11]

In an article published in 2002, Dieter Quast established a list of five motifs of 'warrior depictions' known from the Merovingian period: 'Military saints' (Reiterheilige), the 'Pliezhausen'-motif, 'dancing-warriors', 'wolf-warriors' and depictions of a rider holding a lance.[12] The Reiterheilige-motif refers to depictions of horsemen, who are in some cases haloed, carrying lances or cross-staffs.[13] The 'Pliezhausen'-motif is named after a brooch found in a seventh-century burial in south-western Germany. It features a rider carrying shield and spear and trampling down an enemy, while the latter simultaneously stabs the horse. A smaller figure is holding the rider's spear at the rear. The scene is also depicted on the helmets from Sutton Hoo Mound 1, Valsgärde 7 and Vendel 8 (both Sweden).[14] The 'dancing-warriors' on the sixth- and seventh-century foils from Sutton Hoo Mound 1, Valsgärde 7 and Gamla Uppsala (Sweden) are distinguished by the pose of their legs which seems to imply a 'dance' movement.[15] On a die-plate found in Torslunda (Sweden) and on a fragment of a bronze-foil from Obrigheim (Germany), the 'dancing-warrior' is accompanied by a figure which Quast assigns to the 'wolf-warrior'-motif. Its headgear is commonly interpreted as a wolf's mask and a similar depiction survives on a silver foil attached to a seventh-century sword-scabbard from Gutenstein (Germany).[16] The motif of a single rider holding a lance completes the list.[17] Recently, the 'warrior-procession' has been suggested as an addition to the motifs established by Quast.[18] While depictions of armed figures aligned in rows were already known from Torslunda, Vendel 14 and Valsgärde 7, another example from the seventh century has been found within the hoard from Staffordshire (England).[19] The depictions on the silver strap-ends of a woman's puttee from a grave in Rain (Germany), excavated between 2011 and 2012, have likewise been assigned to this motif.[20] Quast also omits depictions of 'fighting warriors' known from Vendel 11, 12 and 14 from the discussion.[21]

Before analysing the images' interpretation, their archaeological context needs to be considered according to three factors: distribution, burial context and secondary use. While the 'Pliezhausen'-motif was discovered in the burials from Vendel, Valsgärde and Uppsala, only one example has been found in Great Britain and south-western Germany, respectively.[22] Examples of 'dancing-warriors' are more widespread, but again limited to Great Britain, south-western Germany and parts of Scandinavia.[23] 'Wolf-warriors' have not been discovered in Great Britain and, apart from Sweden, only two examples of 'warrior-processions' overall survive in Great Britain and on the Continent (see Figures 19.1 and 19.2). The small number of finds, which leaves considerable gaps in the map of post-Roman Europe, not least with regard to the Merovingian kingdoms, should advise caution when using the images to retrace a process of widespread militarisation.[24]

Although the motifs specified here are addressed as 'warrior' images, they were not all included in male burials, nor were they all attached to helmets or scabbards. The brooch from Pliezhausen and the strap-ends from Rain in Bavaria were each discovered in a richly furnished woman's grave.[25] The Gutenstein scabbard, on the other hand, lacks an archaeological context altogether, since the burial was destroyed during its discovery in 1887.[26] The foil from Obrigheim had been attached to a wooden container, probably a maple bowl.[27] The Gutenstein foil shows traces of a secondary use, since the motif appears again in cropped form in the lower part of the scabbard. The foil appears to have been cut into form to fit the scabbard, while it had previously been attached to a different object, such as a bucket or a drinking horn.[28] The disc from Pliezhausen originally belonged to a three-piece horse-gear (*phalerae*) and was later reworked into a brooch by cutting the foil into form.[29] The presence of objects with a clear reference to Christianity alongside the 'warrior' images, such as the engraved silver spoons in the Sutton Hoo burial or the golden crosses within the Staffordshire Hoard, are indications that these depictions cannot *a priori* be linked to non-Christian beliefs.[30] Finally, die-impressed foils could also feature 'non-military' images. Depictions of figures guiding or fighting animals form part of the iconographic

'Warrior' images and the concept of Gefolgschaft   317

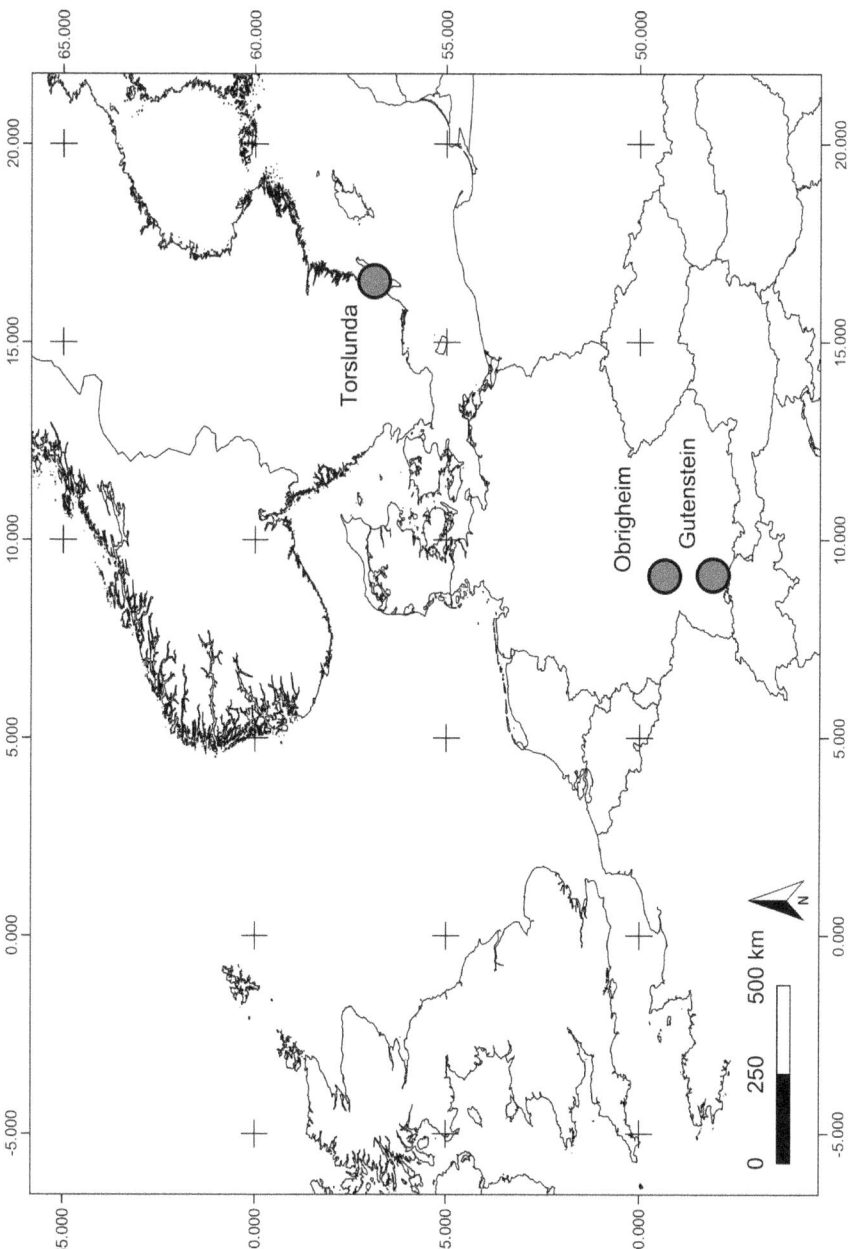

Figure 19.1 Distribution of 'wolf warrior' images

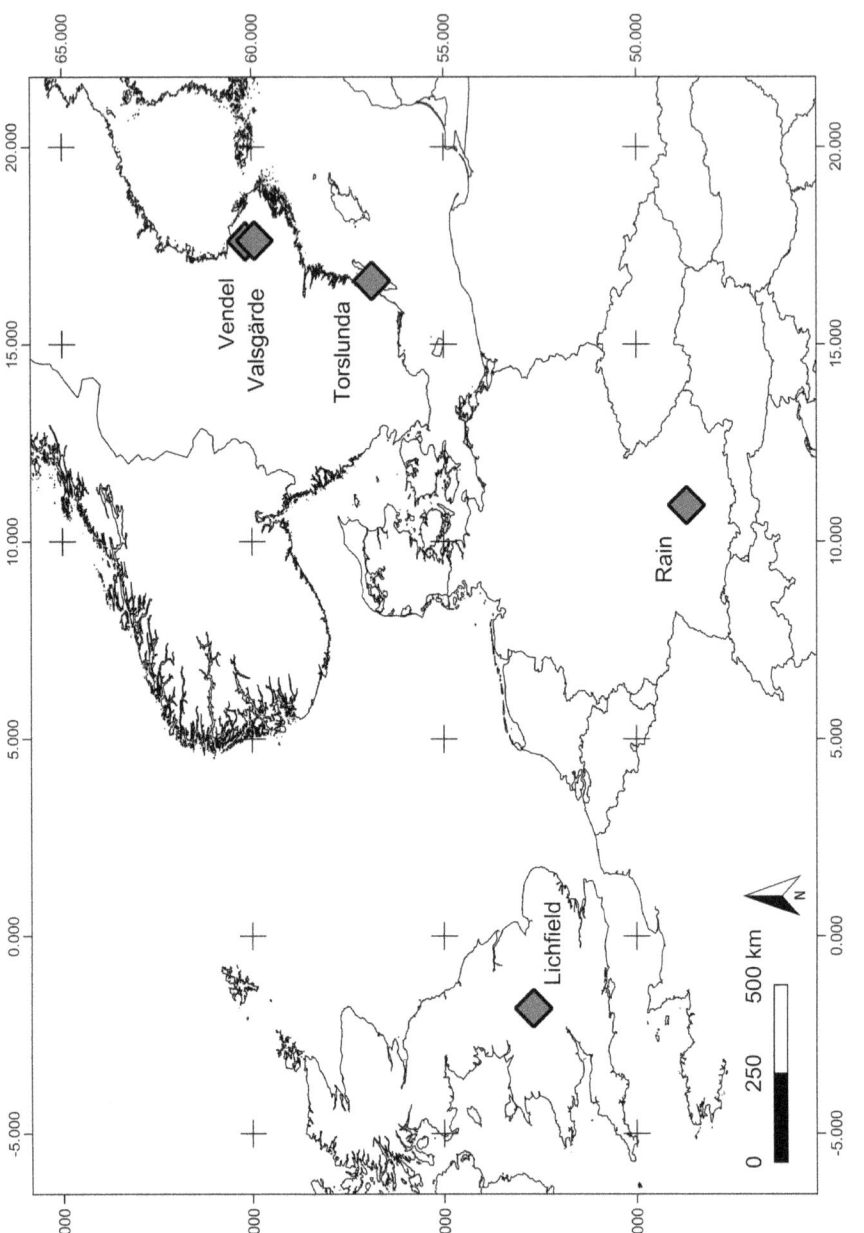

Figure 19.2 Distribution of 'warrior procession' images

repertoire of early medieval helmets.[31] Rather than referring to mythological topics, they seem to tie in with antique depictions of games held in the circus.[32]

This short overview shows that the images' archaeological contexts are diverse. The corpus of 'warrior' images is moreover relatively small. Although certain motifs reoccur in different regions, each image only survives once. While their presence in female burials and their use as a decoration for non-military objects does not preclude a possible 'military' symbolism, the specific burial context should be considered. Archaeological studies, however, have often neglected this aspect in favour of an interpretation that tries to embed the images within a larger context of a 'Germanic' military culture, as the two following historiographical examples demonstrate.

Quast classifies the depictions into a 'Mediterranean' and a 'Germanic' style. He argues that images of *Reiterheilige* constituted an import from the Mediterranean. The other motifs allegedly belonged to a widespread group of 'Germanic depictions' of warriors.[33] Quast concludes that 'in the seventh century, certain motives seem to have been known across the entire Germanic world', which reached from 'Scandinavia to Italy'.[34] In reaction to an advancing 'Christianisation', the 'Germanic elites' supposedly began to 'visualise' mythical and religious motifs that had previously been transmitted orally. These motifs could be adopted within a Christian context, but they nonetheless originated from a 'Germanic' rather than a 'Roman' context, according to Quast.[35] It is noticeable that the establishment of the dichotomy between a 'Germanic' and a 'Roman' cultural context precedes the images' interpretation. Quast doubts that the 'Pliezhausen' motif was influenced by Roman models and presumes that armed horsemen were already in use as a motif in the 'Germanic world' before the seventh century, since riders with lances are depicted on the so-called golden horn from Gallehus (Denmark), dated to *c.* 400.[36] Quast acknowledges that certain forms of representation could have been derived from Roman models, but argues that the images' meaning must have had its origin in an independent tradition, since monuments which could have served as an inspiration were already 'ruins' by the seventh century.[37] The assumption that 'Germanic' oral traditions and motifs survived more or less unchanged through the centuries, while influences from the late Roman Empire allegedly ceased, seems unconvincing when considering the continuity of the *Reiterheilige* motif throughout late antiquity and its presence in early medieval Alamannia, not least suggested by the example of the late sixth/early seventh-century *phalerae* from Hüfingen (Germany) initially dismissed by Quast as an import.[38]

Yet a similar perspective is adopted in an article by Heiko Steuer published in 1987.[39] Steuer points out that in certain depictions of 'wolf-warriors', 'warrior-processions' and armed riders, one or more of the figures carry so-called ring-swords.⁴⁰ The term does not denote a specific type of blade but refers to the fact that these swords have a pair of rings attached to the pommel. Their distribution reached from the Baltic Sea to Lombard Italy between the early sixth and the late seventh centuries.⁴¹ Although ring-swords are not explicitly mentioned by any written source and their combination with helmets in burials is very rare,⁴² Steuer suggests that the spread of 'heroic poetry' and burials containing helmets and ring-swords mirrors 'a distinct Germanic way of life between Antiquity and the Carolingian era'.⁴³ Steuer identifies the rings as gifts which the followers of a king or a lord, such as the Merovingian *antrustiones*, received in return for their service within his retinue. The images attached to the helmets and the scabbards worn by the members of the retinue supposedly helped to underpin a 'warrior ideology'.⁴⁴ According to Steuer, their content could be understood in both Christian and non-Christian societies since they had their common denominator in a Germanic military culture based on the retinue (*Gefolgschaft*).⁴⁵ Steuer concludes that the 'pagan' equivalent of the Frankish *antrustiones* were the *úlfheðnar* ('wolf-skins') of Old Norse literature and links the depictions of 'wolf-warriors' to these literary figures, whose earliest mention in the written sources dates to the second half of the ninth century.⁴⁶

This recapitulation of Quast's and Steuer's articles is necessary to understand the approach that has hitherto been adopted regarding the images discussed here. As their conclusions indicate, a tendency exists in archaeological studies to identify a single cultural context in which the images could be understood and disseminated. Since they appear in areas as far apart from each other as Scandinavia and northern Italy, and since certain motifs are thought to reoccur in the texts of later centuries, the perspective of most studies has been supra-regional and diachronic. Underlying this point of view, however, is the assumption that sources as geographically and chronologically diverse as early medieval grave-goods from Alamannia, Old English Christian poetry, and late medieval texts from Scandinavia are primarily connected through the impact of a fixed 'Germanic' culture on north-western Europe throughout the Middle Ages.⁴⁷

This line of thought is not limited to German-speaking archaeology. Furthermore, it has not been replaced following the criticism of the term 'Germanic' and the concept of an early medieval Germanic identity which has developed since the 1980s.⁴⁸ It has been only recently suggested that the people who spoke a Germanic language were connected through 'common cultural traits' such as religion and shared myths.⁴⁹ The examples of Quast's and Steuer's articles show that such a claim has enabled archaeologists to refer to the sources of historians and philologists with the intent to 'decipher' the allegedly religious or mythological meaning of early medieval images. In the case of the 'warrior' images and the question of whether they reflect a process of militarisation, this method is problematic because it *a priori* subsumes different archaeological contexts under the notion of a pan-Germanic military culture developed on the basis of the written sources.[50] This approach ignores the possibility that the political preconditions for and the degree of militarisation varied considerably across post-Roman Europe.[51]

In German-speaking scholarship, the creation of the concept of *Gefolgschaft* by historians and its adaption by archaeologists is at the heart of the issue.[52] Originally created by legal historians as a translation of the *comitatus* mentioned by the ancient writer Tacitus (d. *c*. 120) in chapters 13 and 14 of his *Germania*, '*Gefolgschaft*' has been the prevailing term to denote the military retinue in German since the late nineteenth century.[53] Scholars now agree that the *comitatus* is a literary notion created by Tactius to suggest that the warlike and stateless character of ancient Germanic societies as perceived by the Romans was balanced by the moral obligations imposed on young warriors who joined the *comitatus* of a high-ranking individual.[54] However, through the distortion of *Gefolgschaft*, the relevance of the *comitatus* as a medieval political phenomenon was subsequently expanded beyond the meaning of military patronage by the so-called *Neue Deutsche Verfassungsgeschichte*, a school of thought which developed during the 1930s and 1940s in German-speaking medieval studies. Its representatives abandoned the notion of a medieval 'state' as the legal historians of the nineteenth century had envisaged it. Turning away from the liberal positions of the previous century, they postulated that medieval society was not founded on public institutions but on personal relationships stemming from a specifically Germanic form of loyalty (*Treue*).[55]

During the dictatorship of the National Socialist Party, a military elite led by a *Führer* was thought to constitute a more effective and dynamic system of leadership than a parliamentary democracy. This contemporary ideal of a polity headed by military retinues was subsequently transferred to the concept of *Gefolgschaft*.[56] In 1939, the archaeologist Friedrich Garscha published an article on the 'wolf-warrior' from Gutenstein.[57] Garscha suggested that the depiction reflects a long tradition of ferocious warriors within Germanic societies which was still remembered in the literature of Anglo-Saxon England and medieval Scandinavia. He furthermore assumed that the ringsword held by the figure was understood as a symbol of the retinue in Germanic societies. According to Garscha, 'cultic male unions' (*kultische Männerbünde*) such as the *einherjar*[58] of Old Norse literature were a special form of the retinue, which in turn constituted the social core around which Germanic life was organised. Drawing a connection to the prevailing political ideology of his own lifetime, Garscha stated that the German state revived its old Germanic origins by promoting the male fellowship next to it's non-military equivalent, the kin (*Sippe*).[59] After 1945, the connection between

Gefolgschaft and *Führer* was dissolved, as the usage of the latter term was discarded. The concept of *Gefolgschaft*, however, remained an essential notion within German-speaking medieval studies during the second half of the twentieth century.[60] It had been established before its ideological deformation and did not originate from the vocabulary of the National Socialist Party. Nonetheless, its development was informed by authoritarian, anti-liberal and racial notions among the representatives of the *Neue Deutsche Verfassungsgeschichte*. Despite being criticised in the post-war period, their conception of the medieval state as being based on reciprocal relations of domination (*Herrschaft*) and loyalty has remained influential beyond the end of the twentieth century.[61] Within this larger model, *Gefolgschaft* was established as a core vocabulary of German-speaking medieval studies during the 1950s.

The debate between the historian Walter Schlesinger and the philologist Hans Kuhn influenced the understanding of *Gefolgschaft* among subsequent generations of archaeologists and historians.[62] Although they each pleaded for a different chronological context in which the phenomenon apparently flourished, both stressed its Germanic origin and the significance of *Treue*.[63] Schlesinger suggested that relations of *Gefolgschaft* constituted the very fabric from which medieval political hierarchies developed and considered them as the origin of the feudal system.[64] Kuhn, on the other hand, assumed that their impact declined during the Merovingian period and that they were rekindled in the Scandinavian kingdoms of the high Middle Ages.[65] Although he demonstrated that not every medieval mention of loyalty can be subsumed under the concept of *Gefolgschaft*, he stated that traces of the 'old spirit' of the Germanic *comitatus*, as described by Tacitus, can be found in the texts of medieval Scandinavia.[66] In defining *Gefolgschaft*, both Schlesinger and Kuhn drew on the same traditional corpus of sources which ranges from Tacitus to Old Norse literature. Schlesinger especially pursued the view that, throughout the centuries, Germanic societies were marked by a continuity of cultural values and institutions such as the *Gefolgschaft* and that the 'heroic poetry' of later centuries could be used to reconstruct its significance during the early Middle Ages.[67] Thereby, a supra-regional and diachronic understanding of Germanic military culture was sustained.[68] The concept of *Gefolgschaft* was subsequently adapted by archaeologists and historians in Anglophone and Francophone publications, moreover in Scandinavian research.[69]

In *The inheritance of Rome*, Chris Wickham states that 'the major change in political culture [between late Antiquity and the early Middle Ages] was not Germanisation but militarisation', thus taking up the criticism of the notion that the post-Roman kingdoms of the early Middle Ages were 'Germanic' in terms of culture and political organisation.[70] This observation leaves out the fact that in German-speaking scholarship, 'militarisation' has traditionally meant 'Germanisation'. As the concept of Gefolgschaft remained in use, the break with the notions prevailing before 1945 was less radical than Kuhn's article suggests.[71] Its enduring influence was not necessarily the consequence of an ideological continuity, although this cannot in every case be excluded.[72] While the ideological misuse of the retinue during the Nazis' reign and the political notions of the *Neue Deutsche Verfassungsgeschichte* have been reassessed, a decided revision of concepts such as *Herrschaft* and *Gefolgschaft* has never taken place.[73] Their use has now become almost arbitrary.[74]

While historians have discarded the notion that the military retinue was an exclusively Germanic phenomenon,[75] the interpretative framework persists even beyond German-speaking studies. The English translations of *comitatus* ('retinue', 'warband') have never directly correlated with the connotation of *Gefolgschaft*, yet Anglophone studies on early medieval Britain in the nineteenth and early twentieth centuries were guided by similar ideological currents with regard to the supposed Germanic origin of the Anglo-Saxons' political culture.[76] Even though the designation 'Germanic' has been mostly abandoned, the example of the 'warrior' images shows that archaeologists and historians still operate within the framework of a pan-Germanic culture, which is predisposed by a corpus of written sources that was established in the nineteenth and early twentieth centuries.[77] Through their dependency on the concepts created by historians and the uncritical use of the traditional terminology, archaeologists continue to reduce the scope of their interpretations to categories such as 'heroic warfare', 'weapon cults' and 'Nordic myths'.[78] Thus, a circular argument is sustained as the archaeological interpretations seem to confirm the assumptions of the historians with regard to the existence of a pan-Germanic (military) culture in the early Middle Ages.[79]

In his article from 1987, Heiko Steuer concludes that the images on early medieval helmets depict 'reality' and that they mirror the existence of a 'pagan warrior ideology'.[80] This chapter argued for a reconsideration of this assumption with regard to two factors: the historical framework employed and its imposition on the archaeological context of the images. As the transformation of the military organisation within the western Roman Empire in the fourth and fifth centuries is no longer seen as the result of a 'Germanisation', the connection of 'warrior' images with notions imported from *Germania* is no longer helpful.[81] Future studies should continue to discern the impact of historical interpretations and focus on the different geographical and chronological contexts in which the images were used. Rather than instantly connecting them with the poetical and idealised representations of warfare in later sources, their function as the decoration of grave-goods should be stressed.[82] The sixth and seventh centuries are marked by furnished inhumation burials and the formation of this pattern across western Europe has been linked to local discourses on power and social status in a post-Roman context.[83] The deposition of weapons and armour does not necessarily imply that the deceased possessed a military identity. It was a 'multilayered symbolic act' most likely undertaken by the descendants to openly perpetuate their capacity to protect the local community. [84] Future studies should consider the potential of 'warrior' images to suggest social status across different religious and political contexts which for centuries had been influenced by a Roman military frame of reference, but on varying scales.[85] In late Antiquity, iconographic programmes of military acclamation and victory in battle were employed in an imperial context to suggest political power.[86] The images discussed in this chapter reference this late antique military iconography, but this observation should not lead to the conclusion that they were 'Roman' (and 'Christian') rather than 'Germanic' (and 'pagan').[87] The establishment of such a dichotomy is not helpful to assess the agency of the images' users in their attempt to negotiate new social identities and forms of representation. The diversity of the archaeological evidence is a reminder that the extent of the Roman military heritage varied considerably across early medieval Europe and that it could be adopted by both men and women of different political status. The use of 'warrior' images should not be regarded as evidence of a pan-Germanic 'militarisation' but as an indicator that this heritage was renegotiated in multiple forms during the sixth and seventh centuries.

Notes

During the writing of this chapter the author was supported by the Luxembourg National Research Fund (Project code: WILL17).

1 J. R. R. Tolkien, '*Beowulf*: the monsters and the critics', in D. Donoghue (ed.), *Beowulf. A verse translation* (New York: W. W. Norton and Company, 2002), pp. 103–30, p. 103 [originally published in *Proceedings of the British Academy*, 22 (1936), 245–95].
2 Tolkien, '*Beowulf*', p. 105.
3 For the crest, see R. M. Liuzza (ed. and trans.), *Beowulf* (Peterborough, Ontario: Broadview Press, 2nd edn 2013), 80 (lines 1030–4); for the boar shapes, see p. 58 (lines 301–6); for the Sutton Hoo helmet, see R. Bruce-Mitford, *The Sutton Hoo ship-burial*. Vol: 2. *Arms, armour and regalia* (London: British Museum Publications, 1978), pp. 138–231.
4 See Liuzza, *Beowulf*, 80 (lines 1020–4); 82 (lines 1110–3); 105 (lines 1900–3).
5 See H. Steuer, 'Helm und Ringschwert. Prunkbewaffnung und Rangabzeichen germanischer Krieger. Eine Übersicht', in H.-J. Häßler (ed.), *Studien zur*

'Warrior' images and the concept of Gefolgschaft   325

Sachsenforschung, 6 (Hildesheim: August Lax, 1987), pp. 190–236, pp. 200–3; M. P. Speidel, *Ancient Germanic warriors. Warrior styles from Trajan's Column to Icelandic sagas* (New York: Routledge, 2004), pp. 144–6, 180.

6 Bruce-Mitford, *The Sutton Hoo ship-burial* 2, pp. 146–50 (figure 110).

7 For an (incomplete) list of 'warrior' images (including other objects besides embossed foils) see D. Quast, 'Kriegerdarstellungen der Merowingerzeit aus der Alamania', *Archäologisches Korrespondenzblatt*, 32 (2002), 267–80, pp. 276–7.

8 See G. Halsall, *Warfare and society in the barbarian west, 450–900* (London: Routledge, 2003), pp. 3–10. Significantly, references to 'heroic' warfare are largely absent from the written sources from Merovingian Francia.

9 For a critique of the gift-giving model see F. Curta, 'Merovingian and Carolingian gift giving', *Speculum*, 81:3 (2006), 696–9.

10 See M. Helmbrecht, *Wirkmächtige Kommunikationsmedien. Menschenbilder der Vendel- und Wikingerzeit und ihre Kontexte* (Lund: Lund University, 2011), p. 405; S. Nygaard, '…nú knáttu Óðin sjá: The function of hall-based, ritualised performances of Old Norse poetry in pre-Christian nordic religion', in M. Bruus and J. Hansen (eds), *The fortified Viking age* (Odense: Odense City Museums and University Press of Southern Denmark, 2018), pp. 26–34, pp. 29–31.

11 E. James, 'The militarisation of Roman society, 400–700', in A. N. Jørgensen and B. L. Clausen (eds), *Military aspects of Scandinavian society in a European perspective, AD 1–1300* (Copenhagen: National Museum, 1997), pp. 19–24, pp. 19–20.

12 Quast, 'Kriegerdarstellungen', pp. 267–9.

13 *Ibid.*, p. 267 (figure 1).

14 K. Böhner and D. Quast, 'Die merowingerzeitlichen Grabfunde aus Pliezhausen, Kreis Reutlingen', *Fundberichte aus Baden-Württemberg*, 19:1 (1994), 383–419, p. 389 (figure 4), 395 (figures 8, 9), 396 (figure 10).

15 M. Helmbrecht, 'Der Gebrauch von anthropomorphen Darstellungen im vendel- und wikingerzeitlichen Skandinavien. Das Beispiel der Motivgruppe "Hörnerhelmträge"' in C. Grünewald and T. Capelle (eds), *Innere Strukturen von Gräberfeldern und Siedlungen als Spiel gesellschaftlicher Wirklichkeit?* (Münster: Verlag Aschendorff, 2007), pp. 163–71, pp. 163–6 (figures 1:1, 1:2); for Sutton Hoo and Uppsala see Bruce-Mitford, *The Sutton Hoo ship-burial* 2, p. 149 (figure 110a), 208 (figure 155).

16 Quast, 'Kriegerdarstellungen', p. 269; Speidel, *Ancient Germanic warriors*, p. 21 (figure 1.3), p. 26 (figure 1.5), p. 28 (figure 1.6).

17 *Ibid.*, p. 268 (figures 2:4, 2:5a, 2:5b); H. Stolpe and T. J. Arne, *Graffältet vid Vendel* (Stockholm: K. L. Beckmans Boktryckeri, 1912), plate VI (figure 1).

18 B. Theune-Großkopf, 'Krieger oder Apostel. Bilderwelt im frühen Mittelalter. Eine vollständig erhaltene Leier aus Trossingen', in B. Päffgen, E. Pohl and M. Schmauder (eds), *Cum grano salis. Beiträge zur europäischen Vor- und Frühgeschichte* (Friedberg: Likias, 2005), pp. 303–15, p. 306.

19 For Torslunda, see Steuer, 'Helm und Ringschwert', p. 224 (figure 14:4); for Vendel 14, see Stolpe and Arne, *Graffältet vid Vendel*, plate XLI (figure 4), plate XLII (figure 1); for Valsgärde 7, see Speidel, *Ancient Germanic warriors*,

p. 99 (figure 10.1); for the Staffordshire Hoard see J. Butterworth, G. Fregni, K. Fuller and P. Greaves (eds), 'The importance of multidisciplinary work within archaeological conservation projects. Assembly of the Staffordshire Hoard Die-impressed sheets', *Journal of the Institute of Conservation*, 39:1 (2016), 29–43, 38 (fig. 7).

20 S. Zintl and M. Blana, 'Krieger auf dem Weg ins Depot. Merowingerzeitliche Riemenzungen mit figürlicher Darstellung aus Rain', *Das archäologische Jahr in Bayern 2016* (2017), 106–8, 108 (figure 172); S. Zintl and M. Helmbrecht, 'Wadenbindengarnitur mit Kriegerdarstellung. Ein Neufund aus Rain am Lech (Lkr. Donau-Ries)', *Archäologisches Korrespondenzblatt*, 50:1 (2020), 107–32. I thank the authors for sending me a copy of their paper in advance.

21 Stolpe and Arne, *Graffältet vid Vendel*, plate XXXVI (figure 5), plate XLI (figure 3); K. Hauck, 'Bildforschung als historische Sachforschung. Zur vorchristlichen Ikonographie der figuralen Helmprogramme aus der Vendelzeit', in K. Hauck and H. Mordek (eds), *Geschichtsschreibung und geistiges Leben im Mittelalter* (Cologne, Vienna: Böhlau, 1978), pp. 27–70, plate V (figure 6a).

22 Quast, 'Kriegerdarstellungen', p. 270 (figure 3a).

23 *Ibid.*, (figure 3b).

24 See Steuer, 'Helm und Ringschwert', p. 196. Steuer assumes that several thousand helmets originally existed, but admits that his calculation is based on speculation only.

25 Böhner and Quast, 'Die merowingerzeitlichen Grabfunde', p. 391; Zintl and Blana, 'Krieger auf dem Weg', p. 106.

26 F. Garscha, 'Die Schwertscheide von Gutenstein', *Volk und Vorzeit. Volkstümliche Hefte für oberrheinische Ur- und Frühgeschichte*, 1 (1939), 1–11, 2.

27 C. Engels, 'Obrigheim', *RGA*, 21 (2002), 516.

28 Steuer, 'Helm und Ringschwert', p. 205.

29 Böhner and Quast, 'Die merowingerzeitlichen Grabfunde', pp. 388–93.

30 R. Bruce-Mitford, 'The Sutton Hoo ship-burial. Comments on general interpretation', in R. Bruce-Mitford (ed.), *Aspects of Anglo-Saxon archaeology. Sutton Hoo and other discoveries* (London: Victor Gollancz limited, 1974), pp. 1–72, p. 26. [Originally published in *Proceedings of the Suffolk Institute of Archaeology and Natural History*, 15 (1949), 1–78]; staffordshirehoard.org.uk/explore-the-hoard/religion/list (accessed 11 February 2019).

31 E. Wamers, 'Von Bären und Männern. Berserker, Bärenkämpfer und Bärenführer im frühen Mittelalter', *Zeitschrift für Archäologie des Mittelalters*, 37 (2009), 1–46, pp. 28–9 (figures 19, 20).

32 See *Ibid.*, pp. 33–42.

33 Quast, 'Kriegerdarstellungen', p. 267.

34 *Ibid.*, p. 269: 'Zunächst einmal kann also festgehalten werden, dass im 7. Jahrhundert einige Motive anscheinend in der gesamten germanischen Welt – teilweise von Schweden bis Italien – bekannt waren.'

35 *Ibid.*, pp. 273–5.

36 *Ibid.*, p. 275.

37 *Ibid.*, pp. 269–71.

38 *Ibid.*, p. 267; A. Eastmond, 'Consular diptychs, rhetoric and the languages of art in sixth-century Constantinople', *Art History*, 33:5 (2010), 743–65, 751 (figures 9, 10).
39 Steuer, 'Helm und Ringschwert', pp. 190–236; For a reception of Steuer's ideas see A. Nørgård Jørgensen, *Waffen und Gräber. Typologische und chronologische Studien zu skandinavischen Waffengräbern 520/30 bis 900 n. Chr.* (Copenhagen: Kongelige Nordiske Oldskriftselskab, 1999), pp. 158–9; A. Wendt, 'Viking age gold rings and the question of "Gefolgschaft"', *Lund Archaeological Review*, 13/14 (2007/08), 75–89, 75–6; V. Samson, *Les Berserkir. Les guerriers-fauves dans la Scandinavie ancienne. De l'âge de Vendel aux Vikings. VIe-XIe siècle* (Villeneuve d'Ascq: Presses Universitaires du Septentrion, 2011), p. 194.
40 Steuer, 'Helm und Ringschwert', pp. 203–6.
41 S. Brather, 'Lokale Herren um 500. Rang und Macht im Spiegel der Bestattungen', in S. Patzold and M. Meier (eds), *Chlodwigs Welt. Organisation von Herrschaft um 500* (Stuttgart: Franz Steiner Verlag, 2014), pp. 567–607, pp. 585–6.
42 See Steuer, 'Helm und Ringschwert', pp. 213–14.
43 *Ibid.*, p. 225: 'Wie die Verbreitung germanischer Heldendichtung, so spiegeln Prunkbestattungen – für die Helm und Ringschwert stehen – eigenständigen germanischen Lebensstil zwischen Antike und Karolingerreich.'
44 *Ibid.*, pp. 221–2.
45 *Ibid.*, pp. 190, 223–5; for a critique of Steuer's thesis see E. Wamers, 'Warlords oder Vasallen? Zur Semiotik der merowingerzeitlichen Bootsbestattungen von Vendel und Valsgärde in Mittelschweden', in S. Brather, C. Merthen and T. Springer (eds), *Warlords oder Amtsträger? Herausragende Bestattungen der späten Merowingerzeit* (Nuremberg: Verlag des Germanischen Nationalmuseum, 2018), pp. 212–37, p. 225. Wamers doubts that ring-swords were symbols of a personal *Gefolgschaft*, yet still argues that they were distributed among 'Germanic' warriors.
46 Steuer, 'Helm und Ringschwert', pp. 205–6; H. Hiltmann, *Vom isländischen Mann zum norwegischen Gefolgsmann. Männlichkeitsbilder, Vergangenheitskonstruktionen und politische Ordnungskonzepte im Island des 13. und 14. Jahrhunderts* (Bamberg: University of Bamberg Press, 2011), pp. 95–7.
47 M. Friedrich, Review of 'W. Heizmann and S. Oehrl (eds), *Bilddenkmäler zur germanischen Götter- und Heldensage* (2015)', *Zeitschrift für Archäologie des Mittelalters*, 44 (2016), 215–21, 215.
48 G. Halsall, *Barbarian migrations and the Roman west, 376–568* (Cambridge: Cambridge University Press, 2007), pp. 10–19; M. Kulikowski, 'Barbarische Identität. Aktuelle Forschungen und neue Interpretationsansätze', in M. Konrad und C. Witschel (eds), *Römische Legionslager in den Rhein- und Donauprovinzen. Nuclei spätantik-frühmittelalterlichen Lebens?* (Munich: Verlag der Bayerischen Akademie der Wissenschaften, 2011), pp. 103–12, p. 111.
49 S. Oehrl, 'Einleitung', in W. Heizmann and S. Oehrl (eds), *Bilddenkmäler zur germanischen Götter- und Heldensage* (Berlin: De Gruyter, 2015), pp. 1–8, p. 1 (note 1).

50 Friedrich, Review of 'W. Heizmann and S. Oehrl', p. 217; see Steuer, 'Helm und Ringschwert', p. 190; Quast, 'Kriegerdarstellungen', pp. 273–5.
51 S. Esders, 'Nordwestgallien um 500. Von der militarisierten spätrömischen Provinzgesellschaft zur erweiterten Militäradministration des merowingischen Königtums', in S. Patzold and M. Meier (eds), *Chlodwigs Welt. Organisation von Herrschaft um 500* (Stuttgart: Franz Steiner Verlag, 2014), pp. 339–61, pp. 339–41.
52 For recent overviews of the development of *Gefolgschaft* as a concept and the interpretation of Tacitus' report, see J. Bazelmans, 'Conceptualising early Germanic political structure. A review of the use of the concept of Gefolgschaft', in N. Roymans and F. Theuws (eds), *Images of the past. Studies on ancient societies in northwestern Europe* (Amsterdam: University of Amsterdam, 1991), pp. 91–129 and K. Kroeschell, 'Führer, Gefolgschaft und Treue', in J. Rückert and D. Willoweit (eds), *Die Deutsche Rechtsgeschichte in der NS-Zeit: Ihre Vorgeschichte und ihre Nachwirkungen* (Tübingen: Mohr Siebeck, 1995), pp. 55–76.
53 G. Waitz, *Deutsche Verfassungsgeschichte*, vol 1 (Kiel: Ernst Homann, 1865), pp. 345–74; O. Gierke, *Rechtsgeschichte der deutschen Genossenschaft* (Berlin: Weidmannsche Buchandlung, 1868), pp. 93–9.
54 Bazelmans, 'Conceptualising early Germanic political structure', pp. 104–6; S. Fanning, 'Tacitus, Beowulf, and the *comitatus*', *The Haskins Society Journal*, 9 (1997), 17–38, 32–5.
55 O. Brunner, 'Moderner Verfassungsbegriff und mittelalterliche Verfassungsgeschichte', *Mitteilungen des Österreichischen Instituts für Geschichtsforschung. Ergänzungsband*, 14 (1939), 513–28, 527; T. Mayer, 'Die Ausbildung der Grundlagen des modernen deutschen Staates im hohen Mittelalter', *Historische Zeitschrift*, 159:3 (1939), 457–87, 466; W. Schlesinger, *Die Entstehung der Landesherrschaft. Untersuchungen vorwiegend nach mitteldeutschen Quellen*, 1 (Dresden: Von Baensch Druckerei, 1941), pp. 113–29.
56 R. Meißner (ed.), *Das norwegische Gefolgschaftsrecht. Hirðskrá* (Weimar: Herman Böhlaus Nachf., 1938), p. XXIII.
57 Garscha, 'Die Schwertscheide von Gutenstein', pp. 1–12.
58 Hiltmann, *Vom isländischen Mann*, pp. 99–102 (note 167). The *einherjar* represent a collective of fallen warriors, who are received by Óðinn. The written sources do not attest any connection between *úlfheðnar*, berserks and *einherjar* before the thirteenth century.
59 Garscha, 'Die Schwertscheide', p. 12.
60 Kroeschell, 'Gefolgschaft und Treue', pp. 73–4; W. Pohl, 'Staat und Herrschaft im Frühmittelalter. Überlegungen zum Forschungsstand', in S. Airlie, W. Pohl and H. Reimitz (eds), *Staat im frühen Mittelalter* (Vienna: Verlag der Österreichischen Akademie der Wissenschaften, 2006), pp. 9–38, pp. 12–13.
61 Pohl, 'Staat und Herrschaft', pp. 11–13; S. Patzold, *Episcopus. Wissen über Bischöfe im Fränkenreich des späten 8. bis frühen 10. Jahrhunderts* (Ostfildern: Jan Thorbecke, 2008), pp. 30–4; for the continuing influence of this notion, see J. W. Busch, *Die Herrschaften der Karolinger 714–911* (Munich: Oldenbourg Verlag, 2011), p. 1.

62 W. Schlesinger, 'Herrschaft und Gefolgschaft in der germanisch-deutschen Verfassungsgeschichte', *Historische Zeitschrift*, 176 (1953), 225–75; H. Kuhn, 'Die Grenzen der germanischen Gefolgschaft', *Zeitschrift der Savigny-Stiftung für Rechtsgeschichte. Germanistische Abteilung*, 73 (1956), 1–83; See also H. Steuer, *Frühgeschichtliche Sozialstrukturen in Mitteleuropa. Eine Analyse der Auswertungsmethoden des archäologischen Quellenmaterials* (Göttingen: Vandenhoeck and Ruprecht, 1982), p. 54.
63 Schlesinger, 'Herrschaft und Gefolgschaft', 235–6; Kuhn, 'Die Grenzen', 12.
64 Schlesinger, 'Herrschaft und Gefolgschaft', 240–6, 269.
65 Kuhn, 'Die Grenzen', 38–40.
66 *Ibid.*, pp. 1–2, pp. 40–1.
67 Schlesinger, 'Herrschaft und Gefolgschaft', 240–6.
68 Kroeschell, 'Gefolgschaft und Treue', pp. 73–4.
69 See Jørgensen, *Waffen und Gräber*, pp. 158–9; R. Le Jan, 'Frankish giving of arms and rituals of power. Continuity and change in the Carolingian period', in F. Theuws and J. L. Nelson (eds), *Rituals of power. From late Antiquity to the early Middle Ages* (Leiden: Brill, 2000), pp. 281–309, pp. 283–7; Samson, *Les Berserkir*, p. 294.
70 C. Wickham, *The inheritance of Rome. A history of Europe from 400 to 1000* (Penguin Books: London, 2010), p. 200.
71 See R. Wenskus, 'Die neuere Diskussion um Gefolgschaft und Herrschaft in Tacitus' Germania', in G. Neumann and H. Seemann (eds), *Beiträge zum Verständnis der Germania des Tacitus* 2 (Göttingen: Vandenhoeck and Ruprecht,1992), pp. 311–31, pp. 316–19.
72 See P. Paulsen, *Alamannische Adelsgräber von Niederstotzingen (Kreis Heidenheim)* (Stuttgart: Müller and Gräff, 1967), p. 142; M. Jelusić, 'Ein Archäologe im Dienste des Endsieges? Peter Paulsen und die SS-Führerschule "Haus Germanien" in Hildesheim', in S. Grunwald, U. Halle, D. Mahsarsk and K. Reichenbach (eds), *Die Spur des Geldes in der Prähistorischen Archäologie. Mäzene – Förderer – Förderstrukturen* (Bielefeld: Transcript, 2016), pp. 173–208. Paulsen, who intended to transform a SS-officers' training school into a 'Germanic research center', suggested that the 'wolf-warriors' from Gutenstein and Obrigheim belong to the *Gefolgschaft* of Woden / Óðinn.
73 Pohl, 'Staat und Herrschaft', 12–13.
74 Patzold, *Episcopus*, pp. 33–4 (note 96).
75 See G. M. Berndt, 'Aktionsradien gotischer Kriegergruppen', *Frühmittelalterliche Studien*, 47 (2013), 7–52, 8 (note 3).
76 Fanning, 'Tactius, Beowulf', pp. 36–8.
77 Friedrich, Review of 'W. Heizmann and S. Oehrl', pp. 220–1.
78 See Wamers, 'Warlords oder Vasallen?', pp. 230–4. Wamers demonstrates that the 'warrior' images have late antique precursors, yet still assumes that antique formulas were used to visualise 'nordic heroic myths'.
79 See Friedrich, Review of 'W. Heizmann and S. Oehrl', p. 215.
80 Steuer, 'Helm und Ringschwert', p. 206: 'Über diese Deutungsmöglichkeiten hinaus ist wichtig ... daß Krieger mit Ringschwertern im Rahmen einer heidnischen

Kriegerideologie gezeigt werden. Die Bildszenen geben Realität wieder'; Wamers, 'Warlords oder Vasallen?', p. 230, shares this assumption.
81 See J. W. P. Wijnendaele, '"Warlordism" and the disintegration of the western Roman army', in J. Armstrong (ed.), *Circum Mare. Themes in ancient warfare* (Leiden: Brill, 2016), pp. 185–203.
82 See R. Frank, '*The Battle of Maldon* and Heroic Literature', in D. Scragg (ed.), *The Battle of Maldon AD 991* (Oxford: Basil Blackwell, 1991), pp. 196–207.
83 D. Petts, *Pagan and Christian. Religious change in Early Medieval Europe* (London: Bristol Classical Press, 2011), pp. 104–5; Brather, 'Lokale Herren', pp. 567–8.
84 F. Theuws and M. Alkemade, 'A kind of mirror for men. Sword depositions in late antique northern Gaul', in F. Theuws and J. L. Nelson (eds), *Rituals of power. From late Antiquity to the early Middle Ages* (Leiden: Brill, 2000), pp. 453–6; Esders, 'Nordwestgallien um 500', p. 401–47, p. 466; S. Brather, 'Nur "Adlige" und "Bauern"? Komplexe Sozialstrukturen der Merowingerzeit und ihre archäologische Rekonstruktion', in T. Kienlin and A. Zimmermann (eds), *Beyond elites. Alternatives to hierarchical systems in modelling social formations*, 2 (Bonn: Dr. Rudolf Habelt GmbH, 2012), pp. 561–72, p. 567.
85 Theuws and Alkemade, 'A kind of mirror for men', pp. 360–1.
86 M. E. Frazer, 'Iconic representations', in K. Weitzmann (ed.), *Age of spirituality. Late antique and early Christian art, third to seventh century* (New York: Metropolitan Museum of Art, 1979), pp. 513–55, pp. 514–15; see Wamers, 'Warlords oder Vasallen?', pp. 229–31.
87 See B. Theune-Großkopf, *Mit Leier und Schwert. Das frühmittelalterliche "Sängergrab" von Trossingen* (Friedberg: Likias, 2010), pp. 72–3; Friedrich, Review of 'W. Heizmann and S. Oehrl', p. 218. In contrast to the *Reiterheilige* motif, most 'warrior' images elude an explicit religious symbolism.

20

Conclusion – militarisation: process or discourse?

Guy Halsall

It was an enormous pleasure to be asked to furnish a conclusion to this substantial collection of studies of a phenomenon in which, in many of its various manifestations, I have been interested throughout my academic career. My studies (monographic and edited) that looked specifically at violence and warfare seem, in 2020, to have receded far into the past and I have never seen myself, or wanted to be pigeonholed, as a 'military historian'. The relationship between broader aspects of early medieval western European society and its martial features has nonetheless never been far from my analysis. These interconnections are in most regards unsurprising. The widespread acceptance of the thesis (to which we will return) that western European society was militarised after the disintegration of the western Roman Empire surely stems from the fact that the military or at least the martial – we may wish to distinguish the two – underpinned so many aspects of society, religion, economics, culture and politics. The chapters in this volume underline that very clearly. Yet, explicit study of warfare and the military has not often engaged serious academic historians of the period.[1] At first sight this seems curious, but it has been just as possible for social historians and archaeologists like myself to have similarly inexplicable blind spots concerning equally, if not more central features of early medieval life, such as belief and the church! The neglect of the broader social history of armies, warfare and militarisation has, since 2002, been addressed by numerous works, discussed in the Introduction.[2] This volume is a milestone in that development.

Including the editors' very useful introduction, the nineteen preceding chapters present close studies of a wide range of aspects of society, economy, religion, culture and politics. They extend in space from the eastern Roman (or Byzantine) Empire to the kingdoms of 'Anglo-Saxon' England, and in time from the last century of the Roman Empire to the ninth and tenth centuries. After reading these analyses there can be no doubt that in countless regards the societies and polities of this period could be considered militarised. The purpose of this conclusion is thus to pose various questions about where the discussion of the martial aspects of late antique and early medieval society might go from here, building upon this base.

The first such question goes back to the very basics. What is a militarised society? Many of the chapters in this volume employ the valuable provisional definition set out by Edward James in 1997,[3] which encompassed nine general points:

1. No clear distinction between soldier and civilian.
2. No clear distinction between a military officer and a government official.
3. The head of state is the commander of the army.
4. All adult free males have the right to carry weapons.
5. Certain classes (notably the aristocracy) are expected to participate in the army.
6. Education includes a military element.
7. The symbolism of weaponry is prominent in official and private life.
8. Warlike and heroic virtues are glorified.
9. Warfare is a major expenditure and source of profit.

Interestingly, and characteristically of his subtle and reflexive scholarship, James is the only contributor to subject his own definition to detailed scrutiny.[4] There can be no doubt that a society could be called militarised if it satisfied all of the criteria listed above, but how do we use definitions like this? How many of the characteristics listed need to be present before a society can be called militarised? Which are the most crucial? Are all of equal weight? Many such problems are not necessarily answerable by a simple yes or no, as much as by 'it depends what you mean by ...'. These questions develop those posed in the Introduction to this volume, and are familiar to everyone who has attempted to establish a workable definition of a particular historical phenomenon, especially a definition like this, which takes the form of a *Kriterienbündel*.[5] The problem facing us is essentially that it is difficult to imagine a society that is *not*, in some way, militarised. Western European society in *c.* 300 would not be much less militarised than that around 700; the first, second and possibly fourth of James' criteria would be the only ones not met by the Roman Empire between the Tetrarchy and the earlier fifth century. The early Empire and, *a fortiori*, the Republic were even less distinguishable, with the state's officials having military and civil responsibilities; the citizen legionary would only really disappear in the later Republic and as a result, ironically perhaps, of the constant warfare of that period.

We must therefore confront the very premise upon which the present volume is founded – and indeed stated in the very first sentence of the

Introduction (although provided with nuance and caveats almost immediately afterwards): is it true that the late Roman Empire was any less militarised than the so-called 'Barbarian west' (to borrow the phrase coined by J. M. Wallace-Hadrill and reused in the title of my own volume on warfare and society)?[6] Michael Summers' excellent Chapter 19 shows how deeply rooted some of the assumptions about post-imperial western society have become, and how important it is to subject these to critical scrutiny. Let us for now, however, return to the issue of what a militarised society is. A late Roman *colonus* or free peasant might see his surplus produce taken by the state, and used, overwhelmingly, to pay for a huge standing army.[7] The main function of the officials of the large imperial bureaucracy was to administer and carry out that taxation, in money and in kind, and organise the distribution of its proceeds to the army as payment and supplies. Although the civil branch of the government was now strictly separated from the military (meaning James' second criterion did not apply) service in that arm was nevertheless referred to as a *militia* and used the same badges of rank as the army. Towns were walled, perhaps to protect the storage of taxation, fortified granaries appeared in some regions, and the army was dispersed throughout various provinces in impressive fortifications which heavily marked the landscape of those regions (and were a further significant governmental expenditure). It is possible that swathes of territory were harnessed by the state to the production of the foodstuffs and other supplies necessary to maintain the army.[8] At the apex of the system, uniting civic and military hierarchies, was an emperor expected to be ever-victorious and a pacifier of foreign nations (*semper victorius, domitor gentium*).[9] It is hard to see this society or any part of this system as anything other than militarised, as organised for war, even if all free men did not automatically have the right to bear arms.[10]

One issue that the studies in this volume raise in various ways is indeed the relationship between soldier and civilian (this is particularly clear in the chapters by Rance (Chapter 2), Whateley (Chapter 6) and Grundmann (Chapter 3).[11] As we saw in the enumeration of the points included in James' definition, the lack of a clear distinction between soldier and civilian seems to be a solid point of departure for thinking about militarisation. A move from a situation where the army and its members are clearly marked out from the non-military, to one where every free male (at least) might be summoned to fight, looks uncontroversially like the militarisation of society. In this context, the disappearance of the Roman Empire's regular army in the west, and some aspects of changes within its organisation in the east, appear to be good grounds for seeing those transformations as tending towards militarisation. And yet ... Part of the problem is those very specific, solid-looking categories themselves: soldier and civilian. They bear with them considerable baggage, associated images and signifieds. If we replace the opposed terms with 'combatant' and 'non-combatant', the problem takes on a different nature. The distinction between a soldier and a civilian might have been clear in the late Roman Empire – though we are still entitled to ask to what extent it really was – but was the boundary between those entitled to join the army and those who were not any less rigid in subsequent centuries? The basis for recruitment may eventually have changed beyond recognition, but was the line between member of the army and those who had no right to participate in its activities any less pronounced? Was it any less policed? It is difficult to read the account, in the *Annals of Saint-Bertin*, of the slaughter, seemingly by local aristocrats, of poor freemen who had presumed to take up arms in defence of their region against the Vikings and not conclude that the maintenance of the boundary between 'soldier' and 'civilian', or 'combatant' and 'non-combatant' was considerably more rigid and violent than it had been in the later empire.[12] The point gains rather than loses its significance if one reads that incident – as I have done[13] – in connection with the contemporary legislation of Charles the Bald attempting to ensure that poorer freemen could join the army and perform their military service without being attacked by wealthier and more powerful warriors.[14] Indeed it is in the issues surrounding the levying of armies that we can find one of the most important dynamics for political change in the period: kings ideally wanted to raise forces which they could use as their own coercive force without being dependent upon the retinues of their leading aristocrats; the existence of such a force could pose a serious threat to powerful noble dynasties. We can trace this dynamic in east and west in the early Middle Ages[15] and it is, I contend, precisely this that we see in the story of the unfortunate Frankish poor freemen and in Charles' attempt to open military service to all those technically liable to perform it. The dividing line between 'soldier and civilian' was thus a locus of politics in a way that it had not been under the empire. Indeed, one might suggest that the line was frequently policed in the opposite direction: under the empire the concern was to keep people *in* the army; in the early medieval west the concern was often to keep people *out*.

On what basis, then, can we accept the idea, as seems generally to have come to be the case,[16] that western society 'became militarised' after the fall of the western empire? This question seems easier to respond to by employing James' list of features not as a checklist but rather as a list of headings under which comparative discussion can take place. In other words, rather than looking at whether or not societies are militarised, we can look at in what areas and in what precise ways they are. Here, James' own chapter is a model of the approach I have in mind, in that it questions the issue of 'warlike and heroic virtues', showing how these might be absent in the forms that we might expect but very present nonetheless, albeit relocated to a different area of society and a different type of evidence. Peter H. Wilson's definition, discussed in the Introduction and employed in Whateley's Chapter 6,[17] similarly points a way to the kind of analysis proposed. The opposition between militarised and non-militarised societies seems too crude; the studies contained in this volume make clear that post-imperial societies changed through time and space in the ways in which they were militarised, not simply in whether or not they were militarised, or in simply moving from a hypothetical 'un-militarised' to a militarised state. The elements of James' and Wilson's definitions provide thematic spaces not only for the comparative discussion of different societies but also for the analysis of change and development through time.

Probably the most important question to ask when thinking about the dynamics of change is whether variations in the evidence necessarily indicate transformations in the degree of militarisation. The presence of weaponry in the burials of northern Gaul is an apposite case study. Weaponry begins to appear in the furnished inhumations of men in that region in the last third or so of the fourth century, at the same time as a range of other changes. What does this mean? Is it a sign of the militarisation of the northern Gallic countryside? Frans Theuws has presented a detailed case against this and the presence of other weapons in burials having anything to do with militarisation, contending that it is unconnected with the military; but the argument seems forced and lacking in clear empirical support.[18] The axe is a weapon that features in late Roman military iconography and is associated with the Gallic legions and their successors, the later fifth- and sixth-century Frankish armies.[19] Judging from the size and weight of the axe-heads, the length of the haft and the wedge angle of the blade, the types of axe found in northern Gallic burials are suitable for cutting wood but not for tree-felling, although they are eminently effective weapons. It is of course possible, as I have argued in the past,[20] that objects could be selected precisely for their ability to signify more than one thing at once, though I maintain that that is more likely with spears than axes. Indeed, one of the key issues in the study of militarisation is precisely that of polysemy: the way in which items associated with warfare or the military come to be used to symbolise other things. I will discuss some possible instances of this later.

If, without assuming that these artefacts had no other symbolic referents, the *primary* symbolism of axes and other weaponry was a link to service in the imperial army, as with the belt-sets and official brooches found in these and similar contemporary burials, to what extent does the deposition of such items indicate militarisation? What would be the symbolic content of weaponry and in what context? In the cemetery associated with the late Roman fort at Oudenburg (Belgium), for example, there is little or no weaponry, but one must ask why there should have been.[21] Demonstrating status to an audience of soldiers and (possibly, in a late Roman military context) their families would be unlikely to involve simple signs that the deceased had been involved in the weapon-using activities of the army. Instead, badges of rank and status within that community – belt-sets and crossbow brooches – are more commonly deposited as one might expect. Away from military bases, where a link to the army might be the basis for local status and power, symbols of such a link, like perhaps the axe associated with the Gallic army, would have much clearer and more practical semiotic content. This need, however, represent no increase in the militarisation of society. One might, for example, think that when the empire and its administration were working properly, the heirs of soldiers who had been given *agri deserti* to retire on (an interpretation which allows a point of contact with Theuws' reading)[22] did not need to demonstrate the basis of their claim to the land when the former *miles* died. In the crisis of state presence in northern Gaul at the end of the fourth and beginning of the fifth century, however, the heirs of such a soldier might not expect to enter into that inheritance so easily. In that context, a display of his military status, and thus his claim to the land, was made to an audience comprising the other members of the community in the ritual context of his funeral. In other words, military status and its relationship to other aspects of social organisation became visible in the evidence in a period of crisis. What might be at stake, if anything, is a *breakdown* of those relations.

An analogous point might be made about the scattered but interesting weapon burials of northern and eastern England in the decades around 900. Again, it would seem that these displays of military equipment are related to the change in political control in the region, with the creation of the Danish kingdom of York, the appearance of new landowners and possibly a crisis in the legitimacy of extant lordship. While the symbolism of the artefacts clearly manifests one of the bases of secular power, an increase in the militarisation of society or its upper echelons is unlikely.[23]

The appearance of military service in the laws of the early medieval west is a similar sign of crisis. A recurrent feature of early medieval western European history in the fifth to tenth century (and I imagine beyond) is the appearance of legislation about military service only at moments when the government of a polity was, for whatever reason, finding difficulty in persuading those who had hitherto regarded military service as a *right* to do their *duty*. Examples of this can be found in numerous places: the late seventh-century laws about military service in the Visigothic Code;[24] the appearance of legislation setting out the required equipment of those attending the army in the last decades of the Lombard kingdom;[25] possibly the laws of Ine of Wessex;[26] most famously the later (post-800) capitularies of Charlemagne and of his successors.²⁷ Do these legal pronouncements represent a change in militarisation or a change in the evidence? What they certainly illustrate is the importance of military service in early medieval politics. Abandonment by the troops was a frequent – and absolute – marker of a ruler's imminent downfall. The classic instance of this is doubtless the so-called Lügenfeld, at which Louis the Pious' troops deserted him *en masse* for his rebellious sons, even as the two armies lined up to face each other.²⁸ It was far from the only such instance of this kind of decisive display of the withdrawal of political consent. Louis' son Charles suffered a similar military collapse when his brother Lothar invaded his kingdom in 858.²⁹ What distinguished these famous Carolingian examples was, rather, the fact that the abandoned ruler survived. Louis retook his throne a year later and Charles bounced back from his setback. Queen Brunhild, deserted by the forces of Austrasia and Burgundy in the face of an invasion by Chlothar II in 613, was less fortunate, being tortured and executed by the Neustrian monarch. Most of her surviving descendants died in the ensuing purge.³⁰ Something similar might have befallen King Oswine of Deira in 651 who was unable to raise a sufficiently strong army to resist an attack by Oswiu of Bernicia, who was said to have disbanded his army as a result, and was killed in the aftermath.³¹ Early medieval legislation about military service does not in itself denote a change in aristocratic militarisation. If anything, it seems to denote periods of crisis, possibly crises of political legitimacy.

One can also think about the presence of weaponry in the furnished cemeteries – the so-called *Reihengräberfelder* – of the post-imperial period, as is discussed in Brather-Walter's Chapter 16. As is mentioned by more than one contributor to this volume, Heinrich Härke pointed out long ago in a hugely important article that the deposition of weaponry with an individual in an Anglo-Saxon cemetery had no necessary bearing on whether or not the deceased person had been a warrior, and that a wide array of other semiotic possibilities was available.³² His argument that the frequency of weapon-graves did not tally with periods of warfare was, however, based upon an uncritical use of very unreliable written data such as Gildas' *De Excidio* and the *Anglo-Saxon Chronicle*.³³ Nonetheless, his general point stands and has been corroborated by many subsequent studies. In other parts of sixth- to seventh-century western Europe one can find, albeit in different ways, a similar lack of correlation between the social groups buried with weapons and those who customarily took part in the activities of armies – still less so with those described as taking evidently legitimate part in violent actions.³⁴ Written sources from Merovingian Gaul, as elsewhere, suggest, for example, that males as young as fifteen could serve in the armed followings of older men and yet weaponry is found very rarely in the burials of men of this age group in northern Gallic cemeteries. On the other hand, the percentage of masculine inhumations containing weaponry increases after *c.* 600, while the written sources suggest a more socially restricted right to serve in the army. It seems reasonable to suppose that the notional right to serve in the army, as a freeman, was important in local politics, even if the actuality of military service was quite different. What we might see here is weaponry as a sign of free status, in a context where graduations of freedom before the law seem to have been of increased significance,[35] rather than any sign of militarisation or otherwise. What would be interesting here, if my interpretation is plausible,[36] is how martial symbolism had become important in discourses of legal freedom or otherwise. Here we can see the polysemy I mentioned earlier: the symbolism of objects relating to one aspect of society (warfare) becomes, in a way, a metaphor for another (legal freedom).

Another intriguing issue concerns the fortification or otherwise of settlements. What is at stake in the appearance of fortifications around already-existing cities or the dwelling places of aristocrats? Famously, the villas of the Roman nobility were rarely fortified, even if they could be defensible. Until *c.* 300, the *civitas*-capitals of Roman Gaul were mostly un-walled, as they had been in Britain until the end of the second century; the non-fortification of Roman cities was widespread before the Tetrarchy. Traditionally, much of the wave of fortification from the end of the third century was attributed to a response to the Barbarian invasions of the third quarter of that century. This explanation has generally been found wanting and other factors have been adduced, such as the need to protect political and administrative centres, especially those where taxation and supplies were gathered. Nonetheless it is difficult to argue that the later empire was characterised by more banditry and civil war than the 'Principate' or the Republic. There was, clearly, something more to the decision to fortify cities and other settlements than simple defensive necessity. Equally, the repair of urban and other fortifications in the Carolingian period was clearly, at least in part, a reaction to the activities of Vikings and Magyars, but the large-scale violence of the pre-Viking period had not evinced a similar response. A similar point can be made for the towns of later 'Anglo-Saxon' England and other areas of the North Sea world.[37] By the same token, before the eighth or ninth century, elite settlements, where they were separate from those of other members of the community, also often lacked any kind of defences.[38] This is something that, again, bears scant relationship to the frequency of warfare or the importance of martial activity in the construction of aristocratic identities.

It is, of course, foolish to deny the practical value of fortifications, but to rely upon a purely functional explanation is to miss the full depth and complexity of the issue. This becomes especially clear when one looks at the full chronological and geographical span of late Antiquity and the early Middle Ages. The decision to fortify a site using the public dues of the realm opened a political dialogue, for it involved the mobilisation of manpower and other resources which might not willingly be provided. It involved the establishment of a right – in practice – for the ruler to call upon the free inhabitants and above all the aristocrats of the realm.[39] Where rulers managed to mobilise such resources it is important to look beyond their strictly functional value and even beyond the (often overlooked) logistics involved to their possibly even more important political role. When landowners were persuaded or coerced into fulfilling their obligations in helping with the construction of fortresses this did not simply divert resources from private to public use, which was important in itself. It also made visible that diversion. Bringing men and material together at a specific point for the purpose of constructing fortifications created a political assembly wherein lords and others saw that the king was able to command them and their men to work for the good of the realm. The very attendance of lords with their men and the required materials was a performance to a political community of the legitimacy of that command. Once built, fortified sites, like the Anglo-Saxon *burhs*,[40] were visible marks on the landscape. In some political contexts, such as the later Anglo-Saxon period in England, the role as a perceptible 'signature' of a particular set of power relationships was reinforced regularly. Men fulfilling their duty to man such fortifications came together – again – as a political gathering whose very reason for being was the ability of the ruler to assemble them to serve the realm. Public fortifications were in a very real sense spaces of the political. Consequently, of course, as with armies themselves, there was no guarantee that such assemblies would do what the king wanted in the way he wanted; they too were sites of action, of debate and even of resistance. The various failures to get the Frankish nobility to build and garrison the defences that Charles the Bald wanted are a good illustration.[41] As with the decision to call together the army, these summonses always represented – to some degree – political wagers.

If one views the attempts to maintain or introduce public duties such as fortress- and bridge-work in this light one can see the relationship between these and private fortifications in a slightly different perspective. Indeed, there is no necessary relationship between kings' attitudes to the two different categories. There is no especially good reason to suppose that kings would automatically see the fortification of aristocratic dwellings as a problem as long as the obligations to the maintenance and garrisoning of public defence works were being observed. In the central Middle Ages, the construction of aristocratic castles close to royal ones (or vice versa) made a very clear gesture but there is nothing to suggest that the building of fortified dwellings in the ninth century made such a pointed or threatening statement. Where problems arose was where such private fortifications were used *instead of* public ones in the defence of the realm; this entirely subverted the role that the latter were intended to play. The other issue that could come into play here was the appropriation of *public* dues for private construction or defence. It has been cogently argued that this was at stake in the building of aristocratic castles in post-Conquest England and made a very powerful political statement about who the new rulers were and their presence in the landscape.[42] Again, however, although it is interesting to speculate, it is difficult to see this as a concern in the attitude of Carolingian kings like Charles the Bald towards aristocratic *castella*.[43] Consideration of the issues set out here might provide a way of exploring the significantly different stories of private and public fortifications in late Anglo-Saxon England and ninth- and tenth-century *Francia*.

The presence or otherwise of aristocratic fortifications is then a topic that goes far beyond indicating the extent of warfare or the militarisation of the secular elite, encompassing issues such as the separation of the aristocracy from the remainder of the free population; the relative importance of town and countryside in aristocratic politics and culture; the existence of fixed *sedes* for the secular elite, as opposed to multiple estate centres between which lords moved; factors determining where surplus was invested and in what types of structure: communal or private, religious or secular. Where powerful lords spent their money and resources on, and made permanent marks on the landscape with, military manifestations of power this was clearly a part of a complex discourse about elite power and culture, which the simple notion of 'militarisation' – especially if envisaged as a straightforward linear process – is wholly insufficient to capture.

That, ultimately, is the most important point I want to make in considering where the study of militarisation goes from here. If one thinks about the aspects of evidence and the changes in it, which I have raised in this conclusion, one sees that, while they do reveal how society, politics and culture were militarised, there is always a crucial something that remains outside the equation if the discussion is limited to the idea of militarisation. Or at least it is if that idea is restricted to seeing militarisation as a process. Instead, I want to draw out the point, which I think emerges from all of the case studies which I have set out above, that militarisation is better seen as a discourse than as a process. Indeed, most if not all of the case studies set out in this book can be read as demonstrations of this point. What we can see, across a wide range of aspects of society, is the way in which martial symbolism, or values, or the army as the locus for particular activities, was the subject of a discourse. In addition to those alluded to already, we can see the debate on the appropriateness or otherwise of warfare in the name of religion,[44] or the ways in which attempts to create a nation depended upon the warlike representation of others.[45] Others can be added, with direct reference to James' criteria. I would include the processes of socialisation (the sixth of James' criteria) and the discourse of masculinity (perhaps encompassing the seventh and eighth of James' criteria).

The ninth and final of James' criteria of militarisation is conspicuous in its absence from the discussions in this volume, and this is especially remarkable because of the importance of the debate on loot and warfare that was started by two classic articles by Timothy Reuter.[46] Even here, though, we can refocus that discussion. I have argued elsewhere that the economic profits from warfare could sometimes be spectacular. The loot taken from the Avars by Charlemagne in the 790s is probably the best-known example, although it is worth remembering that the vast quantities of gold exacted from the eastern Roman Empire by Attila in the 440s were doubtless many times greater. They were, however, more often intangible than material.[47] The economic role of warfare should not be measured by profit and loss in material terms. Again, what is more clearly at stake in early medieval warfare is a discourse about the proper role of a king, whether as victorious war-leader and predator or as the defender of his people, and about the martial virtues of, especially aristocratic, males and the importance of their performance to an audience of peers. This is perhaps nowhere made clearer than in the early medieval discourse of good kingship, which is addressed in Coupland's and Wittkamp's chapters (Chapters 10 and 18 respectively). It is especially important to consider how insecure, how shifting, was the ideal of the militarily successful ruler. Contemporary critique could be made of Charles the Bald's failures as a warrior-king in ways that, as Coupland demonstrates, entirely ignored the realities and actual successes of his actions. Simon MacLean made a similar argument about the even more maligned Charles III 'the Fat'.[48] Inconsequential victories against Vikings could be 'spun' (in modern political parlance) as great triumphs. This argument can be made concerning Asser's story of Æthelræd I's (and, in Asser's view, his brother Alfred's) victory over the Danish Great Army at Ashdown in 871 in the *Vita Alfredi*; the *Ludwigslied*'s tale of how Louis II beat the Vikings at Saucourt in 881 and the *Annals of Fulda*'s account of Arnulf I's defeat of the Vikings at the Dyle in 891.[49] On the other hand, kings who successfully – and in entirely conventional fashion – ensured the departure of a Viking host could be pilloried as ineffectual cowards if the sources were hostile to them. Different sources might ignore the victories and praise the peaceful negotiation but the martial element in the ideals of good kingship remained the same. They were no less, either, in later sixth-century Francia when (like eastern Roman Emperors between Arcadius and the accession of Heraclius) kings rarely led their armies into battle, compared with either the earlier sixth-century or the period around 600, when they did command their forces in person. A good king (or emperor) was always victorious. Quite what counted as a victory and how directly involved the ruler needed to be in the actions of his army shifted interestingly, according to political discourse.

In all of the areas just addressed, late antique and early medieval militarisation cannot simply be discussed as a process or in relative quantifiable terms (i.e. how militarised is this society compared with that?). Militarisation – we might prefer the term martialisation if militarisation has too many connotations of formal, regular, standing armies – is in this period much more interestingly considered as a set of terms within which contemporaries debated the ideals, especially, but also the realities of their world: political, cultural, social, religious, economic, iconographic and so on. Militarisation does not concern a process or socio-political categories; it is a state of mind.

Notes

1 On the reasons for this, see Guy Halsall, *Warfare and society in the barbarian west, 450–900* (London: Routledge, 2003), pp. 10–11.
2 To which I would add, above all, C. Haack, *Die Krieger der Karolinger. Kriegsdienste als Prozesse gemeinschaftlicher Organisation um 800*. Ergänzungsbände zum Reallexikon der Germanischen Altertumskunde, 115 (Berlin: De Gruyter, 2020). Important works which take a different view from mine of Frankish military organisation that have appeared since 2003 include W. Goffart, 'Frankish military duty and the fate of Roman taxation', *Early Medieval Europe*, 16 (2008), 166–90; E. Renard, 'La politique militaire de Charlemagne at la paysannerie franque', *Francia*, 36 (2009), 1–33.
3 E. James, 'The militarisation of Roman society', in A. N. Jørgensen and B. L.Claussen (eds) *Military aspects of Scandinavian society in a European perspective, AD 1–1300* (Copenhagen: National Museum of Denmark, 1997), pp. 19–24.
4 Above, pp. 253–65.
5 *Kriterienbündel* featured heavily, for example, in attempts to define urbanism in the 1970s and 1980s. See, e.g., R. Hodges, *Dark-Age economics. The origins of towns and trade, 600–1000* (London: Duckworth, 1982), pp. 21–5.
6 J. M. Wallace-Hadrill, *The barbarian west* 4th edition (rev. R. Collins) (Oxford: Blackwells, 1996); Halsall, *Warfare and society*.
7 Estimates place the Roman standing army in the region of 400,000 or (quite likely) more: recently, I. N. Wood, *The transformation of the Roman west* (Leeds: Arc Humanities Press, 2018), pp. 15–19. No western European state came anywhere near the mobilisation of military manpower on the scale of the western empire alone before the later eighteenth century.

8 I have argued this in 'From Roman fundus to Carolingian Grand Domaine. Crucial ruptures between late Antiquity and the Middle Ages.' *Revue Belge de Philologie at d'Histoire*, 90 (2012), 273–98
9 See, classically, Michael McCormick, *Eternal victory. Triumphal rulership in Late Antiquity, Byzantium and the early Medieval west* (Cambridge: Cambridge University Press, 1990).
10 Although in practice, as Brent Shaw made very clear, free citizens, especially aristocrats, certainly possessed weapons and were on occasion called upon to use them in the service of the state. B. Shaw, 'Bandits in the Roman Empire', *Past and Present*, 105 (1984), 4–52.
11 G. Halsall, 'The Ostrogothic military', in J. J. Arnold, M. S. Bjornlie and K. Sessa (eds) *A companion to Ostrogothic Italy* (Leiden: Brill, 2016), pp. 173–99, for a somewhat different reading from Grundmann's of the Italian Gothic army between 489 and 561. I am less convinced of the existence of a standing army although, as Grundmann's chapter demonstrates, the evidence will clearly support that interpretation.
12 *Annals of St-Bertin s.a.* 859. J. L. Nelson (trans.), *The Annals of St-Bertin. Ninth-century Histories.* Vol. 1 (Manchester: Manchester University Press, 1991).
13 Halsall, *Warfare and society*, p. 100
14 *Edict of Pîtres*, 26. A. Boretius and V. Krause (eds) *MGH Legum sectio II Capitularia regum francorum 2* (Hanover: Hahnsche Buchhandlung, 1895–7), no. 273.
15 See J. Haldon, *Warfare, state and society in the Byzantine world, 565–1204* (London: Routledge, 1999).
16 Even to some extent by me: G. Halsall, *Barbarian migrations and the Roman west, 376–568* (Cambridge: Cambridge University Press: 2007), p. 495, which downplays the extent of 'militarisation' in the fifth–sixth-century west. Four years previously, I argued (Halsall, *Warfare and society*, pp. 44–5) that the 'demilitarisation' of the provincial Roman aristocracy had been overstressed.
17 Above, pp. 99–114.
18 F. Theuws, 'Gravegoods, ethnicity and the rhetoric of burial rites in late antique northern Gaul' in T. Derks and N. Roymans (eds), *Ethnic constructs in Antiquity. The role of power and tradition* (Amsterdam: Amsterdam University Press, 2009), pp. 283–319. For my critique of this argument, see Guy Halsall, *Cemeteries and society in Merovingian Gaul. Selected studies in history and archaeology, 1992-2009* (Leiden: Brill, 2010), pp. 155–9. Theuws' anti-military argument is repeated, curiously given the theme of the volume, in Hamm's chapter, which seems unaware of my later work on the topic and response to Theuws.
19 Ammianus Marcellinus *Res Gestae* 19.6.7 describes the axes (*securis*) of the Gallic legions. This is the same word used for axe in descriptions of Frankish warriors. J. C. Rolfe (ed. and trans.) *Ammianus Marcellinus* 3 vols. (Heinemann: London 1935–9).
20 Halsall, *Cemeteries and society*, p. 158.
21 For a convenient summary, see J. Mertens, 'La nécropole du castellum de Oudenburg', in S. Applebaum (ed.), *Limeskongress 7* (Tel Aviv: University of Tel Aviv, 1971), pp. 59–70.

22 Halsall, *Cemeteries and society*, pp. 162–3.
23 Guy Halsall, 'The Viking presence in England? The burial evidence reconsidered', in D. M. Hadley and J. Richards (eds) *Cultures in contact. Scandinavian settlement in England in the ninth and tenth centuries*, (Turnhout: Brepols, 2000), pp. 259–76.
24 For the military laws of Wamba and Ervig, see *Visigothic Law* 9.2.8–9: K. Zeumer (ed.) *MGH Legum sectio I*, Vol.1 (Hanover: Hahnsche Buchhandlung, 1902). See Chapter 7 in this volume by Poveda Arias.
25 *Laws of Ratchis* 4; *Laws of Aistulf* 2–3: K. Fischer-Drew (trans.) *The Lombard Laws* (Philadelphia: University of Pennsylvania Press, 1973); see the chapters by Berndt and Gasparri.
26 *Ine's Laws* 50. Important context is provided by *Ine's Laws* 13. D. Whitelock (trans.) *English historical documents*. Vol.1, *c.500–1042*. 2nd edn (London: Methuen, 1979), document 32.
27 The change in Carolingian military legislation after *c*.800 has been the subject of much debate. Classically this included T. Reuter, 'Plunder and tribute in the Carolingian empire', *Transactions of the Royal Historical Society*, 5th series, 35 (1980), 75–94; T. Reuter, 'The end of Carolingian military expansion', in P. Godman and R. Collins (eds), *Charlemagne's heir. New perspectives on the reign of Louis the Pious* (Oxford: Oxford University Press, 1990), pp. 391–405. Halsall, *Warfare and society*, pp. 90–1, for a response.
28 *Annals of St-Bertin*, s.a. 833. 'Astronomer', *Life of Louis* 48: A. Cabaniss (trans.), *Son of Charlemagne. A contemporary Life of Louis the Pious* (Syracuse: Syracuse University Press, 1961); Thegan, *Life of Louis*, 42: P. E. Dutton, *Carolingian civilization. A reader* (Peterborough, Ontario, 1996), pp. 141–55.
29 *Annals of St-Bertin*, s.a. 858.
30 *Vita Columbani* 1.29: A. O'Hara & I. N. Wood (trans.), *Jonas of Bobbio. Life of Columbanus, Life of John of Réomé, and Life of Vedast* (Liverpool: Liverpool University Press, 2017). Fredegar, *Chronicle* 4.42: J. M. Wallace-Hadrill (ed. and trans.), *The fourth book of the Chronicle of Fredegar with its Continuations* (London: Nelson, 1960).
31 Bede, *Ecclesiastical History* 3.14. B. Colgrave and R. A. B. Mynors (ed. and trans.), *Bede's Ecclesiastical History of the English people* (Oxford: Oxford University Press, 1969).
32 H. Härke, '"Weapon graves" The background of the Anglo-Saxon weapon burial rite', *Past and Present*, 126 (1990), 22–43. This point makes the immediate rush to declare female subjects of weapon-burial 'warrior women' very odd. In Anglo-Saxon cemeteries, pre-pubescent subjects were frequently interred with spears, without anyone deducing the existence of 'child soldiers' from that.
33 On which see G. Halsall, *Worlds of Arthur. Facts and fictions of the Dark Ages* (Oxford: Oxford University Press), pp. 51–86, and references.
34 Various social groups excluded from service in the army – not least women and the unfree – were involved in lower level violence without their participation rendering their actions illegitimate.

35 *Ripuarian Law*, of the seventh century, includes much more discussion of various grades of free, semi-free and unfree classes than its sixth-century precursor, *Salic Law*.
36 Esders, Chapter 11 above, reads *Ripuarian Law* in a very different – but interesting – way from me.
37 See Lavelle's Chapter 5, above.
38 See Bourgeois' Chapter 8 for the fortification of sites in the latter part of the period.
39 See Lavelle's Chapter 5 and Coupland's Chapter 10.
40 See Lavelle's Chapter 5.
41 See Coupland's Chapter 10 and the literature cited there.
42 Sarah Speight, 'Violence and the creation of socio-political order in post-conquest Yorkshire', in G. Halsall (ed.), *Violence and society in the early medieval west* (Woodbridge: Boydell, 1998), pp. 157–74.
43 I am grateful to Professor Simon MacLean for discussion of this issue.
44 See Heil's Chapter 12 and Goetz's Chapter 13.
45 See Bennett's Chapter 17. One might, nonetheless, wonder whether the community under construction in some of the pre-Viking sources discussed was that of the English or that of good Christians.
46 Above, note 28.
47 G. Halsall, 'Predatory warfare. The moral and the physical' in R. Keller and L. Sarti (eds), *Pillages, tributs, captifs* (Éditions de la Sorbonne: Paris, 2018), pp. 53–68.
48 S. MacLean, 'Charles the Fat and the Viking Great Army. The military explanation for the end of the Carolingian empire' (876–888), *War Studies Journal*, 3:2 (1998), 74–95; S. MacLean, *Kingship and politics in the late ninth century. Charles the Fat and the end of the Carolingian empire* (Cambridge: Cambridge University Press, 2003).
49 Asser, *Life of Alfred*: S. Keynes and M. Lapidge (trans.), *Alfred the Great* (Harmondsworth: Penguin Classics, 1983), pp. 65–110. *Ludwigslied*: P. E. Dutton, *Carolingian civilization. A reader* (Peterborough, Ontario, 1996), pp. 482–3. *Annals of Fulda*, s.a. 891: T. Reuter (trans.) *The Annals of Fulda. Ninth-century histories*. Vol. 2 (Manchester: Manchester University Press, 1992).

Select bibliography

Abels, R., *Lordship and military obligation in Anglo-Saxon England* (London: University of California Press, 1988).
Abels, R., '"Cowardice" and duty in Anglo-Saxon England', *Journal of Medieval Military History*, 4 (2006), pp. 29–49.
Abels, R., 'Reflections on Alfred the Great as a military leader', in G. I. Halfond (ed.), *The medieval way of war. Studies in medieval military history in honor of Bernard S. Bachrach* (Farnham: Ashgate, 2015), pp. 47–63.
Achard-Corompt, N. and Kasprzyk, M. (eds), *L' antiquité tardive dans l'Est de la Gaule II. Sépultures, nécropoles et pratiques funéraires en Gaule de l'Est. Actualité de la recherche*, Revue archeologique de l'Est Supplément, 41 (Dijon: RAE, 2016).
Alcock, L., 'The site of the "Battle of Dunnichen"', *The Scottish Historical Review*, 75 (1996), pp. 130–42.
Arjava, A., Frösen, J. and Kaimio, J. (eds), *Petra Papyri V* (Amman: ACOR, 2008).
Arjava, A., Buchholz, M., Gagos, T. and M. Kaimo (eds), *The Petra Papyri IV* (Amman: ACOR, 2011).
Arnold, J., Bjornlie, S. and Sessa, K. (eds), *Companion to Ostrogothic Italy* (Leiden: Brill, 2016).
Ausenda, G., Delogu, P. and Wickham, C. (eds), *The Langobards before the Frankish Conquest. An ethnographic perspective* (Woodbridge: Boydell & Brewer, 2009).
Azzara, C. and Gasparri, S., *Le leggi dei Longobardi. Storia, memoria e diritto di un popolo germanico* (Roma: Viella, 2005).
Bachrach, B. S., *Charlemagne's early Campaigns (768–777). A diplomatic and military analysis*, History of Warfare, 82 (Leiden: Brill, 2013).
Bachrach, D. S., *Religion and the conduct of war, c. 300–1215*, Warfare in History (Woodbridge and Rochester: Boydell, 2003).
Baker, J. and Brookes, S., 'From frontier to border. The evolution of northern west Saxon territorial delineation in the ninth and tenth centuries', *Anglo-Saxon Studies in Archaeology and History*, 17 (2011), pp. 108–23.
Baker, J. and Brookes, S., *Beyond the Burghal Hidage. Anglo-Saxon civil defence in the Viking age* (Leiden: Brill, 2012).
Baker, J., Brookes, S. and Reynolds, A. (eds), *Landscapes of defense in early medieval Europe* (Turnhout: Brepols, 2013).

Barbero, A. and Vigil, M., *La formación del feudalismo en la Península Ibérica* (Barcelona: Crítica, 1978).

Barbiera, I., 'Remembering the warriors. Weapon burials and tombstones between Antiquity and the early Middle Ages in northern Italy', in W. Pohl and G. Heydemann (eds), *Post-Roman transitions. Christian and barbarian identities in the early medieval west* (Turnhout: Brepols, 2013), pp. 407–36.

Barnwell, P. S., *Emperor, prefects and kings. The Roman west, 395–565* (London: Duckworth, 1992).

Baumeister, R. F. and Leary, M. R., 'The need to belong. Desire for interpersonal attachments as a fundamental human motivation', *Psychological Bulletin*, 117 (1995), pp. 497–529.

Bayerle, K., 'Einsatzfelder des weltlichen Bannes im Frühmittelalter', in H.-G. Hermann, H. Siems, T. Gutmann, M. Schmoeckel and J. Rückert (eds), *Von den leges barbarorum bis zum ius barbarum des Nationalsozialismus* (Cologne: Böhlau, 2008), pp. 13–34.

Bazelmans, J., 'Conceptualising early Germanic political structure. A review of the use of the concept of Gefolgschaft', in N. Roymans and F. Theuws (eds), *Images of the past. Studies on ancient societies in northwestern Europe* (Amsterdam: University of Amsterdam, 1991), pp. 91–129.

Bennett, E., 'Tagungsbericht. Military organisation and society in the post-Roman world', *H-Soz-Kult*, hsozkult.de/conferencereport/id/tagungsberichte-6886 (accessed 10 February 2019).

Bernstein, M. J., 'Ingroups and outgroups', in J. Stone, R. M. Dennis, P. Rizova, A. D. Smith, X. Hou (eds), *The Wiley Blackwell encyclopedia of race, ethnicity, and nationalism* (Malden: Wiley-Blackwell, 2016).

Bertolini, O., 'Ordinamenti militari e strutture sociali dei langobardi in Italia', in *Ordinamenti militari in Occidente nell'alto medievo*. Settimane di studio del Centro italiano di studi sull'alto medioevo, 15 (Spoleto: Fondazione CISAM, 1968), pp. 429–629.

Bevir, M. and H. E. Bödeker (eds), *Begriffsgeschichte, Diskursgeschichte, Metapherngeschichte* (Göttingen: Wallstein-Verlag, 2002).

Beyerle, F., 'Zum Kleinreich Sigiberts III. und zur Datierung der Lex Ribuaria', *Rheinische Vierteljahrsblätter*, 21 (1956), pp. 357–61.

Bognetti, G. P., 'L'influsso delle istituzioni militari romane sulle istituzioni longobarde del secolo VI e la nature della fara', in G.P. Bognetti (ed.), *L'età longobarda 3* (Milan: Editore Giuffrè, 1967), pp. 3–46.

Borri, F., 'Romans growing beards. Identity and historiography in seventh-century Italy', *Viator*, 15 (2014), pp. 39–72.

Bothe, L., 'From subordination to integration. Romans in Frankish law', in W. Pohl, C. Gantner, C. Grifoni and M. Pollheimer-Mohaupt (eds), *Transformations of Romanness. Early medieval regions and identities* (Berlin: De Gruyter, 2018), pp. 345–68.

Bourgeois, L., '*Castrum* et habitat des élites (France et ses abords, vers 880-vers 1000)', in D. Iogna-Prat, M. Lauwers, F. Mazel and I. Rosé (eds), *Cluny, les moines et la société au premier âge féodal* (Rennes: Presses universitaires de Rennes, 2013), pp. 471–94.

Bourgeois, L., 'La fortification des abbayes et des collégiales aux ixe-xe siècles. Quelques pistes de recherche', in J.-M. Duvosquel and P. Perrin (eds), *Religion, quotidien et animaux au Moyen Âge. Études offertes à Alain Dierkens, RBPH*, 96:1/2 (2018), pp. 193–208.

Brandes, W., *Finanzverwaltung in Krisenzeiten. Untersuchungen zur byzantinischen Administration im 6.-9. Jahrhundert* (Frankfurt: Löwenklau-Gesellschaft, 2002).
Bronisch, A. P., *Reconquista und Heiliger Krieg. Die Deutung des Krieges im christlichen Spanien von den Westgoten bis ins frühe 12. Jahrhundert*, Spanische Forschungen der Görresgesellschaft. Zweite Reihe, 35 (Münster: Aschendorff 1998).
Brown, T. S., *Gentlemen and officers. Imperial administration and aristocratic power in Byzantine Italy, AD 554–800* (Rome: British School at Rome, 1984).
Brubaker, L. and Haldon, J., *Byzantium in the iconoclast era, c. 680–850* (Cambridge: Cambridge University Press, 2011).
Brulet, R., 'Das spätrömische Verteidigungssystem zwischen Mosel und Nordseeküste', in T. Bechert and W. J. H. Willems (eds), *Die römische Reichsgrenze von der Mosel bis zur Nordseeküste* (Stuttgart: Theiss, 1995), pp. 103–19.
Butler, R. M., 'Late Roman town walls in Gaul' *Archaeological Journal*, 116 (1959), pp. 25–50.
Böhme, H. W., *Germanische Grabfunde des 4. bis 5. Jahrhunderts zwischen unterer Elbe und Loire. Studien zur Chronologie und Bevölkerungsgeschichte*, Münchner Beiträge zur Vor- und Frühgeschichte, 19 (Munich: C.H. Beck, 1974).
Castro, M., *The function of the Roman Army in southern Arabia Petraea* (Oxford: Archaeopress, 2018).
Chadwick, H. M., *The heroic age* (Cambridge: Cambridge University Press, 1912).
Charles-Edwards, T. M., 'Wales and Mercia, 613–918', in *Mercia. An Anglo-Saxon kingdom in Europe*, ed. M. P. Brown and C. A. Farr (Leicester: Leicester University Press, 2001), pp. 89–105.
Christie, N., 'Invasion or invitation? The Longobard occupation of northern Italy, AD 568–69', *Romanobarbarica*, 11 (1991), pp. 79–108.
Christie, N., *The Lombards. The ancient Longobards* (Malden, MA: Blackwell, 1995).
Christie, N. and Sarantis, A. (eds), *War and warfare in late Antiquity* (Leiden: Brill, 2013).
Claessen, H. J. M., 'Changing legitimacy', in R. Cohen and J. D. Toland (eds), *State formation and political legitimacy* (Oxford: Transaction Books, 1988), pp. 23–44.
Clauss, M., *Kriegsniederlagen im Mittelalter. Darstellung – Deutung – Bewältigung*, Krieg in der Geschichte 54 (Paderborn: Schöningh, 2010).
Costambeys, M., 'The transmission of tradition. Gregorian influence and innovation in eight-century Italian monasticism', in Y. Hen, M. Innes (eds), *The uses of the past in the early Middle Ages* (Cambridge: Cambridge University Press, 2000), pp. 78–101.
Coupland, S., *Charles the Bald and the defence of the west Frankish kingdom against the Viking invasions, 840–877* (PhD dissertation, Cambridge University, 1987).
Coupland, S., 'Carolingian arms and armor in the ninth century', *Viator*, 21 (1990), pp. 29–50.
Coupland, S., 'The fortified bridges of Charles the Bald', *Journal of Medieval History*, 17 (1991), pp. 1–12.
Coupland, S., 'From poachers to gamekeepers. Scandinavian warlords and Carolingian kings', *Early Medieval Europe*, 7:1 (1998), pp. 85–114.
Coupland, S., 'The Frankish tribute payments to the Vikings and their consequences', *Francia*, 26/1 (1999), pp. 57–75.
Coupland, S., 'The Carolingian army and the struggle against the Vikings', *Viator*, 35 (2004), pp. 49–70.
Coupland, S., *Carolingian coinage and the Vikings. Studies on power and trade in the 9th century* (Aldershot: Variorum, 2007).

Dahmen, K., 'Zum Münzwesen des Merowingerreiches', in A. Greule, B. Kluge, J. Jarnut and M. Selig (eds), *Die merowingischen Monetarmünzen als interdisziplinär-mediaevistische Herausforderung* (Paderborn: Wilhelm Fink, 2017), pp. 71–124.

Dal Santo, M., 'Gregory the Great, the empire and the emperor', in B. Neil and M. Dal Santo (eds), *Companion to Gregory the Great* (Leiden: Brill, 2013), pp. 57–81.

Delogu, P., 'Il regno longobardo', in G. Galasso (ed.), *Storia d'Italia*, I (Torino: Utet, 1980), pp. 2–216.

Di Segni, L., 'The Beersheba tax edict reconsidered in the light of a newly discovered fragment', *Scripta Classica Israelica*, 23 (2004), pp. 131–58.

Díaz, P. C., 'El esquema provincial en el contexto administrativo de la monarquía visigoda', *Mélanges de la Casa de Velázquez*, 49:2 (2019), pp. 77–108.

Díaz, P. C. and Valverde, M. R., 'The theoretical strength and practical weakness of the Visigothic monarchy of Toledo', in F. Theuws and J. L. Nelson (eds), *Rituals of power. From late Antiquity to the early Middle Ages* (Leiden: Brill, 2000), pp. 59–93.

Dutt, C., 'Historische Semantik als Begriffsgeschichte. Theoretische Grundlagen und paradigmatische Anwendungsfelder' in J. Riecke (ed.), *Historische Semantik* (Berlin: De Gruyter, 2011), pp. 37–50.

Ebenbauer, A., 'Heldenlied und "historisches Lied" im Frühmittelalter und davor', in H. Beck (ed.), *Heldensage und Heldendichtung im Germanischen*, Ergänzungsbände zum RGA, 2 (Berlin: De Gruyter, 1988), pp. 15–34.

Ehlers, J., 'Die Sachsenmission als heilsgeschichtliches Ereignis', in F. J. Felten and N. Jaspert (eds), *Vita Religiosa im Mittelalter* (Berlin: Duncker & Humblot, 1999), pp. 37–53.

Esders, S., 'Treueidleistung und Rechtsveränderung im frühen Mittelalter', in S. Esders and C. Reinle (eds), *Rechtsveränderung im politischen und sozialen Kontext mittelalterlicher Rechtsvielfalt* (Münster: Lit, 2005), pp. 25–62.

Esders, S., *Die Formierung der Zensualität. Zur kirchlichen Transformation des spätrömischen Patronatswesens im früheren Mittelalter* (Ostfildern: Thorbecke, 2010).

Esders, S., '"Faithful believers". Oaths of allegiance in post-Roman societies as evidence for eastern and western "visions of community"', in W. Pohl, C. Gantner and R. Payne (eds), *Visions of community in the post-Roman world. the west, Byzantium and the Islamic world, 300–1100* (Aldershot: Ashgate, 2012), pp. 357–74.

Esders, S., 'Nordwestgallien um 500. Von der militarisierten spätrömischen Provinzgesellschaft zur erweiterten Militäradministration des merowingischen Königtums' in M. Meier and S. Patzold (eds), *Chlodwigs Welt. Organisation von Herrschaft um 500*, Roma aeterna 3 (Stuttgart: Franz Steiner, 2014), pp. 339–61.

Esders, S., 'Late Roman military law in the Bavarian Code', *clio@themis. Revue électronique d'histoire du droit*, 10 (2016) (*La forge du droit. Naissance des identités juridiques en Europe, IVe–XIIIe siècles*): cliothemis.com/IMG/pdf/3-_Esders-2.pdf (accessed 25 March 2020).

Esders, S., 'Amt und Bann. Weltliche Funktionsträger (*centenarii, vicarii*) als Teil ländlicher Gesellschaften im Karolingerreich', in T. Kohl, S. Patzold and B. Zeller (eds), *Kleine Welten. Ländliche Gesellschaften im Karolingerreich* (Ostfildern: Thorbecke, 2019), pp. 255–307.

Ewig, E., 'Die *Civitas Ubiorum*, die Francia Rhinensis und das Land Ribuarien' (1954), in E. Ewig, *Spätantikes und fränkisches Gallien. Gesammelte Schriften (1952–1973)*, vol. 1 (Zurich: Artemis, 1976), pp. 472–503.

Ewig, E., 'Waldorf am Vinxtbach. Römisch-fränkische Kontinuität auf dem Lande? Fakten und Fragen', *Rheinische Vierteljahrsblätter*, 59 (1995), pp. 304–13.
Fagerlie, J. M., *Late Roman and Byzantine solidi found in Sweden and Denmark* (New York: American Numismatic Society, 1967).
Fanning, S., 'Tacitus, Beowulf, and the *comitatus*', *The Haskins Society Journal*, 9 (1997), pp. 17–38.
Ferguson, R. B., 'Ten points on war', *Social Analysis*, 52:2 (2008), pp. 32–49.
Fischer, S. and López Sánchez, F., 'Subsidies for the Roman west? The flow of Constantinopolitan solidi to the western empire and barbaricum.' *Opuscula, Annual of the Swedish Institutes at Athens and Rome*, 9 (2016), pp. 249–69.
Foot, S., 'The making of the *Angelcynn*. English identity before the Norman conquest', *Transactions of the Royal Historical Society*, 6 (1996), pp. 25–49.
Fournier, G., *Le château dans la France médiévale. Essai de sociologie monumentale* (Paris: Aubier-Montaigne, 1978).
Frank, R., 'The ideal of men dying with their lord in *The Battle of Maldon*. Anachronism or nouvelle vague?', in I. Wood and N. Lund (eds), *People and places in northern Europe, 500–1600* (Woodbridge: Boydell and Brewer, 1991), pp. 95–106.
Friedrich, M., Review of 'W. Heizmann and S. Oehrl (eds), '*Bilddenkmäler zur germanischen Götter- und Heldensage* (2015)', *Zeitschrift für Archäologie des Mittelalters*, 44 (2016), pp. 215–21.
Frighetto, R., 'Cuando la confrontación genera la colaboración: godos, romanos y el surgimiento del reino hispanogodo de Toledo (siglos V-VI)', *Vínculos de Historia*, 7 (2018), pp. 157–72.
Fuhrmann, M. and Fink, G., 'Erwartungshorizont und Lesersteuerung. Drei Beispiele aus Notkers *Gesta Karoli*', *Der Altsprachliche Unterricht*, 23:3 (1980), pp. 41–52.
Ganz, D., 'Humour as history in Notker's *Gesta Karoli Magni*', in E. B. King, J. T. Schaefer and W. B. Wadley (eds), *Monks, nuns, and friars in medieval society* (Sewanee: Press of the University of the South, 1989), pp. 171–83.
García Moreno, L. A., 'Estudios sobre la organización administrativa del reino visigodo de Toledo', *Anuario de Historia del Derecho Español*, 44 (1974), pp. 1–155.
Gasparri, S., *I duchi longobardi*, Studi Storici, 109 (Rome: Istituto storico italiano per il Medio Evo, 1978).
Gasparri, S., 'La questione degli arimanni', *Bullettino dell'Istituto Storico Italiano per il Medioevo*, 87 (1978), pp. 121–53.
Gasparri, S., 'The fall of the Lombard kingdom. Facts, memory and propaganda', in S. Gasparri (ed.), *774 – ipotesi su una transizione*, Atti del seminario di Poggibonsi, 16–18 febbraio 2006 (Turnhout: Brepols, 2008), pp. 41–65.
Gasparri, S. *Italia longobarda. Il regno, i Franchi, il papato* (Bari-Roma: Laterza, 2012).
Gasparri, S., 'I barbari, l'impero, l'esercito e il caso dei Longobardi', in F. Botta and L. Loschavio, *Civitas, Arma, Iura. Organizzazioni militari, istituzioni giuridiche e strutture sociali alle origini dell'Europa, secc. III–VIII* (Lecce: Edizioni Grifo, 2015), pp. 91–102.
Gasparri, S., 'Compétion ou collaboration? Les Lombards, les Romains et les évêques jusq'au milieu du VIIe siècle', in R. Le Jan, G. Bührer-Thierry and S. Gasparri (éds), *Coopétiton. Rivaliser, coopérer dans les sociétés du Haut Moyen Âge*, HAMA, 10 (Turnhout: Brepols, 2018), pp. 39–47.
Goetz, H.-W., '"Vorstellungsgeschichte": Menschliche Vorstellungen und Meinungen als Dimension der Vergangenheit. Bemerkungen zu einem jüngeren Arbeitsfeld der

Geschichtswissenschaft als Beitrag zu einer Methodik der Quellenauswertung', *Archiv für Kulturgeschichte*, 61 (1979), pp. 253–71.
Goetz, H.-W., *Strukturen der spätkarolingischen Epoche im Spiegel der Vorstellungen eines zeitgenössischen Mönchs. Eine Interpretation der Gesta Karoli Notkers von St. Gallen* (Bonn: Habelt, 1981).
Goffart, W., *The narrators of barbarian history. Jordanes, Gregory of Tours, Bede, and Paul the Deacon* (Princeton: Princeton University Press, 1988).
Goffart, W., 'Conspicuously absent. Martial heroism in the *Histories* of Gregory of Tours and its likes', in K. Mitchell and I. N. Wood (eds), *The world of Gregory of Tours* (Leiden: Brill, 2002), pp. 365–93.
Goldberg, E. J., 'More devoted to the equipment of battle than the splendor of banquets. Frontier kingship, martial ritual, and early knighthood at the court of Louis the German', *Viator*, 30 (1999), pp. 41–78.
Graus, F., 'Der Heilige als Schlachtenhelfer. Zur Nationalisierung einer Wundererzählung in der mittelalterlichen Chronistik', in K.-U. Jäschke and R. Wenskus (eds), *Festschrift für Helmut Beumann zum 65. Geburtstag* (Sigmaringen: Thorbecke, 1977), pp. 330–48.
Graus, F., *Mentalitäten im Mittelalter. Methodische und inhaltliche Probleme* (Sigmaringen: Thorbecke, 1987).
Gregory, S., *Roman military architecture on the eastern frontier* (Amsterdam: Hakkert, 1997).
Gumbrecht, H. U., *Dimension und Grenzen der Begriffsgeschichte* (Paderborn: Fink, 2006).
Gübele, B., *Deus vult, Deus vult. Der christliche heilige Krieg im Früh- und Hochmittelalter*, Mittelalter-Forschungen, 54 (Ostfildern: Thorbecke, 2018).
Haldon, J., 'Military service, military lands, and the status of soldiers. Current problems and interpretations', *Dumbarton Oaks Papers*, 47 (1993), pp. 1–67.
Haldon, J. F., *Byzantium in the seventh century. The transformation of a culture* (Cambridge: Cambridge University Press, 2nd edn, 1997).
Haldon, J. F., *Warfare, state and society in the Byzantine world, 565–1204* (London: University College London Press, 1999).
Haldon, J. F., *The empire that would not die. The paradox of eastern Roman survival, 640–740* (Cambridge, MA: Harvard University Press, 2016).
Halphen, L., 'Le moine de Saint-Gall' (Études critiques sur l'histoire de Charlemagne, IV), *Revue Historique*, 128 (1918), pp. 260–98.
Halsall, G., 'The origin of the Reihengräberzivilisation. Forty years on' in J. Drinkwater and H. Elton (eds), *Fifth-century Gaul. A crisis of identity?* (Cambridge: Cambridge University Press, 1992), pp. 196–207.
Halsall, G., *Warfare and society in the Barbarian west, 450–900*, Warfare and History (London and New York: Routledge, 2003).
Halsall, G., *Barbarian migrations and the Roman west, 376–568* (Cambridge: Cambridge University Press, 2007).
Halsall, G., *Worlds of Arthur. Facts and fictions of the Dark Ages* (Oxford: Oxford University Press, 2013).
Halsall, G., 'Predatory warfare. The moral and the physical' in R. Keller and L. Sarti (eds), *Pillages, tributs, captifs* (Éditions de la Sorbonne: Paris, 2018), pp. 53–68.
Halsall, G., 'Transformations of Romanness. The northern Gallic case', in W. Pohl, C. Gantner, C. Grifoni and M. Pollheimer-Mohaupt (eds), *Transformations of Romanness in the early Middle Ages. Regions and identities* (Berlin: De Gruyter, 2018), pp. 41–58.

Harland, J. M., 'Rethinking ethnicity and "otherness" in early Anglo-Saxon England', *Medieval Worlds*, 5 (2017), pp. 113–42.
Harrison, D., 'The development of élites. From Roman bureaucrats to medieval warlords', in W. Pohl and M. Diesenberger (eds), *Integration und Herrschaft. Ethnische Identitäten und soziale Organisation im Frühmittelalter* (Vienna: Verlag der Österreichischen Akademie der Wissenschaften, 2002), pp. 289–300.
Harrison, D. 'Dark Age migrations and subjective ethnicity. The example of the Lombards', *Skandia* 57 (2008), pp. 19–36.
Haslam, J., 'King Alfred and the Vikings. Strategies and tactics 876–886 AD', *Anglo-Saxon Studies in Archaoleogy and History*, 13 (2006), pp. 122–54.
Heath, C., *The narrative worlds of Paul the Deacon. Between empires and identities in Lombard Italy* (Amsterdam: Amsterdam University Press, 2017).
Heather, P., 'Elite militarisation and the post-Roman west', in G. Bonamente and R. Lizzi Testa (eds), *Istituzioni, carismi ed esercizio del potere (IV-VI secolo d.C.)* (Bari: Edipuglia, 2010), pp. 245–65.
Hill, D., and Rumble, A. R. (eds), *The defence of Wessex. The Burghal Hidage and Anglo-Saxon fortifications* (Manchester: Manchester University Press, 1996).
Holdsworth, C. J., '"An Airier Aristocracy". The saints at war', in R. R. Davies et al. (eds), *Transactions of the Royal Historical Society. Sixth series* (Cambridge: Cambridge University Press, 1996), pp. 103–22.
Holzem, A. (ed.), *Krieg und Christentum. Religiöse Gewalttheorien in der Kriegserfahrung des Westens*, Krieg in der Geschichte, 50 (Paderborn: Schöningh, 2009).
Huntington, S., *The soldier and the state* (Cambridge: Harvard University Press, 1957)
Härke, H., '"Warrior graves"? The background of the Anglo-Saxon weapon burial rite', *Past and Present*, 126 (1990), pp. 22–43.
Härke, H., *Angelsächsische Waffengräber des 5. bis 7. Jahrhunderts*, Zeitschrift für Archäologie des Mittelalters, supplement, 6 (Bonn and Cologne: Rheinland-Verlag, 1992).
Innes, M. J., 'Memory, orality and literacy in an early medieval society', *Past and Present*, 158 (1998), pp. 3–36.
Isaac, B., 'The meaning of the terms *limes* and *limitanei*', *Journal of Roman Studies*, 78 (1988), pp. 125–47.
James, E., 'The militarisation of Roman society, 400–700' in A. N. Jørgensen and B. L. Clausen (eds), *Military aspects of Scandinavian society in a European perspective AD 1–1300*, National Museum Studies in Archaeology and History, 2 (Copenhagen: National Museum, 1997), pp. 19–24.
Jarnut, J., 'Beobachtungen zu den langobardischen arimanni und exercitales', *Zeitschrift der Savigny-Stiftung für Rechtsgeschichte, Germanistische Abteilung*, 88 (1971), pp. 1–28.
Jarnut, J., *Geschichte der Langobarden*, Urban-Taschenbücher, 339 (Stuttgart: Kohlhammer, 1982).
Jarnut, J., 'Die Landnahme der Langobarden in Italien aus historischer Sicht', in M. Müller-Wille and R. Schneider (ed.), *Ausgewählte Probleme europäischer Landnahmen des Früh- und Hochmittelalters. Methodische Grundlagendiskussionen im Grenzbereich zwischen Archäologie und Geschichte*, Vorträge und Forschungen 41 (Sigmaringen: Jan Thorbecke, 1993), pp. 173–94.
Jarnut, J., 'Zum Stand der Langobardenforschung', in W. Pohl and P. Erhart (eds), *Die Langobarden. Herrschaft und Identität*, Forschungen zur Geschichte des Mittelalters, 9 (Vienna: Akademie, 2005), pp. 11–19.

Kahl, H.-D., 'Die ersten Jahrhunderte des missionsgeschichtlichen Mittelalters. Bausteine für eine Phänomenologie bis ca. 1050', in K. Schäferdiek (ed.), *Die Kirche des früheren Mittelalters*, Kirchengeschichte als Missionsgeschichte, 2 (Munich: Chr. Kaiser Verlag, 1978).

Kamp, H. and Kroker, M. (eds), *Schwertmission. Gewalt und Christianisierung im Mittelalter* (Paderborn: Ferdinand Schöningh, 2013).

Kaplan, M., *Les hommes et la terre à Byzance du VIe au XIe siècle. Propriété et exploitation du sol* (Paris: Sorbonne, 1992).

Keller, H., 'Zum Sturz Karls III.', in E. Hlawitschka (ed.), *Königswahl und Thronfolge in fränkisch-karolingischer Zeit* (Darmstadt: Wissenschaftliche Buchgesellschaft, 1975), pp. 432–94.

Kennedy, D., *The Roman army in Jordan* (London: Council for British Research on the Levant, 2004).

King, P. D., *Law and society in the Visigothic kingdom* (Cambridge: Cambridge University Press, 1972).

Kleemann, J., 'Hospes. Archäologische Aspekte zur Integration von Barbaren in das römische Imperium. Eine vergleichende Betrachtung zur Beigabensitte in gallischen und pannonischen Provinzen', in T. Vida (ed.), *The frontier world – Romans, Barbarians and Military Culture* (Budapest: Eötvös Loránd University, 2015), pp. 499–516.

Konrad, M. and Witschel, C. (eds), *Römische Legionslager in den Rhein- und Donauprovinzen – Nuclei spätantik-frühmittelalterlichen Lebens?* (Munich: C.H. Beck, 2011).

Kortüm, H.-H., *Menschen und Mentalitäten. Einführung in die Vorstellungswelten des Mittelalters* (Berlin: De Gruyter, 1996).

Krallis, D., 'Popular political agency in Byzantium's villages and towns', *Byzantina Symmeikta*, 28 (2018), pp. 11–48.

Kroeschell, K., 'Führer, Gefolgschaft und Treue', in J. Rückert and D. Willoweit (eds), *Die Deutsche Rechtsgeschichte in der NS-Zeit. Ihre Vorgeschichte und ihre Nachwirkungen* (Tübingen: Mohr Siebeck, 1995), pp. 55–76.

Kuefler, M., *The manly eunuch. Masculinity, gender ambiguity, and Christian ideology in late Antiquity* (Chicago: University of Chicago Press, 2001).

Körntgen, L. 'Heidenkrieg und Bistumsgründung. Glaubensverbreitung als Herrscheraufgabe bei Karolingern und Ottonen', in A. Holzem (ed.), *Krieg und Christentum. Religiöse Gewalttheorien in der Kriegserfahrung des Westens* (Paderborn: Ferdinand Schöningh, 2009), pp. 281–304.

La Rocca, C., 'L'archeologia e i Longobardi in Italia. Orientamenti, metodi, linee di ricerca', in S. Gasparri (ed.), *Il regno dei Longobardi in Italia. Archeologia, società e istituzioni* (Spoleto: CISAM, 2004), pp. 207–17.

La Rocca, C., 'Rituali di famiglia. Pratiche funerarie nell'Italia longobarda', in F. Bougard, C. La Rocca and R. Le Jan (eds), *Sauver son âme et se perpétuer. Trasmission du patrimoine et mémoire au Haut Moyen Âge* (Rome: Ecole Française de Rome, 2005), pp. 431–57.

Later, C., Helmbrecht, M. and U. Jecklin-Tischhauser (eds), *Infrastruktur und Distribution zwischen Antike und Mittelalter* (Hamburg: Dr. Kovač, 2015).

Lavelle, R., *Alfred's wars. Sources and interpretation of Anglo-Saxon warfare in the Viking age* (Woodbridge: Boydell and Brewer, 2010).

Le Goff, J., 'Les mentalités. Une histoire ambiguë', in J. Le Goff and P. Nora (eds), *Faire de l'histoire*, vol 3 (Paris: Gallimard, 1974), pp. 76–94.

Leicht, P. S., 'König Aistulfs Heergesetze', *Miscellanea Academia Berolinensia*, 11/1 (1950), pp. 97–102.
Le Jan, R., 'Les élites au haut Moyen Âge. Approche sociologique et anthropologique', in F. Bougard, H.-W. Goetz and R. Le Jan (eds), *Théorie et pratiques des élites au haut Moyen Âge. Conception, perception et réalisation* (Turnhout: Brepols, 2012), pp. 69–99.
Le Maho, J., 'Un grand ouvrage royal du ixe siècle. Le pont fortifié dit "de Pîtres" à Pont-de-l'Arche (Eure)', in É. Lalou, B. Lepeuple and J.-L. Roch (eds), *Des châteaux et des sources. Archéologie et histoire dans la Normandie médiévale* (Mont Saint-Aignan: Publications des Universités de Rouen et du Havre, 2008), pp. 143–58.
Lemerle, P., *The agrarian history of Byzantium from the origins to the twelfth century. The sources and the problems* (Galway: Galway University Press, 1979).
Leneghan, F., 'Royal wisdom and the Alfredian context of Cynewulf and Cyneheard', *Anglo-Saxon England*, 39 (2011), pp. 71–104.
Liebeschuetz, J. H. W. G., *The decline and fall of the Roman city* (Oxford: Oxford University Press, 2001).
Löwe, H., 'Das Karlsbuch Notkers von St. Gallen und sein zeitgeschichtlicher Hintergrund', *Schweizerische Zeitschrift für Geschichte*, 20 (1970), pp. 269–302.
MacLean, S., *Kingship and politics in the late ninth century. Charles the Fat and the end of the Carolingian empire* (Cambridge: Cambridge University Press, 2003).
Martin, C., *La géographie du pouvoir dans l'Espagne wisigothique* (Villeneuve d'Ascq: Presses Universitaires du Septentrion, 2003).
McClure, J., 'Bede's Old Testament Kings', in P. Wormald, D. Bullough and R. Collins (eds), *Ideal and reality in Frankish and Anglo-Saxon society* (Oxford: Blackwell, 1983), pp. 76–98.
McCormick, M., *Eternal victory. Triumphal rulership in late Antiquity, Byzantium and the early medieval west* (Cambridge: Cambridge University Press, 1990).
Moisl, H., *Lordship and tradition in barbarian Europe*, Studies in Classics, 10 (Lewiston: Edwin Mellen, 1999).
Müller, E. and F. Schmieder, *Begriffsgeschichte und historische Semantik. Ein kritisches Kompendium*, Taschenbuch Wissenschaft (Berlin: Suhrkamp, 2016).
Murray, A. C., 'From Roman to Frankish Gaul. "Centenarii" and "centenae" in the administration of the Merovingian kingdom', *Traditio*, 44 (1988) pp. 59–100.
Murray, A. C., '*Pax et disciplina*. Roman public law and the Merovingian state', in T. F. X. Noble (ed.), *Roman provinces to medieval kingdoms* (London: Routledge, 2006), pp. 376–88.
Nelson, J. L., *Charles the Bald* (London: Longman, 1992).
Nicholson, H., *Medieval warfare. Theory and practice of war in Europe 300–1500* (Basingstoke: Palgrave Macmillan, 2004).
Nicolay, J., *Armed Batavians. Use and significance of weaponry and horse gear from non-military contexts in the Rhine Delta (50 BC to AD 450)*, Amsterdam Archaeological Studies 11 (Amsterdam: Amsterdam University Press, 2007).
Noethlichs, K. L., 'Krieg', in *Reallexikon für Antike und Christentum*, 22 (Stuttgart: Hiersemann, 2008), pp. 1–75.
Noizet, H., *La fabrique de la ville. Espaces et sociétés à Tours (ixe-xiiie siècles)* (Paris: Publications de la Sorbonne, 2007).
Nonn, U., *Pagus und Comitatus in Niederlothringen. Untersuchungen zur politischen Raumgliederung im früheren Mittelalter* (Bonn: Röhrscheid, 1983).

Oikonomides, N., *Fiscalité et exemption fiscale à Byzance (IXe-XIe s.)* (Athens: EIE, 1996).
Parker, T. (ed.), *The Roman frontier in central Jordan. Final report on the limes arabicus project, 1980–1989* (Washington, DC: Dumbarton Oaks Press, 2006).
Parnell, D., *Justinian's men. Career and relationships of Byzantine army officers 518–610* (London: Palgrave Macmillan, 2017).
Pattison, J. E., 'Is it necessary to assume an Apartheid-like social structure in early Anglo-Saxon England?', *Proceedings of the Royal Society*, 275 (2008), pp. 2423–29.
Petersen, L. I. R., *Siege warfare and military organization in the successor states (400–800 AD). Byzantium, the west and Islam* (Leiden: Brill, 2013).
Pohl, W., 'The empire and the Lombards. Treaties and negotiations in the sixth century', in W. Pohl (ed.), *Kingdoms of the empire. The integration of barbarians in late Antiquity*, The Transformation of the Roman World, 1 (Leiden: Brill, 1997), pp. 75–134.
Pohl, W., 'Invasions and ethnic identity', in C. La Rocca (ed.), *Italy in the early Middle Ages 476–1000*, Short Oxford History of Italy (Oxford: Oxford University Press, 2002), pp. 11–33.
Pohl, W., 'Migration und Ethnogenesen der Langobarden aus Sicht der Schriftquellen', in J. Bemmann and M. Schmauder (eds), *Kulturwandel im Mitteleuropa. Langobarden-Awaren-Slawen* (Bonn: Habelt, 2008), pp. 1–9.
Pratt, D., *The political thought of king Alfred the Great* (Cambridge: Cambridge University Press, 2007).
Prinz, F., *Klerus und Krieg im früheren Mittelalter. Untersuchungen zur Rolle der Kirche beim Aufbau der Königsherrschaft*, Monographien zur Geschichte des Mittelalters, 2 (Stuttgart: Hiersemann, 1971).
Quast, D., 'Kriegerdarstellungen der Merowingerzeit aus der Alamania', *Archäologisches Korrespondenzblatt*, 32 (2002), pp. 267–80.
Rabe, S. A., *Faith, art, and politics at Saint-Riquier. A symbolic vision of Angilbert* (Philadelphia: University of Pennsylvania Press, 1995).
Rance, P., 'The army in peace time. The social status and function of soldiers', in Y. Stouraitis (ed.), *A companion to the Byzantine culture of war ca. 300–1204* (Leiden: Brill, 2018), pp. 394–439.
Reuter, T., 'The recruitment of armies in the early Middle Ages. What can we know?', in A. N. Jørgensen and B. L. Clausen (eds), *Military aspects of Scandinavian society in a European perspective AD 1–1300*, National Museum Studies in Archaeology and History 2 (Copenhagen: National Museum, 1997), pp. 32–7.
Reuter, T., 'Carolingian and Ottonian warfare', in M. Keen (ed.), *Medieval warfare. A history* (Oxford: Oxford University Press, 1999), pp. 13–35.
Richards, J., *Gregor der Große. Sein Leben – seine Zeit* (Graz: Styria, 1983).
Sahlins, M. S., 'Poor man, rich man, big-ban, chief. Political types in Melanesia and Polynesia', *Comparative Studies in Society and History*, 5:3 (1963), pp. 285–303.
Salten, O., *Vasallität und Benefizialwesen im 9. Jahrhundert. Studien zur Entwicklung personaler und dinglicher Beziehungen im frühen Mittelalter* (Hildesheim: Franzbecker KG, 2013).
Sánchez-Albornoz, C., 'El gobierno de las ciudades de España del siglo V al X', in *Estudios sobre las instituciones medievales españolas* (México D.F.: UNAM, 1965), pp. 615–37.
Sarti, L., *Perceiving war and the military in early Christian Gaul (ca. 400–700 A.D.)*, Brill's series on the early Middle Ages, 22 (Leiden: Brill, 2013).

Sarti, L., 'Die spätantike Militärpräsenz und die Entstehung einer militarisierten "Grenzgesellschaft" in der nordwesteuropäischen *limes*-Region' in C. Rass (ed.), *Militärische Migration vom Altertum bis zur Gegenwart*, Studien zur Historischen Migrationsforschung, 30 (Paderborn: Schöningh, 2016), pp. 43–56.

Sarti, L., 'Eine Militärelite im merowingischen Gallien? Versuch einer Eingrenzung, Zuordnung und Definition', *Mitteilungen des Instituts für Österreichische Geschichtsforschung*, 124:2 (2016), pp. 271–95.

Sarti, L., 'Der fränkische *miles*. Weder Soldat noch Ritter', *Frühmittelalterliche Studien*, 52:1 (2018), pp. 99–117.

Sarti, L., 'The military and its role in Merovingian society' in B. Effros and I. Moreira (eds), *Oxford handbook of the Merovingian world* (Oxford: Oxford University Press, 2020), pp. 255–77.

Schaller, D., 'Der Dichter des *Carmen de conversione Saxonum*', in G. Bernt, F. Rädle and G. Silagi (eds), *Tradition und Wertung* (Sigmaringen: Jan Thorbecke, 1989), pp. 27–45, reprinted in D. Schaller, *Studien zur lateinischen Dichtung des Frühmittelalters* (Stuttgart: Hiersemann, 1995), pp. 313–31.

Scharf, R., *Der Dux Mogontiacensis und die Notitia Dignitatum. Eine Studie zur spätantiken Grenzverteidigung* (Berlin: De Gruyter, 2005), pp. 284–98.

Scharff, T., *Die Kämpfe der Herrscher und der Heiligen. Krieg und historische Erinnerung in der Karolingerzeit*, Symbolische Kommunikation in der Vormoderne. Studien zur Geschichte, Literatur und Kunst (Darmstadt: Wissenschaftliche Buchgesellschaft, 2002).

Scharff, T., 'Karolingerzeitliche Vorstellungen vom Krieg vor dem Hintergrund der romanisch-germanischen Kultursynthese', in D. Hägermann, W. Haubrichs and J. Jarnut (eds, with the collaboration of C. Giefers), *Akkulturation. Probleme einer germanisch-romanischen Kultursynthese in Spätantike und frühem Mittelalter*, Ergänzungsbände zum RGA, 41 (Berlin: De Gruyter, 2004), pp. 473–90.

Schlesinger, W., 'Herrschaft und Gefolgschaft in der germanisch-deutschen Verfassungsgeschichte', *Historische Zeitschrift*, 176 (1953), pp. 225–75.

Schreiner, K. (ed., with the collaboration of E. Müller-Luckner), *Heilige Kriege. Religiöse Begründungen militärischer Gewaltanwendung. Judentum, Christentum und Islam im Vergleich*, Schriften des Historischen Kollegs. Kolloquien, 78 (Munich: Oldenbourg, 2008).

Settia, A. A., 'Una "fara" in Collegno', in A. A. Settia (ed.), *Barbari e infedeli nell'alto medioevo italiano. Storia e miti storiografici* (Spoleto: CISAM, 2011), pp. 73–86.

Siegrist, T., *Herrscherbild und Weltsicht bei Notker Balbulus. Untersuchungen zu den Gesta Karoli* (Zürich: Fretz & Wasmuth Verlag, 1963).

Sims-Williams, P., 'The settlement of England in Bede and the *chronicle*', *Anglo-Saxon England*, 12 (1983), pp. 1–41.

Springer, M., 'Jährliche Wiederkehr oder ganz anderes. Märzfeld oder Marsfeld?', in P. Dilg, G. Keil and D.-R. Moser (eds), *Rhythmus und Saisonalität* (Sigmaringen: Thorbecke, 1995), pp. 297–324.

Springer, M., 'Riparii – Ribuarier – Rheinfranken nebst einigen Bemerkungen zum Geographen von Ravenna', in D. Geuenich (ed.), *Die Franken und die Alemannen bis zur 'Schlacht bei Zülpich' (496/97)* (Berlin: De Gruyter, 1998), pp. 200–69.

Steuer, H., 'Helm und Ringschwert. Prunkbewaffnung und Rangabzeichen germanischer Krieger. Eine Übersicht', in H.-J. Häßler (ed.), *Studien zur Sachsenforschung* 6 (Hildesheim: August Lax, 1987), pp. 190–236.

Stoll, O., '"Heeresdiziplin". Vom Einfluß Roms auf die Germanen', in O. Stoll, *Römisches Heer und Gesellschaft. Gesammelte Beiträge 1991–1999* (Stuttgart: Franz Steiner, 2001), pp. 269–79.
Stouraitis, Y. (ed.), *A companion to the Byzantine culture of war ca. 300–1204* (Leiden: Brill, 2018).
Strothmann, J., 'Königsherrschaft oder nachantike Staatlichkeit? Merowingische Monetarmünzen als Quelle für die politische Ordnung des Frankenreiches', *Millennium*, 5 (2008), pp. 353–81.
Theuws, F. and M. Alkemade, 'A kind of mirror for men. Sword depositions in late antique northern Gaul', in F. Theuws und J. L. Nelson (eds), *Rituals of Power. From late Antiquity to the early Middle Ages*, Transformation of the Roman World, 8 (Leiden: Brill, 2000), pp. 401–76.
Theuws, F., '"Terra non est" Zentralsiedlungen der Völkerwanderungszeit', in H. Steuer and V. Bierbrauer (eds), *Höhensiedlungen zwischen Antike und Mittelalter von den Ardennen bis zur Adria* (Berlin: De Gruyter 2008), pp. 765–93.
Theuws, F., 'Grave goods, ethnicity, and the rhetoric of burial rites in late antique northern Gaul', in T. Derks and N. Roymans (eds), *Ethnic constructs in Antiquity. The role of power and tradition*, Amsterdam Archaeological Studies, 13 (Amsterdam: Amsterdam University Press 2009), pp. 283–320.
Thomas, M. G., Stumpf, M. P. H. and Härke, H., 'Evidence for an Apartheid-like social structure in early Anglo-Saxon England', *Proceedings of the Royal Society*, 273 (2006), pp. 2651–57.
Toplyn, M., 'Livestock and *Limitanei*. The zooarchaeological evidence', in T. Parker (ed.), *The Roman frontier in central Jordan. Final report on the* limes arabicus *project, 1980–1989* (Washington, DC: Dumbarton Oaks Press, 2006), pp. 463–507.
Trombley, F., 'War, society and popular religion in Byzantine Anatolia (6th–13th centuries)', in S. Lampakis (ed.), Η Βυζαντινή Μικρά Ασία (6ος-12ος αι.) (Athens: EIE/IBE, 1998), pp. 97–139.
Valverde, M. R., *Ideología, simbolismo y ejercicio del poder real en la monarquía visigoda. Un proceso de cambio* (Salamanca: Ediciones Universidad de Salamanca, 2000).
Van Ossel, P., 'Insécurité et militarisation en Gaul du nord au bas-empire: L'exemple des campagnes', *Revue du Nord* LXXVII (1995), pp. 27–36.
Van Rey, M., *Die Lütticher Gaue Condroz und Ardennen im Frühmittelalter. Untersuchungen zur Pfarrorganisation* (Bonn: L. Röhrscheid, 1977).
Van Thienen, V., 'A symbol of late Roman authority revisited. A socio-historical understanding of the crossbow brooch', in N. Roymans, St. Heeren and W. de Clercq (eds), *Social dynamics in the northwest frontiers of the late Roman Empire. Beyond decline or transformation* (Amsterdam: Amsterdam University Press 2017), pp. 97–126.
Wamers, E., 'Warlords oder Vasallen? Zur Semiotik der merowingerzeitlichen Bootsbestattungen von Vendel und Valsgärde in Mittelschweden', in S. Brahter, C. Merthen and T. Springer (eds), *Warlords oder Amtsträger? Herausragende Bestattungen der späten Merowingerzeit* (Nuremberg: Verlag des Germanischen Nationalmuseum, 2018), pp. 212–37.
Ward-Perkins, B., *From classical Antiquity to the Middle Ages. Urban public building in northern and central Italy AD 300–850* (Oxford: Oxford University Press, 1984).
Ward, W., *Mirage of the Saracen* (Berkeley: University of California Press, 2015).

Wermelinger, O. Bruggisser, P. and Roessli, J.-M. (eds), *Mauritius und die Thebäische Legion* (Fribourg: Academic Press, 2005).

Werner, J., 'Zur Entstehung der Reihengräberzivilisation. Ein Beitrag zur Methode der frühgeschichtlichen Archäologie', *Archaeologia Geographica*, 1 (1950), pp. 23–32.

Werner, M., *Der Lütticher Raum in frühkarolingischer Zeit. Untersuchungen zur Geschichte einer karolingischen Stammlandschaft* (Göttingen: Vandenhoeck & Ruprecht, 1980).

Whately, C., 'Militarization or rise of a distinct military culture? The east Roman ruling elite in the sixth century', in D. Boatright and S. O'Brien (eds), *Warfare and society in the ancient eastern Mediterranean* (Oxford: BAR Archaeopress, 2013), pp. 49–57.

Whately, C., 'Camels, soldiers, and pilgrims in sixth century Nessana', *Scripta Classica Israelica*, 35 (2016), pp. 121–35.

Wijnendaele, J. W. P., '"Warlordism" and the disintegration of the western Roman army', in J. Armstrong (ed.), *Circum mare. Themes in ancient warfare* (Leiden: Brill, 2016), pp. 184–203.

Wilson, P., 'Defining military culture', *The Journal of Military History*, 72 (2008), pp. 11–41.

Wolfram, H., *Die Goten* (Munich: C.H. Beck, 2001).

Wormald, P., 'The *leges barbarorum*. Law and ethnicity in the post-Roman west', in H.-W. Goetz, J. Jarnut and W. Pohl (eds), *Regna and gentes. The relationship between late antique and early medieval peoples and kingdoms in the transformation of the Roman world*, Transformation of the Roman world, 13 (Leiden: Brill, 2003), pp. 21–53.

Yorke, B., *Kings and kingdoms of early Anglo-Saxon England* (London: Routledge, 1990).

Yorke, B., 'The representations of early west Saxon history in the Anglo-Saxon Chronicle', in A. Jorgensen (ed.), *Reading the Anglo-Saxon Chronicle. Language, literature, history* (Turnhout: Brepols, 2010), p. 141–60.

Zerjadtke, M., *Das Amt "Dux" in Spätantike und frühem Mittelalter. Der "ducatus" im Spannungsfeld zwischen römischem Einfluss und eigener Entwicklung*, RGA supplements, 110 (Berlin: De Gruyter, 2019).

Index

adōreia (exemption from military obligation) 40–1
adventus Saxonum 4, 283, 285
Æthelfrith (king of Northumbria, r. 592–616) 288–91, 293
Æthelred (king of Wessex, r. 865–71) 80, 83, 85, 88
Africa 99, 108, 202
  see also Vandal Africa
Agila (Visigothic king, r. 549–55) 117, 119
Agilulf (Lombard king, r. 590–615) 154–5, 166
Agnellus (of Ravenna, priest and historian, fl. 805–46) 79
Aistulf (Lombard king, r. 749–56) 6, 68, 70–1, 79, 153, 157–9
Alahis (duke of Trent and Brescia, Lombard king, r. 689) 67, 155
Alamannia 319–20
Alboin (Lombard ruler, r. c.560–72/3) 65–8, 73, 75–6, 152
Alcuin (of York, scholar, c.735–804) 200, 210, 292
Alfonso III (king of León, Galicia, and Asturias, r. 866–910) 217, 226
Alfred (the Great, king of the Anglo-Saxons r. 871–99) 4, 80–95, 168, 170, 283, 285, 341
  military reforms 4, 80–95
Alps 50, 65, 71, 155, 162, 301
Amalaric (Visigothic king, r. 522–31) 119

Amiens 142, 165, 183, 207
Andernach 170, 182–4, 190
Andreas of Bergamo (ninth-century historian) 154, 160
Angers 2, 167, 171, 176
  Formularies of Angers 2
  siege of 167, 171
Anglo-Saxon Chronicle 82, 84, 168, 285, 337
Anglo-Saxon England 1, 4–5, 13, 257, 296, 321, 331, 338, 340
Anglo-Saxons 4–5, 82, 201, 203, 208, 210, 257, 283–98, 323
Annals of Fulda 213, 215, 341
Annals of Xanten 166
antrustiones 2, 320
Aquitaine 135, 138–40, 165, 175
Arabia 99, 101–14
  Arabia Petraea (Rome's Arabian province) 100
Arabs 100, 216–17
  Arab phylarch 103
  Arab tribes 100
archaeology 12, 136, 142, 234, 247, 238, 315, 320
Argait (eighth-century Lombard *sculdahis* in Friuli) 156–7
arimanni 6, 66
aristocracy 2, 10, 42, 49, 55, 65, 68, 71, 116, 119, 153, 156–61, 233, 238, 242, 253, 256, 263, 332, 340, 343

Arnulf (duke of Carinthia, c. 850–99) 341
Arthur (legendary British hero) 253–4
Arx Cynuit (fortress) 84
Ashdown, Battle of (871) 83, 341
Asia Minor 33, 40
Asser (monk of St David's, bishop of Sherborne in the 890s) 82, 85, 341
  Life of King Alfred 83–5
Athanagild (Visigothic king, r. c.555–67) 117, 119
Athelney (fortification) 84
Attila (the Hun, fl. 406–53) 253, 257, 341
Augustine (archbishop of Canterbury, 597–604) 285, 289
Augustine (saint, bishop of Hippo, 396–430) 198, 200, 206, 208
Augustus (first Roman emperor) 54
Aurelian wall 131
Austrasia 22, 181–2, 185–7, 189, 337
Authari (Lombard king, r. 584–90) 65, 72, 75, 154, 160
Avars 3, 73, 155–6, 160, 208, 224, 300, 341

Balkans 32, 64, 99, 154, 232
baptism 196, 198–9, 203–4, 208, 309
barbarisation 7–8, 245
Bede (the Venerable, Northumbrian monk and scholar, c.672–735) 4, 210, 256
  Historia Ecclesiastica gentis Anglorum 256, 284–98
Beersheba 101–2, 106, 108
Begriffsgeschichte 12
Belgium 130–51, 243, 335
Belisarius (sixth-century Byzantine commander) 51–2, 54, 57
Benevento 6, 66–7, 72, 75, 77, 155
Beowulf 253–4, 257, 314
Bergamo 67, 154, 160
Boethius (sixth-century philosopher) 89
  Consolation of Philosophy (Old English translation) 89
booty 37, 39, 73, 125
border troops 49, 53, 58

Boves (Picardy) 135, 144
Breones (military unit) 49
Brescia 67
Britain 3–4, 14, 19, 244, 283–5, 288, 290, 293, 296, 315–16, 323, 338
Bulgarians 66
Burchard (ninth-century bishop of Chartres) 201, 203
Burghal Hidage 82, 86–90
Burgundians 119, 186, 253
burhs (Anglo-Saxon fortified sites) 90–1, 339
burial rites 231, 236, 239, 246
Byzantine Empire 31–47, 331
Byzantine law codes 39
  see also laws

Cædwalla (king of Gwynedd, d. c.634) 290–1
Caesarea 104–5
Cambrai 140, 183
Carloman (Frankish king, d. 880) 161, 167
Carolingians 3, 164, 210
  armies 3
  Empire 134, 140
  fortifications 130, 135–6, 138, 146
  military organisation 12
Cassiodorus (scholar and statesman, 490–c.585) 50–2, 56
  Variae (letters) 50–1, 56
castellum, castella 139, 145, 189, 234, 340
castra Bonnensia (Bonn) 1
castrum of Noirmoutier 139
castrum of Saint-Martin, Tours 131, 135, 139–41
Caucasus, the 99
cavalry 49, 158
  heavy cavalry 158
  light cavalry 158
  shock cavalry 51
cemeteries 1, 5, 8, 231–52, 266, 337, 344
ceorls (free farmers) 4
Chaldaeans 216–17, 225
Charente 131–2, 145, 171
Charlemagne (first Frankish emperor, r. 800–14) 71–2, 138, 154, 158,

160, 165, 190, 196, 198–200, 203, 207–8, 212, 214–15, 223–4, 255, 299–313, 341
capitularies 336
Charles Martel (*de facto* ruler of Francia, 718–41) 27, 68
Charles the Bald (Frankish emperor, r. 875–77) 135, 138, 164–77, 213, 334, 339–41
Charles the Fat (Frankish emperor, r. 881–88) 138, 168, 172, 299, 306, 309–10
Charles the Simple (king of West Francia, r. 898–922) 139
Château-Thierry (Aisne) 135, 142
Chester, Battle of (615/616) 289, 291, 293
Childebert II (Merovingian king, r.575–96) 182, 184, 186, 190, 260
Chindaswinth (Visigothic king, r. 642–53) 115, 117, 120
Chlothar II (king of the Franks, r. 613–29) 255, 337
Christianity 27, 196–210, 211–28, 284, 290, 297, 316
Cividale del Friuli (*Forum Iulii*) 65
Claudius (Visigothic duke) 121–3, 129
Cleph (Lombard king, r. 572–74) 67
clergy 3, 11, 165, 168, 172, 201
Clovis I (first king of the Franks, r. c.509–11) 2, 255
clusae (Alpine barriers) 153, 160
Cohors Prima Flavia 105
Cologne 71, 182–6, 242
comes 55, 120–1, 128
 comes ciuitatis 120–1
 comes exercitus 120–1
 comites Gothorum 53
 comites provinciarum 53
comitatus 321–3
Constans II (Roman emperor, r. 641–68) 72, 77, 155
Constantine V (Roman emperor, r. 741–75) 34
Constantine VII (Roman emperor, r. 913–59) 41
 Novel on soldiers' landholdings 41
Constantinople 34, 36, 41, 51, 108, 201, 209

Coronate, Battle of (689) 67, 155
Cunincpert (Lombard king, r. 688–700) 67, 72, 155

Dagobert I (Frankish king, r. 629–39) 186, 189
Danube frontier 237
Dead Sea 99
death penalty 185, 187, 303
dekarchs, *dekarchies* 105–6
Desiderius (Lombard king, r. 757–74) 68, 71, 153, 157–60
Domesday Book 20, 88, 90
 folios for Berkshire 20, 90
Domnolinus (Lombard from Pisa) 159
donatiuum 52, 54
dux 65–6, 69–70, 102–3, 121–2, 126, 182
 dux Palaestinae 105

ealdormen 82, 84
East Anglia (Anglo-Saxon kingdom) 297
eastern Roman Empire 57, 341
Ecgfrith (king of Northumbria, r. 670–85) 289–90, 293
Edington, Battle of (878) 88
Edward the Elder (king of the Anglo-Saxons, r. 899–924) 82, 85, 87
Edwin (king of Northumbria, r. 616–33) 289, 291, 297
Egica (Visigothic king, r. 687–702) 117
Egypt 32, 36, 45, 104–5, 107, 215, 242, 251
el-Lejjun 101–4
Elbe river 138
Elusa 105–6
England 80–95, 201–2, 231, 239, 256–7, 283–98, 314, 316, 336, 339–40
Ennodius (Magnus Felix, bishop of Pavia, 514–21) 48, 53, 55
equites 103
 equites Dalmatae Illyriciani 105
 equites promote indigenae 107
 equites Scutarii Illyriciani 105
 equites Thamudeni Illyriciani 105
Ermentarius of Noirmoutier (ninth-century historian) 166, 169

Ermold the Black (Ermoldus Nigellus, Carolingian poet, fl. 824–30) 164
  verse biography of Louis the Pious 164
ethnicity 48, 53–4, 57, 187, 285
Eucherius (bishop of Lyon, c.380-c.449) 196–200
Euric (Visigothic king, r. 466–84) 122
excubitores 48
exercitales 6, 66, 69, 158–9
Exeter 80, 87

faida 156
female burials 266–82
  see also women
Ferdulf (Lombard duke) 156–7
field army (*comitatenses*) 49–52, 54, 56–7
Flavius Dusarius (prefect of Kastron Ammatha) 107–8
Flodoard (of Reims, tenth-century chronicler) 136
  chronicle 142
Flovius, Battle at (664) 155
foederati (auxiliaries) 1, 8, 64, 154, 233, 235
Folcuin (tenth-century abbot of Lobbes) 140
Fontenoy, Battle of (841) 165
Forinus, Battle of (663) 155
fortifications 38, 57, 67, 82, 84, 86–8, 90, 99–102, 130–51, 164, 170, 172, 181, 190, 234, 300–1, 310, 333, 338–40
France 68, 130–52, 238, 239, 242, 244, 269
Francia 68, 138, 159, 167, 170–1, 181–95, 256, 284, 340–1
  East Francia 299
Franks 6, 14, 67, 70, 72, 76–7, 79, 117, 119, 127, 153, 155, 158–61, 164, 167–9, 172, 182–6, 201, 208, 257, 303, 309
  Frankish capitularies 164
  Frankish vassals 160
  Frankish world 1, 136
  regnum Francorum 127
Freya (Norse goddess) 152

Frisia 168, 171–2, 184, 225
fyrdwite (fine for neglecting military service) 4

Gallic provinces 1
gastalds 5, 66, 69
Gaul 1–3, 12–14, 181, 183, 185, 201, 210, 235, 237, 247, 249, 257, 259, 275, 308, 335–8
generalships (*stratēgiai*, *stratēgides*) 33
Gepids 54, 66, 152
Germanisation 7–8, 22–3, 322–3
Germany 1, 152, 231, 241, 243, 266–8, 271, 274–5, 277, 287, 315–16, 319
  warlike Germans 8
Gesaleic (Visigothic king, r. 507–11) 119, 127
Gildas (British monk, fl. 570) 4, 287, 296, 337
Gisulf (duke, nephew of Alboin) 65
Goths 2, 50, 52, 54, 117, 127, 218, 253, 257–9
  exercitus Gothorum 48–62
  Gothic Wars (535–62) 48, 50–1, 54, 57, 64, 74
  see also Visigoths
Granustrum of Aachen Palace 142
grave-goods 5, 156, 231–52, 266–82, 314, 320, 323
Greece 40, 43
Gregory I ('the Great', pope, 590–604) 67, 74, 154, 200
  Dialogi 154
Gregory of Tours 5, 76, 154, 219, 253–65
  Histories 5, 260
Grimoald (Lombard king, r. 662–71) 72, 77, 155
Gumfrid (abbot of St Peter in Monteverdi) 157–8
Gundemar (Visigothic king, r. 610–12) 117
Guntram (Frankish king, r. 561–92) 117
Guthrum (Viking king of East Anglia, r. c.879–90) 83

Hadrian I (pope, 772–95) 159, 215
Heraclius (Roman emperor, r. 610–41) 32, 255, 341

heroism 253–65
　heroic poetry 257, 320, 322
　heroic virtues 10, 253–65, 315, 332, 334
Heruls 54, 73
Hildegar (ninth-century bishop of Meaux) 166, 169
Hincmar (archbishop of Rheims, 845–82) 165, 170, 171
Hincmar (of Laon, 858–71) 165
Hispania 115–29
　see also Spain
Historia Wambae 116
honor 14–16, 28
horse archers 51
Hrotgaud (Lombard duke of Friuli, r. 774–76) 160
Hungarian raids 139, 145
Huns 54, 208, 253

Iconoclasm (730–87, 815–42) 32
Igoville 138–9, 146, 149
Ine (king of Wessex, r. 688–726) 4, 336
　laws 4, 336
Isacius (Byzantine exarch) 77, 155
Isidore of Seville (historian and archbishop, c.631–36) 115, 126, 286
Islam 31–2
　Islamic Spain 217
　Islamic territories 216
Israel 99, 228
iudex (judicial functionary) 121, 128

John of Biclaro (Visigothic chronicler) 115
Jordan 99, 102, 108–9, 114
Julian Alps 65
Justinian (Roman emperor, r. 527–65) 41, 49, 54, 64–5, 73, 101–3, 201, 203
　law 40
　legislation 35
　novels 47
　Pragmatic Sanction 65

Kent (Anglo-Saxon kingdom) 88, 284, 288
Khurramites 39

La Truque de Maurélis 142, 147
laeti (border communities) 1, 8, 235
landlords 38
landowners 32, 41, 66, 70, 158, 202, 238, 336, 339
Laon 142, 151, 165
laws 1, 5–6, 41, 66, 68–70, 128, 158, 198, 336, 344
　leges antiquae 120
　leges Langobardorum 5, 68, 75
　lex Iulia de vi publica 35
　see also Byzantine law codes
Lea (river) 170
Leo VI (Roman emperor, r. 886–912) 35, 38, 40–1, 43
　Taktika 35, 43
Liber Pontificalis 79, 160
Liège (Belgium) 146, 171
limes 2, 8
limitanei 49, 50, 102
Liutprand (Lombard king, r. 712–44) 68, 72, 155, 157–9
Liuva (Visigothic king, r. 567/8–72) 118–19
Liuvigild (Visigothic king, r. 568/9–86) 116–18, 122
Lobbes (monastery) 139, 140
Lombards, *gens Langobardorum* 5, 6, 14, 63–78, 153–62, 259, 320, 336
　Lombard *dux/duces* 5, 6, 63, 65, 67, 69, 70, 74, 77
　Lombard *fara/farae* 65, 66, 74, 75
　Lombard *gasindii* 70
　Lombard *gastaldi* 5, 63, 66, 69, 70
　Lombard Italy 1, 5–7, 13, 63, 65
　rex Langobardorum (king) 5–6, 66, 69
London 84, 288
Lothar I (Frankish emperor, r. 817–55) 164–8, 171–2, 213
Lothar II (Frankish emperor, r. 855–69) 167–8
Lotharingia 139, 166
Louis the German (king of East Francia, r. 843–76) 165, 168, 170, 299, 308–10
Louis the Pious (Frankish emperor, r. 814–40) 136, 139, 164, 213, 306, 309–10, 337

loyalty 17, 57, 68, 69, 181, 189, 190, 287, 292, 321, 322
Lupus (*dux* of Aquitaine) 257, 259
Lupus (Lombard duke of Friuli) 77, 155

Maastricht 182–4, 186
Malmesbury 85, 87
manliness (*virilitas*) 3, 10, 14, 16, 262, 288
  see also masculinity
Marne 138, 144–5, 170, 237
marpahis (lat. *strator*) 65, 69
martiality, martial values 10, 118, 121, 123, 200, 212, 231, 242, 245–7, 256–7, 259, 288, 307–8, 310, 331–2, 338, 340–2
masculinity 7, 232, 261–2, 341
  see also manliness (*virilitas*)
Mayenne 131, 142–3
Mercia 4, 85–6, 88, 90, 284, 286, 291
  Mercians 88, 284, 291–3
Merida 122, 228
Merovingians 12, 14–15, 121, 127, 136, 182, 185, 211, 259, 267, 268, 320, 322, 325, 337
  Merovingian kingdoms 128–9, 181–3, 190, 268, 278, 315–16
Mesopotamia 32–3, 101
Metz 136, 181–4
Milan 55, 56, 66–7, 72
military clothing 37, 53–5, 231, 238–40, 246–7
  cingulum militare (military belt) 53, 272
  habitus militaris (military dress) 53, 234, 241, 243, 246, 247, 278
military saints 22, 212
military service 2, 4, 6, 10, 33, 35–6, 39, 41–2, 51, 69, 78, 90, 94–5, 185, 190, 197–8, 242–5, 305, 334, 336–8
missus 69, 189
Modave (hillfort) 131–2, 147
Muslims 215–16
  Muslim invasions 33
Müstair (Grisons, Switzerland) 140, 142

Near East 32, 108, 109
Negev 99, 102
Nessana 101–2, 105–7, 109, 113
  Nessana papyri 104, 106–7
Neustria 170, 337
Nikephoros I (emperor, r. 802–11) 40–1
Nithard (Frankish historian, c.790–844) 164, 172, 213
Normandy 167
  Norman army 139
Northumbria 4, 288–93
Notitia Dignitatum 103, 105, 108, 238
Notker (the Stammerer, Notger Balbulus, c.840–912) 212, 299–310
numerus (barbarian fighting force) 2, 183

Odda (*ealdorman* of Alfred the Great) 84–5
Old Testament 116, 212, 217–18, 227–8, 289, 292
oppida (fortified settlements) 131, 136
Origo gentis Langobardorum 152
Orléans 136, 169
Ostrogoths 51, 76, 118
  Ostrogothic army 48–9
  see also Goths

paganism 198, 202, 208, 224, 268, 288, 291, 292
palace guards 48–9, 51, 54
Pannonia 64, 66, 73, 269
Paris 138–9, 145, 168, 182, 190
Paul the Deacon (eighth-century historian) 65–7, 72, 79, 154–6, 158, 160, 257
  Historia Langobardorum 5, 7, 64, 152, 159, 255
Pavia 66, 67, 71, 153, 212, 301, 302, 308
pax Romana 2, 9
Pemmo (Lombard duke of Friuli, r. 706–39) 157
Penda (king of Mercia, d. 655) 291–2, 297

pendants 267, 268, 269
Pepin the Short (Frankish king, r. 751–68) 70–2, 135, 138, 308, 310
Périgueux (Dordogne) 133, 136
Persians 100, 258
Petra 100, 106–8, 113
Phoenice Libanensis 102, 103
Picardy 142, 144
Picts 4, 284, 286–7, 289, 290, 293
Pineuilh 133, 145
Pippin II (mayor of the palace of Austrasia, r. 680–714) 146, 158
plunder 77, 121, 165, 166, 169
Poitiers 136, 165, 168
Ponts-de-Cé 138, 170–1
principate 11, 56, 338
priores (officers) 105, 107
Procopius of Caesarea (sixth-century historian) 49, 51, 57
  Historia Arcana (Secret History) 49, 102
Provence 144, 158–9, 306
public order 185, 190, 234, 245

Quentovic 146, 168

Raetia 50, 59
Ratchis (Lombard king, r. 744–9/756–7) 70, 157
rations (*siteresia, siteseis*) 37–8
Ravenna 5, 6, 54, 55, 65, 68, 70–1, 77, 79, 158, 160, 181
  exarchate 6, 65, 158, 208
Recceswinth (Visigothic king, r. 653–72) 115
Reiterheilige (military saints) 315, 319, 330
religious war 213–18, 221–2, 224
Repton 84
retinue 14, 27, 315, 320–1, 323
Rhine (river) 1, 139, 167, 181–4, 186, 225, 237, 271, 301
Ripuarians 184, 186–7
  law-code 186, 188–90
    see also laws
  pagus 187
roads 12, 38, 181, 183, 190, 241

Roman Empire 1, 5, 11, 49, 57, 64, 99, 130, 138, 153, 182–3, 185, 201, 203, 211, 231–2, 235, 246, 267, 315, 319, 323, 331–4, 341
romanitas 3, 89
Romans 1, 8, 10, 49, 52, 54, 77, 78, 100, 109, 154, 185–8, 258, 262, 308, 321
  late Roman *comitatenses* 49, 51
  senatorial elite 2, 52, 65
Roman world 8, 9, 11, 100, 131
  transformation of the 10, 272
Rome 5, 53, 55–7, 71, 89, 131, 139, 159, 160, 201, 203, 204, 254
Rothari (Lombard king, r. 636–52) 68–9, 72, 77, 155
  edict (*Edictum Rothari*) 6, 66, 68–9, 162

sagas 153, 314
Saint-Dizier-Leyrenne (Creuse) 131, 137
Saracens 72
Sarmatians 66
Sasanians 100
Saxons 4, 76, 80, 84, 90, 184, 198–200, 225, 255, 287–8, 290, 297, 300
  conversion of 198, 214
Scandinavia 268, 275, 277, 315–16, 319–22
  Scandinavians 167–72
  berserkers 152
  invaders 172
  see also Vikings
Scoltenna, Battle of (643) 77, 155
Scots 4, 284, 286, 288, 290, 293
Seine 138, 167–71
Septimania 118, 164
  William of 164
servants 38, 73, 85, 197, 304, 309
Sisebut (Visigothic king, r. 612–21) 117–18, 126
slaves 122, 188, 202, 263
Slavs 23, 156–7, 160, 162, 300, 306–7
Soissons, kingdom of 2

soldiers 1, 3, 9, 31–42, 49, 51–4, 56–8, 102–9, 169, 184, 186, 196–8, 204–6, 233, 237–9, 240, 243, 245, 258, 262, 289, 308, 336, 344
   douloi (frontier soldiers) 106
   mercenaries 36, 37, 64
   miles, milites 14, 15, 90, 212, 239, 277, 336
   militia 14, 35, 333
   stratiōtēs 33, 34, 36, 37, 39–41
   see also warriors
Spain 17, 214, 215, 217, 218, 228
   see also Hispania
Spoleto 6, 66, 67, 75, 154, 157
St Denis (Saint-Denis) 135, 139, 147, 149, 168, 170, 213
strateia (military service/obligation) 33, 34, 36–7, 40–2
Suebians 66
Suintila (Visigothic king, r. 621–31) 116–17
Sutton Hoo (ship burial) 5, 20, 314–16, 324, 325
Switzerland 130, 140, 142, 165, 272, 275, 306
syndotai (contributors) 41
Syria 32–3, 100, 101, 104

Tacitus (Roman historian, c.56–c.120) 73, 151, 153, 254, 321–2, 328
tagmata 34, 37
taxes 6, 17, 40, 105–6, 165
   communal tax liabilities 35, 42
   exemptions 34, 39, 42
   hearth-tax (*kapnikon*) 37
   land-tax (*dēmosion telos*) 37
   military tax 37
      heribannum, heribannus 3, 165
      hostilitium 165
Thames (river) 85
thegns 82
thema, themata 33, 36–7, 39
   theme system 31
Theodahad (Ostrogothic king, r. 534–6) 57
Theoderic/Theodoric (Ostrogothic king, r. 493–526) 49–58, 75, 119, 208, 253, 255
Theophilos (Roman emperor, r. 829–42) 57
Theudigisel (Visigothic king, r. 548–9) 117
Theudis (Visigothic king, r. 531–49) 117–19
Tiberius (Roman emperor, r. 14–37) 67, 152, 201, 256
Tiberius II (Roman emperor, r. 578–82) 67, 201
Torksey 84, 93
Toulouse 2, 120, 136
Tours (Indre-et-Loire) 135
tractus Italiae 50
Trent/Trento 67, 154–5, 160
tribute 165–6, 168–72, 215, 308
Turkey 99, 101
Tuscany 72, 154, 157

usefulness (*utilitas*) 3

Valentinianic ban 53
Valsgärde (Sweden) 274–5, 315–16
Vandal Africa 102
   see also Africa
Vegetius (fifth-century Roman writer) 135
   De re militari 131, 164
Velleius Paterculus (first-century Roman historian) 73, 152–3
Venantius Fortunatus (sixth-century poet) 182, 257, 259
Venetian republic 160
Verdun (Meuse) 136, 139
Verona 66, 140, 161, 253
vici 1, 3, 146, 189
Vikings 17, 81–2, 84, 88, 164–77, 215–16, 224, 283, 289, 293, 308–10, 334, 338, 341
   longships 170
   Norsemen 166
   Viking attacks 90, 214
   see also Scandinavians
Visigoths 115–29, 255, 257
   Visigothic kingdom of Toulouse 120
Vorstellungsgeschichte 12
Vouillé 120, 122
VSPE (*Vitas Sanctorum Patrum Emeretensium*) 121–2, 128–9

Walfrid (Lombard founder of St Peter's in Monteverdi, 754) 157, 163
Walprand (eighth-century bishop of Lucca) 159
Wamba (Visigothic king, r. 672–80) 116–17, 126
  military laws 334
  see also Historia Wambae
Wareham 84, 87, 93
warlords 67, 171, 242–3, 245
warriors 6–7, 13, 27, 34, 39, 51, 63–70, 72–3, 75, 77, 116, 152–3, 156, 159–60, 214, 235, 287, 292, 299–313, 314–30, 334, 343
  bellator 14–15, 26, 209
  belliger 14, 27
  depictions of 266–82
    'dancing-warriors' 315–16
    'wolf-warriors' 316, 319–20, 329
  lifestyle of 300
  milites Christi 212, 277
  proeliator 14, 27
  pugnator 14, 27
  see also soldiers
weapon burials 8, 13, 156, 233, 237, 336
weapons 1, 5, 10, 13, 15, 23, 35, 63, 128, 156, 164–5, 199, 231–52, 253, 266–8, 271, 278–9, 292, 308, 314–15, 324, 332, 335, 337, 343
  armour 35, 37, 164–5, 267, 269, 275, 278, 300–1, 310, 314, 324

axes 235, 237, 244, 335, 343
helmets 199, 275, 279, 314–16, 319–20, 323, 326
lances 235, 237–8, 244, 259, 269, 315, 319
shields 158, 199, 244, 267, 275, 301
spears 55, 75, 199, 237–8, 244, 274, 335, 344
swords 156, 164, 247, 267–8, 308–9, 314
  ring-swords 320, 327
wergild 3, 5, 11, 28, 185–90, 279
Wessex 4, 84–6, 88–90, 170, 283–4, 286, 297, 336
William of Malmesbury (twelfth-century English historian) 85–6
  Gesta Regum Anglorum 85
Witteric (Visigothic king, r. 603–10) 117, 119, 128
women 35, 39, 106, 152, 190, 261–2, 266–82, 304, 324, 344
  see also female burials
Worcester 86–8

Yarmuk, Battle of (636) 100

Zangentor-type
  gates 131
  towers 135
Zeeland 145, 150

EU authorised representative for GPSR:
Easy Access System Europe, Mustamäe tee 50,
10621 Tallinn, Estonia
gpsr.requests@easproject.com

www.ingramcontent.com/pod-product-compliance
Lightning Source LLC
Chambersburg PA
CBHW071202240426
43668CB00032B/1866